BIOLOGY
OF THE
REPTILIA

BIOLOGY
OF THE
REPTILIA

Edited By
CARL GANS

The University of Michigan
Ann Arbor, Michigan, U.S.A.

VOLUME 11

MORPHOLOGY F

Coeditor for this volume
THOMAS S. PARSONS

University of Toronto
Toronto, Ontario, Canada

1981
ACADEMIC PRESS

LONDON   NEW YORK   TORONTO   SYDNEY   SAN FRANCISCO
A Subsidiary of Harcourt Brace Jovanovich, Publishers

ACADEMIC PRESS INC. (LONDON) LTD.
24/28 Oval Road
London NW1

United States Edition published by
ACADEMIC PRESS INC.
111 Fifth Avenue
New York, New York 10003

British Library Cataloguing in Publication Data

Biology of the Reptilia.
  Vol. II: Morphology
  1. Reptiles
  I. Gans, C   II. Parsons, Thomas S
  597.9   QL641   68-9113
  ISBN 0-12-274611-2

Filmset by Northumberland Press Ltd, Gateshead, Tyne and Wear
Printed in Great Britain by Fletcher and Son Ltd, Norwich

Contributors to Volume 11

A. d'A. Bellairs, *Department of Anatomy, St. Mary's Hospital Medical School, University of London, Paddington, London W2, England*

J.-P. Gasc, *Laboratoire d'Anatomie Comparée, Muséum National d'Histoire Naturelle, 55 Rue de Buffon, 75005 Paris, France*

K. F. Guthe, *Division of Biological Sciences, The University of Michigan, Ann Arbor, Michigan 48109, USA*

The late A. M. Kamal, *Department of Zoology, University of Cairo, Egypt*

Preface

This volume marks the continuation of the treatment of the musculo-skeletal system of reptiles and indicates something of the diversity of issues important to this topic. The first chapter was begun by the late A. M. Kamal, who unfortunately died before more than the basic framework had been prepared. We are thus grateful and fortunate that Professor Angus d'A. Bellairs was prepared to complete the assignment; not only this, he has taken it far beyond the initial concept. Thus we have here a review of the chondrocranium and also of osteocranial development, as well as an introduction to the basic issues of skull formation and diversity.

Next we have Dr. Gasc's review of the axial musculature, mainly, but not exclusively, of limbless reptiles. It represents the first recent discussion in English of this important and generally neglected group of muscles.

Finally we are pleased to have interested Professor Karl Guthe in summarizing the diverse and disparate literature on the ultrastructure and physiology of reptilian muscle. This first recent summary brings together a disparate literature much of which was only incidentally carried out on reptiles. It offers a basis for comparing the nature of reptilian muscle to that of Recent amphibians on the one hand and of birds and mammals on the other. The chapter is particularly timely because of the recent emphasis on more directly functional studies of reptilian feeding, breathing and locomotor mechanisms; Professor Guthe is providing a first level basis for interpreting the functional characteristics of the tissues comprising these systems.

It may be appropriate again to refer to the problem of species identifications which plagues any project such as this one. With the aid of our colleagues, Heinz Wermuth and George Zug, we constantly attempt to update the nomenclature to that currently accepted and being used in checklists, such as those published under the auspices of *Das Tierreich* (also see chapter 5 of volume 2, and the appendix to chapter 1 of volume 8 of this series). Consequently the names listed for different sections are the current ones rather than the version in vogue at the time a particular study was carried out. In the best of circumstances this avoids the potential for confusion, such as comparisons between *Crocodylus* (*lucius*) and *Alligator* (*mississippiensis*) when both reports refer to the same species.

Our practice assumes that the name was properly applied in the original research report, which may not always be the case. Certain categories of animals (see entry under *Varanus monitor*) have developed catchall names that seem to be assigned to any specimen of the genus likely to be studied. In some such cases, one may assume that the investigator was dealing with the locally available species of the genus. This may not be a safe assumption as the specimen may have been donated by a colleague. For the benefit of those students engaged in ongoing work, it seems useful to stress again that there is one way of avoiding future problems. It is for the investigator to retain some portion of the external anatomy, skeletal remains, and histological slides of the particular specimen being used, or other members of a series from which it was sampled, and later to deposit this material in a natural history museum or other "permanent" reference collection. It then remains possible to determine the species actually used in a particular study and to avoid future confusion due to inadequate identification or changes in the biological concepts reflected by the names.

Drs. W. Auffenberg, B. D. Clark, Alan Crowe, E. S. Gaffney, M. Jollie, K. Kardong, R. Marsh, L. Maxwell, O. Rieppel, T. S. Scanlon, D. M. Secoy, W. W. Tanner, J. F. Waters, and S. Wickler reviewed individual manuscripts and Drs. G. Zug and H. Wermuth critically read the entire set of manuscripts for current usage and accuracy of the Latin names employed. I thank my co-editor for his help with editorial chores. The Division of Biological Sciences of The University of Michigan assisted with postage and copying.

March, 1980   Carl Gans

Contents

1. The Chondrocranium and the Development of the Skull in Recent Reptiles
A. d'A. Bellairs and the late A. M. Kamal

CHAPTER 1

The Chondrocranium and the Development of the Skull in Recent Reptiles

A. d'A. BELLAIRS

*Department of Anatomy, St Mary's Hospital Medical School
and the Zoological Society of London*

and the late

A. M. KAMAL

Department of Zoology, University of Cairo, Egypt

I. Introduction

A. HISTORICAL

During the nineteenth and early twentieth centuries the development of the skull attracted the interest of many biologists. In his famous Croonian lecture, T. H. Huxley (1858) demolished, or at least profoundly transformed, the ingenious but misleading theory, propounded by Goethe, Oken, Owen, and others, that the skull consisted of a series of modified vertebrae (see also Huxley, 1864, 1894; de Beer, 1937). Stimulated by the theory of evolution, many workers, especially in Germany, began to embark on detailed studies of the developing skull in every living class of vertebrates. The reptiles were not neglected, W. K. Parker and Ernst Gaupp being perhaps the two most eminent students in the field during the latter part of the nineteenth century.

Parker's work is of singular interest and in some ways recalls the tradition of the seventeenth century microscopists. He earned a living as a medical practitioner, but somehow managed to make a lifework of morphology (Howes, 1975). His text is idiosyncratic (sometimes charmingly so) and in places obscure, but his copious illustrations are magnificent. For this reason his work has outlasted in some ways that of many of his more professional successors, who all too often tried to make words do the work of pictures. Moreover, his hand-cut sections and dissections display vistas of the skull *in situ* which are hard to reveal by more sophisticated methods. His numerous and substantial papers include accounts of the developing skull in snakes (1879), lizards (1880a), turtles (1880b), and crocodilians (1883).

An immense advance in descriptive embryology was achieved after 1882, when the microtome was invented. It now became possible to build up three-dimensional models from serial sections, and also to plot graphic reconstructions (see Gaunt and Gaunt, 1978). This greatly facilitated an accurate appreciation of such features as the relationship of membrane bones to the chondrocranium, and of muscles, nerves and blood vessels to the frail scaffolding of the developing skull. The new technique was exploited by Born (1879, 1883) in his studies on the nasal capsule of lizards and snakes, and subsequently by Gaupp, Schauinsland, Fuchs and many others. It provided the basis for Gaupp's (1900) important account of the skull of *Lacerta agilis* which did much to establish modern concepts of the reptilian chondrocranium. A further advance was the introduction of methods for staining cartilage and bone in semi-transparent preparations of the whole skeleton (see Dingerkus and Uhler, 1977). Such techniques supplement, though they do not supplant, the more laborious procedures of serial sectioning and reconstruction.

Research on cranial development continued with little abatement into the twentieth century, notable reviews of the subject being contributed by Gaupp (1906), Goodrich (1930) and Versluys and others (1936) in the Bolk *Handbuch*. It culminated in the publication of de Beer's (1937) book *The Development of the Vertebrate Skull* which has provided a baseline for all subsequent workers in the field.* Exhaustively thorough, meticulously accurate and illuminated by years of personal observation, this book is a remarkable monument to its author's erudition and multilinguistic ability. Yet it has certain disadvantages. For the most part the illustrations are confined to views of reconstructed skulls; the serial sections on which the reconstructions are based and which are so important for identification of bones, cartilages and related soft tissues, are seldom figured. Moreover, there is little in the way of general introduction or definition of terms, so that (to paraphrase Huxley, 1894), the neophyte has indeed a long and weary process of initiation before becoming an adept in the arcana of the higher anatomy.

The complexity and over-elaboration of the terminology of the developing skull, the increasing failure of most zoologists to appreciate the significance of the structural approach, and above all the apparently

* A. d'A. B. has a particular affection for this book, which he first read in parallel with the novels of Thomas Hardy. Thus one could balance the harrowing misfortunes of Tess and Jude against the timeless serenity of the cavum epiptericum and the sphenethmoid commissures. This method may be recommended to younger students of the chondrocranium.

limited relevance of cranial embryology to the newer branches of biology, have been important reasons for the decline of the subject since the 1930s, at least in the western world. Indeed, it now seems to have become one of the most esoteric areas of biological knowledge, and in Britain few departments of zoology or anatomy even possess the technical expertise and equipment necessary for the study of the subject. This decline is perhaps remarkable in view of the important recent advances which have been made in the study of fossil skulls, and the all too prevalent separation of palaeontology from the morphology of living forms has benefited neither study.

Nevertheless, work still continues. So far as reptiles are concerned, some notable contributions have been made in what may be called the "post de Beer era", and many more species have been described. Romer's (1956) *Osteology of the Reptiles*, another monumental book, contains an excellent introductory account of the reptilian chondrocranium, as does the article in the present series by Starck (1979), whose work is familiar to students of the developing mammalian skull. One should mention in particular the studies of Brock and subsequently of the Stellenbosch school of cranial morphologists in South Africa, and of the Egyptian school, represented by El-Toubi, Kamal and their collaborators. It is a good augury for the future that important papers by Presley in England and by Rieppel in Switzerland have appeared while this article was being written and prepared for press. In view of these contributions a detailed review of cranial ontogeny in Recent reptiles, dealing with variations among the major groups and covering modern work, is clearly due.

B. RECENT GENERAL LITERATURE

The following references (post de Beer, 1937) deal with aspects of the reptilian chondrocranium in general, or in the larger taxa, rather than with its development in particular families, genera or species. Conditions in Squamata are much better known than in other reptilian orders.

Barry, 1963 (middle ear): Bellairs, 1949a, 1972 (orbitotemporal region): Bellairs and Boyd, 1950 (nasal capsule): El-Toubi and Kamal (Squamata only), 1965 (occipital tectum); 1970 (lizards); El-Toubi, Kamal and Hammouda, 1965a, b, 1968 (snakes): Kamal (Squamata only), 1964b (mandibular arch); 1965e (otic capsule and basal plate); 1965f (fenestra X in snakes); 1965g (interorbital septum); 1965h (cranio-vertebral joint); 1966a (single origin of parachordals); 1966b (sphenoid); 1966c (hypoglossal nerve); 1966d (quadrate of snakes); 1968 (nasal concha); 1968/69 (lizards and snakes); 1969b (trabeculae); 1969c (posterior orbital cartilages); 1969e (glossopharyngeal nerve); 1970 (snakes); 1971 (metotic fissure); 1972 (pterygoquadrate); 1973a (prefacial commissure); 1973b (cranio-vertebral joint): Kamal and Hammouda, 1965g (laterosphenoid of snakes): Kesteven, 1940 (skull base): Malan, 1946 (nasal capsule of lepidosaurs): Pratt, 1948 (nasal capsule of lepidosaurs): Presley and Steel, 1976 (orbitotemporal region); Rieppel, 1976a, b, 1977c (orbitotemporal region); 1978a, 1980, (kinesis): Säve-Söderbergh, 1946, 1947 (brain case of lepidosaurs); Shute, 1956 (middle ear): Torien, 1963, 1965a, b (middle ear and otic capsule); 1967 (experimental approach).

Jarvik (1942) described the snout of crossopterygian fishes and devised an interesting and rational system of nomenclature for the nasal capsule and related structures which can to some extent be applied to tetrapods. This nomenclature was used by Bellairs (1949b) and Bellairs and Boyd (1950) for reptiles, but has not been generally followed by students of the chondrocranium. Because of its unfamiliarity it is not (for the most part) used here.

The development of the osteocranium has been less critically studied than that of the chondrocranium and few workers have tried to integrate the "two skulls" in a significant fashion; in this respect the work of Säve-Söderbergh (1946, 1947) is outstanding. Still less is known about the important changes which occur in early postnatal life involving ossification and growth; this seems a promising area for future work. Study of congenital abnormalities is another neglected field; some cranial features of teratological embryos have been described by Bellairs (1965, 1981), Bellairs and Boyd (1957) and Bellairs and Gamble (1960).

The adult skull has remained a more popular subject because of its relevance to function, palaeontology and evolution. Much of the earlier literature has been ably summarized by Romer (1956). The following, comparatively recent articles are, for the most part, only slightly concerned with ontogeny, but contain much of interest to the cranial morphologist.

Allin, 1975 (evolution of ear): Camp, 1923 (lizards): Frazzetta, 1968 (temporal fenestrae): Haas, 1964, 1968 (Scolecophidia): Groombridge, 1979a (vomer of snakes): Iordansky, 1973 (Crocodilia): Jollie, 1960 (lizards): Kiran, 1979 (Squamata): Langebartel, 1968 (hyoid of snakes): Langston, 1973 (Crocodilia): Lombard and Bolt, 1979 (evolution of ear): McDowell and Bogert, 1954 (Squamata): Parrington, 1979 (evolution of ear): Rieppel, 1977a, b; 1978a–f; 1979a–e (Squamata): Robinson, 1967 (evolution of lizards): Schumacher, 1973 (hyoid and larynx of Testudines and Crocodilia): Starck, 1979 (cranial cavities and membranes): Tanner and collaborators (cranial anatomy and systematics of lizards), see Cox and Tanner, 1977. The skulls of Testudines have been extensively studied by Gaffney (see Gaffney, 1979).

General information on the skull of reptiles is given by Wettstein

(1931–54) and Lüdicke (1962–64), Romer (1956, 1966), Bellairs (1969), Guibé (1970) and Bellairs and Attridge (1975). Some associated structures are described by the following authors. Baird, 1970 (ear): Edgeworth, 1935 (muscles): Gabe and Saint Girons, 1976 (nose): Groombridge, 1979b–d (palate and muscles of snakes): Haas, 1973 (muscles): Parsons, 1970 (nose): Schumacher, 1973 (muscles): Underwood, 1970 (eye). Wever and his associates have published many studies on the anatomy and physiology of the reptilian ear, and Wever (1978) has produced an important mono- graph on the subject. The work of Rieppel (1979b–e) and of Groombridge (1979a–d) has systematic implications.

One significant point of terminology has been raised in a recent review of certain aspects of the vertebrate skeleton (Patterson, 1977). While most workers on higher vertebrates have regarded the terms membrane bone and dermal bone as synonymous, Patterson argues that these terms should be used to distinguish between different types of ossifications. He regards dermal bones as those which are either phylogenetically or ontogenetically associated with ectoderm, such as the bones which form the roof of the skull or which line the jaws; the term membrane bone should be re- stricted to those bones which develop deep in mesoderm without replacing cartilage, but which are, with certain exceptions, homologous with cartilage bones in more primitive vertebrates. Such membrane bones are probably very rare within the skulls of tetrapods, although there are instances where the perichondral ossifications of cartilage bones extend peripherally into membrane, as in the prootic and basioccipital of many Squamata. More- over some bones, such as the mammalian alisphenoid, ossify partly in cartilage and partly in membrane.

While Patterson's distinction between membrane and dermal bones seems of theoretical rather than practical value in descriptive studies of higher vertebrates, we have followed his suggested terminology and refer to bones generally called membrane bones (e.g. by de Beer, 1937) as dermal bones throughout.

C. Problems of Cranial Development

In view of the recondite nature of the subject, it is pertinent to con- sider what kinds of general biological information are likely to be obtained from the study of the development of the skull.

1. Developmental studies of the skull and indeed of any part of the skeleton can provide information on such problems as the ontogenetic and phylogenetic relationships of cartilage to bone, the significance of ad- ventitious or secondary cartilage, and the nature of the cells from which the various types of hard tissues are derived. Much important work has

been done in these areas (see Hall, 1975, 1978; Patterson, 1977; Le Lièvre, 1978), but little of it has involved reptiles.

2. It is impossible to form a rational comprehension of the architecture of even a single skull without some knowledge of its development. Such questions as how the brain, nose and inner ear, which initially develop from the surface of the embryo, come to lie within the skull and influence its shape cannot even be asked without reference to embryology.

3. Embryology is of great assistance in making meaningful comparisons between the skulls of animals belonging to different groups. While it may be possible to establish the homologies of bones by direct examination of the adult condition in living and fossil forms, the interpretation of complex patterns is often facilitated by an embryological approach. The outstanding triumph of this method was the establishment of the homologies of the mammalian auditory ossicles by Meckel, Reichert, Gaupp and others; these inferences have been substantiated by more recent palaeontological studies (see Goodrich, 1930; Shute, 1956; Allin, 1975; Lombard and Bolt, 1979; Parrington, 1979). The homologies of the reptilian and mammalian vomer (Parrington and Westoll, 1940) and the nature of the mammalian alisphenoid and pterygoid bones (Presley and Steel, 1976, 1978) are also problems which have yielded to a synthesis of embryological and palaeontological data (see also Moore, 1981).

4. Cranial development may be a pointer to zoological affinity, and to the recognition of rejection of morphological characters as primitive states (see Rieppel, 1979b). Although the theory of recapitulation in its Haeckelian form has now been more or less discredited, it is generally accepted that embryos, at least at certain stages, tend to resemble each other, and hence a common pattern, more than adults. Any striking divergence from the ontogenetic pattern is likely to indicate phylogenetic divergence more clearly than aberrant features of the adult; the latter are often the hallmarks of comparatively recent adaptive specialization.

Thus, the skulls of amphisbaenians differ radically from those of other Squamata in various features, notably in the configuration of the anterior sphenoid region, which is massively ossified, even in young animals, and difficult to interpret. This is one of the characters which seems to justify the recognition of the Amphisbaenia as a distinct group (suborder or order) of the Squamata (see Gans, 1974, 1978), a practice now quite generally followed. It is possible, however, that this feature, like so many other characters of these reptiles, has been evolved as an adaptive specialization, like the reduction of the eyes. Only the study of embryos at suitable cartilaginous stages can tell us how far and in what way this region of the skull has become modified from a common lepidosaurian pattern. Such information might well be relevant to any re-assessment of the taxonomic status of the group, though it is also possible that forms that are very similar in cranial morphology differ in other respects. The validity of the comparative embryological approach is borne out by consideration of the striking differences in the structure of the orbito-temporal region of the chondrocranium in lizards and snakes. The extent of these differences supports the view that the two groups have been distinct from an early geological period, despite the adaptive resemblance among some of their surviving members.

In this connection it is interesting that parts of the chondrocranium may appear and subsequently regress in some reptiles; thus earlier ontogenetic stages may conform more closely to the common pattern in some respects than later ones. Such regressive changes have been described in the orbitotemporal region of the skink *Eumeces* (Rice, 1920), and occur to a much greater extent in birds (Bellairs, 1958).

It is also possible that in a particular species, certain regions of the skull, present in other forms, never become cartilaginous, but could be detectable in a transient, procartilaginous condition. The use of histo-chemical and perhaps autoradiographic techniques (which have hardly been employed by cranial morphologists) might yield information of interest in this connection.

5. Study of the development of the skull may throw some light on its functional adaptations, which are mainly related to its role in housing the brain, pituitary and principal sense organs, and to the jaws and their muscles. Such adaptations are more likely to be evident in the osteo-cranium than in the chondrocranium, and those familiar only with mammalian anatomy might suppose that the latter has no function in the adult, except in so far as it provides a template which can subsequently be converted into bone. Indeed, Romer (1956 and elsewhere) has suggested that cartilage is a tissue particularly adapted for the growth requirements of the embryo. It is, however, the only endoskeletal material of Recent Agnatha, and of Chondrichthyes, in which, however, it may become calcified (see Halstead, 1974). In extant reptiles considerable areas of the chondrocranium composed of hyaline cartilage, such as the nasal capsule, remain unossified in adult life and form integral parts of the functional skull complex. Many features of cranial structure are most readily appreciated in late embryonic and young postnatal stages, which are much easier to section than are the fully ossified adults. Such immature material shows that the chondrocranium participates in certain adaptations such as kinesis, which involves the presence of movable articulations between cartilaginous surfaces at various sites in the skull (see Rieppel, 1978a, and III–E–7 here). Moreover, it seems unlikely that the typical saurian forms of meso- and metakinesis could have evolved without a substantial reduction of the

cartilages forming the side-walls of the front parts of the brain-case.

6. There appears to be no full account of the ossification and growth of the skeleton in embryonic and post-natal stages of any reptile, though there is evidence of interesting neotenic modification of the skull in certain gekkonid and agamid lizards (Stephenson, 1960). *Lacerta vivipara* would seem particularly suitable for such investigations since its embryos can be raised in culture after removal from the mother (see below), and can be staged by means of the normal table compiled by Dufaure and Hubert (1961). Such embryos are in some respects easier to observe and manipulate than those in the parchment-shelled eggs of oviparous species.

A fairly new, and interesting approach to the study of postnatal growth in reptiles is the examination of natural histological marks in the cranial and other bones, which provide an indication of age (Castanet and Naulleau, 1974; Castanet, 1978).

The importance of mechanical factors such as the influence of the developing eyes on the skull could probably also be investigated by the elaboration of current techniques for the culture of reptilian embryos (see Raynaud, 1959; Holder and Bellairs, 1962; Yntema, 1964; New, 1966; Torien, 1967); such studies have been made on birds (Silver, 1962). Similar methods might also facilitate study of the interrelationships of dermal bones and of their sutural patterns by ablation experiements comparable with those performed on mammalian embryos by Girgis and Pritchard (1958; see also Parrington, 1967). The causal relationships between certain structures such as the otocyst and otic capsule (Torien, 1965a, b), and the nasal placode and nasal capsule (Torien and Rossouw, 1977) provide a further field for the kinds of experimental work which have been neglected in reptiles.

8. The physiology of skeletal development and growth, and the influence of endocrine and nutritional factors upon them have hardly been studied in reptiles. The work of Jenkins and Simkiss (1968) suggests that in marine turtles the calcium required for skeletal development of the embryo is derived from the eggshell, and the same appears to be true for crocodilians and birds. In Squamata, on the other hand the embryo obtains all or almost all the calcium it needs from the yolk. Packard *et al.* (1977) have discussed the physiology of reptilian eggs, and further work in this field would be of great interest.

D. Scope and Plan of Present Account

The following section (II) contains a general account of the reptilian chondrocranium particularly when in the state of maximum development (the "fully formed condition"). Our object here is to discuss the general layout and to define terminology, mainly as used by de Beer (1937); some of this ground has also been covered by Starck (1979) in a valuable article in Volume 9 of this series. The present description is mainly based on conditions in lizards, even though in some respects these may depart further from the basic reptilian condition than do certain other groups.

The names of chondrocranial (and of some related) structures are italicized where they first appear (Section II). Elsewhere names have generally been anglicized (e.g. ascending process for processus ascendens).

Section III presents a detailed account of the chondrocranium in one representative of each group of Recent reptiles and a survey of the known variation among other known forms. It must be emphasized that the supposedly characteristic features listed for the various groups are often based on accounts of a few species only. Further study may well show that some of these characters are invalid for diagnostic purposes, and that the range of variation within the group is wider than is indicated by the present state of knowledge.

It has obviously been difficult to draw a line between the developing and the adult skull. The general principle has been to concentrate on matters of ontogenetic interest and on the chondrocranium at all stages in life; thus the nasal capsule, orbitotemporal chondrocranium and the columellar and hyobranchial apparatus (but not the larynx) of the adult are described. The development of the osteocranium and certain features of the adult skull are summarized, but only conditions which seem of special interest are described in detail. Special emphasis is laid on work which has appeared since the publication of de Beer's book in 1937.

This principle has been followed in the bibliography. The references cited beneath the family headings are mostly concerned with the development of the skull, or with parts of the chondrocranium which persist in the adult. Such work has generally involved the use of sectioning techniques. We have tried to make our bibliography of it reasonably comprehensive, at least in so far as twentieth century publications are concerned.

No attempt has been made to review comprehensively the copious literature on the adult bony skull or to describe in any detail such associated structures as muscles and sense organs. However, some important papers on adult cranial anatomy have been or will be listed in various sections, and some others are cited again under the familial headings where this seemed helpful. In previous papers and in his recent monograph (1978), Wever has described the adult ear in a wide range of reptiles. Reference is made under the familial headings to those species in which the columellar apparatus has been figured in any detail by him.

Work on postnatal growth in fossil reptiles (e.g. growth of the frill in ceratopsian dinosaurs) has not been covered.

All the illustrations, whether taken from our own or others' publications, have been re-drawn and a consistent terminology has been used throughout. All figures which are not acknowledged are the work of A. d'A. B., and are mostly based on his own material.

II. Organization, Development and Ossification of the Chondrocranium

A. DEFINITION

The chondrocranium (primordial cranium of some older authors) may be defined as that part of the skull which is found to consist of cartilage at any stage of life. In higher vertebrates the chondrocranium is, of course, most extensive in the embryo; much of it becomes replaced by cartilage bone at some stage during life. Nevertheless, in reptiles, considerable areas of the chondrocranium, notably the nasal capsule and anterior part of the orbitotemporal region, persist in the adult, though they are surrounded by bones of dermal origin. The terms endocranium and braincase are sometimes used, especially by palaeontologists, to designate some areas of the chondrocranium, or in the adult, the parts of the bony skull which ossify in it.

In some vertebrates regions of cartilage may be found during embryonic life or later within certain dermal bones such as the avian ectopterygoid and the mammalian dentary. They do not appear to belong to designated parts of the chondrocranium and are referred to under the heading of secondary or adventitious cartilage. Such cartilage does not seem to have been described in reptiles, but its distribution and significance has been extensively studied in birds (Murray, 1963; see Patterson, 1977).

The basic components of the chondrocranium (Fig. 1A) are (1) an anterior pair of parallel bars, the *trabeculae cranii*, (2) a posterior pair, the *parachordals*, flanking the notochord (trabeculae and parachordals together form the basicranial axis or central stem), (3) a sphenolateral trough represented by the paired *orbital cartilage* system, (4) the *nasal* or *ethmoid capsules*, (5) the *otic* or *auditory capsules*, and (6) a number of vertebral elements, the *occipital* and *preoccipital arches*, which represent serial homologues of vertebrae packed into the back of the skull. Only the posterior region of the skull can be regarded as being of vertebral origin.

Some visceral arch structures such as the *pterygoquadrate or palato-quadrate*, *Meckel's cartilage* and the *hyobranchial* skeleton are incorporated into or associated with the chondrocranium and can be regarded as components of it. They are sometimes referred to under the heading of the *splanchnocranium*.

B. Trabeculae and Parachordals

The trabeculae may be initially quite separate (Kamal, 1969b); during development they always fuse in the midline (sometimes becoming initially connected by a transient *trabecular plate*) to form a *trabecula communis* throughout some part of their length (Figs. 1B; 12; 13; 14; 26). Anteriorly the fused trabeculae form the *nasal septum*. More posteriorly their fates differ among groups. In most reptiles they fuse between the orbits, forming at least the ventral part of the *interorbital septum*; this is known as the *tropitrabic* or *tropibasic* condition (see de Beer, 1937). In snakes however, the trabeculae remain separate between the orbits, illustrating the *platytrabic* or *platybasic* condition (Fig. 71). Rieppel (1979b) uses a slightly different terminology.

The posterior ends of the trabeculae remain unfused and diverge to enclose a space, the *pituitary fenestra** or *hypophysial fenestra*, which contains the pituitary gland. The cerebral branches of the internal carotid arteries usually enter the cranial cavity through the posterior angles of the fenestra (Figs. 1B, C; 2). At first it is very large but later diminishes to a small triangular vacuity. In many reptiles a prominent *basipterygoid* or *basitrabecular process* grows out laterally from the posterior part of each trabecula, and in the adult articulates with the pterygoid and epipterygoid bones. De Beer (1937, p. 392) states that the basitrabecular process gives rise to the basipterygoid process after ossification. Rieppel (1978a) uses the term basipterygoid process for the ossified structure after the lateral wings of the parasphenoid have contributed to it. We have used the term "basipterygoid" for the process both before and after it has become ossified without distinction. Many vertebrates have a pair of small *polar cartilages* that appear on either side of the pituitary fenestra and become incorporated into the skull base; these appear to be absent in reptiles, except perhaps in Crocodilia.

The parachordals develop on either side of and around the notochord. Although supposedly of paired origin, they are fused with each other from their first appearance in many (perhaps all) reptiles, and form a *basal* or *parachordal plate* beneath the brain. The notochord may be completely or partly embedded in this plate (Kamal, 1966a).

The front of the basal plate fuses with the back ends of the trabeculae just behind the pituitary fenestra (Figs. 1B; 13, p. 41). At a slightly later stage, a vacuity, the *basicranial fenestra*, develops within the anterior part of the basal plate by absorption of preexisting cartilage, and enlarges progressively; contrary to earlier views (de Beer, 1937) it is never confluent with the pituitary fenestra, at least in Squamata. The transverse bar called

* Used interchangeably in the Figs. here with *pituitary fossa*.

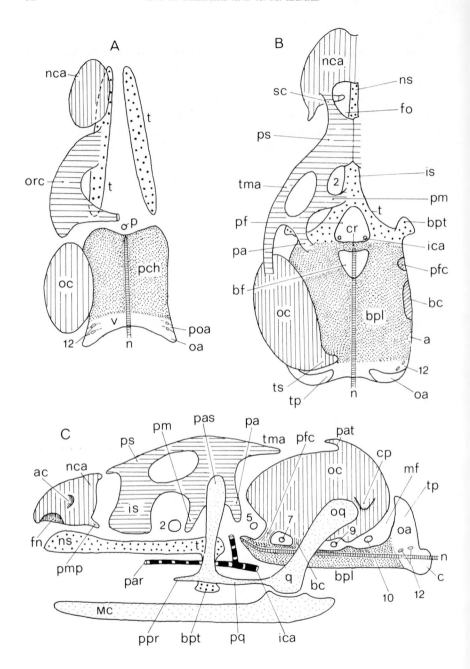

the *crista sellaris* or *acrochordal* which separates the two fenestrae represents the front edge of the fused parachordals or basal plate. It marks the anterior limit of the notochord and eventually becomes ossified to form the dorsum sellae, the posterior wall of the pituitary fossa of the adult. Some workers including Rieppel (1978a) have regarded the crista sellaris as a basic element of the chondrocranium, but this is not borne out by Kamal's (1965f) observations which suggest that it is merely a portion of the front of the basal plate which becomes partly separated from the rest by the development of the basicranial fenestra (see also Kamal and Abdeen, 1972).

The posterior parts of the parachordals, behind the basicranial fenestra, incorporate a number of vertebral elements (Fig. 1); the large hindmost one is called the (main) *occipital arch* which projects from the back of

---

FIG. 1. Schematic diagrams showing basic elements and plan of the chondrocranium of a lizard-like reptile. For the sake of clarity, cranial nerves are designated by arabic numerals throughout. (A) Dorsal view of an early stage. Note the fused parachordals which form most of the basal plate (dark stipple), the paired trabeculae (dotted), and a number of vertebral elements (unshaded), which are attached to the posterior borders of the fused parachordals. The vertebrae consist of a main vertebral element, the occipital arch, and two or more smaller, ill-defined preoccipital arches, recognizable, if at all, in early stages. Other basic elements are the paired nasal capsules (vertical lines), the otic capsules (vertical lines) and the orbital cartilages (horizontal lines), all shown on the left side only. In this diagram and in (B) and (C) the orbital cartilages are shown as a single system (see p. 21). (B) Dorsal view of a later stage. The anterior three-quarters of the trabeculae have fused to form the nasal septum and part of the interorbital septum. The anterior parts of the orbital cartilages are fusing to form the planum supraseptale. The posterior parts of these cartilages have given rise to a system of bars (such as the pila antotica, which form an incomplete side-wall for the cranial cavity). The posterior ends of the trabeculae remain separate and enclose the pituitary fenestra. More posteriorly they have fused with the parachordals which form the basal plate together with the vertebral elements. A basipterygoid (or basitrabecular) process has grown out from each trabecula. The basicranial fenestra has arisen in the basal plate, leaving the crista sellaris (future dorsum sellae) as a bar behind the pituitary. A curved plate of cartilage, the tectum synoticum, has grown posteromedially from each otic capsule and will fuse with a dorsal extension of the occipital arch, the tectum posterius. The two tecta combine to roof over the foramen magnum. (C) Lateral view, also showing (light stipple) the skeleton of the mandibular arch, and the positions of some of the cranial nerves. Some components are shown artificially separated, e.g., of nasal capsule from the septum. (In part after Rieppel, 1978a.)

a, Region of apposition between otic capsule and basal plate; ac, aditus conchae; bc, basicapsular (basicranial) commissure; bf, basicranial fenestra; bpl, basal plate; bpt, basipterygoid process; c, occipital condyle; cp, crista parotica; cr, crista sellaris; fn, fenestra narina; ica, internal carotid artery; is, interorbital septum; fo, fenestra olfactoria; Mc, Meckel's cartilage; mf, metotic fissure; n, notochord (shown as if basal plate was transparent); nca, nasal capsule; ns, nasal septum; oa, occipital arch; oc, otic capsule; oq, otic process of quadrate; orc, orbital cartilage; p, pituitary; pa, pila antotica; par, palatine artery; pas, ascending process of pterygoquadrate (epipterygoid); pat, anterior process of tectum synoticum (not yet formed in B); pch, parachordals; pf, pituitary fenestra; pfc, prefacial commissure; pm, pila metoptica; pmp, posterior maxillary process; poa, preoccipital arches; ppr, pterygoid process of pterygoquadrate; pq, pterygoquadrate (intermediate part); ps, planum supraseptale; q, quadrate; sc, sphenethmoid commissure; t, trabecula; tma, taenia marginalis; tp, tectum posterius; ts, tectum synoticum; v, vertebral elements including occipital and preoccipital arches (unshaded); 2, optic nerve and fenestra; 5, trigeminal nerve root in trigeminal notch (fenestra prootica); 7, 9, 10, 12, facial, glossopharyngeal, vagus and hypoglossal nerves and their foramina.

14 A. D'A. BELLAIRS AND A. M. KAMAL

the basal plate on each side. The smaller ones in front of it are the *preoccipital* arches, and arise from the sides of the parachordals as minute cartilaginous bars, hardly discernible as separate structures. They enclose the roots of the hypoglossal (XII) nerve in separate foramina by fusion, dorsal to the nerve roots, with one another and with the occipital arch. This fusion takes place in postero-anterior sequence (Kamal, 1966c). Reptiles usually have between two and four hypoglossal roots, reflecting the number of preoccipital arches. However, fusion of roots and reduction of hypoglossal foramina may occur during development.

Thus the fully formed chondrocranium of *Crocodylus* has three roots, but earlier embryonic stages sometimes have four (de Beer, 1937).

C. NASAL CAPSULE

The paired *nasal capsules* (Figs. 1–5) invest the nasal sacs and (where present) the organs of Jacobson, and are separated from each other by the nasal septum. The roof and part of the side-wall of each capsule are formed by the *parietotectal cartilage*, which becomes joined on each side to the upper border of the nasal septum. Pratt (1948) believed that the medial part of the capsular roof is morphologically distinct from the rest

FIG. 2. Diagram, dorsal view, of the fully formed chondrocranium of an embryonic lacertid lizard. (Based on Goodrich, 1930.) Parts of the nasal and otic capsules and of the orbitotemporal region on the right side have been cut away to show nerves and other structures. The letters on the right show very approximately the level of sections in Figs. 3, 6, and 8.

ac, Aditus conchae; bc, basicapsular commissure; bf, basicranial fenestra; bpl, basal plate; bpt, basipterygoid process; c, occipital condyle; chy, ceratohyal; cJo', concha of Jacobson's organ; cp, crista parotica; cr, crista sellaris; cu, nasal cupola; ec, ectochoanal cartilage; ef, foramen for endolymphatic duct; ep, epipterygoid; fa, foramen apicale; fe, foramen epiphaniale; fep, fenestra epiotica; fl, fenestra lateralis; fm, fenestra metoptica; fn, fenestra narina; fo, fenestra olfactoria; fop, fenestra optica; fp, foramen for perilymphatic duct; fsu, fenestra superior; g, ophthalmic ganglion; ic, intercalary (processus paroticus of earlier stage); ica, internal carotid artery; ip, insertion plate of extracolumella; is, interorbital septum; jf, jugular foramen; jv, internal jugular vein; lta, lamina transversalis anterior; m, basipterygoid meniscus; Mc, Meckel's cartilage; mf, metotic fissure; n, notochord; nc, nasal concha; ng (lateral) nasal gland; ns, nasal septum; oa, occipital arch; oc, otic capsule; onf, orbitonasal fissure; pa, pila antotica; pacc, pila accessoria; pai, processus alaris inferior; pasu, processus alaris superior; pat, anterior process of tectum; pf, pituitary fossa; pfc, prefacial commissure; pi, internal process of extracolumella; pla, planum antorbitale; pm, pila metoptica; pma, pmp, anterior and posterior maxillary processes; pn, prootic notch; pnc, paranasal cartilage; ps, planum supraseptale; psc, paraseptal cartilage; pt, pterygoid bone (segment only shown); ptc, parietotectal cartilage; q, quadrate; sc, sphenethmoid commissure; si, subiculum infundibuli; sta, stapedial artery; t, trabecula; tc, trabecula communis; te, tectum; tm, taenia medialis; tma, taenia marginalis; 1, olfactory and vomeronasal nerves; 2, optic nerve; 3, oculomotor nerve; 4, trochlear nerve; 5, trigeminal nerve (roots); 5a, ophthalmic nerve; 5al, 5am, lateral and medial ethmoidal branches of ophthalmic nerve; 5b, maxillary nerve; 5c, mandibular nerve; 5g, main trigeminal ganglion; 6, abducens nerve; 7, facial nerve and foramen; 7ct, chorda tympani branch of facial nerve; 7p, a, palatine branch of facial nerve and palatine artery; 8, auditory nerve and foramina; 9, glossopharyngeal nerve; 10, vagus; 12, hypoglossal nerve and foramina.

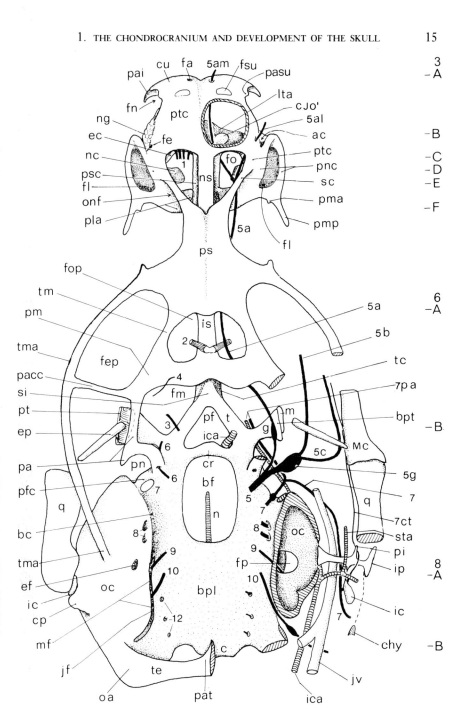

of the parietotectal cartilage and termed it the dorsal plate (see Fig. 38A, III–A–12). This interesting suggestion has not been followed by most recent workers. In many reptiles another cartilage, the *paranasal cartilage*, is said to develop mid way along the side of the capsule, lateral to the parietotectal cartilage with which it becomes fused. The parietotectal and paranasal cartilages may participate in the formation of a cartilaginous nasal concha which projects medially into the nasal cavity (see Kamal, 1968, p. 49 here). A large opening, the *fenestra lateralis*, is often present in the side-wall of this part of the capsule, so that the concha is exposed in lateral view. At the front of the capsule is another large opening, the *fenestra narina*, through which the vestibule of the nose communicates with the external nostril. This fenestra may be bounded anterodorsally and anteroventrally by the *superior* and *inferior* alar *processes*. There may also be a *fenestra superior* in the roof of the capsule, and in addition, there are generally two small foramina for the terminal branches of the medial and lateral ethmoidal nerves; these are called respectively, the *foramen apicale* and *foramen epiphaniale* (Fig. 2).

A large vacuity in the parietotectal cartilage on each side, lateral to the nasal septum, is called the *fenestra olfactoria advehens*. Posterior to these fenestrae two bars of cartilage, the *sphenethmoid commissures*, converge medially to connect the back of the nasal capsule with part of the orbital cartilage system, the *planum* or *solum supraseptale*. Beneath the commissures, the posterior wall of the capsule is formed by the *planum antorbitale* (or lamina orbitonasalis, postnasal wall). The space between the sphenethmoid commissures and the top of the nasal septum is designated the *fenestra olfactoria evehens*, because it carries the olfactory and associated vomeronasal nerves away from the brain. After traversing

---

FIG. 3. *Lacerta vivipara*, late embryo. Transverse sections through nasal and anterior orbital region. The plane of section is somewhat oblique, the right side of each section being posterior to the left. The small arrows in (C) indicate fusion of cartilage slightly behind this level. The retina and associated structures are not shown in (F).

ac, Aditus conchae; cg, choanal groove; cJo', concha of Jacobson's organ; cu, nasal cupola; d, dentary; dJo, duct of Jacobson's organ; dng, duct of nasal gland; e, eye; ec, ectochoanal cartilage; ecp, ectopterygoid; f, frontal; fa, foramen apicale; fs, fenestra in nasal septum; Hg, Harderian gland; is, interorbital septum; j, jugal; Jo, Jacobson's organ; lc, lachrymal canaliculus; ld, lachrymal duct; le, lens; lta, lamina transversalis anterior; Mc, Meckel's cartilage; mx, maxilla; na, nasal; nc, nasal concha; ng, (lateral) nasal gland; npl, plug of epithelium in nostril; ns, nasal septum; nsa, nasal sac (vestibule); o, scleral ossicle; ob, olfactory bulb; pal, palatine; pap, papillary cartilage; pfr, prefrontal; pla, planum antorbitale; pmp, posterior maxillary process; pmx, premaxilla; pmxa, ascending process of premaxilla; pnc, paranasal cartilage; psc, paraseptal cartilage; ptc, parietotectal cartilage; r, lateral (extraconchal) recess of nasal sac; sc, sphenethmoid commissure; scc, scleral cartilage; smx, septomaxilla; sob, superior oblique muscle; tg, tongue; to, tooth; v, vomer; l', olfactory and vomeronasal nerves, 5a, ophthalmic nerve; 5al, 5am, lateral and medial ethmoidal branches of ophthalmic nerve; 5b, maxillary nerve; 5c, mandibular nerve; 7p. palatine nerve.

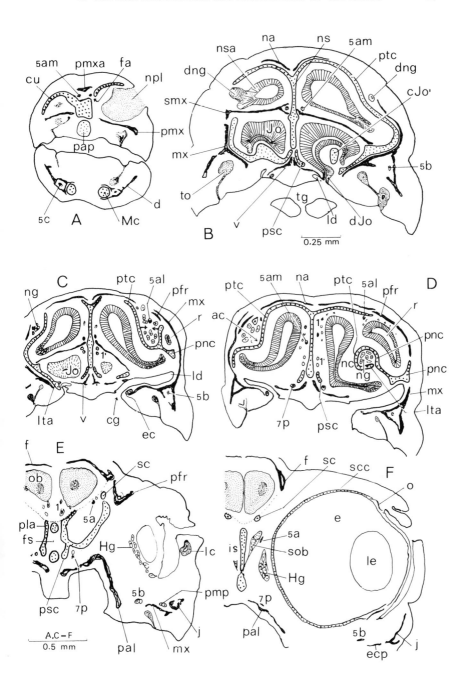

this fenestra on each side, these nerves enter the nasal capsule through the fenestra olfactoria advehens described above (Fig. 4). They then pass forwards to join the sensory cells of the olfactory mucosa and of the dorsal dome of Jacobson's organ respectively (see Parsons, 1970). The fenestra olfactoria advehens and the f. o. evehens together make up the *fenestra olfactoria*.

The main ethmoidal branch of the ophthalmic nerve (Va) passes forwards on each side of the interorbital septum beneath the planum supraseptale and then runs through a space, the *orbitonasal fissure*, between the sphenethmoid commissure and the top of the planum antorbitale. It then enters the nasal capsule with the olfactory nerves through the fenestra olfactoria advehens and soon divides into its medial and lateral branches which leave the nasal capsule through the foramina apicale and epiphaniale respectively. Both the orbitonasal fissure and the space between the fenestrae olfactoria evehens and advehens are outside the nasal capsule.

The back of the planum antorbitale may have a free-ending projection, the *posterior maxillary process*, which extends posteriorly above the palatal shelf of the maxilla (Figs. 2; 3E). It may also have a small anterior projection, the *anterior maxillary process*. The posterior maxillary process appears to be a derivative of the visceral arch skeleton (an anterior extension from the pterygoquadrate) which has become attached to the nasal capsule.

In Squamata the floor of the nasal capsule is less complete than the roof. Indeed, the only part of the floor which may be complete lies just behind the bottom of the fenestra narina. Here a plate of cartilage, the *lamina transversalis anterior*, arises from each side of the nasal septum and may join the parietotectal cartilage laterally, forming a complete ring of cartilage or *zona annularis*. In *Lacerta* the zona is situated at a level slightly anterior to that in Figure 3B (right). The part of the lamina beneath the organ of Jacobson is often called the *cartilage of Jacobson's organ*, from which a small *concha of Jacobson's organ* projects.

Typically in lizards, two processes pass posteriorly on each side horizontally beneath the nasal sac from the rear edge of the lamina transversalis anterior. The medial one is the long, narrow *paraseptal cartilage* which lies along the side of the lower edge of the nasal septum; it may extend posteriorly to join the planum antorbitale. In some forms its origin from the lamina transversalis anterior is narrowed, and it may even occur as a separate cartilage detached from both the lamina and the planum antorbitale. The shorter, more lateral process of the lamina is the *ectochoanal cartilage* which passes posteriorly within the tissues of the palate and supports the palatal part of the lachrymal duct and choanal groove (Figs. 3C; 4). The gap between the paraseptal and ectochoanal cartilages more or less conforms to the gap or fissure between the vomer and maxilla which lie ventral to them. The duct of the organ of Jacobson reaches the palate through the front of the gap, while the nasopharyngeal duct leads down to the internal nostril more posteriorly through the big *choanal vacuity* (*fenestra basalis*) in front of the planum antorbitale (Fig. 18).

The early development of the nasal capsule deserves further study. Skinner (1973) has suggested that in the skink *Mabuya* the entire capsule, except for the sphenethmoid commissures, planum antorbitale, posterior maxillary process and perhaps the paraseptal cartilages, derived from the fused trabeculae or trabecular plate. The distinctiveness of the parieto-tectal and paranasal cartilages is certainly doubtful (p. 51); in the preceding account (p. 16), however, the traditional terminology used by de Beer (1937) has been followed.

The nasal capsule of Testudines and Crocodilia differs considerably from that of Squamata, being more complete ventrally, and therefore more thoroughly investing the nasal sac on each side.

No cartilage bones are known to ossify within the nasal capsule of

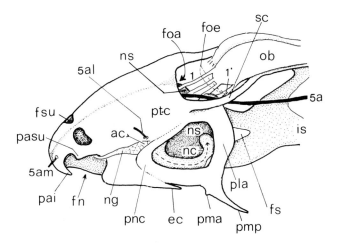

FIG. 4. Diagram of nasal capsule of a lacertid lizard seen obliquely in left lateral view.

ac, Aditus conchae (arrow, partly in broken lines, passes through aditus and cavum conchale); ec, ectochoanal cartilage; fn, fenestra narina; foa, foe, fenestra olfactoria advehens and evehens; fs, fenestra in nasal septum; fsu, fenestra superior; is, interorbital septum; nc, nasal concha seen through lateral fenestra; ng, nasal gland; ns, nasal septum; ob, olfactory bulb; pai, processus alaris inferior; pasu, processus alaris superior; pla, planum antorbitale; pma, pmp, anterior and posterior maxillary processes; pnc, paranasal cartilage; ptc, parietotectal cartilage; sc, sphenethmoid commissure; 1, 1', olfactory and vomeronasal nerves; 5a, ethmoidal continuation of ophthalmic nerve passing through orbitonasal fissure (unlabelled); 5al, 5am, lateral and medial ethmoidal branches of ophthalmic nerve, leaving foramen epiphaniale and foramen apicale respectively.

Recent or fossil reptiles. It is, however, invested by dermal bones such
as the maxilla, nasal, vomer and palatine on each side. One of its associated bones, the septomaxilla, is primarily related to the nasal vestibule,
but in Squamata it extends posteriorly within the capsule and separates
the nose proper from the organ of Jacobson (see Malan, 1946; Fig. 3B
here).

D. ORBITOTEMPORAL REGION

Theoretically, the orbitotemporal region can be envisaged as an open
trough of cartilage (*orbital cartilage* system; sphenolateral plate, Starck,
1979), supporting the forebrain, with an underlying median keel, the
interorbital septum. The trough is roofed over mainly by the dermal
frontal and parietal bones. This seems to have been the condition in
primitive reptiles (see Romer, 1956) and is more or less realized in
Testudines and Crocodilia. It is modified in Squamata, particularly
in snakes. The following account is based on lizards, in which much of
the orbital cartilage system is reduced to a scaffolding of bars enclosing
fenestrae filled with membrane (Figs. 2, 5, 6).

The posterior ends of the sphenethmoid commissures pass backwards
from the roof of the nasal capsule. They unite just posterior to the level
of the olfactory bulbs to form the trough-like planum supraseptale which
supports the olfactory peduncles of the forebrain. Beneath the planum is
the high, thin interorbital septum which usually contains one or more
membrane-filled fenestrae; the oblique muscles of the eye take origin from
its anterior part (Figs. 3F; 23C). The interorbital septum is continuous
anteriorly with the nasal septum; posteriorly its edge falls abruptly and
continues backwards as a short, rod-like trabecula communis. Further
back still, the latter forks into the two trabeculae enclosing the pituitary
fenestra.

Two separate bars arise from the back of the planum supraseptale on
each side. The outer one, the *taenia* marginalis*, passes posteriorly to the
roof of the otic capsule beneath the margins of the frontal and parietal
bones (Figs. 2, 5). The inner one, the *taenia medialis* (taenia parietalis
media), passes back to become connected with a vertical pillar (often
kinked), the *pila* antotica* (or prootica) which joins the side of the basal
plate. The taenia medialis is connected laterally with the taenia marginalis by the *pila accessoria*. It is also joined medially by another bar,
the *pila metoptica*, which joins its opposite fellow in the midline to form
a small trough, the *subiculum infundibuli*; this supports the base of the

* *Taenia* (f) (Latin), a ribbon; *pila* (f), a pillar.

infundibulum of the brain. The front of the subiculum is called the *cartilago hypochiasmatica*, because it underlies the optic chiasma; anteriorly it is continuous with the back of the interorbital septum.

The more anterior cartilages of the orbitotemporal region, particularly the planum supraseptale, are sometimes referred to as the *anterior orbital cartilages*, while the more posterior ones such as the pila antotica and metoptica are called *posterior orbital cartilages* (Kamal, 1969c; Kamal and Abdeen, 1972). The cartilages of the orbitotemporal region give origin to some of the eye muscles and enclose membrane-filled fenestrae through which pass cranial nerves and blood vessels (Goodrich, 1930; Säve-Söderbergh, 1947; Bellairs, 1949a; Underwood, 1970; Starck 1979); see Figs. 5; 9; 19; 33; 41; 46. Thus the optic nerve (II) passes out on each side through the fenestra optica in front of the pila metoptica at the back of the interorbital septum, the oculomotor (III) and trochlear (IV) nerves pass out behind this pila through the fenestra metoptica (which also transmits the pituitary vein and sometimes the ophthalmic artery), while the trigeminal nerve root (V) passes through the *prootic notch* or *fenestra prootica* between the pila antotica and the front of the otic capsule. The fenestra epioptica transmits no structures. In many reptiles the abducens nerve (VI) perforates or grooves the front of the basal plate near its junction with the root of the pila antotica.

Säve-Söderbergh (1947, p. 501) has pointed out that the fenestrae are much larger than the structures which pass through them and has suggested that the configuration of the cartilaginous lattice in lepidosaurs is related to the stresses set up by the contraction of various eye muscles. Although he does not discuss this matter in depth, his suggestion is of considerable interest. It is well known that hollow bones, such as the wing bones of birds, are frequently reinforced by specially oriented struts and trabeculae. However, little if any attention has been given to the influence of mechanical factors on the structure of the large tracts of cartilage which are retained in the adult skeletons of many non-mammalian vertebrates.

In some fossil amphibians and reptiles the anterior part of the orbito-temporal chondrocranium appears to have ossified as a sphenethmoid bone. This is V or Y-shaped in cross section, the arms representing the trough-like planum supraseptale, the apex or vertical bar representing the interorbital septum (Romer, 1956). This bone is well figured in the Carboniferous labyrinthodont *Loxomma* by Beaumont (1977; Fig. 5B) and in the pelycosaur *Dimetrodon* by Romer and Price (1940; Fig. 5C). In such forms the sides of the trough would partly correspond with the orbitosphenoids or lesser sphenoid wings of mammalian anatomy, while the ventral keel derived from the interorbital septum would correspond with

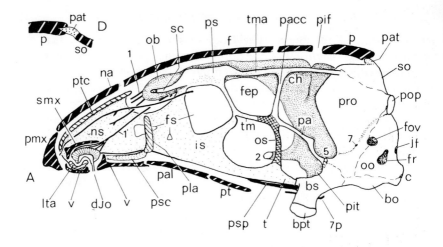

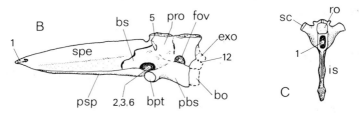

FIG. 5. (A) Diagram showing chondrocranium, cartilage bones, some dermal bones and parts of the brain in a lizard such as a lacertid, seen partly in longitudinal section. The orbitotemporal region of the chondrocranium and ossified brain case are shown intact, as in lateral view. Sectioned cartilages are shown in slanting lines, sectioned dermal bones in slanting white lines on black. (B) Ossified brain-case of the labyrinthodont *Loxomma acutirhinus* from the left side. The nasal capsule anterior to the sphenethmoid was not ossified. After Beaumont (1977). (C) Ossified sphenethmoid of the pelycosaur *Dimetrodon limbatus* in posterior view. After Romer and Price (1940). (D) Median section through skull roof of adult *Varanus*, showing cartilaginous anterior process of tectum fitting into recess in parietal.

bo, Basioccipital; bs, basisphenoid; bpt, basipterygoid process; c, occipital condyle; ch, cerebral hemisphere; dJo, duct of Jacobson's organ; exo, exoccipital; f, frontal; fep, fenestra epiotica; fov, fenestra ovalis; fr, fenestra rotunda; fs, fenestra in nasal or interorbital septum; is, interorbital septum; jf, jugular foramen (for vagus nerve); lta, lamina transversalis anterior; na, nasal; ns, nasal septum; ob, olfactory bulb; oo, otooccipital (opisthotic + exoccipital); os, orbitosphenoid (ossification in pila metoptica); p, parietal; pa, pila antotica (root shown as ossified in A); pacc, pila accessoria; pal, palatine; pat, (cartilaginous) anterior process of tectum; pbs, parabasisphenoid; pif, pineal foramen; pit, stalk of pituitary; pla, planum antorbitale; pmx, premaxilla; pop, paroccipital process; pro, prootic; ps, planum supraseptale; psc, paraseptal cartilage; psp, parasphenoid rostrum (black in A); pt, pterygoid; ptc, parietotectal cartilage; ro, roof of sphenethmoid; sc, sphenethmoid commissure (ossified in C); smx, septomaxilla; so, supraoccipital; spe, sphenethmoid bone; t, trabecula; tm, taenia medialis; tma, taenia marginalis; v, vomer; 1 and 1′, olfactory and vomeronasal nerves, canals for same, and/or in C, for olfactory peduncles; 2, 3, 6, region of foramina for optic, oculomotor, and abducens nerves; 5, approximate position of trigeminal nerve in prootic notch, and opening for nerve in B; 5a, ethmoidal branch of ophthalmic nerve; 7, approximate site of exit of facial nerve; 7p, palatine nerve traversing Vidian canal; 12, foramina for hypoglossal nerve.

the presphenoid. A rather similar ossification occurs in Recent amphisbaenians (p. 130).

In other Recent reptiles the anterior part of the orbitotemporal region, in front of the pituitary fossa, is only lightly, if at all, ossified in the adult. However, in some lizards parts of the taeniae mediales, pila metoptica and perhaps of adjacent regions may ossify (or at least calcify) in mature individuals to form a small orbitosphenoid on each side above and behind the optic nerve (Fig. 5A). The interorbital septum or trabecula communis rarely has a median ossification and if such a separate bone occurs it is best termed a septosphenoid rather than a presphenoid, the latter name being usefully reserved for mammals (see Bellairs, 1949a).

The pila antotica may ossify to form a small bone, here called the pleurosphenoid on each side of the cranial cavity. It's relation to the branches of the trigeminal nerve shows that it is not homologous with the alisphenoid of mammals, which in part at least, represents the reptilian epipterygoid (Fig. 9). Recent lepidosaurs rarely if ever have a pleurosphenoid, but the bone is well developed in crocodilians, in some extinct archosaurs, and in birds. A comparable, though not homologous bone, here called the laterosphenoid, is found in snakes (p. 185), in the skink *Acontias* (p. 70), and perhaps in amphisbaenians.

The more posterior part of the orbitotemporal chondrocranium becomes ossified in all reptiles. The divergent, posterior ends of the trabeculae, the crista sellaris and (when present) the basipterygoid processes ossify to form the basisphenoid in which the pituitary fossa is situated (Figs. 5A; 6B; 9A). In some reptiles the retractor bulbi group of eye muscles takes origin from this fossa and partly fills it (Säve-Söderbergh, 1946); so the size of the fossa may give no true indication of the size of the pituitary gland.

The ventral surface of the ossifying basisphenoid becomes fused with an underlying plate of dermal bone, the parasphenoid (Figs. 6B; 9A). In sectioned material it may be difficult to distinguish between the cartilage-replacement and dermal ossifications, and Kesteven (1940) has denied that a parasphenoid (at least in this position) occurs in Recent reptiles. However, his view has not been confirmed by more recent workers. The combined bone may conveniently be called the parabasisphenoid. In lizards it has a long slender *rostrum* (processus cultriformis) which extends anteriorly beneath the interorbital septum and is probably entirely of dermal origin.

In fusing with the basisphenoid beneath the pituitary region, the parasphenoid encloses the internal carotid arteries and palatine branches of the facial (VII) nerves in the *Vidian* or *parabasal canals*, which in lizards pass through the bases of the basipterygoid processes (Figs. 2; 5;

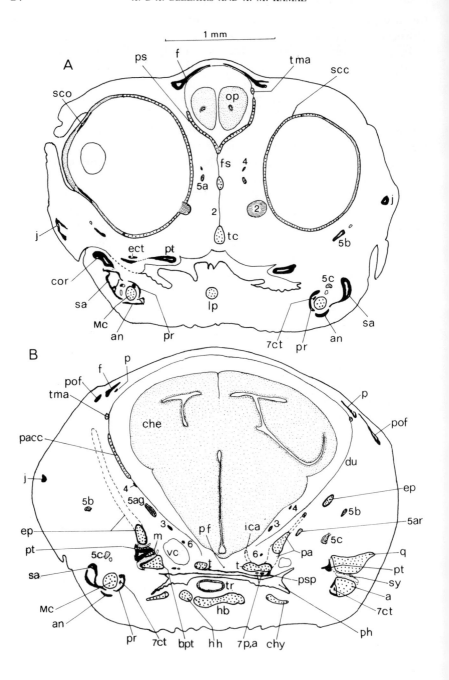

6B). After entering the canal each artery gives off a cerebral carotid branch which curves dorsally to enter the pituitary fossa through the carotid foramen on each side (Figs. 1C; 6B; 9A). The arterial stem typically continues anteriorly with the nerve to issue from the front of the canal as the palatine artery. The cerebral carotid is referred to as the internal carotid artery in the figures and later text of this article.

E. OTIC AND OCCIPITAL REGIONS

The large *otic* (*auditory*) *capsule* chondrifies around the derivatives of the otocyst on each side, enclosing the various inner ear structures in partly separate cavities, the main ones being the *cavum cochleare* and *cavum vestibulare* (see de Beer, 1937). The walls of these cavities are raised up into prominences on the surface of the capsule. The cochlear portion of the capsule (around the cavum cochleare) bulges inwards so that it overlaps the basal plate (Fig. 2). However, the cochlear portion and basal plate appear to develop quite independently although they become connected with each other at an early stage (Kamal and Abdeen, 1972). A conspicuous ridge, the *crista parotica*, develops over the prominence for the lateral semicircular canal. This ridge becomes or contributes to the paroccipital process of the adult, against which the head of the quadrate or otic process abuts.

The ventrolateral wall of the capsule covering the cavum cochleare contains the *fenestra ovalis* (fenestra vestibuli) in which the footplate of the columella auris or stapes rests (Figs. 7; 8A). Kamal (1965f) believed that in Squamata this fenestra arises as the result of regression of the

---

FIG. 6. *Lacerta vivipara*, late embryo. Transverse sections (from same series as Fig. 3) through head. (A) passes behind the middle of the orbits, (B) (on left) through the cavum epiptericum. On this side the distal part of the epipterygoid is reconstructed (in broken lines) as if seen from the front. On the right the cerebral branch of the internal carotid artery is similarly reconstructed to show it entering the cranial cavity at a slightly more posterior level. The junction between the two portions of the right pila antotica is similarly illustrated. The retina and associated structures are not shown in (A), and no muscles are shown.

a, Articular; an, angular; bpt, basipterygoid process; che, cerebral hemisphere; chy, ceratohyal; cor, coronoid; du, dura; ect, ectopterygoid; ep, epipterygoid; f, frontal; fs, fenestra in interorbital septum; hb, hyoid body; hh, hypohyal; ica, internal carotid; j, jugal; lp, lingual process of hyoid; m, basipterygoid meniscus; Mc, Meckel's cartilage; op, olfactory peduncle; p, parietal; pa, pila antotica; pacc, pila accessoria; pf, pituitary fossa (front of); ph, pharynx; pof, postfrontal; pr, prearticular; ps, planum supraseptale; psp, ossifying parasphenoid; pt, pterygoid; q, quadrate; sa, surangular; scc, scleral cartilage; sco, scleral ossicle; sy, synovial cavity of jaw joint; t, trabecula; tc, trabecula communis; tma, taenia marginalis; tr, trachea; vc, vena capitis; 2, optic nerve and fenestra optica; 3, oculomotor nerve; 4, trochlear nerve; 5a, ophthalmic nerve; 5ag, ophthalmic ganglion; 5ar, root of ophthalmic nerve; 5b, maxillary nerve; 5c, mandibular nerve; 6, abducens nerve; 7ct, chorda tympani; 7 p,a, palatine nerve and artery (in Vidian canal, still unclosed).

preexisting cartilaginous wall of the capsule. Perhaps the regression is associated with pressure from the developing columellar footplate; however, the observations of Jaskoll and Maderson (1978) on the chick embryo suggest that more complex factors are involved.

The medial wall of the capsule (Fig. 2) is pierced by one or more foramina for the auditory-vestibular (VIII) nerve, and more posteriorly by the *endolymphatic foramen*, or foramen for the endolymphatic (or otic) duct, which leaves the *cavum vestibuli posterius*. The endolymphatic duct arises from the saccule of the inner ear and passes through its foramen into the cranial cavity where it terminates in the endolymphatic sac (Fig. 8A). In many geckos this sac is greatly enlarged and may issue from the skull between the bones of the vault, or through the jugular foramen. It is probable that the calcareous material which it contains is utilized in the formation of the strongly calcified gekkonid eggshell (see Camp, 1923; Kluge, 1967; Halstead, 1974).

The ventral wall of the otic capsule in the region of the cavum cochleare is pierced by the *perilymphatic foramen* for the perilymphatic or periotic duct (sometimes called the fenestra cochleae) described below.

The medial wall of the otic capsule is partly joined with the basal plate in a somewhat complicated fashion (Figs. 1C; 2). Anteriorly, the capsule and plate are separated by the *prootic* notch in which lies the main ganglion of the trigeminal nerve (V), its root passing inward to the brain. The ophthalmic ganglion is often separate and somewhat anterior to the main ganglion. Behind the prootic notch and often joining the front of the capsule to the basal plate is a bar of cartilage, the *prefacial commissure*; this develops in front of the facial nerve, enclosing it in the facial foramen. Behind this foramen the capsule and plate are joined together by the long anterior *basicapsular* or *basicranial commissure*. Further back still, behind the commissure, and between the otic capsule and basal plate there is a long, narrow gap, the *metotic fissure*. In many reptiles this becomes more or less subdivided into an anterior and a posterior region by apposition of a part of the otic capsule of the adjacent part of the basal plate. This apposition could be regarded as a posterior basicapsular commissure, though Kamal (1965e) is doubtful of this identification. The anterior region of the fissure contains a part of the perilymphatic system within an extra-cranial space, the *recessus scalae tympani* (see below); it also transmits the glossopharyngeal (IX) nerve. The posterior region, generally called the *jugular foramen*, transmits the vagus (X) and (when present) the accessory (XI) nerves (Figs. 2; 7; 8).

It is worth noting that most adult reptiles lack a large vein passing through this "jugular" foramen which in this article is essentially regarded as the foramen for the Xth nerve. However, in early reptilian embryos this foramen is traversed by a vessel corresponding with the internal jugular of mammals. Subsequently this vessel disappears and is functionally replaced by the posterior cerebral vein, which leaves the skull through the foramen magnum and joins the vena capitis lateralis. The latter passes backwards to become the internal jugular vein of the adult (see O'Donoghue, 1920; Brock, 1929; Romer, 1956; Rieppel, 1978c).

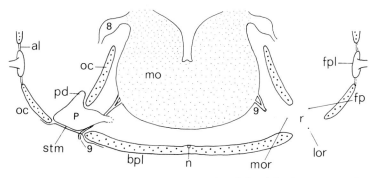

Fig. 7. Diagrammatic transverse section through ear region of a lizard showing recessus scalae tympani. The perilymphatic sac within the recessus is shown on the left side only, with the glossopharyngeal nerve issuing posterior to it. Compare with Fig. 8A (left).

al, Annular ligament of footplate; bpl, basal plate; fp, perilymphatic foramen (for perilymphatic duct); fpl, footplate of columella in fenestra ovalis; lor, lateral opening of recessus scale tympani; mo, medulla oblongata; mor, medial opening of recessus; n, notochord; oc, otic capsule; P, perilymphatic duct; pd, perilymphatic duct; r, recessus scalae tympani; stm, secondary tympanic membrane filling an aperture more or less homologous with the fenestra rotunda of mammals; 8, auditory ganglion and nerve; 9, glossopharyngeal nerve.

The relations of the perilymphatic duct and sac are important in understanding this region of the chondrocranium; they are illustrated by Starck (1979) and in Figures 7 and 8A of this chapter. The duct leaves the ear through the perilymphatic foramen (or foramen cochleae) in the floor of the otic capsule, and then expands to form the perilymphatic sac, extending outside the otic capsule. The extra-capsular space, occupied by the sac, is called the recessus scalae tympani, and represents the most anterior part of the metotic fissure.

The recessus scalae tympani occupies a roughly triangular area; it has a dorsal opening (the perilymphatic foramen), a medial opening (sometimes called the perilymphatic aqueduct), and a lateral opening towards the pharyngo-tympanic cavity. The perilymphatic sac extends through the medial opening towards the brain, and communicates with the subarachnoid space. The lateral or ventrolateral wall of the sac fills the lateral opening of the recessus and lies against the membrane lining the pharyngo-tympanic cavity. The two membranes, and an interposed thin

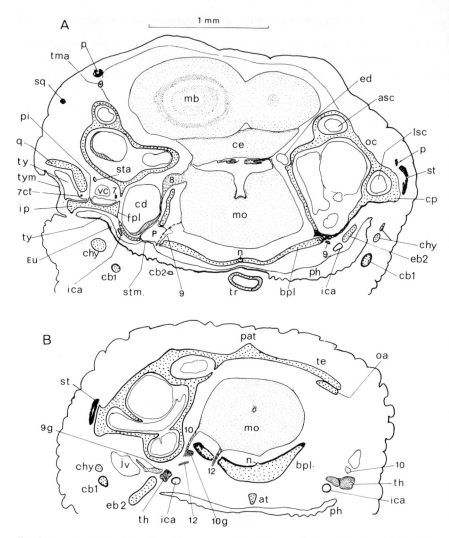

FIG. 8. *Lacerta vivipara*, late embryo. Transverse sections from same series as Figs. 3 and 6, through otic and occipital regions. (A) (left side) shows the columellar apparatus (united medial and lateral rudiments) and the recessus scalae tympani, not labelled as such but occupied by the perilymphatic sac (P). Compare with Fig. 7. Fig. 6B shows a more posterior level, somewhat anterior to the occipital condyle. Muscles are not shown.

asc, Anterior semicircular canal; at, atlas (hypapophysis); bpl, basal plate; cb1, cb2, ceratobranchials 1 and 2; cd, cochlear duct (lagena); ce, cerebellum; chy, ceratohyal; cp, crista parotica; eb2, epibranchial 2; ed, endolymphatic duct; Eu, Eustachian tube; fpl, footplate of columella in fenestra ovalis; ica, internal carotid artery; ip, insertion plate of extracolumella; jv, internal jugular vein; lsc, lateral semicircular canal; mb, midbrain; mo, medulla oblongata; n, notochord; oa, occipital arch; oc, otic capsule; P, perilymphatic sac; p, parietal; pat, anterior process of tectum (base); ph, pharynx; pi, internal process of columellar apparatus; q, quadrate; sq, squamosal; st, supratemporal; sta, stapedial artery; stm, secondary tympanic membrane; te, tectum; th, thymus; tma, taenia marginalis; tr, trachea; ty, tympanic cavity; tym, tympanic membrane; vc, vena capitis; 7, facial nerve; 7ct, chorda tympani; 8, auditory nerve; 9, 9g, glossopharyngeal nerve and ganglion (nerve shown in broken line in A, left, as it emerges at a slightly more posterior level); 10, 10g, vagus nerve and ganglion; 12, rootlets of hypoglossal nerve.

layer of connective tissue, form the secondary tympanic membrane (Figs. 7; 8A, left); the lateral opening of the recessus seems to correspond, at least in part, with the mammalian fenestra rotunda and is often called by this name (Brock, 1929; Goodrich, 1930).

In many reptiles the glossopharyngeal nerve (IX) passes laterally from the brain through the recessus, leaving the skull just behind the secondary tympanic membrane; however, its course varies in different forms (see Fig. 53).

In the adult skull the region of the metotic fissure that contains the recessus scalae tympani, the fenestra rotunda and the secondary tympanic membrane is transformed into the *occipital recess* in the fused opisthotic and exoccipital bones (Fig. 41A); from this the glossopharyngeal nerve generally issues.

Apart from the nasal capsule, the occipital region is the only part of the chondrocranium which has a roof. In some forms such as *Sphenodon* the roof is derived entirely from a process which rises up on each side from the otic capsule and fuses on the midline with its opposite fellow to form the dorsal border of the foramen magnum. Such a roof, derived only from the otic capsule, is called the *tectum synoticum*. *Sphenodon* lacks a *tectum posterius*. However, in many other reptiles the dorsal parts of the occipital arches, which correspond with the neural arches of vertebrae, form one behind the tectum synoticum; the two tecta develop in continuity to produce a tectum synoticum plus posterius, or more simply, an occipital tectum (see El-Toubi and Kamal, 1965; Fig. 1B here). In lizards the tectum has an *anterior* or *ascending process* which projects forwards into or beneath the back of the parietal and remains unossified throughout life (Figs. 2; 5). Fusion between the developing tectum and the posterior part of the basal plate closes the posterior aspect of the metotic fussure.

The otic-occipital region becomes almost entirely ossified, though it may contain areas of cartilage at the time of birth or hatching. The basioccipital ossifies around the notochord in the region of the fused parachordals and eventually closes the basicranial fenestra, while the paired exoccipitals ossify in the occipital arch regions of the basal plate and contain the foramina for the hypoglossal (XII) nerve roots. In many reptiles the single condyle is tripartite, the central portion being formed from the basioccipital, the dorsal or lateral portions from the exoccipitals. The composition of the cranio-vertebral joint differs in the different groups of reptiles (see II–H). The supraoccipital ossifies in the tectum, while the prootic and opisthotic develop in the cartilage of the otic capsule. Some of the adjacent bones developing in various regions of the otic-occipital complex generally fuse, particularly the exoccipital and the opisthotic; the latter forms the greater part of the paroccipital process. Figure 41 shows the main foramina in this region of the skull of an adult lizard (*Varanus*).

F. Visceral Arches

1. *General*

The nomenclature of the visceral arches can be confusing. It is possible that the earliest vertebrates possessed a "premandibular" arch, which is perhaps represented by the trabeculae, at least in part (see de Beer, 1937). Here we refer to the first visceral arch as the mandibular arch, the second visceral arch as the hyoid arch, and the third and fourth visceral arches as the first and second branchial arches, because they correspond with the arches associated with the first and second gill clefts in fishes.

2. *Mandibular Arch*

The skeleton of the mandibular arch (Fig. 1C) comprises the *pterygo-quadrate* (or *palatoquadrate*) *complex* and *Meckel's* (or *mandibular*) *cartilage*. In Squamata these are in continuity during the earlier stages of development (Kamal, 1964b); later they become separated as the jaw joint develops between them. In reptiles the pterygoquadrate is represented mainly by its *ascending process*, which ossifies as the epipterygoid in many forms, by the basal process, which forms the basipterygoid meniscus in lizards, and by the *quadrate* cartilage, which becomes the quadrate bone. The otic process is represented by the postero-dorsal part (cephalic condyle) of the quadrate, which articulates with the otic capsule.

In the generalized reptilian condition, exemplified by *Sphenodon* and many lizards, an extra-cranial space called the *cavum epiptericum* is enclosed by the ascending process (or epipterygoid, when this has ossified) laterally, the basipterygoid process ventrally, and the true side-wall of the skull, here represented by the pila antotica and adjacent cartilages plus the membranes covering the enclosed fenestrae medially (Figs. 6; 9; 46C). The posterior entrance to the cavum and the space posterior to it may be called the cranio-quadrate passage (Goodrich, 1930, p. 267).

The main trigeminal (maxillo-mandibular) ganglion lies slightly posterior to the cavum, and to the level of Figure 6B (right); its root (or roots) enter the cavum through the prootic notch or inferior part of prootic fenestra (Figs. 2; 5; 9C). The ophthalmic ganglion, when separate, is usually situated at a more anterior level, slightly in front of the cavum (Fig. 6B, left). The root of the ophthalmic nerve (Va) runs forwards through the cavum on the way to its ganglion on the medial side of the epipterygoid (Figs. 6B, right, 9A, C); the nerve will continue forwards to the orbit, and ultimately, through its ethmoidal branches, to the snout. The vena capitis* passes posteriorly through the cavum (Figs. 6B; 9C). The maxillary (Vb) and mandibular (Vc) nerves leave their ganglion and pass anteriorly, lateral to the epipterygoid; they supply the more lateral parts of the nose and snout (including the upper teeth), and the lower jaw, teeth and jaw muscles respectively.

In most mammals the cartilaginous pila antotica has disappeared and the ascending process or epipterygoid (or perhaps some adjacent portion of the pterygoquadrate complex) has been incorporated into the alisphenoid, thus walling the cavum epiptericum and trigeminal ganglion into the skull (see Goodrich, 1930; Presley and Steel, 1976; Fig. 9 here). An analogous process seems to have occurred in snakes (p. 188).

Meckel's cartilage is well developed in all reptiles and persists throughout life, becoming more or less invested by the membrane bones of the lower jaw (Fig. 21). Anteriorly it may form a symphysis across the midline during embryonic life; its posterior end ossifies to form the articular (Fig. 6B), which together the quadrate, forms the jaw joint.

3. *Columellar Apparatus*

The columellar apparatus is developed from the more dorsal components of the hyoid arch; its structure has been described by Versluys (1936 and elsewhere), de Beer (1937), and Baird (1970), by Wever and his collaborators in many reptiles (see Wever, 1978), and also by Frank and Smit (1974) in Crocodilia. In a "typical" lizard such as *Lacerta* it consists of a rod running across the tympanic cavity from the tympanic membrane to the fenestra ovalis of the otic capsule (Figs. 8A; 10). It is invested by a thin membrane reflected from the lining of the cavity.

In the adult lizard this rod consists of two parts, an ossified medial *columella* or *stapes*, and a lateral *extracolumella* or *extrastapes* which remains cartilaginous. The medial end of the columella is expanded to form the footplate which is applied to the fenestra ovalis where it is held in place by an annular ligament; a thin layer of cartilage remains around the rim of the footplate. The lateral end of the extracolumella (*insertion plate*) is also expanded and is embedded in the connective tissue of the tympanic membrane; the latter is attached anteriorly to a curved ridge

---

* The main longitudinal head vein in *Sphenodon* and lizards, which drains the orbital sinus and ultimately becomes continuous with the internal jugular vein, is formed as a result of rather complex ontogenetic changes (see O'Donoghue, 1920). The posterior part of this vessel, posterior to the trigeminal ganglion and the entrance of the middle cerebral vein (Fig. 9C) is called the vena capitis lateralis. This name is often applied also to the more anterior portion of the vessel which traverses the cavum epiptericum, but it is uncertain whether this usage is really correct. We follow de Beer (1926) and use the non-committal term vena capitis or head vein for this anterior portion of the main vessel.

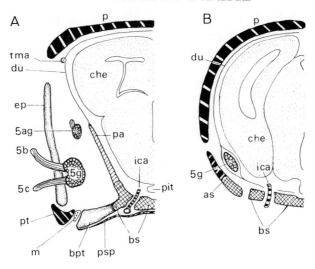

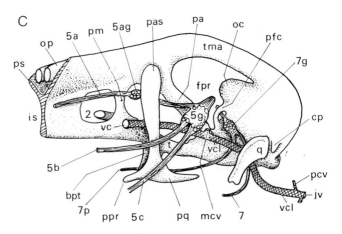

Fig. 9. (A, B) Diagrammatic transverse sections showing relations of cavum epptericum in (A) a lizard (adult) and (B) a primitive mammal. In (A) the basipterygoid process and branches of the trigeminal nerve are reconstructed as if seen from behind. Other nerves and blood vessels are not shown. The epipterygoid of the reptile corresponds with the base of the alisphenoid of the mammal, the rest of the bone being developed in membrane. The pila antotica has disappeared in the mammal (vestiges are found in some forms) but is perhaps represented by the dura dorsal and medial to the trigeminal ganglion, which is actually enclosed in a dural pocket. Cut surfaces are shown as follows: membrane bones in slanting white lines on black, cartilage in slanting lines, cartilage replacement bones cross-hatched, ganglia in small circles. (C) Schematic lateral view of part of embryonic chondrocranium of a primitive *Sphenodon*-like reptile to show the relations of the cavum epptericum and some nerves and blood vessels. After Presley and Steel (1976).

(tympanic crest; Oelrich, 1956) along the front of the quadrate. The junction between the columella and the extracolumella is clearly distinguishable; some lizards have a joint there. The columellar apparatus of other reptiles can be referred to this pattern, though it is often modified; snakes, for example, lack the extracolumella and tympanic membrane at least as distinct structures.

The insertion plate of the extracolumella may bear several processes (Figs. 10A; 19), all attached to the tympanic membrane. The main ones are called the *pars superior* (projecting mainly backwards) and the antero-ventrally projecting *pars inferior*, which is the longer of the two; together they form an elongated, plate-like expansion. The pars superior is attached by the strong *extrastapedial* or *extracolumellar ligament* (which is thought to represent a *laterohyal* element) to the posterior part of the head of the quadrate (*cephalic condyle*) and/or to the intercalary (see below). The smaller *anterior* and *posterior accessory processes* also arise from the insertion plate and are directed mainly upwards and downwards, respectively. Together the four processes give the insertion plate a cruciform appearance when seen from the lateral or medial aspect (Figs. 10A; 28B). Connective tissue may attach the anterior accessory process to the tympanic crest of the quadrate, while in the lizard embryo, the posterior process may be connected with the more ventral, ceratohyal portion of the hyoid arch by a strand of cartilage (*pars interhyalis* or *interhyal*; de Beer, 1937). The interhyal persists as a ligament in some adult lizards and remains chondrified throughout life in *Sphenodon* (III–B–1).

Two further processes, the *dorsal* and *internal processes*, may arise from the medial extremity of the adult extracolumella, just lateral to the point where it joins the bony columella. The short dorsal process (when present) projects posterodorsally. It is at best more or less ligamentous in the adult lizard and the greater part of it may never chondrify, even in the embryo. However, in embryos its dorsal extremity often forms a small cartilaginous nodule, the *processus paroticus* or *intercalary*, which, together with the dorsal process and the extrastapedial ligament, may be regarded

as, Alisphenoid; bpt, basipterygoid process; bs, basisphenoid; che, cerebral hemisphere; cp, crista parotica; du, dura; ep, epipterygoid; fpr, fenestra prootica; ica, internal carotid artery (turning up from Vidian canal in (A); palatine nerve not shown); is, interorbital septum; jv, internal jugular vein; m, basipterygoid meniscus; mcv, middle cerebral vein; oc, otic capsule; op, olfactory peduncle; p, parietal; pa, pila antotica; pas, ascending process of pterygoquadrate; pcv, posterior cerebral vein; pfc, prefacial commissure; pit, pituitary; pm, pila metoptica; ppr, pterygoid process; pq, pterygoquadrate; ps, planum supraseptale; psp, parasphenoid; pt, pterygoid; q, quadrate; t, trabecula; tma, taenia marginalis; vc, vena capitis; vcl, vena capitis lateralis; 2, optic nerve; 5a, b, c, g, ophthalmic, maxillary, and mandibular nerves and main trigeminal ganglion; 5ag, ophthalmic ganglion; 7, facial nerve (hyomandibular branch); 7g, ganglion of facial nerve (chorda tympani not shown); 7p, palatine branch of facial nerve.

as parts of a loop formed by the most dorsal (*epihyal*) elements of the hyoid arch (Shute, 1956; Fig. 10A here).

The fate of the intercalary seems to differ somewhat in different lizards and is not easy to follow in the literature. In some forms it seems to fuse posteriorly with the crista parotica during embryonic life; this probably occurs in *Lacerta*. In other forms it may become incorporated into the cartilage around the paroccipital process (developed partly from the crista parotica), the cephalic condyle of the quadrate and adjacent

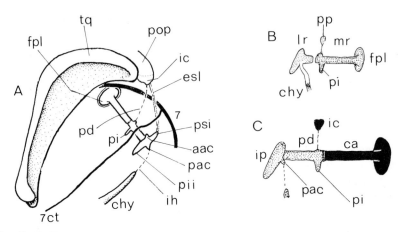

Fig. 10. (A) Diagram of left columellar apparatus of late embryo of lizard showing relationships of facial nerve and its chorda tympani branch. Partly based on Shute (1956). (B) Left columellar apparatus of lizard embryo at intermediate stage. Separate, cartilaginous medial and lateral rudiments are present. (C) Adult stage showing cartilaginous extracolumella, and ossified columella (black). The ligamentous dorsal process, and the internal process are carried on the definitive extracolumella, though they are derived from the medial rudiment, as shown in (B) above. The distal end of the dorsal process, the processus paroticus in (B), has ossified to form the intercalary.

aac, Anterior accessory process of insertion plate; ca, columella auris; chy, ceratohyal; esl, extrastapedial (extracolumellar) ligament (= laterohyal); fpl, footplate; ic, intercalary; ih, ligamentous interhyal; ip, insertion plate; lr, lateral rudiment; mr, medial rudiment; pac, posterior accessory process; pd, ligamentous dorsal process; pi, internal process; pii, pars inferior of insertion plate; pop, paroccipital process; pp, processus paroticus; psi, pars superior; tq, tympanic crest of quadrate; 7, facial nerve; 7ct, chorda tympani.

bones; this is illustrated by Versluys (1936), and by Wever and Werner (1970, in the lizard *Crotophytus*). In some cases, the intercalary may be difficult to distinguish from a cartilaginous epiphysis on the end of the paroccipital process. In the adult skull of some lizards, at least, it can be seen as a small nodule of cartilage wedged between the paroccipital process, the supratemporal and the cephalic condyle; this is the condition noted by Bahl (1937) in *Varanus* and by Jollie (1960) in *Uromastyx*. The latter also figures a second small intercalary nodule dorsomedial to the main one. There may be a synovial cavity between the intercalary and the head of the quadrate. The intercalary may sometimes become ossified.

The internal or quadrate process develops near the columella-extracolumella junction and projects anteroventrally; it may be connected either directly or by a ligament with the posterior surface of the quadrate.

These extracolumellar processes show much variation among reptiles and some or all of them may be absent in any one species. Some of the functional significances are discussed by Wever and Werner (1970), and by Wever (1978).

In the embryo the columellar apparatus is developed from two centres of chondrification which form contiguous medial and lateral rudiments; these unite to form a single rod of cartilage. However, their point of junction does not correspond with the junction between columella and extracolumella in the adult; it lies lateral to it, so that the dorsal and internal processes are derived from the medial rudiment though they are borne by the extracolumella of the adult (Fig. 10B, C).

The terms otostapes and hyostapes are often used to denote the medial and lateral rudiments respectively, but they reflect an early and perhaps erroneous view that the medial rudiment is derived from the otic capsule. More recent work on reptiles seems to indicate that the medial rudiment, including its footplate, is, like the lateral rudiment (Kamal and Hammouda, 1965d), derived entirely from the hyoid arch, although its normal development may depend on the presence of the capsule (Torien, 1965b; see p. 222 here). However, the future application of more sophisticated techniques may lead to some modification of the views expressed above (see Skinner, 1973; Jaskoll and Maderson, 1978).

The main (hyomandibular) branch of nerve VII passes posteriorly, dorsal to the columella and medial to the dorsal process (if present). It then gives off its chorda tympani branch which runs forward again dorsal to the extracolumella but lateral to the dorsal and internal processes. Here it supplies special sensory fibres to the front part of the tongue. The vena capitis lateralis passes dorsal to the columella and the hyomandibular nerve. The stapedial artery arises from the internal carotid and turns dorsally, passing up over the columella, medial to the dorsal process and anterior to the hyomandibular nerve (see Goodrich, 1930). In a few forms, such as geckos, the artery actually pierces the columella just lateral to the footplate, as it does in embryonic mammals; this may be a primitive condition in tetrapods (see Romer, 1956). Further anteriorly the stapedial artery divides into maxillary and superior orbital branches.

4. *Hyobranchial Apparatus*

In reptiles the hyobranchial apparatus lies mainly in the floor of the mouth and throat and gives support and attachment to the tongue and its muscles; its more caudal elements form the larynx with which we are not here concerned. The hyoid consists, typically of a *body* (corpus) derived from the fused, median (copular) parts of the hyoid arch, and sometimes also from the first and second branchial arches, and often of three paired horns (cornua), one from each arch; they consist mainly of ceratohyal and ceratobranchial elements (Figs. 12C; 15B; 29B). At some stage in life the hyoid horn may be connected with the extracolumella. In many reptiles the body bears a median *lingual process* (processus entoglossus) which projects forwards into the tongue. The first cerato-branchial is generally ossified, but the rest of the hyobranchial skeleton often remains cartilaginous throughout life. The hyobranchial apparatus varies considerably among the different reptilian groups; the second branchial arch is often reduced or absent.

G. Epiphyses

Bony epiphyses or secondary centres of ossification are found on a few of the bones of the skull (for example at the dorsal end of the quadrate) in some lizards, but have not been described in other groups of reptiles (see Jollie, 1960; Haines, 1969). It is of interest that a separate quadrate epiphysis, unfused with the rest of the bone, was found in a giant *Varanus* skull, suggesting the possibility of even further growth (Bellairs, 1969).

H. Cranio-vertebral Joint

The composition of the cranio-vertebral joint is a difficult topic which will not be discussed in detail in the present article. The following remarks indicate the nature of the problem.

Three bony elements can be recognized in typical vertebrae of primitive fossil tetrapods: dorsally lies a neural arch and ventrally an *intercentrum* or *hypocentrum* in front and a *pleurocentrum* behind. In reptiles generally, the pleurocentrum is enlarged and forms the centrum proper (Fig. 11A). The intercentra are suppressed or reduced to small elements, typically wedged between adjacent (pleuro-) centra and usually confined to certain regions of the spine such as the neck, and the tail where they are associated with the chevron bones (Romer, 1956).

In most, if not all, lepidosaurian reptiles the occipital condyle appears to be developed from the intercentrum of a vertebral element called the *proatlas*, immediately in front of the atlas (Fig. 11B). The neural arch of the proatlas is usually represented only by the occipital arch of the chondrocranium, though in *Sphenodon* and *Chamaeleo* a part of it seems to have become detached and is found in the adult as a small ossified 'proatlas' or 'proatlas arch' between the atlas and the skull (see Hoffstetter and Gasc, 1969). The pleurocentrum of the proatlas forms the tip of the odontoid process of the second vertebra or axis which articulates with the median dorsal concavity of the occipital condyle. The odontoid process is thought actually to consist of three pleurocentral elements fused together, those of the proatlas (in front, as mentioned), of the atlas and of the axis itself. The intercentrum of the atlas is probably represented by its ventral arch, beneath the odontoid.

In lepidosaurian reptiles the cranio-vertebral joint (often misleadingly called the atlanto-occipital joint) is regarded as lying between the occipital condyle and the tip of the odontoid, i.e. between the intercentrum and the pleurocentrum of the proatlas (de Beer, 1937, p. 223; Fig. 11B here).

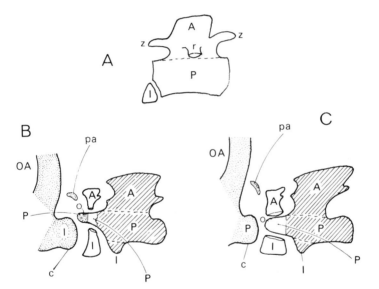

FIG. 11. (A) Typical vertebra of a primitive reptile. The intercentrum (I) is anterior. (B, C) Diagrams showing composition of cranio-vertebral joint according to text of de Beer (1937). Components of the proatlas (stippled), atlas (unshaded) and axis (in slanting lines) are shown in left lateral view. In (B) the joint lies morphologically between the intercentrum of the proatlas (which forms the condyle), and the pleurocentrum of the proatlas (which forms the tip of the odontoid process; hence the joint is said to be intravertebral (i.e. through the proatlas). In (C) the pleurocentrum of the proatlas is incorporated into the condyle and the tip of the odontoid is formed from the pleurocentrum of the atlas; hence the joint is intervertebral (i.e. between proatlas and atlas). In some forms a small portion of the proatlas arch may remain free as the adult "proatlas", as shown here. The fate of the proatlas intercentrum in (C) is not clear. B, condition in lepidosaurs; C, in crocodilians and turtles.

A, Neural arch; c, occipital condyle; I, intercentrum (or hypocentrum); o, odontoid; OA, occipital arch (= arch of proatlas); P, pleurocentrum; pa, free proatlas arch (when present); r, rib facet; z, zygapophysis.

The joint is therefore intravertebral in position. It is also stated to be intersegmental (i.e. developed between two of the original sclerotomal segments from which the vertebrae are derived (de Beer and Barrington, 1934; de Beer, 1937; Kamal, 1965h). However, it is questionable whether the intercentrum and pleurocentrum really correspond to the anterior and posterior half-sclerotomes of adjacent segments which fuse to form the definitive vertebrae.

Werner (1971) states that no derivatives of the proatlas have been found in geckos. However, El-Toubi and Kamal (1961b) and Kamal (1965h) believe that the composition of the cranio-vertebral joint of geckos resembles that of other lepidosaurs, though they give no detailed consideration to the proatlas problem.

De Beer and Barrington (1934) and de Beer (1937) have suggested that, while the cranio-vertebral joint of lepidosaurs resembles that of mammals in its composition, the joint in turtles, crocodilians and birds has a different construction. Here the pleurocentral component of the proatlas forms the occipital condyle (the fate of the intercentrum is uncertain), and the odontoid process is composed only of the pleurocentra of the atlas and axis (Fig. 11C). Thus the joint is intervertebral (i.e., between pro-atlas and atlas) and (supposedly) intrasegmental. The separate "proatlas arch" of crocodiles (p. 238), like that of *Sphenodon*, is regarded as a detached part of the neural arch of the proatlas proper which has not become incorporated into the skull.

De Beer (1937) believed that in lepidosaurs the notochord always runs dorsal to the developing occipital condyle, while in turtles and crocodiles it is embedded in the condyle. He correlated this difference with the intercentral nature of the condyle in lepidosaurs and its pleurocentral nature in other groups. However, Kamal (1965h and elsewhere) has pointed out that the notochord in many Squamata is, in fact, partly embedded in the condyle (though it is much nearer the dorsal surface than the ventral one), so that this distinction in the position of the notochord is not as clear as de Beer supposed. Nevertheless, he agrees with de Beer about the composition of the condyle (i.e., from intercentrum or pleurocentrum) in the various reptilian groups.

Note that the evolution and development of the cartilaginous condyle have been independent of those of the basioccipital and exoccipital bones which ossify in it. Thus, these bones may ossify in an intercentral condyle, as in Squamata, or in a pleurocentral one, as in Testudines (de Beer, 1937).

The distinction between the type of cranio-vertebral joint in lepidosaurs on the one hand and Testudines and Crocodilia on the other does seem to be significant, but the whole problem requires critical reassessment—especially as Gadow's concept of vertebral ontogeny involving arcualia (though used by Shute, 1972) has been shown to be invalid for reptiles (see Romer, 1956; Williams, 1959a; Winchester and Bellairs, 1977). Thus, the term "proatlas interdorsal arch" proposed by de Beer and Barrington (1934) for the free proatlas arch of *Sphenodon* and crocodiles should not be used, at least not without critical definition.

I. Origin of the Skeletal Material

The skeleton of the vertebrate head is derived from two sources, the head mesoderm and the mesoderm of the cranial neural crest; the latter is generally known as mesectoderm or ectomesenchyme. Much experimental work on amphibians has shown that the crest gives rise to the anterior parts of the trabeculae and to the entire visceral arch skeleton except for the second basibranchial. It also gives rise or contributes to certain dermal bones such as the vomer and the splenial, and probably other bones of the jaws; it also contributes to the odontoblasts of the tooth germs (de Beer, 1937; Hörstadius, 1950).

Recent work on avian embryos has shown that the mesectodermal contribution to the skull is much more extensive than had been previously envisaged. Thus, Le Lièvre (1978) found, by grafting distinguishable portions of cephalic neural crest from quail (*Coturnix*) to chick (*Gallus*) embryos, that the crest gives rise, or contributes extensively, to the following structures: the visceral arch skeleton, the dermal bones of the lower jaw, the nasal, premaxilla, maxilla, pterygoid, palatine, vomer, jugal, quadratojugal and squamosal. The nasal capsule, the interorbital septum and the scleral cartilage and ossicles may be of similar origin. The otic capsule, frontal and parasphenoid rostrum arise partly from neural crest and partly from mesoderm, while the basal plate, occipital region and parietal appear to arise entirely from mesoderm.

Some of this work is discussed by Hall (1978) who emphasizes the importance of interactions between mesectoderm and mesoderm with tissues such as the brain and notochord in inducing ossification. These findings may well apply also to reptiles, on which no investigations of this type seem yet to have been made.

III. Development of the Skull in Various Groups

A. Sauria (Lacertilia)

1. Lacertidae (infraorder Scincomorpha)

a. Previous Literature
   Acanthodactylus boskianus, Kamal and Abdeen, 1972. *A.* sp., Shute,

1956 (ear). *Lacerta* (mainly *L. agilis* and *L. vivipara*), Leydig, 1872; Born, 1879 (nasal capsule); Parker, 1880a; Gaupp, 1900, 1906; Cords, 1909 (ear); Goodrich, 1930; de Beer, 1930, 1937; Säve-Söderbergh, 1946 (brain-case); Pratt, 1948 (nasal capsule). *L. sicula*, Rieppel, 1976b (brain-case). *L. muralis*, Wever, 1978 (ear). Duvdevani (1972) has described certain features of nasal anatomy in four species of *Acanthodactylus*.

b. Chondrocranium of Acanthodactylus boskianus

i Earlier stages

Five successive embryonic stages of this species were studied by Kamal and Abdeen (1972), whose work is summarized below. These stages give a very extensive picture of chondrocranial development, stage 1 being relatively earlier than the youngest embryo of *Lacerta* described by de Beer (1937).

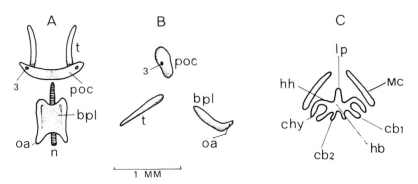

FIG. 12. *Acanthodactylus boskianus*, Stage 1. (A) Dorsal, (B) lateral view of chondrocranium and (C) Hyobranchial apparatus of Stage 2. After Kamal and Abdeen (1972).

bpl, Basal plate; cb1, cb2, ceratobranchials, 1 and 2; chy, ceratohyal; hb, hyoid body; hh, hypohyal; lp, lingual process of hyoid; Mc, Meckel's cartilage; n, notochord; oa, occipital arch; poc, posterior orbital cartilage; t, trabecula; 3, foramen for oculomotor nerve.

At *Stage 1* (15·9 mm total body-length*; Fig. 12), four procartilaginous rudiments can be seen: the trabeculae, which are entirely separate from each other; the basal plate (fused parachordals) with the paired (main) occipital arches fused to its posterior edge; a crescentic plate representing the fused posterior orbital cartilages and perforated by the IIIrd nerve on each side; and Meckel's cartilage, which develops slightly later than the rest.

* It is not clear whether the measurements given by Kamal and Abdeen refer to total length (snout to tail tip), to head plus body-length (snout to vent) or to body length (minus both head and tail).

De Beer (1937) and Rieppel (1977c) found that the trabeculae were fused anteriorly in the earliest stages of *Lacerta agilis* and *L. sicula*, respectively which they examined, but it seems possible that the observations of *Acanthodactylus* by Kamal and Abdeen refer to a relatively earlier stage still.

The trabeculae are separated from the parachordals and are set at an angle of about 100° to them; this angle increases in later stages as the basicranial axis straightens. The notochord is completely embedded in the basal plate. The posterior margin of the plate is connected with the odontoid process of the axis.

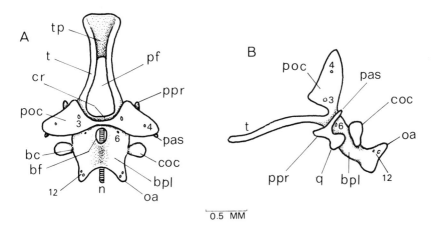

FIG. 13. *Acanthodactylus boskianus*, Stage 2. (A) Dorsal and (B) lateral view of chondrocranium. After Kamal and Abdeen (1972).

bc, Basicapsular commissure; bf, basicranial fenestra; bpl, basal plate; coc, cochlear part of otic capsule; cr, crista sellaris; n, notochord; oa, occipital arch; pas, ascending process of pterygoquadrate; pf, pituitary fossa; poc, posterior orbital cartilage; ppr, pterygoid process of pterygoquadrate; q, quadrate; t, trabecula; tp, trabecular plate; 3, 4, 6, 12, foramina for oculomotor, trochlear, abducens, and hypoglossal nerves.

At *Stage 2* (19·2 mm total body-length; Fig. 13) the structures previously mentioned have all chondrified. The anterior ends of the trabeculae have become joined by a procartilaginous condensation called the trabecular plate; their posterior ends have also fused with the front of the basal plate, enclosing a large pituitary fossa or fenestra. However, they are still unfused at mid-orbital level so that the chondrocranium is platytrabic at this early stage; this appears to be the usual condition in lizards.

A small basicranial fenestra has arisen, probably through degeneration of an area of basal plate cartilage, and is separated from the pituitary fenestra by a transverse bar, the crista sellaris (or acrochordal). The

VIth nerve pierces the front of the basal plate and emerges from its ventral surface. The posterior orbital cartilages have become thin in the midline, where they are now connected by a slender commissure. As in lizards generally, these cartilages originate as a single plate extending across the midline and only later become fenestrated into separate pilae (Kamal, 1969c). As a result of their increasing width the IVth nerve has become enclosed in cartilage on each side.

Only the cochlear portion of the otic capsule is visible as a procartilaginous condensation around the lagena, and this has already fused with the side of the basal plate; the line of fusion constitutes the basicapsular commissure. Two XIIth nerve foramina have become enclosed near the back of the basal plate; this is apparently due to the outgrowth from the plate of small preoccipital arches.

The procartilaginous pterygoquadrate complex is represented by the ascending process, pterygoid process and quadrate, all connected with each other. The quadrate is quite free from the basal plate and otic capsule and articulates with Meckel's cartilage below.

The hyobranchial apparatus consists of a hyoid body with the lingual process extending forwards from it, as well as a hyoid horn and first and second branchial horns, the last very short. Each hyoid horn appears to consist of a hypohyal and a ceratohyal element, while the branchial horns are formed by the ceratobranchials.

At *Stage 3* (23·8 mm total body-length; Fig. 14) the anterior parts of the trabeculae have fused into a trabecula communis as the result of progressive narrowing of the trabecular plate; it is not clear whether the latter ever becomes fully chondrified. The pituitary fenestra is reduced in length and the basipterygoid processes have arisen from the posterior ends of the trabeculae where they join the basal plate.

The front of the trabecula communis projects anteriorly as the rudiment of the nasal septum, which seems to be the first part of the nasal capsule to appear. Further posteriorly the trabecula communis is continuous behind with the interorbital septum, while on the dorsal border of the latter the planum supraseptale has arisen beneath the olfactory parts of the fore-brain. The planum arises as right and left halves, with downturned medial edges which fuse in the midline. The ventral part of the interorbital septum is chondrified and appears to have grown dorsally from the trabecula communis; the dorsal part of the septum, still procartilaginous, is developing from the fused medial edges of the two halves of the planum supraseptale (Fig. 16D–F).

This dual origin of the interorbital septum appears to be characteristic of lizards (Bellairs, 1949a; Kamal, 1965g). It is of interest that an interorbital septum, reduced in size but of fairly normal appearance, was present in teratological embryos of *Lacerta vivipara* and *T. lepida* with severe degrees of microphthalmia as well as cleft palate (Bellairs, 1965; Bellairs and Gamble, 1960; Fig. 16G here). Therefore, pressure from the developing eyes cannot be the critical ontogenetic factor in bringing about the fusion of the septal rudiments. This view has been substantiated by experimental work on chick embryos (Bellairs, 1958; Silver, 1962). A distinct, though abnormally small, interorbital septum develops after ablation of both the eye rudiments. In some reptiles a third element, the intertrabecula (p. 220) participates in the formation of the septum, but this is hardly apparent in lizards.

In *Acanthodactylus* embryos of Stage 3, rudiments of the sphenethmoid commissures have developed at the front of the planum supraseptale. From the posterior edge of the planum a rudiment of the taenia marginalis projects backwards on each side, while more medially the taenia medialis runs backwards to become continuous with the pila metoptica, accessoria and antotica. The pila metoptica is connected with the upper border of the interorbital septum, while the pila antotica joins the anterolateral margin of the basal plate. The newly formed fenestra metoptica is divided into two by the appearance of a slender supratrabecular bar (Fig. 14C). The pilae metoptica, accessoria and antotica and the posterior rudiment of the taenia marginalis (separate at this stage from the anterior rudiment) all appear to be formed as the result of fenestration of the original posterior orbital cartilages, which have now lost their commissure across the midline.

The anterior tip of the notochord terminates just posterior to the crista sellaris. The notochord runs posteriorly in the midline through the enlarged basicranial fenestra and continues on the dorsal aspect of the basal plate, except at the back of the latter, where it is still embedded in cartilage. The VIth nerve tunnels forwards through the basal plate, both entering and emerging on its dorsal surface.

The otic capsule is now partly chondrified, the anterior part being more nearly complete than the posterior one. It is pierced medially by a single foramen for the VIIIth nerve. The floor of the cochlear portion is perforated by a large foramen perilymphaticum which has appeared as a result of regression of preexisting cartilage. The foramen for nerve VII is now enclosed anterior to the cochlear portion of the capsule. Posteriorly, the otic capsule is separated from the basal plate by the metotic fissure, which is not yet closed posteriorly. The most anterior foramen for the XIIth nerve has now been enclosed; the formation of the three definitive hypoglossal foramina has taken place in a postero-anterior sequence (Kamal, 1966c).

The columella auris chondrifies from two centres which form distinct

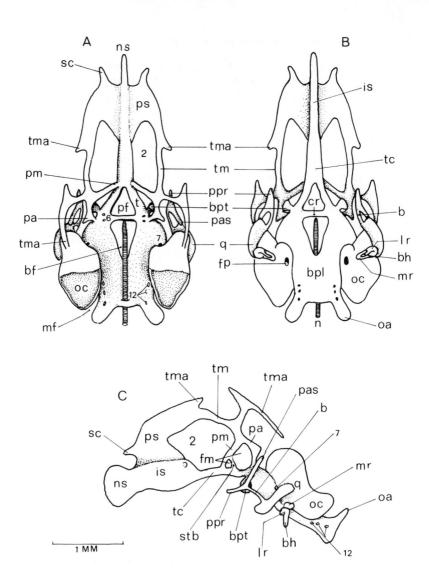

Fig. 14. *Acanthodactylus boskianus*. Chondrocranium of Stage 3, in (A) dorsal, (B) ventral and (C) lateral view. After Kamal and Abdeen (1972).

b, Bar connecting ascending process of pterygoquadrate with quadrate; bf, basicranial fenestra; bh, bar connecting lateral rudiment of columellar apparatus with ceratohyal; bpl, basal plate; bpt, basi-pterygoid process; cr, crista sellaris; fm, fenestra metoptica; fp, foramen for perilymphatic duct; is, interorbital septum; lr, lateral rudiment or portion of columellar apparatus; mf, metotic fissure; mr, medial rudiment or portion of columellar apparatus; n, notochord; ns, nasal septum; oa, occipital arch; oc, otic capsule; pa, pila antotica; pas, ascending process of pterygoquadrate (epipterygoid); pf, pituitary fossa; pm, pila metoptica; ppr, pterygoid process of pterygoquadrate; ps, planum supraseptale; q, quadrate; sc, sphenethmoid commissure; stb, supratrabecular bar (not visible in (A)); t, trabecula; tc, trabecula communis; tm, taenia medialis; tma, taenia marginalis; 2, fenestra optica; 6, foramina for abducens nerve; 7, foramen for facial nerve; 12, foramina for hypoglossal nerve.

medial and lateral rudiments; at this stage, a cartilage transiently connects the lateral one with the ceratohyal element of the hyoid horn.
Both columellar rudiments are derived entirely from the hyoid arch.

At *Stage 4* (total body-length 26·3 mm; Fig. 15A), much of the paired
nasal capsule has developed. The parietotectal cartilage is attached, from
the time of its first appearance, to the dorsal edge of the nasal septum;
the fronts of this cartilage and of the septum participate in the formation
of a concave anterior wall of the capsule called the anterior cupola, which
is perforated by the foramen apicale. The paranasal cartilage (p. 49) has
now chondrified on the lateral aspect of the parietotectal cartilage and is
continuous posterodorsally with the sphenethmoid commissures; these are
now connected posteriorly with the planum supraseptale. The ventral
parts of the parietotectal and paranasal cartilages are continuous with each
other and are pushed into the side of the nasal cavity to form the rudiments of the concha. The lamina transversalis anterior has also developed
beneath the organ of Jacobson on each side and is fused with the
ventral edge of the nasal septum. The planum antorbitale arises as an
independent cartilage and at this stage is separate from the rest of the
capsule.

The two halves of the planum supraseptale have now fused completely,
and a large fenestra has appeared between it and the interorbital septum.
The anterior and posterior rudiments of the taenia marginalis have now
joined on each side, while the pila metoptica has united with its opposite
fellow to form a subiculum infundibuli. The front of this (cartilago
hypochiasmatica) has fused with the interorbital septum. These last
features cannot be seen in ventral view (Fig. 15A).

Much of the otic capsule has now chondrified and the crista parotica
is apparent as a projection from the lateral capsular wall, dorsal to the
swelling for the ampulla of the lateral semicircular canal and just behind
the posterodorsal part (otic process) of the quadrate. There are two
foramina in the medial wall of the capsule for the VIIIth nerve. The
fenestra ovalis has formed as a result of cartilage regression. The occipital
arch has expanded and fused with the posterior end of the otic capsule
so that the metotic fissure is closed behind. The fissure itself has become
partly divided into the anterior recessus scalae tympani (through which
the IXth nerve follows an entirely extra-capsular course) and the posterior
jugular foramen for the Xth and ?XIth nerves. The division of the fissure
is accomplished by the apposition of the prominence for the ampullary
part of the posterior semicircular canal with the basal plate.

The pterygoid process of the pterygoquadrate has begun to regress and
the bar connecting the ascending process and pterygoid process with the
quadrate has broken down. Meckel's cartilage has developed a retro-

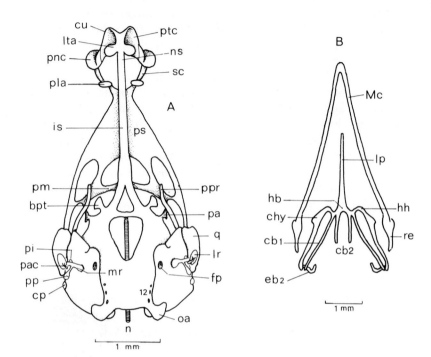

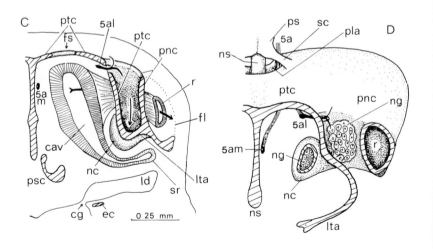

articular process and has fused anteriorly with its opposite fellow to form a symphysis.

The medial and lateral rudiments of the columella have begun to fuse. A small posterior accessory process projects from the lateral rudiment; this is the remnant of the connection (pars interhyalis) between the columella and the ceratohyal observed in earlier stages.

Two processes arise from the lateral end of the medial rudiment of the columella. The first, the processus internus, extends dorsally and closely approaches the ventral surface of the quadrate. The second, the processus dorsalis, is thin and procartilaginous; it extends posterodorsally to end in a rather conspicuous spherical nodule which is well chondrified. This is the processus paroticus which is situated between the posterodorsal aspect of the quadrate in front and the crista parotic behind. The processus paroticus thus originates from the columellar apparatus, not from the crista parotica of the otic capsule.

FIG. 15. (A, B) *Acanthodactylus boskianus.* (A) Chondrocranium of Stage 4 in ventral view. (B) Ventral view of visceral skeleton of Stage 5. After Kamal and Abdeen (1972). (C) *Lacerta vivipara*, late embryo. Reconstructed transverse section through nasal capsule at level of foramen epiphaniale seen from in front. The figure shows the posterior part of the aditus conchae (unlabelled)—which is really the bend in the nasal capsule (see text) with an arrow passing ventrally through it towards the cavum conchale within the nasal concha. The cavum nasi proprium passes posterior to the bend in the nasal capsule to become continuous with the extra-conchal recess, as shown by the broader arrow. The cavum proprium also has a well developed sub-conchal recess. The fenestra lateralis in the paranasal cartilage is shown by dotted lines. The lateral nasal gland is not shown. Cut cartilage is shown in slanting lines, cut nasal epithelium in closer lines. (D) Diagram showing posterior part of nasal capsule of a lizard with an extra-conchal recess but no fenestra lateralis (as in some skinks and geckos). The capsule has been cut transversely and is seen from in front. The level of section, which passes through the lamina transversalis anterior, is anterior to that in (C). The posterior part of the lateral nasal gland is shown *in situ* with the bend of the capsule, and a window has been cut at a more posterior level in the nasal concha to show the gland extending into the cavum conchale. The nasal sac is not shown. Cut cartilage is shown in slanting lines. Conditions in *Lacerta* would be very similar if there were no fenestra lateralis. Compare (C) and (D) here with Fig. 3C, D.

bpt, Basipterygoid process; cav, cavum nasi proprium; cb1, cb2, ceratobranchials 1 and 2; cg, choanal groove; chy, ceratohyal; cp, crista parotica; cu, nasal cupola; eb2, epibranchial 2; ec, ectochoanal cartilage; fl, fenestra lateralis; fp, foramen for perilymphatic duct; fs, fenestra superior; hb, hyoid body; hh, hypohyal; is, interorbital septum; 1d, lachrymal duct; 1p, lingual process of hyoid; lr, lateral rudiment or portion of columellar apparatus; lta, lamina transversalis anterior; Mc, Meckel's cartilage; mr, medial rudiment or portion of columellar apparatus with footplate; n, notochord; nc, nasal concha; ng, lateral nasal gland; ns, nasal septum; oa, occipital arch; pa, pila antotica; pac, posterior accessory process; pi, internal process; pla, planum antorbitale; pm, pila metoptica; pnc, paranasal cartilage; pp, processus paroticus (connected with columella by procartilaginous dorsal process); ppr, pterygoid process of pterygoquadrate; ps, planum supraseptale; psc, paraseptal cartilage; ptc, parietotectal cartilage; q, quadrate; r, extra-conchal recess; re, retroarticular process; sc, sphenethmoid commissure; sr, sub-conchal recess; 5a, ophthalmic nerve; 5al, 5am, lateral and medial ethmoidal branches of ophthalmic nerve (reconstructed in D only); 12, foramina for hypoglossal nerve.

ii. The fully formed chondrocranium

General. The fully formed chondrocranium is seen in embryos of
Acanthodactylus of 40·5 mm (total body-length; Figs. 17; 18; 19). It
appears similar to that of the 31 mm stage of *Lacerta agilis* studied by
Gaupp (1906) and figured by de Beer (1937). The sections of *Lacerta*
(Figs. 3; 6; 8) shown previously will serve to illustrate this account as
Bellairs lacks material of *Acanthodactylus*.

The condition of the fully formed chondrocranium conforms closely
with the general pattern described in the introductory section (II) so that
only points of special note need be dealt with.

Nasal capsule. Embryos of *Lacerta vivipara*, and of certain other lizards
and *Sphenodon*, show a small median nodule of cartilage, the papillary
cartilage, beneath the front of the nasal septum (Fig. 3A). Its significance
is obscure.

In *Acanthodactylus* the roof of the capsule has no fenestra superior, but
there is a small one in *Lacerta*.

In both forms the lamina transversalis anterior is connected medially
to the nasal septum and laterally to the parietotectal cartilage to form a
complete zona annularis. The paraseptal cartilage extends from the lamina
in front to the planum antorbitale behind; an ectochoanal cartilage lies on
its lateral side. This cartilage supports a deep groove in the palate called
the choanal groove with which the lachrymal duct communicates in
lacertids (Figs. 3C; 18). The combined groove and duct pass medially
between the lamina transversalis anterior and the ectochoanal cartilage to
open near the palatal orifice of the duct of Jacobson's organ (see Bellairs
and Boyd, 1950; Parsons, 1970).

In lizards generally the organ of Jacobson is enclosed in a capsule
composed partly of cartilage and partly of bone (Fig. 3C). The medial
wall of this is formed mainly by the nasal septum, and the floor by the
lamina transversalis anterior; the paraseptal cartilage lies ventromedially.
The floor is also reinforced by the horizontal part of the vomer. From
the upper surface of the lamina transversalis anterior a curved cartilaginous
process projects dorsally into the mushroom body of Jacobson's organ.
This process, called the concha of Jacobson's organ or vomeronasal
concha, occurs in almost all Squamata; the part of the lamina from which
it arises is termed the cartilage of Jacobson's organ.

The lateral wall of the capsule of Jacobson's organ is formed by the
parietotectal cartilage and the maxilla. The capsular roof is mostly deficient
of cartilage, but is formed by the septomaxilla. However, the most anterior
part of the organ is completely enclosed in a cartilaginous cupola, formed

by a hollow in the front of the lamina transversalis anterior.

The posterolateral part of the nasal capsule is complicated. The following account is based on *Lacerta vivipara* and differs somewhat in concept from the descriptions of de Beer (1937) of *Lacerta agilis*, and of Kamal and Abdeen (1972) of *Acanthodactylus*, though the actual anatomy of these lacertids is probably very similar.

The posterior end of the cavum nasi proprium of each nasal sac is bent laterally and the shape of the capsule follows it so that a lateral recess or extra-conchal space (Parsons, 1970) of both sac and capsule is formed (Figs. 3C, D; 15C, D; 16A–C). In most lizards the lateral wall of the nasal capsule just in front of this recess is deeply invaginated to form the cartilaginous nasal concha which projects inwards from the lateral wall of the nasal cavity. The opening of the invagination is called the aditus conchae; the extra-capsular cavity within it is the conchal space (cavum conchale) and contains the lateral nasal gland. The duct of this gland passes forward through the aditus conchae and then enters a foramen or notch at the back of the fenestra narina to discharge into the vestibule of the nasal sac near its junction with the cavum (Figs. 4; 16A–C). The outer wall of the lateral recess is largely deficient in lacertids so that in reconstructions of the capsule the concha is exposed from the side. In the intact skull this deficiency (called the lateral fenestra) is covered by the ascending part of the maxilla and by the prefrontal bone (Fig. 3C, D).

The posterior part of the conchal space becomes closed in by the approximation and fusion of the medial wall of the lateral recess with the lateral wall of the main nasal capsule, both dorsal and ventral to the invaginated pocket (Fig. 3C). Thus, the lateral nasal gland becomes enclosed within the cartilage of the concha (Fig. 3D) except at the opening of the invagination (the aditus) in front. However, in many non-lacertid lizards the conchal cartilage is incomplete below so that the conchal space is not completely enclosed.

The cartilage which forms both the medial and the fenestrated lateral wall of the lateral recess is termed the paranasal cartilage by most authors. It is continuous in front with the side of the lamina transversalis anterior, and behind with the planum antorbitale. The parietotectal cartilage forms the lateral wall of the main part of the nasal capsule in this region.

Both paranasal and parietotectal cartilage participate in the formation of the concha, the parietotectal cartilage contributing to its medial wall (Figs. 3D, 15C, D, 16A–C), and the paranasal cartilage to its lateral one. According to Kamal (1968) and Kamal and Abdeen (1972) the inferior wall of the concha is formed by a posterior projection from the lamina transversalis anterior (as labelled in Fig. 3D), but it is difficult to dis-

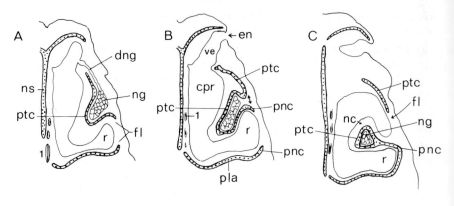

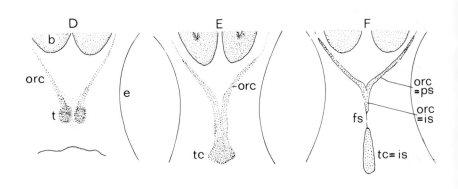

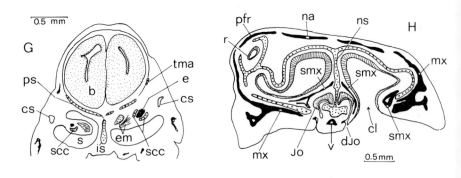

tinguish between regions of cartilage which are all continuous with each other.

At one point the junction between parietotectal and paranasal cartilages is thought to be represented by the site of the foramen epiphaniale. Elsewhere, however, Kamal and Abdeen found them to be continuous at all developmental stages in the great majority of lizards; it therefore seems doubtful, as Skinner's (1973) account suggests, that the paranasal cartilage is really a separate element. It could be regarded as merely the reduplicated side wall of the nasal capsule which results from its lateral bending, but it is provisionally described and labelled as a discrete structure here.

It has been suggested that the conchal infolding is produced by the development of the lateral nasal gland. However, the concha starts to invaginate well before the gland appears. It is more likely that the very early infolding of the olfactory epithelium in this position is the factor responsible for the subsequent invagination of the cartilage (see Kamal and Abdeen, 1972).

In the fully formed chondrocranium of *Acanthodactylus*, the planum antorbitale, which originally chondrified from a separate centre, has become fused with the paraseptal cartilage medially and the paranasal cartilage laterally. The anterior and posterior maxillary processes appear to arise from the paranasal cartilage, as described by Kamal and Abdeen,

---

FIG. 16.   (A–C) Horizontal longitudinal sections in a dorsal to ventral sequence through the nasal capsule of a newborn *Lacerta vivipara* to show the structure of the cartilaginous nasal concha. The paranasal cartilage is here regarded as an entity; arrows in (B) show fusion of the paranasal with the parietotectal cartilage at a slightly more ventral level to enclose the nasal gland within the cavum conchale. (D–F) Diagrammatic transverse sections through the mid-orbital region of lizard embryos at successive developmental stages to show formation of the interorbital septum. In (D) a pro-cartilaginous stage, the trabeculae are still unfused, but are in contact dorsally with the downturned medial edges of the orbital cartilages. In (E) these elements are all fused. In (F) the dorsal parts of the orbital cartilages form the planum supraseptale, while their downturned ventral parts form the interorbital septum, in combination with the trabecula communis below. Based on Bellairs (1949a). (G) Transverse section through head of malformed, microphthalmic embryo of *Lacerta vivipara* showing eye vestiges and the interorbital septum, which is normal in position but greatly reduced in height. The bones are hard to identify and are not labelled. See Bellairs and Gamble (1960) and compare with normal embryo shown in Figs. 3F and 6A here. (H) Transverse section through snout of malformed embryo of *Lacerta lepida* with cleft palate shown on right side. The cleft divides the septomaxilla. See Bellairs (1965) and compare with Fig. 3B, C here.

b, Brain; cl, cleft in palate; cpr, cavum proprium of nasal sac; cs, conjunctival space; dJo, duct of Jacobson's organ; dng, duct of nasal gland; e, eye (consisting only of pigment and scleral cartilage in G); em, eye muscles; en, external nostril; fl, fenestra lateralis; fs, fenestra in interorbital septum; is, interorbital septum; Jo, Jacobson's organ; mx, maxilla; na, nasal; nc, nasal concha; ng, (lateral) nasal gland; ns, nasal septum; orc, (anterior) orbital cartilage; pfr, prefrontal; pla, planum antorbitale; pnc, paranasal cartilage; ps, planum supraseptale; ptc, parietotectal cartilage; r, lateral or extra-conchal recess; s, orbital venous sinus; scc, scleral cartilage; smx, septomaxilla; t, trabecula; tc, trabecula communis; tma, taenia marginalis; v, vomer (? fused vomers); ve, vestibule of nasal sac; 1, olfactory nerves.

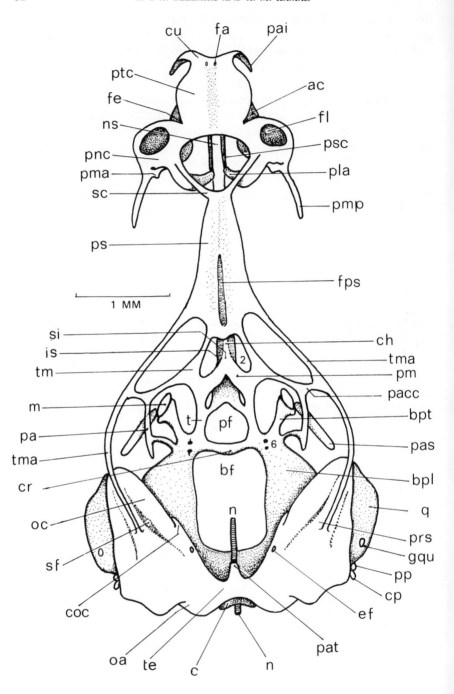

rather than from the planum antorbitale, as described by de Beer (1937) in *Lacerta*. The medial edge of the planum is contact with the nasal septum in *Acanthodactylus* and almost touches it in *Lacerta*.

Orbitotemporal region. The fully formed orbitotemporal region of *Acanthodactylus* (Figs. 17–19) and *Lacerta*, with its planum supraseptale and scaffolding of bars further back, largely conforms to the pattern described on p. 20. However, as noted in stage 3, a small supratrabecular bar connects each pila metoptica with the dorsal surface of the trabecula beneath it (Fig. 19); in *Lacerta* this bar connects the pilae metoptica and antotica. In addition, a long, narrow median slit (absent in *Lacerta*) has appeared along the middle part of the planum supraseptale and the fenestra beneath it has enlarged, separating the planum from the dorsal border of the interorbital septum. Another small fenestra has arisen near the front of the interorbital septum and a third has appeared a little further forwards, in the back of the nasal septum. Except for the split in the planum these fenestrae occur in *Lacerta* as well as *Acanthodactylus* and all appear to arise secondarily by absorption of preexisting cartilage (Fig. 16F). The superior and inferior oblique muscles of the eye take origin from the septal cartilage between the two small fenestrae and from parts of the membrane which fills them.

In the fully formed condition the marked angulation of the basicranial axis seen in the earlier stages has largely disappeared; however, there is still a slight flexure halfway along the lower edge of the interorbital septum, beneath the planum supraseptale.

As in all reptiles, apart from snakes, most amphisbaenians and perhaps a few highly fossorial lizards, the sclera of the eyeball is chondrified.

Otic capsule. The large otic capsules extend the full height of the chondrocranium and converge posteriorly, where they are connected by the front of the occipital tectum (synoticum + posterius). The relations

FIG. 17. *Acanthodactylus boskianus.* Chondrocranium of Stage 5 (fully formed condition) in dorsal view. After Kamal and Abdeen (1972).

ac, Aditus conchae; bf, basicranial fenestra; bpl, basal plate; bpt, basipterygoid process; c, occipital condyle; ch, cartilago hypochiasmatica; coc, cochlear prominence; cp, crista parotica; cr, crista sellaris; cu, nasal cupola; ef, endolymphatic foramen; fa, foramen apicale; fe, foramen epiphaniale; fl, fenestra lateralis; fps, fenestra in planum supraseptale; gqu, gap in quadrate; is, interorbital septum; m, basipterygoid meniscus; n, notochord; ns, nasal septum; oa, occipital arch; oc, otic capsule; pa, pila antotica; pacc, pila accessoria; pai, processus alaris inferior; pas, ascending process of pterygoquadrate; pat, anterior process of tectum; pf, pituitary fossa; pla, planum antorbitale; pm, pila metoptica; pma, anterior maxillary process; pmp, posterior maxillary process; pnc, paranasal cartilage; pp, processus paroticus; prs, prominence for anterior semicircular canal; ps, planum supraseptale; psc, paraseptal cartilage; ptc, parietotectal cartilage; q, quadrate; sc, sphenethmoid commissure; sf, subarcuate fossa; si, subiculum infundibuli; t, trabecula; te, tectum; tm, taenia medialis; tma, taenia marginalis; 2, fenestra optica; 6, foramina for abducens nerve.

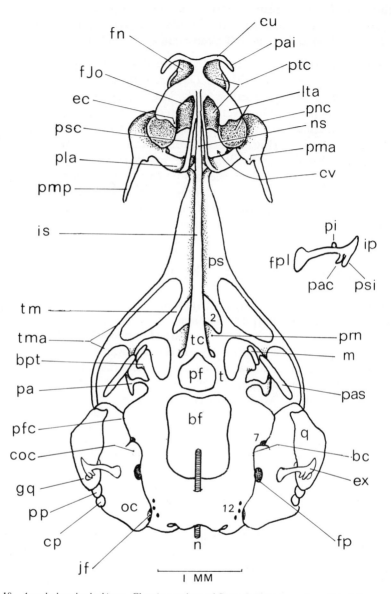

FIG. 18. *Acanthodactylus boskianus.* Chondrocranium of Stage 5 (fully formed condition) in ventral view. The columellar apparatus is shown enlarged on the right. After Kamal and Abdeen (1972). Abbreviations beneath Fig. 19 opposite.

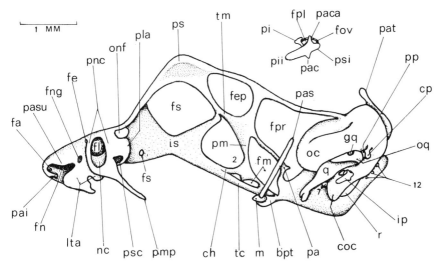

FIG. 19. *Acanthodactylus boskianus*. Chondrocranium of Stage 5 (fully formed condition) in lateral view. Columellar apparatus shown enlarged above. After Kamal and Abdeen (1972). The unlabelled supratrabecular bar separates the larger and smaller portions of the fenestra metoptica.

bc, Basicapsular commissure; bf, basicranial fenestra; bpt, basipterygoid process; ch, cartilago hypochiasmatica; coc, cochlear part of otic capsule; cp, crista parotica; cu, nasal cupola; cv, choanal vacuity; ec, ectochoanal cartilage; ex, extracolumella; fa, foramen apicale; fe, foramen epiphaniale; fep, fenestra epioptica; fJo, fenestra for duct of Jacobson's organ; fl, fenestra lateralis; fm, fenestra metoptica; fn, fenestra narina; fng, foramen for duct of (lateral) nasal gland; fov, fenestra ovalis; fp, foramen for perilymphatic duct; fpl, footplate; fpr, fenestra prootica; fs, fenestra in nasal or interorbital septum; gq, gap in quadrate; ip, insertion plate of extracolumella; is, interorbital septum; jf, jugular foramen; lta, lamina transversalis anterior; m, basipterygoid meniscus; n, notochord; nc, nasal concha; ns, nasal septum; oc, otic capsule; onf, orbitonasal fissure; oq, otic process of quadrate; pa, pila antotica; pac, posterior accessory process; paca, anterior accessory process; pai, processus alaris inferior; pas, ascending process of pterygoquadrate; pasu, processus alaris superior; pat, anterior process of tectum; pf, pituitary fossa; pfc, prefacial commissure; pi, internal process; pii, pars inferior of insertion plate; pla, planum antorbitale; pm, pila metoptica; pma, anterior maxillary process; pmp, posterior maxillary process; pnc, paranasal cartilage; pp, processus paroticus; ps, planum supraseptale; psc, paraseptal cartilage; psi, pars superior of insertion plate; ptc, parietotectal cartilage; q, quadrate; r, recessus scalae tympani; t, trabecula; tc, trabecula communis; tm, taenia medialis; tma, taenia marginalis; 2, fenestra optica; 7, foramen for facial nerve; 12, foramina for hypoglossal nerve.

of the capsule to the metotic fissure are similar to those at the previous stage; in front of the fissure each capsule is joined to the basal plate by the basicapsular commissure.

The external surface of the capsule shows several prominences related to the various parts of the inner ear, the most conspicuous being the prominence for the anterior semicircular canal. The interior of the capsule is subdivided by various cartilaginous septa. Thus the main cavity (cavum vestibulare) is divided by a vertical transverse septum into a cavum vestibulare anterius and a cavum posterius, the latter opening into the cavum cochleare. The semicircular canals themselves are partitioned off from the two vestibular cava by additional septa, their ampullae being lodged in recesses. The foramina in the capsule have been described on p. 26.

Basal plate and occipital region. The VIth nerve does not perforate the basal plate, but tunnels through its dorsal surface just lateral to the crista sellaris. The front of the notochord, which in earlier stages reached forward almost to the crista, has now degenerated so that it ends near the middle of the basicranial fenestra. Posterior to the fenestra the notochord is partly embedded in the substance of the basal plate, but is exposed both dorsally and ventrally over parts of its extent. The kidney-shaped, tripartite occipital condyle has developed from the back of the plate, and consists of a pair of small lateral prominences flanking a median, depressed portion. The notochord passes through the condyle very close to its dorsal surface, and the thin layer of cartilage covering it is prolonged posteriorly to join the tip of the odontoid process, as in earlier stages. The occurrence of this connection supports the view that condyle and odontoid tip belong to a single vertebral element, the proatlas, and that the joint between them is intravertebral (see II–H).

The foramen magnum is now completely enclosed by the junction of the two sides of the occipital tectum, which is derived from both otic capsule and occipital arch and is, therefore, a tectum synoticum plus posterius. A short, thick ascending process projects from the front of the tectum in the midline and lies just dorsal to the two endolymphatic sacs. In lizards generally this process underlies or projects into the back of the parietal bone (Fig. 5). It remains cartilaginous throughout life, allowing metakinetic flexion of the skull roof.

Mandibular arch. The pterygoquadrate cartilage consists of three separate elements; the quadrate cartilage, the ascending process and the basipterygoid meniscus. The pterygoid process found in younger embryos has disappeared. The quadrate cartilage is massive and passes obliquely downwards and forwards. Its lower end articulates with Meckel's cartilage, while its dorsal end (otic process) abuts against the crista parotica of the otic capsule. The ascending process (epipterygoid) is a long narrow rod which passes dorsally to end near the front of the otic capsule; its ventral end is lodged in a notch on the dorsal aspect of the pterygoid bone. The basipterygoid meniscus is an isolated nodule of cartilage intercalated between the prominent basipterygoid process and the ascending process, from which it is more or less separated by the pterygoid (Figs. 6B; 9A, 17; 18). This meniscus is connected with the lower end of the ascending process by a dense strand of connective tissue and represents a detached basal process of the pterygoquadrate.

The two Meckel's cartilages now meet at an extensive symphysis. Each cartilage is a long stout bar, thickened at the region of articulation with the quadrate and possessing a long retroarticular process. This forms part of the articular bone of the adult and in lizards generally gives insertion to the depressor mandibularis and part of the pterygomandibularis muscles (see Oelrich, 1956). In sections of an adult *Lacerta vivipara* the tips of the two Meckel's cartilages do not quite meet in front, so that there may be some post-natal changes in the symphysial region.

Columellar apparatus. The columellar apparatus, formed by the fusion of its two rudiments, is now a long slender rod, still completely unossified, with its footplate fitting into the fenestra ovalis (Figs. 18; 19). All four processes of the insertion plate have now developed, giving the plate the cruciform appearance previously described (p. 33). Further medially, the internal process is connected, not very intimately, with the quadrate. The dorsal process has now regressed completely, except for its processus paroticus; this is a conspicuous nodule, completely separated from the columella and intercalated between the crista parotica posteriorly and the quadrate anteriorly.

Hyobranchial apparatus. All parts of the hyobranchial apparatus (Fig. 15B) have greatly elongated since Stage 2. A hooked second epibranchial element, unconnected with its ceratobranchial, has appeared.

c. Characters of the Lacertid Chondrocranium

So far as can be judged from the only two genera studied, *Lacerta* and *Acanthodactylus*, the following common aspects characterize the lacertids. Many of them occur in other groups of lizards. Features common to lizards in general are listed on p. 194.

1. The nasal capsule contains a large fenestra lateralis.

2. The cavity of the nasal concha (conchal space) is almost or completely enclosed by cartilage except at the aditus conchae in front.

3. A complete zona annularis is present.

4. The planum antorbitale is medially connected with or closely approximated to the nasal septum in the mature chondrocranium. Though of doubtful significance, this character (seen also in skinks) is perhaps unusual in lizards, in which the planum is often further removed from the septum.

5. The scaffolding of the orbitotemporal region is well developed, with its full complement of taeniae and pilae.

6. The IXth nerve has an extracapsular course, passing through the recessus scalae tympani without entering the otic capsule in any part of its course.

7. The columellar apparatus has a cartilaginous internal process and, at an earlier embryonic stage, a procartilaginous dorsal process. Both a processus accessorius anterior and a p.a. posterior are also present.

8. The second branchial arch of the hyobranchial apparatus is composed of two discontinuous segments, a ceratobranchial and an epibranchial.

d. *Osteocranium of* Lacerta

i. *General*

The development of the osteocranium of *Acanthodactylus* has not been studied, though the adult skull is described by El-Toubi and Soliman (1967; Figs. 20, 21A, B here). The following account is therefore taken mainly from de Beer's (1937) description of *Lacerta agilis*, based on the work of Gaupp (1900, 1906). It is unlikely that conditions in *Acanthodactylus* are significantly different, and indeed much of the following account is applicable to lizards in general. All the bones mentioned are paired structures, except where stated to the contrary.

ii. *Cartilage bones*

Most of the cartilage bones arise perichondrally, the ossification starting on the surface and only later replacing the cartilage within. Much of this deeper ossification occurs during postnatal life. Details of the brain-case on an adult lizard (*Varanus*) are shown in Fig. 41, and the bones are shown diagrammatically in Fig. 5 A.

An *orbitosphenoid* may ossify in the pila metoptica and adjacent cartilages in the adult. There appears to be no septosphenoid in Recent lizards (Bellairs, 1949a; Kamal, 1966b), except in the pygopodid *Aprasia* (p. 84). The pleurosphenoid (an ossification of the pila antotica) also seems to be generally absent; however, it is possible that the extreme posterior end of the pila antotica becomes incorporated into the alar process of the basisphenoid. The ossification of this bone (unpaired) is described later with the parasphenoid.

The *epipterygoid* ossifies around the ascending process of the pterygoquadrate. The dorsal end of the epipterygoid may remain cartilaginous. It articulates ventrally with a cartilage-lined depression in the pterygoid by means of a synovial joint (Fig. 6B). Its upper end is attached to the parietal and prootic bones. The slender, strut-like shape of the epipterygoid is a very characteristic feature of the saurian skull. It plays some part in kinesis; Boltt and Ewer (1964) suggest that it prevents the pterygoid from moving dorsally as the snout is raised and thus from compressing the brain, which in this region is hardly protected by the fenestrated chondrocranium.

The *prootic* arises around the front of the otic capsule; its ossification spreads forwards in the membranous lateral wall of the skull.

The *opisthotic* arises around the posteroventral region of the otic capsule.

The *exoccipital* arises on the inner and outer surfaces of the occipital arch and soon fuses with the opisthotic to form a compound *otooccipital*. The lateral portions of the condyle are derived from it. The otooccipital also forms the paroccipital process (formed partly from the crista parotica) which articulates by kinetic joints with the supratemporal, squamosal and quadrate.

The (unpaired) *basioccipital* ossifies on the dorsal and ventral surfaces of the basal plate and around the notochord; it spreads outwards, and by intramembranous extension, forwards to fill in most of the basicranial fenestra from behind.

The (unpaired) *supraoccipital* ossifies on the inner and outer surfaces of the occipital tectum. Some workers (e.g. Jollie, 1960) have described a separate epiotic centre on the dorsal aspect of each otic capsule, which may fuse with the supraoccipital. Further information on this is desirable.

The *quadrate* ossifies around the quadrate cartilage. It is movably attached to the squamosal and paroccipital process above and to the pterygoid and (of course) to the lower jaw below, thus showing the streptostylic condition. The front of the tympanic membrane is attached to the tympanic crest along its lateral surface.

The *articular* is the only cartilage bone in the lower jaw (Figs. 6B; 21). It ossifies around the posterior end of Meckel's cartilage and fuses with a membrane bone, the *prearticular*.

The *columella auris* or *stapes* ossifies in the medial part of the columellar apparatus; the lateral part remains cartilaginous as the extracolumella, which bears all the cartilaginous processes of the adult.

ii. Dermal bones

The *premaxilla* arises around the front of the nasal capsule and has a marked ascending process which terminates between the nasals (Fig. 20A). It fuses during early embryonic life with its opposite fellow and in the late embryo bears a median or paramedian egg-tooth (see de Beer, 1949; Bellairs, 1969). The premaxilla bears teeth in all adult lizards.

The *nasal* arises over the front of the roof of the nasal capsule.

The *septomaxilla* arises within the nasal capsule as a plate of bone between the nasal sac and the organ of Jacobson (Fig. 3B); its medial edge lies against the nasal septum and its lateral edge against the lateral wall of the capsule. In some lizards it has a posterior process which

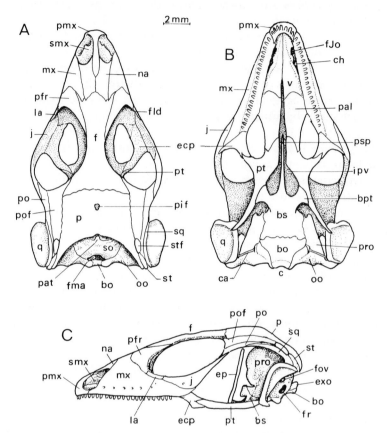

FIG. 20. *Acanthodactylus boskianus*, adult bony skull. (A) Dorsal, (B) ventral and (C) lateral view. After El-Toubi and Soliman (1967).

bo, Basioccipital; bpt, basipterygoid process; bs, basisphenoid (parabasisphenoid); c, occipital condyle; ca, columella auris; ch, choana (internal nostril); ecp, ectopterygoid; ep, epipterygoid; exo, exoccipital; f, frontal; fJo, foramen for duct of Jacobson's organ; fld, foramen for lachrymal duct; fma, foramen magnum; fov, fenestra ovalis; fr, fenestra rotunda; ipv, interpterygoid vacuity; j, jugal; la, lachrymal; mx, maxilla; na, nasal; oo, otooccipital (opisthotic + exoccipital); p, parietal; pal, palatine; pat, ossified part of anterior process of tectum (ossified as supraoccipital); pfr, prefrontal; pif, pineal foramen; pmx, premaxilla; po, postorbital; pof, postfrontal; pro, prootic; psp, parasphenoid (rostrum); pt, pterygoid; q, quadrate; smx, septomaxilla; so, supraoccipital; sq, squamosal; st, supratemporal; stf, superior temporal fossa; v, vomer.

extends into the concha (Fig. 28F). In malformed *Lacerta* embryos showing the anomaly of cleft palate the bone is divided into two parts by the
cleft (Fig. 16H). The embryological implications of this condition are discussed on p. 175.

The tooth-bearing *maxilla* arises lateral and ventral to the nasal capsule
and has ascending and palatine portions.

The *vomer* arises medial and ventral to Jacobson's organ on each side
and beneath the paraseptal cartilage (Fig. 3B, C). This bone has been
shown to be the homologue of the mammalian vomer (Parrington and
Westoll, 1940; Presley and Steel, 1978), and the term prevomer, used by
de Beer (1937) and many other authors, should lapse.

The anterior part of the gap or slit between the maxilla and vomer
transmits the duct of Jacobson's organ (Figs. 3b, 20B). Further back the
slit contains a deep groove of palatal epithelium known as the choanal
groove which receives the lachrymal duct in lacertids and some other
lizards and leads posteriorly into the membranous choana (Fig. 3C, D).
The most posterior part of the slit is the bony choana or internal nostril
(fenestra exochoanalis of Jarvik, 1942; see Bellairs and Boyd, 1950).

Lakjer (1927) introduced a classification of the saurian palate based on
the degree of separation between the bony apertures for the duct of
Jacobson's organ and the internal nostril. In *Sphenodon* and some lizards,
such as agamids and iguanids, these two openings in the bony palate are
completely confluent as a single, long slit (the palaeochoanate condition).
In certain other lizards including lacertids the vomers show a tendency
to approximate with the maxillae behind the openings for the ducts of
Jacobson's organs, thus partly separating their apertures from the internal
nostrils or choanae; this is Lakjer's incomplete neochoanate condition. In
varanids (and perhaps also in certain teiids, Presch, 1976), the approximation between maxillae and vomers is very close and the openings for the
ducts of Jacobson's organs and the choanae are quite distinct from each
other. This is the neochoanate condition, in which a complete secondary
bony palate, separating the mouth from the nasal cavities, is formed. Its
composition differs, however, from that of the secondary palate in
crocodilians or mammals. The term secondary palate is apparently used
in a rather different sense by Greer (1970) who applies it in the case of
certain skinks in which the palatines become nearly approximated beneath
the long nasopharyngeal ducts. It is uncertain how far these variations can be
correlated with the underlying chondrocranium, or whether they have any
functional significance.

The *palatine* separates the mouth from the orbit on each side and forms
the posterior boundary of each internal nostril. Nodules of cartilage found
on its dorsal surface may represent connections between the pterygoid

process of the pterygoquadrate and the posterior maxillary process.

In some lizards (not lacertids) the membranous choana is drawn out into a tubular ductus nasopharyngeus and the palatine of each side arches over it, or even nearly surrounds it.

The *ectopterygoid* (transpalatine) connects the maxilla with the pterygoid.

The pterygoid arises along the ventral aspect of the pterygoid process of the pterygoquadrate and extends forwards to articulate with the palatine; it has a lateral process directed towards the ectopterygoid. It articulates, via the meniscus, with the basipterygoid process of the parabasisphenoid and dorsally with the epipterygoid, a small pad of cartilage intervening between the two (Fig. 6B). In some lacertids such as *Lacerta agilis* (and in certain other lizards) this bone bears a number of small teeth, but these are absent in *L. vivipara* and in *Acanthodactylus boskianus*.

The (unpaired) *parasphenoid* fuses with the basisphenoid to form the *parabasisphenoid* (also unpaired). The basisphenoid ossifies perichondrally around the crista sellaris (and, possibly, the root of each pila antotica), the basipterygoid processes (which grow out from the cartilaginous trabeculae), and the posterior ends of the trabeculae themselves, which become surrounded by cylinders of bone (Fig. 6B). The dermal parasphenoid arises from three centres, one forming a lateral wing beneath each basipterygoid process, and one in the midline for the rostrum; the latter appears as a long slender splint beneath the interorbital septum. The lateral centres seem to grow inwards to fill in the floor of the pituitary fossa, fusing with the perichondrally ossifying basisphenoid as they do so. The combined bone probably also closes the front of the basicranial fenestra, meeting the basioccipital behind. The Vidian canal through the basipterygoid process passes between the basisphenoid above and the parasphenoid below (Figs. 6B; 9A).

Each basipterygoid process articulates with the medial side of the pterygoid. The cartilaginous basipterygoid meniscus intervenes between the two bones, but is firmly attached to the pterygoid. In late embryos of *Lacerta* there is a synovial cavity between the basipterygoid process and the meniscus (Fig. 6B).

In many mammals, elements representing the reptilian ectopterygoid and pterygoid fuse and contribute to the pterygoid process of the sphenoid (Presley and Steel, 1978).

The *frontal* and *parietal* are initially paired elements arising respectively over the planum supraseptale and adjacent regions, and over the hinder part of the cranial cavity. Both bones begin to ossify along their future lateral margins and grow towards the midline to complete the cranial roof. The more medial parts of these bones are barely ossified in newborn *Lacerta vivipara*. The parietals eventually fuse, leaving a foramen anteriorly for the parietal or pineal eye, while the frontals may remain separate. In some lizards of other groups the frontals fuse but the parietals remain paired.

The *prefrontal* arises over the posterolateral part of each nasal capsule.

The *lachrymal* is a tiny bone, absent in some lizards of other groups (e.g., some agamids and chameleons). In *Lacerta* the lachrymal duct passes forwards between it and the prefrontal at the front of the orbit (Fig. 20A).

The *jugal* is well developed and forms most of the postorbital arch. The quadratojugal is absent (or perhaps in some cases, vestigial) in modern lizards.

The *postfrontal* arises in front of the postorbital, with which it may become fused.

The *postorbital* joins the squamosal to form the superior temporal arch. In lacertids and some other lizards it (or the postfrontal) may grow posteriorly to cover the superior temporal fossa.

The *squamosal* arises over the side of each otic capsule, anteroventral to the supratemporal. The homologies of the supratemporal, squamosal and tabular bones have been much discussed (see Brock, 1935; de Beer, 1937; Parrington, 1937). The tabular is regarded here as being absent in Recent reptiles.

The *supratemporal* arises above the crista parotica.

The lower jaw (Fig. 21) contains the following dermal bones on each side: the *prearticular* or goniale (the chorda tympani runs between it and Meckel's cartilage); *angular; surangular; splenial; coronoid;* and the tooth-bearing *dentary*. These bones ossify around Meckel's cartilage, the dentary ossification being lateral to the cartilage initially. Even in the adult, the front of the cartilage is exposed medially in a groove on the medial side of the dentary. The two dentaries are connected at the symphysis by dense connective tissue.

There are about 12 scleral ossicles in each eye, around the rim of the scleral cartilage. Underwood (1970) gives details of these ossicles in reptiles.

There are, in addition, many intradermal ossifications, the *osteoderms* or osteoscutes, which develop in postnatal life and tend to fuse with the underlying bones of the skull. They include the supraocular, supraorbital and supraciliary above the eye (see figures in Parker, 1880a). In conjunction with the underlying postorbital bone, they may grow over the superior temporal fossa in some lizards.

e. General Comments on the Skull of Lacertidae

Both the chondrocranium and the bony skull of lacertids appear to be of a relatively generalized type, as might be expected in view of their

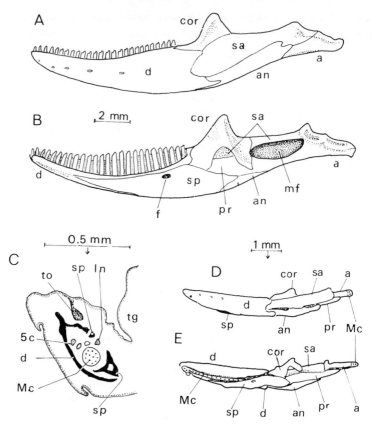

Fig. 21. (A, B) *Acanthodactylus boskianus*. Adult lower jaw from (A) lateral and (B) medial side. After El-Toubi and Soliman (1967). (C) *Lacerta vivipara*, late embryo. Transverse section through lower jaw at level of lingual nerve foramen, and slightly anterior to level of section in Fig. 3F. (D, E) *Lacerta agilis*, 47 mm embryo. Lower jaw from (D) lateral and (E) medial side. After Gaupp (1906).

a, Articular; an, angular; cor, coronoid; d, dentary; f, foramen in splenial for exit of lingual nerve (branch of 5c) + chorda tympani; ln, lingual nerve; Mc, Meckel's cartilage, the groove above the label d in Fig. B probably contains the exposed anterior end of this cartilage; mf, mandibular fossa, contains Meckel's cartilage and transmits 5c; pr, prearticular (fused with articular in B); sa, surangular; sp, splenial; tg, tongue; to, tooth germ; 5c, mandibular nerve (inferior dental branch).

generalized, mainly terrestrial way of life. By comparison with that of the Iguania the nasal capsule is unspecialized, even in the desert-living and otherwise specialized *Acanthodactylus*. The orbitotemporal scaffolding is well developed, while the bony skull shows both superior temporal and postorbital arches, though the former may be covered over, and the latter, as in *Acanthodactylus*, may be slightly reduced. Kinesis is of the amphi-kinetic type characteristic of most lizards (p. 198). One's attitude may, however, be conditioned to some extent by the fact that so much of the important earlier work was carried out on lizards of this family.

2. Scincidae (infraorder Scincomorpha)

a. Previous Literature

Afroblepharus wahlbergii, Malan, 1946 (nasal capsule). *Ablepharus kitaibelii*, Haas, 1935 (sections of adult). *Acontias meleagris*, de Villiers, 1939 (sections of adult); Brock, 1941a; Van der Merwe, 1944; Malan, 1946 (nasal capsule). *Chalcides guentheri*, Haas, 1936 (sections of adult). *C. ocellatus*, El-Toubi and Kamal, 1959a, b; Kamal, 1965a (adult skull). *C. sepsoides*, Kamal, 1969a. *Eumeces fasciatus*, Rice, 1920. *E. schneideri*, Kamal, 1965c. *Lygosoma* sp., Pearson, 1921. *Mabuya brevicollis*, Wever, 1973a, 1978 (ear). *M. capensis*, Malan, 1946 (nasal capsule); Skinner, 1973 (chondrocranium and osteocranium). *M. carinata*, Rao and Ramaswami, 1952 (chondrocranium and osteocranium). *Scelotes bipes*, Malan, 1946 (nasal capsule). *Trachydosaurus rugosus*, Pratt, 1948 (nasal capsule).

The fullest accounts are by Rao and Ramaswami (1952) and Skinner (1973) of *Mabuya*, and of El-Toubi and Kamal (1959a, b) and Kamal (1965a) of *Chalcides ocellatus*. These are fairly generalized skinks with well developed limbs and afford interesting comparisons with the serpentiform *Chalcides sepoides* and *Acontias meleagris*. Aspects of the structure of the otic region in burrowing skinks and other lizards with reduced tympanic membranes are described by Barry (1963) and Torien (1963).

b. Chondrocranium of Scincidae

The chondrocranium of the more generalized skinks (Fig. 22) appears much like that of lacertids. The following features of those members of the family studied are of interest.

1. There is a large fenestra superior in the nasal capsule.
2. The side of the nasal capsule is usually more complete than in lacertids owing to the absence or small size of the fenestra lateralis. In *Chalcides ocellatus* the planum antorbitale comes into contact with the nasal septum during later embryonic life.
3. The scaffolding of the orbitotemporal region may differ from that of lacertids, at least at certain stages. Thus, in early stages of *Eumeces fasciatus* there are two additional bars on each side connecting the taenia medialis with the taenia marginalis, but in later stages these extra bars, together with the pila antotica, are lost (Rice, 1920). In *Lygosoma* sp., at least at the stage studied by Pearson (1921), the taenia marginalis is greatly reduced (Fig. 23C). In late stages of *Mabuya capensis*, however, the condition resembles that of lacertids (Skinner, 1973).

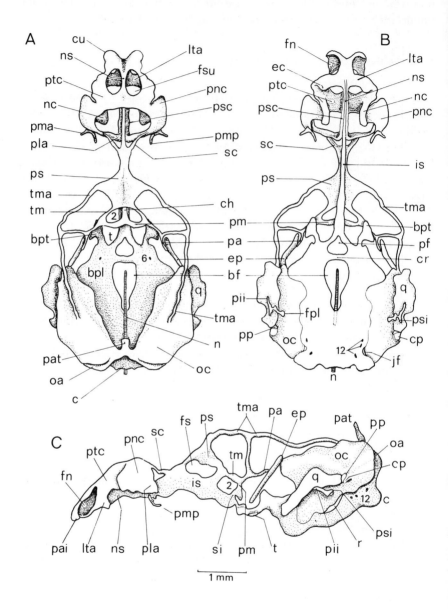

1 mm

In the fossorial, snake-like *Acontias meleagris* (Fig. 23A, B) the interorbital septum is very low, and the planum supraseptale is small and narrow; nearly all the orbitotemporal bars have disappeared except for vestiges of the taeniae marginales—at least in late stages (Brock, 1941a). Similar reduction, though to a lesser extent, is also seen in *Chalcides sepsoides* (Kamal, 1969a). In *Acontias*, at least, this can perhaps be correlated with changes in the bony skull which tend to convert the cranium into a rigid box. In *Voeltzkowia*, another specialized burrower, the interorbital septum may be still further reduced, as in the pygopodid *Aprasia* and in *Dibamus* (Underwood, 1970; Rieppel, personal communication).

4. There is no distinct basipterygoid meniscus in *Mabuya carinata*, *Chalcides ocellatus* or *Acontias meleagris*. In *Mabuya capensis* a thin, mainly fibrous meniscus is present.

5. An interesting, though minor peculiarity of most of the skinks examined is that the IXth nerve appears to pass through the cochlear portion of the otic capsule, differing from the condition in lizards generally (Kamal, 1969e). The nerve enters the capsule through a foramen on its medial aspect and leaves it via the perilymphatic foramen to enter the recessus scalae tympani; from this it emerges laterally from the skull in the usual fasion (Fig. 24B). In *Mabuya capensis*, however, the nerve is extracapsular throughout development (see Skinner, 1973). The significance of this feature is probably trivial.

6. No mesenchymatous or cartilaginous dorsal process connecting the columellar apparatus with the processus paroticus (intercalary) seems to have been described. Except in *Eumeces schneiderii* (Kamal, 1965c) no internal process has been observed in skinks. Although *Acontias* has no true middle ear cavity, it has a tympanic membrane to which the extracolumella is applied (Torien, 1963). The middle ear in *Eumeces* and *Mabuya* is described by Wever (1973a).

FIG. 22. *Chalcides ocellatus*. Fully formed chondrocranium of 42mm embryo. (A) Dorsal, (B) ventral and (C) lateral view. After El-Toubi and Kamal (1959b).

bf, Basicranial fenestra; bpl, basal plate; bpt, basipterygoid process; c, occipital condyle; ch, cartilago hypochiasmatica; cp, crista parotica; cr, crista sellaris; cu, nasal cupola; ec, ectochoanal cartilage; ep, epipterygoid (ascending process of pterygoquadrate); fn, fenestra narina; fpl, footplate of columella; fs, fenestra in interorbital septum; fsu, fenestra superior; is, interorbital septum; jf, jugular foramen (for vagus nerve); lta, lamina transversalis anterior; n, notochord; nc, nasal concha; ns, nasal septum; oa, occipital arch; oc, otic capsule; pa, pila antotica; pai, processus alaris inferior; pat, anterior process of tectum; pf, pituitary fossa; pii, pars inferior of insertion plate of extracolumella; pla, planum antorbitale; pm, pila metoptica; pma, pmp, anterior and posterior maxillary processes; pnc, paranasal cartilage; pp, processus paroticus; ps, planum supraseptale; psc, paraseptal cartilage; psi, pars superior of insertion plate; ptc, parietotectal cartilage; q, quadrate; r, recessus scalae tympani (lateral opening); sc, sphenethmoid commissure; si, subiculum infundibuli; t, trabecula; tm, taenia medialis; tma, taenia marginalis; 2, optic fenestra; 6, foramen for abducens nerve; 12, foramina for hypoglossal nerve (3 on right, two on left).

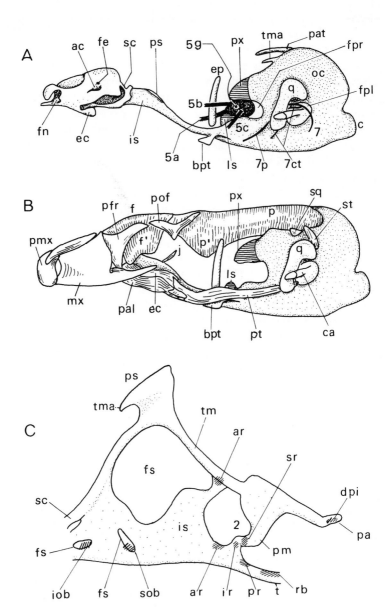

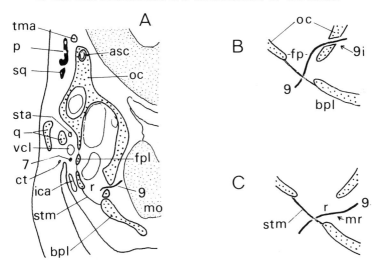

FIG. 24. (A) Transverse section through otic region of late embryo of the skink *Mabuya carinata* showing intracapsular course of the glossopharyngeal nerve. After Rao and Ramaswami (1952). (B, C) Diagrams showing (B) intracapsular course of glossopharyngeal nerve, as in skinks, and (C) extra-capsular course, as in lizards generally (illustrated by transverse sections through left side of head). In (B) the nerve enters the otic capsule through the internal glossopharyngeal foramen and enters the recessus scalae tympani through the perilymphatic foramen. In (C) the nerve enters the recessus directly through its medial opening, as is also shown in Fig. 7. In both (B) and (C) the nerve leaves the recessus through its so-called lateral opening, behind the secondary tympanic membrane. After Kamal (1969e).

asc, Anterior semicircular canal; bpl, basal plate; ct, chorda tympani; fp, foramen perilymphaticum; fpl, footplate of columella; ica, internal carotid artery; mo, medulla oblongata; mr, medial opening of recessus scalae tympani; oc, otic capsule; p, parietal; q, quadrate; r, recessus scalae tympani; sq, squamosal; sta, stapedial artery; stm, secondary tympanic membrane; tma, taenia marginalis; vcl, vena capitis lateralis; 7, facial nerve (hyomandibular); 9, glossopharyngeal nerve; 9i, internal foramen for glossopharyngeal nerve.

FIG. 23. (A) Lateral view of the chondrocranium of a late embryo of the limbless skink, *Acontias meleagris*. (B) Same with membrane bones *in situ*. A, B after Brock (1941a). (C) Lateral view of orbitotemporal chondrocranium of a late embryo of the skink *Lygosoma* sp., showing origins of the eye muscles. After Pearson (1921). Slightly different origins in other species are shown by Säve-Söderbergh (1947) and Underwood (1970).

ac, Aditus conchae; ar, anterior (internal) rectus (2 origins); bpt, basipterygoid process; c, occipital condyle; ca, columella auris; dpi, M. depressor palpebrae inferioris; ec, ectochoanal cartilage; ep, epipterygoid; f, frontal; f′, frontal downgrowth; fe, foramen epiphaniale; fn, fenestra narina; fpl, foot-plate; fpr, fenestra prootica; fs, fenestra in nasal or interorbital septum; iob, inferior oblique; ir, inferior rectus; is, interorbital septum; j, jugal; ls, laterosphenoid; mx, maxilla; oc, otic capsule; p, parietal; p′, parietal downgrowth; pa, pila antotica (absent in *Acontias*); pal, palatine; pat, anterior process of tectum; pfr, prefrontal; pm, pila metoptica; pmx, premaxilla; pof, postfrontal; pr, posterior (external) rectus; ps, planum supraseptale; pt, pterygoid; px, intramembranous extension of prootic; q, quadrate; rb, Mm. retractor bulbi and bursalis; sc, sphenethmoid commissure; sob, superior oblique; sq, squamosal; sr, superior rectus; st, supratemporal; t, trabecula; tm, taenia medialis; tma, taenia marginalis (reduced); 2 optic fenestra; 5a, b, c, g, ophthalmic, maxillary, and mandibular nerves and trigeminal ganglion; 7, facial nerve (hyomandibular branch); 7ct, chorda tympani; 7p, palatine nerve; ec, *also* ectopterygoid.

7. The hyobranchial apparatus resembles that of lacertids, except in *Acontias* in which parts of it are reduced.

8. According to Haas (1935) parts of the chondrocranium, including parts of the otic capsule, of *Ablepharus kitaibelii* remain unfossified to a degree which is noteworthy if the specimen which he examined was truly adult.

c. Osteocranium of Scincidae

The premaxillae are often paired (an unusual saurian feature) and the frontals as well as the parietals may be fused. In some skinks, such as *Acontias*, the palatines are tubular and partly surround the well developed ductus nasopharyngeus; the palatines and pterygoids may become approximated in the midline forming a kind of postchoanal bony secondary palate (see Greer, 1970). In the more generalized skinks the skull arches are present but the superior temporal fossa may become more or less obliterated by the growth of the postfrontal and adjacent bones. Specialized burrowing forms such as *Acontias meleagris* (Fig. 23) show reduction or loss of the arches and smaller circumorbital bones, and the development of downgrowths from the frontals and parietals protecting the forebrain. In this last species there is a laterosphenoid, apparently resembling that of snakes, posterior to the well developed epipterygoid (Brock, 1941a; III–D–11 here; Van der Merwe, 1944).

3. Cordylidae (infraorder Scincomorpha)

a. Previous literature

Chamaesaura anguina, du Plessis, 1945; Pratt, 1948 (nasal capsule). *Cordylus polyzonus*, Van Pletzen, 1946 (sections of adult). *Gerrhosaurus major*, Pratt, 1948 (nasal capsule). *Gerrhosaurus* sp., Malan, 1940, 1946 (nasal capsule).

b. Skull

The nasal capsule of cordylids appears rather like that of lacertids except that the paraseptal cartilage is absent in *Chamaesaura*, while in (adult) *Cordylus* it is discontinuous in the middle. The latter lacks the pilae antotica and has reduced taeniae mediales. Dorsally the lateral parts of the parabasisphenoid are incompletely fused with the basisphenoid, while the parasphenoid rostrum is discontinuous with the rest of the bone, an unusual condition. A remnant of the basicranial fenestra persists in the floor of the adult skull as a foramen between the basisphenoid and the basioccipital. Both *Chamaesaura* and *Cordylus* have a superior temporal arch, but in the latter the superior temporal fossa is almost closed by the approximation of the postorbital, squamosal and parietal bones. In *Cordylus* the orbit is roofed by two rows of osteoderms, those in the upper row being very large.

4. Teiidae (infraorder Scincomorpha)

a. Previous literature

Ameiva lineolata, Wever, 1978 (ear): *A. undulata*, *Cnemidophorus sexlineatus*, *Teius teyou*, Malan, 1946 (nasal capsule). *Tupinambis teguixin*, Pratt, 1948 (nasal capsule); Jollie, 1960 (unsectioned adult); Barbarena *et al.*, 1970 (unsectioned adult). Fisher and Tanner (1970) have described the adult cranial anatomy of certain genera, while Dalrymple (1979) has studied the jaw mechanism of the snail-crushing form, *Dracaena*.

b. Skull

In the three genera studied by Malan (1946) the nasal septum is prolonged forwards as a short rostral process. The paraseptal cartilage is incomplete anteriorly. In *Teius* the organ of Jacobson is partly roofed over by strips of cartilage which lie ventral to the septomaxilla; a more complete roofing cartilage is found among the Iguanidae and in *Sphenodon*. Moreover, the posterior part of Jacobson's organ is enclosed by a cartilaginous cupola presumably derived from the lamina transversalis anterior (Fig. 25C). As in *Lacerta* (Fig. 3B) each side of the nasal septum has a ledge against which rests the inner edge of the septomaxilla. In all three forms the cavum conchale is very large. As in *Tupinambis* (Fig. 25B) there is no fenestra superior but a large fenestra lateralis is present; this is the converse to the condition in skinks.

In *Tupinambis* the columella has a ligamentous dorsal process and an internal process; the lingual process of the hyoid is detached from the basihyal, and the second branchial arch is represented only by the epibranchial (Jollie, 1960).

In the more generalized teiids the temporal arches of the bony skull are complete. Both frontals and parietals in *Tupinambis* are fused, and there is no parietal foramen.

5. Xantusiidae (infraorder Scincomorpha)

a. Previous literature

Lepidophyma flavimaculatum; *Xantusia henshawi*, Wever, 1978 (ear). *Xantusia vigilis*, Young, 1942 (sections of adult); Malan, 1946 and Pratt, 1948 (nasal capsule).

72

A. D'A. BELLAIRS AND A. M. KAMAL

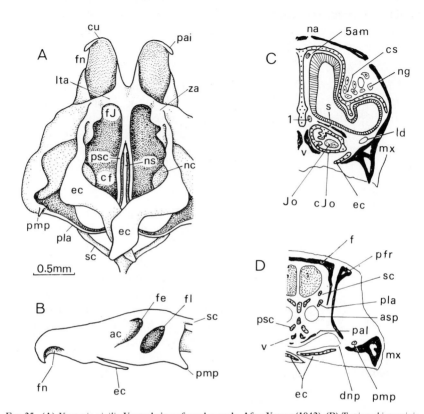

Fig. 25. (A) *Xantusia vigilis*. Ventral view of nasal capsule. After Young (1942). (B) *Tupinambis teguixin*. Lateral view of nasal capsule. After Pratt (1948). (C) *Teius teyou*. Transverse section through conchal region and posterior end of Jacobson's organ, showing the organ surrounded at this level by cartilage. (D) *Xantusia vigilis*. Transverse section through posterior nasal region showing ductus nasopharyngeus and ectochoanal cartilages. (C) and (D) after Malan (1946). All material figured above is postnatal or adult.

ac, Aditus conchae; asp, antorbital space of nasal sac; cf, choanal fenestra; cJo, cartilage surrounding Jacobson's organ; cs, conchal space (cavum conchale); cu, cupola; dnp, ductus nasopharyngeus; ec, ectochoanal cartilage; f, frontal; fe, foramen epiphaniale; fJ, fenestra for duct of Jacobson's organ; fl, fenestra lateralis; fn, fenestra narina; Jo, Jacobson's organ; ld, lachrymal duct; lta, lamina transversalis anterior; mx, maxilla; na, nasal; nc, nasal concha; ng, nasal gland; ns, nasal septum; pai, processus alaris inferior; pal, palatine; pfr, prefrontal; pla, planum antorbitale; pmp, posterior maxillary process; psc, paraseptal cartilage; s, septomaxilla; sc, sphenethmoid commissure; v, vomer; za, zona annularis; 1, vomeronasal nerve; 5am, medial ethmoidal branch of ophthalmic nerve.

b. Skull

The nasal region shows a number of peculiarities such as the great size of the ectochoanal cartilages which overlap in the midline and support the floor of the well developed ductus nasopharyngeus (Fig. 25A, D). The skeleton around the organ of Jacobson shows various adaptations to increase structural solidity. Thus, the paraseptal cartilages are fused anteriorly across the midline beneath the nasal septum and the vomers are also fused, an unusual condition. There is a zona annularis. The septomaxilla is exceptionally well developed, forming a buttress on either side of the nasal septum (Malan, 1946). This strengthening may be necessary to counteract the stress exerted upon the front part of the snout by the enormous ectochoanal cartilages during the bite.

The extracolumella and its processes resemble those in lacertids. The second ceratobranchials are present, but the elements of this arch are not quite continuous, at least not in the adult (Camp, 1923).

The temporal arches are present, but the superior temporal fossa is closed by the union of postfrontal, squamosal and parietal bones. Both frontals and parietals are paired. The adult lower jaw consists of only three separate bones: dentary, splenial, and a coossification of articular, prearticular, angular and surangular (Camp, 1923).

Although *Xantusia* has apparently no stapedial foramen, some of its cranial and other features such as the shape of the basipterygoid region of the brain-case (McDowell and Bogert, 1954) and the presence of post-cloacal bones suggest affinities with the geckos; thus it has been suggested that this family should be classified with the Gekkota. However, Moffat (1973) thinks that it is correctly placed in the Scincomorpha. Further details of the embryonic chondrocranium of these forms would be welcome.

6. Geckonidae (infraorder Gekkota)

a. Previous Literature

Common characters and phylogenetic position of the group, Kamal, 1961b, c. *Gekko gecko*, Werner and Wever, 1972; Wever, (1978) (ear). *Hemidactylus turcicus*, Kamal, 1961a. *Hoplodactylus granulatus*, Pratt, 1948 (nasal capsule). *Lygodactylus capensis*, Brock, 1932a. *Nephrurus levis*, *N. asper*, Stephenson, 1960 (postnatal growth). *Afroedura karroica*, *Palmato-gecko rangei*, Webb, 1951 (sections of adult). *Pachydactylus weberi*, Malan, 1946 (nasal capsule); *Ptyodactylus hasselquistii*, El-Toubi and Kamal, 1961a, b, c (chondrocranium, and osteocranium of late embryo). *Tarentola mauritanica*, Sewertzoff, 1900. *T. annularis*, Hafferl, 1921; Kamal, 1965d:

Tropiocolotes tripolitanus, Kamal, 1960. *T. steudneri*, Kamal, 1964a. *Steno-dactylus sthenodactylus*, Pratt, 1948 (nasal capsule); Kamal, 1965b.

b. Early Stages of Gekkonidae

The early development of the geckonid chondrocranium is best known from the work of El-Toubi and Kamal (1961a) on *Ptyodactylus*. Their figures (Fig. 26 here) show the basic components of the chondrocranium

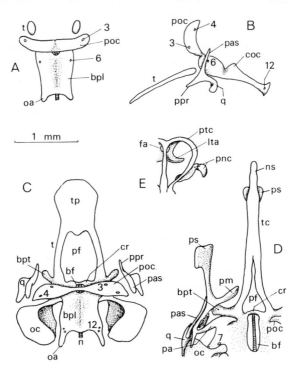

Fig. 26. (A–D) Chondrocranium of *Ptyodactylus hasselquistii*, showing transformation of trabeculae. (A) Dorsal view of Stage 1 (15·2 mm total body length); (B) lateral view of Stage 2 (16·8 mm), with trabeculae still quite separate; (C) dorsal view of Stage 3 (18·9 mm); (D) dorsai view of part of chondrocranium of Stage 4 (21·3 mm) with trabeculae completely fused in front to form trabecula communis. After El-Toubi and Kamal (1961a). (E) *Hemidactylus turcicus*. Dorsal view of nasal capsule of Stage 1 (19·3 mm total body length). The paranasal cartilage is separate from the parietotectal cartilage; they fuse later. After Kamal (1961a).

bf, Basicranial fenestra; bpl, basal plate; bpt, basipterygoid process; coc, cochlear part of otic capsule; cr, crista sellaris; fa, foramen apicale; lta, lamina transversalis anterior; n, notochord; ns, nasal septum; oa, occipital arch; oc, otic capsule; pa, pila antotica; pas, ascending process of pterygoquadrate (epiptery-goid); pf, pituitary fenestra; pm, pila metoptica; pnc, paranasal cartilage; poc, posterior orbital cartilage (regressing across the midline in (D)); ppr, pterygoid process of pterygoquadrate; ps, planum supraseptale (separate anterior and posterior rudiments in D); ptc, parietotectal cartilage; q, quadrate; t, trabecula; tc, trabecula communis; tp, trabecular plate; 3, 4, 6, 7, 12, foramina for oculomotor, trochlear, abducens, facial, and hypoglossal nerves.

very clearly. The general pattern of development follows that described for *Acanthodactylus*. A significant feature is the development, in Stage 3, of a wide trabecular plate, that connects the front ends of the initially separate trabeculae. This plate is still procartilaginous, although the trabeculae themselves are well chondrified. By Stage 4 the plate has regressed completely and the front ends of the trabeculae have fused to form the nasal septum. Another feature of interest is a fenestra lateralis in the paranasal cartilage at Stage 5. This seems to represent an area of retarded chondrification which is later filled in geckos; however, it persists in lacertids. As in lizards generally, the cochlear part of the otic capsule is never separate from the basal plate. In the early stages the notochord is completely embedded in the basal plate.

Early stages of both *Ptyodactylus* and *Hemidactylus turcicus* (Kamal, 1961a) show the planum supraseptale arising from two centres of chondrification on each side. Another unusual feature, seen only in *Hemidactylus*, is the completely separate origin of the paranasal cartilage from the parietotectal cartilage (Fig. 26E). This finding is of interest in suggesting that (contrary to the view expressed on p. 51), the paranasal cartilage may be a distinct element.

c. The Mature Chondrocranium of Gekkonidae

Kamal (1961b) has listed the principal characters of geckos which are mostly shown in Figures 27 and 28 here. There appears to be much variation within the family but it is not yet possible to correlate this with the sub-familial groupings proposed by Kluge (1967) and others.

1. In some geckos at least the foramen apicale is situated in the medial wall of the nasal cupola (Fig. 27C), instead of at the front of the cupola as in most lizards.

2. The superior alar process and anterior maxillary process are absent.

3. *Hoplodactylus* (Pratt, 1948) and *Ptyodactylus* have a superior fenestra in the nasal capsule, unlike other geckos studied. There is no lateral fenestra in the mature paranasal cartilage of these geckos.

4. In mature stages the parietotectal cartilage is usually separated from the lamina transversalis anterior by a lateral nasal fissure which is anteriorly continuous with the fenestra narina (Fig. 27C). Thus there is no complete zona annularis. The fissure continues posteriorly between the parietotectal and paranasal cartilages to the aditus conchae. The duct of the lateral nasal gland passes through this fissure to enter the nasal sac; the lateral edge of the septomaxillary bone fits into the fissure (Fig. 28D). In *Tropiocolotes* (Kamal, 1960, 1961b, 1964a) and *Stenodactylus* (Kamal, 1965b), however, and also perhaps in *Afroedura* and *Palmatogecko* (Webb, 1951), the parietotectal cartilage fuses with the lamina trans-

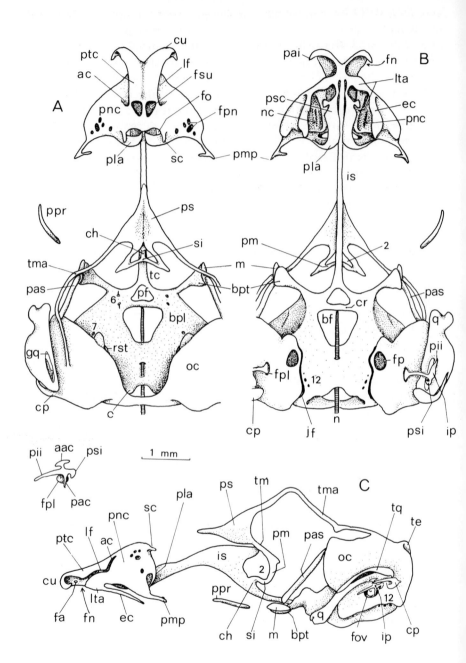

versalis anterior behind the fenestra narina, as in lacertids, so that a zona annularis is present.

5. The cartilaginous nasal concha shows considerable variation. In *Sphaerodactylus argus* (Bellairs unpublished) the concha is very small and consists of little more than a slight invagination of the lateral wall of the capsule at the aditus conchae anteriorly, and a narrow, shelf-like projection at a more posterior level (Fig. 28G, H, I). In *Ptyodactylus* and *Stenodactylus* (Fig. 28E, F), however, and perhaps in the majority of geckos, the morphology of the conchal region essentially resembles that in lacertids (see p. 49), except that there is no lateral fenestra in the paranasal cartilage and that the ventral wall of the cavum conchale is deficient; thus in the posterior part of the conchal region the cartilaginous concha has a simple scroll-like shape in transverse section (Fig. 28F), and does not virtually encircle the cavum as in lacertids (Fig. 3D). The scroll-like shape of the posterior part of the concha is also seen in certain other lizards such as *Xantusia* and *Anguis*, and cannot be regarded as a gekkonid characteristic.

6. The ectochoanal cartilages of geckos are long and flattened.

7. The sphenethmoid commissures are either completely absent as in *Tarentola* (Kamal, 1965d) or reduced, and the front of the planum supraseptale is also reduced. In *Ptyodactylus* (Fig. 27A, C) the commissures fail to reach the planum behind, while in *Pachydactylus*, *Hemidactylus* and *Tropiocolotes* the connection between the commissures and the planum is lost in later embryonic stages. In *Stenodactylus* the posterior end of each commissure is fused with the dorsal aspect of the planum antorbitale, a condition not known in other lizards (Kamal, 1965b). Therefore, in geckos generally the fenestra olfactoria evehens is either absent or without a posterior boundary.

FIG. 27. *Ptyodactylus hasselquistii*. Fully formed chondrocranium in (A) dorsal, (B) ventral and (C) lateral view, with columella shown separately on left above. After El-Toubi and Kamal (1971b).

aac, Anterior accessory process; ac, aditus conchae; bf, basicranial fenestra; bpl, basal plate; bpt, basipterygoid process; c, occipital condyle; ch, cartilago hypochiasmatica; cp, crista parotica; cr, crista sellaris; cu, nasal cupola; ec, ectochoanal cartilage; fa, foramen apicale; fn, fenestra narina; fo, fenestra olfactoria; fov, fenestra ovalis; fp, perilymphatic foramen; fpl, footplate of columella; fpn, foramina in paranasal cartilage; fsu, fenestra superior; gq, gap in quadrate; ip, insertion plate of extracolumella; is, interorbital septum; jf, jugular foramen (for vagus nerve); lf, lateral fissure in nasal capsule; lta, lamina transversalis anterior; m, basipterygoid meniscus; n, notochord; nc, nasal concha; oc, otic capsule; pac, posterior accessory process; pai, processus alaris inferior; pas, ascending process of pterygoquadrate; pf, pituitary fossa; pii, pars inferior of insertion plate; pla, planum antorbitale; pm, pila metoptica; pmp, posterior maxillary process; pnc, paranasal cartilage; ppr, pterygoid process of pterygoquadrate (detached; shown on one side only); ps, planum supraseptale; psc, paraseptal cartilage; psi, pars superior of insertion plate; ptc, parietotectal cartilage; q, quadrate; rst, recessus scalae tympani; sc, sphenethmoid commissure; si, subiculum infundibuli; tc, trabecula communis; te, tectum; tm, taenia medialis; tma, taenia marginalis; tq, tympanic crest of quadrate; 2, optic fenestra; 6, abducens canal; 7, 12, foramina for facial and hypoglossal (three on each side) nerves.

8. The planum antorbitale may closely approach the nasal septum but is not fused with it.

9. The orbitotemporal scaffolding tends to become reduced in later stages, as in certain skinks. Apart from the gap between the upper edge of the interorbital septum and the incomplete planum supraseptale (which probably corresponds to the large fenestra in the septum of lacertids) the interorbital septum is unfenestrated.

In *Tarentola* a fenestra similar to the fenestra X of snakes (p. 139) is developed on each side of the front of the basal plate (Kamal, 1965d).

10. The pterygoquadrate cartilage usually has two pterygoid processes, a short posterior one and a long anterior one. The posterior process, which is fused with the base of the ascending process, only occurs in the early stages. The anterior process chondrifies in late embryos as a slender rod which remains separate from the rest of the chondrocranium (Fig. 27). Its ultimate fate is not clear.

11. In the fully formed chondrocranium the top of the ascending process is either in contact with the anterior wall of the otic capsule or actually

---

Fig. 28. (A) *Coleonyx variegatus*. Hyobranchial skeleton of adult. Cartilage is stippled. After Kluge (1967). (B) *Coleonyx variegatus*. Left columellar apparatus of adult seen from ventromedial aspect. The stapedial artery perforates the footplate in the characteristic gekkonid fashion. After Posner and Chiasson (1966). (C) *Coleonyx variegatus*, adult. Transverse section through otic region showing stapedial artery perforating columellar footplate. (D) *Sphaerodactylus argus*, adult. Transverse section through anterior part of nasal capsule showing Jacobson's organ and lateral fissure. (E, F) *Stenodactylus sthenodactylus*, adult. Transverse sections through conchal region of nasal capsule. (E) is anterior to (F). In (E) the capsule is partly reconstructed (in line shading) as if seen from the front. Arrows show mode of fusion between the parietotectal cartilage and lamina transversalis anterior at a slightly more posterior level, and also the way in which the vestibule communicates with the extra-conchal recess (epithelium within recess not shown). (F) shows the scroll-like shape of the more posterior region of the concha, which does not enclose the nasal gland ventrolaterally. Compare with Fig. 3C, D of *Lacerta* in which the nasal gland is more completely enclosed, but in which there is a large lateral fenestra in the lateral wall of the paranasal cartilage. (G, H, I) *Sphaerodactylus argus*, adult. Successive transverse sections, in anterior to posterior sequence, showing the small, relatively simple nasal concha.

aac, Anterior accessory process; ca, columella auris; cb1, cb2, ceratobranchials 1 and 2; cg, choanal groove; chy, ceratohyal; cJo, cartilage of Jacobson's organ; cri, cricoid cartilage; ct, chorda tympani; eb1, eb2, epibranchials 1 and 2; ec, ectochoanal cartilage; eh, epihyal; ex, extracolumella; exe, extension of external ear cavity; fpl, columellar footplate; hh, hypohyal; ica, internal carotid artery; ip, insertion plate of extracolumella; Jo, Jacobson's organ; ld, lachrymal duct; lf, lateral fissure of nasal capsule; lp, lingual process of hyoid; lsc, lateral semicircular canal; lta, lamina transversalis anterior; mx, maxilla; na, nasal; ng, nasal gland; ns, nasal septum; oc, otic capsule; p, parietal; pac, posterior accessory process; pg, palatine gland; ph, pharynx; pii, pars inferior of insertion plate; pmx, premaxilla; pnc, paranasal cartilage; poa, posterior accessory process of insertion plate; psc, paraseptal cartilage; psi, pars superior of insertion plate; ptc, parietotectal cartilage; q, quadrate; r, extra-conchal recess; smx, septomaxilla; sr, sub-conchal recess of nasal sac; st, supratemporal; sta, stapedial artery; ty, tympanic cavity; v, vomer; vcl, vena capitis lateralis (internal jugular vein); ve, vestibule of nasal sac; 1, 1', olfactory and vomeronasal nerves; 5al, 5am, lateral and medial ethmoidal branches of ophthalmic nerve, in G 5al is about to pass through foramen epiphaniale; 5b, maxillary nerve; 7, facial nerve (hyomandibular branch); 7p, palatine branch of facial nerve.

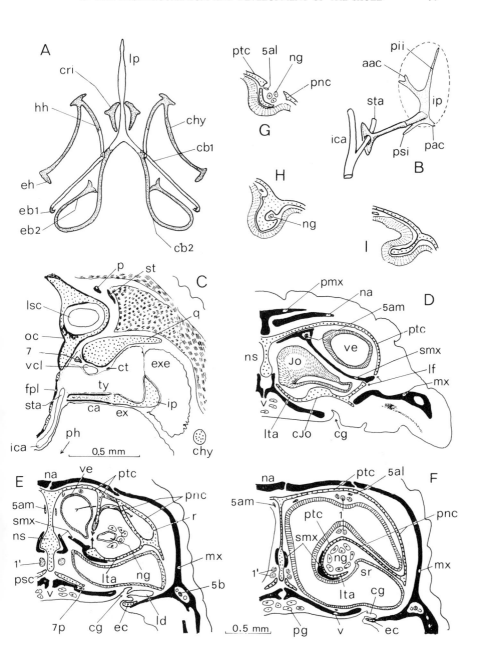

fused with it. This fusion may persist in the adult and is unusual among lizards.

12. The anterior process of the occipital tectum (tectum synoticum plus posterius) is absent or very small.

13. The medial end of the columella auris is pierced by a foramen for the stapedial branch of the internal carotid artery (Fig. 28B, C). This interesting feature is not shared by *Ptyodactylus* or by *Gekko* sp. (one specimen only examined), in which, as in almost all other non-gekkonid lizards, the artery passes dorsal to the columella.

14. The columellar apparatus has no dorsal process, ligamentous or otherwise, apart from a small intercalary, and generally no internal process. The middle ear of *Coleonyx* is described by Posner and Chiasson (1966; Fig. 28B here) and of *Gekko* by Werner and Wever (1972) and Wever (1978). Geckos, and some of their pygopodid relatives, are unusual in having a small extracolumellar muscle which runs from the pars superior of the insertion plate to the ceratohyal and influences sound conduction in some degree.

15. In some geckos, such as *Ptyodactylus*, a cartilaginous connection between the extracolumella and ceratohyal, called the interhyal, persists in late embryonic stages and only disappears before hatching. In other lizards this connection disappears early, though it remains chondrified in postnatal *Sphenodon* (p. 118). The persistence of a well developed extra-stapedial (or extracolumellar) ligament, which represents the laterohyal and connects the pars superior of the insertion plate with the processus paroticus or intercalary (see Fig. 10), is another gekkonid feature; it is uncertain to what extent this condition can be matched in other lizards.

d. Osteocranium of Gekkonidae

Geckos are characterized by the loss of the temporal arches and reduction of the jugal. The single small temporal bone has usually been regarded as a supratemporal (or tabular), the squamosal being supposedly absent, as shown in Figure 29. However, Underwood (1957) has good evidence that the converse is true. In some forms such as *Ptyodactylus*, a tiny splint of bone on the lateral surface of the quadrate can be interpreted as a vestigial quadratojugal (see El-Toubi and Kamal, 1961c, who do not, however, indicate its position in their figures, reproduced as Fig. 29 here). The lachrymal seems to be absent in geckos and the splenial is often reduced. Kluge (1967), who lists many osteological features of the family, states that the angular is generally absent and that the surangular may fuse with the articular and prearticular in the adult. However, these last features are not evident in the embryonic osteocranium of *Ptyodactylus* shown here. In many geckos the frontals fuse while the parietals remain

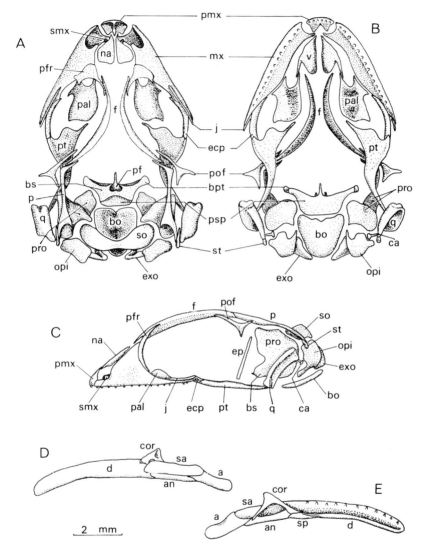

Fig. 29. *Ptyodactylus hasselquistii.* (A) Dorsal, (B) ventral and (C) lateral views of osteocranium of a late embryo. (D) Lower jaw from lateral side, (E) from medial side. After El-Toubi and Kamal (1961c).

a, Articular; an, angular; bo, basioccipital; bpt, basipterygoid process; bs, basisphenoid; ca, columella auris; cor, coronoid; d, dentary; ecp, ectopterygoid; ep, epipterygoid; exo, exoccipital; f, frontal; j, jugal; mx, maxilla; na, nasal; opi, opisthotic; p, parietal; pal, palatine; pf, pituitary fossa; pfr, prefrontal; pmx, premaxilla; pof, postfrontal; pro, prootic; psp, parasphenoid; pt, pterygoid; q, quadrate; sa, surangular; smx, septomaxilla; so, supraoccipital; sp, splenial; st, supratemporal; v, vomer.

82 A. D'A. BELLAIRS AND A. M. KAMAL

separate. There is usually no parietal foramen. Orbitosphenoid ossifications have not been reported.

In most geckos the premaxilla of the late embryo bears paired egg-teeth instead of the single median or paramedian egg-tooth found in other Squamata (de Beer, 1949; Kluge, 1967).

Stephenson and Stephenson (1956) and Stephenson (1960) have drawn attention to the fact that the skulls of some New Zealand and Australian geckos, such as *Nephrurus*, show neotenic features; they believe that neoteny has played a significant part in the evolution of the group. Thus, a particular structure in the adult of one genus may resemble the same structure in a juvenile of another genus.

In some of these geckos, notably *Nephrurus*, the dermis of the skin, though lacking separate osteoderms, becomes intimately fused with the roofing bones of the skull. Moreover, the latter, as in *Nephrurus*, undergo marked growth changes during postnatal life. The supratemporal (? squamosal) bone changes from a splint to a broad plate and the relative width of the posterior skull roof is increased. "These changes indicate that the ultimate shape of the supratemporal and parietal is not exclusively determined by the initial lines along which their rudiments, growing at different rates, or starting to grow at different times, meet" (Stephenson, 1960, p. 296).

e. Supposedly Primitive Features of Gekkonidae

It has been suggested that the geckos possess a significant number of primitive characters, notwithstanding the fact that they are highly specialized in some respects (such as the possession of digital scansors) and that parallel evolution has occurred extensively among them. Supposedly primitive characters found in many, though not in all representatives of the family are the amphicoelous centra of the vertebrae and the persistence of the notochord into adult life, a feature that could be neotenic. Among the various cranial characters which could be regarded as primitive are:

1. The lack of attachment of the planum antorbitale of the nasal capsule to the nasal septum (Kamal, 1961c). This is actually a common condition among lizards.

2. The absence of fenestrae in the interorbital septum.

3. The elongate anterior process of the pterygoquadrate which approaches the processus maxillaris posterior, illustrating a tendency towards the continuation of the pterygoquadrate cartilage (Kamal, 1961c).

4. The persistence into comparatively late embryonic life of a chondrified interhyal, connecting the extra-columella with the ceratohyal (Kamal, 1961c). This persistence could be another neotenic feature.

5. The presence of the stapedial foramen, as in many primitive fossil reptiles (see Romer, 1956; Greer, 1976).

6. The hyobranchial skeleton of *Naultinus* (Stephenson and Stephenson, 1956) and of the eublepharine gecko *Coleonyx* (Kluge, 1962) is perhaps primitive in that the second branchial arch is continuous on each side with no gap between its ceratobranchial and epibranchial elements (Fig. 28A); other geckos such as *Ptyodactylus* show such a gap.

7. The presence of a vestigial quadratojugal in some forms (Brock, 1932a; Kamal, 1961c; El-Toubi and Kamal, 1961c).

Some of these characters sound convincingly primitive, others less so; an equally or more impressive list of gekkonid specializations could be compiled. It seems unlikely that on overall assessment the geckos would seem more (or less) "primitive" than any other surviving members of the ancient and diversified suborder Sauria, which perhaps originated in far-back, Upper Permian times (Carroll, 1977).

7. Pygopodidae (infraorder Gekkota)

a. Previous Literature

No embryos of these snake-like, Australasian relatives of the geckos appear to have been described, but the accounts by Pratt (1948) of the adult nasal capsule of *Lialis burtonis*, and by Underwood (1957) of some cranial features of *Aprasia pulchella*, *A. repens*, *Delma fraseri*, *Lialis burtonis* and *Pygopus lepidopodus* contain relevant information. Adult skulls of some species are figured by McDowell and Bogert (1954) and by Stephenson (1962). Moffat (1973) lists some "primitive" features of the group. The middle ear of *Lialis* is described by Wever (1974, 1978).

b. Skull of Pygopodidae

In *Lialis* the nasal capsule is elongated, conforming with the shape of the snout, and as in geckos there is a long ectochoanal cartilage (Fig. 30C). The nasal concha and paraseptal cartilage are small, the sphenethmoid commissures and orbitotemporal scaffolding are reduced, and the very narrow anterior part of the planum supraseptale is excluded from the cranial cavity by local fusion of the downgrowths from the frontals.

The columellar apparatus is massive and the insertion plate possesses the typical four saurian processes with an extracolumellar muscle attached to the pars superior, as in geckos. There is no internal process (Wever, 1978).

In the highly fossorial *Aprasia repens* the orbitotemporal scaffolding is entirely absent. There is no proper interorbital septum, but the orbits are separated by a rodlike trabecula communis which presumably cor-

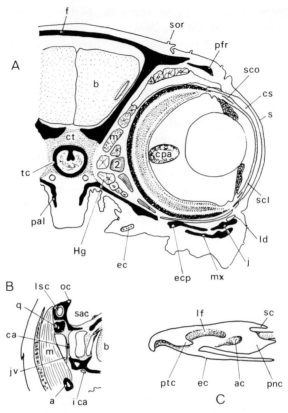

Fig. 30. (A) *Aprasia repens*, adult. Transverse section at mid-orbital level showing ossified trabecula communis. (B) *Aprasia pulchella*, adult. Transverse section through vestigial columella auris embedded in the membrane closing the fenestra ovalis. There is no tympanic membrane and the ear region is covered by muscles. A and B after Underwood (1957). (C) *Lialis burtonis*, adult. Lateral view of nasal capsule. After Pratt (1948).

a, Articular; ac, aditus conchae; b, brain; ca, columella auris; cpa, conus papillaris; cs, conjunctival space; ct, dense connective tissue; ec, ectochoanal cartilage; ecp, ectopterygoid; f, frontal; Hg, Harderian gland; ica, internal carotid artery; j, jugal; jv, internal jugular vein (vena capitis lateralis); ld, lachrymal duct; lf, ? lateral fissure; lsc, lateral semicircular canal; m, eye and jaw muscles; mx, maxilla; oc, otic capsule; pal, palatine; pfr, prefrontal; pnc, paranasal cartilage; ptc, parietotectal cartilage; q, quadrate; s, spectacle; sac, saccule; sc, sphenethmoid commissure; scl, sclera; sco, scleral ossicle; sor, scale organ (? sensory); tc, ossified trabecula communis; 2, optic nerve.

responds with the ventral part of the septum in lizards generally. The posterior part of the trabecula communis is well ossified to form a tubular bone in contact posteriorly with the basisphenoid (Fig. 30A); this remarkable ossification could be regarded as a septosphenoid and has not been described in other lizards. The middle ear of *Aprasia* is highly degenerate and the columella is absent or vestigial (Fig. 30B); this is perhaps a unique condition among lizards (Shute, 1956; Underwood, 1957). The hyoid skeleton is most complete in *Delma*, with the second ceratobranchial separated from its epibranchial by a gap; the latter is connected with the paroccipital process, as in many geckos.

The bony skull of Pygopodidae is characterized by loss of the temporal arches, reduction of the jugal, loss of the lachrymal, and as in geckos, by the presence of frontal downgrowths (Fig. 30A). In the more fossorial forms there are parietal downgrowths also. The columella is not perforated.

8. Dibamidae (? infraorder Gekkota)

The chondrocrania of these serpentiform burrowers are virtually unknown. Greer (1976) confirms previous observations by Underwood (1957) and McDowell (1967) that a stapedial foramen is present in *Dibamus* and *Anelytropsis*; it is, however, absent in the scincid *Feylinia*, where it has been previously reported. Torien (1963) has briefly described the middle ear of *Typhlosaurus*, which he places in the family Anelytropsidae.

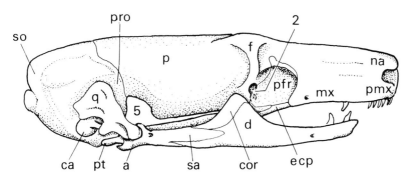

FIG. 31. *Dibamus novaeguineae*, ? subadult. Lateral view of skull. After Gasc (1968).

a, Articular; ca, columella auris; cor, coronoid; d, dentary; ecp, ectopterygoid; f, frontal; mx, maxilla; na, nasal; p, parietal; pfr, prefrontal; pmx, premaxilla; pro, prootic; pt, pterygoid; q, quadrate; sa, surangular; so, supraoccipital; 2, foramen for optic nerve; 5, trigeminal foramen.

In *Dibamus* the fronto-parietal downgrowths are very extensive and the optic nerves apparently issue through a foramen between the frontal and parietal on each side (Fig. 31). The jugal, lachrymal, postorbital, postfrontal and epipterygoid bones are absent (Gasc, 1968). Like the pygopodid *Aprasia*, *Dibamus* lacks a proper interorbital septum. Only a rodlike, unossified trabecula communis is seen in transverse section at mid-orbital level. (Rieppel, in preparation).

9. Iguanidae (infraorder Iguania)

a. Previous Literature

Anolis carolinensis, Willard, 1915 (sections of adult head showing cranial nerves, etc.); Armstrong *et al.*, 1953 (forebrain and olfactory apparatus of adult); Stimie, 1966 (sections of adult skull). *A. roquet*, Pratt, 1948 (nasal capsule). *A. sagrei*, Malan, 1946 (nasal capsule). *Callisaurus draconoides*, *Cophosaurus texana*, Wever, 1973b, 1978 (ear). *Crotaphytus collaris*, Wever, 1978 (ear). *Ctenosaura pectinata*, Oelrich, 1956 (important study of adult cranial anatomy). *Holbrookia maculata*, Wever, 1973b, 1978 (ear). *Iguana iguana*, Malan, 1946 (nasal capsule); Pratt, 1948 (nasal capsule). *Liolaemus pictus*, *Leiosaurus belli*, Born, 1879 (nasal capsule). *Phrynosoma douglassii*, Malan, 1946 (nasal capsule). *P. platyrhinos*, *Sceloporus magister*, Wever, 1973b, 1978 (ear). *S. undulatus*, Born, 1879 (nasal capsule); Malan, 1946 (nasal capsule). *Uta stansburiana*, Malan, 1946 (nasal capsule). Nasal sac (but not the capsule) of some desert-living forms, Stebbins, 1948. Cox and Tanner (1977) and Zalusky *et al.* (1980) deal with the adult cranial anatomy of certain genera.

There appears to be no study of the development of the chondrocranium in any iguanid genus, and the nasal capsule, middle ear and hyobranchial apparatus of the late embryo or adult are the only parts of it which are at all well known.

b. Nasal Capsule of Iguanidae

Clearly the nasal capsule shows much adaptive variation in the different iguanids studied. The most generalized condition is seen in the big iguanas, *Iguana* and *Ctenosaura* (Fig. 32A, B). The general morphology of the capsule is not unlike that in lacertids, with a well developed nasal concha and a large cavum conchale housing the lateral nasal gland. However, unlike lacertids, most iguanids lack a lateral or superior fenestra and possess a rostral or prenasal process, an anterior prolongation of the nasal septum between the cupolae. Malan (1946) and Oelrich (1956) show a lateral nasal fissure like that of geckos passing back from the fenestra narina to the aditus conchae in *Iguana* and *Ctenosaura* respectively. In Pratt's (1948) figure of *Iguana* the fissure is interrupted between the fenestra narina and the aditus. The nasal sac of *Iguana* is illustrated by Parsons (1970) and by Gabe and Saint Girons (1976) in their surveys of this organ. The rostral process and lateral fissure appear to be characteristic of the family.

In *Anolis* the olfactory sense is poorly developed, probably in association with arboreal life (Armstrong *et al.*, 1953). The nasal concha is absent (a rare condition in lizards), while the organ of Jacobson (Fig. 32G) is small and situated relatively far forwards, approaching the situation in chameleons. The paraseptal cartilage is vestigial, but there is a long ecto-choanal cartilage (Fig. 32E) which overlaps the vomer medially and re-inforces the soft tissues of the palate. There is a large lateral fenestra. Malan (1946) found that in *A. sagrei* each ethmoidal nerve divides into lateral and medial branches before it enters the nasal capsule, the lateral branch passing directly to the small nasal gland; she observed no foramen epiphaniale. In *A. carolinensis*, however, Stimie (1966) described the ethmoidal nerve entering and leaving the capsule in the usual fashion; on one side of the head the foramen epiphaniale was continuous with the lateral fissure.

Malan (1946) described striking modifications of the nasal capsule of *Sceloporus*, to which the following account refers, and of *Uta* and *Phrynosoma*, inhabitants of the arid regions of America.

In *Sceloporus*, as in a number of other desert lizards, the vestibule is extremely long and is twisted on the cavum nasi proprium. This flexure is perhaps conditioned by the necessity for accommodating the long vesti-bule within a rather short snout. The elongation of the vestibule appears to be an adaptation to cleansing the inspired air in a dry, dusty habitat (Stebbins, 1948). This modification is reflected in the structure of the nasal capsule.

The nasal vestibule of *Sceloporus* extends back above the cavum and enters it from the dorsal aspect; the cavum has been displaced relatively forwards and outwards so that its front end is lateral to Jacobson's organ. The vestibule is covered by the parietotectal cartilage, while the cavum is covered by the dome-like paranasal cartilage; the two cartilages are separated by the long lateral nasal fissure, which is much more extensive than that in geckos. The lateral nasal gland lies within the fissure, but its duct has been carried back by the elongation of the vestibule, so that it passes backwards instead of forwards as in lacertids and geckos, and enters the capsule through the posterior part of the fissure. There is no lateral or superior fenestra (Fig. 32C, D). *Sceloporus* is one of the few lizards which has no indication of a cartilaginous nasal concha.

The foramina in the roof of the nasal capsule of *Sceloporus* are considerably modified (Fig. 32C). The ethmoidal and olfactory nerves of each side enter it through a single aperture which represents the com-bined orbitonasal fissure and fenestra olfactoria advehens. The opening lies beneath the sphenethmoid commissure which does not extend posteriorly to reach the planum supraseptale. The lateral branch of the ethmoidal nerve leaves the capsule almost immediately by passing through the foramen epiphaniale which is situated close to the medial side of the combined fenestrae. The nerves to the organ of Jacobson (which in most

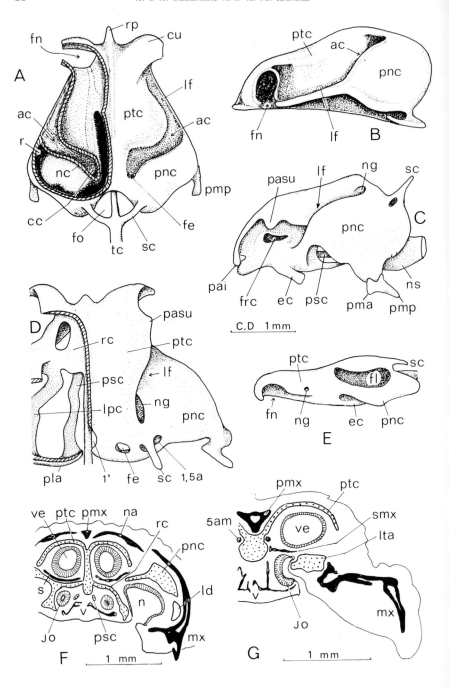

lizards follow the same route as the olfactory nerves) enter the capsule through a separate opening near the midline.

In many lizards, such as lacertids, the most anterior part of Jacobson's organ is embedded in a hollow in the posterior aspect of the lamina transversalis anterior, so that it is roofed over by cartilage. In some teiids (Fig. 25C) and iguanids, notably in *Sceloporus*, the cartilaginous roof over the organ extends much further posteriorly, underlying the septomaxilla (Fig. 32F). This is comparable with the condition in *Sphenodon* (III–B–1), and Malan (1946) regards it as a primitive feature. The roof in *Sceloporus* is not complete, however, since it contains a considerable fenestra (Fig. 32D).

The floor of the nasal capsule in *Sceloporus* is unusually well developed, since a wide band of cartilage, termed the lateral paraseptal cartilage by Malan, extends posterolaterally from the lamina transversalis anterior to the planum antorbitale. This band is separated from the typical paraseptal cartilage by the long fenestra for the duct of Jacobson's organ in front and the choana behind (Fig. 32D). There is also a small ectochoanal cartilage.

As in most of the other iguanids studied, the nasal septum of *Sceloporus* is prolonged forwards as a rostral process. The posterior part of the septum is interrupted by a large notch or incomplete fenestra, open superiorly.

The nasal capsules of *Uta* and *Phrynosoma* on the whole resemble that of *Sceloporus*, with long lateral nasal fissures and well developed roofing cartilages for Jacobson's organs, which are situated well forwards in the snout. Both genera, however, possess a small nasal concha without a cavum

---

Fig. 32. (A, B) *Ctenosaura pectinata*, adult. Dorsal and lateral views of nasal capsule. In (A) the roof of the capsule on the left side has been removed; cut surfaces are shown in slanting lines. After Oelrich (1956). (C, D) *Sceloporus undulatus*, adult. Lateral and dorsal views of nasal capsule. In (D) the roof of the capsule on the left side has been removed to show the roofing cartilage of Jacobson's organ. After Malan (1946). (E) *Anolis roquet*, adult. Lateral view of nasal capsule. After Pratt (1948). (F) *Sceloporus undulatus*, adult. Transverse section through nasal region to show roofing cartilage of Jacobson's organ. After Malan (1946). (G) *Anolis equestris*, adult. Transverse section through organ of Jacobson.

ac, Aditus conchae; cc, cavum conchale; cu, cupola; ec, ectochoanal cartilage; fe, foramen epiphaniale; fl, fenestra lateralis; fn, fenestra narina; fo, fenestra olfactoria; frc, fenestra in roofing cartilage of Jacobson's organ; ld, lachrymal duct; lf, lateral nasal fissure; lp, lateral paraseptal cartilage; lta, lamina transversalis anterior; mx, maxilla; n, nasal sac (opening into front of choana in F); na, nasal; nc, nasal concha; ng, foramen for duct of nasal gland; ns, nasal septum; pai, processus alaris inferior; pasu, processus alaris superior; pla, planum antorbitale; pma, pmp, anterior and posterior maxillary processes; pmx, premaxilla; pnc, paranasal cartilage; psc, paraseptal cartilage; ptc, parietotectal cartilage; r, extra-conchal (lateral) recess; rc, roofing cartilage of Jacobson's organ, Jo; rp, rostral process; smx, septomaxilla; sc, sphenethmoid commissure; tc, trabecula communis; v, vomer; ve, vestibule; l, l′, foramina for olfactory and vomeronasal nerves; 5a, 5am, ethmoidal and medial ethmoidal branches of ophthalmic nerve.

conchale. In *Phrynosoma* there is a large fenestra superior in the parietotectal cartilage where it roofs over the vestibule.

c. Other Regions of the Iguanid Skull

The cartilaginous orbitotemporal scaffolding of adult *Ctenosaura*
(Oelrich, 1956; Fig. 33A here) and *Anolis* (Stimie, 1966) resembles that
in lacertids, but in *Anolis* (Fig. 32E) the sphenethmoid commissures fail
to reach the planum supraseptale, the pilae antotica are reduced, and the
taeniae mediales are absent. There are ossified orbitosphenoids in most
adult iguanids.

The columellar apparatus of *Ctenosaura* (Oelrich, 1956), *Sceloporus*
(Wever, 1973b, 1978) and *Crotaphytus* (Wever and Werner, 1970; Wever,

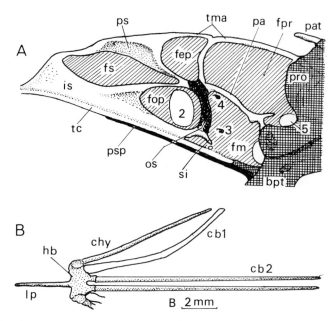

Fig. 33. (A) *Ctenosaura pectinata*, adult. Lateral view of orbitotemporal region. Membranes filling
fenestrae are shown in slanting lines; the bones of the brain-case are cross-hatched. The sphenethmoid
commissures are not shown. After Oelrich (1956). (B) *Anolis chrysolepis*, adult. Hyobranchial skeleton,
shown complete at top of drawing only. The cartilage is stippled. After Langebartel (1968).

bpt, Basipterygoid process of basisphenoid; cb1, cb2, ceratobranchials 1 and 2; chy, ceratohyal; fep,
fenestra epioptica; fm, fenestra metoptica; fop, fenestra optica; fpr, fenestra prootica; fs, fenestra in
interorbital septum; hb, hyoid body; is, interorbital septum; lp, lingual process; os, orbitosphenoid
(ossified pila metoptica) in black; pa, pila antotica; pat, anterior process of tectum; pro, prootic; ps,
planum supraseptale; psp, parasphenoid (rostrum), in black; si, subiculum infundibuli; tc, trabecula
communis; tma, taenia marginalis; 2, 3, 4, 5, fenestrae for optic, oculomotor, trochlear, and trigeminal
nerves.

1978) seems to follow the usual saurian pattern (p. 31). However, in some forms, such as *Holbrookia*, the tympanic membrane has regressed; the small extracolumella, capped with a wedge of cartilage which may represent the internal process, is applied to a depression in the quadrate (Wever, 1973b, 1978).

In Iguanidae the second branchial arch of the hyobranchial skeleton is usually well developed, and in some forms such as *Anolis* (Fig. 33B) the second ceratobranchials are much elongated, lie together near the midline, and can be rotated forwards by muscular action to erect the throat-fan or dewlap (see Von Gueldern, 1919; Bellairs, 1969).

The bony skull of Iguanidae is of a generalized saurian type with complete postorbital and superior temporal arches (see Romer, 1956). Apart from a suggestion of neoteny in very short-snouted forms such as *Phrynosoma* (which may resemble certain geckos and agamids in this respect), the skull appears to show no features of special ontogenetic interest. Both the frontals and parietals may be fused, as in agamids; the postfrontal is small or absent.

1. Agamidae (infraorder Iguania)

a. Previous literature

Agamid chondrocranium in general, Kamal and Zada, 1970. *Agama agama*, Harris, 1963 (adult skull); Wever, 1978 (ear). *A. atricollis*, Pratt, 1948 (nasal capsule). *A. atra*, *A. hispida*, Malan, 1946 (nasal capsule). *A. hispida*, Barry, 1953. *A. mutabilis*, Kamal and Zada, 1973; Zada, 1975 (mature chondrocranium and embryonic osteocranium). *A. stellio*, Eyal-Giladi, 1964. *Amphibolurus barbatus*, Born, 1879 (nasal capsule): *Calotes versicolor*, Gnanamuthu, 1937 (hyoid); Ramaswami, 1946, chondrocranium and osteocranium of hatchling). *Ceratophora stoddartii*, Wever, 1973b, 1978 (ear). *Draco volans*, Born, 1879 (nasal capsule); Wever, 1973b, 1978 (ear); Gnanamuthu, 1937 (hyoid). *Phrynocephalus maculatus*, Wever, 1973b, 1978 (ear).

The nasal glands and associate structures in *Uromastyx* and *Agama* have been studied by Lemire *et al.* (see Lemire and Grenot, 1974).

b. Chondrocranium of Agamidae

The following particulars are based mainly on the work of Malan (1946), and of Kamal and Zada (1973, 1975), though the latters' (1970) interpretation of phylogenetic significance seems questionable in some respects, and is not accepted here. Figures of the fully formed chondrocranium of *Agama mutabilis* from Zada's unpublished thesis (1975) are shown below (Fig. 34), by kind permission.

1. The available data, derived mainly from a few of the smaller species, indicate that the nasal capsule of agamids varies less than that of the iguanids previously described; in some respects the condition resembles that of the iguanid *Sceloporus*. There is a similar tendency towards elongation of the vestibule and ventrolateral displacement of the cavum nasi proprium.

2. The superior and lateral fenestrae are absent or very small. As in most geckos and iguanids, there is a complete lateral fissure, and hence no zona annularis.

3. The organ of Jacobson has no well developed roofing cartilage, unlike the condition in some of the iguanids described. In *Calotes* the rather small organ apparently lacks a vomeronasal concha projecting dorsally from the lamina transversalis anterior (Ramaswami, 1964); this is a very unusual condition.

4. The nasal concha is also absent or much reduced in the agamids studied (except in *Physignathus*; Gabe and Saint Girons, 1976). Thus, there is no cavum conchale and the lateral nasal gland is partly accommodated in the posterior part of the lateral nasal fissure. Kamal and Zada (1970) and Zada (1975) state that there is no paranasal cartilage in *Agama mutabilis*, but in view of the doubtful identity of this cartilage as a separate entity this seems mainly a point of terminology. Zada labels the cartilage covering the cavum as part of the lamina transversalis anterior, but it clearly corresponds with the paranasal cartilage of Malan (1946) and other authors,

---

FIG. 34. *Agama mutabilis*. Fully formed chondrocranium of embryo of 41·2 mm total body length (? total length) seen in (A) dorsal, (B) ventral and (C) lateral view. (D) Transverse section through interorbital septum and planum supraseptale at level shown in (C). After Zada (1975).

bf, Basicranial fenestra; bpl, basal plate; bpt, basipterygoid process; c, occipital condyle; ch, cartilago hypochiasmatica; cJo, cartilage of Jacobson's organ; coc, cochlear part of otic capsule; cp, crista parotica; cpr, cochlear prominence; cu, nasal cupola; D, plane of section in Fig. 34D; ec, ectochoanal cartilage; f, frontal; fa, foramen apicale; fel, foramen for endolymphatic duct; fm, foramen through which medial ethmoidal nerve enters nasal capsule, emerging through fa (there is no foramen epiphaniale); fma, foramen magnum; fn, fenestra narina; fo, fenestra olfactoria; fp, foramen perilymphaticum; fpl, footplate of columella auris; fs, fenestra in interorbital septum; g, gap in otic capsule; is, interorbital septum; lf, lateral nasal fissure; lta, lamina transversalis anterior; m, basipterygoid meniscus; n, notochord; ns, nasal septum; oa, occipital arch; oc, otic capsule; olp, olfactory peduncle; pa, pila antotica; pac, anterior or posterior accessory process; pacc, pila accessoria; pai, processus alaris inferior; pas, ascending process of pterygoquadrate (epipterygoid); pasu, processus alaris superior; pat, anterior process of tectum; pf, pituitary fenestra; pi, internal process of extracolumella; pii, pars inferior of insertion plate; pla, planum antorbitale; pm, pila metoptica; pnc, paranasal cartilage; pp, processus paroticus; ps, planum supraseptale; psc, paraseptal cartilage (posterior vestige); psi, pars superior of insertion plate; ptc, parietotectal cartilage; q, quadrate; sc, sphenethmoid commissure; si, subiculum infundibuli; stb, (incomplete) supratrabecular bar; t, trabecula; te, occipital tectum; tm, taenia medialis; tma, taenia marginalis; 2, optic fenestra; 5a, ophthalmic nerves; 5al, 5am, lateral and medial branches of ethmoidal branch of ophthalmic nerve; 6, foramina for abducens canal; 7, foramen for facial nerve; 12, foramina for hypoglossal nerve.

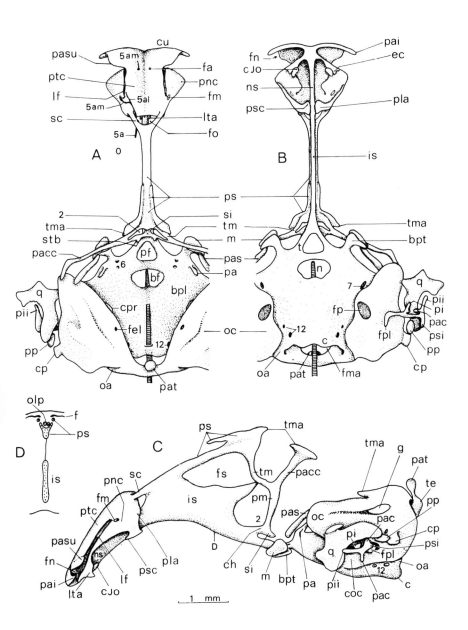

and has been labelled as such in Fig. 34.

5. In *Agama atra* and *A. hispida* (Malan, 1946; Barry, 1953) and in *A. mutabilis* (Zada, 1975) the ethmoidal nerve divides outside the nasal capsule and the lateral branch passes directly to the nasal gland within the lateral fissure. However, the medial branch enters the capsule through a foramen just behind the fissure which might easily be mistaken for a foramen epiphaniale; it then passes anteriorly within the capsule to emerge from the foramen apicale in the usual fashion (Fig. 34A). Thus, as in the iguanid *Anolis sagrei*, there is no true foramen epiphaniale. It is uncertain whether conditions are similar in other agamids.

6. In *Agama atra* and *A. hispida*, as in iguanids again, the courses of the olfactory and vomeronasal nerves may also deviate from the usual saurian condition; the olfactory nerves enter the nasal capsule through several foramina in the back of the planum antorbitale while the vomero-nasal nerves have a separate and more ventral point of entrance, so there is no proper fenestra olfactoria. In *Agama mutabilis*, *A. stellio* and *Calotes* these nerves enter the capsule in the normal fashion (Fig. 4).

7. The floor of the nasal capsule is reduced, and paraseptal cartilages (apart from vestigial posterior portions; Fig. 34B) occur only in *Agama hispida* and *A. stellio*. The ectochoanal cartilages are small, except in *A. atricollis* (Pratt, 1948) and the maxillary processes are lacking except in *Calotes* (Ramaswami, 1946) which has only the anterior one.

8. The planum antorbitale closely approaches, or is in contact with the nasal septum.

9. Even in mature stages the nasal septum is markedly flexed on the interorbital septum behind it, the usual condition in early embryos of other lizards. This could be a neotenic feature.

10. The interorbital septum is long and high, in correlation with the large size of the eyes. The main fenestra septi is very large (Fig. 34C); the other fenestrae are small or absent. The nasal septum is usually unfenestrated.

11. The anterior part of the planum supraseptale is very narrow and the orbitotemporal scaffolding is reduced, the extent of reduction varying in different forms. In *Agama mutabilis* the taenia marginalis of the fully formed chondrocranium consists of three discontinuous parts and the optic fenestra is the only fenestra completely enclosed by cartilage (Fig. 34C).

12. There are two hypoglossal foramina on each side.

13. The pterygoid process of the pterygoquadrate is reduced or absent.

14. In *Calotes* the extracolumella has an internal process and a ligamentous dorsal process; *Agama mutabilis* has the internal process only. Various modifications of the adult middle ear in those agamids which have lost the

tympanic membrane are described by Smith (1935–43) and Wever (1973b, 1978).

15. The second branchial arch is composed of the second cerato-branchial only; this lies alongside its opposite fellow near the midline and depresses the gular fold or throat-fan, as in certain iguanids (see Gnanamuthu, 1937).

c. Osteocranium of Agamidae

In many agamids the snout is markedly shortened, as in some iguanids, but otherwise the bony skull, with its complete arches, follows the typical saurian pattern in most respects. The lachrymal is usually absent. *Lyriocephalus* has a prominent supraorbital crest formed by prolongations of the pre- and postfrontal bones (Smith, 1935–43). Small orbitosphenoids may be present in mature specimens. Ramaswami (1946) states that pleurosphenoids (or laterosphenoids) ossify in the pilae antotica of *Calotes*, but does not show them in his figures; if really present, such ossifications are very unusual in lizards.

The dentition is acrodont except, in most species, at the anterior ends of both jaws, where it is pleurodont. Dentitional phenomena and the postnatal growth of the jaws in certain agamids are described by Robinson (1976) and by Capel-Williams and Pratten (1978).

11. Chamaeleonidae (infraorder Iguania)

a. Previous Literature

Bradypodion pumilus, Parker 1881; Brock, 1941b; Malan, 1946 (nasal capsule); Engelbrecht, 1951 (sections of adult); Visser, 1972 (important account of several embryonic stages). *Chamaeleo bitaeniatus*, Finneman, 1940. *C. bitaeniatus*, *C. chamaeleon*, *C. hoehnelii*, *C. jacksoni*, *C. quilensis*, *C. senegalensis*, Wever, 1968, 1969a, b, 1978 (ear). *C. calyptratus*, Pratt, 1948 (nasal capsule). *C. chamaeleon*, Parker, 1881 (juvenile and adult skull); Haas, 1947 (Jacobson's organ). *Rhampholeon marshallii*, Torien, 1963 (ear). *R. platyceps*, Frank, 1951 (sections of adult).

b. Chondrocranium of Chamaeleonidae

The chondrocranium of chameleons shows striking modifications, especially of the nasal capsule and anterior orbitotemporal region. These are associated with the shortening of the snout, marked reduction of the sensory olfactory apparatus, and the large size of the eyes and of the specialized tongue. The organ of Jacobson is moderately well developed in *Bradypodion* [= *Microsaura*], and apparently also in some *Chamaeleo* (*C. chamaeleon* and *C. dilepis*; see Engelbrecht, 1951); it is vestigial or absent in other members of the family. In *Bradypodion* it is situated very far forwards, anterior to the nostrils, and its opening to the palate is well in front of the opening of the lachrymal duct—a remarkable feature in Squamata, in which this duct normally ends in close proximity to the duct of Jacobson's organ.

The following features are noteworthy in the mature chondrocranium (Fig. 36).

1. The nasal capsule is small and secondarily simplified. Its various elements are difficult to distinguish in early embryonic stages. Its anterior part is compressed dorso-ventrally, the palate here being vaulted to accommodate the retracted tongue. Hence the nasal septum is very low.

2. Only in *Rhampholeon* (Frank, 1951) is there a lateral fissure comparable with that in *Sceloporus*. In *Bradypodion* this fissure has apparently been obliterated by the fusion of the paranasal cartilage with the parietotectal cartilage, leaving only a foramen for the lateral nasal gland and a few small adjacent perforations (Visser, 1972). The gland itself is small and lies in a small groove in the capsule behind the foramen. There appear to be no foramina lateralis or superior.

3. Jacobson's organ in *Bradypodion* is roofed over by cartilage but has no vomeronasal concha (Fig. 35B). There is no nasal concha. The paraseptal cartilage is greatly reduced or absent; the ectochoanal cartilage is bifurcated.

4. The posterior part of the nasal capsule is telescoped anteroposteriorly in association with the size of the eyes, so that the front of the planum supraseptale has become merged with the roof of the capsule. There are no recognizable sphenethmoid commissures.

5. Malan (1946) has described the curious courses of the nerves associated with the nose in *Bradypodion pumilus* (Fig. 35A). The small olfactory (and probably the vomeronasal) nerves enter the nasal capsule on each side through a foramen which represents the fenestra olfactoria advehens. The courses of the ethmoidal nerves become altered during development. Initially they pass forward beneath the planum supraseptale in the usual fashion, but they subsequently become enclosed in a canal, the orbitonasal canal (not to be confused with the orbitonasal fissure) in the capsular roof. This canal is formed by the fusion of the planum supraseptale with the back of the parietotectal cartilage and adjacent part of the planum antorbitale. Within this canal, which incorporates the foramen epiphaniale, the nerves divide into their medial and lateral branches which emerge separately on the roof of the capsule. The medial branch re-enters the capsule through another, more anterior foramen which corresponds with the orbitonasal fissure of the "normal" saurian type and then passes forwards within the capsule to issue from the

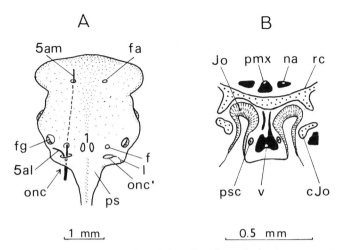

FIG. 35. (A) *Bradypodion pumilus*, adult. Dorsal view of nasal capsule showing courses of ethmoidal nerves, in broken lines where they pass beneath cartilage. The line (l) along which the front of the planum supraseptale fuses with the back of the nasal capsule to enclose the orbitonasal canal is shown in broken lines on the right. The maxillary processes are not shown. (B) *Bradypodion pumilus*, late embryo. Transverse section through organ of Jacobson showing roofing cartilage. (A) and (B) after Malan (1946).

cJo, Cartilage of Jacobson's organ; f, foramen through which medial branch of ethmoidal nerve enters nasal capsule; fa, foramen apicale; fg, foramen for duct of nasal gland; Jo, Jacobson's organ; l, line of fusion between planum supraseptale and nasal capsule; na, nasal; onc, entrance to orbitonasal canal, ventral to roof of nasal capsule; onc', anterior opening of orbitonasal canal; pmx, premaxilla; ps, planum supraseptale; psc, paraseptal cartilage rudiment; rc, roofing cartilage of Jacobson's organ; v, vomer; 1, fenestra olfactoria; 5al, 5am, lateral and medial branches of ethmoidal nerve.

foramen apicale. The lateral ramus passes directly to the lateral nasal gland, having never become truly intracapsular. The ontogenetic changes responsible for these conditions are described by Visser (1972). Some variation is found in other chameleons. Thus, in other examples of Bradypodion (Fig. 36A) the medial ethmoidal nerve passes directly into the nasal capsule from the orbitonasal canal and remains intracapsular until it reaches the foramen apicale (Brock, 1941b). Individual or subspecific variation is possible.

6. The interorbital septum is high and contains a single large fenestra septi; it is surmounted by a long, narrow planum supraseptale. The orbitotemporal scaffolding is reduced, the taenia marginalis being absent or vestigial and the pila antotica reduced to a small stump on the anterolateral corner of the basal plate (Fig. 36).

7. The ascending process of the pterygoquadrate is absent or represented only by a vestige of cartilage on the dorsal surface of the pterygoid (Fig. 36A).

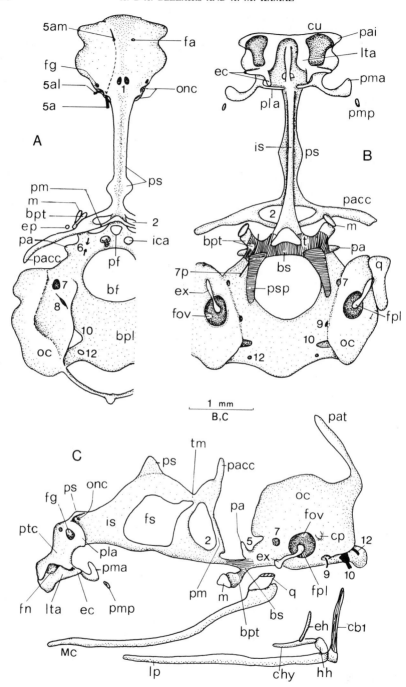

8. In early embryos of *Bradypodion* the carotid arteries enter the cranial through separate canals in the cartilage flanking the pituitary fenestra, instead of passing through the posterolateral corners of the fenestra itself, as in most lizards. When this region has ossified and fused with the parasphenoid, however, the arteries appear to run in the usual fashion, entering the Vidian canal and dividing into their cerebral and palatine branches.

9. As in lizards generally, the metotic fissure is divided into the recessus scalae tympani and the jugular foramen by a region of contact between the otic capsule and basal plate. Visser (1972) terms this contact (or possibly fusion) a posterior basicapsular commissure in *Bradypodion*, although Kamal (1965e) has denied the existence of this commissure in Squamata. The term commissure implies actual fusion, and some clarification is required over this point.

10. As in most lizards, nerve IX passes through the recessus scalae tympani during embryonic life, and is therefore extracapsular. However, in adult *Bradypodion*, this nerve acquires a small separate opening in the prootic, through which it leaves the skull.

11. *Bradypodion* initially has four hypoglossal roots, but in the adult these become reduced by fusion or loss to one anterior root, which passes out through the "jugular" foramen, and one posterior root, which leaves through a foramen of its own in the exoccipital (Visser, 1972).

12. The middle ear of chameleons varies considerably. The tympanic membrane is absent and the tympanic cavity is absent or small. In *Rhampholeon platyceps* the columellar apparatus consists only of a cartilaginous nodule, probably a vestige of the extracolumella (Frank, 1951). *Bradypodion* has both columella and extracolumella, but the latter lacks processes and insertion plate and is embedded distally in the adjacent

---

FIG. 36. (A) *Bradypodion* [= *pumilus*], late embryo. Dorsal view of chondrocranium. After Brock (1941b). (B, C) *Bradypodion pumilus*, embryo (Stage 6; 14 mm snout-vent length). (B) Ventral and (C) lateral views of chondrocranium. Ossified regions in lines; most of quadrate removed in (C). After Visser (1972).

bf, Basicranial fenestra; bpl, basal plate; bpt, basipterygoid process; bs, basisphenoid; cbl, ceratobranchial 1; chy, ceratohyal; cp, crista parotica; cu, nasal cupola; ec, ectochoanal cartilage; eh, epihyal; ep, epipterygoid (vestigial); ex, extracolumella; fa, foramen apicale; fg, foramen for duct of nasal gland; fn, fenestra narina; fov, fenestra ovalis; fpl, footplate of columella; fs, fenestra in interorbital septum; hh, hypohyal; ica, foramen for internal carotid artery; is, interorbital septum; lp, lingual process; lta, lamina transversalis anterior; m, basipterygoid meniscus; Mc, Meckel's cartilage; oc, otic capsule; onc, orbitonasal canal; pa, pila antotica; pacc, pila accessoria; pai, processus alaris inferior; pat, anterior process of tectum; pf, pituitary fenestra; pla, planum antorbitale; pm, pila metoptica; pma, pmp, anterior and posterior maxillary processes; ps, planum supraseptale; psp, parasphenoid; ptc, parietotectal cartilage; q, quadrate; t, trabecula; tm, taenia medialis; 1, fenestra olfactoria; 2, optic fenestra; 5, trigeminal notch; 5a, ophthalmic nerve; 5al, 5am, lateral and medial branches of ophthalmic nerve; 6, abducens canal; 7, 8, 9, 10, 12, facial, auditory, glossopharyngeal, vagus, and hypoglossal nerves and/or their foramina, 10 is the jugular foramen; 7p, palatine nerve.

muscles (Brock, 1941b; Engelbrecht, 1951). As in *Rhampholeon marshallii*, the columellar footplate is reduced (Torien, 1963).

The columellar apparatus is better developed in *Chamaeleo*, which has a tympanic cavity, but no tympanic membrane. In some species the extracolumella is attached by a ligament or a process to the thin, plate-like adjacent region of the pterygoid, which acts as a substitute tympanic membrane; it is also attached to the quadrate, and indirectly to the articular. The anterior and posterior processes which arise from the extracolumella are difficult to homologize with those of other lizards. The auditory sensitivity of chameleons is low as compared with that of most other lizards, due partly to the absence of a typical fenestra rotunda; there is, however, a tortuous alternative route to allow for displacement of the endolymphatic fluid (Wever, 1968, 1969a, b, 1978).

13. The cartilaginous lingual process of the hyoid body is exceedingly long and forms an essential part of the mechanism for the projection of the tongue (see Bellairs, 1969). The second branchial arch is reduced or absent (Fig. 36C).

c. Osteocranium of Chamaeleonidae

The bony skull is considerably modified and shows a number of features of developmental interest (Brock, 1941b). The postfrontal, parasphenoid rostrum, lachrymal and (more surprisingly) the septomaxilla are absent. The loss of the last can be correlated with the reduction and forward displacement, or the absence of Jacobson's organ.

Postorbital and superior temporal arches are present, but the latter is raised above the level of the head of the quadrate as a result of the development, during late embryonic life, of a pedicel at the lower end of the squamosal. Both frontals and parietals are fused in the midline in the adult. The median casque is formed by rapid, late embryonic growth of the parietals. These bones grow posteriorly dorsal to the supraoccipital ossification in the cartilaginous tectum which is itself raised up to form a supraoccipital crest beneath the parietals. The anterior process of the tectum appears to be partly ossified in *Bradypodion* (see Engelbrecht, 1951; Fig. 37C here). Brock (1941b) correlates the presence of the casque with the powerful development of the jaw muscles which attach to it (see Haas, 1973, for detailed account), but it may, of course, also have some ethological function.

Since there is virtually no ascending process of the pterygoquadrate, there is no epipterygoid bone. Basitrabecular processes and menisci are present but the two structures may be partly fused in the adult (Engelbrecht, 1951). Kinetic movement of the maxillary segment of the skull appears to be minimal. In *Chamaeleo* and *Bradypodion* the quadrate

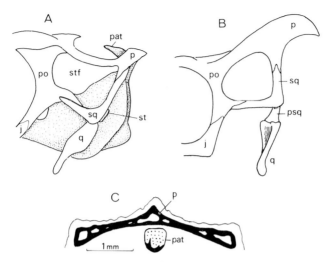

FIG. 37. *Bradypodion pumilus.* (A) Temporal region of late embryo showing early development of casque. Chondrocranium stippled. (B) Temporal region of adult. (A) and (B) seen from right side; after Brock (1941b). (C) Transverse section through casque of adult showing fused parietals and partly ossified anterior process of tectum arising from supraoccipital. After Engelbrecht (1951).

j, Jugal; p, parietal; pat, anterior process of tectum; po, postorbital; psq, pedicel of squamosal; q, quadrate; sq, squamosal; st, supratemporal; stf, superior temporal fossa.

is movable, such movement presumably effecting protraction and retraction of the lower jaw. In *Rhampholeon* the quadrate can have only very limited movement, and the crista parotica, around which the quadrate hinges in other lizards, is hardly developed (Frank, 1951). It is, perhaps, not surprising that the specialized method of feeding practised by chameleons has been associated with loss of kinesis, even though the quadrate may remain streptostylic.

12. Anguidae (infraorder Anguimorpha)

a. Previous Literature

Anguis fragilis, Leydig, 1872; Zimmermann, 1913; Pratt, 1948 (nasal capsule); Bellairs, 1949a (orbitotemporal region); Bellairs and Boyd, 1950 (nasal capsule); Wever, 1973, 1978 (ear). *Diploglossus pleii,* Malan, 1946 (nasal capsule). *Ophisaurus apodus,* Pratt, 1948 (nasal capsule). *O. ventralis,* Malan, 1946 (nasal capsule). Adult skull of anguids, McDowell and Bogert, 1954.

b. Skull of Anguidae

The development of the nasal capsule of *Anguis* has been studied by

Pratt (1948), who observed that at some embryonic stages the cartilage of the medial part of its roof was more mature than that of the lateral regions. He considered that the medial part was a distinct morphological element which grew out from the nasal septum; he termed it the dorsal plate (Fig. 38A). The parietotectal and paranasal cartilages are, in his view, initially developed as independent lateral elements. Study of original sections of *Anguis* does not provide clear-cut evidence that any of these cartilages are really distinct elements, and Pratt's view is not followed by El-Toubi and Kamal (1961b, p. 183), though it is given some support by Visser's work on chameleons (1972, p. 54). The problem could perhaps best be studied by the use of transparency preparations showing the developing nasal capsule in total perspective.

The nasal capsule (Fig. 38) is more like that of Scincomorpha than of Gekkota or Iguania. Conditions in *Anguis* and *Ophisaurus* seem very similar. The posterior parts of the nasal sac and nasal capsule are simply expanded rather than being bent round, as they are in many other lizards. Thus, there is no extra-conchal recess. The concha itself is well developed, but the lateral nasal gland is small and does not extent into the cavum conchale. The floor of the cavum conchale is deficient so that in transverse section the concha has a scroll-like form throughout much of its extent, with the large sub-conchal recess extending into the concavity of the scroll (Fig. 38D, C). The paraseptal cartilage is incomplete

---

Fig. 38. *Anguis fragilis*. (A) Late embryo. Dorsal view of chondrocranium, mainly after Zimmermann (1913). The nasal capsule is modified after Pratt (1948) and the broken lines show his suggested demarcation between the dorsal plate and the more lateral roofing elements. (B) Subadult. Ventral view of nasal capsule, showing also Jacobson's organ and lachrymal duct, after Bellairs and Boyd (1950). The broken lines show the borders of the vomer and of the medial border of the palatal process of the maxilla. (C) Late embryo. Partly reconstructed transverse section at level of foramen epiphaniale seen from in front. Cut cartilage is shown in slanting lines. (D) Late embryo. Transverse section through nasal concha at a more posterior level than (C). The dorsal plate of Pratt (1948) is labelled parietotectal cartilage in (C) and (D). (E) Adult. Section (? horizontal or transverse) through middle ear. After Wever (1973b).

ac, Aditus conchae; Bg, Bowman's gland; bpt, basipterygoid process; ca, columella auris; cd, cochlear duct; cg, choanal groove; dpl, dorsal plate; ec, ectochoanal cartilage; ep, epipterygoid; ex, extra-columella; fa, foramen apicale; fe, foramen epiphaniale; fl, fenestra lateralis; fs, fenestra superior; jm, jaw muscles (M. depressor mandibulae); Jo, Jacobson's organ; lc, lachrymal canaliculi; ld, lachrymal duct; lta, lamina transversalis anterior; mc, vestigial cavity of external auditory meatus; mx, maxilla (medial border of palatal process in B); na, nasal; nc, nasal concha; ng, lateral nasal gland; ns, nasal septum; o, o', anterior and posterior openings of lachrymal duct into choanal groove; oc, otic capsule; oJo, opening of duct of Jacobson's organ; pai, processus alaris inferior; pla, planum antorbitale; pm, pila metoptica; pma, pmp, anterior and posterior maxillary processes; pnc, paranasal cartilage; ps, planum supraseptale; psc, paraseptal cartilage; ptc, parietotectal cartilage; q, quadrate; ro, roof of nasal capsule (region of Pratt's dorsal plate); sc, sphenethmoid commissure; sr, sub-conchal recess; tma, taenia marginalis; ty, tympanic cavity; v, vomer; za, zona annularis; 1, 1', olfactory and vomeronasal nerves; 2, optic fenestra; 5a, ophthalmic nerve; 5al, 5am, lateral and medial ethmoidal branches of ophthalmic nerve; 5b, maxillary nerve.

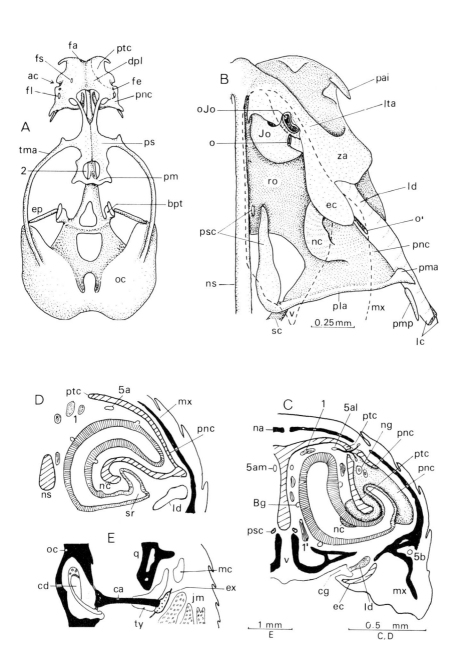

anteriorly ending well behind the lamina transversalis anterior. Isolated nodules of cartilage may be found between the front of the main paraseptal cartilage and Jacobson's organ. The ectochoanal cartilage is large and broad. In *Anguis* the superior and lateral fenestrae are small; there is a broad but rather oblique zona annularis.

In *Anguis* the interorbital septum is fairly low and the orbitotemporal scaffolding, especially the more medial cartilages, is much reduced. Bellairs (1950) found a well defined joint, perhaps of synovial character, across the ascending process of the occipital tectum in an adult specimen. This joint has not been seen in late embryos, but is of interest if constantly present in the adult, since it would presumably facilitate metakinetic flexion of the skull roof.

Anguis has no tympanic membrane and the auditory meatus is absent or, in some specimens, reduced to a tiny pore (see Hochstetter, 1951; Wever, 1978). The extra-columella is small and lies in connective tissue between part of the M. depressor mandibulae and a portion of the middle ear cavity (Wever, 1973, 1978; Fig. 38E here). It has short partes inferior and superior, but no other process.

In *Anguis*, a limbless form slightly adapted for burrowing life, the paired frontals have downgrowths around the olfactory peduncles. Both postorbital and superior temporal arches are complete, but the superior temporal fossa is very narrow. Rieppel (1978d) has described tooth replacement in anguid lizards.

13. Anniellidae (infraorder Anguimorpha)

a. Previous Literature

Anniella pulchra, Malan, 1946 (nasal capsule); Bellairs, 1950 (sections of late embryo and adult); Torien, 1950 (sections of adult), and 1963 (ear); McDowell and Bogert, 1954 (adult skull); Wever, 1973b, 1978 (ear); Rieppel, 1978c (adult brain-case).

b. Skull

Many features of these limbless burrowing lizards suggest close affinity with the Anguidae, and Bellairs (1969) has included them in this family.

The nasal capsule (Fig. 39A) is fairly like that of *Anguis*, though Malan (1946) has emphasized differences in the conchal region. The lateral nasal gland is larger than that of *Anguis* and lies mainly in a groove in front of the aditus conchae. The cavum conchale is small and there is no extraconchal recess. In the floor of the capsule the very large ectochoanal cartilage supports a long ductus nasopharyngeus. The paraseptal cartilage is reduced to a small spur projecting from the planum antorbitale. There is a small nodule of cartilage (papillary cartilage) beneath the front of the nasal septum; this structure may be commoner in lizards than would appear from the literature; it also occurs in *Sphenodon* and crocodilians.

Anniella is of interest in being one of the few specialized burrowing lizards of which the skull structure of both the embryo and adult has been described. Modifications are particularly evident in the orbitotemporal region and middle ear and involve both the chondrocranium and the bony skull.

The orbitotemporal region is elongated and the interorbital septum is very long and low (Fig. 39A, D). It is surmounted by a narrow planum supraseptale which is connected with the roof of the nasal capsule in front by complete sphenethmoid commissures. The dorsal edge of the septum is separated from the planum by a long, narrow fenestra. The orbitotemporal scaffolding is reduced on each side to the taenia marginalis, a vestige of the taenia medialis, and a stump of the pila antotica attached to the front of the basal plate. Despite the small size of the eyes, both scleral cartilage and ossicles are present. There is a basipterygoid process, a meniscus cartilage and a small epipterygoid.

The frontal bones have descending processes that almost meet in the midline, enclosing the sphenethmoid commissures and front of the planum supraseptale within the bony cranial cavity (Fig. 39B, D). Further posteriorly, the very long, fused parietal bones also have descending processes which enclose the lateral two-thirds of the cranial cavity, so that the IIIrd, IVth, VIth and ophthalmic nerves pass extra-cranially through the cavum epiptericum, as in lizards generally. A large vein, either the vena capitis (? lateralis) or the pterygoid vein passes lateral to the epipterygoid, rather than through the cavum (Rieppel, 1978c; personal communication). There may be a parallel with snakes, but the identity of these head veins requires critical re-study.

Rieppel also describes an unusual course of the IXth nerve which enters the recessus scalae tympani through a foramen of its own instead of directly through the medial aperture of the recessus, as in most other lizards. However, the nerve is not partly intracapsular, as it is in skinks. It leaves the skull in the usual fashion, through the lateral aperture of the recessus.

Anniella has no tympanic membrane, and the ear region is covered by skin and by the depressor mandibulae and other muscles (Fig. 39E). A true middle ear cavity is absent, though one is simulated by large fluid-filled cavities which surround the columella; these cavities apparently permit a fluid circuit which enables the footplate to move medially during sound conduction, despite the absence of a fenestra rotunda (Wever,

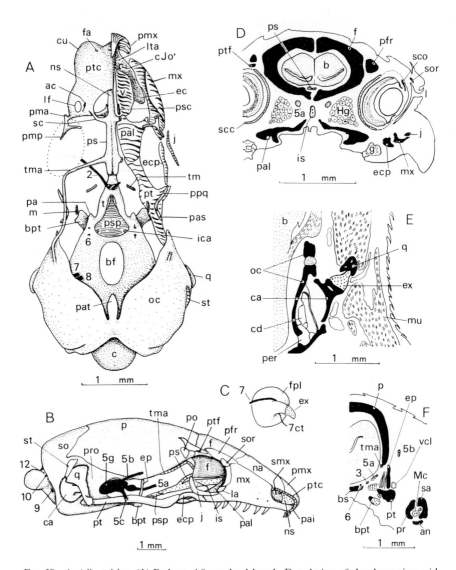

FIG. 39. *Anniella pulchra.* (A) Embryo, 4·8 mm head-length. Dorsal view of chondrocranium with some membrane bones. Outline of eye shown in dotted lines on left. (B) Adult. Lateral view of skull with parts of chondrocranium. A and B after Bellairs (1950). (C) Adult. Right columellar apparatus. After Torien (1950). (D) Adult. Transverse section through mid-orbital region showing interorbital septum. (E) Adult. "Frontal" (? horizontal) section through middle ear. After Wever (1973b, 1978). (F) Adult. Transverse section through cavum epiptericum. The Mm. levator (more lateral) and protractor pterygoidei (unlabelled) are on the medial side of the epipterygoid.

1973b; 1978). The columella is short and stout with a large footplate, as in certain other burrowing lizards such as *Acontias*, and amphisbaenians. The cartilaginous extracolumella (Figs. 39C, E, F) is short, apparently devoid of processes and has its distal end (which perhaps represents the internal process) firmly embedded in the lower end of the quadrate. The chorda tympani passes anteroventrally and medial to it. Auditory sensitivity is poor, but the columellar apparatus presumably plays a major part in the conduction of ground vibrations (see Torien, 1950, 1963; Barry, 1963; Baird, 1970; Wever, 1973b, 1978). There is no fenestra rotunda. The hyoid apparatus is unusual in consisting of a lingual process, basihyal and a single pair of horns, which probably represent first ceratobranchials (Langebartel, 1968).

The superior temporal arch is absent, the postorbital and squamosal are respectively small and vestigial, and there is a small supratemporal; a supraorbital or palpebral bone is present in the upper eyelids (Fig. 39B). The sutures among the various components of the otooccipital complex have disappeared in the adult. Although the suture between the back of the parietal and the supraoccipital is clearly evident, only a little (if any) metakinetic movement appears possible between these bones; the main line of kinetic flexion is situated further forwards, in the frontoparietal plane (mesokinesis). The parietal foramen fails to penetrate the full thickness of the bone.

Both the chondrocranium and the bony skull of *Anniella* resemble those of the burrowing skink *Acontias meleagris* (Brock, 1941a; p. 67 here) in the following respects: the development of frontoparietal downgrowths around the forebrain, the reduction of the orbitotemporal scaffolding, the elongation of the temporal region of the skull, the loss of the superior

---

ac, Aditus conchae; an, angular; b, brain; bf, basicranial fenestra; bpt, basipterygoid process; bs, basisphenoid; c, occipital condyle; ca, columella auris; cd, cochlear duct; cJo', concha of Jacobson's organ; cu, nasal cupola; ec, ectochoanal cartilage; ecp, ectopterygoid; ep, epipterygoid; ex, extracolumella; f, frontal; fa, foramen apicale; fpl, footplate of columella; g, gland; Hg, Harderian gland; ica, internal carotid artery; is, interorbital septum; j, jugal; l, eyelids; la, lachrymal; lf, lateral fenestra; lta, lamina transversalis anterior; m, basipterygoid meniscus; Mc, Meckel's cartilage; mu, muscles; mx, maxilla; na, nasal; ns, nasal septum; oc, otic capsule; p, parietal; pa, pila antotica; pai, processus alaris inferior; pal, palatine; pas, ascending process of pterygoquadrate (epipterygoid); pat, anterior process of tectum; per, perilymphatic recess; pfr, prefrontal; pma, pmp, anterior and posterior maxillary processes; pmx, premaxilla; po, postorbital; ppq, pterygoid process of pterygoquadrate; pr, prearticular; pro, prootic; ps, planum supraseptale; psc, paraseptal cartilage; psp, parasphenoid; pt, pterygoid; ptc, parietotectal cartilage; ptf, postfrontal; q, quadrate; sa, surangular; sc, sphenethmoid commissure; scc, scleral cartilage; sco, scleral ossicle; smx, septomaxilla; so, supraoccipital; sor, supraorbital (palpebral); st, supratemporal; t, trabecula; tm, taenia medialis (vestigial); tma, taenia marginalis; v, vomer; vcl, ?vena capitis lateralis; 2, optic nerve; 3, oculomotor nerve; 5a, b, c, ophthalmic, maxillary, and mandibular branches of trigeminal nerve; 5g, trigeminal (maxillo-mandibular) ganglion; 6, abducens nerve and canal; 7, facial nerve; 7ct, chorda tympani; 8, auditory nerve; 9, 10, 12, foramina for glossopharyngeal, vagus, and hypoglossal nerves.

temporal arch and the reduction of metakinesis. Such features do not necessarily indicate close zoological affinity but appear to be concomitants of fossorial adaptation among Squamata, though some of them are also seen in non-burrowing forms. In some ways they suggest a skull type which may have been present in the ancestors of snakes, though most probably the resemblances are purely convergent (see Bellairs, 1950, 1972, and Rieppel, 1978c, for discussion).

14. Xenosauridae (infraorder Anguimorpha)

The middle ear of *Xenosaurus grandis* is briefly described by Wever (1973b, 1978).

15. Varanidae (infraorder Platynota)

a. Previous Literature

Varanus exanthematicus, Born, 1879 (nasal capsule). *V. niloticus*, Malan, 1946 (nasal capsule). *V.* sp.*, Pratt, 1948 (nasal capsule); Bellairs, 1949a, b (nasal capsule and orbitotemporal region of young); Shrivastava, 1963, 1964a, b (development of chondrocranium and osteocranium of young); Wever, 1978 (ear).

The gross anatomy of the adult skull of *Varanus* has been described by Bahl (1937), Mertens (1942), Säve-Söderbergh (1946, 1947; brain-case), McDowell and Bogert (1954), and Frazzetta (1962; kinesis). Gabe and Saint Girons (1976) have dealt with the nasal sacs and lachrymal ducts.

b. Chondrocranium of Varanidae

In many monitors the external nostrils are set far back on the snout and the large organ of Jacobson lies on level with or even in front of them—as in chameleons, the morphology of which is, of course, very different. As in certain iguanids, the very large nasal vestibule describes a U-turn at the front of the nose, within the cartilaginous cupola. The bony external narial opening is very large so that a considerable part of the nasal capsule has no covering of dermal bone (Bellairs, 1949b).

Some noteworthy features of the varanid chondrocranium (Fig. 40) may be listed as follows.

1. The nasal septum, especially its anterior part, is low and continues anteriorly in front of the large anterior cupolae to form a flattened rostral process with upturned lateral wings which support the medial ethmoidal nerves and vessels. There is no foramen apicale.

---

* Most anatomical papers on *Varanus* are said to be based on "*V. monitor*"; this is a combination of *V. niloticus*, *V. salvator*, and sometimes *V. bengalensis*. We do not here attempt to untangle this situation.

2. The lamina transversalis anterior does not join the parietotectal cartilage, so that there is no zona annularis.

3. The cartilaginous concha of Jacobson's organ, projecting dorsally from the lamina transversalis anterior, is large and is supported by a bony concha (reniform process, Bahl, 1937) derived from the vomer (Bellairs, 1949; Fig. 40A here).

4. The large lateral ("extraconchal") recess formed by the paranasal cartilage which in *Varanus bengalensis* is incomplete dorsally; the concha extends round into it from the main part of the capsule (Fig. 40B, C, D). The cavum conchale and lateral nasal gland are well developed. In the embryo, at least, there is also a ventral nasal gland which is very unusual in lizards (Shrivastava, 1963).

5. The paraseptal cartilage may be long, as in *Varanus* sp., or short, as in *V. niloticus*, but does not join the planum antorbitale behind. In the former case the paraseptal is expanded near its root and fragmented to form a cartilaginous network through which the vomeronasal nerve bundles pass on their way backwards from Jacobson's organ (Fig. 40B). In *V. "monitor"* (= *bengalensis* ?), but not in *V. niloticus*, the planum antorbitale is medially in contact with the nasal septum.

6. The orbitotemporal scaffolding is relatively complete, but the pila antotica is greatly reduced in the fully formed stage, so that the metoptic and prootic fenestrae are confluent (Figs. 40F; 41E). There are two fenestrae in the interorbital septum.

7. In some embryonic stages the basicranial fenestra is divided into anterior and posterior portions by a thin strand of cartilage which lies just in front of the tip of the notochord. Shrivastava believes that this fenestra is present from the beginning and becomes progressively reduced, contrary to the view of Kamal (1965f) that it is formed secondarily as the result of cartilage regression.

8. There is only a single hypoglossal foramen, as the roots of the XIIth nerve fuse during development. This is visible only on the internal surface of the adult skull; the XIIth nerve leaves the occipital aspect of the skull through the "jugular foramen" in common with the vagus and accessory nerves (Bahl, 1937).

9. The processus accessorius anterior of the extracolumella is absent; there is a ligamentous dorsal process in some embryonic stages. McDowell (1967) states that *Varanus* has no intercalary, but Shrivastava (1964b) mentions its precursor, the processus paroticus, a dissociated derivative of the dorsal process, and Bahl (1937) figures a cartilaginous intercalary. As one might expect from their active, predatory mode of life (Auffenberg, 1978), monitor lizards have good hearing (Wever, 1978).

10. The lingual process of the hyoid is elongated (Fig. 40E); the

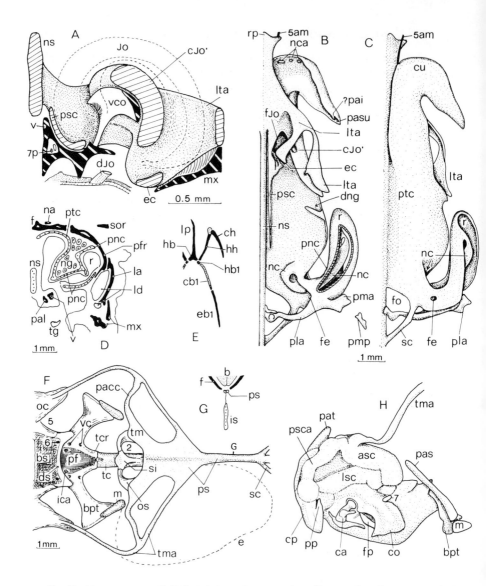

Fig. 40. *Varanus monitor*. (A–F) Subadult. (A) Reconstruction of bones and cartilages associated with Jacobson's organ, seen in transverse section from behind. The outlines of the dorsal dome and mushroom body of the organ are shown in broken lines. (B) Ventral and (C) dorsal view of nasal capsule. In (B) an opening has been cut in the ventral wall of the lateral recess to show the concha. In (C) the posterior maxillary process is not shown. (D) Transverse section through conchal region at approximate level of label nc in (B). (A–D) after Bellairs (1949b). (E) Hyobranchial skeleton. The black structures are ossified, a pattern which apparently differs from that in other lizards. After Shrivastava (1964b). (F) Dorsal view of orbitotemporal region of chondrocranium and of ossified basisphenoid. (G) Transverse section at level of G in F below. F and G after Bellairs (1949a). (H) Embryo, total length 94·2 mm. Lateral view of oto-occipital region of chondrocranium. The prominences for the semicircular canals seem very pronounced. After Shrivastava (1964b).

second branchial arch elements are absent, as in *Heloderma* and *Lanthanotus* (McDowell and Bogert, 1954; Langebartel, 1968).

11. In view of the suggestion that platynotid lizards and snakes are closely related (McDowell and Bogert, 1954), it should be mentioned that the chondrocranium of *Varanus* conforms essentially to the typically saurian pattern and shows no significant approximation to that in snakes (see Bellairs, 1972).

c. Osteocranium of Varanidae

The bony snout is elongated and the ascending (nasal) processes of the premaxillae between the external nostrils are very long. The bony palate is of Lakjer's (1927) neochoanate type with complete approximation between maxilla and vomer behind the opening for the duct of Jacobson's organ on each side. The superior temporal arch is complete, though slender; the postorbital arch is just incomplete dorsally though the gap may be filled by a ligament. Postfrontal and postorbital bones are separate in the young but subsequently fuse. A well developed supraorbital protects the front and upper part of the eyeball. There are two lachrymal ducts on each side (Gabe and Saint Girons, 1976); the larger, dorsal one passes anteriorly between the lachrymal and prefrontal, while the ventral one perforates the lachrymal; this doubled duct also occurs in *Lanthanotus*. The paired frontals have well developed downgrowths surrounding the olfactory peduncles. The parietals are fused. The adult brain-case and its foramina are shown in Figure 41.

---

asc, Prominence for anterior semicircular canal; b, brain (olfactory peduncles); bpt, basipterygoid process; bs, basisphenoid; ca, columella auris; cb1, ceratobranchial 1; ch, ceratohyal; cJo′, concha of Jacobson's organ; co, cochlear prominence; cp, crista parotica; cu, cupola of nasal capsule; dJo, duct of Jacobson's organ; dng, duct of nasal gland; ds, dorsum sellae; e, outline of eye; eb1, epibranchial 1; ec, ectochoanal cartilage; f, frontal; fe, foramen epiphaniale; fJo, fenestra for duct of Jacobson's organ; fo, fenestra olfactoria; fp, foramen perilymphaticum; G, level of section in Fig. 40G; hb, hyoid body; hbl, a small bony nodule representing the first hypobranchial; hh, hypohyal; ica, foramen for internal carotid artery; is, interorbital septum; Jo, outlines of Jacobson's organ; la, lachrymal; ld, lachrymal duct (*Varanus* has both a dorsal and a ventral lachrymal duct; see Gabe and Saint Girons, 1976); lp, lingual process; lsc, prominence for lateral semicircular canal; lta, lamina transversalis anterior; m, basipterygoid meniscus; mx, maxilla; na, nasal; nc, nasal concha; nca, nodules of cartilage; ng, (lateral) nasal gland; ns, nasal septum; oc, otic capsule; os, orbitosphenoid (ossified); pacc, pila accessoria; ? pai, ? processus alaris inferior; pal, palatine; pas, ascending process (epipterygoid); pasu, processus alaris superior; pat, anterior process of tectum; pf, pituitary fossa; pfr, prefrontal; pla, planum antorbitale; pma, pmp, anterior and posterior maxillary processes; pnc, paranasal cartilage; pp, processus paroticus; ps, planum supraseptale; psc, paraseptal cartilage; psca, prominence for posterior semicircular canal; ptc, parietotectal cartilage; r, lateral recess of nasal capsule; rp, rostral process; sc, sphenethmoid commissure; si, subiculum infundibuli; sor, supraorbital; tc, trabecula communis; tcr, trabecular crest; tg, tip of tongue; tm, taenia medialis; tma, taenia marginalis; v, vomer; vc, anterior and posterior openings of Vidian canal; vco, vomerine concha; 2, optic fenestra; 5, trigeminal notch; 5am, medial ethmoidal nerve; 6, posterior opening of abducens canal; 7, facial nerve foramen; 7p, palatine branch of facial nerve.

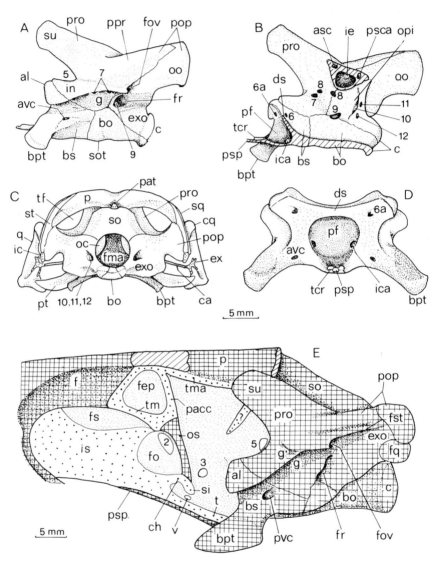

FIG. 41. (A–D) *Varanus monitor*, adult. (A) Ventrolateral view of basisphenoid and oto-occipital region seen from left side. (B) Paramedian section of region shown in (A) seen from medial aspect. (C) Posterior view of skull. (D) Anterior view of basisphenoid. (A–D) after Bahl (1937). (E) *Varanus salvator*, adult. Semi-diagrammatic figure of brain-case with quadrate removed, seen in lateral view. Cut surfaces in slanting lines, bone cross-hatched, cartilage in large dots, membrane in fine stipple. After Säve-Söderbergh (1947). (See footnote, p. 108).

The varanid skull affords a classical example of amphikinesis (Frazzetta, 1962; Rieppel, 1978b), and there is a kind of hinge halfway along the lower jaw, between the dentary and surangular on the outer surface. On the inner surface the very extensive groove for Meckel's cartilage frees the dentary from the splenial. However, this hinge is better developed in *Lanthanotus* and in Cretaceous lizards (the mosasaurs and their allies) (McDowell and Bogert, 1954). The mandibular mechanics associated with postnatal changes in the tooth form of *Varanus niloticus* have been studied by Rieppel and Labhardt (1979).

16, 17. Helodermatidae and Lanthanotidae (infraorder Platynota)

The chondrocranium of the Helodermatidae and Lanthanotidae is almost unknown, but Wever (1978) describes the middle ear of *Heloderma*, which shows no markedly unusual features. McDowell (1967) has described the middle ear of *Lanthanotus borneensis*. The tympanic cavity of the latter is very shallow, and its inner wall is mostly formed by the lateral surface of the quadrate. The rather slender, bony columella apparently lies deep to the cavity, its distal end being attached to the arch of the quadrate. The cartilaginous extracolumella protrudes from the concavity of this bone into the tympanic cavity in a fashion analogous with that in some turtles. There is no tympanic membrane, and the expanded, plate-like extracolumella lies beneath the unmodified skin over the middle ear region. The internal process, the only clearly recognizable

---

al, Alar process of basisphenoid; asc, cavity for anterior semicircular canal; avc, anterior opening of Vidian canal; bo, basioccipital; bpt, basipterygoid process; bs, basisphenoid; c, condyle; ca, columella auris; ch, cartilago hypochiasmatica; cq, cephalic condyle (head) of quadrate; ds, dorsum sellae; ex, extra-columella; exo, exoccipital; f, frontal; fep, fenestra epioptica; fma, foramen magnum; fo, fenestra optica; fov, fenestra ovalis; fq, facet for quadrate; fr, fenestra rotunda and occipital recess; fs, fenestra in interorbital septum; fst, facet for supratemporal; g, groove for vena capitis lateralis; g', groove for middle cerebral vein; ic, intercalary; ica, foramen for internal carotid artery; ie, cavity for inner ear; in, anterior inferior process of prootic; is, interorbital septum; jf, jugular foramen, for 10 in B, for 10, 11, 12 in C on external surface; oc, otic capsule; oo, otooccipital (exoccipital + opisthotic, the latter probably forming much of the paroccipital process); opi, opisthotic; os, orbitosphenoid; p, parietal; pacc, pila accessoria; pat, anterior process of tectum; pf, pituitary fossa; pop, paroccipital process; ppr, posterior process of prootic; pro, prootic; psca, cavity for posterior semicircular canal; psp, parasphenoid; pt, pterygoid; pvc, posterior opening of Vidian canal; q, quadrate; si, subiculum infundibuli; so, supraoccipital; sot, sphenooccipital tubercle; sq, squamosal; st, supratemporal; su, anterior superior process of prootic; t, trabecula; tcr, trabecular crest; tf, postemporal fossa; tm, taenia medialis; tma, taenia marginalis; v, foramen for anastomotic vein; ?, area labelled as cartilage (unidentified) by Säve-Söderbergh; 2, optic foramen; 3, foramen for oculomotor nerve; 5, trigeminal notch and foramen for trigeminal nerve root; 6, 6a, posterior and anterior openings of abducens canal; 7, foramen for facial nerve—in (A) the anterior foramen for the exit of the palatine branch, the posterior foramen for the hyomandibular. 8, foramina for auditory nerve; 9, internal foramen for glossopharyngeal nerve, and in A, region of its exit from recessus scalae tympani; 10, 11, 12, foramina for vagus, accessory, and hypoglossal nerves—these nerves have a single, combined exit foramen in the back of the skull, shown in (C).

one, is in contact with the quadrate throughout its length.

McDowell (1967) compares this condition with that in mosasaurs, in which the columella was also connected with the quadrate. He interprets the supposedly ossified tympanic membrane in one genus of these reptiles (*Plioplatecarpus*) as an ossified extracolumella.

The bony skulls of *Heloderma* and *Lanthanotus* differ from the varanid skull in various features such as the loss of the superior temporal arch and the retention of a complete postorbital arch. Nevertheless, the skulls of all platynotan lizards, living and extinct, show many detailed resemblances. These, and the particularly close similarity between *Lanthanotus* and the Lower Cretaceous dolichosaurs, are discussed by McDowell and Bogert (1954) and McDowell (1967). The relevance of some of this work to the problem of the origin of snakes is summarized by Bellairs (1972).

B. RHYNCHOCEPHALIA

1. Sphenodontidae

a. Previous Literature

Sphenodon punctatus, Howes and Swinnerton, 1901; Schauinsland, 1900, 1903; Fuchs, 1908 (nasal capsule); Broom, 1906 (nasal capsule); Wyeth, 1924 (ear); Hoppe, 1934 (nasal region); de Beer, 1937; Malan, 1946 (nasal capsule); Säve-Söderbergh, 1946, 1947 (adult brain-case); Pratt, 1948 (nasal capsule); Werner, 1962 (late embryo); Wever, 1978 (ear).

The developing skull of *Sphenodon* is remarkably similar to that of lizards and may be dealt with here, before the skull in the other suborders of Squamata. Our account of the early stages is mainly based on the work of Howes and Swinnerton (1901) and de Beer (1937), using the terminology of the latter. The embryonic osteocranium is described by these authors, and also by Schauinsland (1900, 1903) and Werner (1962).

b. Chondrocranium of Sphenodon

i. Early stages

In the youngest relevant stage (Howes and Swinnerton, 1901, Stage P; Fig. 42A, B here) much of the chondrocranium is still procartilaginous. The condition is platytrabic, the trabeculae being wide apart in the orbital region; they are not yet fused with the basal plate posteriorly. Anteriorly they are connected by a trabecular plate which continues forwards as the nasal septum. The roof of the nasal capsule has begun to develop in continuity with the dorsal edge of the septum. The planum supraseptale has

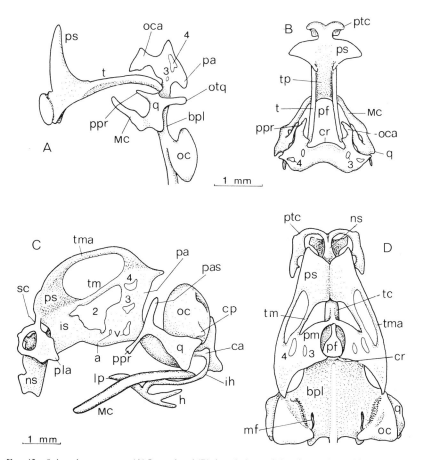

FIG. 42. *Sphenodon punctatus.* (A) Lateral and (B) dorsal views of chondrocranium of Stage P embryo. (C) Lateral and (D) dorsal views of Stage Q. After Howes and Swinnerton (1901).

a, Foramen for ophthalmic artery; bpl, basal plate; ca, columella auris; cp, crista parotica; cr, crista sellaris; h, hyobranchial skeleton; ih, interhyal; is, interorbital septum; lp, lingual process; Mc, Meckel's cartilage; mf, metotic fissure; ns, nasal septum; oc, otic capsule; oca, orbital cartilage; otq, otic process of quadrate; pa, pila antotica; pas, ascending process of pterygoquadrate (epipterygoid); pf, pituitary fenestra; pla, planum antorbitale; pm, pila metoptica; ppr, pterygoid process of pterygoquadrate; ps, planum supraseptale; ptc, parietotectal cartilage; q, quadrate; sc, sphenethmoid commissure; t, trabecula; tc, trabecula communis; tm, taenia medialis; tma, taenia marginalis; tp, trabecular plate; v, foramen for pituitary vein; 2, optic fenestra; 3, 4, foramina for oculomotor and trochlear nerves.

arisen as a pair of wing-shaped processes extending laterally from the dorsal surface of the trabecular plate.

The parachordal plate, traversed by the notochord, is flexed at right angles to the long axis of the trabeculae. The crista sellaris has developed at the front of the basal plate; it is raised at each side to form the pila antotica which is connected to other parts of the posterior orbital cartilage system, enclosing separate foramina for the IIIrd and IVth nerves. The otic capsules are in contact with the lateral edges of the posterior half of the basal plate.

The various components of the mandibular arch—the quadrate and Meckel's cartilage, the pterygoid process, and the processus ascendens (epipterygoid) can all be distinguished, but, as in some lizards of corresponding stages, they are still in continuity with each other.

In the next stage (Q) the chondrocranium is much more advanced (Fig. 42C, D). The trabeculae have fused with the basal plate enclosing a pituitary fenestra, and small basipterygoid processes have developed at their posterior ends. The marked angulation between trabeculae and parachordals seen in the earlier stages has now greatly diminished. There is no basicranial fenestra.

The wide trabecular plate has now disappeared and the trabeculae have fused in the orbital region to form a trabecula communis. This, together with the downturned medial edges of the two halves of the planum supraseptale makes up the interorbital septum. Thus, the initially platytrabic condition has been replaced by the tropitrabic one, as in lizards.

The orbitotemporal scaffolding has now developed and resembles that of lacertid lizards in most respects. However, the pilae metoptica and antotica on each side together make up a broad plate of cartilage which is perforated by four separate foramina. Jointly these correspond to the single fenestra metoptica of lacertid lizards; there is one foramen each for the IIIrd and IVth nerves, the pituitary vein and the ophthalmic artery.

The nasal capsule is now represented by the septum, the parietotectal and paranasal cartilages, the planum antorbitale and the sphenethmoid commissures, the last reaching the planum supraseptale behind.

The auditory capsule has chondrified. Its lateral wall bears a projection, the crista parotica, against which the otic process of the quadrate rests. The prefacial commissure separates the VIIth nerve from the prootic notch. At this stage the two auditory capsules are quite separate from each other as the occipital tectum has not yet developed.

The elements of the pterygoquadrate complex are still fused, but the jaw joint between the quadrate and Meckel's cartilage has differentiated. The processus ascendens has increased in height and encloses an extracranial cavum epiptericum just like that of lizards.

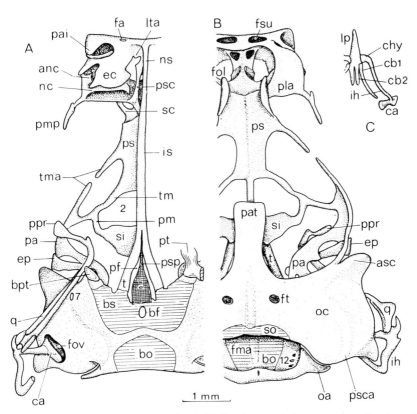

FIG. 43. *Sphenodon punctatus*. (A) Ventral and (B) dorsal views of chondrocranium of embryo of 58 mm total length. After Werner (1962). (C) Hyobranchial skeleton of late embryo. Only the first ceratobranchial is known to ossify. After Schauinsland (1900).

anc, Anterior nasal concha; asc, prominence for anterior semicircular canal; bf, basicranial fenestra; bo, basioccipital; bpl, basal plate; bpt, basipterygoid process; bs, basisphenoid; ca, columella auris; cb1, cb2, ceratobranchials 1 and 2; chy, ceratohyal; ec, ectochoanal cartilage; ep, epipterygoid; fa, foramen apicale; fma, foramen magnum; fol, fenestra olfactoria; fov, fenestra ovalis; fsu, fenestra superior; ft, fenestra in tectum synoticum (? for endolymphatic duct); ih, interhyal; is, interorbital septum; lp, lingual process; lta, lamina transversalis anterior; nc, posterior nasal concha; ns, nasal septum; oa, occipital arch; oc, otic capsule; pa, pila antotica; pai, processus alaris inferior; pat, anterior process of tectum; pf, pituitary fenestra; pla, planum antorbitale; pm, pila metoptica; pmp, posterior maxillary process; ppr, pterygoid process of pterygoquadrate; ps, planum supraseptale; psc, paraseptal cartilage; psca, prominence for posterior semicircular canal; psp, parasphenoid; pt, pterygoid; q, quadrate; sc, sphenethmoid commissure; si, subiculum infundibuli; so, supraoccipital; t, trabecula; tm, taenia medialis; tma, taenia marginalis; 2, optic fenestra; 7, foramen for facial nerve; 12, foramina for hypoglossal nerves.

The columellar apparatus (Fig. 46D) arises as a mass of procartilage which later differentiates into the columella and extracolumella, partly separated by a constriction; it is possible that there is only a single centre of chondrification for the two parts. Wever (1978) found no joint between them in the adult. The lateral extremity (insertion plate) of the extracolumella is expanded and in contact with the poorly differentiated tympanic membrane. It is also in direct cartilaginous continuity with the ceratohyal (anterior hyoid horn) by means of a pars interhyalis, which probably represents part of an epihyal element. In some lizards there is a similar continuity, but it is transient and seldom, if ever, chondrified. In *Sphenodon*, on the other hand, it apparently persists throughout life, at least in some individuals (see Wever, 1978). De Beer (1937) suggests that this feature is not truly primitive but is associated with the degenerate condition of the tympanic membrane. However, lizards such *Anniella*, which retain an extracolumella but have lost the tympanic membrane completely, apparently lack the connection.

Sphenodon also develops a chondrified processus dorsalis on the extracolumella. A nodule of cartilage (processus paroticus or intercalary) arises within the dorsal extremity of this processus and later fuses with the quadrate near its articulation with the crista parotica of the auditory capsule; in lizards the intercalary generally fuses with the crista. A cartilaginous bar, the laterohyal, extends from the intercalary to the extracolumella, enclosing a foramen between itself and the processus dorsalis; this foramen is known as Huxley's foramen (see Huxley, 1869; Fig. 46D here). A ligamentous connection, homologous with the laterohyal, is found in geckos and Crocodilia. The chorda tympani passes lateral to

FIG. 44. *Sphenodon punctatus.* (A) Lateral view of chondrocranium of embryo of 54 mm total length. (B) Lateral view of skull of same embryo. After Werner (1962). The homologies of the extracolumellar processes are not clear from Werner's labelling, which is, however, followed here. It is possible that his "anterior process" corresponds with the dorsal process of de Beer (1937), and that his dorsal process corresponds with the laterohyal.

an, Angular; ap, "anterior process" of extracolumella; asc, prominence for anterior semicircular canal; bpt, basipterygoid process; ca, columella auris; cb1, cb2, ceratobranchials 1 and 2; chy, ceratohyal; cor, coronoid; d, dentary; ec, ectochoanal cartilage; ecp, ectopterygoid; ep, epipterygoid; f, frontal; fep, fenestra epioptica; fn, fenestra narina; fpl, footplate of columella; fs, fenestra in interorbital septum; ih, interhyal; is, interorbital septum; j, jugal; lp, lingual process; lsc, prominence for lateral semicircular canal; Mc, Meckel's cartilage; mx, maxilla; na, nasal; nc, posterior nasal concha; oc, otic capsule; onf, orbitonasal fissure; p, parietal; pa, pila antotica; pai, processus alaris inferior; pal, palatine; pap, papillary cartilage; pasu, processus alaris superior; pat, anterior process of tectum; pd, dorsal process of extracolumella; pfr, prefrontal; pla, planum antorbitale; pm, pila metoptica; pmp, posterior maxillary process; pmx, premaxilla; po, postorbital; pof, postfrontal; pp, processus paroticus; ppr, pterygoid process of pterygoquadrate; ps, planum supraseptale; psca, prominence for posterior semicircular canal; pt, pterygoid; q, quadrate; qj, quadratojugal; sa, surangular; sc, sphenethmoid commissure; si, subiculum infundibuli; smx, septomaxilla; sq, squamosal; t, trabecula; tm, taenia medialis; tma, taenia marginalis; 2, optic fenestra; 12, foramina for hypoglossal nerve (three in this specimen).

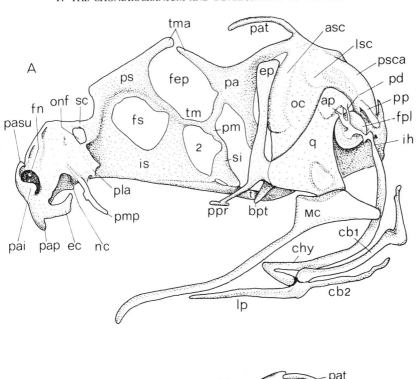

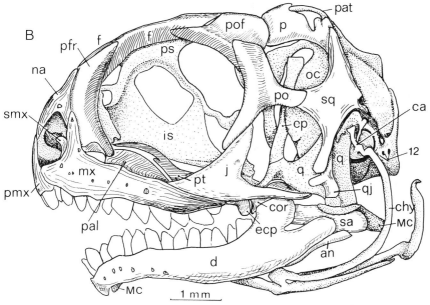

the laterohyal, and does not go through Huxley's foramen, which transmits no structure of importance (see de Beer, 1937, Pl. 141; Fig. 14).

ii. The fully formed chondrocranium of Sphenodon (Figs. 43; 44)

Nasal Capsule. The fully formed chondrocranium is realized in Howes and Swinnerton Stages R, S and T, and in the material described by Schauinsland (1900, 1903), Broom (1906), Malan (1946) and Werner (1962).

The nasal capsule has not been well described, but shows certain interesting features. There is a well developed papillary cartilage, as in a few lizards, crocodiles and some primitive mammals, and the nasal septum is prolonged forwards as a short rostral process. The parietotectal cartilage contains a superior fenestra; the presence of a transient lateral fenestra in the paranasal cartilage is doubtful. A complete paraseptal cartilage runs from the lamina transversalis anterior to the planum antorbitale; there is a zona annularis, a broad ectochoanal cartilage, and a processus maxillaris posterior. The planum antorbitale appears to be in contact with the nasal septum medially.

There are two nasal glands, a lateral one which corresponds with the lateral nasal gland of lizards, and a ventral one, probably homologous with the medial nasal gland of Testudines. Both discharge into the posterior part of the nasal vestibule. The lateral nasal gland of *Sphenodon* lies on a shallow groove in the side of the nasal capsule, but does not invaginate it, so there is no cavum conchale (Fig. 45B, C). Early workers have suggested that there is no cartilaginous nasal concha (see de Beer, 1937); however, others report two of these structures, an anterior concha which commences behind the external nostril, and a larger one further back which is perhaps homologous with the single nasal concha of lizards (see Parsons, 1970; Werner, 1962). In the embryo (Stage R–S) examined by us, the cartilages of the "two" conchae are continuous (Fig. 45D). Although the snout is fairly short, as in many iguanian lizards, the nasal sac has remained relatively simple and there has been no elongation of the vestibule or twisting of the latter on the cavum proprium.

The organ of Jacobson and its neighbouring structures show certain rather striking differences from the usual adult saurian condition. The organ itself is small, devoid of a mushroom body and cartilaginous concha, and opens directly into the front of the very long choana rather than on to the palate (Fig. 45A, B). In some ways it recalls the condition in lizard embryos and, as Broom (1906) pointed out, in the adults of many mammals; however, the presence in the latter of a secondary palate complicates the issue. The lachrymal duct opens into the front of the choana lateral to and slightly behind the duct of Jacobson's organ (Bellairs and Boyd, 1950).

The anterior part of each organ of Jacobson is enclosed within a complete cartilaginous capsule formed by the fusion of the roofing cartilage above, the paraseptal below and the nasal septum medially (Fig. 45 shows a slightly posterior level); further back these elements become separated and the organ is more exposed. The roofing cartilage has already been encountered in certain iguanid lizards (p. 89).

Orbitotemporal region. The fully formed planum supraseptale and orbitotemporal scaffolding are much like those of lacertids, but the edges of the anterior part of the planum are curved medially, and the taenia marginalis is interrupted halfway along its length (Figs. 43, 44, 46E). The interorbital septum is high and contains a single large fenestra between its dorsal edge and the planum supraseptale (Fig. 46B). The pila metoptica meet in the midline to form a substantial subiculum infundibuli. The separate foramina for the IIIrd and IVth nerves, the ophthalmic artery and the pituitary vein have now become confluent, forming a single fenestra metoptica. In very late embryonic stages this is said to become subdivided by a supratrabecular bar, as in lacertids; however, this is not apparent in Werner's (1962) figures.

Basal plate, occipital and otic regions. There is no basicranial fenestra in the earlier stages, but Werner (1962) has shown that this opening occurs in the later embryos. The occipital arches do not meet in the dorsal midline, so that the very broad tectum consists only of the tectum synoticum; there is no tectum posterius. The ascending process of the tectum is extremely broad and massive; it remains cartilaginous throughout life. The composition of the cranio-vertebral joint is similar to that in Squamata (i.e. intravertebral and supposedly intersegmental), but a small part of the proatlas element (the "proatlas arch") chondrifies as an independent structure which is often called a proatlas by students of the adult skeleton. (Hoffstetter and Gasc, 1969). This element is not seen in lizards (other than some chameleons), at least not as a separate structure.

The otic capsule resembles that of lizards in its general structure (except that the cavum vestibulare is single), in its relationship with the basal plate, and in the arrangement of the metotic fissure and recessus scalae tympani. However, each endolymphatic duct emerges through its foramen in the otic capsule, and then continues as a diverticulum which pierces the tectum synoticum through a large foramen; this is an unusual feature. *Sphenodon* appears to be one of the few Recent reptiles in which the internal jugular vein, leaving the skull through the metotic fissure,

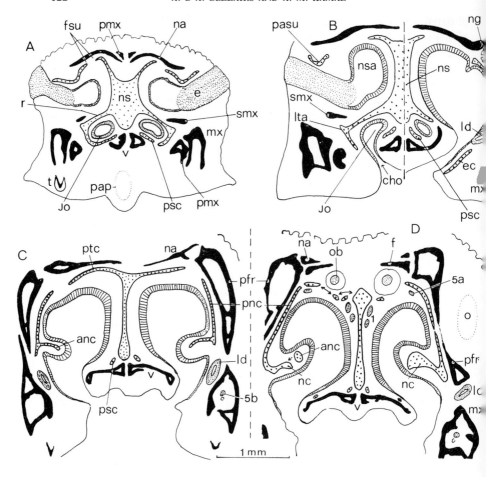

Fig. 45. *Sphenodon punctatus.* Late embryo, Stage R–S (see Howes and Swinnerton, 1901). Transverse sections through nasal capsule. (B) Shows two different sections, that on the right being markedly more posterior. In (D) the cartilage of the anterior nasal concha is about to fuse with the posterior concha, as shown by the small arrow. The right side is slightly more posterior and shows the posterior concha only. More dorsally placed arrows show fusion of cartilage nodules with each other and with the nasal septum to form a continuous anterior border of the fenestra olfactoria.

anc, Anterior nasal concha; cho, front of choana; e, epithelial plug filling vestibule and external nostril; ec, ectochoanal cartilage; f, frontal; fsu, fenestra superior; Jo, Jacobson's organ; ld, lachrymal duct; lta, lamina transversalis anterior; mx, maxilla; na, nasal; nc, posterior nasal concha; ng, lateral nasal gland; ns, nasal septum; nsa, nasal sac (front of cavum proprium); o, front of orbit; ob, front of olfactory bulb; pap, region of papillary cartilage, which is damaged in this embryo; pasu, processus alaris superior; pfr, prefrontal; pmx, premaxilla; pnc, paranasal cartilage; psc, paraseptal cartilage; ptc, parietotectal cartilage; smx, septomaxilla; t, tooth germ; v, vomer; l, olfactory nerves; 5a, 5b, ethmoidal and maxillary branches of trigeminal nerve; r, roofing cartilage of Jo.

persists in late embryonic and adult stages. The fissure is thus a true jugular foramen (O'Donoghue, 1920; Rieppel, 1978c).

The ascending process of the pterygoquadrate and the quadrate cartilage remain in contact with each other (Fig. 44A), whereas in lizards they become separate. The pterygoid process of the pterygoquadrate is at first long and kinked anteriorly, but later becomes reduced. The basal process is represented by the basipterygoid meniscus. The relations of the cavum epiptericum seem essentially lizard-like (Fig. 46C). The columellar apparatus has already been described.

The hyobranchial apparatus (Fig. 43C) is already chondrified at Howes and Swinnerton's Stage Q. It consists of a median basihyal, which is prolonged anteriorly to form a lingual process; of hypohyal and ceratohyal elements, and of first and second ceratobranchials. No derivatives of the third branchial arch are present. The basihyal and first ceratobranchial may become ossified.

The chondrocranium of *Sphenodon* is compared with that of lizards on page 193.

C. *Osteocranium of* Sphenodon

i. *Cartilage bones*

The general pattern of ossification resembles that of lizards; only certain points of interest will be noted her.

The occipital condyle is formed mainly or entirely from the basioccipital. Werner's (1962) figure (43A here) suggests that the small basicranial fenestra is closed by the parabasisphenoid rather than by the basioccipital ossification. Both basisphenoid and basioccipital seem to arise from paired centres. The Vidian canal is not closed ventrally by the parasphenoid, but forms an open groove in the basisphenoid (Fig. 46C); this is perhaps a primitive condition (Rieppel, 1979a).

The epipterygoid, ossifying in the ascending process of the pterygoquadrate, is wider than in lizards and remains attached to the front of the quadrate.

ii. *Dermal bones*

The unfused premaxillae of the late embryo bear no egg-tooth, as they do in lizards, but there is a horny egg-caruncle on the dorsal aspect of the snout, as in turtles, crocodilians and birds (De Beer, 1949).

The septomaxilla lies somewhat laterally, beneath the vestibule; instead of covering Jacobson's organ completely, as in the Squamata, it only forms a partial roof for the most anterior region of the organ (Fig. 45A).

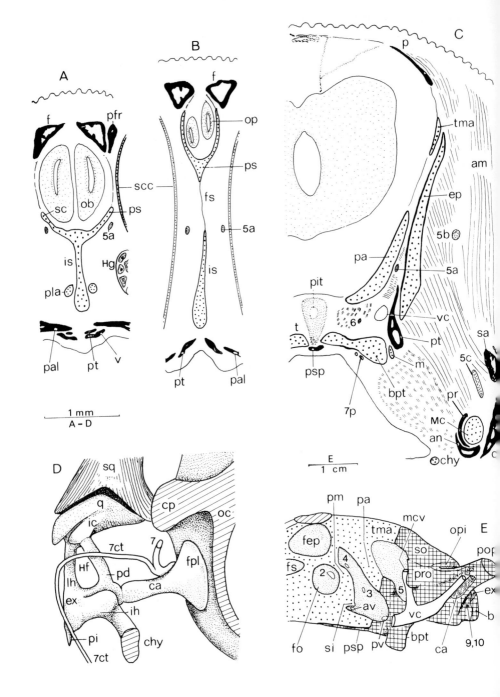

The palatine is toothed, a condition which is very rare among lizards. The very long pterygoid is toothless, and its anterior end contacts the vomer. Both frontals and parietals remain unfused in the adult; there is an elongated parietal foramen near the front of the latter bones. The superior temporal arch is formed from the postorbital and squamosal, as in typical lizards. There is also a complete inferior temporal arch formed by the articulation of the jugal with the quadratojugal; this feature (not yet quite realized in Werner's embryo; Fig. 44B) distinguishes *Sphenodon* from all Squamata. The lachrymal is absent. Despite the presence of basipterygoid joints, kinesis is probably minimal, and the quadrate, being firmly attached to the epipterygoid and quadratojugal, is unable to swing freely as it can in the streptostylic Squamata.

C. AMPHISBAENIA

a. Previous Literature

No real developmental studies have been made on the skulls of these highly specialized burrowing reptiles. In the late embryo of *Leposternon* recently studied by May (1978) the pattern of ossification was essentially complete, so that the origin and nature of certain problematical elements could not be elucidated. All the other references cited below indicate studies of postnatal specimens; many of these articles are based partly or

---

FIG. 46. *Sphenodon punctatus.* (A–C) Late embryo, Stage R–S. (A) Transverse section through anterior part of planum supraseptale. (B) Transverse section through planum at mid-orbital level. (C) Transverse section through cavum epiptericum. (D) Late embryo, Stage S. Reconstruction of left columellar apparatus in posterior view. After Wyeth (1924). (E) Adult brain-case in lateral view. Bones are cross-hatched, cartilage in large dots, membrane in fine stipple. After Säve-Söderbergh (1947).

am, Adductor mandibulae; an, angular; av, transverse anastomotic vein; bo, basioccipital; bpt, basipterygoid process; ca, columella auris; chy, ceratohyal; cp, crista parotica; d, dentary; ep, epipterygoid; ex, extracolumella; exo, exoccipital; f, frontal; fep, fenestra epioptica; fo, fenestra optica; fpl, footplate; fs, fenestra in interorbital septum; Hf, Huxley's foramen; Hg, Harderian gland; ic, intercalary; ih, interhyal; is, interorbital septum; lh, laterohyal; m, basipterygoid meniscus; Mc, Meckel's cartilage; mcv, middle cerebral vein; ob, olfactory bulb; oc, otic capsule; op, olfactory peduncle; opi, opisthotic; p, parietal; pa, pila antotica; pal, palatine; pd, dorsal process of extracolumella; pfr, prefrontal; pi, inferior process of extracolumella; pit, pituitary; pla, planum antorbitale; pm, pila metoptica; pop, paroccipital process; pr, prearticular; pro, prootic; ps, planum supraseptale; psp, parasphenoid; pt, pterygoid; pv, foramen for pituitary vein; q, quadrate; sa, surangular; sc, sphenethmoid commissure; scc, scleral cartilage; si, subiculum infundibuli; so, supraoccipital; sq, squamosal; t, trabecula; tma, taenia marginalis; v, vomer; vc, vena capitis; 2, 3, 4, foramina for optic, oculomotor, and trochlear nerves; 5, trigeminal notch; 5a, b, c, ophthalmic, maxillary, and mandibular branches of trigeminal nerve; 6, abducens nerve; 7, facial nerve, hyomandibular branch; 7ct, chorda tympani branch of facial nerve; 7p, palatine branch of facial nerve; 9, 10, common "jugular" foramen for glossopharyngeal and vagus nerves.

completely on sectioned material. Although four Recent families of these animals are recognized (see Gans, 1978) it is easier to describe their cranial anatomy in a single section.

1. Amphisbaenidae. *Amphisbaena alba*, Pratt, 1948 (nasal capsule). *A. cubana*; *A. fuliginosa*, Zangerl, 1944: *A.* sp., Versluys, 1936 (ear); Kesteven, 1957a (very eccentric terminology). *Chirindia ewerbecki, Geocalamus acutus, Leposternon microcephalum*, Zangerl, 1944. *L. microcephalum*, May, 1978 (late embryo). *Monopeltis capensis*, Kritzinger, 1946; Malan, 1946 (nasal capsule).

2. Bipedidae. *Bipes biporus*, Zangerl, 1944.

3. Rhineuridae. *Rhineura floridana*, Zangerl, 1944.

4. Trogonophidae. *Agamodon anguliceps*, Gans, 1960. *Diplometopon zarudnyi*, Gans, 1960; El-Assy and Al-Nassar, 1976. *Pachycalamus brevis*, Gans, 1960. *Trogonophis wiegmanni*, Fischer, 1900 (nasal capsule); Zangerl, 1944; Bellairs, 1949a, 1950 (brain-case and epipterygoid); Gans, 1960.

The anatomy and physiology of the ear of many species have been described by Wever and Gans (see Gans, 1974, and Wever, 1978). Gabe and Saint Girons (1976) have described the nasal sac and organ of Jacobson of *Blanus* and *Trogonophis*, while Rieppel (1979e) has compared parts of the jaw muscles of amphisbaenians with those of other Squamata. Gans (1978) has reviewed the characters of Amphisbaenia and summarized the available information on the chondrocranium. Sectioned material of *Amphisbaena fuliginosa, Anops kingii, Chirindia rondoensis, Diplometopon zarudnyi, Loveridgea ionidesii, Rhineura floridana*, and *Trogonophis wiegmanni* has been examined.

b. Chondrocranium and Ossified Brain-case of Amphisbaenia

The nasal capsule is known in *Trogonophis* (Fischer, 1900; personal observations), in *Monopeltis* (Malan, 1946; Kritzinger, 1946) and in *Leposternon* (May, 1978). The cartilages, especially those of the roof of the capsule, are reduced, perhaps in correlation with the very compact structure of the surrounding dermal bones; the olfactory and superior fenestrae are large (Fig. 47). In *Trogonophis* (and very possibly in the other two genera mentioned above, though the accounts are not clear) a foramen epiphaniale is present in the usual position, but there is no foramen apicale. The medial ethmoidal nerves leave the nasal capsule by passing through bony canals in the septomaxillae and premaxilla, issuing from the latter to innervate the soft tissues of the snout and, very probably as in *Rhineura*, the premaxilla and its dentition (Smith *et al.*, 1953). The nasal concha consists of a fairly simple invagination of the lateral capsular wall; the lateral nasal gland is situated in its concavity.

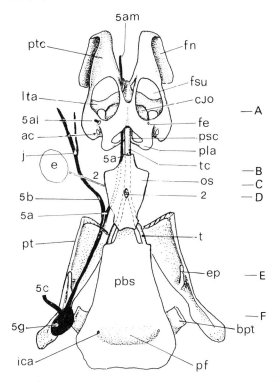

Fig. 47. *Trogonophis wiegmanni*, adult. Dorsal view of nasal capsule and sphenoid complex. Levels of section in Fig. 48 are shown. Based on reconstruction by N. Al-Nassar.

ac, Aditus conchae; bpt, basipterygoid process; cJo, concha of Jacobson's organ; e, outline of eye; ep, epipterygoid; fe, foramen epiphaniale; fn, fenestra narina; fsu, fenestra superior; ica, foramen for internal carotid artery; j, junction between superficial and deep branches of 5b, maxillary nerve; lta, lamina trasversalis anterior; os, orbitosphenoid; pf, pituitary fossa; pla, planum antorbitale; psc, paraseptal cartilage; pt, pterygoid; ptc, parietotectal cartilage; t, trabecula; tc, trabecula communis; 2, optic nerve and foramen; 5a, ophthalmic nerve; 5al, 5am, lateral and medial branches of ophthalmic nerve; 5b, maxillary nerve; 5c, mandibular nerve; 5g, trigeminal ganglion.

The floor of the capsule is represented by the lamina transversalis anterior, the dorsal surface of which bears the substantial concha of Jacobson's organ. In *Monopeltis* the paraseptal cartilage is incomplete and consists only of its anterior and posterior portions. The relationships of the organ of Jacobson to the surrounding skeletal elements and the structure of the organ itself conforms to the usual pattern in Squamata (Fig. 48A). There appear to be no sphenethmoid commissures in the three genera described above.

Other features of the unossified and ossified chondrocranium of amphisbaenians may be illustrated by reference to *Trogonophis*. This genus is primitive in some respects, such as the relatively large size of the eyes (which are still minute by normal saurian standards), and the presence therein of the lens and scleral cartilage, and in some individuals at least, of scleral ossicles. Scleral cartilage occurs in certain other amphisbaenians, such as *Leposternon* (May, 1978), but in many forms the tiny eye, almost buried in the enormous Harderian gland, retains only a capsule of connective tissue (Underwood, 1970).

The nasal septum of *Trogonophis* falls abruptly in height behind the nasal capsule and continues posteriorly into a rod-like trabecula communis. This extends posteriorly behind the level of the eyes and then forks into two separate trabeculae which diverge and ultimately become enclosed within lateral extensions of the parabasisphenoid bone. The front of the trabecula communis is somewhat compressed laterally and forms what can be regarded as a very low interorbital septum (Fig. 48B); May (1978) describes a similar formation in *Leposternon*. Since the trabeculae are fused at the level of the orbits, the condition is technically tropitrabic. However, the interorbital septum lies between the two nasopharyngeal grooves, roofed over by the concave palatine bones, rather than between the orbits proper. The latter are separated by the whole width of the cranial cavity and dermal brain-case, formed here mainly by the frontals.

A conspicuous paired bone appears at mid-orbital level immediately above the trabecula communis and between the well developed frontal and parietal downgrowths (Fig. 48B, C). It extends backwards as an elongated structure with lateral wings and a shallow ventral keel, and ends some distance posterior to the region where the trabecula communis forks into the paired trabeculae. A small foramen in the posterior third of this bone transmits the tiny optic nerve (Figs. 47, 48C, D). Kritzinger (1946) mentions a similar foramen in *Monopeltis*. The ophthalmic nerves pass forward beneath the wings. The usual system of saurian orbital cartilages

---

FIG. 48. *Trogonophis wiegmanni*, adult. Transverse sections through head at levels shown in Fig. 47.

ar, Articular; bpt, basipterygoid process; cJo´, concha of Jacobson's organ; cor, coronoid; d, dentary; dJo, duct of Jacobson's organ; ec, base of ectochoanal cartilage; ecp, ectopterygoid; ep, epipterygoid; ex, extracolumella; f, frontal; Hg, Harderian gland; ld, opening of lachrymal duct; ls, ? laterosphenoid; m, basipterygoid meniscus; mx, maxilla; na, nasal; ng, nasal gland; ns, nasal septum; os, orbitosphenoid; p, parietal; pal, palatine; pbs, parabasisphenoid; pmx, premaxilla; psp, parasphenoid rostrum; pt, pterygoid; ptc, parietotectal cartilage; q, quadrate; sa, surangular (fused with articular); sg, superior labial gland; smx, septomaxilla; t, trabecula; tc, trabecula communis; tg, tip of tongue; to, tooth; v, vomer; 2, optic nerve; 5a, b, c, ophthalmic, maxillary, and mandibular branches of trigeminal nerve; 5al, 5am, lateral and medial ethmoidal branches of ophthalmic nerve; 5g, trigeminal ganglion; 7p, palatine branch of facial nerve.

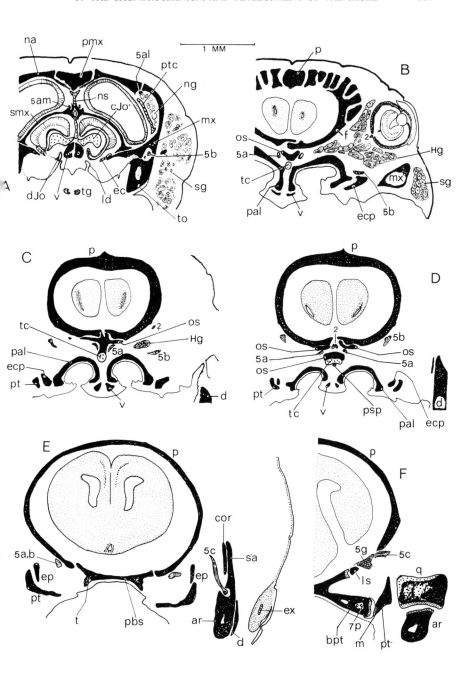

is absent, having apparently been replaced by this bone (see below).

The bone described above is termed a laterosphenoid by May (1978) but can best be regarded as an orbitosphenoid, following the usage of Zangerl (1944) and most later workers. In some ways it recalls the sphenethmoid bone of primitive tetrapods (see Beaumont, 1977) but does not extend so far anterior that it enters the nasal region. One may suppose that it originally ossifies in the planum supraseptale and pila metoptica which are presumably present as cartilaginous structures in the unknown embryonic stages. It is ossified in the late embryo described by May (1978). The low orbitosphenoid keel of *Trogonophis* could represent the downturned medial edges of the fused anterior orbital cartilages (planum supraseptale), which in lizards form the dorsal part of the interorbital septum. The ventral part of the saurian septum could be represented by the trabecula communis, which, together with the paired trabeculae, are the only parts of the orbitotemporal chondrocranium to remain cartilaginous in postnatal *Trogonophis*.

Behind the orbitosphenoid of *Trogonophis* is another unpaired bone in a slightly more ventral plane, the parabasisphenoid (Zangerl, 1944). It lies beneath and between the parietal downgrowths and forms the greater part of the skull base (Figs. 47; 48D, E). Its rostrum extends anteriorly beneath the orbitosphenoid and between the paired parts of the trabeculae which become buried in its margins and merge into the general ossification. Posteriorly, the parabasisphenoid has a suture with the basioccipital. In *Trogonophis*, as in most trogonophine and some other genera, the parabasisphenoid bears distinct basipterygoid processes tipped with cartilage; in sections of *Trogonophis* these can be seen to articulate with the pterygoids by means of synovial joints. A wedge of cartilage, probably the meniscus, is attached to the adjacent surface of the pterygoid (Fig. 48F).

Trogonophis has small, completely ossified epipterygoid bones which articulate with the dorsomedial surfaces of the pterygoids some distance in front of the basipterygoid joints (Bellairs, 1950; Gans, 1960; Figs. 47; 48E here). The presence of these bones appears to be a primitive feature which has not yet been observed in any other amphisbaenian genus.

The relationship of the maxillary nerve to the epipterygoid in *Trogonophis* is of interest. Two main branches of this nerve can be seen around the level of the middle of Jacobson's organ, a deep branch within the maxilla and a superficial branch between the maxilla and the superior labial gland (Fig. 48A). Further posteriorly, the superficial branch enters the bone and joins the deep branch. The single nerve issues from the maxilla anterior to the orbit, gradually approaches the ophthalmic nerve and eventually comes to run alongside it for a considerable distance.

Finally the two nerves become virtually merged together and continue back on the *medial* side of the epipterygoid (Figs. 47; 48E), to reach the trigeminal ganglion lying in a large foramen which represents the prootic notch. In lizards the maxillary nerve always lies lateral to the epipterygoid. Unfortunately, Bellairs (1950) mistakenly labelled the mandibular nerve as the "maxillary" in his Pl. 1B of *Trogonophis*.

In *Trogonophis* and many other amphisbaenians there is a small bone, sometimes divided in two by a suture, between the adjacent margins of the parabasisphenoid and the basioccipital. It was called "element X" by Zangerl (1944). Kesteven (1957a) termed it the prootic, but it probably represents a basioccipital and/or basisphenoid epiphysis (see Gans, 1960, 1978).

Despite its unlizard-like appearance, the anterior part of the brain-case of *Trogonophis* can theoretically be derived from a chondrocranium like that of *Anniella* (Bellairs, 1950; Fig. 39 here). This burrowing anguimorph does not show the extreme fossorial specialization encountered among amphisbaenians, but the rigidity and elongation of the temporal part of the skull so characteristic of *Trogonophis* has been partly achieved. The principal modifications necessary to convert the *Anniella*-like to the *Trogonophis*-like condition would be the removal of the sphenethmoid commissures and taeniae marginales of *Anniella*, and the complete ossification of the long narrow planum supraseptale, which probably takes place in amphisbaenians during embryonic life. The resulting structure would resemble the orbitosphenoid of *Trogonophis*, except that the pila metoptica, lost in *Anniella*, would have to be retained and ossified to form the part of the orbitosphenoid that lies behind the optic foramen. Further ventral extension of parietal downgrowths similar to those of *Anniella* would also have to occur, so that these bones would contact each other or the parabasisphenoid beneath the brain. The ophthalmic nerves would be excluded from the cranial cavity by this contact, instead of being enclosed within it as in snakes. Although no modern worker would claim that *Anniella* has any close taxonomic affinity with the Amphisbaenia, the analogy is of interest; it suggests that the brain-case of amphisbaenians may not be such a unique structure as has been supposed.

The anterior part of the brain-case of other amphisbaenians appears to be basically similar to that in *Trogonophis*, but shows many variations in proportion and detail. In *Monopeltis* the trabecula communis forks at a more anterior level than in *Trogonophis*, quite close to the back of the nasal capsule; thus Kritzinger (1946) regarded the condition as platytrabic. His Fig. 6A, however, shows a trabecula communis (labelled interorbital septum) close to the level of the orbits, much as in *Trogonophis*. In these reptiles with minute eyes the distinction between platytraby and tropitraby is a somewhat arbitrary one. In *Monopeltis* also the parabasisphenoid rostrum extends a long way forwards dorsal to the orbitosphenoid and frontal downgrowths, and forms the floor of the cranial cavity in the region just behind the snout. This anterior extension of the parasphenoid is not found in *Trogonophis*.

In *Rhineura* the trabecula communis becomes ossified and is incorporated into the relatively deep orbitosphenoid keel. In *Loveridgea* and *Chirindia* the nasal septum or trabecula communis ends just posterior to the nasal capsule and no signs of paired trabeculae can be seen, either as separate structures or as rods or cartilage enclosed by the parabasisphenoid. This absence (at least in the adult) of much of the trabecular system is remarkable among Squamata and can perhaps be correlated with the general reduction of cartilage and massive development of the dermal bones. In *Diplometopon*, *Loveridgea*, and *Chirindia* the orbitosphenoid is very wide, suggesting that the planum supraseptale of the embryo formed a great wide plate.

Several authors have described a "laterosphenoid" bone just beneath or just above the foramen for the trigeminal ganglion in certain forms such as *Amphisbaena manni* (Fig. 49A) and *Diplometopon* (El-Assy and Al-Nassar, 1976) but this was difficult to identify with certainty in our sectioned material. Whether this bone is a true laterosphenoid ossified in the region of the pila antotica or a part of the prootic can only be determined by study of embryonic material. A detailed investigation of the brain-case of amphisbaenians by Gans and Bellairs is in preparation.

c. Columella and Hyobranchial Apparatus of Amphisbaenia

The middle ear structures of amphisbaenians are highly specialized. The columella and its footplate are massive, and in most forms there is a cartilaginous extracolumella; this is partly ossified in *Diplometopon* (Gans and Wever, 1975) and in certain other forms. In *Leposternon* the columella is pierced by the stapedial artery, as in geckos (May, 1978). This feature has not been observed in other amphisbaenians. As in snakes and some lizards the tympanic membrane and cavity are absent. However, the extracolumella is not applied to the inner surface of the quadrate, as is usual among "earless" Squamata, burrowing or otherwise. Instead, it passes forwards along the side of the "face" (Figs. 48E, 49A). In *Agamodon* and *Diplometopon* the extracolumella forms a broad plate which extends forwards a little way in front of the jaw joint; it then becomes connected with flat bands of connective tissue which are fused with the dermis covering the posterior part of the upper and lower jaws

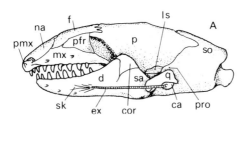

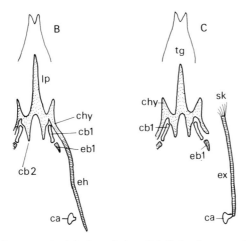

FIG. 49. (A) *Amphisbaena manni*, adult. Lateral view of skull showing extracolumella. After Wever and Gans (1973) and Wever (1978). (B, C) Adult hyobranchial skeleton and columella of (B) *Bipes* sp. and (C) *Amphisbaena* sp. (which resembles most other amphisbaenian genera). In *Bipes* there is a long epihyal, and the columella has no extracolumella attached to it. The epihyal of *Bipes* appears to correspond with the extracolumella of *Amphisbaena*; both are shown in cross lines, and other cartilaginous structures are stippled. After Gans (1974).

ca, Columella auris; cb1, cb2, ceratobranchials 1 and 2; chy, ceratohyal; cor, coronoid; d, dentary; eb1, epibranchial 1; eh, epihyal; ex, extracolumella; f, frontal; lp, lingual process; ls, ? laterosphenoid; mx, maxilla; na, nasal; p, parietal; pfr, prefrontal; pmx, premaxilla; pro, prootic; q, quadrate; sa surangular; sk, skin attachment of extracolumella; so, supraoccipital; tg, tongue.

(Gans, 1960, 1974). In *Amphisbaena manni* (Fig. 49A) and other amphisbaenid species the extracolumella is a long slender rod, while in *Monopeltis* it is a massive beam of cartilage extending along the side of the lower jaw (Kritzinger, 1946); in both cases it is attached to the skin over the lateral surface of the lower jaw. In amphisbaenians generally the columellar apparatus appears to act as a stereophonic amplifying system for the conduction of airborne or earthborne sounds, set up by movements of the little animals on which these reptiles prey (Gans, 1974; Gans and Wever, 1972; Wever and Gans, 1973; Wever, 1978).

In the great majority of amphisbaenians the hyobranchial apparatus consists of the usual hyoid body with a well developed lingual process, ceratohyals (perhaps incorporating hypohyals) forming the hyoid horns, ossified first ceratobranchials (sometimes with cartilaginous epibranchials), and short second ceratobranchials (Fig. 49C). However, *Bipes biporus* and *Blanus cinereus* lack an extracolumella and have the lateral end of the columella connected to a specialized region of skin in the neck, where it acts as a transmittor of sound vibrations. The hyoid arch has an extremely long dorsal horn regarded as an epihyal which passes back to the occipital region, where it ends freely.

On the basis of these findings, Wever and Gans (1972), Gans (1974) and Wever (1978) have suggested that the structure usually (as above) termed the extracolumella in amphisbaenians (other than *Bipes* and *Blanus*) is really the epihyal, which has become detached from the rest of the hyoid skeleton and attached to the columella. Thus it is not homologous with the extracolumella of lizards, which represents the hyomandibular, but with a more dorsal element of the hyoid arch.

d. The Amphisbaenian Skull as a Whole

The skulls of amphisbaenians (Fig. 49A) show many characteristic features of extreme fossorial adaptation in reptiles. The superior temporal and postorbital arches have been lost, with extreme reduction or loss of such elements as the jugal, postorbital, squamosal and supratemporal. In many forms, such as *Trogonophis*, the dermal roofing bones articulate by means of complex interlocking sutures which demarcate the finger-like processes of adjacent bony margins. Both frontal and parietal downgrowths are extremely well developed and articulate firmly beneath the brain with each other and also with the orbitosphenoid and parabasisphenoid which form much of the skull base. The tip of the skull is firmly welded into the nasal region by means of the long ascending process of the premaxilla; this runs back in the midline betwen the nasals, sometimes between the frontals, and in *Trogonophis* even extends so far back as to reach the front of the fused parietal. There is no parietal foramen (see Gans, 1960), except in some species of *Monopeltis* (Kritzinger, 1946; Gans, 1978).

The general proportions of the skull also tend to be modified and, as Zangerl (1944) has suggested, in some ways recall those of certain mammals. Thus the jaw joint is set well forward and the orbital and posterior nasal regions of the skull have become "telescoped" into one another so that the cranial and nasal cavities are close to each other as in mammals. Gans' (1974, p. 134) figure of the skull of a cat above that of the trogonophid *Agamodon* shows a striking apparent similarity, but as he remarks, "The two skulls differ in everything except their solidity and the most superficial proportions".

The presence in adults of some amphisbaenians of a cartilaginous anterior process of the occipital tectum fitting into or beneath the back of the parietal, and of synovial joints between basipterygoid processes and pterygoids, suggests the possibility of kinetic movement. However, the general solidity of the skull would not lead one to believe that such movements could be at all extensive, especially in forms such as *Trogonophis* with complex interlocking sutures (see Gans, 1960; May, 1978).

The premaxilla of amphisbaenians characteristically bears a large median tooth in front, which is perhaps a successor to an egg-tooth. The entire dentition, both in acrodont and pleurodont forms, is surprisingly powerful. The lower jaw is short and massive, with a well developed "coronoid process" formed by the dentary, coronoid and surangular bones; the splenial is small or absent. The symphysial region of the lower jaw is interesting and deserves detailed study. In some forms, such as *Trogonophis*, the two dentaries are connected by dense connective tissue, while in others, such as *Rhineura*, the junction is fibrocartilaginous. In *Trogonophis* the anterior part of Meckel's cartilage is exposed in a groove on the medial aspect of the dentary; in other forms it may be partly embedded in the bone, or apparently absent altogether.

Gans (1974) has emphasized the very marked differences between the overall skull shapes of various amphisbaenians. Thus, the skull may be elongated, particularly in the temporal region, as in *Trogonophis* and *Amphisbaena*, or it may be short and chunky, as in *Leposternon* and *Agamodon*. The snout may be relatively pointed, as in *Trogonophis*, blunt as in many species of *Amphisbaena*, depressed and shovel-shaped as in *Monopeltis* and *Rhineura*, laterally compressed like the prow of a ship as in *Anops*, or furnished with a grotesque dorsal keel, as in *Ancylocranium*. These variations are probably associated with differences in the methods of burrowing.

The development and growth of these strange skulls must present many features of great interest, and a series of well fixed embryos of any amphisbaenian species would be one of the richest prizes that a cranial morphologist could obtain.

D. SERPENTES

1. Colubridae (infraorder Caenophidia). The simple classification of Parker (1977) is used here.

a. Previous Literature

Dasypeltis scabra, *Lamprophis inornatus*, Pringle, 1954. *Lampropeltis getulus*, Wever, 1978 (adult ear). *Crotaphopeltis hotamboeia*, Brock, 1929. *Malpolon monspessulanus*, El-Toubi, Kamal and Zaher, 1973a, b. *Natrix natrix*, Rathke, 1839; Parker, 1879; Möller, 1905 (ear); Gaupp, 1906; de Beer, 1926 (orbitotemporal region); Bäckström, 1931; Tschekanowskaja, 1936; de Beer, 1937. *Nerodia sipedon*, Wever, 1978 (adult ear). *Psammophis sibilans*, Kamal, 1964c (aberrant facial nerve); Kamal, 1966d (rotation of quadrate); Kamal and Hammouda, 1965a, b (chondrocranium); 1965c (embryonic osteocranium); 1965d (columella auris); 1968 (adult skull). *Thelotornis kirtlandii*, Visser, 1961.

Hegazy (1976) has described the cranial nerves of *Psammophis* and certain other snakes from sections of embryonic material, while Auen and Langebartel (1977) have studied the cranial nerves of adult *Elaphe* and *Thamnophis*. Lüdicke (1978) deals with the vascular relations of the columellar apparatus in colubrid and other snakes. Zehr (1962) has illustrated normal embryonic stages of *Thamnophis*.

b. Chondrocranium of Psammophis sibilans

Seven successive stages of this opisthoglyph colubrid have been studied by Kamal and Hammouda (1965a, b, c); their work on this species provides a basic account of the developing ophidian skull.

i. Earlier stages

At Stage 1 (age 15 days of incubation, 47 mm total body-length; Fig. 50A here) four elements are present: the trabeculae, the basal plate (fused parachordals), Meckel's cartilages, and rudiments of the hyobranchial apparatus. The trabeculae are widely separated from each other and from the basal plate. The notochord is embedded in the latter, but its tip slightly projects from the plate in front. The back of the plate is continuous with the rudiment of the occipital arch on each side. There is a single pair of hypoglossal foramina. The hyobranchial apparatus consists of the hyoid body and two short horns, termed ceratohyals by Kamal and Hammouda, but regarded here as second ceratobranchials (p. 150).

At Stage 2 (age 19 days, 61·7 mm total body-length; Fig. 50B, E) the front ends of the trabeculae have fused to form a broad trabecular plate from which the nasal septum will be derived; this septal region is bent at a sharp angle to the more posterior parts of the trabeculae behind. The latter also form an angle with the basal plate. The notochord extends anteriorly only as far as the anterior quarter of the basal plate. The VIth nerve pierces the anterolateral corner of the plate; in *Natrix* de Beer (1937) mentions that it perforates a tiny stump which could represent a vestige of a pila antotica, otherwise absent. There are now two hypoglossal foramina on each side. The posterior margin of the basal plate is fused with the tip of the odontoid process of the axis vertebra. The quadrate cartilage is now visible and represents the only element of the pterygoquadrate complex developed in snakes (except perhaps for the posterior maxillary process of a few forms; p. 169). It is in close contact with Meckel's cartilage and lies nearly in a straight line with it. Behind the jaw joint the posterior end of Meckel's cartilage forms a rudimentary retroarticular process. The lingual process extends anteriorly from the body of the hyoid.

In *Stage 3* (age 22 days, total body length 64 mm; Fig. 50C) the trabecula communis extends anteriorly and ventrally to form the nasal septum, and the posterior parts of the trabeculae have become somewhat closer to each other. The hind tip of each is fused with the anterolateral edge of the basal plate, thus enclosing the pituitary fenestra. The VIth nerve now passes through a tunnel in the basal plate, its two openings being on the dorsal surface of the plate. There are now three pairs of hypoglossal foramina. The otic capsules have begun to chondrify, and the cochlear portion of each is connected to the parachordal plate by a single basicapsular commissure. At this stage the VIIth nerve passes for a short distance through the cavity of the auditory capsule before leaving it through the facial foramen in the ventrolateral aspect of the capsule; the IXth nerve passes through a tunnel in the ventromedial wall of the capsule, but does not actually enter the capsular cavity (see Kamal, 1969e; Fig. 53C here). The columella auris begins to chondrify quite independently of the otic capsule. The lower end of the quadrate cartilage has begun to rotate downwards and backwards so that it now makes an obtuse angle with Meckel's cartilage.

At *Stage 4* (age 26 days, total body length 78·2 mm; Fig. 50F), the medial parts of the nasal cupolae have chondrified and project in front of the nasal septum, which has now increased greatly in height; they have no separate centres of chondrification and appear to have been derived from the plate-like anterior region of the trabecula communis. As in Squamata generally, the lateral parts of the nasal capsule appear relatively late in development. The pituitary fenestra is reduced as the trabeculae are now quite close together. The internal carotid arteries enter the skull through notches at the posterior corners of the fenestra. The occipital arch

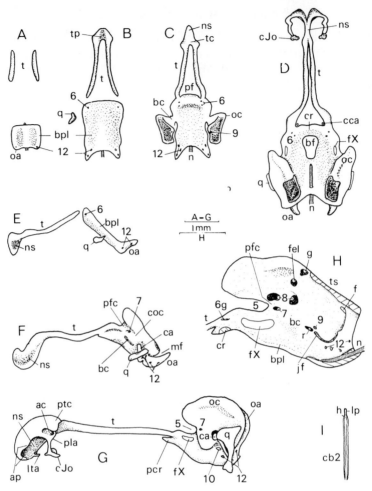

Fig. 50. *Psammophis sibilans*. Chondrocrania of embryos. Dorsal view of (A) Stage 1; (B) Stage 2; (C) Stage 3 and (D) Stage 5. Lateral view of (E) Stage 2; (F) Stage 4; (G) Stage 6. (H) Medial view of right otic capsule after median section (cut regions in slanting lines) of fully formed chondrocranium. (I) Fully formed hyobranchial apparatus (much reduced). (A–G) after Kamal and Hammouda (1965a); (H) and (I) after Kamal and Hammouda (1965b).

ac, Aditus conchae; ap, superior and inferior alar processes; bc, basicapsular commissure; bf, basicranial fenestra; bpl, basal plate; ca, columella auris; cb2, ceratobranchial 2; cca, cerebral branch of internal carotid artery; cJo, cartilage of Jacobson's organ; coc, cochlear part of otic capsule; cr, crista sellaris; f, occipito-capsular fissure; fel, foramen for endolymphatic duct; fX, fenestra X; g, unchondrified gap in otic capsule; h, hyoid body; jf, jugular foramen (for vagus); lp, lingual process; lta, lamina transversalis anterior (anterior rudiment); mf, metotic fissure; n, notochord; ns, nasal septum; oa, occipital arch; oc, otic capsule; pcr, protrusion of crista sellaris; pf, pituitary fenestra; pfc, prefacial commissure; pla, planum antorbitale; ptc, parietotectal cartilage; q, quadrate; r, recessus scalae tympani; t, trabecula; tc, trabecula communis; tp, trabecular plate; ts, tectum synoticum; 5, trigeminal (prootic) notch; 6, foramen of abducens nerve; 6g, groove for abducens nerve; 7, 8, 9, 10, 12, foramina for facial, auditory, glossopharyngeal, vagus, and hypoglossal nerves (four foramina in F).

has increased in size and curves inwards posteriorly. A fourth and final pair of hypoglossal foramina has appeared. Each otic capsule has enlarged and its cochlear portion encroaches slightly on the basal plate. The foramen perilymphaticum is formed. The VIIth nerve is now entirely extracapsular and leaves the chondrocranium through its foramen at the angle between the otic capsule and basal plate, as in reptiles generally. The foramen is separated from the prootic notch by the pre-facial commissure. The nerve describes a short intracapsular course only in the earlier stages; this transient condition has been observed only in *Psammophis* and is not characteristic of snakes in general (see Kamal, 1964c). The columella auris has now developed a footplate and a shaft, apparently from a single centre of chondrification.

At *Stage 5* (age 29 days, 88·3 mm total body length; Fig. 50D), the parietotectal cartilage has appeared as a continuous extension from the anterior cupola and the rudiment of the lamina transversalis anterior can be seen. The latter is represented mainly by the cartilage of Jacobson's organ. Absorption of cartilage appears to have been taking place in the basal plate; much of the notochord is now exposed dorsally and a substantial basicranial fenestra, absent in earlier stages, has appeared. The front of the plate forms the crista sellaris. Lateral to the fenestra at the edge of the basal plate on each side and beneath the front of the otic capsule, is a smaller vacuity called fenestra X by Bäckström (1931) and de Beer (1937); no structures pass through it and in later stages it may become continuous with the prootic notch. The chondrification of the anterior two-thirds of the otic capsule is well established, but the posterior part of the capsular roof is still absent; the metotic fissure remains open posteriorly. The tunnel through the otic capsule for the IXth nerve has now disappeared and the nerve has an extracapsular course.

The fenestra ovalis is formed by a process of degeneration of pre-existing cartilage, perhaps as a result of pressure from the columellar footplate. The lower end of the columellar shaft has now rotated backwards, probably in association with the backward rotation of the lower end of the quadrate. This rotation is characteristic of snakes and is associated with the posterior extension of Meckel's cartilage which displaces the jaw joint progressively further backwards (Kamal, 1966d; Fig. 54 here).

At *Stage 6* (age 35 days, 106·2 mm total body length; Fig. 50G), the parietotectal cartilage has become extensively chondrified and rudimentary inferior and superior alar processes are present. The parietotectal cartilage is continuous behind with the planum antorbitale which has no separate centre of chondrification, contrary to the condition in lizards. The rudiment of a simple infolded type of nasal concha is formed. At this stage the lamina transversalis anterior consists of two separate portions,

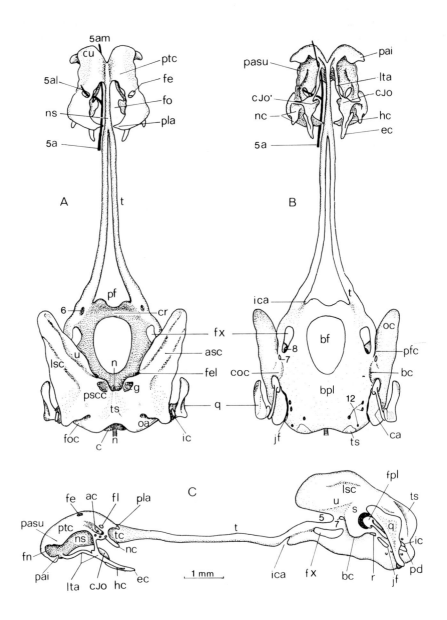

an anterior one continuous with the lateral wall of the nasal capsule, and a posterior one comprising the cartilage of Jacobson's organ and its concha. The metotic fissure is continuous above and behind with the fissure between the otic capsule and the occipital arch, which are fused together posteriorly. The otic capsules have enlarged and the perilymphatic foramen is completely delineated on each side. The occipital arches do not join in the dorsal midline. A rudimentary tectum synoticum entirely of otic origin is present. The hyoid horns (second ceratobranchials) have started to elongate posteriorly.

ii. Fully formed chondrocranium of Psammophis

General. Stage 7 of *Psammophis* (age 44 days, 157·8 mm total body length; Fig. 51) shows the fully formed condition of the chondrocranium. The conditions described by Kamal and Hammouda (1965b) do not appear to differ greatly from those in other colubrids, so that conditions may be illustrated by sections of *Natrix natrix* (Figs. 52; 53). Some differences in detail will be noted later in our accounts of the different genera.

Nasal capsule. The anterior parts of the nasal capsules (cupolae) project well in front of the nasal septum; laterally they bear superior and inferior alar processes which border the fenestra narina; the inferior process is much the longer, as in snakes generally. The fenestra narina is open posteriorly. Anteriorly the nasal cupolae are separated by a deep groove; its floor is formed by the flattened anterior part of the trabecula communis (trabecular plate) which continues posteriorly into the nasal septum (Figs. 51; 52A). The parietotectal cartilage is extensive and forms the roof, side and part of the medial wall of each capsule. As in earlier stages it is continuous

---

Fig. 51. *Psammophis sibilans.* Fully formed chondrocranium (Stage 7) in (A) dorsal, (B) ventral and (C) lateral view. After Kamal and Hammouda (1965b).

ac, Aditus conchae; asc, prominence for anterior semicircular canal; bc, basicapsular commissure; bf, basicranial fenestra; bpl, basal plate; c, occipital condyle; ca, columella auris; cJo, cartilage of Jacobson's organ; cJo′, concha of Jacobson's organ; coc, cochlear prominence; cr, crista sellaris; cu, nasal cupola; ec, ectochoanal cartilage; fe, foramen epiphaniale; fel, foramen for endolymphatic duct; fl, fenestra lateralis; fn, fenestra narina; foc, fissure between occipital arch and otic capsule; fo, fenestra olfactoria; fpl, footplate of columella; fX, fenestra X; g, unchondrified gap in tectum; hc, hypochoanal cartilage; ic, intercalary; ica, notch for internal carotid artery; jf, jugular foramen (for nerves 9 and 10); lsc, prominence for lateral semicircular canal; lta, lamina transversalis anterior; n, notochord; nc, nasal concha and its posterior projection; ns, nasal septum; oa, occipital arch; oc, otic capsule; pai, processus alaris inferior; pasu, processus alaris superior; pd, dorsal process of columella; pf, pituitary fenestra; pfc, prefacial commissure; pla, planum antorbitale; pscc, prominence for posterior semicircular canal; ptc, parietotectal cartilage; q, quadrate; r, opening of recessus scalae tympani; s, prominence for saccule; t, trabecula; tc, trabecula communis; ts, tectum synoticum; u, prominence for utricle; 5, trigeminal notch; 5a, ophthalmic nerve; 5al, 5am, lateral and medial ethmoidal branches of ophthalmic nerve; 6, abducens depression; 7, foramen for facial nerve; 8, anterior foramen for auditory nerve; 12, hypoglossal foramina.

with the dorsal edge of the nasal septum. There is no fenestra superior, but a very small lateral fenestra. Posteriorly the parietotectal cartilage is continuous with the planum antorbitale which curves inwards, approaching the nasal septum but remaining unfused with it; this is the usual condition among snakes.

As there are no sphenethmoid commissures, there is no fenestra olfactoria evehens and no orbitonasal fissure. The large vacuity in the roof of each capsule, bounded medially by the septum and posteriorly by the planum antorbitale, corresponds to the fenestra olfactoria advehens of lizards, but may be termed the fenestra olfactoria (Fig. 51A). The olfactory and vomeronasal nerves enter the nasal capsule through this fenestra, in company with the ethmoidal nerves. The lateral ethmoidal ramus passes outwards through the foramen epiphaniale to supply the lateral nasal gland, while the medial ramus continues anteriorly, dorsal to Jacobson's organ, to issue from the front of the capsule beneath the cupola. There is no foramen apicale.

The nasal sac is comparatively simple. The lateral recess is small, and no paranasal cartilage has been recognized. The concha is formed by the invagination of the parietotectal cartilage, which encloses a small cavum conchale containing a few follicles of the lateral nasal gland (Fig. 52B). The gland lies mainly outside the cavum.

The floor of the nasal capsule is reduced, as in snakes generally. It comprises only the floor of the anterior cupola and the lamina transversalis anterior and associated structures. Ventrally, the lamina forms the cartilage of Jacobson's organ; it is continuous laterally with the side-wall of the capsule. However, the floor of the capsule in this region is deficient medially and there is no zona annularis. The cartilage of Jacobson's organ bears a prominent concha on its dorsal surface which projects into the mushroom body of the organ, as in all snakes and most lizards. Projecting posteriorly from the lamina is a long ectochoanal cartilage; another longitudinal bar called the hypochoanal cartilage lies alongside the ectochoanal and is attached to the latter by its posterior end. These cartilages arise rather late in development. The hypochoanal cartilage is characteristic of snakes, and de Beer (1937) suggests that it is homologous with the processus maxillaris posterior of lizards and therefore probably a derivative of the palatoquadrate (see also McDowell, 1972). There is no paraseptal cartilage.

The marked angulation between the nasal capsule and the more posterior trabeculae, which is characteristic of early stages, has now disappeared so that the lower edge of the septum and the paired trabeculae are almost in a straight line (Fig. 51C). This change seems to be due to upward rotation of the capsule, perhaps associated with the elongation of the maxilla, palatine, ectopterygoid and pterygoid bones (see Pringle, 1954).

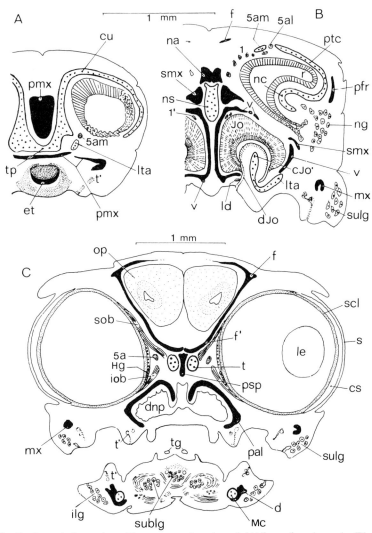

FIG. 52. *Natrix natrix*, late embryo. Transverse sections through (A) front of nasal capsule, (B) organ of Jacobson and (C) orbits (anterior to lens on left; retina, etc., not shown).

cJo′, Concha of Jacobson's organ; cs, conjunctival space; cu, nasal cupola; d, dentary; dJo, duct of Jacobson's organ; dnp, ductus nasopharyngeus, et, egg-tooth, f, frontal, f′, frontal downgrowth; Hg, Harderian gland; ilg, inferior labial gland; iob, inferior oblique muscle; Jo, Jacobson's organ; ld, anterior extremity of lachrymal duct opening into duct of Jacobson's organ; le, lens; lta, lamina transversalis anterior; Mc, Meckel's cartilage; mx, maxilla; na, nasal; nc, cartilaginous nasal concha; ng, nasal gland; ns, nasal septum; op, olfactory peduncle; pal, palatine; pfr, prefrontal; pmx, premaxilla; psp, parasphenoid; ptc, parietotectal cartilage; r, lateral recess; s, spectacle; scl, sclera; sob, superior oblique muscle; smx, septomaxilla; sublg, sublingual glands; sulg, superior labial gland; t, trabecula; t′, tooth; tg, tip of tongue; tp, trabecular plate; v, vomer; 1, olfactory nerve; 1′, vomeronasal nerve; 5a, ophthalmic nerve; 5al, 5am, lateral and medial ethmoidal branches of ophthalmic nerve.

Orbitotemporal region. At the back of the nasal capsule, the nasal septum diminishes in height and becomes continuous with the paired, rodlike trabeculae which run back side by side and quite close together between the orbits (Fig. 51A, B, 52C); as in the earlier stages, the chondrocranium is platytrabic, forming a marked contrast with the tropitrabic condition of lizards. There is no cartilaginous interorbital septum, and no parts of the orbital cartilage system can be recognized. Although, certain other species of snake may have vestigial orbital cartilages the conditions described above are characteristic of snakes in general (see Bellairs, 1972; III-E-8 here). The trabeculae diverge towards the back of the orbits, and enclose the large pituitary fenestra. *Psammophis* lacks carotid foramina in the chondrocranium; the arteries enter the cranium through a notch between the back of the trabecula and the crista sellaris on each side of the pituitary fenestra. Later the arteries become enclosed by bone. The relations of the trigeminal and eye muscle nerves to the skull and the problem of the cavum epioptericum in snakes are discussed on pages 185–190.

Basal plate and occipital region. Anteriorly the basal plate is continuous with the trabeculae. The crista sellaris, which bears two small anterior protrusions, forms the front of the basal plate and separates the pituitary fenestra from the basicranial fenestra. On either side of the latter lies fenestra X, which is now very large. The notochord lies mainly on the dorsal surface of the plate, with its ventral aspect embedded in the cartilage. The tunnel for the VIth nerve has now been converted into a shallow depression in the basal plate into which the nerve dips in its anterior course (Fig. 51A). The tectum synoticum is complete, connecting the otic capsule with its opposite fellow, and roofing over the foramen magnum. Though very broad it lacks the anterior process which is seen in many lizards. Apparently, the occipital arch does not participate in the main part of the tectal roof of *Psammophis*, though different conditions may occur in other snakes (see El-Toubi and Kamal, 1964/65; Kamal and Hammouda, 1965b). The kidney-shaped occipital condyle is formed from the hind part of the basal plate and represents part of the centrum of the proatlas vertebra; thus, as in other lepidosaurs, the cranio-vertebral joint is intravertebral. The condyle and the tip of the odontoid process are still connected at this stage, and the notochord is embedded in the condyle.

Otic capsule. In snakes the surface of the otic capsule shows prominences for structures of the inner ear, similar to those in lizards, except that there is no crista parotica. This reflects the attachment of the quadrate to the supratemporal, rather than directly to the otic capsule. Each capsule is connected to the basal plate by a prefacial commissure anterior to the foramen for the VIIth nerve and, more posteriorly, by a long basicapsular commissure. Behind this the metotic fissure is divided by a strut of cartilage into an anterior recessus scalae tympani and a posterior jugular foramen. The latter transmits the Xth nerve and, apparently, also an accessory (XI) nerve and the internal jugular vein, the latter persisting to this late embryonic stage in *Psammophis*, though not in many other reptiles (Kamal and Hammouda, 1965b, p. 270). The identification of an accessory nerve by Kamal and Hammouda and by Hegazy (1976) is of interest, as Auen and Langebartel (1977) were unable to find such a nerve in *Thamnophis* and *Elaphe*. The jugular foramen continues posteriorly as the occipito-capsular fissure, which is closed behind by the fusion of the occipital arch with the tectum synoticum (Fig. 51A).

The course of the IXth nerve has altered significantly from Stage 3 of *Psammophis* previously described. The glossopharyngeal tunnel through the wall of the otic capsule has disappeared. The nerve now passes ventral to the capsule and penetrates the cartilaginous strut which divides the metotic fissure. It then enters the recessus scalae tympani and leaves the skull through its lateral opening (see Kamal, 1969e; Fig. 53D here). It joins the vagus almost immediately after leaving the skull and participates in a combined ganglion. Conditions in a late embryo of *Natrix* (Fig. 53G, H) appear to be fairly similar. The inner ear of *Psammophis* is described by Kamal and Hammouda (1969).

The lateral opening of the recessus scalae tympani is closed by a membrane called the secondary tympanic membrane by Kamal and Hammouda (1965b). Brock's (1929) account suggests that it is homologous with the similarly named membrane of lizards, although Wever (1978) states that snakes lack a fenestra rotunda.

Mandibular arch. The pterygoquadrate of snakes lacks the normal tetrapod complement of four processes: the otic process (the part of the quadrate which articulates with the crista parotica in lizards), the basal process (forms basipterygoid meniscus in lizards), the pterygoid process (present in earlier lizard embryos, and additionally, perhaps forms the posterior maxillary process which is generally absent in snakes), and apparently the ascending process or epipterygoid (see p. 188). Thus, the ophidian pterygoquadrate is represented mainly or entirely by the body of the quadrate cartilage, which throughout development remains separate from the otic capsule, though in later stages it becomes connected with it by virtue of its articulation with the (dermal) supratemporal bone.

As previously mentioned, the quadrate cartilage and Meckel's cartilage, the two skeletal components of the mandibular arch, intitially lie almost

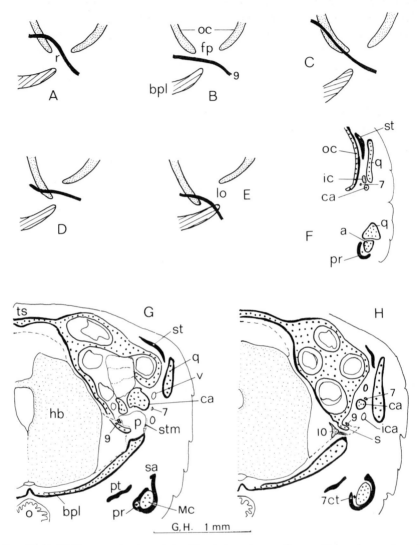

FIG. 53. (A–E) Diagrams showing relationship of glossopharyngeal nerve (9) to otic capsule and recessus scalae tympani in Squamata, as seen in transverse section through right side of head. (A) Intracapsular course characteristic of Scincidae and late stages of *Malpolon*. The nerve penetrates the medial wall of the capsule, passes ventrally through the perilymphatic foramen and leaves the skull through the lateral opening of the recessus. (B) Extracapsular course seen in most lizards. The nerve passes through both the medial and lateral openings of the recessus. (C) Transient condition in which the nerve passes through a tunnel in the medial wall of the capsule, as in earlier stages of the snakes *Psammophis* and *Cerastes*. (D) Condition seen in late stages of *Psammophis*. Conditions in *Natrix* and probably many other snakes are not very different. The nerve passes through a strut of cartilage derived from the ventral wall of the capsule and then traverses the recessus. (E) Resembles

on a straight line (Fig. 54). Subsequently, Meckel's cartilage lengthens, shifting the jaw joint posteriorly. The quadrate then comes to lie nearly at right angles with Meckel's cartilage, and this is their position in the fully-formed stage. Furthermore, the quadrate as a whole moves backwards in relation to the rest of the skull. The process also involves a backward rotation of the lower end of the columella auris (Kamal, 1964b, 1966d, 1972; Kamal and Hammouda, 1965b, d).

Meckel's cartilage now has a well developed retroarticular process. As in snakes generally, its anterior tip does not form a symphysis with its fellow in the midline.

Columella of Psammophis *and other snakes.* Snakes lack a tympanic membrane, and the tympanic cavity is generally stated to be absent also. However, Wever (1978) reports a small, flattened tympanic cavity on the medial aspect of the ophidian columellar shaft. Embryological studies seem necessary to confirm the identity of this cavity.

The columella (described by Kamal and Hammouda, 1965d) is a long slender rod with a large footplate which is deeply sunk into the fenestra ovalis and covered by a membranous sheath. Its distal end is slightly bent on the rest, and its tip is applied to the posteromedial aspect of the quadrate (Figs. 51B, C; 53F). Almost all of the columella ossifies, but the distal end remains cartilaginous and articulates with a cartilaginous facet on the quadrate (Wever, 1978). As in lizards, it is probable that the columella is entirely of hyoid arch origin. Although the footplate becomes transiently attached to the rim of the fenestra ovalis, there is no clear evidence that the otic capsule makes any contribution to it. The footplate has a mesenchymatous connection with the ceratohya for a short period in embryonic life.

In later embryonic stages of *Psammophis* a mass of procartilaginous cells becomes detached from the distal end of the columella and fuses with the back of the quadrate, eventually becoming coossified with it to form a small bony nodule. Similar events occur in other snakes.

Kamal and Hammouda (1965d) follow de Beer (1937) in believing that

---

(D) but the nerve leaves the skull through a foramen in the edge of the basal plate instead of through the lateral opening of the recessus; seen in late stages of *Cerastes*. After Kamal (1969e). (F, G, H) *Natrix natrix*, late embryo. (F) Transverse section through posterior end of columella and intercalary. (G, H) Successive sections anterior to and at a higher magnification than (F) through columella and glossopharyngeal nerve. In (G) the origin of the nerve from the brain is shown in broken lines.

a, Articular; bpl, basal plate; ca, columella auris; fp, perilymphatic foramen; hb, hind-brain; ic, intercalary; ica, internal carotid artery; lo, lateral opening of recessus scalae tympani; Mc, Meckel's cartilage; o, oesophagus; oc, otic capsule; p, perilymphatic sac in recessus scalae tympani; pr, prearticular; pt, pterygoid; q, quadrate; r, recessus scalae tympani; s, strut of cartilage penetrated by glossopharyngeal nerve; sa, surangular (fused with pr in G and H); st, supratemporal; stm, secondary tympanic membrane; ts, tectum synoticum; v, vena capitis lateralis; 7, facial nerve; 7ct, chorda tympani; 9, glossopharyngeal nerve; 10, vagus nerve.

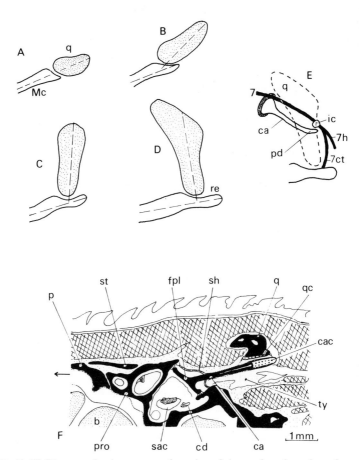

Fig. 54. (A–D) Diagrams showing process of rotation of the quadrate in snake embryos at four successive stages. (E) Diagram showing relation of facial nerve to columella in a snake. The distal part of the columellar shaft and parts of the intercalary and facial nerve lie deep to the quadrate, which is shown in broken lines. (F) *Lampropeltis getulus*, adult. Horizontal longitudinal section showing columella and tympanic cavity. The intercalary may have become incorporated into the quadrate and is not shown. The muscles are cross-hatched. The arrow points anteriorly. After Wever (1978).

b, Brain; ca, columella auris; cac, cartilaginous tip of columella; cd, cochlear duct; fpl, footplate; ic, intercalary; Mc, Meckel's cartilage; p, parietal; pd, dorsal process; pro, prootic; q, quadrate; qc, cartilaginous articular facet of quadrate; re, retroarticular process; sac, saccule; sh, membranous sheath investing footplate; st, supratemporal; ty, tympanic cavity; 7, facial nerve; 7ct, chorda tympani; 7h, hyomandibular branch of facial nerve.

the columella of snakes corresponds with those parts of the saurian columellar apparatus which are derived from the medial rudiment or "otostapes", i.e. the columella itself and the dorsal and internal processes. The structures derived from the lateral rudiment ("hyostapes"), which in lizards forms the greater part of the extracolumella including its insertion plate, are thought to be absent in snakes. The nodule which fuses with the quadrate in snakes is regarded as the intercalary—though in lizards the correspondingly named structure fuses with the crista parotica of the otic capsule (which crista is absent in snakes). If the intercalary of snakes is indeed homologous with that of lizards it must represent a detached part of the dorsal process (processus paroticus) of the medial rudiment; the distal, bent portion of the ophidian columella would correspond with the proximal part of the dorsal process, which in lizards generally fails to chondrify. The relationships of the chorda tympani are perfectly consistent with this view. The nerve loops round behind the distal end of the columella and then runs forward ventral to it, whereas it passes dorsal to the extracolumella of lizards. If the latter (apart from the dorsal process) were to disappear, the nerve could "drop down" and occupy the position it does in snakes (Fig. 54E). This view has been accepted by most recent students of the reptilian chondrocranium.

However, McDowell (1967) has an interesting and rather different interpretation. A strong advocate of the platynotid origin of snakes, he emphasizes certain apparent similarities between the middle ear in *Lanthanotus* and mosasaurs and that in snakes. For example, the columella of mosasaurs and snakes is quite slender and, incidentally, very different from the massive structure found in burrowing lizards, such as *Anniella*, and amphisbaenians. In the mosasaur *Plioplatecarpus* the columella is connected to an ossicle on the inner face of the quadrate which occupies the same position as the supposed intercalary of snakes, but also has the same position as the internal process of the extracolumella in lizards. Thus, McDowell believes that the intercalary of snakes corresponds to the internal process of lizards (plus a small adjacent portion of the base of the extra-columella), rather than to the dorsal process. The relationships of the chorda tympani would be suitable in either case. On this assumption the "intercalary" of snakes is not homologous with that of lizards.

Hyobranchial apparatus. The hyobranchial apparatus of *Psammophis* consists of two very long parallel cornua which are joined anteriorly and extend backward to the level of the 19th vertebra (Fig. 50I). A lingual process projects forwards from the junction (the hyoid body) which may be regarded as a basihyal element. As in the great majority of snakes, all these structures remain cartilaginous throughout life.

Many workers (e.g., de Beer, 1937) regard the cornua as ceratohyals and this view is followed by Kamal and Hammouda (1965a) who found that the cornua were in continuity with the basihyal in the earliest developmental stage examined. However, Langebartel (1968) has suggested that one or more of the more caudal visceral arches may have contributed to the blastema of the hyobranchial primordium. From comparison with the adult morphology of lizards, he regards the caenophidian horns as being the second ceratobranchials; these resemble the parallel, second ceratobranchial horns of a generalized saurian hyobranchial apparatus, for example that of *Acanthodactylus* (Fig. 15B), and are so labelled here. An alternative view, suggested by McDowell (1972), is that the cornua of all snakes correspond with parts of the first branchial arch.

c. Osteocranium of Psammophis

i. General

The osteocranium of the late embryonic and adult skull has been described by Kamal and Hammouda (1965c, 1968; Figs. 55; 56 here). All bones are paired unless stated to the contrary. The pattern of ossification in most other snakes is probably very similar.

ii. Cartilage bones

There is no orbitosphenoid bone. The problem of the epipterygoid and laterosphenoid bones is discussed on page 185.

The unpaired *basisphenoid* ossifies from a single centre in the front of the basal plate, in the crista sellaris and around the back ends of the trabeculae. It fuses with the underlying parasphenoid to form the *parabasisphenoid* (see later). In *Psammophis*, as in the majority of Caenophidia, it does not bear basipterygoid processes (at least distinct ones) comparable with those of lizards and some Henophidia.

The *prootic* arises perichondrally in the anterior part of the otic capsule and extends into the prefacial commissure. This bone also extends forwards intramembranously on the side of the skull, where it fuses ventrally with the small laterosphenoid which separates the foramina for the maxillary and mandibular branches of the trigeminal nerve.

The *opisthotic* arises perichondrally on the inner and outer surfaces of the posterolateral region of the otic capsule. Together with the prootic it participates in forming the boundary of the fenestra ovalis. The sutures between it and the prootic and exoccipital appear to persist in adult *Psammophis*.

The unpaired *basioccipital* ossifies on the dorsal and ventral surfaces of the basal plate. Posteriorly, it forms the median part of the occipital condyle.

The *exoccipital* ossifies before the other cartilage bones in perichondral lamellae on the inner and outer surfaces of the occipital arch and encloses the four hypoglossal foramina. An anterior protrusion from it forms the floor of the jugular foramen. As in snakes generally, and in contrast to the condition in lizards, the approximation of the two exoccipitals in the dorsal midline forms a roof over the foramen magnum and excludes the supraoccipital from the margins of this foramen. The exoccipitals form the lateral portions of the tripartite occipital condyle. The foramina in the caenophidian brain-case have not been adequately described.

The unpaired *supraoccipital* arises very late from the inner and outer perichondrium of the tectum synoticum and extends laterally on to the roof of the otic capsule. There is no evidence that the lateral parts of this bone are derived from separate, epiotic centres, which cannot be certainly identified.

The *quadrate* ossifies in the perichondrium of the quadrate cartilage and intercalary nodule. It is movably attached to the supratemporal and highly streptostylic.

The *columella auris* or stapes eventually becomes completely ossified and articulates with the intercalary nodule on the quadrate.

The *articular* ossifies in the posterior end of Meckel's cartilage, including the retroarticular process; it fuses with the prearticular and surangular to form a composite bone. As in other reptiles, the anterior part of Meckel's cartilage remains unossified and becomes invested by the dermal bones of the lower jaw, except in front where it is partly exposed in a groove on the inner aspect of the dentary.

iii. Dermal bones

Dermal bones first appear in embryos of *Psammophis* at 35 days of incubation, shortly before there are any signs of ossification in the chondrocranium (Kamal and Hammouda, 1965c). This finding confirms the observations of Franklin (1945), who showed by alizarine staining that the palatine and pterygoid were the first bones to ossify in *Nerodia* and other colubrid snakes.

The *premaxilla* arises beneath the front of the nasal cupola on each side and fuses with its opposite fellow during embryonic life to form a single bone. This has an ascending process which lies in the groove between the two cupolae, paired lateral wings and short palatine processes. The bone is not in contact with the maxilla in the more advanced types of snakes. The tiny premaxilla is toothless in adult Caenophidia, but in the late embryo it bears the median egg-tooth and also some vestigial toothlets, at least in certain species (Smith *et al.*, 1953).

The *nasal* develops over the medial part of the nasal capsule on each side and has a well developed descending process which dips into the groove between the two capsules but does not fuse with its opposite fellow. In the adult skull it remains out of contact with the maxilla, frontal, and prefrontal, an arrangement which allows mobility of the anterior part of the snout. This bone articulates only with the premaxilla and septomaxilla.

The *septomaxilla* first develops as a small plate posterodorsal to the premaxilla and extends back to form the roof, lateral wall and lateral part of the floor of the bony capsule of Jacobson's organ; it extends from the side wall of the nasal capsule to the nasal septum, above the organ of Jacobson and beneath the nasal sac. The gap on the palate between the septomaxilla and vomer (fenestra vomeronasalis) transmits the duct of Jacobson's organ and the anterior part of the lachrymal duct which enters the medial aspect of the duct of Jacobson's organ (Bellairs and Boyd, 1950). The concha of Jacobson's organ, a dorsal projection from the adjacent part of the lamina transversalis anterior (the cartilage of Jacobson's organ; see p. 18) also passes through this gap to support the mushroom body (Fig. 52B). The septomaxilla has a lateral process which extends outwards and projects forwards to terminate beneath the processus alaris superior.

The *vomer* forms the medial part of the front of the bony palate. Anteriorly it forms the floor and medial wall of the bony capsule surrounding Jacobson's organ; its posterior part roofs over the organ as well, ventral to the septomaxilla, and forms a kind of pocket in which the back of the organ is lodged (Figs. 52B; 59). Groombridge (1979a) has shown that in Caenophidia generally, the dorsal part of the vomer is pierced by multiple foramina for the vomeronasal nerves, whereas in Henophidia (other than Acrochordidae), there are, as a rule, only one or two large foramina.

The *maxilla* ossifies rather early and has a prominent palatal process which, in the adult skull, makes contact with the palatine. The maxilla also makes contact with the ectopterygoid behind and, by a movable articulation, with the prefrontal above. These contacts are incompletely established in the late embryonic stage studied by Kamal and Hammouda (1965C; Fig. 55 here). In *Psammophis* the posterior maxillary teeth are enlarged and grooved, representing the opisthoglyphous condition.

The *palatine* has a well developed medial process anteriorly; this arches over the ductus nasopharyngeus in the region of the choana (Fig. 52C). The palatine bears teeth in nearly all snakes, apart from Scolecophidia.

The *ectopterygoid* (or transpalatine) connects the posterior end of the maxilla with the pterygoid. It is toothless, at least in the adult. However, in late embryos of *Natrix* tooth germs (presumably transient) are related to its anterior extremity (Fig. 68A).

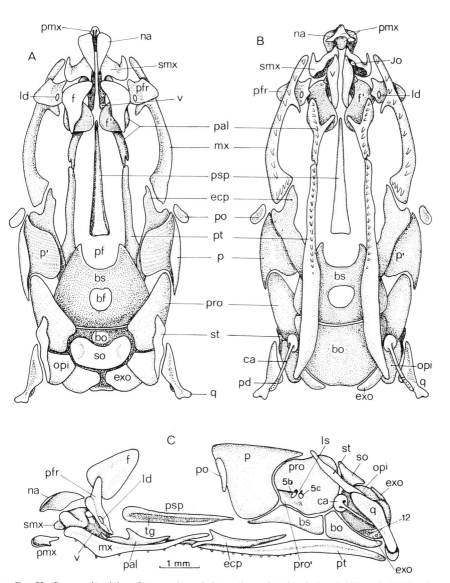

FIG. 55. *Psammophis sibilans*. Osteocranium of a late embryo of total body-length 190 mm in (A) dorsal, (B) ventral and (C) lateral view. After Kamal and Hammouda (1965c).

bf, Basicranial fenestra; bo, basioccipital; bs, basisphenoid; ca, columella auris; ecp, ectopterygoid; exo, exoccipital; f, frontal; f′, frontal downgrowth; Jo, foramen for duct of Jacobson's organ; ld, foramen for lachrymal duct; ls, region of laterosphenoid; mx, maxilla; na, nasal; opi, opisthotic; p, parietal; p′, parietal downgrowth; pal, palatine; pd, dorsal process of columella; pf, pituitary fenestra; pfr, prefrontal; pmx, premaxilla; po, pôstorbital; pro, prootic; pro′, prootic extension; psp, parasphenoid; pt, pterygoid; q, quadrate; smx, septomaxilla; so, supraoccipital; st, supratemporal; tg, trabecular groove; v, vomer; 5b, 5c, foramina for maxillary and mandibular branches of trigeminal nerve; 12, foramina for hypoglossal nerve.

The *pterygoid* develops as a slender bar in front of the quadrate and elongates anteriorly until it reaches the posterior tip of the palatine. In the adult skull its hind end appears to be attached by ligaments to the inner aspect of the ventral extremity of the quadrate. In view of the supposed independence of pterygoid and quadrate movements in snakes (see Boltt and Ewer, 1964) the nature of this attachment deserves further study. Only the anterior part of the very long pterygoid bone bears teeth.

The median *parasphenoid* arises rather late as a long, rostral splint beneath and between the trabeculae, so that in the adult skull the persistent trabecular cartilages run in grooves along each side of the bone, which is then quite massive (Figs. 52C; 55C). A ridge developed from the dorsal edge of the parasphenoid rises up between the trabeculae to make contact anteriorly with the frontal downgrowths and forms a kind of bony interorbital septum (Fig. 52C). The bony septum is, of course, quite different from the cartilaginous interorbital septum of lizards and other reptiles which is absent in snakes.

The parasphenoid fuses posteriorly with the basisphenoid to form the parabasisphenoid, but the territorial limits of the two bones are difficult to determine. Traced posteriorly, the parasphenoid rostrum of *Natrix*, first lying entirely between the trabeculae, seems to extend laterally both above and below each trabecula, and to fuse with the thin perichondral shell of basisphenoid which surrounds the latter. Thus the posterior part of the trabecula becomes ossified as a bony cylinder which ends abruptly at the back of the trabecular groove in the dry skull. The thin lamella of bone which forms the floor of the pituitary fossa between the trabeculae and fills in the fenestra could be derived from the parasphenoid, basisphenoid, or a combination of both. The basicranial fenestra, further back, is probably filled in by the basisphenoid alone.

De Beer (1937) states that in *Natrix* the lateral wings of the parasphenoid, which ossify in such close relationship to the basisphenoid in lizards, are absent, and that the internal carotid artery on each side passes through the basisphenoid only, rather than between the basisphenoid and parasphenoid. This view is supported by the figure of Kamal and Hammouda (1965c) who show only the rostral portion of the parasphenoid in a late embryo of *Psammophis* (Fig. 55A). However, Rieppel (1979a) states that the parasphenoid does have lateral wings and participates in the formation of the Vidian canal in *Natrix*. The mode of ossification of the skull base in snakes remains somewhat obscure, and, as Pringle (1954) suggests, the pattern may vary in different species. Some observations on the adult anatomy of the Vidian canal in caenophidians are given by Underwood (1967).

In *Natrix* the VIth nerve passes through a canal in the basisphenoid which is quite distinct from the Vidian canal (Fig. 68).

Each *frontal* arises over the planum antorbitale and extends medially, posteriorly and ventrally. In the late embryo of *Psammophis* the two frontals are not yet approximated in the midline dorsally, but their ventral downgrowths are well developed. These downgrowths will, in the adult, make contact with each other in the ventral midline above the trabeculae and, further back, articulate with the dorsal edge of the parasphenoid. They completely enclose the olfactory peduncles of the forebrain, but remain unfused in the dorsal midline, as in snakes generally (Fig. 52C).

The *parietals* (paired in the embryo) are very large and form the roof and side-walls of the orbitotemporal region. In the great majority of snakes they fuse dorsally during postnatal life to form a single bone. There is no parietal foramen (or parietal eye) in Serpentes.

Like the frontals, the parietals have well developed descending processes which develop very early; they also ossify in the membranous side-wall of the cranial cavity, which lacks the orbitotemporal scaffolding found in lizards. However, the parietal downgrowths do not become approximated in the midline, but come into contact with the sides of the parasphenoid rostrum in front and the parabasisphenoid and prootic behind, thus enclosing the cerebral hemispheres. In growing ventrally to meet the latter, each parietal downgrowth encloses an extracranial and extradural space through which pass the IIIrd, IVth, VIth and ophthalmic nerves, closely approximated to form a common orbital trunk (Auen and Langebartel, 1977); this space appears to correspond with the cavum epiptericum of lizards (Fig. 68A). The nerves pass forwards to enter the orbit in company with the optic nerve through a foramen orbitale magnum which is usually situated between the frontal and parietal bones in the orbit, and above the parasphenoid rostrum (Fig. 67). Certain variations in the position of this foramen in snakes are described by Underwood (1967). The boxlike orbitotemporal region of the bony skull in snakes is paralleled by that in amphisbaenians (which, however, show significant differences in the nerve relationships) and to a lesser extent by that in certain burrowing lizards.

The *prefrontal* arises over the posterolateral surface of the nasal capsule, forming the anterior margin of the orbit; it covers the lateral nasal gland, nasal concha and planum antorbitale. It is perforated by the lachrymal duct. Snakes lack a *lachrymal* bone.

A single small bone behind the orbit in snakes has been variously regarded as a *postfrontal* or a *postorbital* by different authors. Kamal and Hammouda (1965c, 1968) incline to the latter alternative (as labelled in Fig. 55C) and consider that the postfrontal is absent in *Psammophis*. There are no temporal arches.

The narrow, splint-like bone which ossifies over the postero-lateral aspect of each otic capsule is here regarded as the *supratemporal*. Other workers have homologized it with the squamosal or with the tabular bone of other reptiles (see Kamal and Hammouda, 1965c, 1968). In the adult skull of *Psammophis* it projects well behind the exoccipital and articulates laterally with the dorsal end of the quadrate.

The *jugal* and *quadratojugal* bones appear to be completely absent in snakes.

The *dentary* begins to ossify in 35 day embryos of *Psammophis* on the lateral and ventral surfaces of the anterior part of Meckel's cartilage, which it fails to enclose medially (Fig. 56).

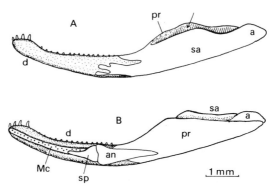

FIG. 56. *Psammophis sibilans.* Lower jaw of late embryo seen in (A) lateral and (B) medial view. The arrow in (A) points to a gap above the surangular which leads to the mandibular canal for the inferior dental branch of the mandibular nerve. After Kamal and Hammouda (1965c).

a, Articular (partly fused with surangular); an, angular; d, dentary (stippled); Mc, Meckel's cartilage; pr, prearticular; sa, surangular; sp, splenial.

The *splenial* arises along the medial side of Meckel's cartilage opposite the posterior part of the dentary. There is a kind of intramandibular joint (though not synovial in character) between the dentary and splenial in front and the other jaw bones behind; this allows considerable flexion and rotation between the front and back halves of the mandible (see Albright and Nelson, 1959). This joint is characteristic of snakes and has been compared with the similar joint in platynotid lizards (McDowell and Bogert, 1954).

The posterior part of each ramus of the adult lower jaw is a massive composite bone formed by the fusion during embryonic life of the *surangular, prearticular* and the *articular*, the last ossifying in the posterior part of Meckel's cartilage. The mandibular nerve (Vc) enters its canal in the groove between the upper edges of the prearticular and surangular bones (Fig. 56A). Caenophidian snakes lack a *coronoid*.

The sclera of the ophidian eye has neither cartilage nor *ossicles*. Snakes have no *osteoderms*.

d. Chondrocranium of other Colubridae

The chondrocrania of other Colubridae which have been studied show considerable minor variation, as might be expected in this large and diverse assemblage. It is as yet impossible to recognize characters particular to the various new subfamilial groups listed by Parker (1977), nor is it really possible to find basic characters which separate the Colubridae from other families of advanced snakes. Possibly some of the apparent differences reported between species are due merely to the fact that the embryos studied by various investigators happened to be at different growth stages. The following points relating to the fully formed chondocranium of Colubridae may be noted.

1. As in snakes generally the floor of the nasal capsule is reduced; there are no paraseptal cartilages, but the cartilage of Jacobson's organ and the ectochoanal and hypochoanal cartilages are always present. In *Crotaphopeltis* (Brock, 1929) the lamina transversalis anterior is represented only by its posterior part, the cartilage of Jacobson's organ (Fig. 57C); in *Lamprophis* (Pringle, 1954) only a small remnant of its anterior part remains, attached to the ventral wall of the cupola and unconnected with the cartilage of Jacobson's organ behind. Conditions in *Dasypeltis* (Pringle, 1954) and *Malpolon* (El-Toubi, Kamal and Zaher, 1973a, b; Fig. 57A here) appear to be similar to *Lamprophis*. However, in *Natrix* (Bäckström, 1931; de Beer, 1937), *Psammophis* (Kamal and Hammouda, 1965b) and *Thelotornis* (Visser, 1961) the anterior part of the lamina is complete, connecting the cupola with the cartilage of Jacobson's organ.

In *Dasypeltis*, *Malpolon*, and *Thelotornis*, and probably in *Crotaphopeltis*, the cartilage of Jacobson's organ is not connected laterally with the parietotectal cartilage. In *Psammophis* and *Natrix* these structures are connected, but on the ventral aspect of the capsule the connection between the cartilage of Jacobson's organ and the nasal septum is in the longitudinal rather than the transverse plane (Fig. 51B). Thus, the nasal sac is not really encircled by cartilage in anything approaching the transverse plane, and the use of the term zona annularis (de Beer, 1937, p. 248) seems inappropriate.

2. The invagination of the parietotectal cartilage, which forms the nasal concha, is less extensive than in many lizards; in some colubrids at least the lateral (extraconchal) recess of the nasal sac does not extend so far anteriorly and so does not appear as a separate cavity in transverse sections

(Figs. 3D; 15D: 16B; 52B). Thus it is stated that the paranasal cartilage is usually absent in snakes (Kamal, 1968). However, this region of the nasal capsule in Squamata, and the whole concept of the paranasal cartilage as a distinct entity, is in need of re-assessment.

In *Dasypeltis* Pringle (1954) describes a curious rod of cartilage arising from the posterior end of the nasal concha which loops forward around the posterior margin of the lachrymal duct (Fig. 57B). This structure, which Pringle calls the paranasal process, is also present in *Malpolon* (Fig. 57A).

3. A small lateral fenestra in the parietotectal cartilage is found in *Natrix* and *Psammophis*, but not in the other colubrids studied. There is no superior fenestra.

4. In *Crotaphopeltis*, *Lamprophis* and *Dasypeltis* the planum antorbitale is attached medially to the nasal septum, but it is free from the septum in other colubrids, as in most reptiles.

5. Parker (1879) described a pair of small cartilaginous "orbitosphenoid" nodules above the trabeculae in the mid-orbital region of an embryo of *Natrix natrix*. Similar structures have been described in an embryo of the opisthoglyph colubrid *Thelotornis* by Visser (1961), and in certain other non-colubrid snakes. In *Thelotornis* these cartilages lie posterior to the optic nerves and internal to the parietal downgrowths (Fig. 58C). They may be regarded as vestiges of the pila metoptica or other adjacent parts of the orbital cartilage system, and may be termed orbital cartilages. It is uncertain whether these structures are transient and regress in late embryonic or postnatal life, whether they can be seen constantly in certain species, or whether they occur as individual variations and when present persist throughout life, as Pringle (1954) suggested.

6. In embryos of *Natrix*, *Lamprophis* and *Thelotornis* the internal carotid artery becomes enclosed in a canal in the basal plate on each side of the pituitary fenestra; in other colubrids, however, the artery enters the cranial cavity through the posterior corner of the fenestra, as in most lizards. In all cases, however, the artery eventually becomes enclosed by the ossifying basisphenoid (with or without a parasphenoid contribution) and runs through part of the Vidian canal, turning upwards to enter the pituitary fossa. The palatine nerves continues forward through the canal to emerge from its anterior foramen.

There appears to be no palatine continuation of the internal carotid artery in snakes, other than typhlopids (Rieppel, 1979a).

7. Distinct basipterygoid processes are absent in the forms described.

8. In *Crotaphopeltis*, *Natrix* and *Thelotornis* the abducent nerve passes through a canal in the basal plate which persists in the fully formed chondrocranium and bony skull; the cartilage in front of the canal may incorporate a vestige of the pila antotica. In *Psammophis* the canal present

in the earlier embryonic stages (Fig. 50D) is later transformed into a mere depression in the cartilage (Fig. 51A). In *Dasypeltis*, *Lamprophis* and *Malpolon* no canal forms, and there is only an abducens depression.

9. The course of the glossopharyngeal nerve shows minor variations in different species and may also vary at different developmental stages of the same species (Kamal, 1969e). In *Psammophis*, as previously described, the nerve initially tunnels very obliquely through the medial wall of the otic capsule, but later shifts its course ventral to the capsule before it enters the recessus scalae tympani (Fig. 53C, D). Conditions in the late embryo of *Natrix* studied (Fig. 53G, H) and probably in other snakes such as *Dasypeltis* (Pringle, 1954) appear to be fairly similar to those in the late stages of *Psammophis*. In *Malpolon* the course of the nerve at first resembles that in early stages of *Psammophis*, but later becomes distinctly intra-capsular, as in scincid lizards (El-Toubi, Kamal and Zaher, 1973a, b). It seems likely that these differences are not as clear-cut as Kamal's (1969e) account suggests, as they could be caused by very small variations in the growth pattern. However, in *Leptodeira* the IXth nerve passes out directly through the basal plate without entering the recessus at all (Brock, 1929).

10. Fenestra X is present in all colubrids with the possible exception of *Dasypeltis*.

11. The number of hypoglossal foramina varies between two and four in different species.

12. The tectum appears to be formed mainly from the otic capsules in *Malpolon*, *Natrix*, *Psammophis* and *Thelotornis*, whereas in *Lamprophis*, *Crotaphopeltis* and *Dasypeltis* the occipital arches make the principal contribution. These apparent variations in the development of the tectum in snakes are at least partly the result of different interpretations by different workers.

13. The hyobranchial apparatus of Colubridae and of other Caenophidia is of Langebartel's (1968) "parallel" type, with long second ceratobranchials (ceratohyals, etc. of other authors) lying parallel with each other and joined in front (Fig. 50I). In some forms the lingual process is reduced, or as in *Natrix natrix* and *Nerodia sipedon*, absent (Fig. 57D).

e. Osteocranium and Kinesis of Colubridae

Few, if any significant differences between the development of the osteocranium of *Psammophis* and that of other colubrids have been reported. General characters of the adult skull have already been mentioned in the section on *Psammophis*; Underwood (1967) has described interesting variations in certain regions, notably the brain-case.

The functional anatomy of colubrid skulls is reviewed by Albright and

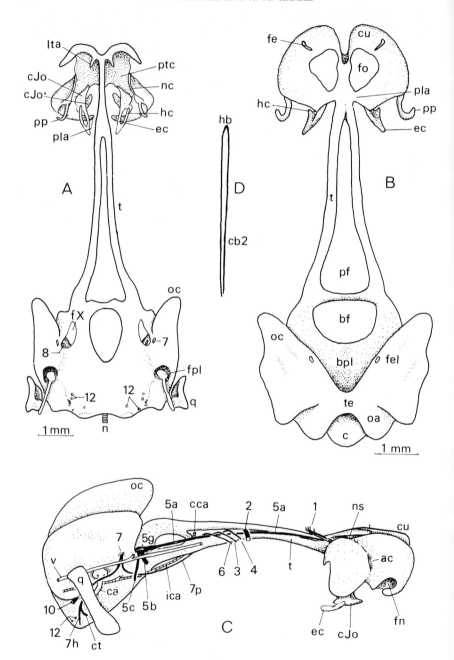

Nelson in *Elaphe* (1959a, b), a generalized form, and by Gans (1952) in the specialized egg-eater *Dasypeltis*. Kinesis in the Henophidia (Rieppel, 1980) and in Caenophidia depends on such factors as the extreme mobility of the jaw bones, the mobility of the nasal region (see Pringle, 1954), and the high degree of streptostyly (often enhanced by the mobility of the supratemporal); it is associated with the loss of the middle ear cavity (Berman and Regal, 1967), and, of course, with the elaboration of the jaw muscles. There is little, if any movement between the components of the brain-case behind the nasal region, such as occurs in mesokinetic and meta-kinetic lizards. The rigidity of the ophidian brain-case and the reinforce-ment of its floor by the strongly developed parasphenoid rostrum prevents injury to the brain during the engulfment of relatively large prey.* The adult chondrocranium will, therefore, hardly be involved in kinetic movement, except where the nasal capsule joins the orbitotemporal region. Here dorsoventral bending will presumably occur through the short region of trabecula communis that lies between the nasal capsule and the paired trabeculae. This rodlike cartilage probably offers little resistance as the bones of the nasal region (premaxilla, nasals, septomaxilla and vomer) are rotated upwards to increase the gap at the front of the mouth. The loss of the sphenethmoid commissures may be an additional factor which

---

*Parker (1879, p. 407, footnote) wrote 'Most solid in its *cranial*, yet the Snake's skull is, of all others, the most elastic and mobile in its *facial* parts; no foot must bruise its head, for it is doomed to go on its belly all the days of its life, yet its throat must be, practically, "unhidebound;" devouring, as it does, prey, whose girth is many times its own.'

FIG. 57. (A) *Malpolon monspessulana*. Dorsal view of fully formed chondrocranium. After El-Toubi, *et al.* (1973b). (B) *Dasypeltis scabra*. Dorsal view of chondrocranium of embryo of 7 cm total length. After Pringle (1954). (C) *Crotaphopeltis hotamboeia*. Lateral view of chondrocranium of late embryo with some nerves and vessels shown. After Brock (1929). (D) *Nerodia sipedon*, adult. Hyobranchial apparatus. After Langebartel (1968).

ac, Aditus conchae; bf, basicranial fenestra; bpl, basal plate; c, condyle; ca, columella auris; cb2, ceratobranchial 2; cca, cerebral branch of internal carotid; cJo, cartilage of Jacobson's organ; cJo', concha of Jacobson's organ; ct, chorda tympani; cu, nasal cupola; ec, ectochoanal cartilage; fe, foramen epiphaniale; fel, foramen for endolymphatic duct; fn, fenestra narina; fo, fenestra olfactoria; fpl, footplate of columella; fx, fenestra x; hb, hyoid body; hc, hypochoanal cartilage; ica, internal carotid artery; lta, lamina transversalis anterior; n, notochord; nc, nasal concha; ns, nasal septum; oa, occipital arch; oc, otic capsule; pf, pituitary fenestra; pla, planum antorbitale; pp, posterior projection from nasal concha; ptc, parietotectal cartilage; q, quadrate; t, trabecula; te, tectum; v, vena capitis lateralis; 1, olfactory and vomeronasal nerves; 2, optic nerve; 3, oculomotor nerve; 4, trochlear nerve; 5a, 5b, 5c, 5g, ophthalmic, maxillary, and mandibular branches of trigeminal nerve and trigeminal ganglion; 6, abducens nerve; 7, facial nerve and foramen; 7h, hyomandibular branch of facial nerve; 7p, palatine branch of facial nerve; 8, anterior foramen for auditory nerve; 10, vagus nerve; 12, foramina for hypo-glossal nerve.

162   A. D'A. BELLAIRS AND A. M. KAMAL

facilitates such movement. It is also possible that the fusion of the planum antorbitale with the nasal septum in certain colubrids is associated with some modification of facial kinesis (Pringle, 1954).

It is well known that in the majority of snakes the two sides of the lower jaw have great independent mobility, and that this is a basic adaptation to the swallowing of large prey (see Gans, 1961). Neither the two dentaries nor the anterior parts of Meckel's cartilages meet in a symphysis, as they do in lizards. In some snakes, at least, an elongated nodule of dense connective tissue lies in the ventral midline between the dentary tips, and part of the intermandibularis anterior muscle is attached to it. This nodule or intermandibular "ligament" (Groombridge, 1979c) deserves further study.

2, 3. Elapidae and Hydrophiidae (infraorder Caenophidia)

a. Previous Literature

Hemachatus haemachatus, Pringle, 1954 (chondrocranium and embryonic osteocranium). Naja haje, El-Toubi et al., 1970 (chondrocranium). Kamal et al., 1970a, b, c (embryonic and adult osteocranium). Pseudechis porphyriacus, de Beer, 1926 (orbitotemporal region). Bogert (1943) has described the bony skull of cobras (Naja, etc.) with special reference to the fangs.

Cranial development in the Hydrophiidae has not been studied, but Kathariner (1900) and Gabe and Saint Girons (1976) have described some aspects of the nasal anatomy of sea snakes.

b. Skull of Elapidae

The development and morphology of the chondrocrania of Hemachatus and Naja closely resemble those of colubrids, but the following features of the mature chondrocranium may be noted.

1. The anterior part of the lamina transversalis anterior is separated from the cartilage of Jacobson's organ, and the latter is separate from the lateral wall of the nasal capsule (Fig. 58A, B).

2. In Naja the extra-conchal recess of the nasal sac appears to project forwards far enough to form a blind recess, as in many lizards. El-Toubi et al. (1970) report the presence of a paranasal element covering the recess; they regard this as unusual in snakes.

3. The planum antorbitale is fused medially with the nasal septum (Fig. 58B).

4. In the early embryonic stages of Naja, the VIth nerve passes through a tunnel in the basal plate; this tunnel is converted into a mere abducens depression in the mature condition; there is a similar depression in mature Hemachatus. After leaving the depression the VIth nerve passes forwards

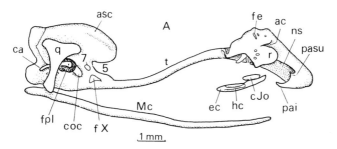

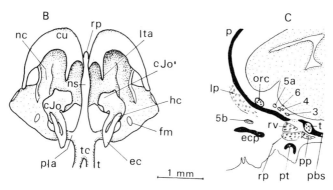

FIG. 58. (A) *Hemachatus haemachatus*, embryo of 10·2 cm total length. Lateral view of chondrocranium. After Pringle (1954). (B) *Naja haje*. Ventral view of fully formed nasal capsule. After El-Toubi *et al.* (1970). (C) *Thelotornis capensis*, late embryo. Transverse section posterior to orbit showing orbital cartilage. After Visser (1961).

ac, Aditus conchae; asc, prominence for anterior semicircular canal; ca, columella auris; cJo, cartilage of Jacobson's organ; cJo′, concha of Jacobson's organ; coc, cochlear prominence; cu, nasal cupola; ec, ectochoanal cartilage; ecp, ectopterygoid; fe, foramen epiphaniale; fm, fenestra for medial part of prefrontal bone; fpl, footplate of columella; fX, fenestra X; hc, hypochoanal cartilage; lp, M. levator pterygoidei; lta, lamina transversalis anterior; Mc, Meckel's cartilage; nc, nasal concha; ns, nasal septum; orc, orbital cartilage; p, parietal; pai, processus alaris inferior; pasu, processus alaris superior; pbs, parabasisphenoid; pla, planum antorbitale; pp, M. protractor pterygoidei; pt, pterygoid; q, quadrate; r, lateral recess; rp, retractor pterygoidei; rv, M. retractor vomeris; t, trabecula; tc, trabecula communis; 3, 4, oculomotor and trochlear nerves; 5, prootic notch containing trigeminal ganglion; 5a, 5b, ophthalmic and maxillary branches of trigeminal nerve; 6, abducens nerve; 7, foramen for facial nerve; rp, rostral process.

between the dura mater and the parietal downgrowth in company with nerves III, IV and Va, eventually reaching the orbit through the foramen orbitale magnum. This is the usual condition in snakes.

5. In the embryo the internal carotid arteries enter the cranial cavity through the corners of the pituitary fenestra, and are not enclosed in cartilaginous canals.

6. In *Hemachatus* the course of the IXth nerve is extra-capsular,

as it passes out through the jugular foramen, as may sometimes occur in *Natrix*. In *Naja* it is intracapsular as in *Malpolon*.

7. The lingual process of the hyoid is reduced or absent.

The development of the osteocranium also seems very like that in *Psammophis*, though doubtless there are special features (undescribed) associated with the development of the venom apparatus. Kamal *et al.* (1970a, b) mention that in *Naja* the fangs and other maxillary teeth are not completely anchylosed with the bone in embryos about four days before the time of hatching. These authors (1970b) regard the small bone behind the orbit in *Naja* as a postfrontal, although Kamal and Hammouda (1968) considered the rather similar bone in adult *Psammophis* to be a postorbital. This distinction is apparently based on the fact that in *Naja* the bone is in contact with the frontal, whereas in *Psammophis* it is not.

Underwood (1967) has noted an extreme development of the bony interorbital septum in the Australian elapid *Demansia*; the parasphenoid has a very high, thin crest which supports the frontals far above the level of the trabeculae. This is remarkable since there is no bony interorbital septum in any other elapid which he examined.

Basipterygoid processes are generally thought to be lacking in caenophidian snakes (Kamal and Hammouda, 1965f). Such processes, short but distinct, are present, however, on the parabasisphenoid of an available skull of *Bungarus fasciatus*.

Bogert (1943) gives excellent figures of the skulls of various cobras, though his account is primarily concerned with the venom apparatus.

4. Viperidae (infraorder Caenophidia)

a. Previous literature

Azemiops sp., Liem *et al.*, 1971 (adult cranial anatomy). *Trimeresurus* sp., Okajima, 1915 (ear). *Causus rhombeatus*, Pringle, 1954 (chondrocranium and embryonic osteocranium); Sülter, 1962 (sections of adult). *Cerastes vipera*, Kamal and Hammouda, 1965e. *Vipera aspis*, Möller, 1905 (ear); Peyer, 1912. *V. russelii*, Srinivasachar, 1955. Hubert and Dufaure (1968) have described normal embryonic stages of *V. aspis*. Kinesis in the adult crotaline skull has been studied by Dullemeijer and Povel (1972), and by Kardong (1977).

b. Chondrocranium of Viperidae

The following characteristics of the later chondrocranium may be noted.

1. As in most other Caenophidia, the floor of the nasal capsule is reduced. The anterior part of the lamina transversalis anterior is absent or vestigial and is not connected with its posterior part, the cartilage of Jacobson's

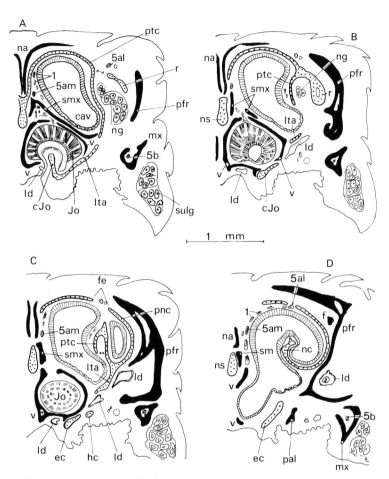

FIG. 59. *Vipera berus*, newborn. (A–D) Transverse sections through nasal region showing structure of the concha. The curved lachrymal duct is cut three times in (C). Small arrows in (A) and (C) indicate where cartilages fuse at slightly more posterior levels.

cav, Cavum proprium of nasal sac; cJo, cartilage and cartilaginous concha of Jacobson's organ; ec, ectochoanal cartilage; f, frontal; fe, foramen epiphaniale; hc, hypochoanal cartilage; Jo, Jacobson's organ; ld, lachrymal duct; lta, lamina transversalis anterior; mx, maxilla; na, nasal; nc, nasal concha; ng, nasal gland; ns, nasal septum; pal, palatine; pfr, prefrontal; pnc, paranasal cartilage; ptc, parietotectal cartilage; r, lateral recess of nasal capsule and sac; sm, smx, septomaxilla; sulg, superior labial gland; v, vomer; 1, 1′, olfactory and vomeronasal nerves; 5al, 5am, lateral and medial ethmoidal branches of ophthalmic nerve; 5b, maxillary nerve.

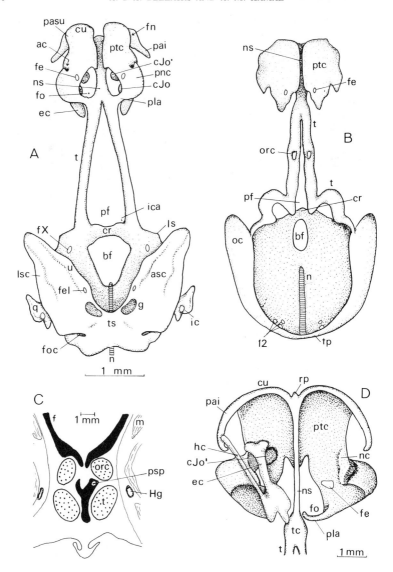

Fig. 60. (A) *Cerastes vipera*. Embryo of total body-length 64·8 mm. Dorsal view of fully formed chondrocranium. After Kamal and Hammouda (1965e). (B) *Vipera russelii*. Embryo of 4·2 mm head-length. Dorsal view of chondrocranium. After Srinivasachar (1955). (C) *Causus rhombeatus*. Newborn. Transverse section through orbit showing orbital cartilages. After Pringle (1954). (D) *Causus rhombeatus*. ? juvenile. Ventral view of nasal capsule. After Sülter (1962). Some structures shown on one side only.

ac, Aditus conchae; asc, prominence for anterior semicircular canal; bf, basicranial fenestra; cJo, cartilage of Jacobson's organ; cJo', concha of Jacobson's organ; cr, crista sellaris; cu, nasal cupola; ec, ectochoanal organ. Similarly, the latter is not connected with the parietotectal cartilage laterally except (in some cases) by fragments of cartilage which regress in the fully formed condition. The floor of the capsule is therefore represented only by the cartilage of Jacobson's organ and by the ectochoanal and hypochoanal cartilages (Fig. 60D).

2. Kamal and Hammouda (1965e) describe in *Cerastes* (Fig. 60A) a massive paranasal cartilage; however, this has no separate centre of chondrification and is continuous from the beginning with the parietotectal cartilage. Their figures suggest that conditions are very similar to those in *Naja* (El-Toubi *et al.*, 1970) and in *Vipera berus* (Fig. 59). Their labelling has been followed here, but the main difference between these forms and other snakes in which no paranasal cartilage has been described seems to be that the lateral or extra-conchal recess extends further forward to form a blind space. In transverse section the cartilage covering this space reduplicates the side-wall of the nasal capsule and gives the impression of being an entity of its own. Thus, the occurrence of the paranasal cartilage in snakes, as in lizards, is doubtful in the general absence of separate chondrification. Its supposed presence or absence seems to depend only on the extent to which the cavum proprium of the nasal sac is flexed on itself.

3. The planum antorbitale is fused with the nasal septum in *Cerastes*, but not in *Causus*, *Vipera berus* or *V. russelii*. In late embryos of *Causus* (Fig. 60D) the nasal septum is prolonged forwards as a small rostral process which projects into a cavity in the premaxilla.

4. Paired, elongated nodules of cartilage have been found above the trabeculae in the mid-orbital region of some embryos of *Vipera berus* (Bellairs, 1949c), *V. russellii* (Fig. 60B), and *Causus*; these may be termed

cartilage; f, frontal; fe, foramen epiphaniale; fel, foramen for endolymphatic duct; fn, fenestra narina; fo, fenestra olfactoria; foc, occipito-capsular fissure; fX, fenestra X; g, unchondrified gap in tectum; hc, hypochoanal cartilage; Hg, duct of Harderian gland; ic, intercalary; ica, notch for internal carotid artery; ls, laterosphenoid extension from basal plate; lsc, prominence for lateral semicircular canal; m, eye muscle; n, notochord; nc, nasal concha; ns, nasal septum; oc, otic capsule; orc, orbital cartilage; pai, processus alaris inferior; pasu, processus alaris superior; pf, pituitary fenestra; pla, planum antorbitale; pnc, paranasal cartilage; psp, parasphenoid; ptc, parietotectal cartilage; q, quadrate; rp, rostral process; t, trabecula; tc, trabecula communis; tp, tectum posterius (from occipital arches); ts, tectum synoticum; u, utricular prominence; 12, foramina for hypoglossal nerve.

orbital or orbitosphenoid cartilages. In a 106 day embryo of *Causus*, Pringle (1954) found these cartilages nearly equal to the trabeculae in cross-sectional diameter (Fig. 60C). In these vipers the orbital cartilages appear to lie anterior to the optic nerves, not behind them as in the colubrid *Thelotornis*, and may, therefore, represent vestiges of the planum supraseptale rather than of the pila metoptica. In some cases the cartilage occurs only on one side; in others they may be asymmetrical in size. The presence of a unilateral cartilage in a juvenile, postnatal specimen of *Causus* (Sülter, 1962) tends to support Pringle's view that in those individuals in which these cartilages develop at all they persist throughout life (but see p. 158).

5. In the viperid embryos studied, the internal carotid artery enters the cranial cavity through the corner of the pituitary fossa on each side, sometimes through a notch but not through a cartilaginous canal.

6. In *Vipera russelli* Srinivasachar describes a curious lateral bowing of the posterior ends of the trabeculae where they meet the basal plate (Fig. 60B) and suggests that polar cartilages (unknown in other lepidosaurs) may possibly be incorporated in these regions of the trabeculae. This seems doubtful, but study of additional material of this species would be of interest.

7. Fenestra X has not been observed in the described stages of *Vipera aspis* or *V. russelli*, but occurs in the other viperid species.

8. There is an abducens depression in the mature chondrocranium of *Causus*, but *Cerastes* lacks both a tunnel and a depression; the VIth nerve passes forwards freely over the dorsal surface of the basal plate.

9. In *Cerastes* the course of the IXth nerve follows the same developmental pattern as in *Psammophis*, being first intramural and then extracapsular. However, the nerve leaves the skull through a small foramen of its own instead of issuing from the lateral aperture of the recessus scalae tympani. In *Causus*, and probably in *Vipera*, the nerve follows an intracapsular course, as in mature *Dasypeltis* and *Malpolon* (see Kamal, 1969e).

10. The hyobranchial apparatus in late embryonic and postnatal vipers is of the parallel type. The lingual process is variable in length. In early stages of *Cerastes* the second ceratobranchial horns are short and divergent.

c. Osteocranium of Viperidae

No features of special remark in the development of the osteocranium of vipers seem to have been described, though of course the adult skull shows many important modifications, especially in connection with the venom apparatus. Some aspects of the development of the venom glands are described by Kochva (1978). The abnormal occurrence of a bifurcated egg-tooth on the premaxilla in embryos of *Vipera berus* is described by

Smith *et al.* (1953). The mature egg-tooth in this viviparous form is of problematic function and normally points backwards and downwards, rather than forwards as in oviparous forms such as *Natrix natrix*. The functional anatomy of the head and the mechanism of fang erection in vipers are dealt with by Dullemeijer (1959), Boltt and Ewer (1964), and by Haas in many papers on various groups of snakes (see Haas, 1973).

5. Boidae (infraorder Henophidia)

a. Previous literature

Corallus annulatus, C. enydris, Eryx johnii, Wever, 1978 (ear). *Eryx jaculus,* Kamal and Hammouda, 1965f). *Eunectes murinus,* Bellairs and Boyd, 1957 (nasal capsule). *Sanzinia madagascariensis,* Genest-Villard, 1966). Aspects of the adult bony skull in Boidae and other primitive snakes are described by Underwood (1976), Rieppel (1977a; 1978e, f; 1979c, d; 1980) and Groombridge (1979a, b).

b. Chondrocranium of Boidae

The fully formed chondrocranium of the Boidae studied shows a number of interesting features.

1. In *Eryx* and *Eunectes* (but not in *Sanzinia*) there is a short rostral process embedded in the premaxilla.

2. In all three boid genera the floor of the nasal capsule is more extensive than in the Caenophidia described. The lamina transversalis anterior is complete; it is connected with the nasal septum medially, and laterally by a broad band of cartilage with the outer wall of the nasal capsule. Thus there is quite a wide, though somewhat oblique zona annularis. Rather similar conditions are seen in late embryos of *Trachyboa boulengeri* and *Boa constrictor* (Bellairs, unpublished). The retention of a rather extensive floor of the nasal capsule seems a genuinely primitive feature of Boidae, as Kamal and Hammouda (1965f) suggest—although of course further representatives of the family should be studied.

3. The ectochoanal and hypochoanal cartilages join posteriorly to form a broad plate (labelled ectochoanal cartilage here).

4. Kamal and Hammouda describe a short posterior projection from the planum antorbitale of *Eryx jaculus* which they regard as a posterior maxillary process. If this corresponds with the projection doubtfully labelled posterior maxillary process in *E. conicus* (Fig. 61D), it seems to lie more medially than the corresponding structure in lizards. A smaller, but apparently similar projection is present in *Eunectes*, and in *Xenopeltis* (Fig. 63), but not in *Sanzinia*. De Beer (1937, p. 248) has suggested that the posterior maxillary process of lizards (probably a pterygoquadrate

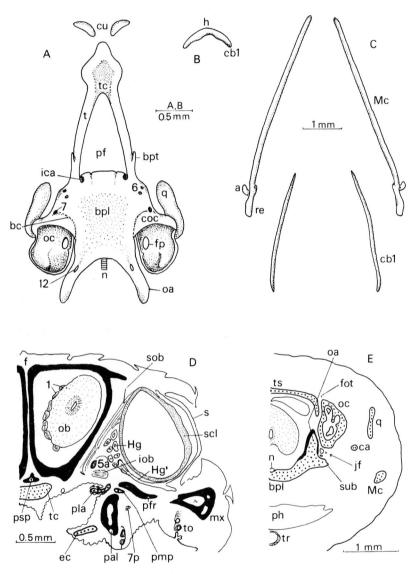

Fig. 61. (A, B) *Eryx jaculus*, embryo 48·4 mm total body length. (A) Dorsal view of chondrocranium. (B) Hyobranchial apparatus. (C) *Eryx jaculus*, embryo 92·2 mm total body length. Ventral view of Meckel's cartilage and hyobranchial apparatus of fully formed chondrocranium. (D) *Eryx conicus*, newborn. Transverse section through front of orbit showing structure perhaps regarded as the posterior maxillary process by Kamal and Hammouda (1965f). The frontals completely surround the brain at this level. (E) *Eryx jaculus*, embryo 92·2 mm total body length. Transverse section through otic region showing subcapsular ledge. A, B, C, E after Kamal and Hammouda (1965f).

derivative) is homologous with the hypochoanal cartilage of snakes. This cannot be so if Kamal and Hammouda are correct, since *Eryx* would then have both structures (see also McDowell, 1972).

5. In *Eunectes*, *Sanzinia* and *Xenopeltis* there is an irregular mass of cartilage situated above and medial to the posterior part of Jacobson's organ on each side, and within the bony capsule of the organ formed by the septomaxilla and vomer. This was regarded by Bellairs and Boyd (1957) and Genest-Villard (1966) as a vestigial paraseptal cartilage, but perhaps corresponds with parts of the roofing cartilage of Jacobson's organ described by Malan (1946) in certain lizards. This cartilage is not described in *Eryx jaculus*; something like it, however, can be seen in sections of a juvenile *E. conicus*.

6. In *Eryx* the nasal concha is small and formed by a fairly shallow infolding of the parietotectal cartilage. In *Eunectes*, and probably in *Sanzinia* which appears to have on the whole a similar nasal capsule, the concha is bigger and there is an extra-conchal recess enclosed by a cartilage which could be regarded as a paranasal element. The cavum conchale of *Eunectes* is well developed.

7. In *Eunectes* and *Sanzinia* the planum antorbitale closely approaches the nasal septum medially but is not attached to it. In *Eryx* the planum is separated from the septum by a considerable gap.

8. In *Eryx* a pair of orbital cartilages, probably lying in front of the optic nerves, is present; they become fused in the midline at their posterior ends (Fig. 62). These cartilages were absent in a somewhat later embryonic stage, and Kamal and Hammouda (1965f) follow the suggestion of Bellairs (1949c) that they are transient structures. Rather similar cartilages having a mesenchymatous connection with the trabeculae are described by Genest-Villard (1966) in certain stages of *Sanzinia*. Bellairs (1949c) has observed a single cartilaginous nodule in the midline above the trabeculae of an embryo *Python*. These cartilages appear to be relics of the anterior orbital cartilage system of other reptiles and deserve further study. They cannot

---

a, Articular facet on dorsal projection from Meckel's cartilage for articulation with quadrate; bc, basi-capsular commissure; bpl, basal plate; bpt, basipterygoid process; ca, columella auris; cbl, cerato-branchial 1; coc, cochlear part of otic capsule; cu, rudiment of nasal cupola; ec, ectochoanal cartilage; f, frontal; fot, fissure between otic capsule and tectum; fp, foramen for perilymphatic duct; h, hyoid body; Hg, Harderian gland; Hg', duct of Harderian gland; ica, notch for internal carotid artery; iob, inferior oblique muscle; jf, jugular foramen for vagus and, possibly accessory nerve and jugular vein; Mc, Meckel's cartilage; mx, maxilla; n, notochord; oa, occipital arch; ob, olfactory and accessory olfactory bulb; oc, otic capsule; pal, palatine; pf, pituitary fenestra; pfr, prefrontal; ph, pharynx; pla, planum antorbitale; pmp, ? posterior maxillary process; psp, parasphenoid rostrum; q, quadrate; re, retroarticular process of Meckel's cartilage; s, spectacle; scl, sclera; sob, superior oblique muscle; sub, subcapsular process; t, trabecula; tc, trabecula communis; to, tooth germs; tr, trachea; ts, tectum synoticum; 1, olfactory/vomeronasal nerves; 5a, ophthalmic nerve; 6, abducens canal; 7, foramen for facial nerve; 7p, palatine branch of facial nerve; 12, foramen for hypoglossal nerve.

be regarded as primitive characters peculiar to Boidae, since they have also been described in certain caenophidian snakes.

9. In the adult skull of *Eunectes*, *Python* and many other boid snakes the basisphenoid or parabasisphenoid possesses a pair of short but distinct basipterygoid processes which appear to be homologous with those of lizards. Such processes are also present in the Upper Cretaceous henophidian *Dinilysia* (Estes *et al.*, 1970; Frazzetta, 1970) and may reasonably be regarded as primitive in snakes—though they may occasionally crop up among the Caenophidia.

In the earlier embryonic stages of *Eryx* a small cartilaginous projection appears in continuity with the lateral border of the posterior part of the trabecula on each side and appears to be of trabecular origin (Fig. 61A). In later stages each process becomes, larger, oval, and detached from its trabecula (Fig. 62). Kamal and Hammouda (1965f) regard these structures as basipterygoid (basitrabecular) processes, and they are labelled as such here. However, their eventual fate, which would presumably involve re-attachment to the ossifying skull base is not described, while Rieppel (1978e) states that distinct basipterygoid processes are lacking in adult *Eryx jaculus*.

In the light of Genest-Villard's work (1966) it seems possible that these structures in *Eryx jaculus* are not really basipterygoid processes, but correspond with the subtrabecular nodules which she describes in *Sanzinia*; these oval nodules lie in close relationship to the lateral borders of the posterior parts of the trabeculae and may perhaps represent vestiges of the pterygoquadrate complex, possibly pterygoid processes. In later embryonic stages of *Sanzinia* a structure which looks considerably more like a basipterygoid process, and has the appropriate neurovascular relationships, arises posterior to each subtrabecular nodule from the lateral edge of the chondrocranium in the region where the trabeculae and the basal plate join. It is unfortunate that these important papers, on *Eryx* and *Sanzinia* respectively, appeared too close together in time for cross-reference; further study is necessary to clarify the development of this interesting region of the boid chondrocranium.

10. In the fully formed chondrocranium of *Eryx* (Fig. 62) the notochord traverses the greater part of the basicranial fenestra, as in many lizards. This differs from the condition observed in most other snakes where, at comparable embryonic stages, the notochord ends behind the posterior margin of the fenestra. It would thus appear that degeneration of the front part of the notochord in *Eryx* is delayed until a comparatively late growth stage.

11. In *Eryx* fenestra X is present in the usual position and appears to arise by degeneration of preexisting cartilage; it is absent in *Sanzinia*.

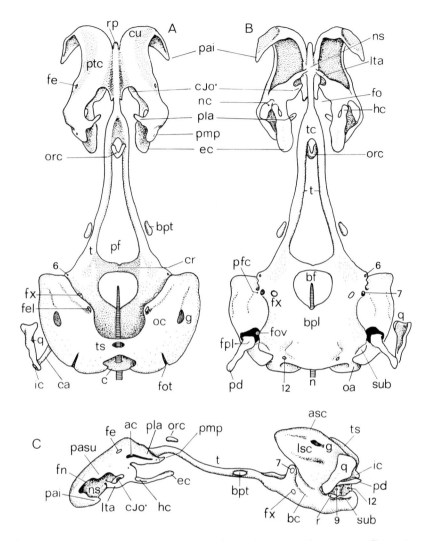

FIG. 62. *Eryx jaculus*, embryo 92·2 mm total body length. (A) dorsal, (B) ventral and (C) lateral view of fully formed chondrocranium. After Kamal and Hammouda (1965f).

ac, Aditus conchae; asc, prominence for anterior semicircular canal; bc, basicapsular commissure; bf, basicranial fenestra; bpl, basal plate; bpt, basipterygoid process; c, occipital condyle; ca, columella auris; cJo', concha of Jacobson's organ; cu, nasal cupola; ec, ectochoanal cartilage; fe, foramen epiphaniale; fel, foramen for endolymphatic duct; fn, fenestra narina; fo, fenestra olfactoria; fot, fissure between otic capsule and tectum; fov, fenestra ovalis; fpl, columellar footplate; fX, fenestra X; g, unchondrified gap; hc, hypochoanal cartilage; ic, intercalary; lsc, prominence for lateral semicircular canal; lta, lamina transversalis anterior; n, notochord; nc, nasal concha; ns, nasal septum; oa, occipital arch; oc, otic capsule; orc, orbital cartilage; pai, processus alaris inferior; pasu, processus alaris superior; pd, dorsal process; pf, pituitary fenestra; pfc, prefacial commissure; pla, planum antorbitale; pmp, posterior maxillary process; ptc, parietotectal cartilage; q, quadrate; r, recessus scalae tympani; rp, rostral process; sub, subcapsular process; t, trabecula; tc, trabecula communis; ts, tectum synoticum; 6, 7, 9, 12, foramina for abducens, facial, glossopharyngeal, and hypoglossal nerves.

12. In earlier stages of *Eryx* the VIth nerve passes through an abducens tunnel in the dorsal surface of the basal plate (Fig. 61A). Later, however, the nerve comes to penetrate the plate from its dorsal to its ventral surface; on emerging from the latter it lies in an extension of the cranial cavity (Kamal and Hammouda, 1965f, p. 180).

13. In earlier embryos of *Eryx* the IXth nerve has an intracapsular course; later it becomes extracapsular, perforating the strut of cartilage which divides the recessus scalae tympani from the jugular foramen. It leaves the skull through the lateral opening of the recessus (Kamal, 1969e; Fig. 53D here).

14. From the ventrolateral border of each side of the basal plate of *Eryx* there projects a stout cartilaginous ledge (Figs. 61E; 62C). This forms the floor of the recessus scalae tympani and lies beneath the jugular foramen. Such a ledge has not apparently been described in *Sanzinia* or other snakes, but a similar structure, usually called the subcapsular process, occurs in crocodilians and perhaps also in Testudines.

15. According to Kamal and Hammouda (1965f) the tectum of *Eryx* is entirely derived from the otic capsule. It contains an oval, medial fenestra which has not been observed in other snakes.

16. There is only one pair of hypoglossal foramina in *Eryx*; in most other snakes the number varies between two and four.

17. The cochlear portion of the otic capsule of *Eryx* encroaches on or overlaps the lateral margin of the basal plate to a greater extent than is usual in snakes.

18. In *Eryx*, *Sanzinia* and adult *Corallus*, one or more cartilages, probably intercalaries of dorsal process origin, are interposed between the distal end of the columella and the quadrate; functionally these provide a series of sliding joints within a common capsule (see Wever, 1978).

19. In earlier stages of *Eryx* the cornua of the hyobranchial apparatus are fused anteriorly and diverge posteriorly (Fig. 61B), but in the late embryonic and postnatal condition this fusion is lost owing to resorption of the hyoid body region (Fig. 61C). The horns diverge posteriorly and the condition represents a modification of Langebartel's "inverted V" type. This latter is characteristic of Boidae, in which the horns are often joined in front but in which there is no lingual process. By analogy with lizards, Langebartel (1968) regards the hyobranchial horns of boids as first ceratobranchials. In the boid subfamily Tropidophinae the horns are of the parallel type, as in caenophidians.

c. *Osteocranium of Boidae*

The developing osteocranium of *Sanzinia* is described by Genest-Villard (1966), while Bellairs and Boyd (1957) figure and comment on the bones of the snout in a late embryo of *Eunectes*. This specimen is of considerable interest in showing the teratological condition of unilateral cleft lip and palate, resembling the well known congenital malformation in mammals.

Neither the chondrocranium nor the osteocranium of this embryo is grossly affected by the abnormality. However, the zona annularis of the nasal capsule is interrupted on the side of the cleft (Fig. 63A, C). The septomaxillary bone is divided by the cleft. The similar presence of this last abnormality in embryos of *Lacerta* (Bellairs, 1965; Bellairs and Gamble, 1960) and of *Natrix* and *Vipera* (Bellairs and Boyd, 1957) which also had cleft palate malformations suggests that in Squamata the septomaxilla may have a dual origin. The main, medial part associated with Jacobson's organ appears to arise within the tissues of the frontonasal process, while the lateral extension of this bone arises within the maxillary process. It is not known whether such a dual origin is reflected in the pattern of ossification, but it is likely that the fusion of frontonasal and maxillary processes to form the "face" would have occurred at a stage considerably earlier than that at which the bone begins to ossify.

A remarkable feature of this embryo of *Eunectes*, which appears unrelated to its malformation, is the presence of a small vertical plate of bone in the midline between the frontals and prefrontals. This "interfrontal" element is figured, but not labelled, by Gadow (1901) in an adult skull of *Eunectes*.

The skulls of Boidae retain certain primitive characters such as the presence, in most species, of the coronoid bone in the lower jaw, and often of basipterygoid processes. Boid skulls also show many advanced features, notably those associated with the mobility of the jaws and kinesis (see Frazzetta, 1966). Members of the subfamily Pythoninae possess a distinct postfrontal bone (often called a supraorbital) in addition to the postorbital. The majority of the Pythoninae have premaxillary teeth. Some cranial features of Boidae which are significant in classification are listed by Underwood (1967, 1976). For example, the Vidian canals are often asymmetrical, being larger on the left in Pythoninae and on the right in Erycinae and Boinae. The adult skulls of boid snakes are described and figured by McDowell and Bogert (1954) and Frazzetta (1959), while Frazzetta (1975) has discussed the phylogenetic significance of certain features of the premaxilla. Rieppel (1977a; 1978e, f; 1979c, d) and Groombridge (1979a, b, c) have made important studies on the adult cranial anatomy of this and other groups of primitive snakes.

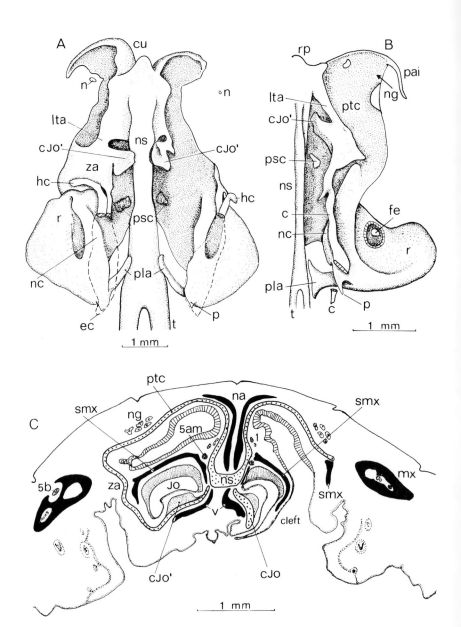

6. Xenopeltidae (infraorder Henophidia)

a. Previous Literature

No developmental studies of the skulls of Henophidia other than Boidae are available, but Bellairs (1949b) used sections to describe the nasal capsule and bones of the snout of an adult *Xenopeltis unicolor*. The systematic status of this form is doubtful. Underwood (1976) places it in the Boidae.

b. Nasal Capsule of Xenopeltis (Fig. 63B)

The following features were observed.

1. There is a short rostral process.

2. The lamina transversalis anterior is connected anteriorly with the flattened anterior part of the nasal septum, but not laterally with the parietotectal cartilage. Hence there is no zona annularis. This last feature contrasts rather strikingly with the condition in *Eryx* and *Eunectes*.

3. As in *Eunectes* there is a small nodule of cartilage within the bony capsule of Jacobson's organ; this may represent a vestigial paraseptal cartilage or a part of the roofing cartilage of the organ found in certain lizards.

4. The nasal concha is well developed. There is an extra-conchal recess enclosed by a paranasal(?) cartilage.

5. The long "choanal cartilage" bears a short medial projection; it is uncertain whether the choanal cartilage represents the ectochoanal or the hypochoanal cartilage of other snakes.

6. A small projection from the back of the nasal capsule (labelled by

---

FIG. 63. (A) *Eunectes murinus*, late embryo. Ventral view of nasal capsule. This specimen shows the congenital malformation of cleft "lip" and palate (see text). Structures on the left side (of figure) are normal. The chondrocranium on the right side is comparatively little affected, except that the zona annularis is absent. The ectochoanal cartilages are shown in broken lines. After Bellairs and Boyd (1957). (B) *Xenopeltis unicolor*, subadult. Ventral view of nasal capsule. (After Bellairs, 1949b.) A segment has been removed from the posterior part of the choanal cartilage, and a window has been cut in the floor of the lateral recess to show the foramen epiphaniale. (C) *Eunectes murinus*, late embryo with cleft palate. Transverse section through organs of Jacobson, showing duct on the malformed side (right in figure), and the position of the cleft, which divides the septomaxilla into two parts. The duct of Jacobson's organ on the "normal" side (left in figure) is at a level slightly posterior to that shown. The concha of Jacobson's organ has been reconstructed on both sides, as if seen from in front.

c, Choanal cartilage (? ectochoanal); cJo, cJo′, cartilage and concha of Jacobson's organ; cu, nasal cupola; ec, ectochoanal cartilage; fe, foramen epiphaniale; hc, hypochoanal cartilage; Jo, Jacobson's organ; lta, lamina transversalis anterior; mx, maxilla; n, nodule of cartilage; na, nasal; nc, nasal concha; ng, nasal gland, and course of its duct in B; ns, nasal septum; p, projection from planum antorbitale (? posterior maxillary process); pai, processus alaris inferior; pla, planum antorbitale; psc, paraseptal cartilage; ptc, parietotectal cartilage; r, cartilage of lateral recess; rp, rostral process; t, trabecula; v, vomer; za, zona annularis; 1, olfactory nerves; 5am, medial ethmoidal branch of ophthalmic nerve; 5b, maxillary nerve.

Bellairs, 1949b, as part of the paranasal cartilage) may correspond to the structure in *Eryx* which Kamal and Hammouda (1965f) regard as a posterior maxillary process.

7. The hyobranchial apparatus is of the inverted V type, with the first ceratobranchial horns joined anteriorly (Langebartel, 1968).

c. Osteocranium of Xenopeltis

The bony skull of *Xenopeltis*, described by Rieppel (1977a), shows interesting features. The premaxilla bears teeth. The coronoid is absent, or much reduced. The palatine bears a long, slender vomerine process which curves medially above the vomer and enters the medial wall of the nasopharyngeal duct (see also Bellairs, 1949b). This process is a special feature of *Xenopeltis*, and Rieppel (1977a) suggests that it may be involved in kinesis. *Xenopeltis* is unusual in possessing a distinct intercalary bone (Smith, 1943; Rieppel, 1977a).

7. Aniliidae (infraorder Henophidia).

Sections through the anterior part of the head of an adult *Anilius scytale* have been examined by A. d'A. B. There is a short rostral process and a somewhat oblique zona annularis. The nasal concha and cavum conchale are well developed, but the cartilaginous floor of the latter is deficient, so that the nasal gland is in contact with the nasal epithelium (Fig. 64A). There are no paraseptal vestiges and the planum antorbitale is free from the nasal septum (Fig. 64B).

The nasal capsule and orbitotemporal region (Fig. 64C) of *Anilius* show certain apparently primitive features such as the zona annularis and basipterygoid processes. However, Rieppel (1977a) doubts whether these processes are homologous with those in Sauria.

The hyobranchial apparatus is of the inverted V type with the horns (formed from the first ceratobranchials) joined anteriorly; there is no lingual process. In *Cylindrophis* the horns do not meet anteriorly (Langebartel, 1968). The nasal sac of Aniliidae is described by Gabe and Saint Girons (1976) and the adult bony skull by Rieppel (1977a, b; 1980).

8. Uropeltidae (infraorder Henophidia)

Sections through the anterior part of the head of adult *Uropeltis pulneyensis* and *Rhinophis philippinus* have been examined by A. d'A.B. *Rhinophis* has a long rostral process, perhaps correlated with the elongation of the snout, and a narrow, oblique zona annularis. In both forms the cartilaginous nasal concha consists of a simple shelf of cartilage without invagination or cavum conchale (Fig. 64D). *Rhinophis* is remarkable for the great reduction of the cartilage of the nasal capsule, which recalls the

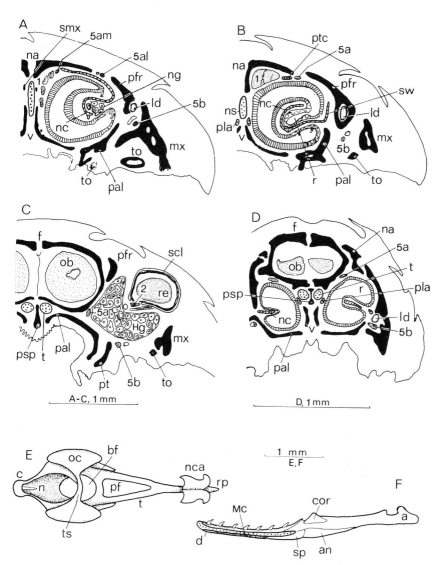

Fɪɢ. 64. (A, B, C) *Anilius scytale*, adult. (A) and (B) Transverse sections through nasal concha. (C) Section through posterior part of orbit, slightly behind region where trabeculae diverge. (D) *Rhinophis philippinus*, adult. Transverse section through nasal concha. (E) *Rhinophis philippinus*, juvenile. Dorsal view of chondrocranium. Details of nasal capsule are not shown but the roof cartilage seems more extensive than in the specimen figured in 64D. (F) *Rhinophis philippinus*, subadult. Medial view of lower jaw. E, F, after Baumeister (1908).

a, Articular (probably fused with prearticular and surangular); an, angular; bf, basicranial fenestra; c, occipital condyle; cor, coronoid; d, dentary; f, frontal; Hg, Harderian gland; ld, lachrymal duct; Mc, Meckel's cartilage; mx, maxilla; n, notochord; na, nasal; nc, nasal concha; nca, nasal capsule; ng, nasal gland; ns, nasal septum; ob, olfactory bulb; oc, otic capsule; pal, palatine; pf, pituitary fenestra; pfr, prefrontal; pla, planum antorbitale; psp, parasphenoid; pt, pterygoid; ptc, parietotectal cartilage; r, lateral recess of nasal sac; re, retina; rp, rostral process; scl, sclera; smx, septomaxilla; sp, splenial; sw, side-wall of nasal capsule (? paranasal cartilage); t, trabecula; to, tooth; ts, tectum synoticum; v, vomer; 1, olfactory and vomeronasal nerves; 2, optic nerve; 5a, ethmoidal and ophthalmic nerve; 5al, 5am, lateral and medial branches of ethmoidal nerve; 5b, maxillary nerve.

condition in some amphisbaenians. In *Uropeltis* the reduction is mainly evident in the posterior part of the capsule. The small, isolated planum antorbitale of both forms is closely applied to, though not actually fused with, the trabecula communis and the adjacent region of the trabecula (Fig. 64D).

The hyobranchial apparatus is of the inverted "V" type, but the first ceratobranchial horns do not meet anteriorly (Langebartel, 1968).

The bony skull and some features of the chondrocranium of *Rhinophis philippinus* (Fig. 64E, F) are described in a remarkable monograph by Baumeister (1908); Rieppel (1977a) figures the skull of *Uropeltis brevis*. Peculiarities of the cranio-vertebral joint are described by Williams (1959b) and by Hoffstetter and Gasc (1969). The curious middle ear structure of *Rhinophis drummondhayi* is described by Wever (1978).

9, 10. Typhlopidae (including Anomalepinae) and Leptotyphlopidae (infraorder Scolecophidia)

a. Previous Literature

No developmental studies of the skull have been made on members of these families, which are highly specialized for burrowing, but which also retain many primitive ophidian features. The Scolecophidia differ in many respects from each other, but apparently form a natural group (Underwood, 1967). Sections through adult or subadult skulls of the following species have been described.

Typhlopidae: *Anomalepis aspinosus*, Haas, 1968: *Liotyphlops albirostris*, Haas, 1964. *Typhlops delalandii*, Smit, 1949. *T. pusillus*, Wever, 1978 (ear). *T. vermicularis* and other species, Rieppel, 1979a.

Leptotyphlopidae: *Leptotyphlops macrorhynchus*, Haas, 1959. *Leptotyphlops nigricans*, Brock, 1932b. *L. scutifrons*, Rieppel, 1979a.

Unsectioned skulls of scolecophidians have been described by McDowell and Bogert (1954) and by List (1966), while Gabe and Saint Girons (1976) have described the nasal organs. A. d'A. B. has examined sections through the head of an adult *Typhlops jamaicensis*. The information available is not adequate for any general assessment of the chondrocranium, and further studies, especially on embryos, are badly needed.

b. Chondrocranium of Scolecophidia

Smit's (1949) reconstruction of the nasal capsule of *Typhlops* shows that it definitely follows the ophidian rather than the saurian pattern (Fig. 65A, B). The nasal cupolae are large and project well in front of the nasal septum, and there are long inferior alar processes. There is no rostral process. The roof and side-wall of the capsule are well developed, though the fenestra

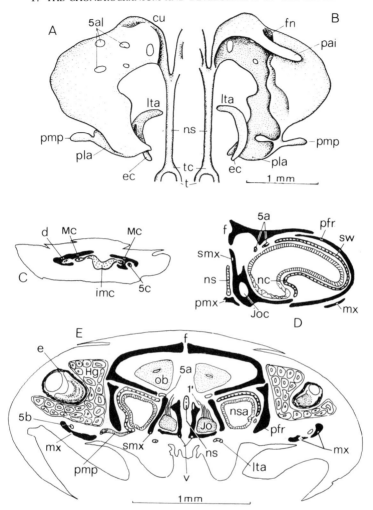

FIG. 65. (A, B) *Typhlops delalandii*, subadult. (A) dorsal and (B) ventral views of nasal capsule. After Smit (1949). (C, D, E) *Typhlops jamaicensis*, adult. (C) Transverse section through front of lower jaw showing intermandibular cartilage. (D) Section through nasal concha, just anterior to organ of Jacobson. (E) Section through orbits showing structure regarded by Smit (1949) as posterior maxillary process, here reconstructed from four adjacent sections.

cu, Nasal cupola; d, dentary; e, eye; ec, ectochoanal cartilage; f, frontal; fn, fenestra narina; Hg, Harderian gland; imc, intermandibular cartilage; Jo, Jacobson's organ; Joc, cavity in septomaxilla for Jacobson's organ; lta, lamina transversalis anterior; Mc, Meckel's cartilage; mx, maxilla; nc, nasal concha; ns, nasal septum; nsa, nasal sac; ob, olfactory bulb; pai, processus alaris inferior; pfr, prefrontal; pla, planum antorbitale; pmp, ? posterior maxillary process; pmx, premaxilla; smx, septomaxilla; sw, side-wall of nasal capsule; t, trabecula; tc, trabecula communis; v, vomer; 1', vomeronasal nerves; 5a, ethmoidal nerve; 5al, foramina for lateral branches of ethmoidal nerve; 5b, maxillary nerve; 5c, mandibular nerve.

olfactoria is large and the roofing cartilage is perforated by several big foramina for the lateral ethmoidal nerves. The floor of the capsule is much reduced and there is no zona annularis. The lamina transversalis anterior consists only of the cartilage of Jacobson's organ, from which the ectochoanal cartilage projects posteriorly. There is no hypochoanal cartilage. The planum antorbitale does not reach the nasal septum medially. Smit describes a lateral projection from the back of the lateral capsular wall as a posterior maxillary process; this process is also present in *Typhlops jamaicensis* (Fig. 65E) and, apart from its lateral inclination, seems to resemble the posterior maxillary process of lizards. The only other snake in which such a process has been described is *Eryx* (Kamal and Hammouda, 1965f) though its identification, like that of the small projections from the back of the nasal capsule in *Eunectes* and *Xenopeltis*, is in need of confirmation.

Typhlops jamaicensis, and probably other species, has an extensive but relatively simple infolded type of concha resembling that of many other snakes (Fig. 65D). There is no extra-conchal recess. The concha is absent in *Typhlops braminus* (Haas, 1964; Gabe and Saint Girons, 1976).

A striking feature of the scolecophidian skull is the tendency to telescope the nasal and orbital regions into each other. Thus, in a single transverse section of *Leptotyphlops macrorhynchus* or *Typhlops braminus* (Haas, 1959, 1964), or of *T. jamaicensis* (Fig. 65E) one can see the eye, the olfactory bulb of the brain, the organ of Jacobson and the nasal sac, which is situated lateral to the organ rather than above it, as in more "normal" snakes (Fig. 63C). This telescoping is less pronounced in *Liotyphlops albirostris* and *Anomalepis aspinosus*, which are placed in the subfamily Anomalepinae (sometimes elevated to separate familial status). In this and perhaps other respects the Anomalepinae seem to be more primitive than the subfamily Typhlopinae (genus *Typhlops*).

In some species of *Typhlops* at least the nasal septum or the trabecula communis is seen at the level of the middle of the tiny orbits; the trabeculae diverge a little further back so that the chondrocranium is technically tropitrabic (Fig. 65E). However, this condition may be ascribed to "telescoping" and to changes in the proportions of the front of the head rather than to any fundamental difference between the chondrocranium of *Typhlops* and other snakes.

The columella auris of *Typhlops* (Fig. 66A) has a large spoon-shaped footplate somewhat like that of *Rhinophis*, and a short shaft which is attached to the quadrate by a strong ligament. The bony relationships of the footplate are modified. In snakes generally the margins of the fenestra ovalis are raised up into a ridge, the circumfenestral crest. In *Typhlops* and certain other burrowing snakes this ridge is greatly enlarged so that the footplate is almost enclosed within a space, the juxtastapedial fossa or recess, which contains an extension of the perilymphatic space. Similar enclosure of this fossa is seen in *Rhinophis* and *Leptotyphlops*, but in *L. scutifrons*, the columella has no distinct footplate (see Baird, 1970; Wever, 1978; Rieppel, 1979a).

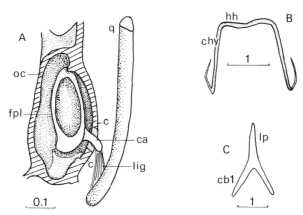

FIG. 66. (A) *Typhlops pusillus*, adult. Reconstruction of columella auris in (probably) dorsal view. Cut surfaces in slanting lines. Top of figure faces anteriorly, quadrate is lateral. After Wever (1978). (B) *Liotyphlops albirostris*, adult. All-cartilaginous, hyobranchial apparatus of "M" type. (C) *Typhlops schlegeli mucruso*, adult. Ossified hyobranchial skeleton. B and C after Langebartel (1968). Scales are in millimetres.

c, Circumfenestral crest; ca, columella auris; cb1, ceratobranchial 1; chy, ceratohyal; fpl, columellar footplate; hh, hypohyal; lig, ligament; lp, lingual process; oc, otic capsule; q, quadrate.

The hyobranchial apparatus of the Anomalepinae is of a unique "M" shaped type (Langebartel, 1968; Fig. 66B here). It has a concave transverse portion which probably represents a median basihyal (body) plus hypohyals, and posteriorly directed ceratohyals with recurrent ends. The entire complex is thus derived from the hyoid (second) arch. The remaining Typhlopidae (subfamily Typhlopinae) and the Leptotyphlopidae have a hyobranchial apparatus of the inverted "Y" type, usually with a long lingual process incorporating the basihyal, and always with a single pair of horns regarded by Langebartel as the first ceratobranchials (Fig. 66C). Members of the genus *Typhlops* appear to be the only snakes in which all or parts of the hyobranchial skeleton are liable to ossify with age, at least in some species.

c. Osteocranium of Scolecophidia

The bony skulls of scolecophidians (well figured in Parker, 1977) show many peculiarities which separate them from other snakes, and which almost constitute a study in themselves.

In most or all scolecophidians the optic foramen is in the frontal rather than between the frontal and parietal, the coronoid is present in the lower jaw, and the supratemporal (squamosal or tabular of some authors) is vestigial or absent (Underwood, 1967). There appears to be no laterosphenoid.

In the Typhlopinae the tooth-bearing region of the mobile maxilla is disposed more or less in the transverse plane of the head. The postorbital (? postfrontal) and ectopterygoid are absent and the dentary is toothless. In some forms the parietal is paired.

In the Anomalepinae (at least in *Anomalepis* and *Liotyphlops*) the nasals are fused and their fused descending processes form a bony nasal septum which projects ventrally between the cupolae, and lies dorsal to the low, cartilaginous nasal septum (Haas, 1964, 1968). The nasal also participates, together with the septomaxilla, in forming a bony support for the nasal concha; there is also a conchal cartilage. The ectopterygoid is present. Various interpretations of the circumorbital bones have been proposed, and it is possible that they are vestiges of the saurian postorbital and superior temporal arches (see McDowell and Bogert, 1954; Haas, 1964, 1968). The splenial is absent, and the parietals remain unfused in *Liotyphlops*; the dentary bears teeth only at its anterior tip. In *Typhlops* this bone is toothless.

Typhlops is of special interest in possessing a relatively rigid mandibular symphysis, in contrast to the condition in snakes generally. The tips of the dentaries are not themselves fused, but the anterior ends of the two Meckel's cartilages are connected by a mass of cartilage (Fig. 65C).

In *Leptotyphlops* the maxilla is relatively immobile and lacks teeth. The dentigerous lower jaw has a well developed hinge between the dentary and the more posterior bones (McDowell and Bogert, 1954), and has no firm connection anteriorly with its fellow.

Rieppel (1979a) has described certain features characteristic of the braincase of scolecophidians, notably the more or less enclosed juxtastapedial recess and the Vidian canal, which unlike that of other snakes is for the most part represented only by a groove in the basisphenoid. He regards the almost unclosed condition of the canal as a primitive feature, also found in *Sphenodon*, and due to the absence of the lateral wings of the parasphenoid.

McDowell and Bogert (1954) suggested that the Typhlopidae are really lizards, but Underwood (1967) and Rieppel (1979a) consider them to be essentially snakes, albeit aberrant ones, and possibly having a monophyletic origin. Papers by Rieppel (1979c) and Groombridge (1979d), which have appeared too late for detailed consideration here, deal with aspects of the adult cranial anatomy of the Scolecophidia and their phylogenetic implications.

11. The Laterosphenoid of Snakes

Parker (1879) described a small bone on each side of the head in "ripe" embryos of *Natrix natrix*, situated between the basisphenoid, parietal downgrowth, and front of the prootic; he called it the alisphenoid. Gaupp (1902) described a similar bone in certain adult snakes, de Beer (1926) found it in embryos of *Natrix* and *Pseudechis*, and Brock (1929) described it in embryos of *Crotaphopeltis*, in which she referred to it as "Gaupp's bone". Peyer (1912) regarded it as merely an extension of the prootic in *Vipera*, but most workers have considered it to be an individual element, at least in the embryo. It has been variously called alisphenoid (Parker, 1879), epipterygoid (Brock, 1929; de Beer, 1937), and laterosphenoid (de Beer, 1926; Brock, 1941a; Kamal and Hammouda, 1965g; Rieppel, 1976a). The nature and homologies of this bone, here provisionally called the

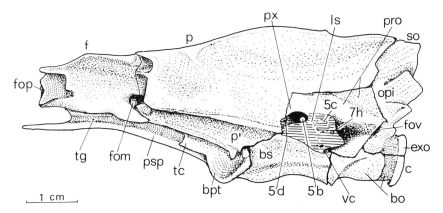

FIG. 67. *Eunectes murinus*, adult. Left lateral view of braincase. The main part of the laterosphenoid is shown in horizontal lines, and this bone also forms part of the small recessed area anterior to the foramen for the maxillary nerve. The foramina for the mandibular nerve and for the hyomandibular branch of the facial nerve lie deep to the bone and their positions are shown in broken lines; they emerge from the groove posterior to the bone. The small foramen anterodorsal to the Vidian canal probably transmits the palatine branch of the facial nerve, en route for the canal. The columella auris is missing.

bo, Basioccipital; bpt, basipterygoid process; bs, parabasisphenoid; c, occipital condyle; exo, exoccipital; f, frontal; fom, foramen orbitale magnum for ophthalmic nerve and nerves to eye muscles; fop, foramen for olfactory peduncle; fov, fenestra ovalis; ls, laterosphenoid; opi, opisthotic (fused with exoccipital); p, p′, parietal and parietal downgrowth; pro, prootic; psp, parasphenoid; px, prootic extension; so, supraoccipital; tc, trabecular crest (ossified posterior end of trabecula); tg, groove for trabecula; vc, Vidian canal (posterior opening); 5b, c, d, foramina for maxillary and mandibular nerves, and for nerve to M. constrictor dorsalis; 7h, foramen for hyomandibular branch of facial nerve.

laterosphenoid, have been much discussed and call for separate treatment in this chapter.

The laterosphenoid can be recognized in the skulls of many adult snakes, though it is rarely labelled in diagrams, being regarded as part of the prootic, with which it may be more or less fused. Its relations are shown in the boid *Eunectes* (Fig. 67). Here it is separated from the basisphenoid below by a distinct suture, but is partly fused with the prootic above. The large foramen in its anterior part transmits the maxillary nerve, while the foramen just posterior to it transmits the mandibular nerve; the main trigeminal ganglion lies medial to it and the ophthalmic nerve passes forwards on its deep surface. The mandibular foramen and the smaller foramen for the facial nerve behind it are almost covered by a spur arising from its posterior edge. This spur is demarcated by a faint groove (probably not a suture) from the rest of the bone. Similar conditions are seen in other snakes, though there are minor variations.

Embryological studies have shown that the laterosphenoid develops in the prootic notch in association with the edge of the basal plate, dorsal to fenestra X (when present) and anterior to the prefacial commissure which becomes incorporated into the prootic. In some snakes the laterosphenoid has two constituents, an initially cartilaginous one and another, much larger one which develops as an intramembranous ossification. The cartilage arises as a small spur or crest on the edge of the basal plate, with which it is continuous (Figs. 68D; 69A). This cartilage becomes surrounded and ultimately replaced by bone which extends anterodorsally into a sheet of membrane (the spheno-obturator membrane), which in the embryo connects the basal plate with the front of the prootic and the parietal downgrowth. The ossification makes contact anteriorly with an intramembranous downgrowth of the prootic (prootic extension, Kamal and Hammouda, 1965g) and may fuse with it. It also spreads posteriorly, between the maxillary and mandibular branches of the trigeminal nerve, enclosing the trigeminal ganglion.

The cartilaginous constituent of the laterosphenoid has been observed in *Natrix* and *Pseudechis* (de Beer, 1926), *Vipera* (Presley, personal communication), *Cerastes* (Kamal and Hammouda, 1965e, g) and probably in *Dasypeltis* (Pringle, 1954). It has not been identified, however, in *Crotaphopeltis* (Brock, 1929), *Lamprophis* and *Hemachatus* (Pringle, 1954), or *Psammophis* (Kamal and Hammouda, 1965g) or in *Sanzinia* (Genest-Villard, 1966). In these forms the laterosphenoid appears to be entirely a membrane bone (in the sense of Patterson, 1977; see p. 5), though its general position and relations are similar to those in snakes in which the laterosphenoid cartilage is initially developed.

Snakes possess no obviously recognizable epipterygoid or cavum epip-

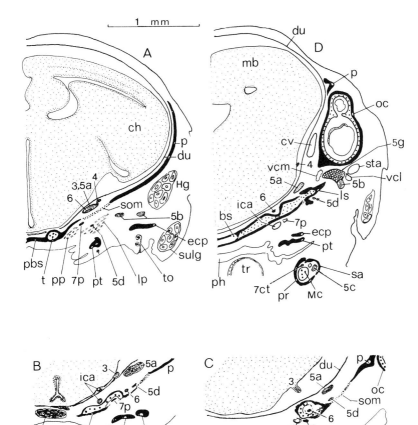

Fig. 68. *Natrix natrix*, late embryo, c. 10 mm head-length. Successive transverse sections through orbitotemporal region. Veins are shown in D only. (A) Level somewhat anterior to pituitary showing ophthalmic nerve and nerves to eye muscles passing forwards within cranial cavity. (B) Through pituitary showing palatine nerve passing through Vidian canal, which is not yet closed ventrally. It is uncertain whether the skull base (labelled basisphenoid) contains any parasphenoid component at this level. (C) Slightly posterior to B showing internal carotid artery passing through foramen in the ossifying skull base, and abducens nerve passing through its canal in the lateral part of the basisphenoid. (D) Posterior to pituitary, showing laterosphenoid and abducens nerve leaving its canal. The otic capsule, like the skull base, is undergoing perichondral ossification.

bs, Basisphenoid; ch, cerebral hemisphere; cv, cerebral vein; du, dura; ecp, ectopterygoid; Hg, Harderian gland; ica, internal carotid artery; lp, M. levator pterygoidei; ls, laterosphenoid with enclosed cartilage constituent; mb, mid-brain; Mc, Meckel's cartilage; oc, otic capsule; p, parietal; pbs, para-basisphenoid; ph, pharynx; pi, pituitary; pp, M. protractor pterygoidei; pr, prearticular; pt, pterygoid; sa, surangular; som, spheno-obturator membrane (later replaced by ossifying parietal downgrowth); sta, stapedial artery; sulg, superior labial gland; t, trabecula; to, tooth related to ectopterygoid; tr, trachea; vcl, vena capitis lateralis; vcm, vena capitis medialis; 3, oculomotor nerve; 4, trochlear nerve; 5a, ophthalmic nerve; 5b, maxillary nerve; 5c, mandibular nerve; 5d, branch of trigeminal nerve supplying constrictor dorsalis musculature (M. protractor pterygoidei, etc.); 5g, trigeminal ganglion; 6, abducens nerve; 7ct, chorda tympani nerve; 7p, palatine nerve.

tericum, but the position of the laterosphenoid does suggest an epipterygoid which has become incorporated into the cranium with the loss (in most forms) of the basipterygoid processes. Moreover, it has similar relationships to the branches of the trigeminal nerve (Figs. 68D; 70). One branch of the main head vein (labelled vena capitis lateralis in Fig. 68D) passes lateral to it, while another branch (labelled vena capitis medialis) is seen on its medial aspect, at least in some embryonic stages. It is possible that this medial vein corresponds with the vein (termed vena capitis in this article) which passes medial to the epipterygoid and through the cavum in lizards.

On the other hand, the laterosphenoid lies too far posteriorly to be a typical epipterygoid; in the adult skull, it lies well posterior to the basipterygoid process of boid snakes such as *Eunectes* (Fig. 67), in which this process is well developed. Presley (personal communication) has suggested that the cartilage bone constituent of the laterosphenoid is a derivative of some part of the pterygoquadrate complex posterior to the epipterygoid which has largely disappeared, but which still retains some chondrogenic activity. It would thus follow that the space between the laterosphenoid and the dura, which contains the ophthalmic nerve root and trigeminal ganglion, is broadly homologous with the saurian cavum epiptericum (see Fig. 70). This view is consistent with the observations of Brock (1929) and de Beer (1937) who refer in these works to the bone as an epipterygoid; however, both authors have expressed different views elsewhere (de Beer, 1926; Brock, 1941a), a fact which has led to some confusion in the literature.

The membrane bone constituent of the laterosphenoid—the only constituent in some forms—appears to be a structure peculiar to snakes and perhaps to amphisbaenians, in which it has not been studied embryologically. It is also present in the burrowing skink *Acontias*, in which it develops posterior to an epipterygoid of typical saurian character (Brock, 1941a).

It would seem that in snakes the skeleton of the original lateral wall of the cranial cavity (pila antotica, etc.) has disappeared, except for inconstant orbitosphenoid vestiges, so that this side-wall is represented only by the layer of dura mater around the brain (Figs. 68, 70). A new side-wall, external to the old one, has been formed by the parietal downgrowths, which give the cranium its rigid, box-like character and enclose the ophthalmic nerves and nerves to the eye muscles. The laterosphenoid, apparently a neomorph superimposed in some snakes on a vestigial pterygoquadrate derivative, helps to complete the new side-wall at a more posterior level, filling in the prootic notch and enclosing the trigeminal ganglion.

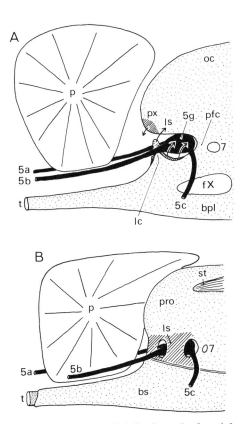

FIG. 69. Diagrams of orbitotemporal region of skull of a snake from left side, showing laterosphenoid. In (A) the cartilaginous component of the laterosphenoid (lc) is projecting dorsally from the basal plate, as in embryos of *Natrix* (Fig. 68B). Arrows indicate where intramembranous ossification will extend ventrally from the otic capsule (prootic extension), and dorsally from the laterosphenoid cartilage, and from the region of the basal plate behind it. The oculomotor, trochlear and abducens nerves pass deep to the parietal with 5a, but are not shown. (B) shows a later stage. The cartilaginous component of the laterosphenoid has been obliterated by intramembranous ossification which merges anteriorly with the prootic extension, and also extends posteriorly to separate the maxillary and mandibular nerves and to cover the trigeminal ganglion. The approximate extent of the membrane bone is shown in slanting lines; it becomes more or less fused with the prootic but remains separated from the basisphenoid by a suture. Further posterior extension of the membrane bone may cover the facial foramen.

bpl, Basal plate; bs, basisphenoid; fX, fenestra X; lc, laterosphenoid (cartilage component); ls, laterosphenoid; oc, otic capsule; p, parietal; pfc, prefacial commissure; pro, prootic; px, intramembranous extension of prootic; st, supratemporal; t, trabecula; 5a, 5b, 5c, 5g, ophthalmic, maxillary, and mandibular nerves and trigeminal ganglion; 7, foramen for facial nerve.

This view, originally proposed in its essentials by Gaupp (1902) and apparently accepted by de Beer (1937, p. 430) remains an attractive and reasonable hypothesis. De Beer (1926), however, has previously advanced a more complicated interpretation: that the original cranial side-wall does not consist only of the dura, but includes both the laterosphenoid and the space between it and the dura which contains the ophthalmic nerve root and the trigeminal ganglion. He regarded these structures as intramural (i.e., within the original side-wall) and not extra-cranial like the epiptery-

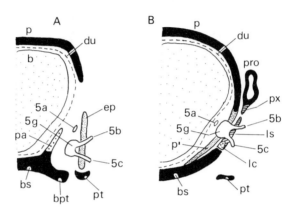

Fig. 70. Diagrams showing morphology of temporal region of skull in a lizard (A) and a snake (B). The dura is shown in broken lines, and the space occupied by the trigeminal ganglion and ophthalmic nerve in the snake is regarded as homologous with the cavum epiptericum of the lizard. Likewise, the epipterygoid of the lizard is regarded as broadly homologous with the cartilaginous component of the ophidian laterosphenoid. (A) Transverse section through cavum epiptericum of lizard with incipient parietal downgrowths. (B) Transverse section through skull of snake at a slightly more posterior level showing the prootic extension and the intramembranous constituent of the laterosphenoid in slanting lines. This section shows a partial reconstruction, seen from behind. The parasphenoid ossification, Vidian canal, and the nerves to the eye muscles are not shown.

b, Brain; bpt, basipterygoid process; bs, basisphenoid; du, dura mater; ep, epipterygoid; lc, laterosphenoid cartilage or cartilage bone constituent; ls, membranous laterosphenoid; p, p', parietal and parietal downgrowth; pa, pila antotica; pro, prootic; pt, pterygoid; px, prootic extension; 5a, 5b, 5c, 5g, ophthalmic, maxillary and mandibular nerves, and trigeminal ganglion.

goid and the cavum epiptericum in lizards. If one follows this view, it would seem that the cavum epiptericum has entirely disappeared in snakes. De Beer's (1926) remarks are reiterated by Kamal and Hammouda (1965g), who do not, however, cite the different views expressed in his book (1937). Further research is needed to clarify the problem.

The obvious parallel of the laterosphenoid of snakes is with the alisphenoid of eutherian mammals; this develops partly as a cartilage bone replacing a derivative of the pterygoquadrate (the ala temporalis), and partly as an intramembranous ossification (see de Beer, 1937 on *Homo*; Presley and Steel, 1977). It might well be appropriate to revive Parker's (1879) usage of alisphenoid for the bone in snakes, but more recent workers have generally reserved this term for the bone in mammals. In so far as terminology is concerned, we provisionally follow the recommendation of Rieppel (1976a) who points out that two alternative terms, laterosphenoid and pleurosphenoid, have been used for ossifications of the original cranial sidewall in the region of the pila antotica, such as occur in crocodilians. The ophidian laterosphenoid cannot be homologous with this bone since it lies lateral and not medial to the ophthalmic nerve, and hence cannot be an ossified pila antotica. It is therefore suggested that the term pleurosphenoid be reserved for the bone in crocodilians and other descendants of the archosaurian stock, leaving the name laterosphenoid available for the bone so designated here in snakes. We may also continue to apply the same name to the bone so designated in amphisbaenians, at least until the brain-case of these reptiles is more fully understood.

E. THE REPTILIAN CHONDROCRANIUM AND THE FEATURES OF THE LEPIDOSAURIA

1. General

Theoretically, the chondrocranium should provide as rich material for phenetic analysis as the adult skull—if only it were easier to display and interpret. Moreover, embryos of some of the most interesting forms such as amphisbaenians are extremely difficult to collect and even adult specimens suitable for serial sectioning may not be easy to come by. Nevertheless, the chondrocrania of a considerable number of reptilian (or rather lepidosaurian) genera are now tolerably well known. It is thus possible to make some kind of comparison of conditions in different families and also to evaluate the significance of certain chondrocranial characters. Initially, however, it is useful briefly to consider the common features of the chondrocranium in the class Reptilia and in its major subdivisions.

2. Common Features of the Reptilia

While mature reptilian chondrocrania can be distinguished fairly easily by their general pattern from those of other vertebrates, it is difficult to find many significant characters which are common to reptiles and absent among other classes of vertebrates. De Beer (1937) listed the following features as being characteristic of reptiles and it is difficult to think of any further additions today; indeed, we have had to omit or modify some of his particulars in the light of recent work.

1. One or more nasal conchae (except in Testudines and a very few Squamata).

2. An ectochoanal cartilage (except in Crocodilia).

3. Peculiar structure of orbitotemporal region, including interorbital septum, planum supraseptale, pila, etc. (except in Serpentes and possibly Amphisbaenia; see Fig. 70).

4. Basipterygoid processes with or without meniscus cartilages, at least at some stage in embryonic life (except in some Amphisbaenia, and most Serpentes).

5. An intercalary (processus paroticus) derived from the dorsal process of the columellar apparatus which becomes attached to the crista parotica or the quadrate (except, doubtfully, Testudines and Amphisbaenia).

6. Autodiastylic jaw suspension with pterygoquadrate apposed to but not fused with cartilaginous brain-case, and possessing ascending, pterygoid and otic processes.

Of these characters, number six is common to all amniote vertebrates, while number one is also seen in birds and mammals; character number two seems of dubious weight. It would seem that this type of simple, quantitative assessment of reptilian class characters is not very practical.

3. The Chondrocranium of Lepidosauria

Lists of the features common to the major groups of reptiles (subclasses, orders, suborders) are also unimpressive. The characters of the Testudines and Crocodilia are given in sections III F and G.

The features common to the Lepidosauria (Rhynchocephalia, Sauria, Amphisbaenia, Serpentes) are:

1. A single (perhaps two in *Sphenodon*) nasal concha (except in a very few lizards and snakes).

2. A tendency towards reduction of the floor of the nasal capsule.

3. Basipterygoid processes distinct in mature chondrocrania of *Sphenodon*, most if not all lizards, some amphisbaenians, and a few snakes.

4. Pleurocentrum of the proatlas fused with the odontoid process; a median, intercentral occipital condyle.*

Scrutiny of the general pattern of the chondrocranium, especially of the nasal and otic capsules and of the branchial arch derivatives, does suggest a substantial similarity among the chondrocrania of the various lepidosaurian groups, though this is difficult to express as a simple tabulation of isolated characters.

4. The Chondrocranium of *Sphenodon*

As El-Toubi and Kamal (1970) have pointed out, the range of differences

---

* The position of the notochord in relation to the condyle and basal plate is not as significant as de Beer (1937) believed, as Kamal and his associates (see Kamal, 1965h) have shown that in Squamata the notochord may be partly embedded in the condyle and basal plate.

between *Sphenodon* and lizards hardly exceeds that between the different saurian families. In particular, the tuatara shares with the more generalized lizards the overall pattern of the tropitrabic orbitotemporal chondrocranium. However, the lone rhynchocephalian stands apart from all or almost all the lizards in the following respects.

1. Two nasal conchae—assuming that these really are distinct (p. 120).

2. No concha for Jacobson's organ, which has a different morphology from that of Squamata.

3. The ascending process of the pterygoquadrate (epipterygoid) is continuous with the quadrate cartilage; the adult quadrate is not streptostylic.

4. The occipital tectum arises entirely from otic elements (as is probably the case in snakes); the occipital arches fail to meet in the midline.

5. Certain cartilaginous connections (interhyal and laterohyal) in the middle ear region persist throughout life (these connections are transient or ligamentous in lizards).

6. A horny egg-caruncle, as in Testudines and Crocodilia, instead of a true egg-tooth as in Squamata. This is a puzzling feature in a primitive lepidosaur; as other extant lepidosaurs have egg-teeth, one would expect to find teeth, rather than caruncles, in *Sphenodon*.

Almost all of these characters could be interpreted as primitive and their presence is not inconsistent with the view that *Sphenodon* is a surviving representative of the primitive diapsid stock, not very far removed from the common ancestors of Squamata.

5. The Chondrocranium of Squamata

In general plan, the nasal capsules of lizards, amphisbaenians and snakes show a distinct resemblance, though they also exhibit hallmarks of adaptive radiation, especially among the lizards. The structure of the highly elaborated organ of Jacobson and its associated cartilages is relatively constant, though the organ is reduced or virtually absent in a few arboreal lizards. The otic capsule has, perhaps, been more conservative than the nasal capsule, though it is possible that further work will display differences in detail, perhaps correlated with adaptive modification as, for example, to burrowing life. The columellar and the hyobranchial apparatus certainly show considerable variation within the order. The orbitotemporal region, however, probably shows more extensive variation than any other part of the chondrocranium in Squamata. The following features of the group as a whole may be listed, though it is uncertain whether some of them are found in the Amphisbaenia.

1. The trabeculae cranii are either separate from each other (Kamal, 1969b) or fused at their anterior tips (Rieppel, 1977c, 1979b) in the earliest embryonic stages examined. Later, their anterior parts fuse directly or

become connected by a trabecular plate which (at least in lizards) diminishes in width until it disappears.

2. The parachordals first appear as a single procartilaginous mass (basal plate) in which the notochord is embedded. The paired origin of the parachordals cannot be detected at any stage.

3. In early embryonic stages the long axis of the trabeculae is almost at right angles to that of the basal plate. Subsequently this angulation diminishes progressively until it is almost obliterated.

4. The nasal septum has no separate centre of chondrification but develops from some part of the fused trabeculae (trabecula communis) or from the trabecular plate, when present.

5. There is, with very few exceptions, a single nasal concha.

6. The floor of the nasal capsule is reduced but nearly always contains parts of the lamina transversalis anterior, in particular the cartilage of Jacobson's organ with its vomeronasal concha.

7. According to Kamal and his associates (see Kamal, 1965f) the basicranial fenestra is formed by degeneration of a part of the previously formed cartilage of the basal plate. Thus, the crista sellaris merely represents the remaining front edge of the plate. The large fenestra between the trabeculae laterally and the basal plate posteriorly, which is seen in early stages, represents the pituitary fenestra only, not the coalesced pituitary and basicranial fenestrae.

8. Two commissures, the prefacial and the anterior basicapsular (Kamal, 1965e), lie between the otic capsule and basal plate. The posterior end of the metotic fissure is formed by the junction of the otic capsule with the occipital arch.

9. In both lizards and snakes the IXth nerve may follow either an extracapsular or an intracapsular course.

10. The quadrate cartilage and Meckel's cartilage develop in contact with each other and initially arise from a continuous mass of blastema (Kamal, 1964b).

6. The Chondrocranium of Sauria

a. General Characters

The chondrocrania of lizards show the following characters in addition to those listed in section 4 above.

1. The nasal septum usually contains one or more fenestrae.

2. Usually there are paraseptal cartilages, that chondrify separately from the rest of the nasal capsule.

3. There are posterior maxillary processes, that chondrify independently.

4. The planum antorbitale usually chondrifies independently; it may or may not be attached to (or fused with) the nasal septum.

5. Sphenethmoid commissures, joining the roof of the nasal capsule with the planum supraseptale, are usually present. When these are present and complete it is possible to distinguish a fenestra olfactoria advehens, fenestra olfactoria evehens, and an orbitonasal fissure on each side.

6. The trabeculae fuse throughout the greater part of their length. In the orbital region the fused trabeculae (trabecula communis) form the ventral part of the interorbital septum, which usually contains one or more fenestrae. The fusion of the trabeculae at the level of the orbits constitutes the tropitrabic condition (Fig. 71A, B). This may be regarded as the primitive reptilian state (Rieppel, 1979b).

7. The dorsal region of the interorbital septum is formed by the fusion of the downturned medial edges of the anterior orbital cartilages, which spread out dorsolaterally to form the two wings of the planum supraseptale, supporting the olfactory peduncles of the forebrain (see Kamal, 1965g; Fig. 16D–F here). In a few specialized burrowers such as *Dibamus* this dorsal component of the interorbital septum is missing; indeed there is no septum as such and only a rodlike trabecula communis is present between the orbits.

8. In early embryos, fused posterior orbital cartilages, consisting of two lateral portions joined by a transverse commissure are characteristically seen. The commissure is perforated on each side by nerves III and IV and soon becomes connected with the front of the basal plate (Fig. 13). Parts of it then regress, leaving behind the scaffolding of pila and taeniae which is characteristic of the orbitotemporal region of the saurian chondrocranium.

9. The ascending process of the pterygoquadrate (palatoquadrate) is usually well developed (except in chameleons) and ossifies to form the epipterygoid.

10. Basipterygoid (basitrabecular) processes grow out from the posterior ends of the trabeculae. The basal process of the pterygoquadrate forms the basipterygoid meniscus, through which the basipterygoid process articulates with the epipterygoid and pterygoid bones.

11. In later embryos the metotic fissure is divided into an anterior recessus scalae tympani and a posterior jugular foramen by the approximation of the prominence for the ampulla of the posterior semicircular canal with the basal plate.

12. In the embryos of at least some lizards the anterior tips of the two Meckel's cartilages meet in the midline in a symphysis. It is uncertain whether the cartilaginous connection persists during postnatal life.

13. The columellar apparatus consists of a columella and an extra-

columella which arise from separate rudiments. The distal extremity of the extracolumella (insertion plate) typically bears four processes attached to the tympanic membrane and arranged in a cruciform fashion: the pars inferior, the pars superior, and the anterior and posterior accessory processes. There may also be a processus internus and a processus dorsalis, developed from the medial (columellar) rudiment near its junction with the (lateral) extracolumellar rudiment. These processes are associated with the extracolumella of the adult rather than with the columella, the only part of the apparatus which becomes ossified.

The greater part of the dorsal process usually (if not always) remains unchondrified but a nodule of cartilage, the processus paroticus or intercalary, appears in its dorsal end. In the majority of lizards this fuses with the crista parotica of the otic capsule.

14. The hyobranchial apparatus consists typically of a hyoid body with lingual process, hypohyals, ceratohyals, and parts of the 1st and 2nd branchial arches; there is much variation, especially of the 2nd branchial arch. Only the 1st ceratobranchials usually become ossified.

b. Major Variation within the Sauria

i. General

The chondrocranium shows many variations among lizards, as might be expected in a group which originated in the Permian and was already becoming diversified by the end of the Triassic (Carroll, 1977; Robinson, 1967). Many of these variations are of a minor character and some have already been noted in our account of the different families. Here only variations of a major character, or ones which have been emphasized in the literature will be discussed.

ii. Nasal capsule

The nasal capsule naturally becomes modified in association with the nasal sac. As previously mentioned, the reduplication of the side-wall of the capsule and the presence of a supposed paranasal element is a concomitant of bending of some part of the nasal sac which is almost universal among lizards. This bending is particularly marked in *Varanus*, and in agamids and many iguanids in which it is associated with the presence of a long lateral fissure. The nasal concha also shows much variation in size and morphology, being small in many Iguania and absent in *Anolis* and some chameleons.

The number and size of the fenestrae in the nasal capsule, and the completeness of its floor, vary considerably. On the whole, a rather complete capsule with fenestrae small or absent, a broad zona annularis and well developed paraseptal and ectochoanal cartilages, as seen in *Sphenodon*, may be regarded as the primitive condition. A large fenestra lateralis (as in lacertids) and loss of the zona annularis (as in *Varanus*), or of the paraseptal cartilage (as in some agamids) could perhaps be regarded as specialized or derived conditions. The reduction or loss of the sphenethmoid commissures, as in many geckos and chameleons, also seems a specialization. The relationship of the planum antorbitale to the nasal septum is another variable. Kamal (see Kamal and Abdeen, 1972) regards complete separation of the planum from the septum (as in geckos and some skinks) as primitive, but the phylogenetic significance of this character is questionable.

iii. Orbitotemporal region

Sphenodon and lacertid lizards appear to have the fullest complement of pilae and taeniae in the orbitotemporal region, a deep interorbital septum and a broad planum supraseptale. This condition (i.e., retention of the greatest amount of cartilage) may perhaps be regarded as primitive, and is, incidentally, closest to that in Testudines (p. 210). Reduction of cartilage has occurred in many saurian groups, doubtless for different reasons, and is evident on the one hand in the very large-eyed chameleons (in which the planum supraseptale is reduced), and on the other in small-eyed burrowers, such as *Acontias* and *Anniella*, in which the planum is very narrow and the interorbital septum very low (Figs. 36; 39; 71B). Reduction or loss of the ascending process of the pterygoquadrate (epipterygoid) is another striking modification of chameleons, and (at the opposite extreme of divergent specialization) perhaps also of a few worm-like burrowers, such as *Dibamus* and all but one amphisbaenian.

iv. Otic and occipital regions

The course of the glossopharyngeal (IX) nerve in relation to the otic capsule is variable (Fig. 53A–E). The purely extracapsular course seen in lacertids and geckos is probably the commonest. Here the nerve leaves the cranial cavity through the medial opening of the recessus scalae tympani, passes through the recessus and leaves the skull through the lateral aperture of the recessus. In most skinks the IXth nerve takes an intracapsular course; it enters the otic capsule through an internal glossopharyngeal foramen and then leaves it through the foramen perilymphaticum, traverses the lateral part of the recessus and finally issues through its lateral aperture. Slight variations of these principal types of IXth nerve course are also found among other Squamata (see Kamal, 1969e; Starck, 1979).

In most lizards, including lacertids, geckos and agamids, the occipital tectum is derived from both otic capsules and occipital arches and is, therefore, a tectum synoticum plus posterius.

Geckos appear to be the only lizards in which the tectum has no anterior (ascending) process.

The definitive number of hypoglossal foramina varies between two and four pairs in different genera; it may also change during the development of any species, as separate XIIth nerve roots become enclosed in separate foramina in the cartilage.

v. Columellar and hyobranchial apparatus

The stapes is perforated in most geckos and a very few other lepidosaurs. This feature, common among early tetrapods, can perhaps be regarded as primitive. The bone tends to be curiously massive in specialized burrowers, such as *Anniella*.

The various processes of the extracolumella vary considerably, but without obvious pattern. The internal process is absent in geckos, and in these and other forms the ligamentous base of the dorsal process may be absent. Some geckos have a ligamentous or transiently cartilaginious laterohyal connection between the extra-columella and the crista parotica, and also a connection between the latter and the ceratohyal (Kamal, 1961b). These connections, in a more permanent form, are found in the adult *Sphenodon* and may be regarded as primitive.

The hyobranchial apparatus varies from the almost complete form containing more than one derivative of the hyoid and first and second branchial arches, as in the eublepharine gecko *Coleonyx* (Kluge, 1967), to a condition similar to that in *Anniella* which has only the hyoid body and lingual process, and short first ceratobranchials (Langebartel, 1968). Again, certain geckos appear to show a primitive condition of the hyobranchial apparatus, but it would be unwise to conclude that the Gekkonidae emerge from an overall assessment of chondrocranial characters as a manifestly primitive group of lizards.

7. Kinesis in Sauria

A critical discussion of kinesis is beyond the scope of this chapter, but certain comments seem relevant. Significant recent observations on the subject have been made by Frazzetta (1962), Boltt and Ewer (1964), Iordansky (1970), and in particular by Rieppel (1978a, b) who discusses the evolution and ontogeny of kinesis in lizards. Rieppel (1978a, b) follows earlier workers in emphasizing that the majority of lizards are amphikinetic, i.e., they possess both mesokinesis and metakinesis, in combination with streptostyly (mobility of the quadrate). Neither of these types of kinesis is directly homologous with the kinesis thought to have occurred in extinct crossopterygian fishes, except in so far as the latter possessed a joint between the upper jaw and the skull comparable with the basipterygoid articulation.

Mesokinesis implies bending of the skull across the plane of the fronto-parietal suture, and also across certain articulations in the upper jaw and palate. Unlike metakinesis, it involves interaction between dermal elements only. It appears to be a unique feature of lizards.

Metakinesis implies a more posterior plane of flexion in the cranial roof, between the back of the parietal and the supraoccipital. The persistently cartilaginous, anterior process of the tectum can apparently slide backwards and forwards in the notch or recess in the posterior edge of the parietal (Fig. 5A, D), and perhaps also bend across its length. Other joints involved in metakinesis are (2) the basipterygoid joint, (3) the joint between epipterygoid and pterygoid, (4) the joint between the paroccipital process and the supratemporal and squamosal via the intercalary, (5) the joints between the cephalic condyle of the quadrate and the supratemporal and squamosal, and (6) the joint between the posterior end of the pterygoid and the lower part of the shaft of the quadrate. All of these, except the tecto-parietal joint in the skull roof, are synovial in character and all contain synovial cavities related to cartilaginous surfaces which originate from the visceral arch skeleton, and hence, probably, from cells of the neural crest, at least by inference from work on the chick embryo (Le Lièvre, 1978). Thus, the basipterygoid meniscus, the cartilage lining the pterygoid concavity at the epipterygoid articulation (Fig. 6B) and the persistent cartilage on the articular regions of the quadrate are derived from the mandibular arch, while the intercalary is a hyoid arch derivative. The histology of these joints in lizards is described by Rieppel (1978a).

The mechanical significance of chondrocranial structure in kinesis is hard to assess. However, it seems likely that raising of the snout, during either mesokinetic or metakinetic movement, will produce some bending of the orbitotemporal pila, and also of the interorbital septum. Such bending might occur through the low, posterior part of the septum, anterior to the pila metoptica and beneath the optic nerve, or more anteriorly between the big septal fenestra and the planum supraseptale. Indeed this could be the functional explanation for the fenestration of the orbital cartilage system and the septum, rather than the effects of eye muscles, as Säve-Söderbergh envisaged (p. 21). The role of the slender parasphenoid rostrum attached to the back part of the inferior edge of the interorbital septum is problematical; it may be flexible enough to bend with the septum, or flexion may only occur anterior to it.

8. The chondrocranium of Amphisbaenia

In the present state of knowledge, only a few general comments on the chondrocrania of Amphisbaenia can be made. The following features are apparent.

1. The cartilage in the nasal region is reduced, especially in the capsular roof.

2. The trabeculae are fused around the level of the tiny orbits, so that the condition may vary between the strictly tropitrabic and platytrabic (p. 182), as in Scolecophidia. In *Trogonophis* (Fig. 48B) the trabecula communis is nearly oval in cross-section at mid-orbital level, but in some other forms it is more compressed and may be regarded as a very low interorbital septum (Fig. 71).

3. The orbitotemporal region of the chondrocranium (planum supra-septale, pila metoptica, antotica, etc.) apparently shows precocious and massive ossification to form the orbitosphenoid; this bone is well ossified, even in young specimens.

4. The basipterygoid processes and probably the meniscus cartilages are absent in many genera. The epipterygoid is only known in *Trogonophis*.

5. The columella is massive and the extracolumella large, specialized and perhaps of a different derivation from that in lizards. Variations of this and of the hyobranchial apparatus are described in section IIIC.

9. The Chondrocranium and its Variations in Serpentes

The chondrocrania of snakes vary less than those of lizards, at least if the Scolecophidia are excluded from consideration. The characteristics of snakes tabulated below are additional to those given on page 193 as common to the Squamata in general, and for the most part indicate features in which the snakes differ from the lizards. This list is mainly based on the articles by Kamal (1968–69) and El-Toubi *et al.* (1965b and 1968). Many of these features may occur in Scolecophidia, but the chondrocrania of these "blind snakes" are too little understood to allow generalization, despite the various studies which have been made of them. Therefore, the particulars cited do not necessarily apply to Scolecophidia, but certain known peculiarities of the Serpentes in general are mentioned.

1. The nasal cupolae generally project well anterior to the nasal septum, and are separated dorsally by a deep groove that lodges the ascending process of the premaxilla and the descending processes of the nasals.

2. There is no foramen apicale. The ethmoidal ramus of Va leaves the front of the capsule by passing beneath the cupola.

3. The nasal septum is unfenestrated. As in a few lizards, it may continue anteriorly between the cupolae as a rostral process.

4. In early embryonic stages the ventral edge of the nasal septum is bent downwards at nearly a right angle to the trabecula communis behind it (Fig. 50). This flexure is quite independent of the flexure further back between the trabeculae and parachordals, which is characteristic of Squamata in general. Later, both flexures straighten out.

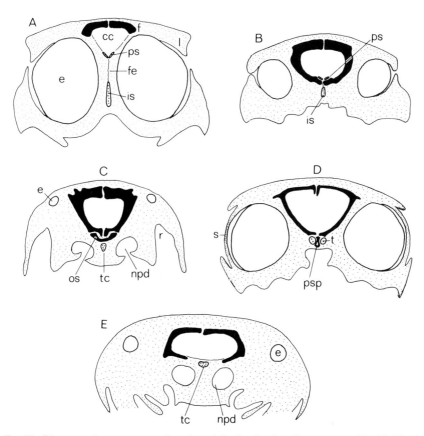

Fig. 71. Diagrammatic transverse sections through heads of various Squamata at mid-orbital level, showing relations of interorbital septum, planum supraseptale, trabeculae, etc. The bones around the cranial cavity are the frontals in each case. (A) Typical lizard, illustrating tropitrabic condition (see also Figs. 3F and 6A). Conditions are basically similar in *Sphenodon*, Testudines, and Crocodilia. (B) Small-eyed, burrowing lizard. Based on *Anniella* (see also Fig. 39D). (C) Amphisbaenian. Based on *Amphisbaena*. The bony orbitosphenoid may correspond with the planum supraseptale, the trabecula communis corresponds with the inferior part of the interorbital septum. See also Fig. 48B of *Trogonophis*, however, the bones around the cranial cavity are differently arranged. (D) Typical snake, illustrating platytrabic condition (see also Fig. 52C). (E) Scolecophidian. Based on an unidentified species of *Typhlops* in which the telescoping of the front of the head is not so marked as in *T. jamaicensis* (Fig. 65E). The trabeculae will diverge from the trabecula communis at a level slightly posterior to that shown above.

cc, Cranial cavity; e, eye; f, frontal; fe, membrane-filled fenestra in interorbital septum; is, interorbital septum; l, eyelid; npd, nasopharyngeal duct of nasal sac; os, orbitosphenoid; ps, planum supraseptale; psp, parasphenoid rostrum; r, recess for lower jaw; s, spectacle; t, trabecula; tc, trabecula communis.

5. The inferior alar process is characteristically long.

6. There is no fenestra superior, except perhaps in the Uropeltidae in which the nasal capsule is much reduced.

7. Flexure of the nasal sac may or may not be sufficiently marked to produce a well developed lateral recess. Where it is marked, as in *Vipera*, *Cerastes* and *Naja*, the side-wall of the capsule is reduplicated and the cartilage surrounding the lateral recess is termed by some authors the paranasal cartilage (Kamal, 1968; El-Toubi *et al.*, 1970).

8. Except in certain Henophidia, the floor of the nasal capsule of snakes is more reduced than is that of lizards; the ophidian zona annularis, if present, is narrow and disposed in an oblique plane. In some snakes the anterior part of the lamina transversalis anterior is absent or discontinuous, and the lamina is represented only by the cartilage of Jacobson's organ with its vomeronasal concha and projecting ectochoanal cartilage. This reduction is most noticeable in elapid and viperid snakes (Fig. 60) and can be regarded as an advanced character of these groups (Kamal, 1969d; El-Toubi *et al.*, 1965a).

9. There is no paraseptal cartilage except for a doubtful vestige in some Henophidia, but the hypochoanal cartilage lies lateral to the ectochoanal cartilage and usually joins it posteriorly.

10. There are no anterior or posterior maxillary processes, though the latter are claimed to occur in *Eryx* and *Typhlops* (and perhaps other Henophidia), on somewhat questionable grounds.

11. The planum antorbitale chondrifies in continuity with the parieto-tectal cartilage, rather than from a separate centre as in lizards.

12. Snakes lack sphenethmoid commissures. A single fenestra olfactoria transmits the olfactory, vomeronasal, and ethmoidal nerves on each side. No fenestrae olfactoriae advehens or evehens or orbitonasal fissure can be recognized.

13. In Scolecophidia, and perhaps also to some extent in the uropeltid *Rhinophis*, there has been a kind of "telescoping" of the orbital and nasal regions.

14. The mature chondrocranium is platytrabic. Only the anterior (nasal) parts of the trabeculae fuse; behind the nose they remain unfused and run back through the long orbitotemporal region as a pair of parallel rods. This statement requires slight qualification, as the Scolecophidia, which have telescoped the nasal and orbital regions, show the rodlike, unpaired trabecula communis at the level of the orbits, as in a very few burrowing lizards, and some amphisbaenians. However, platytraby remains a general distinction between snakes and lizards (Fig. 71).

Although all reptiles pass through a platytrabic condition during early ontogeny, the persistence of platytraby in snakes cannot be regarded as a primitive feature, but is perhaps a manifestation of neoteny or paedo-morphosis (see Rieppel, 1979b).

15. Generally speaking, the planum supraseptale and orbitotemporal scaffolding, so noticeable in other reptiles, have disappeared entirely in snakes. There may, however, be vestigial orbital cartilages. The sporadic and perhaps transitory appearance of these cartilages in representatives of the Colubridae (*sensu* Parker, 1977) and Viperidae, as well as the Boidae, suggest that, in contrast to the views of Kamal (1969d) and El-Toubi *et al.* (1965a), these cartilages do not represent a primitive feature.

16. In contrast to all (or almost all) lizards, snakes have neither scleral cartilages nor scleral ossicles.

17. Most snakes lack basipterygoid processes, both in the embryonic chondrocranium and the adult skull. However, these processes are well developed in *Eryx* and many other Boidae (probably as a primitive feature) and also occur, though they are smaller, in the Aniliidae and perhaps in a few caenophidians.

18. Snakes lack the epipterygoid and the basipterygoid meniscus car-tilage (see also item 26). However, many snakes possess, at least in early life, a bone here called the laterosphenoid (III–D–11). Much of this bone is developed in membrane, but it may have a cartilaginous basal core in the embryo (Fig. 68). The latter can perhaps be interpreted as a derivative of the palatoquadrate complex posterior to the epipterygoid. Most lizards lack such a bone, though it has been reported in the burrowing skink *Acontias* (Brock, 1941a).

19. The VIth nerve may tunnel through the basal plate in early embryonic stages, but in the mature condition the tunnel is often converted into a mere depression. The relationship of this in the adult skull requires investigation, but in some snakes at least, the tunnel penetrates the basisphenoid.

20. In most snakes a transient fenestra called fenestra X develops in the embryo as a result of cartilage regression in each side of the front of the basal plate.

21. In lizards the cochlear part of the otic capsule extends antero-ventrally and "encroaches on" the basal plate so that it forms the inferior boundary of the facial foramen. In snakes such encroachment does not occur to the same extent, and the inferior border of the foramen is formed by the basal plate rather than by the otic capsule. A few lizards such as *Acanthodactylus* and *Agama* approach the ophidian condition in this respect (Kamal, 1968–69). This feature is unlikely to have phylogenetic signi-ficance.

22. In lizards a septum divides the main cavity of the otic capsule (cavum vestibulare) into two parts, the cavum vestibulare anterius and cavum

posterius. However, snakes lack the septum and have a single spacious chamber (Kamal, 1968–69).

23. Snakes lack a crista parotica of the otic capsule.

24. The metotic fissure is divided into a recessus scalae tympani and jugular foramen by a cartilaginous strut developed from the medial wall of the otic capsule. Lizards effect division by apposition of the ampullary prominence to the basal plate. In many snakes the metotic fissure is continuous posterodorsally with a narrow occipitocapsular fissure which is eventually closed by the junction of the occipital arch to the tectum synoticum (Fig. 51A). This fissure is absent in lizards.

25. The occipital tectum has no ascending process.

26. The pterygoquadrate process of snake embryos is represented only by the quadrate cartilage. There is no ascending, pterygoid or basal process (see item 18).

27. During embryonic life the quadrate cartilage undergoes a remarkable process of rotation through about 90° (Fig. 54). In early stages it is directed forwards and slightly downwards, its long axis being in much the same line as Meckel's cartilage. Subsequently, the lower end of the quadrate swings posteriorly bringing the jaw-joint with it; the quadrate finally becomes almost perpendicular to Meckel's cartilage. This rotation is facilitated by the freedom of the quadrate from the otic capsule owing to the absence of the crista parotica; rotation is much less noticeable in lizards (Kamal, 1966d, 1968–69).

28. The anterior tips of Meckel's cartilages do not form a symphysis, except in the Typhlopidae.

29. The columella auris chondrifies and ossifies from a single centre which forms both footplate and shaft. There is no clearly recognizable extracolumella, except in so far as this is represented by the intercalary (detached dorsal process) which fuses with the quadrate, and not with the crista parotica as in lizards. At no stage is there a cartilaginous connection between the columella and the hyoid. The shaft of the columella initially points almost vertically downwards; later it rotates backwards and becomes attached to the quadrate via the chondrifying intercalary. This rotation is associated with the rotation of the quadrate.

30. The hyobranchial skeleton is reduced and possesses only one pair of horns. In Caenophidia these are regarded as second ceratobranchials by Langebartel (1968), but many workers have believed them to be ceratohyals. Variations of the apparatus are found in other groups of snakes, etc.

F. TESTUDINES

1. General

It is remarkable that so few studies of the developing skull in Testudines and Crocodilia should have been made in recent years, especially since so many species of Squamata have been investigated. As commercial turtle and crocodile farming is being attempted in some parts of the world (see Bustard, 1972; Pooley, 1973) embryos of some species should be readily available. Shaner's (1926) study of *Chrysemys* seems to contain the only account of the early development of the entire testudinian chondrocranium; his terminology has been ably modernized by de Beer (1937), but unfortunately the illustrations are inadequate. Kunkel's (1912a) study of *Emys* remains the definitive account of the mature chondrocranium, at least in English; the works of Nick (1912) and Fuchs (1915) on marine turtles are inordinately long and difficult to follow. More recent authors, such as de Beer (1926), have dealt only with particular regions of the skull. Gaffney (1972, 1975, 1976, 1977, 1979) has provided valuable data on the anatomy and terminology of the adult testudinian skull, while Albrecht (1976) has dealt with the morphology of the cranial arterial canals; Schumacher (1973) has reviewed the hyobranchial apparatus. The eye, nose and ear are described by Underwood, Parsons, and Baird respectively (all 1970), and by Wever (1978; ear).

2. Emydidae and Testudinidae (suborder Cryptodira)

a. Previous Literature

Chrysemys picta, Smith, 1914 (ear); Shaner, 1926; de Beer, 1937 (development of chondrocranium and embryonic osteocranium). *Emys orbicularis*, Noack, 1907 (ear); Kunkel, 1912a; 1912b (ear); de Beer, 1937. *Testudo graeca*, Seydel, 1896 (nasal capsule); Bender, 1911 (ear).

b. Chondrocranium of Chrysemys (*earlier stages*)

The earliest stages examined by Shaner (1926) were around 6–7 mm (? total; no details given) length. The trabeculae are separate throughout most of their length (Fig. 72A, B), but are posteriorly connected behind by a mesenchymatous bridge (acrochordal) that forms the crista sellaris; it is raised up on either side to form a pila antotica. This bridge appears to correspond with the fused posterior orbital cartilages of early lizard embryos (p. 40). Also present at this stage are the procartilaginous otic capsules, two pairs of preoccipital arches and the paired occipital arches, rudiments of Meckel's cartilage, the quadrate, columellar apparatus, ceratohyal and first ceratobranchial.

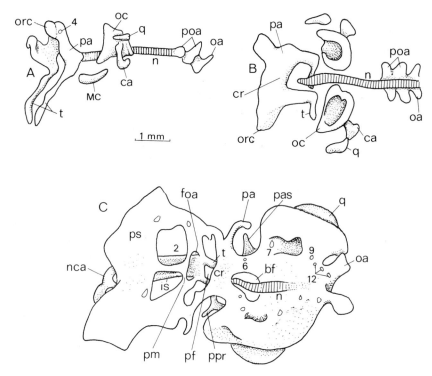

FIG. 72. *Chrysemys picta*. (A) 6 mm stage, lateral view of chondrocranium with hyobranchial skeleton omitted. (B) 6 mm stage, dorsal view. (C) 8 mm stage, oblique dorsal view. After Shaner (1926).

bf, Basicranial fenestra; ca, columella auris; cr, crista sellaris; foa, foramen for ophthalmic artery; is, interorbital septum; Mc, Meckel's cartilage; n, notochord; nca, nasal capsule; oa, occipital arch; oc, otic capsule; orc, posterior orbital cartilage; pa, pila antotica; pas, ascending process of pterygoquadrate (epipterygoid); pf, pituitary fenestra; pm, pila metoptica; poa, preoccipital arch; ppr, pterygoid process of pterygoquadrate; ps, planum supraseptale; q, quadrate; t, trabecula; 2, optic fenestra; 4, 6, 7, 9, 12, foramina for trochlear, abducens, facial, glossopharyngeal and hypoglossal nerves.

The chondrocranium has undergone important changes by the 8 mm stage (Fig. 72C). The trabeculae have fused in front to form the nasal septum and much of the nasal capsule has developed. The large, flattened planum supraseptale has arisen on each side beneath the forebrain. The medial edges of each half of the planum are turned downwards and fuse in the midline, forming the dorsal part of the interorbital septum. Beneath this, the trabeculae have fused beneath the orbits, forming the ventral part of the interorbital septum, so that, as in *Sphenodon* and lizards, the chondrocranium passes from a platytrabic to a tropitrabic condition. Shaner (1926: 346) hints at the presence of a third rudiment between the trabeculae which contributes to the septum. This is most probably the intertrabecula, an element characteristic of turtles and later described in *Chrysemys* and other forms by Pehrson (1945). However, it was not clearly recognized at the time when Shaner or even de Beer (1937) were writing (see p. 220 and Fig. 78). Posteriorly the trabeculae diverge to enclose the pituitary fenestra.

As in Squamata, the parachordals are not seen as separate structures; they seem to arise as a common basal plate in which the notochord, at first lying dorsally, becomes embedded. A small basicranial fenestra appears behind the dorsum sellae; this is thought to represent a persistently unchondrified area, rather than a site of cartilage regression as Kamal (1965f) regarded this vacuity in Squamata. The basal plate becomes connected laterally with the otic capsule and posteriorly with the occipital arches, which seem to incorporate the preoccipital arches (Fig. 72C) to form a single large process on each side, enclosing the metotic fissure. The VIIth nerve, which runs partly through the otic capsule, leaves the skull through the facial foramen, bounded anteriorly by the prefacial commissure. The IXth nerve also becomes enclosed within the capsule as it chondrifies. A region (the "stapes inferior" of Kunkel, 1912b) of the wall of the capsule posteroventral to the fenestra ovalis appears to chondrify independently, later fusing with the rest. This region may perhaps be derived from the basal plate and in some ways resembles the operculum of urodele amphibians.

The pterygoquadrate is represented by the quadrate cartilage which develops in contact with the otic capsule, the pterygoid process and the ascending process. Meckel's cartilage fuses anteriorly with its fellow in the midline.

The columellar apparatus—columella, extracolumella, and interhyal process—are laid down as a single piece of procartilage. The columella and extracolumella chondrify as separate rudiments; the interhyal has a transient connection with Meckel's cartilage, but never chondrifies.

c. *Fully Formed Chondrocranium of* Emys orbicularis

i. General

The chondrocranium of *Emys* has been described by Kunkel (1912a) from an embryo of 11 mm carapace-length, with reference to some earlier stages. His account has been summarized by de Beer (1937) and may be used to exemplify the general morphology of the chondrocranium in Testudines (Figs. 73; 74). Conditions are also illustrated by sections of *Chrysemys* (Fig. 75D, E) and of *Chelydra* (Fig. 76).

ii. Nasal capsule

The nasal capsule shows many differences from the lepidosaurian condition, being both more complete (especially ventrally) and simpler in construction. Even in relatively mature chondrocranial stages, it is bent at a considerable angle to the rest of the basicranial axis. The snout is fairly short so that the posterior part of the capsule lies posterior to the orbits.

The roof is formed by a complete parietotectal cartilage which is fused with the dorsal edge of the nasal septum over some of its extent. There is no fenestra superior, but a slit in the midline (Kunkel's fenestra septi nasi), towards the front of the capsule, separates each parietotectal cartilage from the septum. Further posteriorly there is an oval fenestra olfactoria on each side bounded medially by the septum and laterally by the sphenethmoid commissure, which reaches the front of the planum supraseptale. The morphology of the fenestrae olfactoriae advehens and evehens and of the orbitonasal fissure seems essentially similar to those of lacertid lizards. The lateral branch of the ethmoidal nerve leaves the capsule through a foramen epiphaniale, but the course of the medial branch is unclear, as no foramen apicale seems to have been described. The roof of the capsule is continued posteroventrally into the planum antorbitale, which is not attached to the nasal septum.

The floor and side-walls of the capsule are also remarkably complete, as in Testudines generally, and much of the nasal sac is surrounded by cartilage. Each side shows a large anteroventrally facing fenestra narina; alar processes are lacking. Posterior to the fenestra narina the floor is made up by the lamina transversalis anterior, which forms a bridge between the parietotectal cartilage and the ventral edge of the nasal septum, so that there is a broad zona annularis. Study of stages earlier than that figured shows that the posterior part of the capsular floor is formed by fusion of the paraseptal cartilages medially with the nasal septum and laterally with the ectochoanal cartilages. Like the paraseptals, these initially arise as short projections from the posterior edge of the lamina transversalis anterior (Fig. 74B). A slit between the paraseptal and the septum remains on each side as the foramen prepalatinum. These changes appear in the fully formed chondrocranium (Figs. 73B, 75B) so that the foramen prepalatinum is isolated in the floor of the nasal capsule on each side. This foramen presumably corresponds in position with the similarly named foramen in the bony skull which lies between the vomer and premaxilla on either side. It transmits the anterior nasal vessels from the palate to the interior of the nose (Albrecht, 1976). There seems to be no evidence that this foramen has any developmental similarity to the foramen for the duct of Jacobson's organ in Squamata or the incisive foramen of mammals, which lie in a similar position. The choanal or internal narial apertures face posteriorly rather than ventrally, and are situated posterolateral to the paraseptal cartilages in the mature chondrocranium (Fig. 73B).

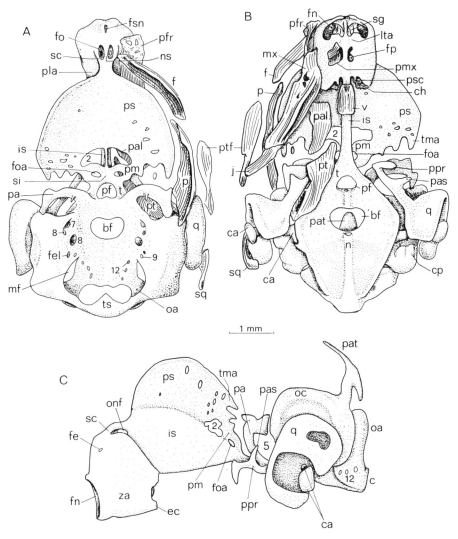

Fig. 73. *Emys orbicularis*, embryo, 11 mm carapace-length. (A) Dorsal, (B) ventral and (C) lateral views of chondrocranium, with some dermal bones in (A) and (B). After Kunkel (1912a).

bf, Basicranial fenestra; c, occipital condyle; ca, columella auris; ch, choanal opening; cp, crista parotica; ec, ectochoanal cartilage; f, frontal; fe, foramen epiphaniale; fel, foramen for endolymphatic duct; fn, fenestra narina; fo, fenestra olfactoria; foa, foramen for ophthalmic artery; fp, foramen pre-palatinum; fsn, fenestra septi nasi; is, interorbital septum; j, jugal; lta, lamina transversalis anterior; mf, metotic fissure; mx, maxilla; n, notochordal swelling; ns, nasal septum; oa, occipital arch; oc, otic capsule; onf, orbitonasal fissure; p, parietal; pa, pila antotica; pal, palatine; pas, anterior process of pterygoquadrate; pat, anterior process of tectum synoticum; pf, pituitary fenestra; pfr, prefrontal; pla, planum antorbitale; pm, pila metoptica; pmx, premaxilla; ppr, pterygoid process of pterygo-quadrate; ps, planum supraseptale; psc, paraseptal cartilage; pt, pterygoid; ptf, postfrontal; q, quadrate; sc, sphenethmoid commissure; sg, pila supraglandularis; si, subiculum infundibuli; sq, squamosal; t, trabecula; tma, taenia marginalis (incomplete); ts, tectum synoticum; v, vomer; za, zona annularis; 2, optic fenestra; 5, prootic fenestra; 7, foramen for facial nerve; 8, anterior and posterior foramina for auditory nerve; 9, foramen for glossopharyngeal nerve; 12, foramina for hypoglossal nerves.

The interior of the nasal capsule is simpler than that of lepidosaurs, as there is no well developed nasal concha or capsule of Jacobson's organ, the latter being represented by parts of the ventral region of the nasal sac (Parsons, 1970). However, a longitudinal ridge, of variable prominence according to species, and covered by a fold of mucosa, runs along the lateral wall of the capsule (parietotectal cartilage); this ridge resembles a kind of rudimentary concha and may be called the conchal ridge (Fig. 75C).

A longitudinal bar of cartilage, the pila supraglandularis, develops along each side of the nasal septum and fuses with it medially to form a shelf over the medial nasal gland (Fig. 75A). This gland occurs in many Testudines and lies between the nasal cavity and the septum; its duct enters the medial wall of the front of the cavum of the nasal sac. The lateral nasal gland, the only gland present in the great majority of Squamata, seems to occur in all Testudines. It lies outside the dorsolateral aspect of the front of the nasal capsule; the duct of the lateral nasal gland enters the nasal sac in the region where the vestibule joins the cavum (see Seydel, 1896; Parsons, 1970). The relationships of the ducts of these glands to the nasal capsule in Testudines requires further study.

iii. Orbitotemporal region

In *Emys* and other Testudines the orbitotemporal region consists of a wide planum supraseptale surmounting a high interorbital septum which (at least in *Emys*) is unfenestrated (Figs. 73A; 75D).

In *Emys* (Fig. 73) the wings of the planum contain a number of small perforations. Posteriorly, between it and the upper border of the interorbital septum on each side, is the large optic foramen. This is enclosed behind by the pila metoptica; each pila joins the trabecula below, and also joins its opposite fellow in the midline to form a subiculum infundibuli. The subiculum is connected with the posterior edge of the interorbital septum and is perforated by the ophthalmic artery on each side.

In the mature chondrocranium of *Emys*, the taenia marginalis is represented only by a short projection from the back of the planum supraseptale, and the pila antotica is not connected with the planum. Thus there is a gap between the anterior and posterior orbital cartilage systems which corresponds with the fenestra metoptica and transmits the IIIrd and IVth nerves. The Vth nerve (which has a combined ophthalmo-maxillo-mandibular ganglion; Soliman, 1964) leaves the chondrocranium between the otic capsule and the pila antotica. The VIth nerve tunnels through the base of the latter (Fig. 77).

A short ridge is developed from the posterior end of each trabecula, and a small, initially separate cartilage may become attached to it. This ridge represents the basipterygoid process of lizards; in Testudines

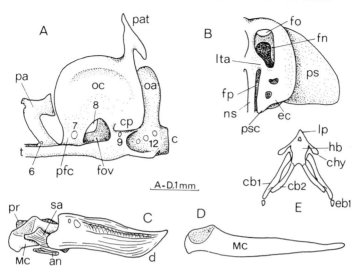

Fig. 74. *Emys orbicularis*. Embryo, 11 mm carapace-length. (A) Left lateral view of oto–occipital region of chondrocranium with quadrate removed. (B) Embryo, 7 mm carapace-length. Ventral view of nasal capsule at stage before paraseptal cartilage fuses with nasal septum to enclose foramen prepalatinum posteriorly. (C) and (D) embryo, 11 mm carapace-length. Right lateral views of lower jaw (C) with dermal bones. A–D after Kunkel (1912a). (E) Hyobranchial skeleton of late embryo. After Fuchs (1907).

an, Angular; c, occipital condyle; cb1, cb2, ceratobranchials 1 and 2; chy, ceratohyal; cp, crista parotica (? subcapsular process); d, dentary; eb l, epibranchial l; ec, region of ectochoanal cartilage (fused with paraseptal); fn, fenestra narina; fo, fenestra olfactoria; fov, fenestra ovalis; fp, foramen prepalatinum; hb, hyoid body; lp, lingual process; lta, lamina transversalis anterior; Mc, Meckel's cartilage; ns, nasal septum; oa, occipital arch; oc, otic capsule; pa, pila antotica; pat, anterior process of tectum; pfc, prefacial commissure; pr, prearticular; ps, planum supraseptale; psc, paraseptal cartilage; sa, surangular; t, trabecula; 6, 7, foramina for abducens and facial nerves; 8, posterior foramen for auditory nerve; 9, 12, glossopharyngeal and hypoglossal foramina.

it does not articulate with the ascending process of the pterygoquadrate (epipterygoid) but is in contact laterally with the pterygoid bone. The separate cartilage has been regarded as the equivalent of the saurian basipterygoid meniscus; however, Rieppel (1977c) denies that the two structures are homologous.

In the testudinian embryo, the internal carotid artery and palatine nerve pass forwards beneath the basipterygoid process, the artery giving off its palatine branch and continuing upwards to the pituitary fenestra. In the adult the artery and nerve become enclosed in bony canals by the ossification of the skull base.

iv. Otic capsule

The two otic capsules are united by a tectum synoticum from which

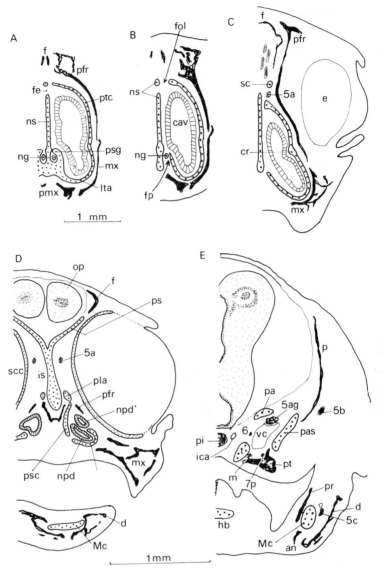

FIG. 75. (A–C) *Emys orbicularis*, embryo, 13·5 mm carapace-length. Transverse sections through nasal capsule in anterior to posterior sequence. After Kunkel (1912a). (D, E) *Chrysemys picta*, late embryo. Transverse sections (D) through anterior orbital region, and (E) through cavum epiptericum.

an, Angular; cav, cavum of nasal sac; cr, conchal ridge; d, dentary; e, eye; f, frontal; fe, fenestra in nasal septum; fol, fenestra olfactoria; fp, foramen prepalatinum; hb, hyoid body; ica, internal carotid artery; is, interorbital septum; lta, lamina transversalis anterior; m, ? region of basipterygoid "meniscus"; Mc, Meckel's cartilage; mx, maxilla; ng, medial nasal gland; npd, nasopharyngeal duct; npd', diverticulum from nasopharyngeal duct; ns, nasal septum; op, olfactory peduncle; p, parietal; pa, pila antotica; pas, ascending process of pterygoquadrate (epipterygoid); pfr, prefrontal; pi, pituitary; pla, planum antorbitale; pmx, premaxilla; pr, prearticular; ps, planum supraseptale; psc, paraseptal cartilage; psg, pila supraglandularis; pt, pterygoid; ptc, parietotectal cartilage; sc, sphenethmoid commissure; scc, scleral cartilage; t, trabecula; vc, vena capitis; 5a, 5ag, ophthalmic nerve and ophthalmic portion of trigeminal ganglion; 5b, maxillary nerve; 5c, mandibular nerve; 6, abducent nerve; 7p, palatine branch of facial nerve.

arises a short anterior process. The cavum vestibuli is not subdivided by an intervestibular septum, and the anterior of the two foramina for the VIIIth nerve lies close to the VIIth nerve foramen. The outer side of the capsule bears a short crista parotica (?, see p. 222), just posterior to the head of the quadrate.

The posteroventral part of the capsule shows a number of striking peculiarities which are characteristic of Testudines in general. The anterior portion of the recessus scalae tympani and the IXth nerve are apparently incorporated into the capsule (Fig. 76D, E). The nerve enters the capsule quite high up through the internal glossopharyngeal foramen, passes across the cavum cochleare, and issues through a foramen at the front of the metotic fissure which corresponds with the lateral opening of the recessus. In the adult this foramen lies within the cavum acustico-jugulare (Gaffney, 1972), partly in the opisthotic. The Xth and XIth nerves (see Soliman, 1964) issue further back, through a separate jugular foramen (foramen jugulare anterius), between the opisthotic and exoccipital in the adult.

The lagena (terminal part of the cochlear duct) and the perilymphatic duct extend posteriorly rather than ventrally and the latter enters a canal in what appears to be either the floor of the otic capsule or the adjacent part of the basal plate. Arising ventrally from this canal is a small diverticulum termed by Nick (1912) the hypoperilymphatic canal, which opens into a groove, called the sulcus supracristularis, along the lateral edge of the basal plate (see Fig. 76E, F of *Chelydra*). The hypoperilymphatic canal contains an extension from the perilymphatic duct and can perhaps be regarded as an outlying portion of the recessus scalae tympani (de Beer, 1937).

v. Basal plate and occipital region

The notochord continues forward to the front of the crista sellaris. It passes across the basicranial fenestra and is embedded in the basal plate and occipital condyle. As Kamal (1965h) has shown, this condition does not differ so radically from that in Squamata as de Beer (1937) believed. However, as Kamal states, his own findings do not necessarily invalidate the generally accepted view that the occipital condyle and occipital arch together represent the entire proatlas in Testudines. The cranio-vertebral joint is thus intervertebral (i.e., between proatlas and atlas) in position (II–H).

The occipital arches are well developed, but do not meet in the midline above the foramen magnum to form a tectum posterius. The base of each arch (probably incorporating two preoccipital arches) is pierced by three hypoglossal foramina in *Emys*. Some other forms, such as *Chelonia*, have only two.

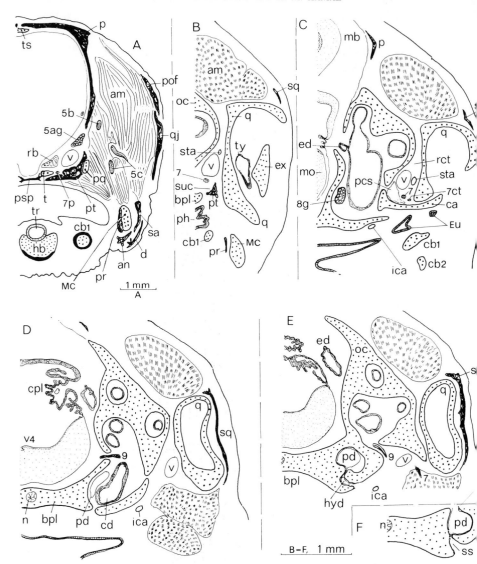

FIG. 76. (A) *Chelydra serpentina*, late embryo. Transverse section through cavum epiptericum. After Soliman (1964). (B–F) *Chelydra serpentina*, late embryo 14·5 mm carapace-length, but somewhat earlier stage than (A). Transverse sections through otic region in anterior to posterior sequence. (F) shows part of basal plate only, with sulcus supracristularis. The region ventral to the 9th nerve in (D) and (E) represents the recessus scalae tympani.

am, M. adductor mandibulae (part of); an, angular; bpl, basal plate; ca, columella auris (shaft); cb1, cb2, ceratobranchials 1 and 2; cd, cochlear duct (lagena); cpl, choroid plexus; d, dentary; ed, endolymphatic duct; Eu, Eustachian tube; ex, extracolumella; hb, hyoid body; hyd, hypoperilymphatic *vi. Visceral arches, etc.*

As in Recent Testudines generally, the concave posterior margin of the large quadrate extends backwards to form a kind of septum across the space which in other reptiles is occupied by the tympanic cavity, dividing it into two compartments. The medial one is called the recessus cavi tympani and lies between the quadrate and the otic capsule (see Romer, 1956, p. 101). It is essentially a part of the cranio-quadrate passage and transmits, dorsal to the stapes, the facial nerve, vena capitis lateralis and stapedial artery (Fig. 76C). The lateral compartment is the tympanic cavity proper. The tympanic membrane (attached to the concave posterior margin of the quadrate) shows varying degrees of development in different forms and is not evident as a distinct structure in the *Chelydra* embryo shown in Figure 76B. The columellar apparatus passes across both compartments, traversing a notch or foramen in the posterior margin of the quadrate. Its medial portion, within the recessus cavi tympani, is partly surrounded by a fluid-filled space, the pericapsular (or paracapsular) sinus, which is perhaps derived from the tympanic cavity (Baird, 1970).

The columellar apparatus has no dorsal or internal processes; the large insertion plate has only a ventral interhyal process connected with the posterior end of Meckel's cartilage by a ligamentous strand. As in Squamata, the medial part of the apparatus ossifies as the columella while the lateral part (extracolumella) remains cartilaginous. The junction between the two in the adult is situated within the tympanic cavity proper.

The ascending process of the pterygoquadrate (epipterygoid) is described later.

The hyobranchial apparatus (Fig. 74E) consists of a broad body or corpus composed partly of the basihyal element. To this are attached a pair of short ceratohyals in front and two pairs of posterior horns formed by the first ceratobranchials and epibranchials, and the second ceratobranchials respectively. The lingual process is usually small or absent. There is, however, a unique structure, a leaf-like cartilaginous plate in the floor of the mouth and ventral to the tongue called the hypoglossum or entoglossum.

---

duct and canal; ica, internal carotid artery; mb, mid-brain; Mc, Meckel's cartilage; mo, medulla oblongata; n, notochord; oc, otic capsule; p, parietal; pcs, pericapsular sinus; pd, perilymphatic duct; ph, pharynx; pof, postfrontal; pq, pterygoquadrate cartilage (probably just posterior to ascending process); pr, prearticular; psp, parasphenoid; pt, pterygoid; q, quadrate; qj, quadratojugal; rb, M. retractor bulbi; rct, recessus cavi tympani; sa, surangular; sq, squamosal; ss, sulcus supracristularis; sta, stapedial artery; suc, sulcus cavernosus; t, trabecula; tr, trachea; ts, tectum synoticum; ty, tympanic cavity; v, vena capitis lateralis; v4, 4th ventricle; 5ag, ophthalmic part of trigeminal ganglion; 5b, maxillary nerve; 5c, mandibular nerve; 7, facial nerve; 7ct, chorda tympani nerve; 7p, palatine branch of facial nerve; 8g, auditory ganglion; 9, glossopharyngeal nerve.

This chondrifies from connective tissue in the very late embryo; it is quite distinct from the hyobranchial apparatus and lies ventral to it. The hyoid body ossifies partly or entirely in most forms, from several centres which are mostly paired. The first and second ceratobranchial also ossify. Variations of the apparatus within the Testudines are described by Schumacher (1973).

The cartilago transiliens is a cartilaginous plate found in the external tendon of the adductor mandibulae externus muscle, where it passes round the pulley-shaped trochlear process formed from the protruding anterior edges of the quadrate and prootic in crypodires, within the temporal fossa. An analogous cartilage is found in crocodilians (Schumacher, 1973; Gaffney, 1975). We have no information about its development.

d. Development and Morphology of the Osteocranium of Testudines

i. General

The ontogenetic data below refer mainly to *Chrysemys* and *Emys*, those on adult morphology to Testudines in general. Conditions in this order are less well known than in Squamata. However, critical comparative studies on the adult skull in various fossil and Recent groups have been undertaken by Gaffney (1975, 1976, 1977, 1979).

ii. Cartilage bones

There appear to be no orbitosphenoid, laterosphenoid or pleurosphenoid ossifications.

The *basisphenoid* (unpaired in the adult) arises from paired centres in the crista sellaris and the posterior end of each trabecula. It subsequently fuses with the underlying parasphenoid to form a parabasisphenoid (see later). The small basipterygoid processes recognizable in the embryo become obliterated in the adult skull, where the parabasisphenoid is in contact along its whole length with the pterygoid on each side.

The epipterygoid ossifies in the ascending process of the pterygoquadrate as a small flattened bone lying dorsal to the pterygoid and ventral to the descending process of the parietal. This bone may also have an anterior process extending forwards dorsal to the pterygoid; this is probably an ossification of the pterygoid process. If the epipterygoid extended further dorsally its relationships to the branches of the Vth nerve similar to those of the rod-like epipterygoid of lizards (Figs. 75E, 77). The epipterygoid is recognizable in nearly all adult cryptodires, but is absent in pleurodires (Gaffney, 1975).

The *prootic* and *opisthotic* ossify in the otic capsule and remain suturally distinct. Together they form a massive parocciptal process which is firmly attached laterally to the quadrate in the adult skull. The Vth nerve foramen

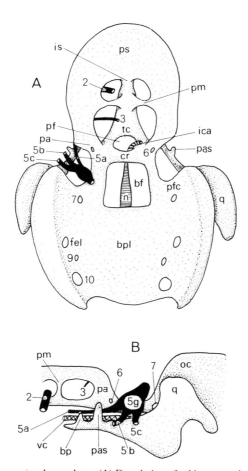

FIG. 77. *Chelydra serpentina*, late embryo. (A) Dorsal view of orbitotemporal region and basal plate showing some nerves. (B) Lateral view of orbitotemporal region from left side showing ascending process of pterygoquadrate. After de Beer (1926).

bf, Basicranial fenestra; bp, basal process of pterygoquadrate; bpl, basal plate; cr, crista sellaris; fel, foramen for endolymphatic duct; ica, internal carotid artery; is, interorbital septum; n, notochord; oc, otic capsule; pa, pila antotica; pas, ascending process of pterygoquadrate; pf, pituitary fossa; pfc, prefacial commissure; pm, pila metoptica; ps, planum supraseptale; q, quadrate; tc, trabecula communis; vc, vena capitis; 2, optic nerve; 3, oculomotor nerve; 5a, 5b, 5c, 5g, ophthalmic, maxillary, and mandibular nerves, trigemina ganglion; 6, 7, 9, 10, foramina for abducens, facial, glossopharyngeal, and vagus nerves.

lies between the prootic and the epipterygoid and is bounded dorsally by the descending process of the parietal (Fig. 76A). The medial surface of the prootic is perforated by the foramina for the VIIth and VIIIth nerves and that of the opisthotic by the internal glossopharyngeal foramen. The internal aspect of the jugular foramen lies between the opisthotic and exoccipital (see Gaffney, 1972).

The *basioccipital* ossifies from paired centres in the basal plate but is unpaired in the adult.

The *exoccipital* ossifies in the occipital arch and contains the XIIth nerve foramina. It forms the greater part of the condyle on each side.

The *supraoccipital* ossifies in the tectum synoticum, which may, however, remain partly cartilaginous. The bone extends posteriorly to form a conspicuous sagittal crest in forms which show marked emargination of the skull roof.

The *quadrate* ossifies in the quadrate cartilage; its peculiar shape and relationship to the middle ear have already been noted. In the adult it is firmly attached to the paraoccipital process and to the squamosal and pterygoid bones. It is thus quite immobile and illustrates the monimostylic condition (see de Beer, 1937).

The *articular* ossifies in the back end of Meckel's cartilage and forms much of the retroarticular process of the lower jaw, when present.

iii. Dermal bones

The small *premaxillae* often remain paired and lack ascending processes so that the external nostrils are confluent. Instead of an egg-tooth there is a horny egg-caruncle (see de Beer, 1949).

The nasal is absent except in certain Chelidae. Its place is occupied by a part of the *prefrontal*, which is, however, a much more extensive bone.

The *vomer* is initially paired but later fuses with its fellow. It is absent or reduced in some pleurodires. In *Emys* and many other forms the vomer separates the internal nostrils, which are bounded laterally by the horn-covered palatal shelves of the *maxillae* and posteriorly by the *palatines*. In some forms such as the cheloniid turtles, a bony secondary palate is formed and the internal nostrils lie behind the vomer and are partly enclosed by the palatines. This and other variations of the palate are described by Romer (1956) and Gaffney (1979).

The septomaxilla, lachrymal and ectopterygoid are absent. Testudines lack a lachrymal duct.

The *pterygoid* is large, and firmly sutured to neighbouring elements, in particular to the parabasisphenoid. In some forms, such as *Emys*, it meets its fellow in the midline. There are no interpterygoid vacuities.

The dorsal surface of the pterygoid is grooved by the sulcus cavernosus (Fig. 76B) which leads back into a canalis cavernosus, bounded laterally by the pterygoid and quadrate and medially by the bones of the otic capsule. This canal continues posteriorly into the recesses cavi tympani, crossed by the columella, and ultimately into the large postotic fenestra which opens on the back of the skull. The sulcus and canalis cavernosus are mainly occupied by the vena capitis lateralis which leaves the skull posteriorly through the postotic fenestra. The anterior part of the sulcus which lies medial to the epipterygoid and parietal downgrowth (see below), corresponds with the cavum epiptericum of lizards, while the rest of the sulcus, the canalis, the recessus cavi tympani and the postotic fenestra represent the cranio-quadrate passage (see McDowell, 1961; Gaffney, 1972).

In most Testudines the *parasphenoid* develops rather late as a thin plate of bone beneath and behind the pituitary fenestra and between the trabeculae; it fuses with the basisphenoid. The internal carotid arteries and palatine arteries and nerves may become partly enclosed between this ossification and the pterygoids, with which the lateral edge of the para-basisphenoid becomes fused (see Rieppel, 1977c). In the adult the internal carotid and palatine nerve appear to pass somewhat lateral to the edge of the parabasisphenoid through a canal (or separate canals in some forms) mainly in the pterygoid. The artery (at least) enters the latter bone through a foramen beneath the postotic fenestra. The precise relationship between the internal carotid artery and the palatine nerve in its Vidian canal varies among forms (Romer, 1956). The bony canals have been studied in considerable detail by McDowell (1961), Gaffney (1972, 1975), and Albrecht (1976), but certain basic points about the courses of the structures they transmit still require clarification.

Pehrson (1945) has described a most interesting condition in embryos of *Chrysemys*, *Lepidochelys* and *Dermochelys*. Here, an additional and quite distinct parasphenoid rudiment appears beneath the interorbital septum and in front of the pituitary fenestra. Its anterior end lies dorsal to the vomer (Fig. 79B, C). This anterior parasphenoid probably corresponds with the parasphenoid rostrum of Squamata and disappears completely in the late embryo, when the definitive posterior parasphenoid is developing. The posterior parasphenoid is present in the adult of *Dermochelys* and many other Testudines, but is transient in cheloniid turtles such as *Lepidochelys*, adults of which seem to lack a parasphenoid.

The paired *frontals* lie above the orbits and may bear ventral flanges which enclose the olfactory nerves (Fig. 75C).

The *parietal* is a large bone which remains paired; posteriorly it may form the anterior part of the sagittal crest. There is no parietal foramen. In front of the trigeminal foramen each parietal usually sends down a strongly developed process (Fig. 75E) which meets the epipterygoid (when present) and the dorsal crest of the pterygoid below. In this region, therefore, the cranial cavity is enclosed by dermal bone in a fashion analogous with that in snakes.

Postfrontal, jugal, squamosal and (usually) *quadratojugal* bones are present. There is no supratemporal.

In most Testudines the lower jaw contains the following membrane bones: *dentary* (toothless), which usually fuses with its fellow in front, *surangular, angular, prearticular* and *coronoid*. The *splenial* is generally absent, but may be present in an atypical position in a few Recent forms (Romer, 1956).

The chondrified sclera has 6–13 *scleral ossicles* (Underwood, 1970).

3. Chelydridae (suborder Cryptodira)

a. Previous Literature

Chelydra serpentina, Nick, 1912 (aspects of chondrocranium); Dohrer, 1919 (ear); de Beer, 1926 (orbitotemporal region); Bellairs, 1949a (orbito-temporal region); Soliman, 1964 (cranial nerves); Torien, 1965a, b (ear); Gaffney, 1972, 1975 (adult skull); Rieppel, 1976b, 1977c (orbitotemporal region and base of cranium compared with *Lacerta*). Yntema (1968) has compiled a normal table of developmental stages of this species.

b. Orbitotemporal Region of the Chondrocranium

i. General

The development and morphology of the chondrocranium of *Chelydra* appears to be similar to that of emydid turtles, but several more or less recent studies have revealed points of interest, especially concerning the orbitotemporal region (Fig. 77) and the columella auris.

The development of the interorbital septum has been studied by Bellairs (1949a). In early stages the procartilaginous trabeculae are continuous dorsally with the downturned medial edges of the anterior orbital cartilages, both trabeculae and cartilages being quite wide apart. The trabeculae are connected across the midline by a mass of condensed mesenchyme which projects ventrally between them to form a conspicuous wedge, as seen in transverse section (Fig. 78A). This wedge of mesenchyme was first noted in *Chelonia* by Parker (1880b), who termed it the intertrabecula. In subsequent stages of *Chelydra*, the intertrabecular tissue appears to extend dorsally between the orbital cartilages, fusing with them and the trabeculae to form a high, thin interorbital septum, which in the stages examined contains no fenestrae. Dorsally, the orbital cartilages fan out sideways as the wings of the planum supraseptale; ventrally, the lower edge of the septum loses its ridged appearance and becomes modelled into a smooth, rounded expansion (Fig. 78B, C). The interorbital septum resembles that of lizards in that both orbital cartilages and trabeculae contribute to its formation; however, it differs in containing a third, partly distinct median element, the intertrabecula, which soon loses its identity and becomes merged with the others in the cartilaginous septal plate. The intertrabecula is also seen in some embryonic stages of crocodilians and certain birds, and perhaps, in a less definite form, in certain lizards, where it hardly deserves recognition on existing evidence (see Lindahl, 1946; Bellairs, 1958).

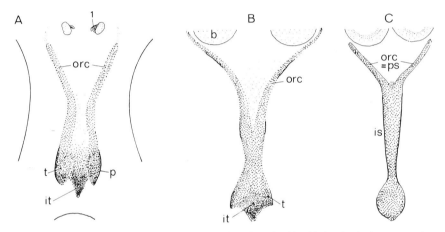

Fig. 78. (A–C) *Chelydra serpentina*. Transverse sections through mid-orbital region in three successive embryonic stages, showing development of interorbital septum from trabeculae, intertrabecula and orbital cartilages. Based on Bellairs (1949a).

b, Brain; is, interorbital septum; it, intertrabecula; orc, orbital cartilage; p, dark-staining perichondrium; ps, planum supraseptale; t, trabecula; 1, olfactory nerves.

ii. Otic capsule and visceral arches

Torien's (1965a, b) experimental studies on the development of the otic capsule and columellar apparatus are of great interest. Following the techniques of Yntema (1964), he removed one otic placode or otocyst from *Chelydra* embryos and one *Chrysemys* embryo of 12 to 20 somites. In successful experiments, the otic capsule on the operated side was completely absent, except for the part of its floor behind the VIIIth nerve foramen which included the ventral rim of the fenestra ovalis. This region, therefore, can be regarded as a derivative of the basal plate which has become assimilated by the capsule. The lateral part of the floor included the partly separate "stapes inferior" region; its development after the operation is evidence against its supposed homology with the operculum of amphibians (see de Beer, 1937), since the latter is derived from the otic capsule. On the other hand the cartilaginous bar which separates the IXth nerve from the recessus scalae tympani and the walls of the perilymphatic and hypoperilymphatic ducts were absent, as were the ducts themselves. This finding suggests that these cartilages are not derived from parts of preoccipital ribs, as de Beer (1937) suggested, but that they either arise from the otic capsule or are induced by the inner ear.

Torien also considered that the structure regarded as a crista parotica by Kunkel (1912a; Fig. 74A here) is actually a metotic process; according to de Beer (1937), the structure also represents a cranial rib. Elsewhere, the metotic cartilage or subcapsular process is seen only in crocodilians and birds, and perhaps in the snake *Eryx*. In Crocodilia it is better developed than in Testudines, and somewhat differently placed. In Torien's experiments on *Chelydra*, this cartilage developed after the operation either as independent structure or in association with the columella, tectum synoticum or quadrate; it is thus not merely an outgrowth from the otic capsule, as one would expect a crista parotica to be.

Torien (1965a, b) also studied the effects of extirpation of the otic placode or otocyst on the development of the columella. After this operation the footplate was defective and irregular in shape, though seldom completely absent. The remainder of the medial columellar rudiment, which chondrifies from the same centre as the footplate, was unaffected. Torien concludes that the footplate is probably not derived from the otic capsule, as some early workers have maintained, but is perhaps induced or partly induced by it. Therefore, his observations tend to confirm the views of Kamal (see Kamal and Abdeen, 1972) which are based on purely descriptive studies of Squamata.

Torien (1965b) also found that removal of the anterior cranial neural folds (and hence of neural crest material) was followed by absence of the quadrate and Meckel's cartilage, the main cartilaginous components of the mandibular arch. The development of the tympanic membrane was also inhibited. The columella was virtually unaffected.

Removal of the posterior cranial neural folds led to absence of the columella and other derivatives of the hyoid arch. No loose footplates (such as might have been derived from the otic capsule) were found. The fenestra ovalis was often irregular when the columella was absent.

4. Trionychidae (suborder Cryptodira)

Ogushi (1911) described the adult skeleton of *Trionyx sinensis* and gave a short account of the persistent chondrocranium, which consists of the nasal capsule, a small planum supraseptale, and a low interorbital septum which divides posteriorly into paired trabeculae. The front of the nasal capsule is elongated and may lie within the snorkel-like proboscis. Dalrymple (1977) has described intraspecific variation in the form of the jaws. The diversity and importance of this family make it an obvious group deserving further study.

5, 6. Cheloniidae and Dermochelydidae (suborder Cryptodira)

a. Previous Literature
  Chelonia mydas, Parker, 1880b; Gaupp, 1906; Nick, 1912; Wever, 1978 (ear). *Dermochelys coriacea*, Nick, 1912; Pehrson, 1945 (orbitotemporal region); Wegner, 1959 (adult bony skull); *Eretmochelys imbricata*, Fuchs, 1915; Soliman, 1964 (cranial nerves, with figures of sections through embryo). *Lepidochelys olivacea*, Pehrson, 1945 (orbitotemporal region). Earlier work on all these forms is reviewed by de Beer (1937).

b. Skull
  Some interesting features of the sea turtles, mainly relating to the orbitotemporal region of the mature chondrocranium, have been described. This region forms a remarkably complete trough beneath the forebrain. Anteriorly the trough is connected with the otic capsule and basal plate by a broad taenia marginalis laterally and pila antotica medially (see Fuchs, 1915; de Beer, 1937; Fig. 79 here).
  A noteworthy feature of these turtles is the division of their pituitary fenestra into two longitudinal halves by a median bar, the taenia inter-trabecularis, which is developed partly from an anterior extension of the crista sellaris and partly from a posterior extension of the trabecula communis. The internal carotid arteries enter the cranial cavity through foramina between the taenia and the back of the trabecula on each side (Fig. 79F).
  The taenia intertrabecularis has been sometimes misleading called the intertrabecula, a term which should be reserved for the median component of the interorbital septum (see Pehrson, 1945, p. 220 here). This component is well developed in *Lepidochelys* and probably also in *Chelonia*; however, it is less evident in *Dermochelys*.
  A curious structure, the "rostral cartilage", occurs in embryos of *Lepidochelys* and *Dermochelys*; it appears to be a prolongation of the front of the nasal septum which has become recurved ventral to the main septum (Pehrson, 1945; Fig. 79E, F). It never becomes fully chondrified and disappears in late embryonic life. It is uncertain whether it corresponds with the uncurved rostral process of some Squamata or with the papillary cartilage seen in a few Squamata, *Sphenodon*, and some mammals.

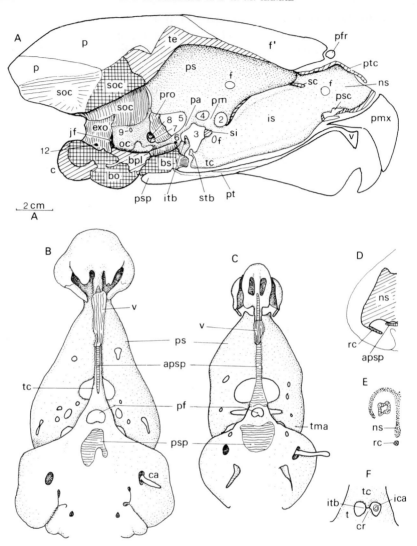

FIG. 79. (A) *Dermochelys coriacea*. Adult, head-length 22 cm. Paramedian section through skull showing persistent regions of cartilage. Cut cartilage in slanting lines, cut cartilage bone crosshatched, intact cartilage in fine stipple, intact cartilage bone in line shading, dermal bones unshaded. Modified from Nick (1912). (B) *Dermochelys coriacea*. Embryo, 29 days incubation. Ventral view of chondrocranium with vomer and anterior and posterior parasphenoid rudiments. Occipital region not shown. (C) *Lepidochelys olivacea*. Embryo, 22 days. Ventral view of chondrocranium with vomer and anterior and posterior parasphenoid rudiments. Occipital region not shown. (D) *Lepidochelys olivacea*. Embryo, 18 days. Median longitudinal section through front of snout showing rostral cartilage. (E) *Lepidochelys olivacea*. Embryo, 17 days. Transverse section through front of snout showing rostral cartilage. (F) *Lepidochelys olivacea*. Embryo, 26 days. Ventral view of region of pituitary fossa which is divided longitudinally by anterior and posterior cartilaginous processes which unite to form the intertrabecular

In these sea turtles considerable areas of the chondrocranium in addition to those in the nasal and interorbital regions may persist into adult life. This is particularly evident in *Dermochelys*, where, as Nick (1912) has shown, much of the basal plate, the medial wall of the otic capsule, and the very large, forwardly projecting tectum synoticum were all cartilaginous in a female specimen with a total length of 1·5 m (Fig. 79A). This aberrant genus has neither epipterygoid nor descending process of the parietal, so that the cavum epiptericum is not incorporated into the skull.

7. Family Pelomedusidae (suborder Pleurodira)

There are few studies of the developing skull or of the chondrocranium in pleurodires; however, Fuchs (1931) has described the ontogeny of the lower jaw of *Podocnemis expansa*, and Van der Merwe (1940) has described the adult anatomy of *Pelomedusa subrufa* from serial sections. Gaffney (1975, 1977) has published important studies of the adult skull in several pleurodiran genera.

8. The Chondrocranium of Testudines

The characters of the mature chondrocranium may be tabulated as follows.

1. The nasal sacs are more completely invested by cartilage than in lepidosaurian reptiles. Lateral and superior fenestrae are small or absent. There is a very broad zona annularis; in mature stages paraseptal and ectochoanal cartilages hardly appear as separate structures but are blended with the rest of the capsular floor.

2. The organ of Jacobson is probably represented by parts of the inferior region of the nasal sac and is not a separate organ, as in Squamata. Consequently, it has no separate cartilaginous capsule.

3. The mature chondrocranium is tropitrabic, usually with a high,

---

bar. The posterior contribution is derived from the region of the crista sellaris. The internal carotid artery is shown on one side only. B–F after Pehrson (1945).

apsp, Anterior parasphenoid rudiment; bo, basioccipital; bpl, basal plate; bs, basisphenoid; c, occipital condyle (cartilaginous); ca, columella auris; cr, crista sellaris; exo, exoccipital; f, fenestrae in nasal and interorbital septa; f', frontal; ica, internal carotid artery; is, interorbital septum; itb, intertrabecular bar; jf, jugular foramen; ns, nasal septum; oc, otic capsule; p, parietal; pa, pila antotica; pf, pituitary fenestra; pfr, prefrontal; pm, pila metoptica; pmx, premaxilla; pro, prootic; ps, planum supraseptale; psc, paraseptal cartilage; psp, posterior rudiment of parasphenoid (definitive parasphenoid in *Dermochelys*); pt, pterygoid; ptc, parietotectal cartilage; rc, rostral cartilage; sc, sphenethmoid commissure; si, subiculum infundibuli; soc, supraoccipital; stb, ? supratrabecular bar; t, trabecula; tc, trabecula communis; te, tectum; tma, taenia marginalis; v, vomer; 2, optic fenestra; 3, fenestra for oculomotor nerve; 4, foramen for trochlear nerve; 5, fenestra for trigeminal nerve; 6, foramen for abducens nerve; 7, foramen for facial nerve; 8, foramen for branch of auditory nerve; 9, foramen for glossopharyngeal nerve; 12, foramen for hypoglossal nerve.

unfenestrated interorbital septum. In some forms at least, a partly distinct median element called the intertrabecula enters the composition of that septum in early embryonic stages.

4. The planum supraseptale is well developed and its fenestrations are less extensive than those of lizards. However, the taenia marginalis of some forms is incomplete (Fig. 73) so that there is a gap between the back of the planum supraseptale and the pila antotica and otic capsule.

5. The VIIth nerve passes through the front of the otic capsule.

6. The posteroventral part of the otic capsule is modified and incorporates a large portion of the recessus scalae tympani, through which the IXth nerve passes.

7. The structure described as a crista parotica may be a metotic cartilage or subcapsular process (Torien, 1965a).

8. There is a tectum synoticum but no tectum posterius.

9. The cranio-vertebral joint is intervertebral, lying between derivatives of the proatlas and the atlas.

10. The quadrate is much modified. It extends posteriorly to form a kind of septum across the middle ear cavity, dividing it into a tympanic cavity proper and an inner recessus cavi tympani.

11. The pterygoquadrate generally has an ascending process which ossifies to form a small epipterygoid partly enclosing the cavum epiptericum; the latter is also enclosed dorsolaterally by a downgrowth from the parietal bone. In early stages there is a small basipterygoid process which subsequently becomes obliterated.

12. The columella auris has neither dorsal nor internal processes. The insertion plate of the extracolumella has only an interhyal process which is transiently connected with the back of Meckel's cartilage. The two Meckel's cartilages are fused anteriorly.

13. The hyobranchial apparatus has a broad body probably derived from basihyal and first and second basibranchial components. There is a separate cartilaginous plate, the hypoglossum, beneath the tongue.

9. The Testudinian Skull as a Whole

The short snouted, massive skull of Testudines can be regarded as a derivative of the primitive reptilian (cotylosaurian) pattern, though it shows numerous and diverse modifications. Since the most ancient Testudines of the Upper Triassic had skulls with a complete roof, devoid of temporal vacuities, the group can be formally classified in the subclass Anapsida.

In some Recent forms, such as the sea turtles, the dermal roof and temporal side-wall are still nearly complete, though it is possible that this extensive covering has been secondarily re-evolved. However, in most Recent forms the posterior and/or inferior margins of the roof and sides of the temporal region have been emarginated to a greater or lesser extent, often exposing a marked sagittal crest to which jaw muscles are attached. The precise nature of this emargination varies in different forms (see Romer, 1956).

In striking contrast to the lepidosaurian condition is the welding of the upper jaw, palate and quadrate with the brain-case and surrounding dermal bones. Skull roof and palate are firmly connected (except in *Dermochelys*) by the descending processes of the parietal, and there is no movable basipterygoid articulation. Thus the skull of all Testudines is completely akinetic, irrespective of their feeding habits. Differences in the detailed relationships between jaws and brain-case in different groups are discussed by Gaffney (1975, 1979).

We have seen that in the fully formed embryonic chondrocranium the nasal capsule and orbitotemporal cartilages are very extensive, more so than in Squamata. The fate of these structures in later life is interesting, and apparently varies in different groups. In very late embryonic or post-natal stages of *Chrysemys* most of this cartilage apparently degenerates and the chondrocranium is represented by the nasal septum, the extracolumella and parts of the hyobranchial apparatus. Other regions of the nasal capsule, the planum supraseptale and interorbital septum are apparently reduced to membranes which retain the shape of the former cartilages; in places a few isolated cartilage cells, devoid of matrix, may remain (Shaner, 1926). It is uncertain how general among testudinians this degeneration of the anterior chondrocranium may be; the nasal capsule, interorbital septum and planum supraseptale are well developed in a juvenile *Testudo graeca* of which sections are available. Moreover, in some marine turtles very extensive tracts of the chondrocranium persist in the adult, even ones posterior to the pituitary region. This persistence is perhaps a neotenic feature, here devoid of functional significance in view of the akinetic nature of the skull. However, the heavy development of the dermal bones suggests that the skull as a whole is not neotenous.

The complete cartilaginous investment of the nasal sacs and the extensive development of the trough-like planum supraseptale in testudinian embryos can perhaps be regarded as primitive reptilian features. On the other hand, the modifications of the otic capsule and of the quadrate seem to represent specialized or derived characters.

Some interesting resemblances between the skeleton of Testudines and Crocodilia are discussed on page 246.

G. CROCODILIA

1. Crocodilidae (suborder Eusuchia)

a. Previous Literature

Alligator mississippiensis, Parker, 1883; Goldby, 1925 (columella); Bellairs, 1949a, 1958 (orbitotemporal region). *Crocodylus cataphractus* (mainly), Müller, 1967. *C. niloticus*, Frank and Smit, 1974 (columella). *C. palustris*, Parker, 1883. *C. porosus*, Meek, 1911 (nasal capsule); Shiino, 1914; Kesteven, 1957b. *C.* sp., Goldby, 1925 (columella); de Beer, 1926 (orbitotemporal region); de Beer and Barrington, 1934.

De Beer (1937) and Iordansky (1973) have reviewed earlier work on the embryonic and adult crocodilian skull respectively, while Langston (1973) has dealt with certain phylogenetic aspects. Baird, Parsons, and Underwood (all 1970), Bellairs (1969, 1971), Saint Girons (1976b) and Martin and Bellairs (1977) have described various aspects of the sense organs. Schumacher (1973) deals with the head muscles and hyobranchial apparatus. Voeltzkow (1902) has described embryonic growth stages of *Crocodylus niloticus*, while Reese (1915) and Ferguson (manuscript) have described certain features of the embryology of the American alligator. Various aspects of postnatal growth are discussed by Kälin (1933), Wegner (1958), Wermuth (1964) and Dodson (1975).

Sectioned material of a 26 mm head-length embryo of the American alligator has been available.

It is likely that there are only minor variations in the embryonic cranial development of the various crocodilian species studied; conditions in *Gavialis*, which could be rather different, have not been investigated. Data are not yet adequate for significant correlation between many features of the embryonic and adult skull in crocodilians, especially in so far as the nasal region and paranasal sinuses are concerned. Study of early postnatal stages is badly needed.

FIG. 80. (A–I) *Crocodylus cataphractus*. Views of chondrocranium; oto–occipital region not shown. (A–C) Stage 2. (A) Ventral, (B) dorsal and (C) lateral view. (D–F) Stage 3; ?6·5 mm head-length. (D) Ventral; (E) dorsal and (F) lateral view. (G–I) Stage 4; 7·8 mm head-length. (G) Ventral, (H) dorsal and (I) lateral view. After Müller (1967). (J) *Crocodylus* sp. Transverse section through developing interorbital septum showing trabeculae and intertrabecula. After Bellairs (1958).

b, Brain; bpl, basal plate; cr, crista sellaris; fn, fenestra narina; foa, foramen or gap for ophthalmic artery; inp, infrapolar process; is, interorbital septum; it, intertrabecula; n, notochord; nca, nasal capsule; ns, nasal septum; oc, otic capsule (cut off); pa, pila antotica; pf, pituitary fossa; pk, Polknorpel (supposed polar cartilage); pm, pila metoptica; ps, planum supraseptale; psc, paraseptal cartilage; sp, suprapolar process; t, trabecula; tc, trabecula communis; tm, taenia medialis; tma, taenia marginalis; 3, 4, foramina for oculomotor and trochlear nerves.

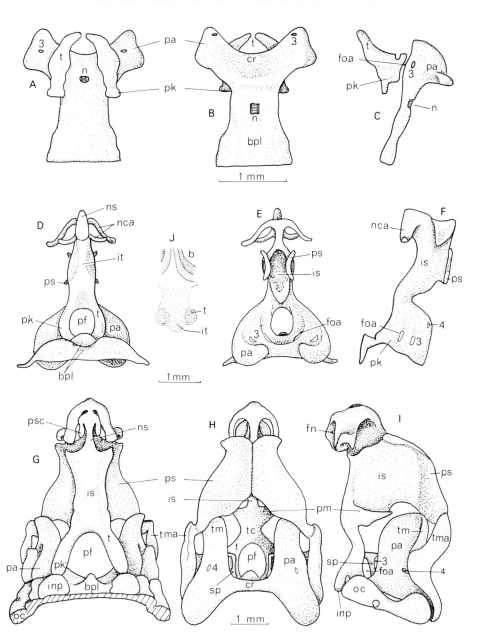

b. Chondrocranium of Crocodilia

Early stages of *Crocodylus* are described by Müller (1967) and by Frank and Smit (1974). The dorsum sellae and basal plate are perhaps the first parts of the chondrocranium to appear, the latter being initially represented by intercellular matrix among the cells surrounding the notochord. Somewhat later, as in Müller's *Stage 2* (? head-length), one can see the trabeculae as separate structures, not yet fused with each other anteriorly or with the basal plate (Fig. 80A, C). A protuberance on the outer side of the base of each trabecula is termed by Müller a polar cartilage (*Polknorpel*), but it is uncertain whether this is originally a separate structure which fuses later with the trabecula, as it does in some birds. As in other early reptilian embryos the trabeculae are strongly flexed in relation to the basal plate; a little later the flexion becomes more marked, but diminishes after Stage 4.

In Müller's *Stage 3* (Fig. 80D–F), the trabeculae have fused in front to form the nasal septum, and more posteriorly to form a thick interorbital septum which probably includes an intertrabecular component (Bellairs, 1958; Fig. 80J here). The septum is surmounted on each side by a narrow rudiment of the planum supraseptale; the two halves of this structure are still quite separate from each other. Further back the trabeculae diverge on either side of the pituitary fenestra and are attached posteriorly to the basal plate. Rudiments of the cochlear portions of the otic capsules have become attached to the latter.

At *Stage 4* (7·8 mm head-length; Fig. 80G–I) the chondrocranium shows a much closer approximation to the fully formed condition. The roof and floor of the nasal capsule are well developed, the latter bearing a distinct paraseptal cartilage. The interorbital septum is still remarkably thick; above it is the broad planum supraseptale with its two wings now contiguous in the midline. The pila metoptica is incomplete, so that the optic foramen is open posteriorly. The crista sellaris forms a bridge between the two large "sphenolateral" plates of cartilage (pierced by the IVth nerve on either side) which appear to be derived from the pilae antoticae. Lateral to each of these plates a broad taenia marginalis passes back from the planum supraseptale to the otic capsule. There is now a well developed infrapolar process on each side. Dorsal to the base of each trabecula, lies a suprapolar process or cartilage (recognized by Müller, 1967, for the first time in Crocodilia), homologous to the one in birds. This process fuses dorsally with the region of the pila antotica and ventrally with the trabecula; however, a foramen for the passage of the ophthalmic artery forms between it and the trabecula.

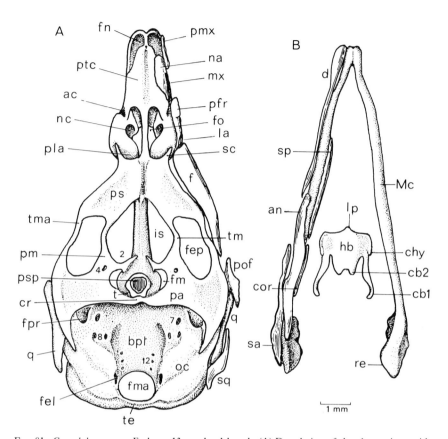

FIG. 81. *Crocodylus porosus*. Embryo, 13 mm head-length. (A) Dorsal view of chondrocranium, with some dermal bones. (B) Ventral view of visceral skeleton with dermal bones of lower jaw. After Shiino (1914).

ac, Aditus conchae; an, angular; bpt, basal plate; cb1, cb2, ceratobranchials 1 and 2; chy, ceratohyal; cor, coronoid; cr, crista sellaris; d, dentary; f, frontal; fel, foramen for endolymphatic duct; fep, fenestra epioptica; fm, fenestra metoptica; fma, foramen magnum; fn, fenestra narina; fo, fenestra olfactoria; fpr, fenestra prootica; hb, hyoid body; is, interorbital septum; la, lachrymal; lp, lingual process; Mc, Meckel's cartilage; mx, maxilla; na, nasal; nc, nasal concha; oc, otic capsule; pa, pila antotica; pfr, prefrontal; pla, planum antorbitale; pm, pila metoptica; pmx, premaxilla; pof, postfrontal; ps, planum supraseptale; psp, parasphenoid; ptc, parietotectal cartilage; q, quadrate; re, retroarticular process; sa, surangular; sc, sphenethmoid commissure; sp, splenial; sq, squamosal; t, trabecula; te, tectum (synoticum with perhaps an occipital arch contribution); tm, taenia medialis; tma, taenia marginalis; 2, fenestra optica; 4, 7, 8, 12, foramina for oculomotor, trochlear, facial, auditory, and hypoglossal nerves.

The otic capsule and mandibular arch derivatives are not completed in Müller's reconstructions.

c. The Fully Formed Chondrocranium of Crocodylus

i. General

This has been described by Shiino (1914) and de Beer (1937) from a 13 mm head-length embryo (and later stages) of *Crocodylus porosus*. Many sections through the nasal region of a 27 mm head-length embryo of the same species are figured by Meek (1911), but despite this and the later paper by Bertau (1935), the nasal capsule of crocodilians has not yet been clearly delineated.

ii. Nasal capsule

At 13 mm the nasal capsule is long and narrow with a nearly complete roof formed by the parietotectal cartilage, which is continuous in the ventral midline with the nasal septum (Figs. 81, 82). The septum extends forwards as a short rostral process ventral to the nasal cupolae. The fenestra narina faces dorsally in front and laterally further back. Its posterior edge is bounded by the junction of the parietotectal cartilage and the long lamina transversalis anterior. Owing to the great length of this fenestra the zona annularis is quite narrow. In the 13 mm *Crocodylus* the sphenethmoid commissures are incomplete and do not reach the back of the nasal capsule. The lateral ethmoidal branch of the ophthalmic nerve is given off behind the capsule, so that there is no foramen epiphaniale. In 19·5 and 26 mm head-length *Alligator* embryos, however, the sphenethmoid commissures are complete and the lateral ethmoidal nerve passes forwards through a foramen epiphaniale in the roof of the capsule (Bertau, 1935; Figs. 83C; 85B here).

The floor of the capsule, mainly formed by the lamina transversalis anterior, is also extensive. It is pierced anteriorly on each side by the foramen apicale for the medial ethmoidal nerve. In these later stages the paraseptal cartilage is reduced to a small projection from the back of the lamina transversalis, alongside the nasal septum. The broad planum antorbitale is fused medially with the septum.

The organ of Jacobson is represented (if at all) by a transient vestige in the early embryo, and thus has no cartilaginous capsule. As in most Squamata, there is only a single nasal gland, the lateral one; it is situated on the dorsolateral aspect of the front of the parietotectal cartilage and (at least in the late embryo) does not invaginate any of the conchae (see below), as does the nasal gland in many lizards. Its duct enters the medial side of the nasal sac, near the junction of the cavum with the short vestibule (Bellairs and Shute, 1953; Fig. 83A here).

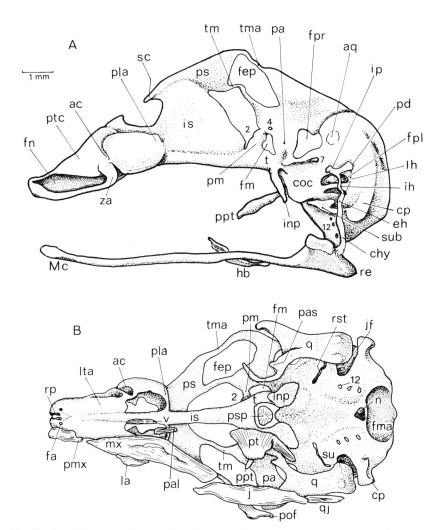

FIG. 82. *Crocodylus porosus*. Embryo, 13 mm head-length. (A) Lateral and (B) ventral view of chondrocranium. The quadrate is not shown in (A). After Shiino (1914).

ac, Aditus conchae; aq, region of attachment by connective tissue of quadrate with otic capsule; chy, ceratohyal; coc, cochlear prominence; cp, crista parotica; eh, epihyal; fa, foramen apicale; fep, fenestra epioptica; fm, fenestra metoptica; fma, foramen magnum; fn, fenestra narina; fpl, footplate of columella; fpr, fenestra prootica; hb, hyoid body; ih, interhyal (pars interhyalis); inp, infrapolar process; ip, insertion plate of extracolumella; is, interorbital septum; j, jugal; jf, jugular foramen (for nerves 9 and 10); la, lachrymal; lh, ligamentous laterohyal; lta, lamina transversalis anterior; Mc, Meckel's cartilage; mx, maxilla; n, canal for notochord; pa, pila antotica; pal, palatine; pas, ascending process of pterygoquadrate; pd, dorsal process; pla, planum antorbitale; pm, pila metoptica; pmx, premaxilla; pof, postfrontal; ppt, pterygoid process; ps, planum supraseptale; psp, parasphenoid; pt, pterygoid; ptc, parietotectal cartilage; q, quadrate; qj, quadratojugal; re, retroarticular process; rp, rostral process; rst, recessus scalae tympani; sc, sphenethmoid commissure; su, sub, subcapsular process; t, trabecula; tm, taenia medialis; tma, taenia marginalis; v, vomer; za, zona annularis; 2, fenestra optica; 4, 7, 12, foramina for trochlear, facial, and hypoglossal nerves.

The cavum proprium of the nose and the cartilaginous nasal structures associated with it are different from and more complicated than the condition in other reptiles. Three conchae project from the lateral wall of the nasal capsule (Figs. 83; 85B); an anterior concha or preconcha, a middle concha or nasal concha, and a postconcha. These are the anterior, middle and posterior turbinals of Meek (1911), the anterior concha being almost continuous with the middle one. The middle concha has been regarded as homologous with the single concha of lizards (de Beer and Barrington, 1934), but the evidence for this seems unconvincing.

The lachrymal duct opens into the nasal sac beneath the anterior concha (Fig. 83B), passing through the side-wall of the capsule. It may be noted that the definitive lachrymal duct of crocodilians is a true lachrymonasal duct like that of mammals, whereas in adult Squamata, the duct opens not into the nasal sac, but in close relationship to the palate and to the opening of the duct of Jacobson's organ.

In the fully formed crocodilian chondocranium, the long nasopharyngeal duct passes posteriorly through the choanal or basal fenestra, bounded by the lamina transversalis anterior in front, the planum antorbitale behind, the septum medially, and the postconcha laterally. Its opening, the choana, lies on level with the back of the orbits in the 26 mm head-length *Alligator* embryo. Bertau (1935) and Müller (1967) have described the development of this duct, which separates itself off from the buccal cavity in an anteroposterior direction so that the choana is shifted to a progressively more caudal position. According to Müller, this process recapitulates the changes seen during crocodilian evolution from the mesosuchian to the eusuchian condition. The skeletal investment of the nasopharyngeal duct is entirely bony and no part of the chondrocranium is immediately related to it. There is no distinct ectochoanal cartilage, such as supports the nasopharyngeal duct in some Squamata (p. 73). In earlier stages the two ducts form a single median tube, but later they become separated by a septum of soft tissue which extends back to the choanae and is partly reinforced by bone. M. J. W. Ferguson (manuscript) is currently studying palatogenesis in the alligator.

iii. Orbitotemporal region

The nasal septum falls in height in the region of the planum antorbitale, but more posteriorly the interorbital septum has become thin and high, though its inferior edge is swollen. Dorsally it is continuous with the two wings of the planum supraseptale (Figs. 82A, 84A). The posterior edge of the planum is connected by the taenia medialis with the pila metoptica medially, and by the taenia marginalis with the broad "sphenolateral plate" formed by the pila metotica laterally. The posterior margins of this plate

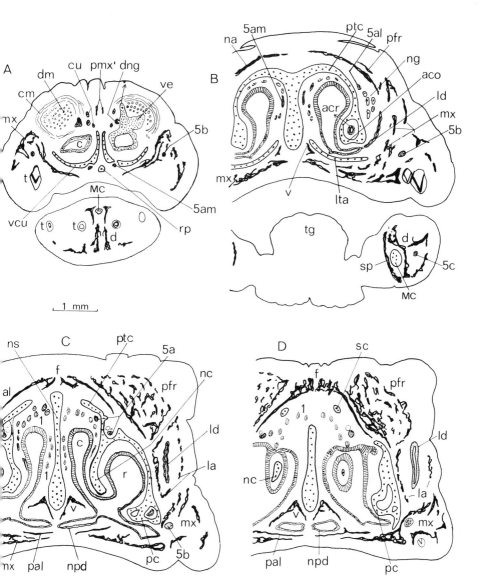

FIG. 83. *Alligator mississippiensis.* Embryo, 26 mm head-length. (A–D) Transverse sections through snout in anterior to posterior sequence.

aco, Anterior concha (preconcha); acr, anterior conchal recess (arrow shows course of communication with nose); c, cavum nasi proprium; cm, M. constrictor naris; cu, nasal cupola (edge of); d, dentary; dm, M. dilator naris; dng, duct of nasal gland; f, frontal; la, lachrymal; ld, lachrymal duct; lta, lamina transversalis anterior; Mc, Meckel's cartilage; mx, maxilla; na, nasal; nc, (middle) nasal concha; ng, nasal gland; npd, nasopharyngeal duct; ns, nasal septum; pal, palatine; pc, posterior concha; pfr, prefrontal; pmx, premaxilla; pmx′, ascending process of premaxilla; ptc, parietotectal cartilage; r, extra-conchal recess; rp, rostral process; sc, sphenethmoid commissure; sp, splenial; t, tooth germ; tg, tongue; v, vomer; vcu, ventral wall of nasal cupola; ve, vestibule of nasal sac (arrow shows line of communication with external nostril); 1, olfactory nerves; 5a, ophthalmic nerve; 5al, 5am, lateral and medial branches of ophthalmic nerve (the cartilaginous tunnel for 5al is partly reconstructed in C, left); 5b, maxillary nerve; 5c, mandibular nerve.

extend posteriorly on each side above the otic capsule. Optic, metoptic, epioptic and prootic fenestrae are now enclosed, much as in lizards, though the IVth nerve has a separate foramen as in *Sphenodon* and Testudines. The suprapolar process, which lay above the foramen for the ophthalmic artery in earlier stages, now seems to have disappeared, so that the artery issues from the single metoptic fenestra in company with the IIIrd and VIth nerves (see Müller, 1967).

In many respects the orbitotemporal region of the mature crocodilian chondrocranium resembles the transient condition in birds before the regression of the anterior orbital cartilages (planum supraseptale, etc.; see Bellairs, 1958).

The basitrabecular region shows interesting differences from that in other reptiles. In place of typical basipterygoid processes, which project more or less laterally on each side, the crocodilian embryo develops a pair of conspicuous plates of cartilage which grow backwards from the base of each trabecula and come to lie beneath the basal plate (Figs. 82A, B, 84B, 86B). These are the infrapolar processes, also found in birds. A space corresponding with the Vidian or parabasal canal is enclosed between each process and the basal plate; it contains the internal carotid artery (before it turns upwards to reach the pituitary fenestra), the palatine nerve and the anterior diverticulum or canal of the Eustachian tube system. As de Beer (1937), Kesteven (1957b) and Müller (1967) have pointed out, the artery and nerve pass dorsally to the infrapolar process itself so that the latter is not strictly homologous with the basipterygoid process of other reptiles (Kesteven's views on basipterygoid processes in general are idiosyncratic). However, the root of the process, where it arises from the trabecula, lies dorsolateral to the nerve and thus seems to correspond with the basipterygoid process, from which the infrapolar process could be merely a posteroventral extension. This process eventually ossifies to form that part of the basisphenoid (ventral presphenoid of Müller) which forms

---

FIG. 84. *Alligator mississippiensis*. Embryo, 20 mm head-length. Transverse sections through (A) anterior orbital region, (B) pituitary fossa and (C, D) otic region.

a, Articular; an, angular; ap, auricular plate (dense connective tissues); bo, basioccipital; ce, cerebellum; chy, ceratohyal; ef, superior ear-flap; Et, Eustachian tube; Eu, anterior diverticulum of Eustachian tube; exo, exoccipital; f, frontal; ica, internal carotid artery; inp, infrapolar process; ip, insertion plate of extracolumella; is, interorbital septum; j, jugal; lag, lagena; mb, midbrain; Mc, Meckel's cartilage; mo, medulla oblongata; mx, maxilla; n, notochord; nm, nictitating membrane; npd, nasopharyngeal duct; oc, otic capsule; op, olfactory peduncle; opi, opisthotic; p, parietal; pa, pila antotica; pal, palatine; pbs, parabasisphenoid; pd, dorsal process; pi, pituitary; po, postorbital; pq, pterygoquadrate cartilage; ps, planum supraseptale; pt, pterygoid; q, quadrate; qj, quadratojugal; s, siphonium; sa, surangular; sq, squamosal; stm, secondary tympanic membrane; sub, subcapsular process; t, trabecula; tym, tympanic membrane; 3, oculomotor nerve; 4, trochlear nerve; 5a, ophthalmic nerve; 5b, maxillary nerve; 5c, mandibular nerve; 5g, trigeminal ganglion; 6, abducens nerve; 7, facial nerve (hyomandibular branch); 7p, palatine nerve; 8g, auditory nerve ganglion; 10, vagus nerve.

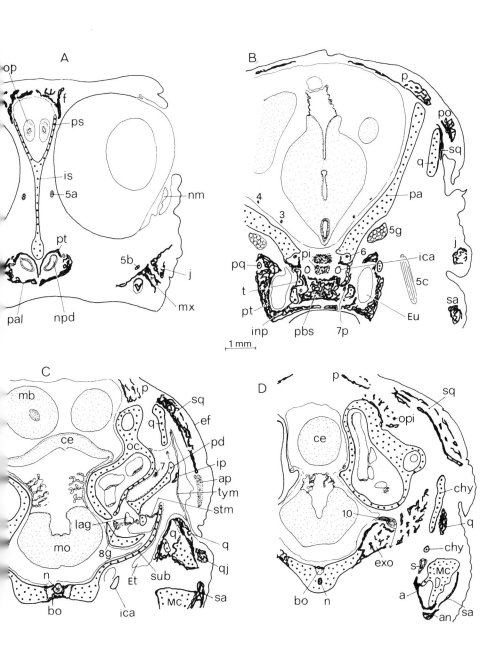

the anterior boundary of the anterior Eustachian canal (see Müller, p. 268).

iv. Occipital and otic regions

No basicranial fenestra has been described, and the notochord is completely surrounded by the basal plate (fused parachordals) and pierces the substance of the occipital condyle. The cranio-vertebral joint is supposedly intervertebral and intrasegmental, as in Testudines and birds. There is a small, free proatlas arch (p. 38; Figs. 11, 85A). The large occipital arch is pierced by three hypoglossal foramina; it fuses with the tectum synoticum and may perhaps contribute a posterius component to the definitive tectum.

The otic capsule shows similar divisions to these of other reptiles, and contains similar foramina. However, the vestibular part has apparently been "rotated" (de Beer, 1937) behind the cochlear part, and the conspicuous crista parotica has come to lie in a vertical rather than a horizontal plane on its lateral surface (Fig. 82A). A cartilaginous process arises from the outer aspect of each occipital arch and extends forwards beneath the otic capsule and anterior part of the metotic fissure. This is the metotic cartilage or subcapsular process, present also, according to Torien (1965b), in Testudines and also found in birds. This process underlies the recessus scalae tympani. The secondary tympanic membrane, which faces dorsally rather than laterally is stretched across a "fenestra pseudorotunda" between the subcapsular process and the otic capsule (Baird, 1970; Fig. 84C here). De Beer (1937) has suggested that the process represents a cranial rib associated with the proatlas. It is uncertain whether the subcapsular process of Crocodilia is homologous with that of Testudines; its homology with the similarly named structure in the snake *Eryx* seems doubtful. The IXth, Xth and XIth (if present) nerves pass out behind the otic capsule through the more posterior part of the metotic fissure, or jugular foramen.

v. Mandibular arch

The pterygoquadrate consists of a large quadrate cartilage and a slender pterygoid process. The fate of the latter, and that of the vestigial ascending process which arises from it (at least at certain stages) is uncertain. No distinct epipterygoid bone is developed and the region lateral to the pila antotica, which corresponds with the cavum epiptericum, is not enclosed (Figs. 84B; 86B). Meckel's cartilage fuses with its fellow in the anterior midline (Fig. 81B).

vi. Columellar apparatus

The development of the columella in Crocodilia has been well described by Goldby (1925). As in reptiles generally, it arises from initially separate lateral and medial rudiments. The medial rudiment has a well developed

dorsal process ("suprastapedial") that chondrifies from a separate (? intercalary) centre and becomes attached to the posterodorsal aspect of the
quadrate, unlike its fusion to the crista parotica of the otic capsule in lizards.
There is no internal (quadrate) process. During early development the
region of the footplate may be almost blended with the otic capsule, but
it is not possible to determine by purely descriptive methods whether the
capsule actually contributes to the footplate.

The original division between medial and lateral rudiments disappears
and the lateral extremity of the continuous structure so formed grows
laterally to constitute the insertion plate or tympanic process, which is
partly applied to the tympanum. At the same time an interhyal process
("infrastapedial") arises from the insertion plate and passes ventrally to
become connected with the developing ceratohyal. As in geckos, an extracolumellar muscle is partly inserted on the interhyal. A region of cartilage
in the fully formed structure, between the interhyal and ceratohyal, is
interpreted as an epihyal. At some stages the epihyal region may have a
transient ligamentous connection (laterohyal) with the tip of the dorsal
process; this encloses a Huxley's foramen between itself and the dorsal
process (Fig. 82A). The ceratohyal is itself for a time continuous with the
retroarticular process of Meckel's cartilage (much as in Testudines), but
later on it degenerates, its remnants blending with the fibrous sheath of
the siphonium. The relationships of the facial nerve and chorda tympani
to the columellar apparatus are similar to those in lizards.

In late embryos the apparatus rotates so that the interhyal is directed
posteriorly rather than ventrally. The medial part of the columellar rod
ossifies as the definitive columella or stapes, while the lateral part, including
the dorsal process, remains cartilaginous as the extracolumella. As in lizards,
the final boundary between bony and cartilaginous regions is medial to the
original division between the two rudiments.

More recently, the development of the columellar apparatus has been
reinvestigated by Frank and Smit (1974). They propose rather different
homologies for some of the processes, which are partly based on comparison
with the crossopterygian hyomandibula, and suggest a new and somewhat
complex terminology. Thus, they regard the medial rudiment and the basal
part of the dorsal process as a pharyngohyal, the tip of the dorsal process
and the tympanic part of the insertion plate as of laterohyal derivation,
and the remainder of the lateral rudiment as epihyal.

vii. Hyobranchial apparatus

The embryonic hyobranchial apparatus of crocodilians consists of a
broad plate, the corpus or hyoid body, with a short lingual process. There
are short ceratohyal and second branchial horns which virtually disappear

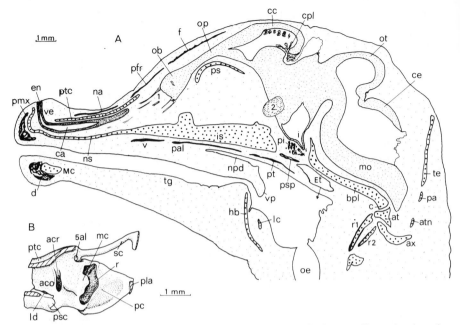

FIG. 85. (A) *Crocodylus niloticus*, embryo 21 mm head-length; longitudinal, paramedian section through head. (B) *Alligator mississippiensis*, embryo 19·5 mm head-length; posterior part of right nasal capsule in paramedian section, seen from medial aspect (after Bertau, 1935).

aco, Anterior concha; acr, opening of anterior conchal recess; at, atlas (centrum); atn, atlas (neural arch); ax, axis; bpl, basal plate; c, occipital condyle; ca, cavum nasi proprium; cc, cerebral cortex; ce, cerebellum; cpl, choroid plexus; d, dentary; en, external nostril; Et, Eustachian tube (arrow shows line of entrance to pharynx); f, frontal; hb, hyoid body (supporting basihyal valve which is not clearly demarcated from the tongue); i, infundibulum; is, interorbital septum; lc, laryngeal cartilage; ld, foramen for lachrymal duct; mc, middle concha; Mc, Meckel's cartilage; mo, medulla oblongata; na, nasal; npd, nasopharyngeal duct; ns, nasal septum (inferior edge); ob, olfactory bulb; oe, oesophagus; op, olfactory peduncle; ot, optic tectum of midbrain; pa, proatlas; pal, palatine; pc, posterior concha; pfr, prefrontal; pi, pituitary; pla, planum antorbitale; pmx, premaxilla; ps, planum supraseptale; psc, paraseptal cartilage; psp, parasphenoid; pt, pterygoid; ptc, parietotectal cartilage; r, extraconchal recess; r1, r2, first and second ribs; sc, sphenethmoid commissure; te, occipital tectum; tg, tongue; v, vomer; ve, vestibule; vp, velum palatini; 1, olfactory nerves; 2, optic chiasma; 5al, foramen epiphaniale for lateral ethmoidal nerve.

in the adult, and a much longer pair of horns derived from the first ceratobranchials. The latter are the only parts of the apparatus to ossify in the adult, where they may have epibranchial cartilages at their tips (Schumacher, 1973). The body of the hyoid turns dorsally and supports the basihyal valve (Fig. 85A). The embryonic ceratohyal horn is unconnected with the portion of the ceratohyal associated with the columella.

d. *Characters of the Crocodilian Chondrocranium*

The characters of the mature chondrocranium may be tabulated as follows.

1. The walls of the nasal capsule are well developed. The paraseptal cartilage is small and the ectochoanal cartilage is probably absent. There is no organ of Jacobson and hence no capsule for it. There are three nasal conchae.

2. The mature chondrocranium is tropitrabic with a high, unfenestrated interorbital septum. Earlier embryos may show an intertrabecular component.

3. The planum supraseptale and the pila antotica are well developed.

4. There are suprapolar and infrapolar processes associated with the bases of the trabeculae. The roots of the infrapolar processes probably correspond with the basipterygoid processes found in many other reptiles.

5. There is a subcapsular process or metotic cartilage beneath the otic capsule which forms part of the floor of the recessus scalae tympani.

6. The cranio-vertebral joint is intervertebral, as in Testudines. There is a free proatlas arch.

7. The ascending process of the pterygoquadrate is vestigial or absent, so that there is no enclosed cavum epiptericum.

8. The columellar apparatus has no internal process. The insertion plate is connected with the ceratohyal.

9. The hyobranchial apparatus has a broad body and a pair of long first ceratobranchial horns, with much smaller ceratohyal and second ceratobranchial horns.

e. Osteocranium of Crocodilia

i. Bone structure

The developing cranial bones of crocodilians, and to a lesser extent those of Testudines, show a loose trabecular structure which resembles that of the mammalian embryo and contrasts with the more compact appearance of bone in lepidosaurian embryos. There are also similarities between crocodilians and turtles in the histological structure of adult long bones, and in their mode of ossification (see Enlow, 1969; Haines, 1969).

ii. Cartilage bones

As in reptiles generally, the nasal capsule is unossified. Occasionally, small *septosphenoid* ossifications in the posterior part of the interorbital septum have been reported, presumably in mature individuals (see Romer, 1956). No orbitosphenoid ossifications in the planum supraseptale appear to have been described.

The extensive sphenolateral cartilage (pila antotica) ossifies to form a large *pleurosphenoid* bone, which may, by virtue of its position in the adult just behind the optic nerve, includes an ossification in the pila metoptica.

The pleurosphenoid (Fig. 86A) lies mainly medial to the ophthalmic nerve, but during later embryonic life a splint of bone develops lateral to the nerve so that the latter issues through a canal in the adult pleurosphenoid—at least in some species. It is possible that this splint corresponds with the pila antotica spuria of the avian chondrocranium (see de Beer, 1926, 1937).

A pleurosphenoid bone of generally similar type is found in birds and occurred in many extinct archosaurs. It is often called a laterosphenoid but this term is perhaps best reserved for the rather different bone in snakes (III–D–11). The pleurosphenoid has been generally regarded (e.g. by Goodrich, 1930) as an ossification of the true side-wall of the cranial cavity and is therefore not homologous with the mammalian alisphenoid which corresponds (more or less) with the reptilian epipterygoid, a bone which is never ossified in crocodilians. Kesteven (1957b), however, has always rejected this concept (on grounds which seem somewhat obscure) and believed that the bones in this region are homologous in all amniote vertebrates. He therefore refers to this bone in *Crocodylus* as the ali-sphenoid, as did Parker (1883) and some earlier workers.

The *basisphenoid* ossifies in the front part of the basal plate, the dorsum sellae, the posterior ends of the trabeculae, the infrapolar processes, and the low, most posterior part of the interorbital septum. It projects forwards as a compressed rostrum beneath the pleurosphenoid (Fig. 86A). Müller (1967) regards the rostral part of the basisphenoid and the infrapolar ossification as comprising a presphenoid, but is is uncertain whether this is really a separate bone at any stage in life.

The otic capsule ossifies from separate *prootic, epiotic* and *opisthotic* centres; the trigeminal foramen lies between the prootic and the back of the laterosphenoid. Epiotic and opisthotic fuse with the small *supraoccipital* (in the tectum) and *exoccipital* respectively; the latter ossifies in the lateral part of the basal plate behind the metotic fissure, the occipital arch and the metotic cartilage. The entire occipital condyle is formed by the basioccipital (Müller, 1967).

During later embryonic life the basisphenoid and basioccipital become occupied by extensions from the very complex system of Eustachian tubes; the development and anatomy of these have been described by Colbert (1946), Simonetta (1956), Romer (1956) and Müller (1967). Romer (1956) and Iordansky (1973) give good general accounts of the crocodilian skull and its foramina.

The *quadrate* ossifies in the quadrate cartilage. It comes to articulate firmly with the bones of the brain-case and otic capsule (thus nearly obliterating the cranio-quadrate passage), and of the palate and temporal region so that it is completely immovable (monimostylic). Together with

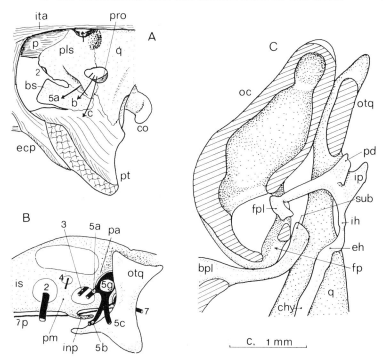

FIG. 86. *Crocodylus niloticus*. (A) Adult. Lateral view of left side of braincase showing pleurosphenoid and lines of exit of branches of trigeminal nerve (5a, b, c). (B) Late embryo. Reconstruction of orbito-temporal region in lateral view. A, B, after de Beer (1926). (C) Late embryo. Thick section through right otic capsule showing columellar apparatus from behind. Cut surfaces in slanting lines. After Frank and Smit (1974), with altered labelling.

bpl, Basal plate; bs, basisphenoid rostrum; chy, ceratohyal; co, occipital condyle; ecp, ectopterygoid; eh, epihyal; fp, foramen for perilymphatic duct; fpl, footplate of columella; ih, interhyal (pars inter-hyalis); inp, infrapolar process; ip, insertion plate; is, interorbital septum; ita, inferior temporal arcade (arrow beneath it leads into superior temporal fenestra); oc, otic capsule; otq, otic process of quadrate; p, parietal; pa, pila antotica; pd, dorsal process; pls, pleurosphenoid; pm, pila metoptica; pro, prootic; pt, pterygoid; q, quadrate; sub, subcapsular process; 2, optic nerve (notch for same in A); 3, oculo-motor nerve; 4, trochlear nerve; 5a, b, c, ophthalmic, maxillary, and mandibular branches of trigeminal nerve; 5g, trigeminal ganglion; 7, facial nerve (hyomandibular branch); 7p, palatine nerve.

the squamosal and opisthotic it forms a recess for the tympanic cavity and also for the cavity of the external meatus which in life is closed by the superior ear-flap, attached along the edge of the squamosal.

The quadrate contains a pneumatic extension from the tympanic cavity which continues downwards from it as the ductus pneumaticus or sipho-nium into the *articular*, ossifying in the rear end of Meckel's cartilage. The siphonial foramen in the articular is situated near the postero-medial border of the joint surface (Fig. 84D).

iii. Dermal bones

The following dermal bones are present; only some of them call for special comment below: *premaxilla, maxilla, nasal, vomer, palatine, ecto-pterygoid, pterygoid, parasphenoid*(unpaired), *lachrymal, jugal, quadratojugal, frontal,* and *parietal* (both become fused across the midline), *postorbital, squamosal, dentary, splenial, angular surangular,* and *coronoid.* In young *Alligator* there may be a small median *postparietal* (dermosupraoccipital) which later fuses with the parietal. In some forms (e.g. *Osteolaemus*) there is a well developed *palpebral* or supraciliary in the upper eyelid. There is no septomaxilla or supratemporal; the prearticular also appears to be absent unless it is fused either with the articular, or, as Liem and Smith (1961) suggest, with the angular. The chondrified sclera has no ossicles, though these were present in the Mesozoic marine crocodiles (Langston, 1973).

The premaxillae support the horny egg-caruncle of the hatchling (see de Beer, 1949). They also underlie the narial excrescence which develops in mature male *Gavialis* but do not participate in the composition of this curious structure (Martin and Bellairs, 1977). These bones remain paired in the adult. In most crocodilians the bony external nares are confluent, forming a single foramen, but in *Alligator* and *Osteolaemus* the premaxillae have small pre-narial ascending processes which meet anterior extensions from the nasals to form a bony septum which divides the narial aperture.

During later embryonic life the premaxillae, maxillae, palatines and pterygoids develop palatal processes which become approximated in the midline and form a complete bony floor beneath the nasal sacs, and beneath the two membranous tubes which constitute the nasopharyngeal ducts (Fig. 84A). In hatchling crocodilians the internal nostrils open near the middle of the pterygoids, but they become shifted towards the posterior margins of these bones during later life (Iordansky, 1973).

The suturing of the pterygoids in the midline occurs well before the end of embryonic life and covers the parabasisphenoid from below (Fig. 84B). In some crocodilians the pterygoids and palatines become dilated in maturity, and probably accommodate pneumatic outgrowths of the naso-pharyngeal ducts; the conspicuous pterygoid bullae seen in many large skulls of *Gavialis* are the best known examples of this modification (see Wegner, 1958; Iordansky, 1973; Martin and Bellairs, 1977).

The outer surface of the lateral flange of each pterygoid is covered by a thin layer of cartilage which plays against a similarly covered groove in the medial face of the angular, thus providing a kind of supplementary jaw joint which is important in the biting mechanism (Schumacher, 1973). De Beer (1937) suggested that this pterygoid cartilage is derived from the pterygoid process of the embryo. These pterygoid flanges are not fully developed in the 26 mm head-length *Alligator* embryo examined.

The vomers (prevomers of de Beer, 1937) arise as splints on the ventro-lateral aspect of each side of the nasal septum, towards the posterior parts of the nasal capsules. They do not fuse, but participate in the formation of the incomplete septum of the bony nasopharyngeal tube. They become covered ventrally by the maxillae and palatines (Fig. 83C, D).

The parasphenoid ossifies beneath the pituitary as a small plate which is in contact ventrally with the pterygoids. It fuses dorsally with the ossifying basisphenoid to form a parabasisphenoid beneath the pituitary fossa (Fig. 84B). De Beer (1937) regarded the small parasphenoid plate as corresponding with the base of the parasphenoid rostrum of lizards. The supposed wings of the bone, often termed basitemporals as in birds, develop separately in a more lateral position, beneath the Vidian canals. Müller (1967) believes that these plates are, in fact, ossifications of the infrapolar processes which later become parts of the basisphenoid (her presphenoid) and are not dermal parasphenoid elements. Her findings indicate the difficulty of distinguishing between perichondral and membranous ossification, a problem raised by Kesteven (1940) whose views on bone homologies have not, however, found general acceptance.

2. The Affinities of the Crocodilian Skull

The crocodilian skull conforms to the archosaurian diapsid type, though the superior temporal fenestra tend to be reduced in some Recent forms. The most notable modifications are the elongation of the jaws and the evolution of the very long secondary palate. As in Testudines, the pterygoids and quadrates are firmly attached to the brain-case; the basipterygoid articulation has been completely lost, even in the embryo. Thus the skull of Recent crocodilians show no trace of streptostyly or kinetism.

Despite obvious differences the crocodilian skull shows many deep-seated resemblances to that of birds, as emphasized in a perceptive paper by Walker (1972). Further characters could be added to his list, and include the presence of three nasal conchae or turbinals (though these may not be strictly homologous), the shape of the planum supraseptale (before it regresses in birds), the presence of suprapolar and infrapolar processes, the substantial development of the pleurosphenoid (perhaps a common archosaurian feature), the presence of subcapsular or metotic cartilages, the pattern of pneumatization by the tympano-Eustachian system and the presence of a siphonium (see Bellairs and Jenkin, 1960; Langston, 1973), the mode of articulation of the head of the quadrate with the otic capsule, and the position of the cranio-vertebral joint. So far as can be ascertained, the osteological similarities are even more marked in primitive protosuchian crocodilians such as the Upper Triassic *Sphenosuchus*, which still retained vestiges of kinetism.

Walker's observations have been extended by Whetstone and Martin (1979), who have demonstrated further resemblances between crocodilians and birds in the arrangement of the perilymphatic duct and the position of the secondary tympanic membrane, attached to the subcapsular process and filling in the fenestra pseudorotunda. The lateral displacement of the tip of the perilymphatic duct contrasts strikingly with the condition in *Sphenodon* and lizards, the primitive reptilian condition, in which the duct terminates in relationship to the anterior end of the metotic fissure. The typical crocodilian condition was apparently present in both *Sphenosuchus* and in the Cretaceous toothed bird *Hesperornis*.

Study of well preserved endocrania and endocranial casts shows that these crocodilian-avian conditions were not present in early thecodonts or in saurischian or ornithischian dinosaurs, which in this respect conformed to the primitive, *Sphenodon*-like pattern. The pneumatization of the bones surrounding the middle ear is another common feature of crocodilians and birds which was not shared by dinosaurs.

It would thus seem that some, apparently fundamental, resemblances among crocodilians and birds are not merely parts of a common archosaurian heritage, but indicate a close phylogenetic affinity between the two groups, which may well have been descended from a common pseudosuchian ancestor. However, this conclusion has been reassessed by Tarsitano and Hecht (1980).

It is also noteworthy, as de Beer (1937) has pointed out, that the developing skulls of Crocodilia and Testudines resemble each other more than either resembles the lepidosaurian condition. Among the similarities are the histological structure of developing bone, the composition of the craniovertebral joint (which is also like that in birds), the presence of a subcapsular or metotic cartilage (if Torien's, 1965a, views on this structure in Testudines are correct), the connection of the interhyal with Meckel's cartilage (a somewhat dubious feature), and the occurrence of a horny eggcaruncle. De Beer (1937, pp. 462, 463) interpreted these features as indicating that the Testudines must have been derived from a diapsid stock, and that the lack of temporal fenestrae (as opposed to emargination) in recent and fossil forms is a secondary, or derived character. The origins of the Testudines are still obscure, but few modern palaeontologists would support this view; it seems much more likely that the Testudines were directly descended from anapsid cotylosaurs. The significance of their chondrocranial resemblances with crocodilians therefore remains problematical.

Acknowledgments

A. d'A. B. is most grateful to Drs C. Gans, T. S. Parsons, R. Presley and O. Rieppel for their helpful comments, and to the Library Staff of the Zoological Society of London for much bibliographic assistance.

References

Albrecht, P. W. (1976). The cranial arteries of turtles and their evolutionary significance. *J. Morph.* **149**, 159–182.

Albright, R. G. and Nelson, E. M. (1959). Cranial kinetics of the generalized colubrid snake *Elaphe obsoleta quadrivittata*. I. Descriptive morphology. II. Functional morphology. *J. Morph.* **105**, 193–240; 241–292.

Allin, E. F. (1975). Evolution of the mammalian middle ear. *J. Morph.* **147**, 403–438.

Armstrong, J. A., Gamble, H. J. and Goldby, F. (1953). Observations on the olfactory apparatus and the telencephalon of *Anolis*, a microsmatic lizard. *J. Anat. Lond.* **87**, 288–307.

Auen, E. L. and Langebartel, D. A. (1977). The cranial nerves of the colubrid snakes *Elaphe* and *Thamnophis*. *J. Morph.* **154**, 205–222.

Auffenberg, W. (1978). Social and feeding behaviour in *Varanus komodoensis*. *In* "Behaviour and Neurology of Lizards." (N. Greenberg and P. D. MacLean, eds). National Institute of Mental Health, Maryland, pp. 301–331.

Bäckström, K. (1931). Rekonstruktionsbilder zur Ontogenie des Kopfskeletts von *Tropidonotus natrix*. *Acta zool. Stockh.* **12**, 83–143.

Baird, I. L. (1970). The anatomy of the reptilian ear. *In* "Biology of the Reptilia." (C. Gans and T. S. Parsons, eds). Academic Press, London and New York, **2**, 193–275.

Bahl, K. N. (1937). Skull of *Varanus monitor* (Linn.). *Rec. Indian Mus.* **39**, 133–174.

Barbarena, M. C., Gomes, N. M. B. and Sanchotene, L. M. P. (1970). Osteologia craniana de *Tupinambis teguixin* (Lacertilia, Teiidae). *Publ. Esp. Esc. Geol.* No. 21; Univ. Fed. Rio Grande do Sul [Brazil], 1–32.

Barry, T. H. (1953). Contributions to the cranial morphology of *Agama hispida* (Linn.). *Ann. Univ. Stellenbosch* **29**, 55–77.

Barry, T. H. (1963). On the variable occurrence of the tympanum in recent and fossil tetrapods. *S. Afr. J. Sci.* **59**, 160–175.

Baumeister, L. (1908). Beiträge zur Anatomie und Physiologie der Rhinophiden. *Zool. Jb. Anat.* **26**, 423–526.

Beaumont, E. H. (1977). Cranial morphology of the Loxommatidae (Amphibia: Labyrinthodontia). *Phil. Trans. R. Soc. B.* **280**, 29–101.

Bellairs, A. d'A. (1949a). The anterior brain-case and interorbital septum of Sauropsida, with a consideration of the origin of snakes. *J. Linn. Soc. (Zool.).* **41**, 482–512.

Bellairs, A. d'A. (1949b). Observations on the snout of *Varanus*, and a comparison with that of other lizards and snakes. *J. Anat.* **83**, 116–146.

Bellairs, A. d'A. (1949c). Orbital cartilages in snakes. *Nature, Lond.* **163**, 106.

Bellairs, A. d'A. (1950). Observations on the cranial anatomy of *Anniella*, and a comparison with that of other burrowing lizards. *Proc. zool. Soc. Lond.* **119**, 887–904.

Bellairs, A d'A. (1958). The early development of the interorbital septum and the fate of the anterior orbital cartilages in birds. *J. Embryol. exp. Morph.* **6**, 68–85.

248 A. D'A. BELLAIRS AND A. M. KAMAL

Bellairs, A. d'A. (1965). Cleft palate, microphthalmia and other malformations in embryos of lizards and snakes. *Proc. zool. Soc. Lond.* **144**, 239–251.
Bellairs, A. [d'A.] (1969). "The Life of Reptiles." Weidenfeld and Nicolson, London.
Bellairs, A. d'A. (1971). The senses of crocodilians. *Proc. first working meeting of crocodile specialists, I.U.C.N.* Vol. 1, Paper 19, 181–189.
Bellairs, A. d'A. (1972). Comments on the evolution and affinities of snakes. *In* "Studies in Vertebrate Evolution." (K. A. Joysey and T. S. Kemp, eds). Oliver and Boyd, Edinburgh. pp. 157–172.
Bellairs, A. d'A. (1981). Congenital and developmental [malformations, etc]. *In* "Diseases of the Reptilia." (J. E. Cooper and O. F. Jackson, eds). Academic Press, London (in press).
Bellairs, A. d'A. and Attridge, J. (1975). "Reptiles." Hutchinson, London.
Bellairs, A. d'A. and Boyd, J. D. (1950). The lachrymal apparatus in lizards and snakes. -II. The anterior part of the lachrymal duct and its relationship with the palate and with the nasal and vomeronasal organs. *Proc. zool. Soc. Lond.* **120**, 269–310.
Bellairs, A. d'A. and Boyd, J. D. (1957). Anomalous cleft palate in snake embryos. *Proc. zool. Soc. Lond.* **129**, 525–539.
Bellairs, A. d'A. and Gamble, H. J. (1960). Cleft palate, microphthalmia and other anomalies in an embryo lizard (*Lacerta vivipara* Jacquin). *Br. J. Herpet.* **2**, 171–176.
Bellairs, A. d'A. and Jenkin, C. R. (1960). The skeleton of birds. *In* "Biology and Comparative Physiology of Birds." (A. J. Marshall, ed.). Academic Press, New York and London, **1**, 241–300.
Bellairs, A. d'A. and Shute, C. C. D. (1953). Observations on the narial musculature of Crocodilia and its innervation from the sympathetic system. *J. Anat.* **87**, 367–378.
Bender, O. (1911). Ueber Herkunft und Entwicklung der Columella auris bei *Testudo graeca. Anat. Anz.* **40**, 161–177.
Berman, D. S. and Regal, P. J. (1967). The loss of the ophidian middle ear. *Evolution* **21**, 641–643.
Bertau, M. (1935). Zur Entwicklungsgeschichte des Geruchsorgans der Krokodile. *Z. Anat. EntwGesch.* **104**, 168–202.
Bogert, C. M. (1943). Dentitional phenomena in cobras and other elapids with notes on adaptive modifications of fangs. *Bull. Am. Mus. nat. Hist.* **81**, 285–360.
Boltt, R. E. and Ewer, R. F. (1964). The functional anatomy of the head of the puff adder, *Bitis arietans* (Merr.). *J. Morph.* **114**, 83–106.
Born, G. (1879). Die Nasenhöhlen und der Thränennasengang der amnioten Wirbelthiere. I. *Morph. Jrb.* **5**, 62–140.
Born, G. (1883). Die Nasenhöhlen und der Thränennasengang der amnioten Wirbelthiere. III. *Morph. Jrb.* **8**, 188–232.
Brock, G. T. (1929). On the development of the skull of *Leptodeira hotamboia. Q. J. microsc. Sci.* **73**, 289–334. [*Leptodeira* = *Crotaphopeltis*].
Brock, G. T. (1932a). Some developmental stages in the skulls of the geckos, *Lygodactylus capensis* and *Pachydactylus maculosa*, and their bearing on certain important problems in lacertilian craniology. *S. Afr. J. Sci.* **29**, 508–532.
Brock, G. T. (1932b). The skull of *Leptotyphlops* (*Glauconia*) *nigricans. Anat. Anz.* **73**, 199–204 [of reprint].
Brock, G. T. (1935). The temporal bones in lizards, birds and mammals. *Anat. Anz.* **80**, 266–284.
Brock, G. T. (1941a). The skull of *Acontias meleagris*, with a study of the affinities between lizards and snakes. *J. Linn. Soc.* (*Zool.*). **41**, 71–88.
Brock, G. T. (1941b). The skull of the chameleon, *Lophosaura ventralis* (Gray); some developmental stages. *Proc. zool. Soc. Lond.* **110**, 219–241. [*Lophosaura* = *Bradypodion*].

Broom, R. (1906). On the organ of Jacobson in *Sphenodon*. *J. Linn. Soc. (Zool.)*. **29**, 414–420.

Bustard, [H.] R. (1972). "Sea Turtles." Collins, London and Sydney.

Camp, C. L. (1923). Classification of the lizards. *Bull. Am. Mus. nat. Hist.* **48**, 289–481.

Capel-Williams, G. and Pratten, D. (1978). The diet of adult and juvenile *Agama bibroni* (Reptilia: Lacertae) and a study of the jaw mechanisms in the two age groups. *J. Zool., Lond.* **185**, 309–318.

Carroll, R. L. (1977). The origin of lizards. *In* "Problems in Vertebrate Evolution." (S. M. Andrews, R. S. Miles and A. D. Walker, eds). *Linn. Soc. Symp. Ser.* Academic Press, London. (4), 359–396.

Castanet, J. (1978). Les marques de croissance osseuse comme indicateurs de l'âge chez les lézards. *Acta zool. Stockh.* **59**, 35–48.

Castanet, J. and Naulleau, G. (1974). Données expérimentales sur le valeur des marques squelettiques comme indicateur de l'age chez *Vipera aspis* (L.) (Ophidia, Viperidae). *Zoologica Scripta* **3**, 201–208.

Colbert, E. H. (1946). The Eustachian tubes in the Crocodilia. *Copeia* **1946**, 12–14.

Cords, E. (1909). Die Entwickelung der Paukenhöhle von *Lacerta agilis*. *Anat. Hefte* **38**, 219–319.

Cox, D. C. and Tanner, W. W. (1977). Osteology and myology of the head and neck regions of *Callisaurus, Cophosaurus, Holbrookia* and *Uma* (Reptilia: Iguanidae). *Great Basin Nat.* **37**, 35–56.

Dalrymple, G. H. (1977). Intraspecific variation in the cranial feeding mechanism of turtles of the genus *Trionyx* (Reptilia, Testudines, Trionychidae). *J. Herpet.* **11**, 255–285.

Dalrymple, G. H. (1979). On the jaw mechanism of the snail-crushing lizards, *Dracaena* Daudin 1802 (Reptilia, Lacertilia, Teiidae). *J. Herpet.* **13**, 303–311.

De Beer, G. R. (1926). Studies on the vertebrate head. II. The orbitotemporal region of the skull. *Q. J. microsc. Sci.* **70**, 263–370.

De Beer, G. R. (1930). The early development of the chondrocranium of the lizard. *Q. J. microsc. Sci.* **73**, 707–739.

De Beer, G. R. (1937). "The development of the Vertebrate Skull." The Clarendon Press, Oxford. [The 1971 reprint is virtually unchanged apart from the addition of some references.]

De Beer, G. R. (1949). Caruncles and egg-teeth: some aspects of the concept of homology. *Proc. Linn. Soc. Lond.* Session 161, 1948–49. 218–224.

De Beer, G. R. and Barrington, E. J. W. (1934). The segmentation and chondrification of the skull of the duck. *Phil. Trans. R. Soc. B*, **223**, 411–467.

De Villiers, C. G. S. (1939). Über den Schädel des südafrikanischen schlangenartigen Scinciden *Acontias meleagris*. *Anat. Anz.* **88**, 320–347 [of reprint].

Dingerkus, G. and Uhler, L. D. (1977). Enzyme clearing of alcian blue stained whole small vertebrates for demonstration of cartilage. *Stain Technol.* **52**, 229–232.

Dodson, P. (1975). Functional and ecological significance of relative growth in *Alligator*. *J. Zool. Lond.* **175**, 315–355.

Dohrer, J. (1919). Die Entwicklung der Paukentasche bei *Chelydra serpentina*. *Morph. Jb.* **97**, 103–112.

Dufaure, J. P. and Hubert, J. (1961). Table de développement du lézard vivipare: *Lacerta* (*Zootoca*) *vivipara* Jacquin. *Archs. Anat. microsc. Morph. exp.* **50**, 309–328.

Dullemeijer, P. (1959). A comparative functional-anatomical study of the heads of some Viperidae. *Morph. Jb.* **99**, 881–985.

Dullemeijer, P. and Povel, G. D. E. (1972). The construction for feeding in rattlesnakes. *Zool. Meded., Leiden*, **47** (Feestbundel L. D. Brongersma), 561–578.

Du Plessis, S. S. (1945). Cranial anatomy and ontogeny of the South African cordylid *Chamaesaura anguina*. *S. Afr. J. Sci.* 41, 245–268.

Duvdevani, I. (1972). The anatomy and histology of the nasal cavities and the nasal salt gland in four species of fringe-toed lizards, *Acanthodactylus* (Lacertidae). *J. Morph.* 137, 353–364.

Edgeworth, F. H. (1935). "The Cranial Muscles of Vertebrates." Cambridge University Press.

El-Assy, Y. S. and Al-Nassar, N. A. (1976). Morphological study of the cranial osteology of the amphisbaenian *Diplometopon zarudnyi*. *J. Univ. Kuwait (Sci.)*. 3, 113–141.

El-Toubi, M. R. and Kamal, A. M. (1959a). The development of the skull of *Chalcides ocellatus*. I. The development of the chondrocranium. *J. Morph.* 104, 269–306.

El-Toubi, M. R. and Kamal, A. M. (1959b). The development of the skull of *Chalcides ocellatus*. II. The fully formed chondrocranium and the osteocranium of a late embryo. *J. Morph.* 105, 55–104.

El-Toubi, M. R. and Kamal, A. M. (1961a). The development of the skull of *Ptyodactylus hasselquistii*. I. The development of the chondrocranium. *J. Morph.* 108, 63–94.

El-Toubi, M. R. and Kamal, A. M. (1961b). The development of the skull of *Ptyodactylus hasselquistii*. II. The fully formed chondrocranium. *J. Morph.* 108, 165–192.

El-Toubi, M. R. and Kamal, A. M. (1961c). The development of the skull of *Ptyodactylus hasselquistii*. III. The osteocranium of a late embryo. *J. Morph.* 108, 193–202.

El-Toubi, M. R. and Kamal, A. E. M. (1965). The origin of the tectum of the occipito-auditory region in Squamata. *Proc. Egypt. Acad. Sci.* 18, 73–75.

El-Toubi, M. R. and Kamal, A. M. (1970). The origin of lizards in the light of the developmental study of the skull. *Z. zool. Syst. Evolforsch.* 8, 47–52.

El-Toubi, M. R., Kamal, A. M. and Hammouda, H. G. (1965a). The phylogenetic relationship between the ophidian families Boidae, Colubridae and Viperidae in the light of the developmental study of the skull. *Zool. Anz.* 175, 289–294.

El-Toubi, M. R., Kamal, A. M. and Hammouda, H. G. (1965b). The origin of the Ophidia in the light of the developmental study of the skull. *Z. zool. Syst. Evolforsch.* 3, 94–102.

El-Toubi, M. R., Kamal, A. M. and Hammouda, H. G. (1968). The common characters of the ophidian chondrocranium. *Bull. Fac. Sci. Egypt. Univ.* 41, 109–118.

El-Toubi, M. R., Kamal, A. M. and Mokhtar, F. M. (1970). The chondrocranium of late embryos of the Egyptian cobra, *Naja haje*. *Anat. Anz.* 127, 233–289.

El-Toubi, M. R., Kamal, A. M. and Zaher, M. M. (1973a). The development of the chondrocranium of the snake, *Malpolon monspessulana*. I. The early and intermediate stages. *Acta Anat.* 85, 275–299.

El-Toubi, M. R., Kamal, A. M. and Zaher, M. M. (1973b). The development of the chondrocranium of the snake, *Malpolon monspessulana*. II. The fully formed stage. *Acta Anat.* 85, 593–619.

El-Toubi, M. R. and Soliman, M. A. (1967). Studies on the osteology of the family Lacertidae in Egypt. I. The skull. *Proc. zool. Soc. United Arab Republic* 2, 219–257.

Engelbrecht, D. van Z. (1951). Contributions to the cranial morphology of the chamaeleon *Microsaura pumila* Daudin. *Ann. Univ. Stellenbosch* 27 (A), 3–31. [*Microsaura* = *Bradypodion*.]

Enlow, D. H. (1969). The Bone of Reptiles. *In* "Biology of the Reptilia." (C. Gans, A. d'A. Bellairs and T. S. Parsons, eds). Academic Press, London and New York, 1, 45–80.

Estes, R., Frazzetta, T. H. and Williams, E. E. (1970). Studies on the fossil snake *Dinilysia patagonica* Woodward: Part I. Cranial morphology. *Bull. Mus. comp. Zool. Harv.* 140, 25–74.

Eyal-Giladi, H. (1964). The development of the chondrocranium of *Agama stellio*. *Acta Zool. Stockh.* 45, 139–165.

Fineman, G. (1941). Zur Entwicklungsgeschichte des Kopfskeletes bei *Chamaeleon bitaeniatus ellioti. Morph. Jb.* **85**, 91–114.

Fisher, D. L. and Tanner, W. W. (1970). Osteological and myological comparisons of the head and thorax regions of *Cnemidophorus tigris septentrionalis* Burger and *Ameiva undulata parva* Barbour and Noble (family Teiidae). *Brigham Young Univ. Sci. Bull. Biol.* **11**, 1–41.

Fischer, E. (1900). Beiträge zur Kenntniss der Nasenhöhle und des Tränennasenganges der Amphisbaeniden. *Arch. mikrosk. Anat. Entwicklungsmech.* **55**, 441–478.

Frank, G. H. (1951). Contributions to the cranial morphology of *Rhampholeon platyceps* Günther. *Ann. Univ. Stellenbosch* **27** (A), 33–67.

Frank, G. H. and Smit, A. L. (1974). The early ontogeny of the columella auris of *Crocodilus niloticus* and its bearing on problems concerning the upper end of the reptilian hyoid arch. *Zool. Africana* **9**, 59–88.

Franklin, M. A. (1945). The embryonic appearance of centres of ossification in the bones of snakes. *Copeia* **1945**, 68–72.

Frazzetta, T. H. (1959). Studies on the morphology and function of the skull in the Boidae (Serpentes). Part 1. Cranial differences between *Python sebae* and *Epicrates cenchris. Bull. Mus. comp. Zool. Harv.* **119**, 453–472.

Frazzetta, T. H. (1962). A functional consideration of cranial kinesis in lizards. *J. Morph.* **111**, 287–320.

Frazzetta, T. H. (1966). Studies on the morphology and function of the skull in the Boidae (Serpentes). Part 2. Morphology and function of the jaw apparatus in *Python sebae* and *Python molurus. J. Morph.* **118**, 217–296.

Frazzetta, T. H. (1968). Adaptive problems and possibilities in the temporal fenestration of tetrapod skulls. *J. Morph.* **125**, 145–158.

Frazzetta, T. H. (1970). Studies on the fossil snake *Dinilysia patagonica* Woodward. *Forma et Functio* **3**, 205–221.

Frazzetta, T. H. (1975). Pattern and instability in the evolving premaxilla of boine snakes. *Amer. Zool.* **15**, 469–481.

Fuchs, H. (1907). Über das Hyobranchialskelett von *Emys lutaria* und seine Entwicklung. *Anat. Anz.* **31**, 33–39.

Fuchs, H. (1908). Untersuchungen über Ontogenie und Phylogenie der Gaumenbildung bei den Wirbeltieren. Zweite Mitteilung. Über das Munddach der Rhynchocephalen, Saurier, Schlangen, Krokodile und Säuger und den Zusammenhang zwischen Mundund Nasenhöhle bei diesen Tieren. *Z. Morph. Anthrop.* **11**, 153–248.

Fuchs, H. (1915). Über den Bau und die Entwicklung des Schädels der *Chelone imbricata.* Ein Beitrag zur Entwicklungsgeschichte und vergleichenden Anatomie des Wirbeltierschädels. Erster Teil: Das Primordialskelett des Neurocraniums und des Kieferbogens. *In* "Reise in Ostafrika in den Jahren 1903–1905. Wissenschaftliche Ergebnisse." (A. Voeltzkow, ed.). Vol. 5. E. Schweizerbart, Stuttgart, pp. 1–325.

Fuchs, H. (1931). Über den Unterkiefer und die Unterkiefernerven (Ramus tertius nervi trigemini et Chorda tympani) der Arrauschildkröte (*Podocnemis expansa*), nebst Bemerkungen zur Kiefergelenksfrage. *Z. Anat. Entw.* **94**, 206–274.

Gabe, M. and Saint Girons, H. (1976). Contribution à la morphologie comparée des fosses nasales et de leurs annexes chez les lépidosoriens. *Mém. Mus. natn. Hist. nat., Paris* (A), **98**, 1–87.

Gadow, H. (1901). "Amphibia and Reptiles." (Cambridge Natural History). Macmillan, London.

Gaffney, E. S. (1972). An illustrated glossary of turtle skull nomenclature. *Am. Mus. Novit.* (2486), 1–33.

Gaffney, E. S. (1975). A phylogeny and classification of the higher categories of turtles. *Bull. Am. Mus. nat. Hist.* 155, 387–436.

Gaffney, E. S. (1976). Cranial morphology of the European Jurassic turtles *Portlandemys* and *Plesiochelys*. *Bull. Am. Mus. nat. Hist.* 157, 487–544.

Gaffney, E. S. (1977). The side-necked turtle family Chelidae: a theory of relationships using shared derived characters. *Am. Mus. Novit.* (2620), 1–28.

Gaffney, E. S. (1979). Comparative cranial morphology of Recent and fossil turtles. *Bull. Am. Mus. nat. Hist.* 164, 65–376.

Gans, C. (1952). The functional morphology of the egg-eating adaptations in the snake genus *Dasypeltis*. *Zoologica, N. Y.* 37, 209–244.

Gans, C. (1960). Studies on amphisbaenids (Amphisbaenia, Reptilia). 1. A taxonomic revision of the Trogonophinae, and a functional interpretation of the amphisbaenid adaptive pattern. *Bull. Am. Mus. nat. Hist.* 119, 129–204.

Gans, C. (1961). The feeding mechanism of snakes and its possible evolution. *Am. Zool.* 1, 217–227.

Gans, C. (1974). "Biomechanics: An Approach to Vertebrate Biology." J. B. Lippincott, Philadelphia and Toronto.

Gans, C. (1978). The characteristics and affinities of Amphisbaenia. *Trans. zool. Soc. Lond.* 34, 347–416.

Gans, C. and Wever, E. G. (1972). The ear and hearing in Amphisbaenia (Reptilia). *J. exp. Zool.* 179, 17–34.

Gans, C. and Wever, E. G. (1975). The amphisbaenian ear: *Blanus cinereus* and *Diplometopon zarudnyi*. *Proc. natn. Acad. Sci. U.S.A.* 72, 1487–1490.

Gasc, J.-P. (1968). Contribution à l'ostéologie et à la myologie de *Dibamus novaeguineae* Gray (Sauria, Reptilia). *Annls Sci. nat. (Zool.)* 10 (12), 127–150.

Gaunt, P. N. and Gaunt, W. A. (1978). "Three Dimensional Reconstruction in Biology." Pitman Medical Publishing, Tunbridge Wells.

Gaupp, E. (1900). Das Chondrocranium von *Lacerta agilis*. Ein Beitrag zum Verständnis des Amniotenschädels. *Anat. Hefte* 15, 433–595.

Gaupp, E. (1902). Über die Ala temporalis des Säugerschädels und die Regio orbitalis einiger anderer Wirbeltierschädel. *Anat. Hefte* 19, 155–230.

Gaupp, E. (1906). Die Entwickelung des Kopfskelettes. *In* "Handbuch der vergleichenden und experimentellen Entwickelungslehre der Wirbeltiere." (O. Hertwig, ed.). G. Fischer, Jena, 3, 573–873.

Genest-Villard, H. (1966). Développément du crâne d'un boidé: *Sanzinia madagascariensis*. *Mém. Mus. natn. Hist. nat.* 40A, 207–262.

Girgis, F. G. and Pritchard, J. J. (1958). Effects of skull damage on the development of sutural patterns in the rat. *J. Anat.* 92, 39–51.

Gnanamuthu, C. P. (1937). Comparative study of the hyoid and tongue of some typical genera of reptiles. *Proc. zool. Soc. Lond.* 1–63.

Goldby, F. (1925). The development of the columella auris in the Crocodilia. *J. Anat.* 59, 301–325.

Goodrich, E. S. (1930). "Studies on the Structure and Development of Vertebrates." Macmillan, London.

Greer, A. E. (1976). On the occurrence of a stapedial foramen in living non-gekkonid lepidosaurs. *Copeia*, 1976, 591–592.

Greer, A. E. (1970). A subfamilial classification of scincid lizards. *Bull. Mus. comp. Zool. Harv.* 139, 151–183.

Groombridge, B.[C.] (1979a). On the vomer in Acrochordidae (Reptilia: Serpentes), and its cladistic significance. *J. Zool. Lond.* 189, 559–567.

Groombridge, B. C. (1979b). Variations in morphology of the superficial palate of henophidian snakes and some possible systematic implications. *J. nat. Hist.* **13**, 447–475.

Groombridge, B. C. (1979c). Comments on the intermandibular muscles of snakes. *J. nat. Hist.* **13**, 477–498.

Groombridge, B. C. (1979d). A previously unreported throat muscle in Scolecophidia (Reptilia: Serpentes), with comments on other scolecophidian throat muscles. *J. nat. Hist.* **13**, 661–680.

Guibé, J. (1970). Le squelette céphalique. *In* "Traité de Zoologie." (P.-P. Grassé, ed.). Masson, Paris, **14** (2), 78–143.

Haas, G. (1935). Zum Bau des Primordialcraniums und des Kopfskelettes von *Ablepharus pannonicus*. *Acta zool. Stockh.* **16**, 409–429.

Haas, G. (1936). Über das Kopfskelett von *Chalcides guentheri* (*Seps monodactylus*). *Acta zool. Stockh.* **17**, 55–74.

Haas, G. (1947). Jacobson's organ in chameleon. *J. Morph.* **81**, 195–208.

Haas, G. (1959). Bemerkungen über die Anatomie des Kopfes und des Schädels der Leptotyphlopidae (Ophidia), speziell von *L. macrorhynchus* Jan. *Vjschr. naturf. Ges. Zürich* **104**, Festschrift. Steiner. 90–104.

Haas, G. (1964). Anatomical observations on the head of *Liotyphlops albirostris* (Typhlopidae, Ophidia). *Acta zool. Stockh.* **45**, 1–62.

Haas, G. (1968). Anatomical observations on the head of *Anomalepis aspinosus* (Typhlopidae, Ophidia). *Acta zool. Stockh.* **49**, 63–139.

Haas, G. (1973). Muscles of the jaws and associated structures in the Rhynchocephalia and Squamata. *In* "Biology of the Reptilia." (C. Gans and T. S. Parsons, eds). Academic Press, London and New York, **4**, 285–490.

Hafferl, A. (1921). Das knorpelige Neurocranium des Gecko (*Platydactylus annularis*). *Z. Anat. EntwGesch.* **62**, 433–518.

Haines, R. W. (1969). Epiphyses and sesamoids. *In* "Biology of the Reptilia." (C. Gans, A. d'A. Bellairs and T. S. Parsons, eds). Academic Press, London and New York, **1**, 81–115.

Hall, B. K. (1975). Evolutionary consequences of skeletal differentiation. *Am. Zool.* **15**, 329–350.

Hall, B. K. (1978). "Developmental and Cellular Skeletal Biology." Academic Press, New York and London.

Halstead, L. B. (1974). "Vertebrate Hard Tissues." Wykeham Publications, London.

Harris, V. A. (1963). "The Anatomy of the Rainbow Lizard *Agama agama* (L.)." Hutchinson Tropical Monographs, London.

Hegazy, M. A. (1976). "Comparative Anatomical Studies on the Cranial Nerves of Ophidia." Ph.D. thesis, University of Cairo.

Hochstetter, F. (1951). Über die Rückbildung der Ohröffnung und des äusseren Gehörganges bei der Blindschleiche (*Anguis fragilis*). *Denksch. Öst. Akad. Wiss. math. nat. Kl.* **108**, 1–35.

Hoffstetter, R. and Gasc, J.-P. (1969). Vertebrae and ribs of modern reptiles. *In* "Biology of the Reptilia." (C. Gans, A. d'A. Bellairs and T. S. Parsons, eds). Academic Press, London and New York, **1**, 201–310.

Holder, L. A. and Bellairs, A. d'A. (1962). The use of reptiles in experimental embryology. *Br. J. Herpet.* **3**, 54–61.

Hoppe, G. (1934). Das Geruchsorgan von *Hatteria punctata*. *Z. EntwGesch.* **102**, 434–461.

Hörstadius, S. (1950). "The Neural Crest." Oxford University Press.

Howes, G. B. (1975). William Kitchen Parker (1823–1890). *In* "The Compact Edition of the Dictionary of National Biography." (Complete text reproduced microphotographically). Oxford University Press, Vol. 2, p. 1592.

Howes, G. B. and Swinnerton, H. H. (1901). On the development of the skeleton of the tuatara, *Sphenodon punctatus*; with remarks on the egg, on the hatching, and on the hatched young. *Trans. zool. Soc., Lond.* **16**, 1–86.

Hubert, J. and Dufaure, J. P. (1968). Table de développement de la vipère aspic: *Vipera aspis*. L. *Bull. Soc. zool. Fr.* **93**, 135–148.

Huxley, T. H. (1858). On the theory of the vertebrate skull. *Proc. R. Soc.* **9**, 381–457.

Huxley, T. H. (1864). "Lectures on the Elements of Comparative Anatomy." J. Churchill, London.

Huxley, T. H. (1869). On the representatives of the malleus and the incus of the Mammalia in the other Vertebrata. *Proc. zool. Soc. Lond.* 391–407.

Huxley, T. H. (1894). Owen's position in the history of anatomical science. *In* "The Life of Richard Owen," by his Grandson the Rev. Richard Owen, M.A. With the Scientific Portions Revised by C. Davies Sherborn. John Murray, London, Vol. 2.

Iordansky, N. N. (1970). Structure and biomechanical analysis of functions of the jaw muscles in lizards. *Anat. Anz.* **127**, 383–413.

Iordansky, N. N. (1973). The skull of the Crocodilia. *In* "Biology of the Reptilia." (C. Gans and T. S. Parsons, eds). Academic Press, London and New York. **4**, 201–262.

Jarvik, E. (1942). On the structure of the snout of crossopterygians and lower gnathostomes in general. *Zool. Bidr. Uppsala* **21**, 235–675.

Jaskoll, T. F. and Maderson, P. F. A. (1978). A histological study of the development of the avian middle ear and tympanum. *Anat. Rec.* **190**, 177–200.

Jenkins, N. K. and Simkiss, K. (1968). The calcium and phosphate metabolism of reproducing reptiles with particular reference to the adder (*Vipera berus*). *Comp. Biochem. Physiol.* **26**, 865–876.

Jollie, M. J. (1960). The head skeleton of the lizard. *Acta zool. Stockh.* **41**, 1–64.

Kälin, J. A. (1933). Beiträge zur vergleichenden Osteologie des Crocodilidenschädels. *Zool. Jb. Abt. Anat.* **57** (4), 535–714.

Kamal, A. M. (1960). The chondrocranium of *Tropiocolotes tripolitanus*. *Acta zool. Stockh.* **41**, 297–312.

Kamal, A. M. (1961a). The chondrocranium of *Hemidactylus turcica*. *Anat. Anz.* **109**, 89–108.

Kamal, A. M. (1961b). The common characters of the geckonid chondrocranium. *Anat. Anz.* **109**, 109–113.

Kamal, A. M. (1961c). The phylogenetic position of the Geckonidae in the light of the developmental study of the skull. *Anat. Anz.* **109**, 114–116.

Kamal, A. M. (1964a). Notes on the chondrocranium of the gecko, *Tropiocolotes steudneri*. *Bull. zool. Soc. Egypt* **19**, 73–83.

Kamal, A. M. (1964b). Note on the relation between the dorsal and ventral components of the mandibular arch in early embryos of Squamata. *Bull. zool. Soc. Egypt* **19**, 84–86.

Kamal, A. M. (1964c). Note on an aberrant intracapsular course of the facial nerve in early stages of the snake *Psammophis sibilans*. *Bull. zool. Soc. Egypt* **19**, 87–88.

Kamal, A. M. (1965a). The cranial osteology of adult *Chalcides ocellatus*. *Anat. Anz.* **117**, 338–370.

Kamal, A. E. M. (1965b). The chondrocranium of the gecko *Stenodactylus sthenodactylus*. *Proc. Egypt. Acad. Sci.* **18**, 59–69.

Kamal, A. M. (1965c). The fully formed chondrocranium of *Eumeces schneideri*. *Proc. Egypt. Acad. Sci.* **19**, 13–20.

Kamal, A. M. (1965d). Observations on the chondrocranium of *Tarentola mauritanica*. *Proc. Egypt. Acad. Sci.* **19**, 1–9.

Kamal, A. M. (1965e). The relation between the auditory capsule and the basal plate, and the commissures between them in Squamata. *Zool. Anz.* **175**, 281–285.

Kamal, A. M. (1965f). The mode of formation of the fenestrae basicranialis, X and ovalis in Squamata. *Zool. Anz.* **175**, 285–288.

Kamal, A. M. (1965g). The origin of the interorbital septum of Lacertilia. *Proc. Egypt. Acad. Sci.* **18**, 70–72.

Kamal, A. M. (1965h). On the cranio-vertebral joint and the relation between the notochord and occipital condyle in Squamata. *Proc. Egypt. Acad. Sci.* **19**, 11–12.

Kamal, A. M. (1966a). The single origin of the parachordal plate in Squamata. *Zool. Anz.* **176**, 3–5.

Kamal, A. M. (1966b). The sphenoid bone in Lacertilia. *Anat. Anz.* **118**, 82–86.

Kamal, A. M. (1966c). On the hypoglossal foramina in Squamata. *Anat. Anz.* **118**, 91–96.

Kamal, A. M. (1966d). On the process of rotation of the quadrate cartilage in Ophidia. *Anat. Anz.* **118**, 87–90.

Kamal, A. M. (1968). On the concha nasalis of Squamata. *Bull. Fac. Sci. Egypt. Univ.* **41**, 97–108.

Kamal, A. M. (1968–1969). The differences between the lacertilian and ophidian chondrocrania. *Bull. zool. Soc. Egypt* (22), 121–129.

Kamal, A. M. (1969a). The development and morphology of the chondrocranium of *Chalcides* species. *Proc. Egypt. Acad. Sci.* **22**, 37–48.

Kamal, A. M. (1969b). On the trabeculae cranii and trabecula communis in early embryos of Squamata. *Proc. Egypt. Acad. Sci.* **22**, 49–51.

Kamal, A. M. (1969c). The fused posterior orbital cartilages of lizards. *Proc. Egypt. Acad. Sci.* **22**, 53–55.

Kamal, A. M. (1969d). The phylogenetic position of the family Elapidae in the light of the developmental study of the skull. *Z. zool. Syst. Evolforsch.* **7**, 254–259.

Kamal, A. M. (1969e). The relation between the glossopharyngeal nerve and the chondrocranium in Squamata. *Proc. zool. Soc. United Arab Republic* **3**, 23–29.

Kamal, A. M. (1970). The distinctive characters of the elapid chondrocranium. *Anat. Anz.* **127**, 171–175.

Kamal, A. M. (1971). On the fissura metotica in Squamata. *Bull. zool. Soc. Egypt* (23), 53–57.

Kamal, A. M. (1972). The pterygoquadrate cartilage in Squamata. *Z. wiss. Zool.* **185**, 69–75.

Kamal, A. M. (1973a). The position of the prefacial commissure and facial foramen in Squamata. *Anat. Anz.* **133**, 283–286.

Kamal, A. M. (1973b). On the connection between the chondrocranium and vertebral column in embryos of Squamata. *Anat. Anz.* **133**, 287–290.

Kamal, A. M. and Abdeen, A. M. (1972). The development of the chondrocranium of the lacertid lizard, *Acanthodactylus boskiana*. *J. Morph.* **137**, 289–334.

Kamal, A. M. and Hammouda, H. G. (1965a). The development of the skull of *Psammophis sibilans*. I. The development of the chondrocranium. *J. Morph.* **116**, 197–246.

Kamal, A. M. and Hammouda, H. G. (1965b). The development of the skull of *Psammophis sibilans*. II. The fully formed chondrocranium. *J. Morph.* **116**, 247–296.

Kamal, A. M. and Hammouda, H. G. (1965c). The development of the skull of *Psammophis sibilans*. III. The osteocranium of a late embryo. *J. Morph.* **116**, 297–310.

Kamal, A. M. and Hammouda, H. G. (1965d). The columella auris of the snake, *Psammophis sibilans*. *Anat. Anz.* **116**, 124–138.

Kamal, A. M. and Hammouda, H. G. (1965e). Observations on the chondrocranium of the snake, *Cerastes vipera*. *Morph. Jb.* **107**, 58–98.

Kamal, A. M. and Hammouda, H. G. (1965f). The chondrocranium of the snake *Eryx jaculus*. *Acta zool. Stockh.* **46**, 167–208.

Kamal, A. M. and Hammouda, H. G. (1965g). On the laterosphenoid bone in Ophidia. *Anat. Anz.* **116**, 116–123.

Kamal, A. M. and Hammouda, H. G. (1968). The cranial osteology of adult *Psammophis sibilans*. *Bull. Fac. Sci. Egypt Univ.* **41**, 119–149.

Kamal, A. M. and Hammouda, H. G. (1969). The structure of the inner ear (membraneous labyrinth) and secondary tympanic membrane in a late embryo of the snake *Psammophis sibilans*. *Proc. zool. Soc. United Arab Republic* 3, 31–40.

Kamal, A. M. and Zada, S. K. (1970). The phylogenetic position of the family Agamidae in the light of the study of the chondrocranium. *Zool. Anz.* 184, 327–335.

Kamal, A. M. and Zada, S. K. (1973). The early developmental stages of the chondrocranium of *Agama pallida*. *Acta morph. neerl.-scand.* 11, 75–104.

Kamal, A. M., Hammouda, H. G. and Mokhtar, F. M. (1970a). The development of the osteocranium of the Egyptian cobra. I. The embryonic osteocranium. *Acta zool. Stockh.* 51, 1–17.

Kamal, A. M., Hammouda, H. G. and Mokhtar, F. M. (1970b). The development of the osteocranium of the Egyptian cobra. II. The median dorsal bones, bones of the upper jaw, circumorbital series and occipital ring of the adult osteocranium. *Acta zool. Stockh.* 51, 19–30.

Kamal, A. M., Hammouda, H. G. and Mokhtar, F. M. (1970c). The development of the osteocranium of the Egyptian cobra. III. The otic capsule, palate, temporal bones, lower jaw and hyoid apparatus of the adult osteocranium. *Acta zool. Stockh.* 51, 31–42.

Kardong, K. V. (1977). Kinesis of the jaw apparatus during swallowing in the cottonmouth snake, *Agkistrodon piscivorus*. *Copeia*, 1977, 338–348.

Kathariner, L. (1900). Die Nase der im Wasser lebenden Schlangen als Luftweg und Geruchsorgan. *Zool. Jb. (Syst.)* 13, 415–442.

Kesteven, H. L. (1940). The osteogenesis of the base of the saurian cranium and a search for the parasphenoid bone. *Proc. Linn. Soc. N.S.W.* 65, 447–467.

Kesteven, H. L. (1957a). Notes on the skull and cephalic muscles of the Amphisbaenia. *Proc. Linn. Soc. N.S.W.* 82, 109–116.

Kesteven, H. L. (1957b). On the development of the crocodilian skull. *Proc. Linn. Soc. N.S.W.* 82, 117–124.

Kiran, U. (1979). Evolutionary significance of the relative disposition of the bones in the jaw complex of snakes and lizards. *Ann. Zool.* [Agra]. 15, 59–78.

Kluge, A. G. (1962). Comparative osteology of the eublepharid genus *Coleonyx* Gray. *J. Morph.* 110, 299–332.

Kluge, A. G. (1967). Higher taxonomic categories of gekkonid lizards and their evolution. *Bull. Am. Mus. nat. Hist.* 135, 1–59.

Kochva, E. (1978). Oral glands of the Reptilia. *In* "Biology of the Reptilia." (C. Gans and K. A. Gans, eds). Academic Press, London and New York, 8, 43–161.

Kritzinger, C. C. (1946). The cranial anatomy and kinesis of the South African amphisbaenid *Monopeltis capensis* Smith. *S. Afr. J. Sci.* 42, 175–204.

Kunkel, B. W. (1912a). The development of the skull of *Emys lutaria*. *J. Morph.* 23, 693–780.

Kunkel, B. W. (1912b). On a double fenestral structure in *Emys*. *Anat. Rec.* 6, 267–280.

Lakjer, T. (1927). Studien über die Gaumenregion bei Sauriern im Vergleich mit Anamniern und primitiven Sauropsiden. *Zool. Jb. (Anat.)* 49, 57–356.

Langebartel, D. A. (1968). "The Hyoid and its Associated Muscles in Snakes." Illinois Biological Monographs 38. University of Illinois Press, Urbana, Chicago and London.

Langston, W. (1973). The crocodilian skull in historical perspective. *In* "Biology of the Reptilia." (C. Gans and T. S. Parsons, eds). Academic Press, London and New York, 4, 263–284.

Le Lièvre, C. S. (1978). Participation of neural-crest derived cells in the genesis of the skull in birds. *J. Embryol. exp. Morph.* 47, 17–37.

Lemire, M. and Grenot, C. (1974). Développement et structure de la glande = (à sels) = du lézard saharien *Agama mutabilis* Merrem (Agamidae). *C. r. hebd. Séanc. Acad. Sci., Paris*, 278, 61–64.

Leydig, F. (1872). "Die in Deutschland lebenden Arten der Saurier." H. Laupp, Tübingen.

Liem, K. F. and Smith, H. M. (1961). A critical reevaluation of the so-called "angular" in the crocodilian mandible. *Turtox News* **39**, 146–148.

Liem, K. F., Marx, H. and Rabb, G. B. (1971). The viperid snake *Azemiops*: its comparative cephalic anatomy and phylogenic position in relation to Viperinae and Crotalinae. *Fieldiana, Zoology,* **59**, 65–126.

Lindahl, P. E. (1946). On some archaic features in the developing central stem of the mammalian chondrocranium. *Acta zool. Stockh.* **27**, 91–100.

List, J. C. (1966). "Comparative osteology of the snake families Typhlopidae and Leptotyphlopidae." Illinois Biological Monographs 36. University of Illinois Press, Urbana and London.

Lombard, R. E. and Bolt, J. R. (1979). Evolution of the tetrapod ear: an analysis and reinterpretation. *Biol. J. Linn. Soc.* **11**, 19–76.

Lüdicke, M. (1962–1964). Ordnung der Klasse Reptilia, Serpentes. *In* "Handbuch der Zoologie." (J.-G. Helmcke, H. V. Lenserken, D. Starck, eds). de Gruyter, Berlin. 7 (1) 5; 1–128, 129–298.

Lüdicke, M. (1978). Die Blutgefässe und Kapillarnetz der Columella, des Sinus pericapsularis und der Cisterna perilymphatica der Serpentes. *Zool. Jb. (Anat.),* **99**, 437–459.

Malan, M. E. (1940). Cranial anatomy of the genus *Gerrhosaurus*. *S. Afr. J. Sci.* **37**, 192–217.

Malan, M. E. (1946). Contributions to the comparative anatomy of the nasal capsule and the organ of Jacobson of the Lacertilia. *Ann. Univ. Stellenbosch,* **24**, 69–137.

Martin, B. G. H. and Bellairs, A. d'A. (1977). The narial excrescence and pterygoid bulla of the gharial, *Gavialis gangeticus* (Crocodilia). *J. Zool. Lond.* **182**, 541–558.

May, E. (1978). Zur Kenntnis der Entwicklung des Schädels von *Leposternon microcephalum* Wagler 1824 (Reptilia: Amphisbaenia). *Senckenberg. biol.* **59**, 41–69.

McDowell, S. B. (1961). On the major arterial canals in the ear-region of testudinoid turtles and the classification of the Testudinoidea. *Bull. Mus. comp. Zool. Harv.* **125**, 23–39.

McDowell, S. B. (1967). The extracolumella and tympanic cavity of the "earless" monitor lizard, *Lanthanotus borneensis*. *Copeia* **1967**, 154–159.

McDowell, S. B. (1972). The evolution of the tongue of snakes, and its bearing on snake origins. *In* "Evolutionary Biology." (T. Dobzhansky, M. K. Hecht and W. C. Steere, eds). Appleton-Century-Crofts, New York, **6**, 191–273.

McDowell, S. B. and Bogert, C. M. (1954). The systematic position of *Lanthanotus* and the affinities of the anguinomorphan lizards. *Bull. Am. Mus. nat. Hist.* **105**, 1–142.

Meek, A. (1911). On the morphogenesis of the head of the crocodile (*Crocodilus porosus*). *J. Anat. Physiol.* **45**, 357–377.

Mertens, R. (1942). Die Familie der Warane (Varanidae). Zweiter Teil: Der Schädel. *Abh. senckenberg. naturf. Ges.* **465**, 117–234.

Moffat, L. A. (1973). The concept of primitiveness and its bearing on the phylogenetic classification of the Gekkota. *Proc. Linn. Soc. N.S.W.* **97**, 275–301.

Möller, W. (1905). Zur Kenntnis der Entwicklung des Gehörknöchelchens bei der Kreuzotter und der Ringelnatter nebst Bemerkungen zur Neurologie dieser Schlangen. *Arch. Mikr. Anat.* **65**, 439–497.

Moore, W. J. (1981). "The Mammalian Skull." Cambridge Univ. Press.

Müller, F. (1967). Zur embryonalen Kopfentwicklung von *Crocodylus cataphractus* Cuv. *Rev. suisse Zool.* **74**, 189–294.

Murray, P. D. F. (1963). Adventitious (secondary) cartilage in the chick embryo, and the development of certain bones and articulations in the chick skull. *Aust. J. Zool.* **11**, 368–430.

New, D. A. T. (1966). "The Culture of Vertebrate Embryos." Logos Press, Academic Press, New York and London.

Nick, L. (1912). Das Kopfskelet von *Dermochelys coriacea*. *Zool. Jb. (Anat.)* **33**, 1–238.

258   A. D'A. BELLAIRS AND A. M. KAMAL

Noack, H. (1907). Uber die Entwicklung des Mittelohres von *Emys europaea* nebst Bemerkungen zur Neurologie dieser Schildkröte. *Arch. mikr. Anat.* **69**, 457–490.

O'Donoghue, C. H. (1920). The blood vascular system of the tuatara, *Sphenodon punctatus*. *Phil. Trans. R. Soc. B.* **210**, 175–252.

Oelrich, T. M. (1956). The anatomy of the head of *Ctenosaura pectinata* (Iguanidae). *Misc. Publs. Mus. Zool. Univ. Michigan* (94), 1–122.

Ogushi, K. (1911). Anatomische Studien an der japanischen dreikralligen Lippenschildkröte (*Trionyx japonicus*). *Morph. Jb.* **43**, 1–106.

Okajima, K. (1915). Beiträge zur Entwickelungsgeschichte und Morphologie des Gehörknöchelchens bei den Schlangen. *Anat. Hefte*, **53**, 325–347.

Packard, G. C., Tracy, C. R. and Roth, J. J. (1977). The physiological ecology of reptilian eggs and embryos, and the evolution of viviparity within the class Reptilia. *Biol. Rev.* **52**, 71–105.

Parker, H. W. (1977). "Snakes—a Natural History." 2nd Ed. Revised and enlarged by A. G. C. Grandison. British Museum (Natural History), Cornell University Press, Ithaca and London.

Parker, W. K. (1879). On the structure and development of the skull in the common snake (*Tropidonotus natrix*). *Phil. Trans. R. Soc.* **169**, 385–417.

Parker, W. K. (1880a). On the structure and development of the skull in the Lacertilia. Part I.—On the skull of the common lizards (*Lacerta agilis, L. viridis*, and *Zootoca vivipara*). *Phil. Trans. R. Soc.* **170**, 595–640.

Parker, W. K. (1880b). Report on the development of the green turtle (*Chelone viridis*). *Challenger Rpts. Zoology*, **1**, 1–58.

Parker, W. K. (1881). On the structure of the skull in the chameleons. *Trans. zool. Soc. Lond.* **11**, 77–105.

Parker, W. K. (1883). On the structure and development of the skull in the Crocodilia. *Trans. zool. Soc. Lond.* **11**, 263–310.

Parrington, F. R. (1937). A note on the supratemporal and tabular bones in reptiles. *Ann. Mag. nat. Hist.* **20**, 69–76.

Parrington, F. R. (1967). The identification of the dermal bones of the head. *J. Linn. Soc. (Zool.).* **47**, 231–239.

Parrington, F. R. (1979). The evolution of the mammalian middle and outer ears: a personal review. *Biol. Rev.* **54**, 369–387.

Parrington, F. R. and Westoll, T. S. (1940). On the evolution of the mammalian palate. *Phil. Trans. R. Soc. B*, **230**, 305–355.

Parsons, T. S. (1970). The nose and Jacobson's organ. *In* "Biology of the Reptilia." (C. Gans and T. S. Parsons, eds). Academic Press, London and New York, **2**, 99–191.

Patterson, C. (1977). Cartilage bones, dermal bones and membrane bones, or the exoskeleton versus the endoskeleton. *In* "Problems in Vertebrate Evolution." (S. M. Andrews, R. S. Miles and A. D. Walker, eds). *Linn. Soc. Symp. Ser.* Academic Press, London and New York, (4), 77–121.

Pearson, H. S. (1921). The skull and some related structures of a late embryo of *Lygosoma*. *J. Anat.* **56**, 20–43.

Pehrson, T. (1945). Some problems concerning the development of the skull in turtles. *Acta zool. Stockh.* **26**, 157–184.

Peyer, B. (1912). Die Entwicklung des Schädelskeletes von *Vipera aspis*. *Morph. Jb.* **44**, 563–621.

Pooley, A. C. (1973). Conservation and management of crocodiles in Africa. *J. Sth. Afr. Wildl. Mgmt. Ass.* **3**, 101–103.

Posner, R. B. and Chiasson, R. B. (1966). The middle ear of *Coleonyx variegatus*. *Copeia* **1966**, 520–524.

Pratt, C. W. M. (1948). The morphology of the ethmoidal region of *Sphenodon* and lizards. *Proc. zool. Soc. Lond.* **118**, 171–201.

Presch, W. (1976). Secondary palate formation in microteiid lizards (Teiidae, Lacertilia). *Bull. S. Calif. Acad. Sci.* **75**, 281–283.

Presley, R. and Steel, F. L. D. (1976). On the homology of the alisphenoid. *J. Anat.* **121**, 441–459.

Presley, R. and Steel, F. L. D. (1978). The pterygoid and ectopterygoid in mammals. *Anat. Embryol.* **154**, 95–110.

Pringle, J. A. (1954). The cranial development of certain South African snakes and the relationship of these groups. *Proc. zool. Soc. Lond.* **123**, 813–865.

Ramaswami, L. S. (1946). The chondrocranium of *Calotes versicolor* (Daud.) with a description of the osteocranium of a just-hatched young. *Q. Jl. microsc. Sci.* **87**, 237–297.

Rao, M. K. M. and Ramaswami, L. S. (1952). The fully formed chondrocranium of *Mabuya* with an account of the adult osteocranium. *Acta zool. Stockh.* **33**, 209–275.

Rathke, H. (1839). "Entwickelungsgeschichte der Natter (*Coluber natrix*)." Bornträger, Königsberg.

Raynaud, A. (1959). Une technique permettant d'obtenir le développement des oeufs d'orvet (*Anguis fragilis* L.) hors de l'organisme maternel. *C. r. Acad. Sci. Paris*, **249**, 1715–1717.

Reese, A. M. (1915). "The Alligator and its Allies." Putnam, New York.

Rice, E. L. (1920). The development of the skull in the skink, *Eumeces quinquelineatus* L. *J. Morph.* **34**, 119–216.

Rieppel, O. (1976a). The homology of the laterosphenoid bone in snakes. *Herpetologica* **32**, 426–429.

Rieppel, O. (1976b). Die orbitotemporale Region im Schädel von *Chelydra serpentina* Linnaeus (Chelonia) und *Lacerta sicula* Rafinesque (Lacertilia). *Acta anat.* **96**, 309–320.

Rieppel, O. (1977a). Studies on the skull of the Henophidia (Reptilia: Serpentes). *J. Zool. Lond.* **181**, 145–173.

Rieppel, O. (1977b). The naso-frontal joint in *Anilius scytale* (Linnaeus) and *Cylindrophis rufus* (Schlegel): Serpentes, Aniliidae. *J. nat. Hist.* **11**, 545–553.

Rieppel, O. (1977c). Über die Entwicklung des Basicranium bei *Chelydra serpentina* Linnaeus (Chelonia) und *Lacerta sicula* Rafinesque (Lacertilia). *Verhandl. Naturf. Ges. Basel* **86**, 153–170.

Rieppel, O. (1978a). The phylogeny of cranial kinesis in lower vertebrates, with special reference to the Lacertilia. *N. Jb. Geol. Paläont. Abh.* **156**, 353–370.

Rieppel, O. (1978b). Streptostyly and muscle function in lizards. *Experientia* **34**, 776–777.

Rieppel, O. (1978c). The braincase of *Anniella pulchra* Gray (Lacertilia: Anniellidae). *Rev. suisse Zool.* **85**, 617–624.

Rieppel, O. (1978d). Tooth replacement in anguinomorph lizards. *Zoomorphologie* **91**, 77–90.

Rieppel, O. (1978e). A functional and phylogenetic interpretation of the skull of the Erycinae (Reptilia: Serpentes). *J. Zool. Lond.* **186**, 185–208.

Rieppel, O. (1978f). The evolution of the naso-frontal joint in snakes and its bearing on snake origins. *Z. zool. Syst. Evolforsch.* **16**, 14–27.

Rieppel, O. (1979a). The braincase of *Typhlops* and *Leptotyphlops*. *Zool. J. Linn. Soc. Lond.* **65**, 161–176.

Rieppel, O. (1979b). Ontogeny and the recognition of primitive characters. *Z. zool. Syst. Evolforsch.* **17**, 57–61.

Rieppel, O. (1979c). A cladistic classification of primitive snakes based on skull structure. *Z. zool. Syst. Evolforsch.* **17**, 140–150.

Rieppel, O. (1979d). The classification of primitive snakes and the testability of phylogenetic theories. *Biol. Zbl.* **98**, 537–552.

Rieppel, O. (1979e). The external jaw adductor of amphisbaenids (Reptilia: Amphisbaenia). *Rev. suisse Zool.* **86**, 867–876.

Rieppel, O. (1980). The evolution of the ophidian feeding system. *Zool. Jb. Anat.* **103**, 551–564.

Rieppel, O. and Labhardt, L. (1979f). Mandibular mechanics in *Varanus niloticus* (Reptilia: Lacertilia). *Herpetologica* **35**, 158–163.

Robinson, P. L. (1967). The evolution of the Lacertilia. *In* "Problèmes Actuels de Paléontologie (Évolution des Vertébrés)." *Colloques int. Cent. natn. Rech. Scient.* No. 163 (1966), 395–407.

Robinson, P. L. (1976). How *Sphenodon* and *Uromastyx* grow their teeth and use them. *In* "Morphology and Biology of Reptiles." (A. d'A. Bellairs and C. B. Cox, eds). *Linn. Soc. Symp. Ser.* Academic Press, London and New York, (3), 43–64.

Romer, A. S. (1956). "Osteology of the Reptiles." University of Chicago Press, Illinois.

Romer, A. S. (1966). "Vertebrate Paleontology." University of Chicago Press, Illinois.

Romer, A. S. and Price, L. W. [= Price, L. I.] (1940). Review of the Pelycosauria. *Geol. Soc. Am., Spec. Pap.* (28), 1–538.

Saint Girons, H. (1976a). Comparative histology of the endocrine glands, nasal cavities and digestive tract in anguimorph lizards. *In* "Morphology and Biology of Reptiles." (A. d'A. Bellairs and C. B. Cox, eds). *Linn. Soc. Symp. Ser.* Academic Press, London and New York, (3), 205–216.

Saint Girons, H. (1976b). Données histologiques sur les fosses nasales et leurs annexes chez *Crocodylus niloticus* Laurenti et *Caiman crocodilus* (Linnaeus) (Reptilia, Crocodylidae). *Zoomorphologie* **84**, 301–318.

Säve-Söderbergh, G. (1946). On the fossa hypophyseos and the attachment of the retractor bulbi group in *Sphenodon*, *Varanus* and *Lacerta*. *Ark. Zool.* **38A**, 1–24.

Säve-Söderbergh, G. (1947). Notes on the brain-case in *Sphenodon* and certain Lacertilia. *Zool. Bidr. Uppsala* **25**, 489–516.

Schauinsland, H. (1900). Weitere Beiträge zur Entwicklungsgeschichte der *Hatteria*. Skelettsystem, schalleitender Apparat, Hirnnerven etc. *Arch. mikr. Anat.* **56**, 747–867.

Schauinsland, H. (1903). Beiträge zur Entwicklungsgeschichte und Anatomie der Wirbeltiere. *Sphenodon, Callorhynchus, Chamaeleon. Zoologica, Stuttgart* **16**, 1–98.

Schumacher, G.-H. (1973). The head muscles and hyolaryngeal skeleton of turtles and crocodilians. *In* "Biology of the Reptilia." (C. Gans and T. S. Parsons, eds). Academic Press, London and New York, **4**, 101–199.

Sewertzoff, A. N. (1900). Zur Entwicklungsgeschichte von *Ascalabotes fascicularis*. *Anat. Anz.* **18**, 33–40.

Seydel, O. (1896). Über die Nasenhöhle und das Jacobson'sche Organ der Sumpfschildkröten. *Festschr. C. Gegenbaur* **2**, 385–486.

Shaner, R. F. (1926). The development of the skull of the turtle, with remarks on fossil reptile skulls. *Anat. Rec.* **32**, 343–367.

Shiino, K. (1914). Studien zur Kenntnis des Wirbeltierkopfes. I. Das Chondrocranium von *Crocodilus* mit Berücksichtigung der Gehirnnerven und der Kopfgefässe. *Anat. Hefte* **50**, 254–381.

Shrivastava, R. K. (1963). The structure and the development of the chondrocranium of *Varanus*. Part I. The development of the ethmoidal region. *Folia anat. Japonica* **39**, 53–83.

Shrivastava, R. K. (1964a). The structure and development of the chondrocranium of *Varanus*. II. The development of the orbito-temporal region. *J. Morph.* **115**, 97–108.

Shrivastava, R. K. (1964b). The structure and development of the chondrocranium of *Varanus*. Part III. The otic and occipital regions, basal plate, viscerocranium and certain features of the osteocranium of a juvenile. *Morph. Jb.* **106**, 147–187.

Shute, C. C. D. (1956). The evolution of the mammalian eardrum and tympanic cavity. *J. Anat.* **90**, 261–281.

Shute, C. C. D. (1972). The Composition of vertebrae and the occipital region of the Skull. *In* "Studies in Vertebrate Evolution." (K. A. Joysey and T. S. Kemp, eds). Oliver and Boyd, Edinburgh. Pp. 21–34.

Silver, P. H. S. (1962). *In ovo* experiments concerning the eye, the orbit, and certain juxta-orbital structures in the chick embryo. *J. Embryol. exp. Morph.* **10**, 423–450.

Simonetta, A. (1956). Organogenesi e significato morfologico del sistema intertympanico dei Crocodilia. *Archo ital. Anat. Embriol.* **61**, 335–372.

Skinner, M. M. (1973). Ontogeny and adult morphology of the skull of the South African skink, *Mabuya capensis* (Gray). *Ann. Univ. Stellenbosch*, **48**, 1–116.

Smit, A. L. (1949). Skedelmorfologie en -Kinese van *Typhlops delalandii* (Schlegel). *S. Afr. J. Sci.* **45**, 117–140.

Smith, L. W. (1914). The origin and development of the columella auris in *Chrysemys marginata*. *Anat. Anz.* **46**, 547–560.

Smith, M. A. (1935–1943). "The Fauna of British India. Reptilia and Amphibia. Vol. II.—Sauria (1935): Vol. III.—Serpentes (1943)." Taylor and Francis, London.

Smith, M. A., Bellairs, A. d'A. and Miles, A. E. W. (1953). Observations on the premaxillary dentition of snakes with special reference to the egg-tooth. *J. Linn. Soc. (Zool.).* **42**, 260–268.

Soliman, M. A. (1964). Die Kopfnerven der Schildkröten. *Z. wiss. Zool.* **169**, 216–312.

Srinivasachar, H. R. (1955). Observations on the development of the chondrocranium in *Vipera*. *Anat. Anz.* **101**, 219–225.

Starck, D. (1979). Cranio-cerebral relations in recent reptiles. *In* "Biology of the Reptilia." (C. Gans, R. G. Northcutt and P. Ulinski, eds). Academic Press, London and New York, **9**, 1–38.

Stebbins, R. C. (1948). Nasal structure in lizards with reference to olfaction and conditioning of the inspired air. *Am. J. Anat.* **83**, 183–222.

Stephenson, N. G. (1960). The comparative osteology of Australian geckos and its bearing on their morphological status. *J. Linn. Soc. (Zool.)* **44**, 278–299.

Stephenson, N. G. (1962). The comparative morphology of the head skeleton, girdles and hind limbs in the Pygopodidae. *J. Linn. Soc. (Zool.)* **44**, 627–644.

Stephenson, N. G. and Stephenson, E. M. (1956). The osteology of the New Zealand geckos and its bearing on their morphological status. *Trans. R. Soc. N.Z.* **84**, 341–358.

Stimie, M. (1966). The cranial anatomy of the iguanid lizard *Anolis carolinensis* (Cuvier). *Ann. Univ. Stellenbosch* **41A**, 239–268.

Sülter, M. M. (1962). A contribution to the cranial morphology of *Causus rhombeatus* (Lichtenstein) with special reference to cranial kinesis. *Ann. Univ. Stellenbosch* **37 A**, 3–40.

Tarsitano, S. and Hecht, M. K. (1980). A reconsideration of the reptilian relationships of *Archaeopteryx*. *Zool. J. Linn. Soc.* **69**, 149–182.

Torien, M. J. (1950). The cranial morphology of the Californian lizard—*Anniella pulchra* Gray. *S. Afr. J. Sci.* **46**, 321–342.

Torien, M. J. (1963). The sound-conducting systems of lizards without tympanic membranes. *Evolution* **17**, 540–547.

Torien, M. J. (1965a). An experimental approach to the development of the ear capsule in the turtle, *Chelydra serpentina*. *J. Embryol. exp. Morph.* **13**, 141–149.

Torien, M. J. (1965b). Experimental studies on the columella-capsular interrelationship in the turtle *Chelydra serpentina*. *J. Embryol. exp. Morph.* **14**, 265–272.

Torien, M. J. (1967). Experimental embryology and cranial morphology. *S. Afr. J. Sci.* **63**, 278–281.

Torien, M. J. and Rossouw, R. J. (1977). Experimental studies on the origin of the parts of the nasal capsule. *S. Afr. J. Sci.* **73**, 371–374.

Tschekanowskaja, O. V. (1936). Die Entwicklung des Schädels von *Tropidonotus natrix*. *Archs. Russe Anat. Hist. Embriol.* **15**, 3–33 (Russian); 123–134 (German).

Underwood, G. (1957). On lizards of the family Pygopodidae. A contribution to the morphology and phylogeny of the Squamata. *J. Morph.* **100**, 207–268.

Underwood, G. (1967). "A Contribution to the Classification of Snakes." British Museum (Natural History), London.

Underwood, G. (1970). The eye. *In* "Biology of the Reptilia." (C. Gans and T. S. Parsons, eds). Academic Press, London and New York, **2**, 1–97.

Underwood, G. (1976). A systematic analysis of boid snakes. *In* "Morphology and Biology of Reptiles." (A. d'A. Bellairs and C. B. Cox, eds). *Linn. Soc. Symp. Ser.* Academic Press, London and New York, (3), 151–175.

Van der Merwe, N. J. (1940). Die Skedelmorfologie van *Pelomedusa galeata* (Wagler). *Tydskr. Wetenskap. Kuns* **1** (19), 67–86.

Van der Merwe, N. J. (1944). Die Skedelmorfologie van *Acontias meleagris*. (Linn.). *Tydskr. Wetenskap. Kuns* **5**, 59–88.

Van Pletzen, R. (1946). The cranial morphology of *Cordylus* with special reference to cranial kinesis. *Ann. Univ. Stellenbosch* **24**, 41–68.

Versluys, J. (1903). Entwicklung der Columella auris bei den Lacertiliern. Ein Beitrag zur Kenntnis der schalleitenden Apparate und des Zungenbeinbogens bei den Sauropsiden. *Zool. Jb. (Anat.)* **19**, 107–188.

Versluys, J. (1936). Kranium und Visceralskelett der Sauropsiden. 1. Reptilien. *In* "Handbuch der vergleichenden Anatomie der Wirbeltiere." (L. Bolk, E. Göppert, E. Kallius, and W. Lubosch, eds). Urban und Schwarzenberg, Berlin and Vienna. **4**, 699–808.

Visser, J. G. J. (1961). The cranial anatomy and kinesis of the bird snake *Thelotornis capensis* (Smith). *Ann. Univ. Stellenbosch* **36 A**, 147–174.

Visser, J. G. J. (1972). Ontogeny of the chondrocranium of the chamaeleon, *Microsaura pumila pumila* (Daudin). *Ann. Univ. Stellenbosch* **47 A**, 1–68. [*Microsaura = Bradypodion*].

Von Geldern, C. E. (1919). Mechanism of the production of the throat-fan in the chameleon, *Anolis carolinensis*. *Proc. Calif. Acad. Sci.* **9**, 313–329.

Voeltzkow, A. (1902). Biologie und Entwicklung der äusseren Körperform von *Crocodilus madagascariensis*. *Abh. Senckenberg nat. Ges.* **26**, 1–150.

Walker, A. D. (1972). New light on the origin of birds and crocodiles. *Nature, Lond.* **237**, 257–263.

Webb, M. (1951). The cranial anatomy of the South African geckoes *Palmatogecko rangei* (Andersson) and *Oedura karroica* (Hewitt). *Ann. Univ. Stellenbosch* **27 A**, 131–165.

Wegner, R. N. (1958). Die Nebenhöhlen der Nase bei den Krokodilen (Studien über Nebenhöhlen des Schädels, 2. Teil). *Wiss. Z. E. M. Arndt-Univ. Greifswald (Math.-Nat.).* **7**, 1–39.

Wegner, R. N. (1959). Der Schädelbau der Lederschildkröte *Dermochelys coriacea* Linné (1766). *Abh. Dtsch. Akad. Wiss. Kl. Chem. Geol. Biol.* (4), 1–80.

Wermuth, H. (1964). Das Verhältnis zwischen Kopf-, Rumpf- und Schwanzlänge bei rezenten Krokodilen. *Senckenb. Biol.* **45**, 369–385.

Werner, G. (1962). Das Cranium der Brückenechse, *Sphenodon punctatus* Gray, von 58 mm Gesamtlänge. *Z. Anat. EntwGesch.* **123**, 323–368.

Werner, Y. L. (1971). The ontogenetic development of the vertebrae in some gekkonoid lizards. *J. Morph.* **133**, 41–92.

Werner, Y. L. and Wever, E. G. (1972). The function of the middle ear in lizards: *Gekko gecko* and *Eublepharis macularius*. *J. exp. Zool.* **179**, 1–16.

Wettstein, O. von (1931–54). Sauropsida: Allgemeines—Reptilia [Rhynchocephalia and

Crocodilia]. *In* "Handbuch der Zoologie." (J.-G. Helmcke and H. V. Lengerken, eds). de Gruyter, Berlin. **7** (1), 1–2; 1–4; 1–320, 321–424.

Wever, E. G. (1968). The ear of the chameleon: *Chamaeleo senegalensis* and *Chamaeleo quilensis*. *J. exp. Zool.* **168**, 423–436.

Wever, E. G. (1969a). The ear of the chameleon: the round window problem. *J. exp. Zool.* **171**, 1–6.

Wever, E. G. (1969b). The ear of the chameleon: *Chamaeleo höhnelii* and *Chamaeleo jacksoni*. *J. exp. Zool.* **171**, 305–312.

Wever, E. G. (1973a). The function of the middle ear in lizards: *Eumeces* and *Mabuya* (Scincidae). *J. exp. Zool.* **183**, 225–240.

Wever, E. G. (1973b). The function of the middle ear in lizards: divergent types. *J. exp. Zool.* **184**, 97–126.

Wever, E. G. (1974). The ear of *Lialis burtonis* (Sauria: Pygopodidae), its structure and function. *Copeia*, 297–305.

Wever, E. G. (1978). "The Reptile Ear. Its Structure and Function." Princeton University Press.

Wever, E. G. and Gans, C. (1972). The ear and hearing in *Bipes biporus*. *Proc. Nat. Acad. Sci. USA*. **69**, 2714–2716.

Wever, E. G. and Gans, C. (1973). The ear in Amphisbaenia (Reptilia); further anatomical observations. *J. Zool. Lond.* **171**, 189–206.

Wever, E. G. and Werner, Y. L. (1970). The function of the middle ear in lizards: *Crotaphytus collaris* (Iguanidae). *J. exp. Zool.* **175**, 327–342.

Whetstone, K. N. and Martin, L. D. (1979). New look at the origin of birds and crocodiles. *Nature* **279**, 234–236.

Willard, W. A. (1915). The cranial nerves of *Anolis carolinensis*. *Bull. Mus. comp. Zool. Harv.* **59**, 15–116.

Williams, E. E. (1959a). Gadow's arcualia and the development of tetrapod vertebrae. *Q. Rev. Biol.* **34**, 1–32.

Williams, E. E. (1959b). The occipito-vertebral joint in the burrowing snakes of the family Uropeltidae. *Breviora*, No. 106, 1–10.

Winchester, L. and Bellairs, A. d'A. (1977). Aspects of vertebral development in lizards and snakes. *J. Zool. Lond.* **181**, 495–525.

Wyeth, F. J. (1924). The development of the auditory apparatus in *Sphenodon punctatus*; with an account of the visceral pouches, aortic arches, and other accessory structures. *Phil. Trans. R. Soc. B.* **212**, 259–368.

Yntema, C. L. (1964). Procurement and use of turtle embryos for experimental procedures. *Anat. Rec.* **149**, 577–586.

Yntema, C. L. (1968). A series of stages in the embryonic development of *Chelydra serpentina*. *J. Morph.* **125**, 219–252.

Young, E. A. E. (1942). The cranial morphology of the Californian lizard *Xantusia vigilis*. *S. Afr. J. med. Sci.* **7** (Biol. Suppl.), 19–32.

Zada, S. K. (1975). "The Fully Formed Chondrocranium, Embryonic and Adult Osteocranium of *Agama pallida*." Ph.D. thesis, University of Cairo.

Zangerl, R. (1944). Contributions to the osteology of the skull of the Amphisbaenidae. *Am. Midl. Nat.* **31**, 417–454.

Zalusky, S. B., Gaudin, A. J. and Swanson, J. R. (1980). A comparative study of cranial osteology in the North American sand lizards, genus *Uma* (Reptilia: Iguanidae). *Copeia*, 1980, 296–310.

Zehr, D. R. (1962). Stages in the normal development of the common garter snake, *Thamnophis sirtalis sirtalis*. *Copeia* **1962**, 322–329.

Zimmermann, S. (1913). Das Chondrocranium von *Anguis fragilis*. *Anat. Anz.* **44**, 594–606.

CHAPTER 2

Reptilian Muscle:
Fine Structure and Physiological Parameters

KARL F. GUTHE

*Division of Biological Sciences, The University of Michigan, Ann Arbor, Michigan,
U.S.A.*

I. Introduction

Muscle is a familiar tissue, and the history of its investigation is long. Reptilian muscles were studied often in the nineteenth and early twentieth centuries (see reviews by Regaud and Favre, 1904; Hines, 1927; Lindhard, 1931; Hinsey, 1934). Most light microscopic studies of fine structure (reviewed by Tiegs, 1953; Cole, 1955b) became obsolete with the advent of electron microscopy. Most earlier physiological studies were also superseded when new paradigms arose between 1950 to 1965 for contraction (sliding filaments), excitation potentials, and the coupling of excitation to contraction (sarcotubules). Details of this early work are not discussed in the body of this review, but references are provided in Appendix II.

Muscles in vertebrates are commonly classified as skeletal, cardiac, and smooth; the muscles of a given type are much alike in all vertebrates. There are recognized minor structural variations within types; these presumably represent adaptations to specific functions. Comparisons among muscles are usually based on homologous muscles from species "typical" of the classes of vertebrates. Differences among species or among functionally different muscles of the same species are just beginning to be explored.

The present review considers skeletal muscle, the contractile process, smooth muscle, and finally the sensory organs of skeletal muscle. Reptilian muscles are compared with those of amphibians and homeotherms where possible, and emphasis is given to the reported interspecific and intermuscular differences. Attention is drawn to some special features of reptilian muscle.

Muscles of tortoises are slow enough to permit sharp temporal resolution of the rapid events of contraction. Muscles of tortoises also use chemical energy more efficiently than do the more familiar muscles of frogs and mammals (Walsh and Woledge, 1970). Many muscle fibers are tonic in reptiles, birds, and amphibians, but tonic fibers are rare in mammals. The tonic fibers of reptiles are not identical to amphibian and avian tonic fibers, and some reptilian twitch fibers are unlike mammalian twitch fibers. Muscle spindles of squamates offer a simple structure for studying sensory function because each spindle contains only a single intrafusal muscle fiber, unlike the spindles of other terrestrial vertebrates.

Current information about muscle is discussed in a four-volume series (Bourne, 1972–73), a short book (Carlson and Wilkie, 1974), and a chapter in Prosser's textbook (1973). There are monographs on the motor end-plate (Zacks, 1973) and on the comparative aspects of the action of neurotransmitters on smooth muscle (Fischer, 1971). Hess (1970) has reviewed slow (tonic) skeletal muscle in the various classes of vertebrates. Reviews are available on reptilian muscle (Proske and Ridge, 1974), its autonomic innervation (Burnstock and Berger, 1979), and its muscular dystrophies (Stolk, 1962a, b) as well as on the study, using tissue culture techniques, of myogenesis in regenerating tails of *Anolis carolinensis* (Chlebowski *et al.*, 1973). In order to limit the length of this review, I have reluctantly omitted many topics. Among them are the properties of cardiac muscle, the role of muscles in thermogenesis, the development and regeneration of reptilian muscle, and the metabolism and ionic concentrations of muscle fibers.

II. Skeletal Muscle

A. GENERAL

The fibers of skeletal muscles of vertebrates vary considerably in their ultrastructural, histochemical, and physiological properties. In addition to the usual extrafusal fibers that are responsible for contraction, muscles also include muscle spindles (with their intrafusal fibers; see Section V) and satellite cells, which supply 5 to 8% of the nuclei in caudal muscles of the lizards *Anolis* and *Scincella* (Kahn and Simpson, 1974). The present discussion is concerned with the varieties of extrafusal fibers.

The skeletal muscle fiber described in textbooks is a mammalian twitch fiber. In most mammalian muscle, three types of twitch fibers are recognized, based on their speed and their metabolic machinery (Close, 1972; Peter *et al.*, 1972); they are fast-glycolytic (FG), fast oxidative-glycolytic (FOG), and slow-twitch-oxidative (SO). Then there are the tonic fibers (= slow fibers, Hess, 1970).

Mammalian fast-twitch fibers, whether FG or FOG, are well adapted for speed. They are innervated by large neurons which conduct impulses rapidly. At the neuromuscular junction infolding of the sarcolemma forms a robust end plate, which increases the junctional area and speeds excitation. Rapid communication to all parts of the fiber is achieved longitudinally by propagated action potentials and transversely by an extensive tubular (T) system which is continuous with the surface membrane. The T system comes into contact with an extensive sarcoplasmic reticulum, which in turn facilitates rapid exchange of calcium ions with the sarcomeres, in which calcium ion concentration controls the activity of sliding filaments. The sarcoplasmic reticulum and the T system together form the sarcotubular system, which divides the array of myofilaments into regular bundles or myofibrils (Fibrillenstruktur). The myosin of the thick filaments cycles rapidly from one site on a thin filament to another, and the ATPase activity of the myosin is correspondingly high (Bárány, 1967).

Fast-twitch fibers use ATP quickly and must rely on a high energy flux to replenish it. Some fast-twitch fibers (FG) depend on glycolysis; other fibers (FOG) depend on both glycolysis and reoxidation. If fibers are active for brief periods, it may be advantageous for them to depend on glycolysis as this will reduce immediate oxygen demand. FG fibers are less well vascularized than are FOG fibers, which diminishes their demand on the cardiovascular system. Fast fibers that are active for longer periods supplement glycolysis with oxidation. More mitochondria, more myoglobin, and a higher capillary density make FOG fibers redder than FG. The two types can be distinguished histochemically by demonstrating the activities of oxidative and glycolytic enzymes and by measuring contents of glycogen and lipid.

The third type of mammalian fiber is slow-twitch (SO) and relies on oxidative metabolism. Its sarcotubular system is less extensive than that of fast-twitch fibers (Eisenberg and Kuda, 1976), and its ATPase is about one-third as fast (Bárány, 1967). Myosins from fast-twitch and slow-twitch fibers of the same animal comprise different light and heavy polypeptide chains (Weeds, 1976), so that different genes are expressed. Myosins from slow-twitch fibers are more labile to alkali and more stable to acid which makes them distinguishable histochemically. Whether a fiber possesses a fast or a slow myosin is a major distinction among types of vertebrate fibers.

As in mammals, fibers in reptiles, birds, and amphibians are usually divided into three types: broad white, narrow red, and intermediate in both size and color. That the three size classes are distinct and not simply part of a continuum has long been assumed by most students of reptilian muscle. For Amphibia, this has recently been supported by a careful study of fibers from the tail of *Ambystoma* (Totland, 1976), and for Reptilia by a study of amphisbaenids (Maxwell and Gans, personal communication). Whether these classes of fiber represent categories equivalent to those of mammals, remains unclear.

In non-mammalian tetrapods slow-twitch fibers have not been unambiguously identified, although they may be present in turtles. Even slower tonic fibers play the role of effecting slow movements and maintaining prolonged tension. In these very slow tonic fibers (Fig. 1), the sarcotubular system is much less extensive than even in slow-twitch fibers of mammals, and myofilaments are so poorly bundled into fibrils that in cross-section they blend into a featureless field (Felderstruktur). Tonic fibers occur in mammals, but only in extraocular and a few other special muscles (Hess, 1970).

Although Hess (1970) terms these slow fibers, they are often called tonic fibers, as they are here, to avoid confusion with slow-twitch fibers. Membranes of such tonic fibers do not propagate action potentials, but support only junctional potentials, and the fibers accordingly show graded rather than all-or-none contraction. Some degree of synchrony of contraction of sarcomeres is achieved by the presence of multiple motor terminals, but rapid influx of ions at the terminals is no longer required, and the terminals are fine grade endings rather than robust end plates (Fig. 2). En grappe (or grape endings) and en plaque (or end plate) are the terms used for different types of terminals; the usage of "end plate" to include both will be avoided here, as it was by Hess (1970) and Tiegs (1953). Tonic and twitch fibers of birds and amphibians are indistinguishable histochemically on the basis of the activity of succinic dehydrogenase or the content of glycogen and lipid (Lee, 1971). Conceivably mammalian slow-twitch fibers may be regarded as tonic fibers that have acquired characteristics of fast-twitch fibers while retaining a relatively low ATPase. Speed is obviously increased by sarcolemmal infolding to produce larger terminal areas and by more rapid communication by means of action potentials and an extensive sarcotubular system.

The terms twitch and tonic are used differently by physiologists than by histologists. Twitch fibers respond to a single stimulus with an action potential that propagates regeneratively along the muscular membrane. As the name implies, their mechanical response is a twitch, that is, a brief contraction and rapid relaxation. Their tension is independent of the strength of the stimulus. Tonic fibers respond to a single stimulus with a graded, slow junctional potential that is not propagated regeneratively. The ensuing contracture is much slower and more prolonged than the twitch of even a slow-twitch fiber; furthermore, a stronger stimulus produces a greater tension. Morphological and physiological properties usually correlate, but sometimes there is a discrepancy and sometimes a fiber

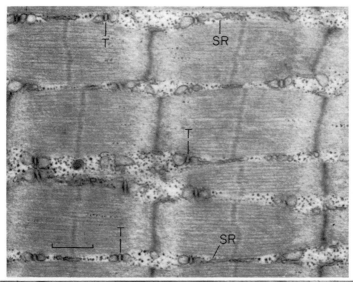

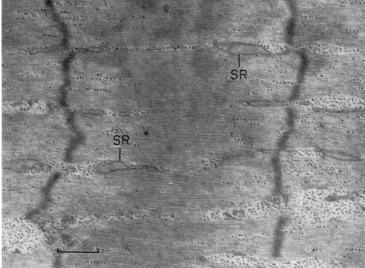

FIG. 1. Electron micrographs of longitudinal sections of fibers from M. costocutaneus of the garter snake (*Thamnophis sirtalis*). Scale lines represent 0·5 μm. A twitch fiber (*top*) shows regular triads (T) at the level of junction of A and I bands. The central transverse tubule of the triad lies between two cisternae of the sarcoplasmic reticulum (SR). Fibrils are distinct and well–separated. Z lines are relatively straight, and M lines are present in the middle of the A bands. A tonic fiber (*bottom*) shows no triads and much less sarcoplasmic reticulum. Filaments are not well separated into fibrils. Z lines zigzag, and M lines are absent. (Both figures from Hess, 1965)

270 KARL F. GUTHE

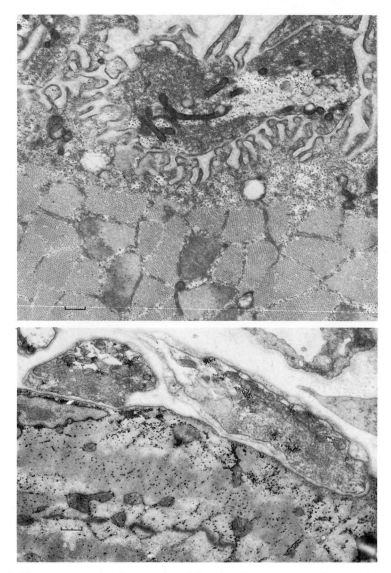

FIG. 2. Electron micrographs of cross-sections of fibers from M. costocutaneus of *Thamnophis sirtalis* to show the structure of the motor terminals. Scale lines represent 0·5 μm. Vesicles fill the nerve terminals. The twitch fiber (*top*), with distinct fibrils, shows the structure of a typical end plate, with many postjunctional folds in the sarcolemma. The tonic fiber (*bottom*), with poorly separated fibrils, shows the structure of a typical grape ending, with postjunctional folds essentially absent. (Both figures from Hess, 1965)

shows intermediate properties. In snakes and frogs, tonic fibers are defined as those:

(1) that respond to a stimulus with a junctional potential and a graded contracture rather than an action potential and an all-or-nothing twitch;

(2) that are innervated by fine axons terminating in multiple grape endings rather than coarse axons terminating in single end plates as shown in Figure 3 (Hess regards the multiplicity of endings as the major diagnostic feature of tonic fibers); and

(3) that show indistinct, irregular, and sometimes confluent fibrils under the light microscope (Felderstruktur) because they possess only a small amount of the sarcotubular system (Fig. 1).

Electron microscopy adds additional morphological distinctions, and histochemistry provides information about the energy utilization of both tonic and twitch fibers.

A discussion of all relevant papers on the structure, innervation and physiology of reptilian fibers follows, and the results are compared with those from some recent reports for other vertebrates. In addition to Hess's review (1970), there are reviews on muscle fibers of reptiles (Proske and Ridge, 1974) and mammals (Close, 1972). A representative but not exhaustive list of papers on the muscle fibers of the various classes of tetrapods is given in Table I.

TABLE I

Literature on the fiber patterns in the classes of tetrapods

	Ultrastructure	Types of fibers	Physiology
Mammals	Eisenberg and Kuda, 1975, 1976 Eisenberg et al., 1974	Peter et al., 1972 Burke et al., 1973	Luff and Atwood, 1972 Wells, 1965
Birds	Page, 1969	George and Berger, 1966 Hikida and Bock, 1974 Khan, 1976	Rall and Schottelius, 1973 Canfield, 1971 Fedde, 1969
Reptiles	Page, 1968 Hess, 1963, 1965	Ridge, 1971 Proske and Vaughan, 1968 Levine, 1966	Woledge, 1968 Walsh and Woledge, 1970
Amphibians	Page, 1965	Gradwell and Walcott, 1971 Totland, 1976 Smith and Ovalle, 1973	Floyd and Smith, 1971 Adrian and Peachey, 1965

Most studies of reptilian muscle use the easily accessible muscles of the legs of turtles or lizards, of the autotomized tail of certain lizards, or of the body wall of snakes. Some other muscles offer special advantages for certain kinds of work. Examples are the internal and external oblique muscles of lizards and snakes, the costocutaneous muscles of snakes, and the scalenes and the rectus abdominis of lizards. A whole row of any of these thin segmental muscles can be removed for study; each muscle consists of only a few layers of fibers, in which motor terminals and muscle spindles are easily observed (Asmussen and Lindhard, 1933). It is easy to study the properties of tonic fibers in the M. costocutaneus inferior of *Natrix* (Ridge, 1971), because the muscles are supplied by a motor nerve that enters near the equator of the muscle. It then forks into a thick branch that continues into the muscle, supplying both twitch and tonic fibers, and a thin branch toward the rib that supplies only tonic fibers. The short cutaneous muscles between the scales of *Thamnophis* contain only a few fibers, so that the responses of individual fibers are readily observed (Heistracher and Hunt, 1969a, b, c). They are particularly useful in studying the electrical properties of membranes because an applied potential decays only slightly over their length of $1·0$ to $1·5$ mm.

The suitability of the M. retractor penis of turtles for mechanical studies was originally recognized by Hoffmann (1913), and its advantages were described by Bishop and Kendall (1928). It is a long, narrow striated muscle that runs bilaterally from its origin on the vertebral column to its insertion on the anterior surface of the cloaca. The muscle is easily dissected without damage. Its fibers are parallel, it is up to 7 cm or more long in large males of *Pseudemys*, and its cross-section is small enough to assure ready exchange of oxygen and carbon dioxide. Its fibers conduct impulses and it contracts slowly, the contractions fusing into a tetanus at stimulation rates of a few hertz. It fatigues more slowly than do the muscles of frogs, and its tension remains constant throughout a tetanus of several seconds. The muscle is extremely durable and develops good tension even three or four days after excision. It extends under slight tension to at least three times its length *in situ*, which interferes with some kinds of experiments.

Hill (1950a, b) chose the M. iliotibialis of the tortoise (*Testudo*) for thermal studies because it is very flat on one side, enabling it to lie well on a thermocouple. It resembles the M. gastrocnemius of the frog, but is softer and more extensible, containing less tendinous material.

B. MORPHOLOGY

1. *Ultrastructure*

In general, skeletal muscles of vertebrates are alike in myofibrillar structure, but differ in the length of their sarcomeres. The sarcomeres of the M. iliofibularis and other muscles of tortoises (*Testudo*) are about 2·6 μm long, of frogs (*Rana*) about 2·1 μm. The longer sarcomeres may be characteristic of slower muscles and may also contribute to the ability of the muscle of tortoises to operate over a greater range of lengths than that of frogs (Page, 1968). Within the sarcomeres, the thick filaments (A bands) are nearly the same length in the snake *Boa constrictor*, the lizard *Tupinambis teguixin*, the crocodilian *Caiman latirostris* (Edwards et al., 1954), and the turtle *Testudo* (Page, 1968) as in other vertebrates. The thin filaments of frogs and tortoises show fine periods of identical length (38·5 nm), but the filaments of tortoises have 29 periods per half-sarcomere (total length of thin filament per sarcomere 2·35 μm) while those of frogs have 24 (1·95 μm). The length of thin filaments and sarcomeres is not always correlated with the speed of contraction. Fast-twitch fibers from the snake *Natrix* also show 29 fine periods (Y. Fukami, unpublished; quoted by Proske and Ridge, 1974). In chickens, the slow M. latissimus dorsi anterior and the fast posterior one both have 26 fine periods (Page, 1969), and in frogs the slow and the fast fibers of the M. rectus abdominis have sarcomeres of the same length (Page, 1965). The longer thin filaments of *Testudo* may, however, account for the greater range of lengths over which the muscle works (Page, 1968).

In fibrils of fast vertebrate muscles, T tubules come together with two cisternae of the sarcoplasmic reticulum (SR) to form triads at regular intervals. In fast fibers of leg muscles of the lizard *Anolis*, two triads occur regularly for each sarcomere, situated at the two boundaries between the A band and its neighboring I bands (Robertson, 1956a). In leg muscles of *Lacerta* the same region of the sarcomere is most sensitive to electrical stimulation (Huxley and Straub, 1958). Huxley (1971) described how these two findings were brought together to suggest that triads are important in excitation–contraction coupling. The sarcotubular system of the sartorius of *Anolis* has recently been visualized by a new technique (Forbes et al., 1977).

Although many twitch muscles that contract slowly often have only one triad per sarcomere, the M. iliofibularis of *Testudo* has two (Page, 1968). The tubules of the two triads on each side of a Z line (at the A-I boundaries) are interconnected. The location of the triads on the sides of the Z line may allow calcium ions to be released nearer their site of action in the long sarcomere than if there were a single triad at the Z line. The resemblance of the M. iliofibularis to fast-twitch muscles is imperfect because the interfacial area between the T tubule and the neighboring cisternae is smaller. The smaller area may reduce the rate at which calcium ions enter the fibril after excitation, delaying the rise in their fibrillar concentration (Page, 1968). The relatively slow activation of the muscles of tortoises may be the result of this ultrastructural difference. Page found only one ultrastructural type of fiber in the M. iliofibularis, but she examined only its superficial layers. The M. rectus femoris (M. iliotibialis) and the M. retrahens capitis collique were not obviously different from the M. iliofibularis.

In addition to the twitch fibers that have just been considered, most reptilian muscles also contain tonic fibers. In the tonic fibers of *Thamnophis* the sarcotubular system is much less highly organized than in twitch fibers (Hess, 1963, 1965; Hoyle *et al.*, 1966), although the myofilaments are the same. As a consequence of the less extensive sarcotubular system, fibrillar structure is not obvious, and in cross-section a fiber shows a field-like appearance (Felderstruktur). Tonic fibers are usually narrower than twitch fibers, their Z lines are broader and more convoluted, and if M lines occur they are less conspicuous. Tonic fibers have few triads, and the T tubules are often associated with only a single sarcoplasmic cisterna rather than the usual pair, forming dyads, rather than triads. These differences are also evident in muscles of *Emys* (Lebedinskaya, 1973). The development of the sarcotubular system varies in different tonic fibers, ranging from a dyad near every fifth or sixth sarcomere in the tonic fibers of frogs (Page, 1965) to a dyad or triad per sarcomere in fibers of the M. latissimus dorsi anterior of chickens (Page, 1969). Sarcotubular systems of tonic fibers are less organized in squamates than in chickens.

In many reptilian muscles twitch and tonic fibers can also be distinguished by light microscopy (Köhler, 1938). Twitch fibers show distinct myofibrils, which range in diameter from 0·3 μm to 1·3 μm. In tonic fibers the bundles of filaments are less regular and larger (up to 3·5 μm), and stain more deeply with iron-hematoxylin. Tonic fibers are generally smaller than twitch fibers. In the trunk muscles of snakes (*Natrix*, *Coronella*, *Vipera*) 30% to 40% of the fibers are tonic, the proportion declining slightly from the middle of the body toward the head and tail. Head and neck muscles have fewer tonic fibers. The muscles of the lizard *Lacerta* show fewer tonic fibers than do most muscles of snakes (from none to 25%). Tonic fibers are more abundant in postural muscles, such as the Mm. deltoideus and sternomastoideus. In *Lacerta* tonic fibers are randomly distributed through particular muscles, but in a gecko (*Tarentola*) they form bundles, especially in leg muscles. In slowworms (*Anguis*) tonic fibers are more frequent, approaching the proportions noted in the functionally similar muscles of snakes.

Twitch and tonic fibers are not as easily distinguished in other reptilian muscles (Köhler, 1938). In *Alligator* the M. scalenus is purely twitch but in some other muscles up to 30% of the fibers are tonic, and tonic fibers form bundles in the Mm. sternomastoideus and splenius capitis. The larger tonic component in the alligator than in lizard may be related to slower movements of the larger animals. In addition a large proportion of fibers, up to 50% of the fibers in some muscles, in the alligator contain filamentary bundles that are intermediate in both size and staining. Squamate muscles contain a low percentage of intermediate fibers. Presumably the sarcotubular system of intermediate fibers is less well developed than that of twitch fibers, but better developed than that of tonic fibers of (frogs and) squamates. In the turtle *Emys* typical tonic fibers are quite common in the Mm. retrahens capitis collique (= M. dorso-occipitis) and spinalis cervicis (= M. testo-cervicalis) but relatively rare in the Mm. deltoideus and sartorius. Intermediate fibers are also common, and here there is physiological evidence (see below) that some tonic fibers behave like the tonic fibers of the M. latissimus dorsi anterior of the chicken (Lebedinskaya and Nasledov, 1977).

Close examination with the electron microscope often permits the division of twitch and tonic fibers into sub-types. Finol and Ogura (1972) recognized two types of twitch fibers in several muscles of the teiid lizard *Cnemidophorus*. One type has abundant mitochondria, a relatively broad Z line (110 nm), small axonal terminals, and end plates with relatively shallow junctional folds. The other is mitochondrion-poor, its end plates show deep junctional folds, and its Z lines are narrower (50 nm). Both types show good sarcotubular systems with two triads per sarcomere. The two types probably correspond to the FOG and the FG fibers of mammals. In a later study on the Mm. soleus, iliofibularis, and gastrocnemius of *Iguana* (Finol and Ogura, 1977), the same two types of twitch fibers were observed ("white" and "red I"). Two types of tonic fibers were also recognized ("red II" and "slow"), both with multiple en grappe innervation, poorly developed sarcotubular systems (no triads were found), and thick zig-zag Z lines. "Red II" had a clear M line. "Slow" had no M line, less sarcoplasmic reticulum, and more sarcoplasm. Its fibrils were more poorly aligned with each other. Table II shows the proportions of the four types.

Twitch and tonic fibers also differ in innervation; a twitch fiber typically receives a single motor terminal, while tonic fibers receive multiple terminals. In fact, Hess (1970) regards this as the best way to distinguish end plates from grape endings. In some muscles of the garter snake,

TABLE II

Proportions of Fiber Types in Iguana. (*Finol and Ogura, 1977*)

	White	Red I	Red II	Slow
M. gastrocnemius	3	2	1	0
M. soleus	1	2	1	0
M. iliofibularis				
White part	1	2	1	0
Red part	0	2	1	1

Thamnophis sirtalis, thick axons supply large twitch fibers (Hess, 1963, 1965; Hoyle *et al.*, 1966), and fine axons supply tonic fibers. In general, coarse fibers conduct impulses more rapidly than fine ones and are more suitable for fast action. It is interesting that mammalian slow-twitch fibers may be innervated by smaller axons than fast-twitch fibers (Burke, 1978).

Twitch fibers have end plates but tonic fibers have grape endings. The classical description by electron microscopy of vertebrate end plates (Robertson, 1956b) is based on leg and intercostal muscles of *Anolis carolinensis*. The axonal terminal contains many mitochondria and synaptic vesicles, and a synaptic cleft of 50 nm separates it from the muscle fiber. The sarcolemmal membrane folds extensively into synaptic troughs with complex branches and anastomoses, producing the robust appearance of a typical end plate (Fig. 2, top). Similar terminals occur in twitch fibers of the costocutaneous muscles of *Thamnophis sirtalis* (Hess, 1963, 1965; Hoyle *et al.*, 1966), but tonic fibers in the same muscles receive much finer and more delicate grape endings, the sarcolemmal folds of which

TABLE III

Ultrastructural differences between twitch and tonic fibers

Twitch	Tonic
Muscle fibers broad. [In *Natrix* (Ridge, 1971), diameter is 59 ± 23 μm.]	Muscle fibers narrow. (In *Natrix*, diameter is 35 ± 8 μm.)
Extensive and regular sarcoplasmic reticulum with triads dividing filaments into myofibrils (Fibrillenstruktur).	Sparse and irregular sarcoplasmic reticulum; triads irregular or absent; poorly recognizable fibrils (Felderstruktur).
Straight and narrow Z line.	Zigzag and broad Z line.
Prominent M line.	M line less prominent or absent.
Terminals single with extensively folded sarcolemmas (end plates) and strong cholinesterase staining.	Terminals multiple with few if any sarcolemmal folds (grape endings) and weak cholinesterase staining.
Innervated by coarse axons.	Innervated by fine axons.

are greatly reduced or absent (Fig. 2 bottom). Table III summarizes the ultrastructural differences.

2. *Innervation*

The location of motor terminals on the muscle fibers has long received attention, because the endings are found at the ends of the muscle fibers in amphibians and near the middle in comparable mammalian fibers. In the caudal muscles of the scincid *Chalcides ocellatus*, they are located in the middle of the muscle fiber (Bacchi and Sassu, 1973); in the regenerating tail, motor terminals first appear at or near the ends and gradually shift toward the middle. Terminals have also been observed at both locations in other reptiles, such as *Lacerta* (Filogamo and Marchisio, 1961; Mackay and Peters, 1961; Gabella, 1966). *Anolis* (Szepsenwol, 1959), *Natrix* (Mackay and Peters, 1961), and *Coluber* (Rahman *et al.*, 1974).

Both end plates and grape endings occur in many reptilian muscles

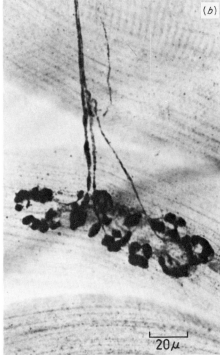

FIG. 3. Teased fibers from M. scalenus of the blue-tongued lizard (*Tiliqua nigrolutea*), stained with gold chloride. Scale line represents 20 μm. (a) Plate ending, supplied by a coarse axon. (b) Cluster of grape endings, supplied by a fine axon. (From Proske and Vaughan, 1968)

(Fig. 3). According to Hess (1970), terminals with the robust ultra-structure of end plates often appear grape-like in the light microscope, which probably accounts for early reports that most reptilian endings are "en grappe". The earlier work has often been reviewed (e.g., Tiegs, 1953; Mavrinskaya, 1962). In a light-microscopic study of paravertebral muscles of many vertebrates, Cole (1951, 1955b) found both end plates and grape endings in *Pseudemys*, *Anolis*, *Phrynosoma* and *Coluber* but only end plates in *Alligator* and *Crotaphytus*. The shapes as well as the proportions of the two types of terminals differ among species, and re-examination with the electron microscope might be rewarding. In lizards, only plates were seen in the pectoral muscles of *Calotes*, *Chamaeleo* and *Varanus* (Chinoy and George, 1965). Both types of endings were reported in muscles from the legs and body wall of *Anolis* (Szepsenwol, 1959), and they were said to occur on the same fiber.

It now seems established that end plates and grape endings rarely if ever occur on the same muscle fiber. Careful searches in the dorsal longitudinal muscles of *Thamnophis* (Hess, 1963) and M. scalenus of the blue-tongued lizard *Tiliqua* (Proske and Vaughan, 1968) failed to show any fiber that had both types of terminals. It is also clear that in squamates the end plates occur singly while the grape endings are multiple, as in *Iguana* (Finol and Ogura, 1977). In *Tiliqua* end plates are present in about 60% of the fibers. Proske and Vaughan (1968) examined more than 800 fibers with plate endings; only one of them received more than one ending, and it had a second plate. More than 500 tonic fibers received 3 to 16 grape endings per fiber (mean 8) and the mean separation of the terminals was 1·2 mm. Each ending appeared to come from a different axon. Fine axons are often interwoven, and they frequently end near each other on the same muscle fiber. In intercostal muscles of *Lacerta* (Witalinski, 1974), end plates occur singly on large fibers 50 to 85 μm in diameter which show distinct fibrils and straight narrow Z lines, as expected of twitch fibers. Smaller fibers 20 to 35 μm in diameter are also present. These smaller fibers have less distinct fibrils and receive two or three grape endings, as do tonic fibers. However, the smaller fibers have regular triads and distinct M lines, and their Z lines are straight and not wide; these traits are those of twitch fibers.

In snakes, some fibers receive single end plates while other adjacent fibers receive multiple grape endings, as seen in the costocutaneous muscles of *Boa* (Candiollo and Englielmone, 1968), *Python* (Panzica Viglietti and Panzica, 1978), *Thamnophis* (Hess, 1963, 1965; Hoyle *et al.*, 1966; Ridge, 1971), *Natrix* (Ridge, 1971), and *Coluber* (Rahman *et al.*, 1974). In *Natrix* the diameters of fibers with end plates ranges from 30 to 160 μm; those with grape endings are smaller, 20 to 50 μm. In M. obliquus externus of

Thamnophis (Kuffler and Yoshikami, 1975a, b) it is easy to distinguish the large nerve fibers that supply compact end plates. The scale elevators of *Thamnophis* (Heistracher and Hunt, 1969a) apparently contain only end plates.

In *Pseudemys* the paravertebral muscles show both kinds of motor terminals (Cole, 1955b), and in *Testudo* the M. extensor digitorum brevis I (Crowe and Ragab, 1970a) receives both coarse axons terminating in end plates and fine axons terminating in grapes. The M. testocervicalis of *Emys*, which draws the head of the animal into the shell, has readily distinguished bundles of red and white fibers (Lebedinskaya and Nasledov, 1977). The white bundle is made up of twitch fibers with appropriate ultrastructural and innervational characteristics. The red bundle contains some twitch fibers, but most of its fibers are tonically innervated, with multiple grape endings. Some of the other properties of the tonic fibers are unexpectedly twitch-like: their Z lines are straight but broad, their M lines distinct, and their sarcotubular system comparatively well developed. They conduct action potentials when stimulated directly. According to an earlier report (Lebedinskaya, 1973) some fibers of *Emys* and particularly *Testudo* are "transitional" between tonic and twitch in their properties, whereas in the lizards *Agama* and *Varanus* tonic and twitch fibers are easily distinguished from each other. In the M. retrahens capitis collique of *Pseudemys* and *Testudo* (Levine, 1966) all the fibers seem to be twitch fibers and receive end plates. Nevertheless the motor supply to fibers of the M. retrahens is polyneuronal and even plurisegmental, from cervical nerves 3 and 4 in *Pseudemys* and from 3, 4, and 5 in *Testudo*. Each single fiber is apparently supplied by all three spinal nerves and will contract briskly when any one of them is stimulated. More than one axon from a nerve trunk is effective, but Levine did not determine whether an axon supplies more than one end plate on the same fiber. Conducted potentials, measured intracellularly in a muscle fiber, show that different end plates respond to different axons. Diameters of the twitch fibers of the M. retrahens range widely with a mean of 64 μm, which is comparable to the diameters of twitch fibers of squamates.

3. *Histochemistry*

Before considering histochemical studies of reptilian muscle, it is appropriate to describe the types of fibers in mammals. Tonic fibers are rare in mammals, limited to certain extraocular and middle ear muscles and a few others. Before 1960, twitch fibers were usually classified as narrow red, intermediate and broad white. This classification persists in studies of other vertebrates but has been abandoned in mammals in favor of a more functional one. That a fiber is red means little by itself; the

TABLE IV

Properties and synonymies of classes of fibers

Contraction time (ms)	20	19	82
Myofibrillar ATPase	high	high	low
NADH-D or SDH	low	high	moderate
Phosphorylase	high	high	low
Myoglobin	low	high	high
Synonymous classifications:			
Dubowitz and Pearse (1960)	II	II	I
Stein and Padykula (1962)	A	C	B
Romanul (1964)	I	II	III
Padykula and Gauthier (1966)	White	Red	Intermediate
Brooke and Kaiser (1970)	IIB	IIA	I
Peter *et al.* (1972)	FG	FOG	SO
Burke *et al.* (1973)	FF	FR	S

M. soleus of rodents is red and slow, while some diaphragmatic muscles are red and fast. In uropeltid snakes serially homologous muscles drift from red to white along the column (Gans *et al.*, 1978).

It is now generally agreed that there are three main types of mammalian twitch fibers (Close, 1972; Burke, 1978). The histochemical demonstration of myofibrillar ATPase separates fibers into fast (α) and slow (β) types, whereas NADH diaphorase (NADH-D) or succinic dehydrogenase (SDH) measures the oxidative capacity of a fiber. Table IV shows the contraction times and the histochemical properties of the three classes in muscles of guinea pigs (Peter *et al.*, 1972) and the synonymy of various common classifications (see Close, 1972 and Peter *et al.*, 1972 for a more complete list of properties and synonymies).

The last two classifications are more descriptive than the others. Burke *et al.* (1973) describe their types as fast-twitch fatigue-sensitive (FF), fast-twitch fatigue-resistant (FR) and slow-twitch very resistant to fatigue (S), whereas the terms of Peter *et al.* denote fast-twitch-glycolytic (FG), fast-twitch-oxidative-glycolytic (FOG) and slow-twitch-oxidative (SO). The terms of Brooke and Kaiser (1970) are commonly used for human muscles, but for most mammals and other vertebrates the designations of either Peter *et al.* or Burke *et al.* have replaced the earlier ones of Padykula and Gauthier (1966). I use terms of Peter *et al.* (1972), because fatigue is not usually measured in reptilian muscles.

FOG fibers are generally also rich in mitochondrial enzymes other than NADH-D and SDH, in myoglobin, and in fat droplets. FG fibers, with few mitochondria, are rich in phosphorylase and glycogen and in other glycolytic enzymes. Apparently FOG fibers rely on both oxidation and glycolysis as sources of metabolic energy, whereas FG fibers rely primarily on glycolysis. Biochemical assays of the muscles of guinea pigs confirm the histochemical findings (Peter *et al.*, 1972). Fibers in muscles of cats are similar except that SDH and NADH-D are more active in SO fibers than in FOG fibers (Burke, 1978). Burke (1978) also identifies fast inter- mediate F(int) fibers, which show intermediate sensitivities to fatigue. In the cat, the slow-twitch fibers of the M. soleus differ from those of the M. gastrocnemius in several respects (Burke, 1978). They contract more slowly although their ATPase is more active, they are larger in diameter, and they show post-tetanic potentiation less clearly. Obviously the tripartite classification is only a convenient first approximation to a probably large number of different types of fibers, and there are discernible variants within each type.

The different properties of the types of fibers match them to different functions. FG fibers, which are white because their contents of myoglobin and mitochondria are low, rely on glycolysis and consequently require little oxygen during activity. The aerobic fibers (FOG and SO) require oxygen from the blood, are more highly vascularized, and have a smaller diameter, thereby reducing the diffusion distance between blood and central fibrils and increasing the ratio of surface to volume. Vascularization in the M. trapezius of *Testudo*, the Mm. biceps brachii and extensor digitorum communis of the lizards *Eremias* and *Varanus*, and muscles of other vertebrates is more extensive for the aerobic muscles (Ivanova, 1973).

Fast or slow movement implies fast or slow contraction, which correlates with the rate of ATPase activity (Bárány, 1967). FG fibers seem to be adapted for fast movements that are brief, FOG for fast movements that are longer lasting, and SO for slow, prolonged contractions in which speed is less important than economy.

In mammals FOG fibers are often narrow and red, FG fibers are broad and white, and SO fibers are intermediate, although many exceptions make these descriptions imprecise, especially for interspecific comparisons. Slow- twitch fibers have not been found in reptiles, and fibers with the slow type of myofibrillar ATPase should be tonic. Tonic fibers are small in reptiles and there are two types of twitch fibers, mitochondrion-rich and mitochondrion-poor. This suggests the very tentative assignment of broad white fibers as FG, intermediate fibers as FOG and narrow red fibers as tonic. However, some narrow red fibers may be FOG. As we shall see, some reptilian fibers are poorly described and others do not fit into their expected types. It is premature to convert from types established on the basis of size and color to the FOG, FG, and SO classification until more data are available.

In several muscles from the legs and trunk of *Draco*, the diameters of red fibers are 35 to 45 μm, intermediate fibers 50 to 65 μm, and white fibers 70 to 100 μm (John, 1970). In thigh muscles of *Calotes*, the corresponding diameters are 16 to 30 μm, 45 to 60 μm, and 65 to 85 μm (Momin, 1975). The diameters of narrow red fibers compare satisfactorily to those described for fibers identified as tonic in other species on the basis of multiple grape endings. However, although most tonic fibers are narrow, it is unlikely that all narrow fibers are tonic, and further investigation is necessary.

Ultrastructural studies by Finol and Ogura (1977) differentiate two types of tonic fibers as well as both mitochondrion-rich and mitochondrion-poor fibers in leg muscles of *Iguana*. These fibers may be compared with the two types of tonic and three types of twitch fibers reported in frogs (Smith and Ovalle, 1973). Histochemical characterization of these types is more difficult.

In neither amphibians nor birds can twitch and tonic fibers be distinguished from each other by demonstration of SDH activity or content of glycogen and lipid (Lee, 1971). If slow-twitch fibers are absent, measurement of the activity of myofibrillar ATPase should permit distinction between tonic and twitch fibers. Unfortunately such measurements have rarely been made in reptiles. There may also be technical difficulties. Although the ATPase of slow-twitch fibers is less active, its histochemical demonstration depends strongly on the lability of the enzyme to alkali at pH 9·4, in contrast to the stability of the ATPase of fast-twitch fibers at this pH. A modified technique depends on the lability of the fast-twitch enzyme to acid. The correlation between activity and stability may not hold for all species of vertebrates. Mammalian histochemical methods sometimes demonstrate high myofibrillar activities both for tonic and twitch fibers of avian muscles, and methods are still being improved.

A careful study of the fiber types in trunk and tail muscles of the snake *Xenochrophis* (Talesara and Mala, 1976) poses problems in matching reptilian size-color types with the mammalian classification (Table V). The red fibers are apparently tonic and oxidative, the intermediate ones are FOG, and the low activity of mitochondrial enzymes in the white fibers implies that they are FG. In this snake, the activity of oxidative enzymes is higher in the apparently slow fibers than in the FOG fibers; it is thus similar to the condition in cats and pigs but not to that in guinea pigs. However, the activities of phosphorylase in fibers of trunk muscle are unexpected. The "glycolytic" white fibers show little phosphorylase activity and the "oxidative" red fibers show much. Biochemical studies suggest that, at least in the turtle *Emys*, the fibers are really different (Lebedinskaya and Ogorodnikova, 1978). The low glycolytic activity of the

TABLE V

Fiber types in Xenochrophis. (*Talesara and Mala, 1976*)

	White	Tail muscle inter- mediate	Red	White	Trunk muscle inter- mediate	Red
Mean diameter (μm)	73	44	36	96	77	43
Myofibrillar ATPase	high	high	low	high	high	low
SDH or NADH-D	low	moderate	high	low	moderate	high
Phosphorylase	high	high	low	low	high	high

broad white fibers in trunk muscle has no mammalian parallel. Similar variety appears in the muscles of the lizards *Hemidactylus* and *Uromastyx* and of the turtle *Lissemys* (Talesara and Mala, 1978).

In costocutaneous muscles of *Natrix* (Pallot and Taberner, 1974), as in the tail muscles of *Xenochrophis*, twitch fibers show high phosphorylase activity and the largest have less SDH activity. Tonic fibers show little phosphorylase activity. In muscles of several other reptiles, as in the trunk muscles of *Xenochrophis*, red fibers are the richest in both glycolytic and oxidative enzymes and white fibers are the poorest. This is true for turtles (*Trionyx*: Ogata and Mori, 1963, 1964), lizards (*Calotes*: Momin, 1975; *Eumeces* and *Gekko*: Ogata and Mori, 1963, 1964; *Calotes* and *Draco*: John, 1966, 1970; *Hemidactylus*: Shah and Chakko, 1966a, b, 1967a, b, 1968, 1969, 1971, 1972; Shah and Magon, 1969; Shah and Ramachandran 1972; *Hoplodactylus* and *Leiolopisma*: Pollock and MacAvoy, 1978), and snakes (*Agkistrodon*: Ogata and Mori, 1963, 1964; *Xenochrophis*: Talesara, 1972; Talesara and Mala, 1976).

Still another variation from the mammalian types is shown in the body musculature of the uropeltid snake *Rhinophis* (Gans *et al.*, 1978). Fibers of the anterior axial muscles are rich in triads and mitochondria (FOG?), whereas those of more posterior serial homologues are poor in both triads and mitochondria, suggesting that they are tonic and glycolytic. There is no regional difference in the activity of glycolytic enzymes, but biochemical evidence confirms the regional difference in oxidative capacity. In contrast, fibers of amphisbaenid muscles (*Bipes, Rhineura, Amphisbaena, Cynisca, Mesobaena*) fall readily into the mammalian histochemical types (Maxwell and Gans, personal communication).

There is other biochemical evidence that reptilian fibers range widely in oxidative capacity. The concentration of cytochromes in the red M. coracohyoideus of *Pseudemys* is like that of the M. sartorius of frogs and toads, whereas it is only a tenth as high in the white M. retrahens capitis collique of these turtles (Jöbsis, 1963a, b). Histochemical studies of these muscles of turtles would be rewarding.

4. *Summary*

In snakes and lizards twitch and tonic fibers are easy to distinguish morphologically. Twitch fibers with typical ultrastructural features apparently receive single end plates from coarse axons, whereas tonic fibers receive multiple grape endings from fine axons. There is no evidence that any extrafusal fiber ever receives both. Single innervation and the presence of distinct fibrils are useful indicators that a fiber is a twitch fiber. The two types of fibers are mixed in many muscles of squamates, although some muscles may contain only twitch fibers. Twitch fibers in squamates can be divided into those which are richer or poorer in mitochondria and oxidative enzymes, but some low-oxidative twitch fibers apparently also have unusually low glycolytic capacity, unlike any mammalian FG fiber.

The muscle fibers of turtles have received less attention. Only twitch fibers have been observed in the M. retrahens capitis collique, but the fibers are unusual in receiving multiple end plates. The sarcotubular system is extensive in tortoises, but contact areas between the T system and the sarcoplasmic reticulum are reduced in *Testudo*, which may help to account for the slowness of the muscle. Both end plates and grape endings occur in the M. extensor digitorum brevis I of *Testudo* and paravertebral muscles of *Pseudemys*, implying that the muscles contain both twitch and tonic fibers. In many muscles of *Emys* light microscopy shows numerous fibers that are structurally intermediate between twitch and tonic fibers, which suggests intermediate development of the sarcotubular system.

C. PHYSIOLOGY

1. *Properties of Reptilian Fibers*

The physiological responses of twitch and tonic fibers to single stimuli are clear cut, at least in principle, whereas the distinction between fast-twitch and slow-twitch is strictly a matter of speed. Twitch fibers respond with a propagated action potential and the tension they develop is independent of the strength of the stimulus. Tonic fibers lack a regenerative membrane and respond with a graded junctional potential that increases with increasing strength of the stimulus. The tension they develop is correspondingly graded, rises much more slowly, and is often referred to as a contracture rather than a twitch. Resistances are higher and capacitances lower for membranes of tonic fibers.

In M. costocutaneus of the snakes *Natrix* and *Thamnophis* (Ridge, 1971;

TABLE VI

Contraction and relaxation times of various muscle fibers

Animal	Muscle	Temp. (C)	TTP (ms)	RT$_{\frac{1}{2}}$ (ms)	Reference
Pseudemys	M. retractor penis	20	400		Gilson *et al.*, 1947
Testudo	M. iliofibularis	0	4000		Woledge, 1968; Hill, 1950b
	M. iliotibialis	0	3000–5000		Hill, 1938
Thamnophis	scale elevator	20	40	30	Heistracher and Hunt, 1969a
Thamnophis and *Natrix*	M. costocutaneus:				
	twitch fibers	20–23	25–56	fast	Ridge, 1971
	tonic fibers	20–23	120–200	slow	Ridge, 1971
Crotalus	shaker	18	8–10		Martin and Bagby, 1973
Rana	M. sartorius	0	250		Hill, 1938
	tonic bundle of M. iliofibularis	20	1200*		Floyd and Smith, 1971
Gallus	M. latissimus dorsi posterior	21	79	82	Rall and Schottelius, 1973
	M. latissimus dorsi anterior	21	320	508	Rall and Schottelius, 1973
Rattus	M. extensor digitorum longus	37	9·8	9·5	Drachman and Johnston, 1975
	M. soleus	37	31	32·2	Drachman and Johnston, 1975

TTP: time to peak of twitch tension; RT$_{\frac{1}{2}}$ time for tension to fall to half maximum; *time to reach half-maximal tension when stimulated at 40 Hz

Hammond and Ridge, 1978a), twitch fibers are identified by their single innervation and ability to conduct action potentials. At 20°C it takes from 25 to 56 ms to reach maximum contraction (Table VI). Neither speed nor membrane constants clearly distinguish a fast-twitch from a slow-twitch population, and all fibers may simply be considered twitch. In addition, the muscles contain tonic fibers, identified by the presence of junctional potentials without action potentials and by multiple innervation from one or more fine axons that conduct impulses at only a third of the speed of the coarse axons that supply twitch fibers. The contraction time of the tonic fibers is 120 to 200 ms, about five-fold slower than that of the twitch fibers. Miniature junctional potentials in tonic fibers decay more slowly and with less sensitivity to membrane potential than do those of twitch fibers of the same costocutaneous muscle of *Thamnophis* (Dionne and Parsons, 1978). Post-tetanic potentiation occurs in twitch fibers of both lizards (Hammond and Ridge, 1978b) and snakes (Hartzell *et al.*, 1975; Hammond and Ridge, 1978b).

Twitch fibers in the M. scalenus of the lizard *Tiliqua* (Proske and Vaughan, 1968) conduct typical action potentials and rarely fail to spike. Their electrical responses never summate, and their junctional potentials rise rapidly and decay with half-times of 3 to 10 ms at 20° to 15°C. In contrast, tonic fibers show only non-propagated junctional potentials that rise rapidly but repolarize slowly, with half-times of 40 to 70 ms. The potentials summate at rates of stimulation above 10 Hz, and the extent of depolarization and the resulting tension continue to increase up to frequencies of more than 100 Hz. Nervous input is distributed over the surface of the fibers, supporting the morphological evidence for multiple innervation. These two types of fibers are like those of snakes and show comparable membrane constants (Table VII). A few fibers (8%) in *Tiliqua* may represent a distinct third type of slow-twitch fibers, characterized by dependence of the latent period on strength of stimulus or by evidence of dual innervation. If the innervation is dual, the endings are probably en grappe, because nearly all fibers with end plates (99.9%) are singly innervated.

There is morphological evidence that tonic fibers occur in the M. extensor digitorum I of *Testudo* (Crowe and Ragab, 1970a, b) and in the paravertebral muscles of *Pseudemys* (Cole, 1955b), but their physiology is unknown. Fibers in the red and white bundles of the M. testocervicalis of *Emys* have been compared (Lebedinskaya and Nasledov, 1977), as examples of twitch and tonic fibers in turtles. Those of the white bundle contain little lipid, and are thus similar to the twitch fibers of frogs. Their action potentials rise in 1·0 to 1·5 ms at 20° to 22°C, and a depolarizing pulse of 400 ms produces a volley of impulses. The red bundle contains a few twitch fibers similar to those of the white bundle, but most fibers of the red bundle are tonic. Upon direct stimulation, action potentials rise in 1·6 to 2·1 ms, and the fibers respond to a long intra-cellular pulse with only a single action potential. Their response to indirect stimulation via nerves is tonic. Presumably the motor terminals, like those in the M. latissimus dorsi anterior of chickens, release too little neuro-transmitter to reach the threshold for the action potential. As in other tonic (but not in twitch) fibers, depolarizing drugs produce a prolonged contracture. The resting potentials of tonic fibers are − 65 mV, those of twitch fibers are − 80 mV. The twitch fibers conduct impulses at 1·3 meters per second, tonic fibers at 0·6 meters per second. All the fibers in the M. retrahens capitis collique of *Pseudemys* and *Testudo* (Levine, 1966) have end plates and respond with action potentials and twitches, even to indirect stimulation, as expected from their ultrastructure. Nevertheless they are multiply innervated. The possibility that stimulation at multiple points on the membrane mimics an action potential has been ruled out by curariza-tion. At 15° to 24°C the action potentials rise in 1·1 ms and decay with a half-time of 1·9 ms. In hibernating tortoises, the time of rising is tripled and that of decay doubled. The spikes are conducted along the muscle

TABLE VII

Membrane constants of various muscle fibers

Animal	Muscle	Temp. (°C)	RP mV	Space constant mm	R_m Ωcm²	C_m μF cm⁻²	Time constant (ms)	Reference
Testudo	M. retrahens capitis collique	15–24	80	1·5	4860	7·9	34	Levine, 1966
Tiliqua	M. scalenus twitch fibers	20–25	>65		800–4800	6·0–9·6	6–40	Proske and Vaughan, 1968
	tonic fibers	20–25	45–55		9000–50000	1–3	18–70	Proske and Vaughan, 1968
Thamnophis and *Natrix*	M. costocutaneus twitch fibers	20–23	85	1·8	3000–4000	3–4	8–14	Ridge, 1971
	tonic fibers	20–23	70	4·4	38000	1·0	37	Ridge, 1971
Thamnophis	scale elevator	20	70–90	2				Heistracher and Hunt, 1969a
Rana	M. iliofibularis twitch fibers	20–22	91		3140	6·8	21·5	Adrian and Peachey, 1965
	tonic fibers	20–22	64		29000	2·5	46	Adrian and Peachey, 1965
Gallus	M. latissimus dorsi posterior	22	57	0·7	560	7·0	3·7	Fedde, 1969
	M. latissimus dorsi anterior	22	51	1·8	4400	8·2	35	Fedde, 1969
Mus	M. extensor digitorum longus (fast-twitch)	37	83	0·55	708	5·2	2·8	Luff and Atwood, 1972
	M. soleus (slow-twitch)	37	83	0·93	2170	3·1	4·4	Luff and Atwood, 1972

RP: resting potential; Space constant (λ): distance for applied voltage to decay to $1/e$ of initial value. $V_x = V_0 e^{-x/\lambda}$. R_m: membrane resistance; C_m: membrane capacitance; Time constant (τ): time for membrane charge to decay to $1/e$ of initial value. $Q_1 = Q_0 e^{-1/\tau}$.

fibers at 1·3 meters per second in active animals and at 0·8 meters per second in hibernators. Miniature end-plate potentials in both *Pseudemys* and *Testudo*, like those in twitch fibers of frogs, rise in about 2 ms and decay with a half-time of 4 to 9 ms. They are less frequent in *Testudo* than in *Pseudemys*. The contraction time for leg muscles of *Testudo* at 0°C is very slow (Hill, 1950b). Curiously, the M. iliotibialis of the tortoise contracts more slowly in the summer (4 to 5 s) than in the winter (3 to 4 s). The contraction time of the M. retractor penis of *Pseudemys* is 400 ms at 20°C (Gilson *et al.*, 1947), making it nearly as slow as that of the muscle of tortoises (after correction for temperature). Other muscles of *Pseudemys* are as fast by other criteria as is the M. sartorius of the toad (Goodall, 1957), and their contraction times are comparable (Wiencek and Guthe, unpublished). Rates of contraction may be measured isotonically as rates of shortening or isometrically as rates of increase of tension. Among reptiles such values are available only for *Pseudemys* and *Testudo* (discussed in Section III). The M. retrahens capitis collique of *Pseudemys* is as fast as the M. sartorius of the toad, but the M. retractor penis of *Pseudemys*, also a twitch muscle, is only a quarter as fast and is as slow as the M. iliofibularis of the tortoise (Goodall, 1957). It is interesting that the M. retractor penis of *Testudo* (Katz, 1939) appears to be as fast as are leg muscles (Woledge, 1968).

Rates of relaxation are usually reported as the interval between attainment of peak tension and the time at which tension falls to half its maximal value (Table VI). Times of relaxation and of contraction are comparable but only approximately correlated. Both times may depend not only on the properties of the contractile machinery but also on the speeds of release and uptake of calcium ions by the sarcotubular system. As Page (1968) suggested, the slow contraction of the muscles of tortoises may depend on the unusually small area of the interface between the tubules and the sarcoplasmic reticulum. Because the rate of flow is proportional to the area across which the flow occurs, the small area might limit the release of calcium and thus slow the rise of tension. The fall of tension in relaxation starts slowly and ends exponentially. The half-time of the exponential phase at $0°$ is 0·06 s in *Rana* (Jewell and Wilkie, 1960) and 2·5 s in *Testudo* (Woledge, 1968).

Not only are the contraction times of tonic fibers slower than those of twitch fibers (by a factor of five in snakes), but their membrane constants are different. In twitch fibers of turtles, lizards, and snakes (Table VII), resistances are a few thousand ohms-cm^2, whereas in tonic fibers they are greater by an order of magnitude. Capacitances are about three-fold greater in twitch fibers. This is to be expected because the membranes of the T tubules, which are characteristically more extensive in twitch fibers, are in parallel with the surface membrane. Capacitances of tonic fibers, with their smaller T system, are nearly as low as the capacitance of an axon, which of course lacks a tubular system. In the M. retrahens capitis collique of tortoises, both resistance and capacitance are high for twitch fibers, and their product, the time constant, is high enough to fall into the range typical of tonic fibers. Tonic fibers generally have slightly smaller resting potentials and larger space and time constants.

2. Comparison with Fibers of Other Vertebrates

Tables VI and VII also contain values for frogs, chickens, and rodents. Twitch (M. sartorius) and tonic fibers of *Rana* can be compared to their reptilian counterparts. Studies of rates of shortening of muscles of *Xenopus* (Lännergren, 1978) suggest that the tabulated contraction time for tonic fibers of *Rana* may be much too long. In chickens, the fibers of the M. latissimus dorsi posterior are twitch in morphology, but those of the M. latissimus dorsi anterior are tonic in ultrastructure and receive multiple grape endings (Ginsborg and Mackay, 1961; Hess, 1961). However, the fibers of the latter twitch in response to direct stimulation, like the fibers of the M. testocervicalis of *Emys*. They develop an action potential when stimulated directly but respond tonically to indirect stimulation via motor nerves, apparently because the terminals release too little transmitter to reach the threshold for the action potential (Bennett *et al.*, 1973). In mammals, the M. soleus is a slow-twitch muscle, about a quarter as fast as the fast-twitch M. extensor digitorum longus. Although the resistance of the avian M. latissimus dorsi anterior is lower than in the tonic fibers of snakes and frogs, it is still seven times that of the M. latissimus dorsi posterior, supporting a tonic classification for the former. Capacitances are lower in tonic fibers, but high in the M. latissimus dorsi anterior. Both twitch and tonic fibers have larger space constants and smaller capacitances in snakes than in other vertebrates. The resting potentials of both muscles of chickens are unusually low and so are the resistances of both muscles of mice.

3. Effects of Drugs

The scale elevators of *Thamnophis* respond to many drugs as do twitch fibers of other vertebrates (Heistracher and Hunt, 1969a, b, c; Washio, 1973, 1974). They are composed of only 3 to 12 parallel fibers, so that responses of individual fibers are easily observed. The fibers are so short that an applied potential does not decay much along their length, making them useful in studying electrical responses as affected by voltage clamp, drugs, glycerol extraction, neurotransmitters, varying calcium concentrations and temperature. After denervation, there is little change in the ionic movements that accompany depolarization (Wilson, 1975).

Drugs have been used in a few other studies on reptilian muscle. The drug ryanodine produces rigor in the M. biceps brachii of alligators, as it does in other vertebrate skeletal muscles (Haslett and Jenden, 1961). Typical twitch and tonic fibers differ in their responses to acetylcholine or to high concentrations of potassium ion. Both types of fibers contract initially, but twitch fibers soon relax again whereas tonic fibers maintain contracture for long periods. By this criterion, tonic and twitch fibers are intermingled in the Mm. gastrocnemius and semitendinosus of *Testudo*, only twitch fibers occur in the M. sartorius (Zhukov, 1965, 1967), and only tonic fibers in the M. retrahens capitis collique (Ginetzinsky and Itina, 1938). Nevertheless the M. retrahens twitches, implying that twitch can only be distinguished from tonic responses by means of additional data, which have been supplied by other Russian studies (Itina, 1938; Lebedinskaya, 1963, 1964, 1965, 1973; Lebedinskaya and Nasledov, 1977; Zhukov, 1965, 1967). All or nearly all fibers of the M. latissimus dorsi of chickens (Page, 1969) are tonic ultrastructurally, but high concentrations of potassium ion produce both an initial twitch-like transient peak and a prolonged tonic plateau in tension.

Although muscles of frogs and mammals classically respond only to nicotinic and not muscarinic agents, muscles of tortoises respond to both (Lebedinskaya 1963, 1964; Lukomskaya and Rozhkova, 1970). Muscles of lizards show responses intermediate between those of frogs and tortoises.

The membrane of the M. retrahens capitis collique of *Testudo* is sensitive to acetylcholine even at large distances from neuromuscular junctions (Ginetzinsky and Shamarina, 1942). In *Testudo* the extra-junctional sensitivity is lower by 3 to 5 orders of magnitude (Levine, 1966), whereas in *Pseudemys* it is not detectable at all. Levine also found that sensitivity falls by an order of magnitude within 150 μm of the junction in tortoise and 100 μm in terrapins, corresponding to 227 μm in the M. latissimus dorsi posterior of chickens and 142 μm in their M. latissimus dorsi anterior (Fedde, 1969). In the M. obliquus externus of *Thamnophis* and the M. cutaneus pectoris of *Necturus* and *Rana* (Hartzell et al., 1975; Kuffler and Yoshikami, 1975a, b) the sensitivity is reduced by several orders of magnitude at 20 to 30 μm from the end plate.

4. *Summary*

The physiological data reinforce the morphological evidence that two kinds of fibers occur in squamates, with the characteristics of twitch and tonic fibers of frogs. In snakes the speeds of twitch fibers are continuously distributed, and tonic fibers are five times slower than twitch. In *Tiliqua* there may be a distinction between a fast and a slow population of twitch fibers, but the properties of the membranes of the putative slow-twitch fibers were not determined, and further study is needed. In *Testudo*, only twitch fibers have been studied in the Mm. retractor penis and iliofibularis. They have membranes with twitch-like characteristics despite the slow rate at which they contract. In *Pseudemys* the M. retractor penis is as slow as muscles of tortoises, but its M. retrahens capitis collique is as fast as the M. sartorius of toads. The M. retrahens is a fast-twitch muscle, and the M. retractor penis contracts four times more slowly, just as in mammals slow-twitch muscles contract four times more slowly than fast-twitch.

Tonic fibers in *Emys* resemble fibers of the chicken's M. latissimus dorsi anterior in twitching when stimulated directly, but not when stimulated via nerves. Tonic fibers of squamates never twitch, suggesting that their membranes lack this capacity.

The muscles of reptiles respond to drugs in the same way as do those of other vertebrates except that reptilian muscles are unusually responsive to muscarinic agents. Extra-junctional receptors for acetycholine appear to be more diffusely distributed in testudinian muscle than in that of squamates or amphibians.

D. PROTEINS AND SPECIAL COMPOUNDS

Proteins of muscle have occasionally been compared among animals belonging to different classes of vertebrates. Extracts of muscles from rabbits, chickens, or pigeons contain more protein than those from tortoises, frogs, or carp (Renard, 1952). After removal of the albumins, there are fewer electrophoretic components in extracts from muscles of tortoises or frogs than in those from rabbits, birds, or carp. Myosin from rabbits or frogs salts out at an ionic strength of 0·35, that from *Testudo* at 0·45, and that from carp at 0·50 (Dubuisson, 1953). Myosins from lizards are less labile to high temperatures in species that live in hotter environments (see Licht *et al.*, 1969, which includes references to earlier papers), but the thermolability is also related to resting potential (Ushakov, 1969). The myosins must differ in structure to account for their differences in solubility, ATPase activity, and alkaline lability. A myosin molecule consists of two heavy polypeptide chains and four light ones. The heavy chains of myosins from lobsters, frogs, turtles, chickens, and man are very similar (Brivio and Florini, 1972), but the light chains differ electrophoretically. Apparently the light chains are more susceptible to evolutionary modification. Although heavy chains from fast and slow mammalian muscles do not differ electrophoretically, their tryptic peptides are different (Weeds, 1976), and their light chains differ in both respects. Immunological differences are also demonstrable (Gauthier and Lowey, 1977). Some slow fibers in *Testudo* and *Lacerta* (Pierobon Bormioli *et al.*, 1980) stain more strongly with antibody to slow twitch myosin, whereas others stain more strongly with antibody to tonic myosin.

The calcium-binding proteins of the troponin complex are very similar in amino acid composition, primary structure, immunological properties, and sensitivities to calcium whether isolated from fishes, frogs, reptiles (*Varanus, Python*), or rabbits (Demaille *et al.*, 1974). Other calcium-binding proteins of low molecular weight (parvalbumins) are found in muscles of turtles (*Pseudemys*), chickens, rabbits and men (Lehky *et al.*, 1974; Blum *et al.*, 1977), despite earlier reports that they were restricted to cyclostomes, selachians, fishes and amphibians (Focant and Pechère, 1965). A newly discovered protein, connectin, occurs in muscles of various vertebrates, including *Cyclemys* (Maruyama *et al.*, 1977).

Information on other proteins is even scarcer. Although the cardiac and skeletal muscle isoenzymes of lactic dehydrogenase in turtles are more alike than they are in rats (Miller and Hale, 1968; Altman and Robin, 1969), this makes the heart of turtles better adjusted for anaerobiosis during diving and is probably not a phylogenetic difference. Specific activities of glycolytic enzymes of skeletal muscle from a range of aquatic and terrestrial snakes also correlate with the probable exposure of the snake to temporary anoxia during normal patterns of activity (Baldwin and Seymour, 1977). Proteins from the caudal muscles of the house lizard *Hemidactylus leschenaultii* show different electrophoretic bands during regeneration and during acclimation to a new temperature (Pushpendra and Eapen, 1972). Different multiple forms of esterases occur in muscles, livers, and kidneys of different species of turtles (Pakhomov *et al.*, 1973), but the patterns are too complex to permit separation of the effects of adaptive features, phylogenetic differences, and tissue specificity. The ratio of the amounts of two isoenzymes of phosphorylase in muscle tissue is different in *Testudo* than in fish (Serebrenikova and Lyzlova, 1977).

Various special small molecules have been found in reptilian muscle. The O-phosphodiester of serine and ethanolamine occurs in several reptilian tissues, especially in cardiac and skeletal muscle, but not in the same tissues of mice and chicks (Roberts and Lowe, 1954). Although muscles of many vertebrates (Crush, 1970) contain carnosine (β-alanylhistidine) and anserine (β-alanyl-1-methylhistidine), ophidine (β-alanyl-3-methylhistidine) has thus far been found only in snakes and whales (Takeda, 1965; Tsunoo *et al.*, 1964; Crush, 1970). The occurrence of these compounds in a long list of reptiles has been documented by Crush (1970).

E. Special Muscles

The structure of the fibers in the shaker muscle of the rattlesnake *Crotalus*, despite its unusual speed (Martin and Bagby, 1973), resembles that of other fast fibers. They have the usual mitochondria, sarcoplasmic reticulum, M line and large transverse tubules lying just within the A-I boundaries (Martin, 1972).

Muscles of the tongue of the chameleon (*Chamaeleo?*) (Rice, 1973) can contract to one-sixth of their extended length. Such extreme shortening is prevented in other muscles by the Z lines, which bring the thick filaments up short. In the tongue of the chameleon the Z lines are discontinuous, permitting thick filaments to slide into adjacent sarcomeres. Otherwise, the ultrastructure of the muscle is apparently conventional. It is said to have the force and speed of skeletal muscle. Its force-velocity and length-tension curves should be interesting. Another study finds no ultrastructural differences between Z lines of the tongue of the unrelated American chameleon (*Anolis?*) and of the M. sartorius of frog (Ullrick *et al.*, 1977a, b).

Muscles of the lizards *Draco* and *Calotes* were compared to see whether the gliding habit of the former led to any apparent specializations (John, 1966, 1970). Broad white, intermediate, and narrow red fibers occur in the Mm. pectoralis major, rectus abdominis, triceps brachii, biceps brachii, and gastrocnemius of both species. Only end plates are evident, and they are similar for the different muscles except that they are more numerous and unusually closely spaced in the Mm. pectoralis and rectus abdominis. In *Draco*, perhaps because the animal is less active, acetylcholinesterase is also less active, suggesting that *Draco* has fewer terminals or less sarcolemmal infolding than does *Calotes*. In *Draco*, broad and intermediate fibers outnumber narrow ones, except in the M. rectus abdominis in which their numbers are equal. The muscles therefore look white and are probably fast. Fibers of the same type cluster together only in the M. pectoralis, where mixed fibers surround a small central band of narrow fibers, and in the M. triceps, where a peripheral layer of narrow fibers surrounds a central core of mixed fibers. Unlike the fibers of other reptilian muscles, the narrow central fibers of the M. pectoralis, although red, apparently contain much phosphorylase and glycogen, no demonstrable succinic dehydrogenase, and little fat or myoglobin. John (1970) suggests that the gliding habit is associated with reduction of the abdominal muscles. Their role may have been usurped by the M. pectoralis, which is probably not used in gliding. The M. pectoralis may thus resemble abdominal rather than pectoral muscles of birds.

Extraocular muscles of *Lacerta agilis* show three ultrastructural types of fibers as well as the usual three histochemical types (Kaczmarski, 1969, 1974). Some fibers are typical large twitch fibers with extensive and regular sarcoplasmic reticula, clear M lines, and end plates, but most of them are multiply innervated. Others are typical small tonic fibers with a scanty sarcoplasmic reticulum, broad Z lines, and multiple grape endings. Fibers of a third type resemble twitch fibers in showing a fairly regular sarcoplasmic reticulum, but they possess multiple, slightly folded terminals that are oval and button-like and may be modified grape endings. Their Z lines are broad and their M lines absent. The three types are segregated within the muscles: the twitch fibers are nearest the eyeball, and the tonic ones in a thin superficial layer, separated from the twitch fibers by fibers of the third type. A companion study (Witalinski, 1974) emphasizes the ultrastructural differences between fibers of the extraocular muscles and those of the intercostal muscles. The extraocular muscles of *Natrix* are ultrastructurally like those of *Lacerta* (Witalinski and Loesch, 1976).

Venom is expelled from the venom gland of the cobra upon contraction of the associated M. adductor externus superficialis (see review by Haas, 1973). The fibers of the muscle show well developed triads and many mitochondria (Gopalakrishnakone and Jayatilaka, 1978) and are probably fast-twitch oxidative glycolytic (FOG).

Although the pupillary constrictors of mammals are smooth, those of birds and reptiles include some striated fibers. In alligators (Reger, 1966), striated fibers are often directly apposed to apparently typical smooth muscle fibers, separated by interspaces of 100 to 200 nm, and there is an intermixture of immature striated muscle cells (myoblasts). The striated fibers resemble tonic fibers in possessing irregular triads.

In several classes of vertebrates the thymus contains myoid cells. Their appearance is similar in the snake *Natrix*, the turtle *Pseudemys*, and the pigeon *Columba* (Raviola and Raviola, 1967). Striated myoid cells are more numerous in the thymus of lizards (*Eumeces* and *Heloderma*), snakes (*Crotalus* and *Lampropeltis*), and turtles (*Trionyx*) than they are in the thymus of man (Bockman, 1968). The reptilian cells are spheroidal or elongate, with large characteristic nuclei. Marked vesiculation and continuity of protoplasm between myoid cells are evident, as are branching networks of sarcoplasmic reticulum or transverse tubules. The thymus of reptiles also contains immature myoid cells more similar to thymic epithelial cells.

F. Summary and Discussion of Types of Reptilian Fibers

The muscle fibers of reptiles may be classified as either twitch or tonic. Tonic fibers are common in many muscles of reptiles, birds, and amphibians, in which they are apparently used for slow movements. In mammals, tonic fibers are limited to extraocular muscles and a few others, and most slowly-contracting mammalian fibers are slow-twitch. Both slow-twitch and tonic fibers contain myosin that has two distinguishable light polypeptide chains whereas the chemically distinct myosin of fast-twitch fibers has three. A tonic fiber differs from a slow-twitch fiber primarily in that it responds to a stimulus with a junctional potential rather than with an action potential. Its innervation is by multiple terminals en grappe rather than by a single end plate. Although speeds of twitch fibers of squamates range widely, overlapping those of avian, amphibian, and mammalian fibers, there do not seem to be separate populations of fast-twitch and slow-twitch fibers. Perhaps the slow-twitch fibers of mammals developed from tonic fibers.

Twitch and tonic fibers are as easily distinguished in snakes as in frogs, for which they were originally described. In many muscles singly innervated twitch fibers with end plates intermingle with multiply innervated tonic fibers with grape endings. Only twitch fibers have action potentials. Their resistances are lower, their time constants shorter and they are supplied by coarser axons. Twitch fibers have extensive sarcotubular systems, prominent M lines, and straight and narrow Z lines. The tonic fibers of snakes are a fifth as fast as their twitch fibers. Tonic fibers have only a small sarcotubular system, their Z lines are broader and less straight, and their M lines are less distinct if present at all. The more extensive sarcotubular system of a twitch fiber divides the array of myofilaments into regular, distinct fibrils (Fibrillenstruktur), whereas in tonic fibers less complete division produces larger, irregular, and indistinct fibrils (Felderstruktur). Tonic fibers in lizards are less frequent, but very like those in snakes. A few twitch fibers of lizards behave as though they are innervated by more than one axon. They may possibly be slow-twitch fibers with grape endings.

Fibers of turtles differ in several respects from those of squamates. There is suggestive but not conclusive evidence that the tubular system of tonic fibers is better developed in *Emys* than in squamates. In both instances, the fibers are supplied by fine axons terminating en grappe. In *Emys* they develop tonic contractures in response to nervous stimulation, but show true action potentials and twitches when stimulated directly. Twitch fibers in the M. retrahens capitis collique of turtles are innervated by several axons, but the terminals are en plaque, not en grappe as in other instances of multiple innervation. The electrical properties of membranes of twitch fibers in *Testudo* are typical of twitch fibers except that the time constant is long. Tortoises may be considered either to possess no fast-twitch but only slow-twitch fibers or to possess unusually slow fast-twitch fibers. In

Pseudemys, the M. retrahens capitis collique is as fast as the M. sartorius of toads, but the M. retractor penis is only a quarter as fast. In *Testudo* the M. retractor penis is no slower than other muscles.

This survey of reptilian muscle raises many questions, some of which may be considered further.

1. *Why are some reptilian junctions different from those of other vertebrates?*

Extrajunctional receptors for acetylcholine are more diffusely distributed in testudinian muscles than in those of squamates or amphibians. Reptilian junctions respond to both muscarine and nicotine, amphibian and mammalian junctions respond only to nicotine (Section II.C.3).

2. *What energy sources do different reptilian fibers use?*

Histochemical methods identify three common types of fibers in reptiles as they do in amphibians and birds. Although evidence is rarely complete, most broad white fibers are probably low-oxidative twitch fibers (like mammalian FG fibers), intermediate are high-oxidative twitch fibers (like FOG fibers), and narrow red fibers are tonic, slow, and oxidative (like slow-twitch fibers except that they do not twitch). Some narrow red fibers may be twitch fibers. Unexpectedly, broad white fibers in many reptilian muscles do not show the high glycolytic activity that is characteristic of mammalian FG fibers. Further histochemical and biochemical studies are obviously required. Some of the fibers in uropeltid snakes are apparently low-oxidative tonic fibers (Section II.B.3).

3. *Why are muscles of tortoises so slow?*

The slowness of muscles in tortoises may be explained by their sarcotubular structure and the low activity of their myofibrillar ATPase. Although the T system is extensive and apparently contributes electrically to the membrane constants, its area of contact with the sarcoplasmic reticulum is very much reduced. The reduced area of contact may slow the release of calcium ions by the sarcoplasmic reticulum; these ions couple excitation to contraction. The membranes of the sarcotubular system themselves may also be different. Comparisons with the much faster homologous muscles of *Pseudemys* might help to untangle the relative roles of these possible mechanisms (Sections II.B.1, C.1).

4. *Is the M. retractor penis of* Pseudemys *a slow-twitch muscle in the mammalian sense?*

The M. retractor penis of *Pseudemys* is only a quarter as fast as other muscles of the animal, just as in mammals slow-twitch muscles are a quarter as fast as fast-twitch. The retractor certainly twitches, but its structure and innervation are unknown. Its fibers might possibly resemble tonic fibers of birds in behavior, twitching only in response to direct stimulation. On the other hand, the muscle might comprise true twitch fibers, and it would be desirable to know whether its ATPase follows the fast, slow or tonic pattern of polypeptide chains. Slow-twitch fibers have not been demonstrated except in mammals (see Section III).

5. *Why is the M. retrahens capitis collique of turtles multiply innervated although its motor terminals are end plates?*

The M. retrahens capitis collique in both *Testudo* and *Pseudemys* is unusual because it comprises twitch fibers with typical end plates, but multiple, plurisegmental innervation. Multiple innervation is not correlated with speed of contraction, because in *Pseudemys* the muscle is fifteen-fold faster than in *Testudo*. A single fiber of the M. retrahens of *Testudo* receives multiple innervation from three spinal cervical nerves and from more than one axon in a nerve. It seems possible that multiple innervation in this muscle is important for the central control of muscular activity and that its fibers are like other twitch fibers except for these special control features. It is important to investigate the innervation of other testudinian twitch muscles (Sections II, B.2, C.1).

6. *Why do tonic fibers in the M. testocervicalis of* Emys *respond to nervous stimuli with tonic contractures, but to direct stimuli with a propagated action potential (Lebedinskaya and Nasledov, 1977)?*

Unlike most fibers with multiple grape endings, those of the M. testocervicalis and of the avian M. latissimus dorsi anterior (ALD) both conduct action potentials. The latter has received much more attention. Apparently its multiple grape endings ordinarily release too little transmitter to reach the threshold of the action potential. Its fibers show many of the other ultrastructural characteristics of tonic fibers, and its myosin shows the slow pattern of polypeptide chains. The M. latissimus dorsi anterior seems to consist of fibers that are on the verge of becoming slow-twitch fibers. An action potential synchronizes the contraction of the sarcomeres of a fiber along its length, and the action potential suggests that changes may be present in the sarcotubular system that synchronize contraction transversely. The sarcotubular system of the M. latissimus dorsi anterior is less extensive than in twitch muscles, but it is much more extensive than in the tonic fibers of frogs and snakes, and the contacts between its T system and its sarcoplasmic reticulum are much more frequent. Köhler's (1938) study of reptilian muscle suggests that a rather extensive sarcotubular system may also be characteristic of tonic fibers of turtles (and perhaps alligators). It is notable that the sarcotubular system of mammalian slow-twitch fibers is less extensive than that of fast-twitch fibers (Eisenberg and Kuda, 1976), although it is certainly better developed than that of the M. latissimus dorsi anterior. The extensive sarcotubular system of that muscle suggests that its synchronized contraction may be important at times. The ability of the fiber to conduct action potentials may be more than a curiosity or a relic of its twitch nature in an ancestral form. Perhaps further study of testudinian tonic fibers and of the M. latissimus dorsi anterior will suggest what selective pressures helped to produce slow-twitch fibers in mammals.

Reptilian muscle certainly differs from amphibian muscle, and that of squamates from that of turtles. Additional information about more muscles and more species is needed before any adaptive or phylogenetic significance can be even tentatively assigned. In all terrestrial vertebrates, fast movements are accomplished by twitch muscles. Slower movements are apparently accomplished by tonic muscles in most ectotherms. Perhaps the endothermal condition makes even slow movements too fast for tonic muscles, for they are rare in mammals, which use slow-twitch muscles for most slow movements. As already discussed, tonic fibers of turtle muscles and the avian M. latissimus dorsi anterior can twitch, although they have many other properties of tonic muscles. Many muscles of *Testudo* are slow muscles that twitch, and their contractile and energetic properties are considered in detail in the next section.

III. Mechanics and Energetics

A. GENERAL

Muscles of tortoises have been objects of special study because their slowness makes it possible to resolve contractile events that follow each other too rapidly in faster muscles. More recently they have attracted attention for their comparatively efficient use of chemical energy. The present section examines information related to energetics and mechanism in these muscles.

It is convenient to begin by describing the present theory of the contractile process (Carlson and Wilkie, 1974). Contraction depends on the activity of cross-bridges that link the thick to the thin filaments in active muscle. The bridges become active when the concentration of calcium ions rises above threshold following the impulse-triggered release of the ions by the sarcoplasmic reticulum. When the bridges become active, they begin to cycle. A cross-bridge (the head of a myosin molecule) binds to a site on the thin filament and somehow provides an impulsive force in a power stroke. It then detaches and recovers. It reattaches and repeats the cycle at a new site on the thin filament. Each cycle lasts about 10 ms in the M. sartorius of the frog *Rana*, and during it the bridge moves about 10 nm (1% of a half-sarcomere) or less and a single molecule of ATP is hydrolyzed. Rates of shortening should correlate with rates of cycling and of hydrolysis of ATP. Leg muscles of tortoises (*Testudo*) shorten about six times more slowly than those of frogs, and their myofibrils hydrolyze ATP about fifteen times more slowly (Bendall, 1964). About the same difference is found in the activities of purified myosins from the two sources (Bárány, 1967). However, there is growing evidence that some mammalian muscles contract at different speeds because their sarcoplasmic reticula release calcium ions at different rates (Brody, 1976; Briggs et al., 1977). It is hard to decide which of the two factors is limiting. The present section describes the evidence from muscles of tortoises that relates to the foregoing scheme of contraction.

The total energy released in a contraction includes heat as well as work, and it must be obtained by conversion of chemical energy. Muscles of tortoises produce remarkably little heat in comparison to work, so that they convert chemical energy to work very efficiently. The advantages to the tortoise are obvious, but possible mechanisms are still elusive.

Available evidence about contraction in a muscle includes its rate of contraction, its strength and stiffness, the heat it produces, and its utilization of chemical energy. Some additional evidence may be obtained by studying the rapid transient changes in tension or length that follow quick stretch or release of the muscle. The present section considers these topics in order.

B. MECHANICAL PROPERTIES

Rate of contraction can be measured isotonically as rate of shortening, in units of muscle lengths per second. The maximal rate of shortening (v_{max}) is reached when the load is zero. The rate of contraction can also be measured isometrically either as time to the peak tension of a twitch (*TTP*) or as the rate of development of tension (dP/dt) in units of P_0 per second, where P_0 is the maximal tension the muscle can develop. According to Close (1965) the isometric and isotonic rates are usually well correlated, with the product of v_{max} and *TTP* being constant in a variety of muscles, but the correlation is imperfect. Rate of relaxation too may depend either upon activity of the cross-bridges or on the rate of uptake of calcium ions by the sarcoplasmic reticulum. Not only contraction, but also changes in the pH of a muscle during contraction are much slower in tortoises than frogs (Distèche, 1960a, b).

Rough estimates of maximal shortening rates may be obtained by allowing the muscle to shorten without added load, but the rate of shortening depends very much upon the load. A precise determination requires measurement of a force-velocity curve. The curve can then be fitted by Hill's empirical equation (1938), which, when normalized, is

$$\frac{v}{v_{max}} \left(\frac{a}{P_0} + \frac{P}{P_0} \right) = \frac{a}{P_0} \left(1 - \frac{P}{P_0} \right) = \frac{b}{v_{max}} \left(1 - \frac{P}{P_0} \right)$$

where v is the rate of shortening, in lengths s^{-1},

   P is the load in kg cm^{-2},

   v_{max} is the maximal rate of shortening,

   P_0 is the maximal isometric load, and

   a and b are constants characteristic of a given muscle.

Of the four constants, only three are independent, and these are usually chosen to be v_{max}, P_0, and a/P_0 $(= b/v_{max})$.

Rates of shortening (v_{max}) in Table VIII show nearly the same sort of variation as the times to peak tension discussed earlier, provided allowance is made for different temperatures. It is interesting that the Mm. sartorii of frogs and toads shorten isotonically at nearly the same rate although isometrically the M. sartorius of toads is only half as fast. The difference still lacks an explanation. In *Xenopus* tonic fibers are only six times slower than twitch fibers (Lännergren, 1978), and technical problems may account for the very slow rates tabulated for tonic fibers of *Rana*.

Maximal tensions (P_0), which are independent of temperature, vary little among the muscles tabulated. The agreement may be fortuitous, and P_0 may vary more when other muscles have been examined. The maximal tension of the medial shaker muscle of the rattlesnake is only 0·25 kg cm^{-2} (Martin and Bagby, 1973), but only 33% of the cross-section is fibrillar. The muscle may also have been weakened by possible damage during dissection. Allowing for these two factors, the tension is still only 1 kg cm^{-2}, about the same as for the muscles of chickens in Table VIII. Both larger and smaller tensions have been reported for various mammalian muscles. P_0 for the M. costocutaneus of *Thamnophis* is more than 1 to 2 kg cm^{-2} (Heistracher and Hunt, 1969a). It is about the same for twitch fibers of the homologous muscle in *Natrix* but at least 3 kg cm^{-2} for tonic fibers in *Natrix* (Ridge, 1971). These results for *Natrix* suggest that tonic fibers develop somewhat more tension than twitch fibers (see also data from *Rana* and *Xenopus* in Table VIII). In mammals, the slow-twitch M. soleus develops more tension than the fast-twitch M. tibialis anterior (Wells, 1965).

Related to maximal tension are the elastic properties of muscles. It has long been known that muscles differ in stiffness. Early workers (Bishop and Kendall, 1928; Fischer, 1935) noted that the resting M. retractor penis of turtles could be stretched more easily than could muscles of frogs, extending up to three times its length *in situ*. In contrast, the shaker muscle of rattlesnakes is unusually resistant to stretching at rest; its passive stiffness may represent 30% of the total tension in a contracted muscle at normal length. Martin and Bagby (1973) suggest that it is stiff because it has so much non-fibrillar sarcoplasm and its extensive vascularization adds additional less compliant tissue.

TABLE VIII

Some mechanical properties of muscle fibers

Animal	Muscle	T °C	P_0 (kg cm^{-2})	v_{max} (l_0^{-1})	TPT (s)	$\dfrac{dP}{dt}$ (P_0 s^{-1})	a/P_0	Stiffness (P_0/l_0)	Reference
Pseudemys	M. retrahens capitis	0		1·05		4·5	0·22	70	Goodall, 1957
	M. retractor penis	0		0·23		0·64	0·15	95–135	Katz, 1939
	penis	10		0·48		1·28	0·18	23–110	Katz 1939
Testudo	M. retractor penis	16		0·29 (summer)			0·11		Woledge, 1968
				0·6 (winter)			0·11		Woledge, 1968
	M. iliofibularis	0	1·9	0·23	4		0·07		Abbott and Lowy, 1957
		15					0·14		Hill, 1949
		20		0·33					
Bufo	M. sartorius	0	1·9	1·27	0·6	5·5	0·22	75	Bressler and Clinch, 1974
		0		1·05			0·21		Hill, 1938
Rana	M. sartorius	0	2·0	1·3	0·25		0·25		Katz, 1939
		0		1·3			0·26		Hill, 1970 p. 101
		2				10		75	Jewell and Wilkie, 1958
		22		10					Hill, 1938
Xenopus	M. iliofibularis tonic[1] fibers	20	2·6	0·11	1·2	0·2			Floyd and Smith, 1971
	M. iliofibularis twitch fibers	22	2·2	6·3			0·38		Lännergren, 1978
	tonic[2] fibers	22	3·0	1·1			0·10		Lännergren, 1978
Rattus	M. tibialis anterior	38	2·8	5·7		0·36			Wells, 1965
	M. soleus	38	3·3	2·0		0·21			Wells, 1965
Gallus	M. latissimus dorsi posterior	21	1·1	9·8	0·079		0·27		Rall and Schottelius, 1973
	M. latissimus dorsi anterior	21	0·5	1·9	0·32		0·11		Rall and Schottelius, 1973

P_0: isometric tension; v_{max}: maximal shortening rate; TPT: time to peak of isometric tension; $\dfrac{dP}{dt}$: maximal rate of development of tension; a/P_0: force-velocity constant; l_0: initial length

[1] stimulated at 40 Hz; [2] stimulated by bathing with solution containing high concentration of K$^+$

The stiffness of a muscle corresponds to Hooke's constant, $\Delta P/\Delta l$, where P is load and l is length. It is the reciprocal of the compliance. After conversion to tension per unit cross-section, the stiffness in kg cm^{-2} cm^{-1} is proportional to P/l_0, if one varies both the initial load (P) and the initial length (l_0). The proportionality constant is the same for resting and active muscles of the legs of tortoises (Reichel and Bleichert, 1955, 1958; Reichel and Zimmer, 1956; Reichel et al., 1956, 1958), although both the initial tension and the stiffness are of course much smaller at rest. The constant is about 75 for Mm. sartorii of toads and frogs (Bressler and Clinch, 1974; Jewell and Wilkie, 1958), 70 for the M. retrahens of *Pseudemys* (Goodall, 1957), and 95 to 135 for its M. retractor penis. In the M. gastrocnemius of *Testudo* (Fowler and Crowe, 1976) it is 68 at 5°C and 34 at 30°C. In *Tiliqua*, tonic fibers are stiffer than twitch fibers (Proske and Rack, 1976), and this is also true in *Rana* (Gregory et al., 1978). In the cat, Rack and Westbury (1974) report about 100 for both the Mm. gastrocnemius and soleus. Whenever careful comparisons are made in the same study, tonic fibers are stiffer than twitch in terms of P/l_0. Gregory et al. (1978) believe tonic fibers are stiffer because the turnover rate of cross-bridges is slower and the number of sarcomeres per muscle fiber is smaller. Like maximal tension, stiffness may vary more when other muscles are examined. Stiffness depends to some extent on the rate of shortening (Julian and Sollins, 1975), and it may vary during different parts of the contractile cycle. Further developments are to be expected, especially as more attention is paid to the rapid transients in tension that are discussed in Section III.D.

An additional unexplained peculiarity of the M. retractor penis of *Testudo* needs re-examination. When the applied load is increased above its

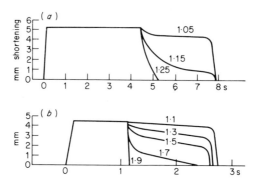

FIG. 4. Superimposed records of isotonic lengthening; values of P/P_0 as marked. The contractions were isometric until the load was increased to make P greater than P_0, when the muscle lengthened again. Note the more pronounced lengthening at small overloads for (a) M. retractor penis of *Testudo graeca* (17°C) than for (b) M. sartorius of *Rana temporaria* (0°C). (From Katz, 1939)

isometric value (Fig. 4), the muscle lengthens much more than does the M. sartorius of frogs (Katz, 1939). Perhaps this behavior is related to the low resistance of resting tortoise muscle to stretch.

If forces and velocities are normalized, the force-velocity curves for different muscles will coincide unless a/P_0 varies. The value of a/P_0 is 0·25 or more in anuran twitch fibers (Table VIII) and in fast-twitch mammalian muscles (Close, 1972). In slow-twitch mammalian muscles, the muscles of tortoises, the M. retractor penis of *Pseudemys*, the avian M. latissimus dorsi anterior, anuran tonic fibers, and slow-twitch mammalian muscles it is lower. In a muscle with a lower value of a/P_0 the speed of shortening decreases more sharply with increasing load (Fig. 5). As discussed later, there is some evidence that a lower value makes the contraction more economical.

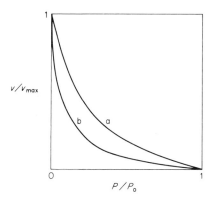

FIG. 5. The effect of different values of a/P_0 on the shape of the relative force-velocity curve calculated from Hill's equation. P/P_0 is the force as a fraction of the isometric force P_0, and v/v_{max} is the velocity as a fraction of the maximal velocity v_{max}. Curve a: $a/P_0 = 0·25$, as in M. sartorius of *Rana;* curve b: $a/P_0 = 0·072$, as in M. retractor penis of *Testudo*. Note that the observed rate of shortening v is much less for the muscle of the tortoise, because its v_{max} is only one-fifth that of the M. sartorius.

If a muscle becomes fully active immediately upon stimulation, the time course of its development of tension should be calculable from the partial differential $(\delta P/\delta t)_l = (dP/dl)(\delta l/\delta t)_p$, where the first term may be obtained from the stiffness of the muscle as a function of length and the second from the force-velocity relation. The calculated initial isometric rate is faster than the observed rate for frogs, and the difference between calculated and observed rates is even worse for tortoises (Jewell and Wilkie, 1958; Katz, 1939). A good fit can be obtained by assuming that activation is slow enough to be rate-limiting (Julian, 1969).

The rapidity of initial activation may also be shown by investigating the development of tension in a fully active muscle, such as one in tetanus. If activation does not limit the initial rate, tension will redevelop at the initial rate after a quick release from tetanus; if activation is slow, redevelopment should be faster in the already activated muscle. In 1939, Katz measured shortening initially and also when the muscle was released to shorten isotonically after it had been tetanized at a fixed length for 5 s. The two rates were not very different in muscles of frogs, but muscles of tortoises shortened as much as 30% faster after delayed release, indicating that the initial shortening rate was limited by the slow onset of the active state. Isometric rates also change. After a quick release to zero tension, tension redevelops 20% faster than it did initially in the M. sartorius of *Rana* (Jewell and Wilkie, 1958) and the M. retrahens of the turtle *Pseudemys* (Goodall, 1957). Slow activation is a much more severe limit in the slow M. retractor penis of *Pseudemys* (Goodall, 1957), wherein tension redevelops 240% faster after a delayed release. Slow activation may have a morphological bases (Page, 1968); the reduced area of the interface between the T tubules and the neighboring cisternae in fibers of *Testudo* may slow the rate at which calcium ions are released to the fibrils, delaying activation. It would be interesting to discover whether a similar arrangement exists in the M. retractor penis of *Pseudemys*.

C. ENERGY FLUXES AND ECONOMY

1. *Introductory*

The energy released on contraction includes the heat produced as well as the work done. The heat produced during contraction may be divided into initial heat and delayed (recovery) heat (Hill, 1938; reviewed by Abbott and Howarth, 1973; Carlson and Wilkie, 1974; Homsher and Kean, 1978).

In an isometric twitch, the rate of production of initial heat after stimulation follows the equation (discussed in the above reviews)

$$\dot{H} = \dot{h}_\alpha e^{-t/t_\alpha} + \dot{h}_a e^{-t/t_a} + \dot{h}_b, \text{ in mcal g}^{-1} \text{ s}^{-1}.$$

The dot signifies the derivative of the heat h with respect to time, and the overall heat production is divided into three components. The time constants in the sartorius of frogs at $0°$ are t_α 35 ms and t_a 1·2 s. Integration yields the total amounts of heat produced:

$$H = \dot{h}_\alpha t_\alpha + \dot{h}_a t_a + \dot{h}_b t, \text{ in mcal g}^{-1}$$

The first term is a rapid burst of *activation heat* accounting for 20 to 30% of the initial heat produced in a twitch (Abbott and Howarth, 1973). The rest is maintenance heat. In isometric tetanus, heat is produced as long as tension is maintained, but the rate of production slowly decreases toward a constant value. The second and third terms of the heat equation are the labile and stable *maintenance heats*. If the isometric constraint is removed and the muscle allowed to shorten, it produces additional *shortening heat*. Finally, after contraction and relaxation are complete, *delayed heat* is produced for many minutes at a low rate. This delayed *recovery heat* accompanies restoration of the steady state concentrations of high-energy phosphates and metabolites. It is produced at a low rate, but for so long that the total amount of heat produced during recovery approximately equals the sum of work and initial heat in both tortoises (Woledge, 1968) and frogs (Hill, 1939). The energy lost initially as work and initial heat is replaced by the chemical work during recovery. The efficiency of the recovery processes must be about 50% in both muscles.

2. Heat of Activation

Immediately after stimulation, a muscle becomes less extensible, and after a latent period it begins to contract. The initial release of heat is attributed to activation rather than development of tension because the rate of release is maximal during the latent period before tension develops. Tension drops slightly during the latent period (latency relaxation) to an extent that depends on the strength of the stimulus in the M. retrahens of *Pseudemys* and even more in its M. retractor penis (Goodall, 1958b, 1960). In Mm. sartorii of frogs and toads (Hill, 1965) the latent period lasts only 4 to 8 ms, too short to measure conveniently extensibility by quick stretch. In the M. iliotibialis of tortoises at 0°C it is much longer (Hill, 1950a, b, 1951). Muscles from animals in summer reach peak tension in 4 to 5 s, and their resistance to stretch increases at 100 ms. Both times are only 60 to 70% as long in muscles from animals in winter. In these muscles of tortoises, resistance to stretch begins to increase at about the same time as the heat of activation is produced. Activation heat probably accompanies the release of calcium ions from the sarcoplasmic reticulum that initiates contraction. In muscles of frogs, the time course of the change in extensibility closely follows that of the intrafibrillar concentration of calcium ions (Jöbsis and O'Connor, 1966). The precise origin of activation heat is still debatable, but it is probably related to sarcotubular activity and not to the contractile process *sensu stricto*. In reptilian muscle, heats of maintenance and shortening have received more attention and will be discussed in more detail.

3. Maintenance Heat

Both the labile and stable components of maintenance heat vary among species. In the M. sartorius, the time constant for labile heat of toads (*Bufo*) is about twice that for this muscle in *Rana temporaria*, comparable to the two-fold difference in isometric rates but not to the approximately equal rates of isotonic shortening. For *R. pipiens* the stable heat rate (h_b) is probably only half that of *R. temporaria* (Abbott and Howarth, 1973). Such variation within a single genus compels caution in drawing conclusions about phylogenetic differences. However, the leg muscles of tortoises are very different, for their labile heat is not measurable and their stable heat only 2·3% as much as in frogs (Table IX). Muscles of tortoises not only lack labile heat, but they relax at the same rate after a tetanus as after a twitch (Woledge, 1968). Muscles of frogs have a high labile heat and relax 2·5 times more slowly after a tetanus, and the two phenomena may be related (Abbott, 1951). Rats and chickens also lack a labile heat (Homsher and Kean, 1978). There is increasing evidence that labile heat, like activation heat, may depend at least in part on the extent and rate at which calcium ions cycle between the fibrils and the sarcoplasmic reticulum.

The stable heat of maintenance reflects the energy cost of maintaining constant tension once it has been established. A muscle in tetanus does its work when it initially shortens. Thereafter it maintains tension without doing additional work, and it continues to produce heat as its cross-bridges continue their cycles of attachment, force generation, and reattachment. The *economy* of a muscle, or the cost of maintaining tension, can be measured by dividing the tension by the stable heat rate. Economy should be distinguished from efficiency, which is equal to work/(heat plus work) and does not directly involve rates of either work or heat production. If maximal tensions are nearly the same, the muscle with the lower stable heat is the more economical. During a tetanus, interfilamentary bridges are continually forming and breaking, and the stable heat rate presumably measures the energy cost of this bridge activity. A muscle that has a slow cycle of activity, will have a low stable heat rate and a high economy, but it will also shorten slowly. A fast muscle, with cross-bridges that repeat cycles more rapidly, will necessarily produce stable heat at a high rate and maintain tension less economically. During a prolonged tetanus, the M. iliotibialis of a tortoise maintains the same tension as the M. sartorius of a frog, but it produces only 2·3% as much stable heat. The energy flux of M. iliotibialis is thus much less and its economy (tension/ maintenance heat rate) about forty times that of the M. sartorius. The M. iliotibialis of the tortoise maintains tension for many minutes at 0°C (Hill, 1950a) provided the frequency of stimulation is low, but the M. sartorius of the frog can only do so for less than a minute. In other words, the lower energy flux of the former muscle provides it with greater resistance to fatigue. Stable heat rates for various muscles are shown in Table IX. The high stable rates for chicken muscles despite their smaller maximal tensions need correction for the higher temperature of measurement.

TABLE IX

Mechanical and thermal constants for selected muscles

Animal	Muscle	T °C	P_0 (kg cm^{-2})	v_{max}	a/P_0 mech.	a/P_0 therm.	Stable (g-cm g^{-1} s^{-1})	ab (g cm g^{-1} s^{-1})	$\dfrac{W}{H\ \&\ W}$	Reference
Testudo	M. iliofibularis	0°	1·88	0·23	0·072	0·039	3·7	2·3	0·77	Woledge, 1968
Rana	M. sartorius	0°	2·00	1·3	0·25	(0·25)	160	160	0·45	Hill, 1938
	M. iliofibularis (tonic bundle)	20°	2·6	0·11	0·2		60	11	0·2	Floyd and Smith, 1971
Gallus	M. latissimus dorsi posterior	21°	1·12	9·8	0·27	0·14	286	800	0·44	Rall and Schottelius, 1973
	M. latissimus dorsi anterior	21°	0·46	1·9	0·11	0·07	46	10	0·55	Rall and Schottelius, 1973

$\dfrac{W}{H + W}$ = enthalpic efficiency = work/(initial heat plus work)

In twitch muscles of *Rana*, the stable heat rate is equal to the product ab, where a and b are determined from force-velocity measurements by Hill's (1938) equation. In Table IX, ab and the stable heat rate for leg muscles of tortoises are not significantly different, because their probable errors are large (Woledge, 1968), but the stable heat rate differs from ab in other muscles as well.

4. *Shortening Heat*

If a muscle shortens a distance x at a rate v, it produces extra heat ax at a rate av. The amount of shortening heat ax is nearly independent of both the rate of shortening and the load on the muscle. Hill pointed out that expanding the left side of his force-velocity equation produces two shortening-dependent terms: $av/P_o v_{max}$ and $Pv/P_o v_{max}$. The second is the rate of doing mechanical work (power output) and the first might therefore represent the rate of releasing energy non-mechanically, i.e., as heat. The parameter a/P_o should therefore be obtainable from either mechanical or termal measurements. For frog muscles, the two values are about the same at most values of P/P_o, although Hill (1964) later found that the thermal value varied with P/P_o. In Table IV, the thermal values for other muscles, including the M. iliofibularis of tortoises, are less than the mechanical values, a discrepancy with no clear explanation.

5. *Discussion*

Reducing the rate of the cyclic activity of cross-bridges should lower maintenance energy and increase economy. With a smaller energy flux, the muscle should hydrolyze less ATP and produce less stable heat. If cross-bridges take longer to complete their cycles, the speed of shortening decreases. A muscle must therefore compromise. It may either contract rapidly and fatigue quickly, like the jumping muscles of frogs, or it may contract slowly and maintain tension economically, like the muscles of tortoises. Both heat production and speed of contraction may be reduced further if the sarcoplasmic reticulum is less active in releasing and taking up Ca^{++}. Whatever the explanation, muscles of tortoises produce stable heat of maintenance at a remarkably low rate and therefore maintain tension very economically. The ratio of the rate of production of stable heat to the maximal isometric tension is the usual measure of the economy of a muscle.

Although the economy of a muscle increases and its rate of work decreases if its cross-bridges take longer to complete a cycle of activity, the energy that the muscle requires to do work is not necessarily changed. To do work the muscle must shorten, not simply maintain tension at a fixed length, and its work varies with load. Mechanical efficiency is calculated as the ratio of the maximal work done by the muscle to its total enthalpy production (heat plus work). It depends on the proportion of enthalpy released as work in each cycle. Slower cycling without other changes would use ATP more slowly but no more efficiently. Muscles of tortoises, however, are more efficient as well as more economical than frogs (Table IX). For each kilocalorie of enthalpy, muscles in tortoises produce 0·77 kcal of work (Woledge, 1968), in frogs only 0·45. Conversely, in doing 1 kcal of work, the M. iliofibularis of tortoises produces only 1·3 kcal of heat (total energy flux 2·3 kcal), whereas in frogs the M. sartorius produces 2·2 kcal of heat (total energy flux 3·2 kcal). Fast muscle may be inefficient (Woledge, 1968) because bridges remain attached long enough at the end of their power stroke to exert force on the thin filament that opposes the forward movement of the filament or because the length of the power stroke is reduced by either late attachment or early detachment. If attachment, the power stroke and detachment were slower, either rate constants or binding constants could be changed enough to reduce one or more of these possible causes of inefficiency. The muscle would then not only maintain tension more economically but also be more efficient.

If maintenance of tension becomes more efficient and economical, several possible strategies are open (Woledge, 1968). The maximum continuous power output (heat plus work) of an aerobic muscle is limited by the rate at which oxygen can be supplied to it (Wilkie, 1960). With better economy and unchanged oxygen supply, a muscle could increase its maximal mechanical power. Alternatively, without changing its power, it could use less energy per minute, and the animal could reduce the amount of food it ate and the size of its lungs and heart. Local storage of energy-rich compounds could also be reduced. It is interesting that muscles contain only about half as much high-energy phosphate in *Testudo* as in *Rana* (Caldwell, 1953; Walsh and Woledge, 1970) although the ratio of total creatine to adenine nucleotides remains the same. Reduced energy flux might also lower the need for rapid oxidation, at least in oxidative fibers, but there is little evidence on this point. Yakovlev (1965) reports that the ratio of creatine phosphate to total adenine nucleotides is not unusual in the back muscles of *Natrix* but that this ratio and the content of cytochrome oxidase are low in the M. gastrocnemius of the turtle *Emys orbicularis*.

The relatively high cost of maintaining tension in fast muscles appears to be a price paid to permit a relatively rapid rate of shortening and the associated large power output.

The chemical processes underlying these energy fluxes were investigated in testudinian muscle (Munch-Petersen, 1953; Mommaerts 1954, 1955; Mommaerts *et al.*, 1962) because its slowness offers the possibility of

observing chemical changes at various times during contraction. Unfortunately the energy flux is so small that chemical changes during a twitch
are barely detectable in the M. rectus femoris (iliotibialis) of *Pseudemys*
and unmeasurable in the M. sartorius (Mommaerts *et al.*, 1962;
Mommaerts, 1969, p. 454). Heat, work, and chemical changes can, however
be measured after repeated twitches. Although hydrolysis of ATP is the
immediate source of energy, the ADP produced is rapidly rephosphorylated
from creatine phosphate (CP) and the concentration of ATP is kept
essentially constant. The total release of enthalpy (heat plus work) is
proportional to the amount of CP hydrolyzed, as expected. The proportionality constant should be the enthalpy change ($-\Delta H$) for the hydrolysis
of CP, which is about 8·1 kcal/mole after correction for side reactions likely
to occur *in vivo* (Woledge, 1972). The observed constants are larger: 11·9
for the M. sartorius of *Rana pipiens* (Rall *et al.*, 1976) and 13·2 for the
M. iliofibularis of *Testudo* (Walsh and Woledge, 1970). Correspondingly,
the hydrolysis of CP accounts for 0·68 and 0·61 respectively of the total
change in enthalpy. The explained fraction is still lower in *R. temporaria*
(Rall *et al.*, 1976). Interpretation is not easy (Homsher and Kean, 1978).
Perhaps there are other energy-yielding reactions, especially connected with
the sarcoplasmic reticulum (reviewed by Kushmerick, 1977). Whatever
their energy source, in tortoises the M. iliofibularis converts 77% of the
enthalpy to work, in frogs, the M. sartorius converts only 45%. Rapid
progress in elucidating the energetics is to be expected, especially as
methods for exploring the dependence of various heats on tension and
length are improved and other chemical reactions are explored.

D. RAPID TRANSIENTS IN TENSION

When resting leg muscles of *Testudo* are stretched, they develop tension
that decays only gradually; this differs from the muscles of frogs and toads
which show little tension when stretched (Hill, 1950b). Stretch does not

TABLE X

Decay of tension after stretch of resting muscle. (Abbott and Lowy, 1957)

Animal	Muscle	Half times of decay component		Maximal shortening rate
		Fast	Slow	
Testudo	M. iliofibularis (20°)	0·23 s	6·2 s	0·33 length s^{-1}
Bufo	M. sartorius (10°)	0·02	1·5	1·5

stimulate tortoise muscle, for the muscle responds to stretch immediately but to electrical stimulation only after 60 to 90 ms. The decay after stretch (Table X) shows a slow and a fast component (Abbott and Lowy, 1957). The proportions are the same for the rates of slow recovery and the maximal rates of shortening, but not for the rates of quick recovery. These results suggest that slow recovery and shortening are related, but that quick recovery has a different basis.

Goodall (1957) recognized the importance of his observation that active muscles of turtles recover tension in two steps, but did not study the phenomenon in detail. Quick recovery of active muscle has received attention only recently (Huxley and Simmons, 1971; Huxley, 1974; Ford et al., 1977). Figure 6 shows schematically the effects of small, rapid changes

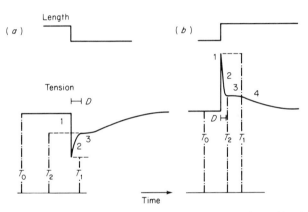

FIG. 6. Schematic records of changes in tension following (a) quick release; (b) quick stretch. T_0: isometric tension; T_1: extreme tension reached during length step; T_2: tension at end of quick recovery. (From Heinl et al., 1974)

in length. After a quick release, tension falls elastically from T_0 to T_1, rapidly recovers to T_2, and rises more slowly to its new isometric value. With the slowly responding transducers characteristic of earlier instruments, the quick recovery component was usually unresolved and the elastic drop in tension truncated so that the earliest measured tension was between T_1 and T_2. Stiffness was underestimated and studies of the rate of redevelopment of tension were restricted to the slow recovery component.

Huxley (1974) and Ford et al. (1977) suggest mechanisms for the two stages of recovery. Slow recovery, like ordinary isometric contraction, depends on detachment and reattachment of the cross bridges linking thin and thick myofilaments. The elastic response is referred to the segment AB of Fig. 7. Quick recovery occurs as the heads of the cross-bridges move without detachment, in steps A_1, A_2, ... that are much shorter than

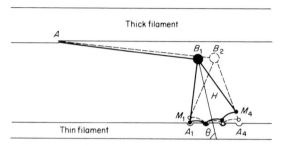

Fɪɢ. 7. Diagram showing cross-bridge properties postulated by Huxley and Simmons (1971). "The myosin head H is connected to the thick-filament by a link AB containing the undamped elasticity which shows up as T_1 [Fig. 8] in the whole fibre. Full line shows head in position where M_1A_1 and M_2A_2 attachments are made; broken lines show position where M_2A_2 and M_3A_3 attachments are made." Quick recovery is attributed to a change in position from the full line to the broken line. (From Huxley and Simmons, 1971)

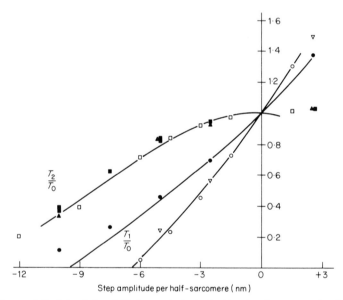

Step amplitude per half-sarcomere (nm)

Fɪɢ. 8. Curves of T_1 (triangles) and T_2 (squares) obtained with a length step complete in 0·2 ms, (open symbols), and with a step complete in 1·0 ms (filled symbols). Single fibers from M. tibialis anterior of *Rana temporaria*; length of sarcomere 2·1 μm; temperature 1·3°C. (From Ford *et al.*, 1977)

the power stroke. The T_1 and T_2 curves (Fig. 8) do not change relative to T_0 when T_0 is altered by changes in initial length. The inference is that both the change in elastic tension and the quick recovery process are intimately connected with the sarcomere itself and not with structures in series with it.

Similar studies have been made in muscles from *Testudo* and *Rana* that

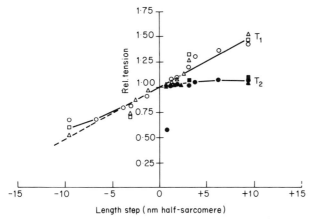

FIG. 9. Curves of T_1 (open symbols) and T_2 (filled symbols) for a thin bundle of glycerinated fibers from M. iliofibularis of *Testudo graeca*; length of sarcomere 2·1 μm; temperature 3°C. (From Heinl *et al.*, 1974)

have been briefly glycerinated (Heinl *et al.*, 1974), a treatment that disrupts the transverse tubular system and destroys the coupling between excitation and contraction. Glycerinated fibers contract when bathed in ATP, and, as in living muscle, their tension recovers after stretch or release (Fig. 9). Times to complete quick recovery of tension following small changes in length in bundles of contracting glycerinated muscle fibers (3°) are longer for tortoises than in frogs (Table XI). Heinl *et al.* (1974) suggest that the heads of the cross-bridges step more slowly during quick recovery in the muscle of *Testudo*. In rigor solution (ATP absent), neither phase of recovery is present, as expected if the bridges are inactive in the absence of ATP.

TABLE XI

Times for recovery of tension in contracting muscle. (Heinl et al., 1974)

Animal	Muscle	After stretch	After release
Rana	M. sartorius	30 ms	20 ms
Testudo	M. iliofibularis	300	400

The ten-fold differences in quick recovery rates of glycerinated fibers compares to the ten-fold difference in quick recovery of resting live muscle to the two species (Abbott and Lowy, 1957). Perhaps a few bridges remain attached even in resting muscle, as has been suggested on other grounds (e.g., by D. K. Hill, 1968; Moss *et al.*, 1976; and others).

E. Summary

Because they are slow, the muscles of tortoises (*Testudo*) have been the subject of many mechanical and energetic investigations. Their strength and stiffness are typical of most muscles that have been studied. They are unusually compliant at rest but not in action. The characteristic force-velocity constant a/P_0 is small in these muscles as in other slow-twitch muscles. Their efficiency (77% compared to 45% for M. sartorius of frogs) is probably related to their ability to maintain tetanic tension for long periods of time while producing very little heat. They are therefore economical as well as efficient. Both efficiency and economy should reduce the chemical cost of muscular activity. Reduced energy flux during activity reduces fatigue. It also reduces both oxygen and nutrient requirements, clearly an advantage to the animal. Slower cycling and greater efficiency may reflect changes in rate constants and binding constants. The molecular basis of these changes offers a fruitful subject for further investigation. Rapid transient changes after quick stretch or quick release are apparently also slower in muscles of tortoises, as would be expected if such changes also depend on activity of the cross-bridges. There is no energetic information on the M. retrahens and leg muscles of *Pseudemys*, which are much faster, with speeds like those of the sartorius of *Bufo*. The M. retractor penis of *Pseudemys*, however, is as slow as muscles of *Testudo*.

Muscles of other reptiles have received less attention. Twitch muscles in the snakes *Natrix* and *Thamnophis* are as strong and as stiff as those in *Rana*. In the lizard *Tiliqua* tonic fibers are stiffer than twitch fibers. The very fast muscle that shakes the rattle of *Crotalus* is unusually weak; perhaps strength has been sacrificed for speed. The muscle contains much non-fibrillar tissue, which may account for its high stiffness at rest.

IV. Smooth Muscle

Early electron microscopists found no difference in fine structure of intestinal smooth muscle from chickens and turtles (Weinstein and Ralph, 1951). The innervation of smooth muscles and its evolution in the various vertebrate classes have been reviewed at length (Burnstock, 1969, 1972; Fischer, 1971). The effects of drugs on the oviduct of the iguanid *Liolaemus* have been reported (Lemus *et al.*, 1970; Paz de la Vega-Lemus *et al.*, 1971). Membrane potentials have been observed in vascular muscle of turtles (Roddie and Kirk, 1961; Roddie, 1962).

In the vascular smooth muscle of mammals calcium ions play an essential role in excitation-contraction coupling (reviewed by Somlyo and Somlyo,

1968, 1970). Nevertheless the aorta of turtles contracts after it has been in a calcium-free bath for an hour or more (Isojima and Bozler, 1963; Bozler, 1969), even when the bath contains EGTA to chelate free calcium ions. Apparently the aorta retains enough calcium intra-cellularly, presumably in the sarcoplasmic reticulum (SR), to permit it to contract spontaneously or when drugs are added. Contractility also persists after treatment with EGTA in the oviduct of turtles, and even in mammalian smooth muscle if the latter is studied at 25°C and not the conventional 37° (Somlyo *et al.*, 1971).

The volume of the sarcoplasmic reticulum in the muscle fibers of the arteries and veins of the turtle *Malaclemys* is hard to measure because other spaces are also present (Somlyo *et al.*, 1971). Extracellular space is invaded by cellular processes, methods of preparation leave spaces that were originally occupied by glycogen, and pinocytotic vesicles are numerous. These complications are less severe in turtle oviducts (Fig. 10).

Just within the surface membrane of the muscle fibers of arteries, veins and oviduct of turtles are large surface vesicles that communicate with

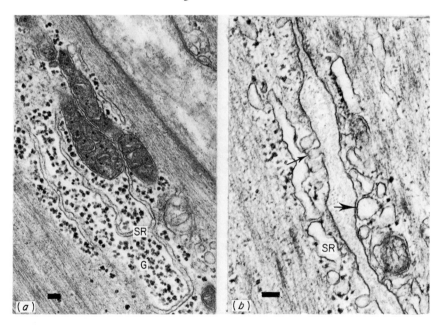

FIG. 10. Electron micrographs of longitudinal sections of smooth muscle cells from the oviduct of *Malaclemys* sp. Scale lines represent 0·1 μm. (a) Glycogen particles (G) are surrounded by longitudinal loops of sarcoplasmic reticulum (SR). Mitochondria and myofilaments are also apparent. (b) Parts of two muscle cells showing SR running longitudinally. Portions of SR come close to surface vesicles (small arrow) and the cell membrane (large arrow). Somlyo *et al.* suggest that these appositions are sites of electromechanical coupling. (From Somlyo *et al.*, 1971)

the extracellular space and are thus not part of the sarcoplasmic reticulum. They vary in shape: some are characteristic flasks, others are tubular invaginations of the surface, and still others are multilobed. Ferritin penetrates throughout the vesicles, implying that they are not divided into compartments. Unlike their mammalian counterparts, they lack diaphragms at their necks, showing instead electron-opaque striations at 10 nm intervals, perpendicular to their long axes. Beneath the vesicles, a peripheral layer of true SR parallels the long axis of the fiber and communicates via radial connections with a central reticulum. A lacy network of SR often surrounds surface vesicles, and SR tubules often dilate into cisternae as they approach these vesicles or the surface membrane. Close contacts are apparent at these appositions, and occasional small electron-opaque bridges occur, but there is no evidence that T-tubules, dyads, or triads are present in smooth muscle. The gaps at the appositions are 8 to 10 nm, like those within the triads of skeletal muscle, and excitation may release calcium at these sites.

The relative importance of intracellular and extracellular calcium stores probably differs among muscles, and the former seem to be important in the oviduct of turtles. The volume of SR averages about 4% of the non-nuclear, non-mitochondrial volume of a fiber. Although the volume of SR and the tension were not measured for the same fibers, Somlyo et al. (1971) estimate that the SR can store enough calcium to cause contraction. Myofilaments of smooth muscles from mammals and turtles are alike in structure and arrangement except that fewer thick filaments are seen in turtles. Thick filaments are probably really less abundant, but they may only be more easily disrupted during fixation.

In summary, the smooth muscle of *Malaclemys* seems to be similar to that described in mammals. Thick filaments may be relatively less abundant in testudinian muscle, but it is too early to assign any physiological importance to this difference. A strong reliance on intracellular stores of calcium ions may reduce the dependence of the muscle on the circulatory system for a continuing supply of calcium ions.

V. Sensory Organs

A. GENERAL

Among the sense organs associated with vertebrate muscle are muscle spindles, Golgi tendon organs, and joint receptors. Only the spindles have received much attention in reptiles, although a few papers on tendon organs are discussed later.

Muscle spindles are sensors of muscle length in all groups of terrestrial vertebrates. Under the light microscope, they look similar in muscles from the backs and legs of many vertebrates, including *Alligator mississippiensis*, *Anolis carolinensis*, *Crotaphytus collaris*, *Coluber constrictor*, and *Nerodia* sp., (Cole, 1955a). Muscle receptors of fish appear to be less specialized, and true spindles are lacking. Vertebrate spindles have been subjects of early reviews (Hines, 1927) and later ones (e.g., Cooper, 1960; Barker *et al.*, 1974). A review of reptilian muscle includes an extensive discussion of spindles by two active investigators in the field (Proske and Ridge, 1974). Extraocular muscles are a special case. In reptiles (*Pseudemys*, *Dipsosaurus*, *Lampropeltis*) as well as birds and some mammals, they lack encapsulated spindles although other length sensors may be present (Maier *et al.*, 1974). Two types of sensory endings occur in extraocular muscles of turtles (*Testudo*, *Emys*) and snakes (*Lampropeltis*, *Natrix*); one ending is like those in frogs, the other like those in mammals, and both are more regular and robust than in frogs (Subbasow *et al.*, 1964).

B. Morphology

The structure of spindles in more usual muscles varies in the different vertebrate classes (Fig. 11). A typical mammalian spindle (Boyd, 1976) contains 5 to 10 intrafusal muscle fibers of three kinds. There is one fiber of each of the two kinds of "nuclear bag" fibers; at their equators they are swollen, contain clusters of nuclei and lack fibrils. There are also several "nuclear chain" fibers; these are not swollen at their equators which contain fibrils. The nuclei of these fibers form a string that is not restricted to the equator. Afferent impulses leave the spindle via a single primary and zero to five secondary afferent axons. The primary afferent has an-nulospiral endings from all fibers, and it carries information on changes in length and also on the rate of change on length. A secondary afferent has mostly annulospiral but some flower-spray endings, and it arises mostly from chain but sometimes from bag fibers. Motor innervation is by axons that form a separate fusimotor system (gamma axons), but there are also some axons that are collaterals of nerves supplying extrafusal fibers (beta axons). The motor endings are plates or trails, which can occur on any kind of intrafusal fiber. Avian spindles often contain three to six intrafusal fibers that are apparently alike (James and Meek, 1973; Ovalle, 1976), although spindles with single intrafusal fibers are fairly common (Maier and Eldred, 1971). Anuran spindles contain two types of intrafusal fibers: broad ones supplied with plates, and narrow ones supplied with grapes. Spindles of alligators (Hines, 1930) and caimans (Palmieri *et al.*, 1977) contain a bundle of two to five intrafusal fibers, and spindles of tortoises (Crowe and Ragab, 1970a) contain two to seventeen, with a mean of ten.

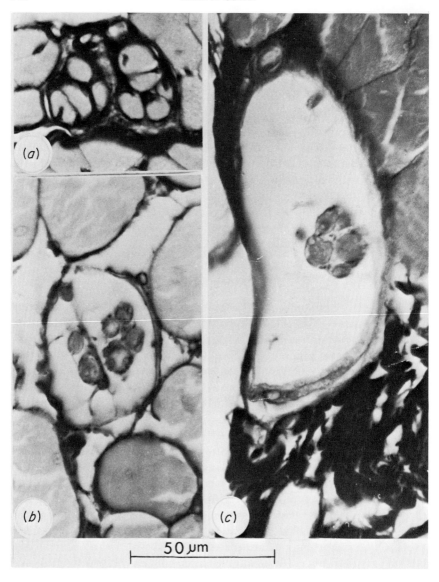

FIG. 11.   Transverse sections at the capsular regions of spindles of (a) a tortoise (*Testudo graeca*), (b) a frog, and (c) a rat. Scale line represents 50 μm. (a) is stained with Masson's triple chrome and (b) and (c) are stained with orcein. In all three, intrafusal fibers are smaller than extrafusal fibers. Spindles of tortoises lack the large fluid-filled spaces found in the other two animals (From Crowe and Ragab, 1970a).

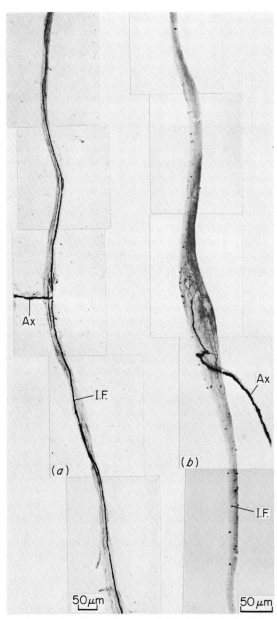

FIG. 12. Composite photographs of (a) a "long capsule" spindle and (b) a "short capsule" spindle of the lizard *Tiliqua nigrolutea*. Scale lines 50 um. Stained with silver. Sensory axons (Ax) and intrafusal fibers (I.F.) are marked. In (a), striations are visible in the intrafusal fiber throughout its length. In (b), the intrafusal fiber is grossly distorted within the capsule and loses its striations. (From Proske, 1969b)

Squamates, unlike other vertebrates, have two distinct types of spindles, and each contains only a single intrafusal fiber (Tschiriew, 1879a, b; reviewed by Barker *et al.*, 1974).

The two types of squamate spindles are distinguished by the length of their capsules (Fig. 12). Both types are usually associated with satellite cells, and their mitochondria and vesicles show no unusual features. In the garter snake *Thamnophis*, sixteen Mm. costocutanei contained 28 long and 18 short capsules (Fukami and Hunt, 1970). A typical long capsule is 15 to 20 μm in diameter and 250 to 300 μm long; a short capsule is 40 μm wide and 100 to 150 μm long. An intrafusal fiber in either capsule is much narrower (7 to 10 μm) than an extrafusal fiber and about 1 cm long. Sarcomere lengths are sometimes reported to be longer in intrafusal fibers and sometimes the same length. Perhaps the spindles are stretched more in some investigations than others. Spindles of *Boa* (Candiollo and Guglielmone, 1968), *Coluber* (Rahman *et al.*, 1974) and *Natrix* (Pallot, 1974) are like those of *Thamnophis*. In the leg muscles of *Tiliqua* (Proske, 1969a, b) many spindles are often adjacent. Two long capsule spindles often occur in tandem along a single intrafusal fiber and are supplied by separate sensory axons; short capsules are single, but occasionally receive

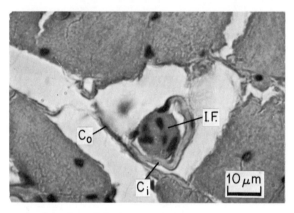

Fig. 13. Transverse section of a spindle from M. iliofibularis of *Tiliqua nigrolutea*. Stained with haematoxylin and eosin. Note the single, narrow intrafusal fiber (I.F.), the fluid-filled space, and the inner (C_i) and outer (C_o) capsules. (From Proske, 1969b)

two axons. Intrafusal fibers are again about 10 μm wide (Fig. 13). In the M. extensor digitorum brevis I of *Testudo* (Crowe and Ragab, 1970a, b) spindles are usually single but often (30%) occur in tadem. Capsules of tortoises resemble the long capsules of squamates in length and breadth, and none were seen that were like short capsules. The intrafusal fibers are 11 μm in diameter. In the M. extensor digitorum longus I of the turtle

Chelodina longicollis, there are usually six to ten spindles per muscle, but there may be only one or two (Proske and Walker, 1975).

The intrafusal fibers from the two types of squamate spindles also differ. In *Thamnophis* (Fukami and Hunt, 1970) and *Natrix* (Pallot, 1974) intrafusal fibers of long capsules contain fibrils and nuclei throughout their length and have distinct M lines, so that they resemble nuclear chain fibers. Their myosin is highly active and their histochemistry is oxidative-glycolytic (Pallot and Taberner, 1974). Fibers of short capsules lack fibrils, have a high density of nuclei in their sensory regions, and lack M lines. In these characteristics they are like nuclear bag fibers, but they also possess thick Z lines, that are straight rather than zigzag (Pallot, 1974). They show no clear sarcotubular structure, although tubules unlike the usual T tubules

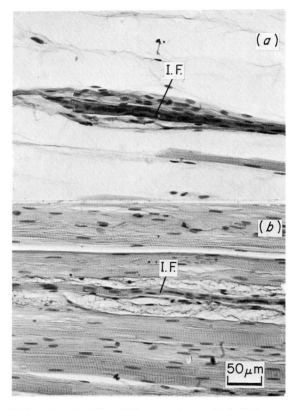

FIG. 14. Longitudinal sections of spindles of *Tiliqua nigrolutea*, stained with haematoxylin and eosin. (*a*) A short capsule spindle from M. scalenus. The intrafusal fiber (I.F.) "shows a distinct accumulation of nuclei and there are no fibre striations in the centre of the capsule". (*b*) A long capsule spindle from M. iliofibularis. "There is a slight increase in the number of nuclei and the muscle fibre striations are clearly visible." (From Proske, 1969b)

are seen in *Natrix* (Cliff and Ridge, 1973; Pallot, 1974). Their myosin is less active, but succinic dehydrogenase is moderately active (Pallot and Taberner, 1974). In lizards (*Tiliqua*) intrafusal fibers of long and short capsules (Fig. 14) resemble their counterparts in snakes (Proske, 1969a, b). In *Testudo*, the structure of intrafusal fibers resembles that in long capsules of squamates (Crowe and Ragab, 1970a, b). The intrafusal fibers

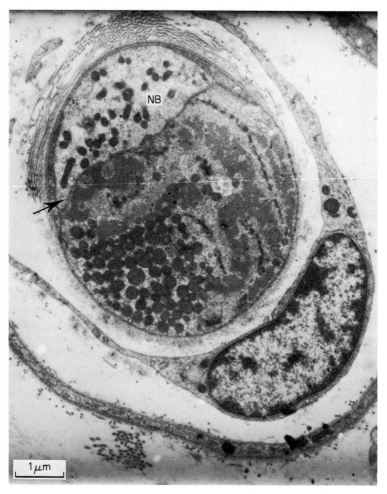

Fig. 15. Electron micrograph of a transverse section of the sensory region of a long-capsule spindle from M. costocutaneus of *Natrix* sp. The single intrafusal fiber (center) contains a nerve bulb (NB) which the sensory nerve has just joined (arrow). Both inner and outer capsules show collagen fibers, and a nucleus is present in the inner capsule. (From Pallot and Ridge, 1972)

show prominent M lines. Fibrils continue through the capsules, and nuclear density increases only slightly in the sensory region. Staining for phosphorylase, ATPase, succinic dehydrogenase and lipid reveals only one histochemical type of intrafusal fiber (Crowe and Ragab, 1972). Light microscopy revealed no difference in the appearance of spindles of the M. extensor digitorum brevis I of *Emys* and *Testudo* (Naeije and Crowe, 1974).

The intrafusal fiber in lizards is surrounded by inner and outer capsules (Fig. 13). The capsule in snakes (*Natrix*) has a continuous outer layer covered by a basal lamina and an interrupted inner layer (Cliff and Ridge, 1973). The inner layer has only a single lamella in a long capsule, but two or three in a short capsule. Within the capsular space, many fine fibrils (elastin?) occur together with the collagen fibers, the collagen layer being especially dense near the sensory apparatus (Fig. 15). Collagen is also associated with avian and mammalian spindles; it may reduce slipping between the intrafusal fiber and the sensory ending, thereby improving mechanical coupling. The elastin filaments may speed recovery from stretch. The capsule of *Python* has now been described (Panzica, 1979).

In *Testudo* (Crowe and Ragab, 1972) intrafusal fibers extend the length of the relatively short M. extensor digitorum brevis I, and connective tissue fills the space between them (Fig. 16). Capsules are composed of several layers of connective tissue, and the outer sheath often embraces one or more extrafusal fibers, recognizable by their greater width. Although apposed fibers do not fuse, they show apparent bridges of electron-dense material. Intrafusal fibers are often surrounded by a basement membrane. Capsules are closely apposed to the intrafusal fibers (Fig. 11), and the fluid-filled space found in squamates and other vertebrates is missing, a feature which limits possible mechanisms of sensitivity to pressure. The capsule lacks elastic tissue, suggesting that the spindle may recover more slowly than the elastin-containing spindles of other terrestrial vertebrates.

The sensory apparatus in snakes (Pallot and Ridge, 1972, 1973) consists of a variable number of bulbs connected together by small links. It is superficially like that of frogs but much less regular. The terminal itself is separated by a 20-nm gap from the intrafusal fiber, and is strikingly different from the terminal of either frogs or mammals (Fig. 15). Its cross-section is crescentic, and the intrafusal fiber lacks the socket-like indentations found in frogs. Sensory terminals branch more frequently in short capsules than in long, and they cover more of the muscular surface. Detailed serial reconstructions suggest that short capsules should be more sensitive to small displacements. Each spindle in the M. costocutaneus of *Thamnophis* is innervated by a single sensory axon (Hunt and Wylie, 1970). Sensory endings in snake spindles are stained by zinc iodide-osmium (Fukami,

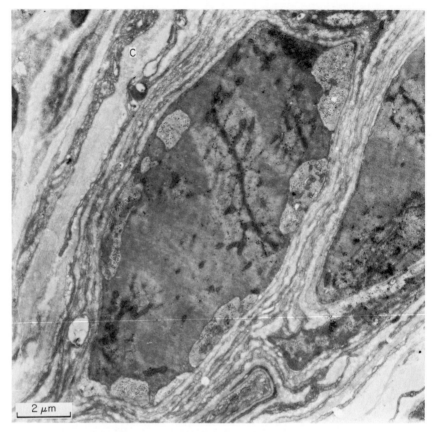

FIG. 16. Electron micrograph of a transverse section of the sensory region of a simple intrafusal fiber from M. extensor digitorum brevis I of *Testudo graeca*. Several sensory endings are seen (low density). "The fibre is completely surrounded by several layers of connective tissue. This section was not stained with uranyl acetate, but collagen fibres (C) can be seen between the cells of connective tissue." (From Crowe and Ragab, 1970b)

1977), a stain originally thought to be specific for synaptic vesicles. In *Tiliqua* (Proske, 1969a, b) sensory axons end in small filaments closely applied to the intrafusal fiber; these filaments cover only a small part of the fiber. In *Testudo* (Crowe and Ragab, 1970a, b) each spindle contains several intrafusal fibers, but it receives only one sensory axon. All sensory axons are alike in size and appearance and probably belong to a single class. There is only one type of sensory ending. An axon ramifies to supply each intrafusal fiber, and sensory endings are not folded. They are found in troughs, separated from the muscular surface by 20 nm, and they are roughly elliptical; their long axis is perpendicular to the long axis of the muscle. The sensory apparatus is relatively simple, resembling neither the annulospiral ending of mammals nor the relatively straight varicose threads (flower-spray) of frogs. Instead there are less well-defined varicosities that meander haphazardly over the muscular surface.

In summary, lizards and snakes each have spindles of two different types that show the usual sorts of specializations in intrafusal fibers and have a normal fluid-filled capsule. In *Testudo*, the intrafusal fibers resemble those of long capsules of squamates and the capsules lack the fluid-filled space found in all other terrestrial vertebrates.

C. INNERVATION

The intrafusal fibers of reptilian muscles are innervated by collaterals of the same motor axons that supply extrafusal fibers (Fig. 17), as shown for alligators (Hines, 1930), tortoises (Crowe and Ragab, 1970a, b), lizards (Proske, 1969a, b) and snakes (Fukami and Hunt, 1970; Pallot and Ridge, 1972, 1973), although Berndt *et al.* (1969) identified collateral innervation of only a few spindles in *Boa constrictor* by their method and assumed that others were supplied by a separate fusimotor system. Such innervation by collaterals resembles the beta system of mammals. If a separate independent fusimotor system like the mammalian gamma system exists, it has not yet been demonstrated conclusively.

In *Anolis* (Szepsenwol, 1960), spindles in multiply innervated muscle are commonly supplied by collaterals from axons that have extrafusal grape terminals, whereas in focally innervated muscles the spindles are supplied by axons that give rise to extrafusal endplates. This is also true in *Tiliqua nigrolutea* (Proske, 1969a, b), where there is no clear evidence that any intrafusal fiber receives both plate and grape innervation. Plate endings on intrafusal fibers are always single, but there may be as many as 16 grape endings on a single fiber. Grape endings were found in either type of capsule, but plates only in the long. Both terminals resemble their extrafusal counterparts but are slightly smaller. Proske found only one type of end-plate; a second described by Szepsenwol may be an earlier developmental stage. Multiply innervated muscles had multiply innervated spindles of both capsular types; focally innervated muscles showed only long capsules with plate endings. Motor and sensory portions of the nerve can be distinguished by tracing the nerve to the dorsal and ventral roots; this makes it possible to avoid antidromic stimulation of afferents. When the nerve trunk is split into five motor filaments, stimulating any one of the five elicits both an extrafusal twitch and an afferent volley from the same spindle, but the patterns of discharge evoked are different, strongly suggesting polyneuronal innervation. Muscles of *Tiliqua* vary in their

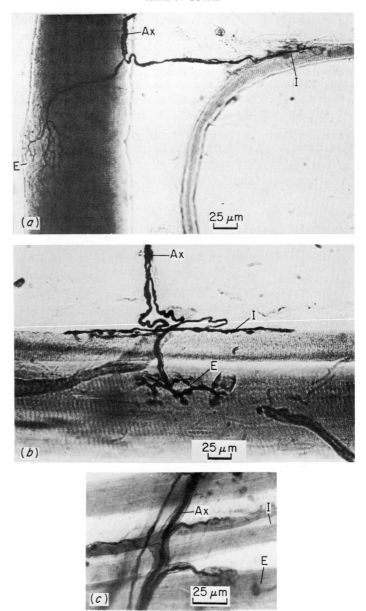

FIG. 17. Silver-stained motor terminals. (a) An axon branches to supply an extrafusal and an intrafusal muscle fiber with end plates. (b) An axon branches to supply an extrafusal and an intrafusal muscle fiber with grape endings. (c) An axon sends a branch to supply an extrafusal fiber and then two branches to supply an intrafusal fiber with end plates. [(a) and (b) *Tiliqua nigrolutea*, from Proske, 1969b; (c) *Natrix* sp., from Pallot, 1974.]

innervation and the nature of their spindles (Proske, 1969a, 1973). The M. iliofibularis (predominantly twitch) has long spindles with both plate and grape endings; the M. scalenus (twitch) has only short capsules and grapes, and the M. semitendinosus (mostly tonic) is multiply innervated. The M. semimembranosus is solely twitch in *Tiliqua scincoides*, but partly tonic in *T. nigrolutea*; it has mostly long capsules in both.

Single spindles in the M. costocutaneus inferior of *Natrix* can be easily identified under dark field illumination (Cliff and Ridge, 1973). Motor endplates occur principally on one side of the spindle and are separated from the intrafusal fiber by a 50-nm cleft. In fine structure they generally resemble extrafusal end-plates. Physiological studies showed that 7 of 14 spindles are polyneuronally innervated by both twitch and tonic axons and sometimes several of each. Cliff and Ridge (1973) quote supporting evidence (Konishi, unpublished) that in *Elaphe* a fiber in a long capsule may receive endings derived from both extrafusal plate and grape units. In *Natrix* (Pallot, 1974) both kinds of extrafusal fibers receive two to twelve nerve terminals which in short capsules are innervated solely by collaterals of coarse axons that supply extrafusal grape endings and in long capsules either only from fine grape-supplying axons or from axons of both kinds.

In the hind leg of *Testudo graeca*, the M. extensor digitorum brevis I and its nerve supply are readily accessible (Crowe and Ragab, 1970a, b). Although both types of motor endings occur on intrafusal fibers (Fig. 18), plates are more numerous and were seen in all of 21 spindles. Eight spindles had end-plates only, but both plates and grapes occurred together on the poles of the other thirteen spindles. In these multifascicular spindles it is not clear whether the same intrafusal fiber receives both types of terminals, as in snakes but not lizards. The plates resemble those of frogs more than those of lizards.

D. PHYSIOLOGY

Responses of spindles are characterized by measuring the frequency of afferent impulses from resting and active spindles. Like other terrestrial vertebrates, reptiles possess spindles that respond characteristically to stretch, and the response is altered by stimulation of motor nerves to the intrafusal fibers, which thereupon contract and stretch the sensory apparatus. The responses have been studied in snakes (*Thamnophis*, Hunt and Wylie, 1970; Fukami, 1970a, b; *Natrix*, Cliff and Ridge, 1973), lizards (*Tiliqua*, Proske, 1969a, 1973) and turtles (*Testudo*, Ottoson, 1972; *Emys*, Naeije and Crowe, 1974; *Chelodina*, Proske and Walker, 1975). They have

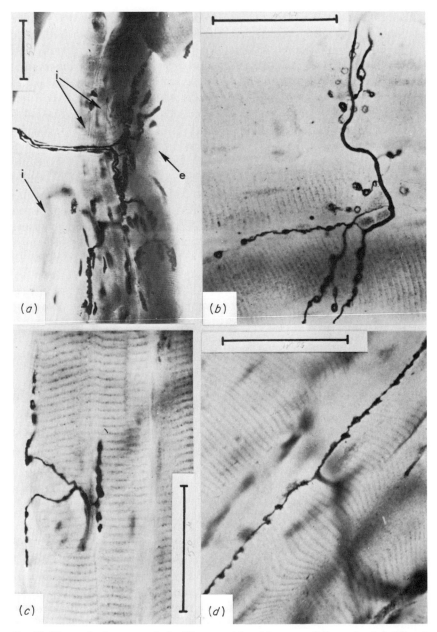

Fig. 18. Silver-stained motor terminals of fibers teased from M. extensor digitorum brevis I of *Testudo graeca*. Scale lines represent 50 μm. (*a*) An axon supplying a number of endings to both intrafusal and extrafusal fibers. (*b*) Grape endings on extrafusal fibers. (*c*) Plate endings on intrafusal fibers. (*d*) Plate endings on extrafusal fibers. (From Crowe and Ragab, 1970a)

also been studied in mammals (reviewed by Boyd, 1976) and amphibians (Brown, 1971). Their physiological role is still debated.

There are two characteristic kinds of responses to stretch in squamate spindles (Fig. 19). Phasic spindles show a sharp burst of activity as the muscle is stretched, then activity slows to a lower tonic frequency characteristic of the new length. Tonic spindles reach peak frequency more slowly without an obvious burst of activity, and they adapt less. They are accordingly primarily sensitive to length, whereas phasic spindles are sensitive partly to length, but especially to change of length. The extent

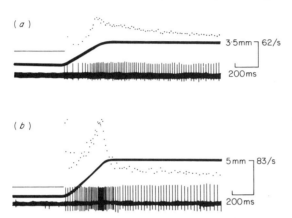

FIG. 19. Responses from spindles of *Tiliqua nigrolutea* during slow stretch of the muscle. "The spindle in (a) (tonic) is from the semi-membranosus muscle, while in (b) (phasic) it is from the scalenus muscle. In each set of records the bottom trace represents the afferent discharge from the spindle while the line above it represents the signal from the displacement transducer monitoring the movement. The dots in the upper trace represent a reciprocal interval display of spindle firing. Each dot in the display corresponds to an action potential, and its height above the zero line (uppermost line on the left of the figure) is proportional to the reciprocal of the time interval between it and the previous action potential." (From Proske and Ridge, 1974; see also Proske, 1969a)

of adaptation is measured by the *dynamic index*, which is the difference between the peak frequency and the frequency 0·5 s later, at which time the response has not quite reached the tonic level characteristic of its new length. Tonic spindles therefore have a smaller dynamic index.

There are also two types of responses to motor stimulation: dynamic, in which the initial burst is increased, as it is in spindles of tonic muscles of frogs, and static, in which the firing increases at a given length of the muscle but phasic responsiveness is not altered. Because in reptiles the same axons supply both extrafusal and intrafusal fibers, complications from extrafusal contractions are usually avoided by critical curarization, i.e., by adding enough tubocurarine to block extrafusal neuromuscular junctions, but not the less sensitive intrafusal junctions.

In both the M. costocutaneus of garter snakes (*Thamnophis*, Fukami, 1970a) and leg muscles of lizards (*Tiliqua*, Proske, 1969a) spindles with short and long capsules respond differently to stretch (Fig. 20). Sensory afferents from short capsules show a strong initial burst and a large dynamic index, responding to change in length, like the primary afferents of mammalian spindles. Long capsules fire less frequently during the rising phase of the stretch with no obvious burst, and they respond to length like the secondary-afferents of mammals. Their dynamic index is low. In both snakes and lizards, the dynamic indices of the two types of spindles depend differently on the rate of stretch, and the shapes of their response curves are not the same (Fig. 20).

The pattern of response is characteristic of an individual spindle in *Thamnophis* (Hunt and Wylie, 1970; Fukami, 1970a); it does not change in repeated experiments on single spindles. After the spindle and its nerve supply are isolated from the rest of the muscle, the spindle becomes more sensitive, but its pattern of response is unchanged. In the snake *Elaphe* (Fukami, 1970b), the receptor potential rises more rapidly, during a stretch, in spindles with short capsules than in spindles with long capsules. In response to stimulation of the sensory regions not by stretch but by depolarizing pulses of electrical current, the two types of spindles are very similar, implying that the different responses to stretch are not due to differences in the electrical properties of the membranes. The cause of the different responses remains elusive (Fukami *et al.*, 1976; Fukami and Hunt, 1977).

Chronic denervation alters the properties of the spindles of the M. costocutaneus of *Thamnophis* (Fukami and Ridge, 1971, 1972). After four days, electron micrographs show degeneration and debris, and phasic receptors fire more slowly or not at all. Tonic spindles respond normally up to five days after denervation, but thereafter their adaptation is prolonged and they fire less often than do normal spindles. Their response never reaches a tonic plateau and sometimes even disappears. The time course of adaptation is unaffected by dinitrophenol. In *Elaphe*, adaptation of denervated spindles depends strongly on the electrical properties of the sensory terminal (Fukami, 1972).

The effects of fusimotor stimulation have also been studied in squamates. In *Thamnophis*, the intrafusal fiber in either type of capsule can apparently twitch and stretch the spindle. A single efferent stimulus triggers a train of afferent impulses (Hunt and Wylie, 1970), as it does in frogs but not mammals. This is consistent with the ability of all intrafusal fibers to conduct action potentials (Fukami, 1970a). *Thamnophis* has two to four spindles in each muscle, and a single stimulus during stretch does not significantly alter the afferent response from either type of spindle, except

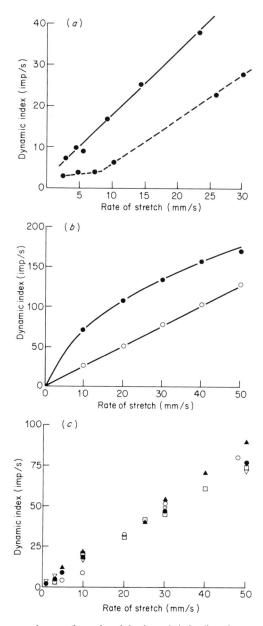

Fig. 20. Relation between the rate of stretch and the dynamic index (impulses per second) for various types of spindles. (*a*) The garter snake (*Thamnophis* sp.). Upper line: results for phasic spindles (short capsule) from M. costocutaneus; lower line: results for tonic spindles (long capsule) from the same muscle. (*b*) The lizard *Tiliqua nigrolutea*. Upper line: results for phasic spindles (short capsule) from M. scalenus; lower line: results for tonic spindles (long capsule) from M. semimembranosus. (*c*) The turtle *Chelodina longicollis*; results for spindles from M. extensor digitorum longus. The single type of spindle responds like the tonic spindles of squamates. (*a*) from Fukami, 1970a; (*b*) from Proske, 1969a; (*c*) from Proske and Walker, 1975)

for the effect of added stretch upon intrafusal contraction. In *Tiliqua* (Proske, 1973), tetanic stimulation of resting spindles greatly increases the firing rate of focally innervated spindles, which do not show a sustained sensitivity to succinyl choline. Both the drug and tetanic stimulation have only a moderate effect on multiply innervated spindles. Tetanic stimulation during stretch does not affect the firing rate of focally innervated spindles, but greatly increases both the phasic and tonic components of the responses of multiply innervated spindles. All intrafusal fibers of both snakes and lizards apparently twitch despite minor differences in innervation. In response to a single shock, the afferent burst is delayed longer in tonic spindles than in phasic spindles and this presumably indicates a slower mechanical response of the intrafusal fiber.

In Mm. costocutanei of *Natrix* (Cliff and Ridge, 1973) a single motor unit may be identified as twitch or tonic by its extrafusal response. The twitch units are easily distinguished from each other because they develop quite different tensions, often at different speeds. One M. costocutaneus contains seventy or so extrafusal fibers, five or fewer twitch units, and a number of tonic units. Of fourteen intrafusal fibers in long capsules, half were multiply innervated, often by collaterals of both twitch and tonic units. The response of a polyneuronally innervated spindle is not recognizably different whether its twitch or tonic supply is stimulated. Never does the same twitch or tonic unit supply more than one spindle. A spindle in the M. iliofibularis of *Tiliqua* (Proske, 1969a, b), which is a twitch muscle, responds only to a single motor filament after division of the motor nerve. In the M. semitendinosus, a tonic muscle, a spindle responds similarly to any of several filaments. There is no obvious difference between responses to stimulation of twitch and tonic motor units. Thus neither of the two spindle types seems to be associated exclusively with tonic or twitch muscle. However, it is true that in a predominantly tonic muscle, intrafusal fibers show a pattern of motor innervation typical of slow tonic extrafusal fibers while in a twitch muscle the pattern is of the twitch type. The intrafusal fibers are of the twitch type in all cases.

The spindles of turtles are not only multifascicular, but they lack the fluid-filled space of other spindles, and connective tissues wrap closely around their intrafusal fibers and sensory neurons. Their physiological properties have been studied in the M. extensor digitorum brevis I of *Testudo graeca* (Ottoson, 1972) and of *Emys orbicularis* (Naeije and Crowe, 1974, 1977a) and in the M. extensor digitorum longus I of *Chelodina longicollis* (Proske and Walker, 1975). The responses to steady stretch and the dynamic index are like those of tonic spindles of lizards and snakes, with little or no burst at the beginning of stretch. Adaptation *in situ* is greater than in frogs, but about the same as in the isolated spindles. Because the mechanical factors are so different, this supports the hypothesis that adaptation depends on properties of the sensory membranes. Motor nerves were divided into smaller filaments until further division was impossible, in the hope of obtaining responses to single axons. Usually 4 or 5 of the split filaments produced firing attributable to the same intrafusal twitch. Different filaments usually produced the same response in a given spindle. Responses to stimulation were equally likely to be static or dynamic, according to Proske and Walker (1975). Naeije and Crowe (1977a) found a wide range of responses with no clear dichotomy, and combined a visco-elastic model with a force generator to simulate their results (Naeije and Crowe, 1977b).

E. Tendinal Organs

The detailed structure of tendon organs in *Caiman* is similar to that of mammals (Palmieri *et al.*, 1977).

In the lizard *Tiliqua*, a separate branch of a nerve supplies the tendons of the M. caudofemoralis (Gregory and Proske, 1975), and afferent impulses from stretch-sensitive mechanical receptors near the myotendinal junction can be recorded. Unlike mammalian tendon organs, the 16 to 20 receptors per tendon are apparently not encapsulated and lie further from the myotendinal junction. In these respects and in their response, they resemble the Ruffini endings in the connective tissue of mammalian joint capsules more than they do mammalian tendon organs. Like spindles, the organs fire rapidly during the dynamic phase of stretch and then more slowly as long as stretch is maintained. At low tensions the firing rate is proportional to tension, but it reaches a plateau at high tensions. The dynamic index rises slowly at low rates of increase of tension and much more steeply at high rates. The results for the lizard were obtained from an isolated segment of tendon, but the receptors apparently respond at lower tensions than do mammalian ones and increase their firing rate rather more steeply. Afferent frequencies of the receptors continue to fall throughout the period during which tension is maintained. There is no obvious structural specialization of the tendon that might account for this adaptation.

An afferent axon typically has four branches, each receiving input from a cluster of unmyelinated terminals (Proske and Gregory, 1976). A cut within the stretch-sensitive area of one cluster abolishes the cluster's input and alters the response. The authors propose that the organ's discharge is a composite response to which several terminals contribute. Interactions among the terminals may extend the range of stretch to which the organ can respond.

F. Summary

Spindles of squamates are unique in containing only a single intrafusal fiber, although a few unifascicular spindles have been reported in birds. The squamate spindles are of two types: some have long capsules and some short ones. Intrafusal fibers with short capsules have swollen equators that lack myofibrils. Spindles with short capsules respond during a stretch with a burst of afferent impulses and adapt to a lower frequency at the new length. Intrafusal fibers with long capsules have less swollen equators and myofibrils continue through them. The response of such long-capsuled spindles is generally tonic, depending on their length and not their rate of change. The sensory apparatus is also different in the two types of spindles and differs in detail from spindles in other classes of vertebrates. Testudinian spindles are unique as they lack a fluid-filled space, but their responses are those of squamate spindles of the long-capsule type. Their intrafusal fibers are also similar to those in long capsules. The mammalian spindle is much more complex and its responses differ in detail, whereas avian spindles seem simple.

It is not yet clear whether the different kinds of spindles seen in different reptiles offer different advantages or whether they represent alternate ways of achieving similar results. Reptiles and birds apparently lack the separate fusimotor system of mammals; motor innervation is always by collaterals of the motor axons that supply the ordinary extrafusal fibers. The results of stimulating the motor axons suggest that all reptilian intrafusal fibers are able to twitch, but that, in a number of other respects, two types of responses can be recognized which resemble tonic and twitch extrafusal fibers.

VI. Conclusion

Reptilian muscles offer a plethora of interesting problems. Their accessibility and their viability make them useful in studying basic physiological mechanisms. The slowness of muscles of tortoises presents interesting problems about differences in mechanisms of slow-twitch muscle fibers. The simplicity of squamate spindles makes them especially suitable for studying the functional properties of stretch receptors in muscles.

The proportions of twitch and tonic fibers differ in different reptilian muscles, and the muscles of turtles apparently have relatively few tonic fibers. The tonic fibers of squamates are faster than the tonic fibers of frogs. Further information about the properties of different fibers is badly needed. Histochemically, three types of fibers are distinguished, but their relation to the three physiological types is obscure, and they are not necessarily the same in different muscles or different species. All three histochemical types seem unspecialized, so far as their relative reliance on aerobic and anaerobic metabolism is concerned. None seems comparable to the specialized glycolytic fibers of mammals. The M. retrahens capitis collique of *Testudo* is especially interesting because its innervation is polyneuronal, which is rare in twitch fibers. Too little information is available for speculation about adaptive advantages of differences in the structure and function of reptilian muscles, although some information is available about histochemical differences in *Draco*. Reports on the responses of reptilian neuro-muscular junctions to cholinergic drugs are fragmentary and incomplete. Clarification is needed.

The muscle fibers of *Testudo* are slower than those of *Pseudemys*, but very little comparative study has been carried out. Studies of other slow-twitch fibers suggest that the contractile mechanism is altered enough to increase efficiency and economy. The increases offer obvious advantages to animals that subsist on a low flux of energy. Although changes in the structure of the sarcotubular system may, perhaps, contribute to slowing contraction, the reduced activity of myofibrillar myosin ATPase certainly does slow it. The molecular differences between myosins from fast-twitch and slow-twitch muscle fibers have just begun to be studied by methods for investigating isozymes. Again, it seems likely that further information will show that the differences have adaptive advantages. It should also be stressed that such experiments should be performed at the temperature at which these reptiles normally perform, rather than at the "room" temperature preferred by the investigators.

Reptilian smooth muscle is generally similar to that of birds and mammals. Scanty information suggests that different smooth muscles rely to different extents on intracellular stores of calcium ions. Why thick filaments are less frequent in reptilian than mammalian smooth muscle is not obvious.

Spindles in birds and testudines apparently contain only one type of intrafusal fiber whereas in frogs and mammals they contain two or three. Squamate spindles are unique because each spindle contains only a single fiber, but the spindles are of two kinds, each with a different type of intrafusal fiber and sensory apparatus. Much has already been learned from studies of squamate spindles, and more information can be safely anticipated. Again possible adaptive advantages of the different kinds of spindles are obscure.

Obviously reptilian muscle offers excellent material for elucidating basic mechanisms as well as for identifying modifications that may have adaptive advantages.

Appendix I

INDEX OF GENERA

The name of each genus considered in the text is followed by a list of the sections in which it is considered.

Turtles
Chelodina (V)
Cyclemys (II.D)
Emys (II.B.1, 2; C; III, B.3; V)
Lissemys (II.B.3)
Pseudemys (II.B.2, 3, C, D, E; III: V)
Testudo (II.B.1, 2, 3, C, D; III: V)
Trionyx (II.B.3, E)

Crocodilians
Alligator (II.B.1, 2, C, D; V)
Caiman (II.B.1; V)

Lizards (II.B.2)
Anguis (II.B.1)
Anolis (II.B.1, 2; V)
Calotes (II.B.2, 3, E)
Chalcides (II.B.2)
Chamaeleo (II.B.3, E)
Cnemidophorus (II.B.1)
Crotaphytus (II.B.2)*Tarentola* (II.B.1)
Dipsosaurus (V)
Draco (II.B.3, E)
Eremias (II.B.3)
Eumeces (II.B.3, E)

Gekko (II.B.3)
Heloderma (II.E)
Hemidactylus (II.B.3, D)
Hoplodactylus (II.B.3)
Iguana (II.B.1, 2)
Lacerta (II.B.1, 2, D, E)
Leiolopisma (II.B.3)
Phrynosoma (II.B.1)
Tiliqua (II.B.2, 3, C; III; V)
Tupinambis (II.B.1)
Uromastyx (II.B.3)
Varanus (II.B.2, 3, D)

Amphisbaenia
II.B.3 refers to *Amphisbaena, Bipes, Cynisca, Mesobaena, Rhineura.*

Snakes
Agkistrodon (II.B.3)
Boa (II.B.1; 2, V)
Coluber (II.B.2; V)
Coronella (II.B.1)
Crotalus (II.C, E; III)
Elaphe (V)
Lampropeltis (II.E; V)

Natrix (II.B.1, 2, 3, C, E; III; V)
Nerodia (V.A)
Python (II.B.2, D; V)
Rhinophis (II.B.3)
Thamnophis (II.B.1, 2, 3, C; III; V)
Vipera (II.B.1)
Xenochrophis (II.B.3)

Appendix II

Morphology

Most of the older morphological work has been superseded by the electron microscopic and histochemical studies discussed in Section II. The early morphologists were especially interested in the structure of nerve endings. Studies in reptiles include those of Boeke (1909, 1922), Bremer (1882, 1883), Dogiel (1890), Gemelli (1905), Giacomini (1898), Haswell (1889), Kühne (1883, 1887), Mayeda (1890), Mays (1884, 1893), Miura (1886), Perroncito (1901, 1902), Rouget (1862), Sihler (1895), and Tschiriew (1879a, b). More recent studies include Rojas *et al.* (1939), Bruni (1942) and Couteaux (1947). The presence of large nerve fibers and small nerve fibers in muscles of reptiles and other vertebrates led to further work on innervation of reptilian muscle by Boeke (1913, 1922, 1927, 1930), Dart (1924), Garven (1925), Hines (1930, 1932), Smith (1926), Tiegs (1932a, b), and Wilkinson (1929). Reptilian spindles were investigated by Bremer (1883), Cipollone (1898), Giacomini (1898), Huber and DeWitt (1897), Kerschner (1888), Kulchitsky (1924), Ruffini (1894), Sihler (1900), Trinchese (1891), and Franqué (1890). Fine structure was studied by Rossi (1902), van Gehuchten (1888) and especially by Verratti (1902), who was able to observe what is now recognized as the sarcoplasmic reticulum. There are several good reviews (Huber and DeWitt, 1897; Hines, 1927; Couteaux, 1947; Tiegs, 1953) and several papers with extensive discussions and bibliographies (Dart, 1924; Garven, 1925; Wilkinson, 1929).

Physiology

The earlier physiological work has largely become obsolescent with the development of greatly improved apparatus and more detailed theoretical models. Neuromuscular junctions were studied in *Lacerta* by Asmussen (1934), Asmussen and Lindhard (1933), Buchthal and Lindhard (1934, 1935, 1937, 1942), Buchthal and Knappeis (1938), Buchthal *et al.* (1936) and Lindhard (1931) and conclusions were summarized by Buchthal and Lindhard (1939, 1942). Electrical activity at testudinal neuromuscular junctions drew the attention of Bishop and Kendall (1928), Hansen (1927),

Hoffmann (1913), Lapicque (1933), Lapicque and Lapicque (1927), Müller (1927), Nothmann (1932), Patzl (1932), Plattner and Krannich (1932), Rosemann (1936), Rückert (1931, who also worked with lizards), Suzdalskaya and Kiro (1957), Wachholder (1931) and Wachholder and von Ledebur (1930).

Mechanics and energetics of testudinian muscle received attention from Brown (1934, 1936, 1957), Brown and Goodall (1956), Fischer (1935), Gilson *et al.* (1947), Hartree (1926), Hartree and Liljestrand (1926), Hill (1926a, b), Jöbsis (1956), Levin and Wyman (1927), Schoepfle and Gilson (1945, 1946), and Wyman (1926).

M. retractor penis of *Pseudemys* provided material for some early studies on the coupling of excitation to contraction (Csapo, 1960; Conway and Curtis, 1960; Conway and Sakai, 1960a, b). In M. retrahens capitis collique of the same species, depletion of calcium ions slows the initial rate of contraction (Goodall, 1957), and M. retractor penis contracts more slowly in heavy water (Goodall, 1958a). In both of these muscles the amount of relaxation during latency (immediately after stimulation) depends on the voltage applied, and the relationships are different for the two muscles (Goodall, 1960).

Miscellaneous

Effects of drugs on the iris of reptiles and birds were described by Meyer (1893). No unusual features were found in the production of heat and work in smooth muscle of *Malaclemys* by Snyder (1927) and Snyder and Light (1928). Little lactic acid accumulates aerobically in the isolated stomach of *Testudo*, as expected from its slow metabolism (Evans, 1925). Denervation produces similar reactions in tortoises and amphibians (Reid, 1941). The time course of contraction for the stomach and intestine of "the turtle" is like that of the sartorius of *Rana* but 100 times slower (30 s at 20°C) (Gilson *et al.*, 1947). Circular constrictions are found as non-specific reactions in muscles of *Vipera* and other vertebrates (Jonecho, 1962).

Acknowledgements

I thank U. Proske, A. Crowe, and R. S. Hikida for their comments on a preliminary version of this paper, R. L. Marsh and T. C. Scanlon for stimulating discussions, and S. K. Schaerer for her patience in typing many versions of the manuscript. I also appreciate the kindness of those who furnished the micrographs for the figures.

References

Abstracts and preliminary reports are cited only when the material was not superseded by more extensive publication

Abbott, B. C. (1951). The heat production associated with a prolonged contraction and the extra heat produced during large shortening. *J. Physiol., Lond.* **112**, 433–445.

Abbott, B. C. and Howarth, J. V. (1973). Heat studies in excitable tissues. *Physiol. Rev.* **53**, 120–158.

Abbott, B. C. and Lowy, J. (1957). Stress relaxation in muscle. *Proc. R. Soc.* **B146**, 280–288.

Adrian, R. H. and Peachey, L. D. (1965). The membrane capacity of frog twitch and slow muscle fibres. *J. Physiol., Lond.* **181**, 324–336.

Altman, M. and Robin, E. D. (1969). Survival during prolonged anaerobiosis as a function of an unusual adaptation involving lactate dehydrogenase subunits. *Comp. Biochem. Physiol.* **30**, 1179–1187.

Asmussen, E. (1934). Untersuchungen über die mechanische Reaktion der Skelettmuskelfaser. *Skand. Arch. Physiol.* **70**, 233–272.

Asmussen, E. and Lindhard, J. (1933). Potentialschwankungen bei direkter Reizung von motorischen Endplatten. *Biol. Meddr.* **11**, 3–31.

Bacchi, A. B. and Sassu, G. (1973). On the fine structure of the motor end-plates during muscular regeneration in *Gongylus ocellatus. Acta anat.* **85**, 580–592.

Baldwin, J. and Seymour, R. S. (1977). Adaptation to anoxia in snakes: Levels of glycolytic enzymes in skeletal muscle. *Aust. J. Zool.* **25**, 9–13.

Bárány, M. (1967). ATPase activity of myosin correlated with speed of muscle shortening. *J. gen. Physiol.* **50**, suppl. 197–218.

Barker, D., Hunt, C. C. and McIntyre, A. K. (1974). "Muscle Receptors." Springer-Verlag, Berlin.

Bendall, J. R. (1964). The myofibrillar ATPase activity of various animals in relation to ionic strength and temperature. *In* "Biochemistry of Muscle Contraction." (J. Gergely, ed.) Little-Brown, Boston, pp. 448–451.

Bennett, M. R., Pettigrew, A. G. and Taylor, R. S. (1973). The formation of synapses in reinnervated and cross-reinnervated adult avian muscle. *J. Physiol., Lond.* **230**, 331–357.

Berndt, J. M., Oswaldo-Cruz, E. and Rocha-Miranda, C. E. (1969). Identification of beta fibres at spindle entry. *J. comp. Neurol.* **136**, 419–422.

Bishop, G. H. and Kendall, A. I. (1928). Action of formalin and histamine on tension and potential curves of a striated muscle, the retractor penis of the turtle. *Am. J. Physiol.* **88**, 77–86.

Blum, H. E., Lehky, P., Kohler, L., Stein, E. A. and Fischer, E. H. (1977). Comparative properties of vertebrate parvalbumins. *J. biol. Chem.* **252**, 2834–2838.

Bockman, D. E. (1968). Fine structure of myoid cells in human and reptilian thymus. *Anat. Rec.* **160**, 319 (Abstr.).

Boeke, J. (1909). Die motorische Endplatte bei den höheren Vertebraten, ihre Entwickelung, Form, und Zusammenhang mit der Muskelfaser. *Anat. Anz.* **35**, 193–226.

Boeke, J. (1913). Die doppelte (motorische und sympathische) efferente Innervation der quergestreiften Muskelfasern. *Anat. Anz.* **44**, 343–356.

Boeke, J. (1922). Zur Innervation der quergestreiften Muskeln bei den Ophidiern. *In* "Libro en Honor de Ramon y Cajal." Privately published, Madrid, **1**, 113–123.

Boeke, J. (1927). Die morphologische Grundlage der sympathischen Innervation der quergestreiften Muskelfasern. *Z. mikrosk.-anat. Forsch.* **8**, 561–639.

Boeke, J. (1930). Die angebliche doppelte (sympathische und spinale) Innervation der quergestreiften Muskelfaser bei Reptilien, besonders bei *Python. Z. mikrosk.-anat. Forsch.* **21**, 597–613.

Bourne, G. H., ed. (1972–73). "The Structure and Function of Muscle." 2nd edn., Academic Press, New York, 4 vols.

Boyd, I. A. (1976). The response of fast and slow nuclear bag fibers and nuclear chain fibres in isolated cat muscle spindles to fusimotor stimulation, and the effect of intrafusal contraction on the sensory endings. *Q. Jl exp. Physiol.* **61**, 203–254.

Bozler, E. (1969). Role of calcium in initiation of contraction in smooth muscle. *Am. J. Physiol.* **216**, 671–674.

Bremer, L. (1882). Über die Endigungen der markhaltigen und marklosen Nerven im quergestreiften Muskel. *Arch. mikrosk. Anat.* **21**, 165–201.

Bremer, L. (1883). Über die Muskelspindeln nebst Bemerkungen über Structur, Neubildung, und Innervation der quergestreiften Muskelfaser. *Arch. mikrosk. Anat.* **22**, 318–356.

Bressler, B. H. and Clinch, N. F. (1974). The compliance of contracting skeletal muscle. *J. Physiol., Lond.* **237**, 477–493.

Briggs, F. N., Poland, J. L. and Solaro, R. J. (1977). Relative capabilities of sarcoplasmic reticulum in fast and slow mammalian skeletal muscles. *J. Physiol., Lond.* **226**, 587–594.

Brivio, R. P. and Florini, J. R. (1972). Myosin: a comparative study. *Comp. Biochem. Physiol.* **41B**, 99–104.

Brody, I. A. (1976). Regulation of isometric contraction in skeletal muscle. *Expl. Neurol.* **50**, 673–683.

Brooke, M. H. and Kaiser, K. K. (1970). Muscle fiber types: How many and what kind? *Archs Neurol.* **23**, 369–379.

Brown, D. E. S. (1934). The effect of rapid changes in hydrostatic pressure upon the contraction of skeletal muscle. *J. cell. comp. Physiol.* **4**, 257–281.

Brown, D. E. S. (1936). The effect of rapid compression upon events in the isometric contraction of skeletal muscle. *J. cell. comp. Physiol.* **8**, 141–157.

Brown, D. E. S. (1957). Temperature-pressure relation in muscular contraction. *In* "The Influence of Temperature on Biological Systems." (F. H. Johnson, ed.). Am. Physiol. Soc., Washington, D.C. pp. 83–110.

Brown, D. E. S. and Goodall, M. C. (1956). Reversal of relaxing mechanism in muscle fibre systems by hydrostatic pressure. *Nature, Lond.* **178**, 1470–1471.

Brown, M. C. (1971). The responses of frog muscle spindles and fast and slow muscle fibres to a variety of mechanical inputs. *J. Physiol., Lond.* **218**, 1–17.

Bruni, A. C. (1942). Le placche motrici studiate a fresco. *Rc. Ist. lomb. Sci. Lett.* **76**, 67–77.

Buchthal, F. and Knappeis, G. G. (1938). Untersuchungen über die Doppelbrechung der einzelnen lebenden quergestreiften Muskelfaser. *Skand. Arch. Physiol.* **78**, 87–116.

Buchthal, F., Knappeis, G. G., and Lindhard, J. (1936). Die Struktur der quergestreiften, lebenden Muskelfaser des Frosches in Ruhe und während der Kontraktion. *Skand. Arch. Physiol.* **73**, 163–198.

Buchthal, F. and Lindhard, J. (1934). Elektrostatische Messungen an einzelnen motorischen Endplatten und Muskelfasern. *Skand. Arch. Physiol.* **70**, 227–232.

Buchthal, F. and Lindhard, J. (1935). Elektrostatische Messungen an einzelnen motorischen Endplatten und Muskelfasern. II. Wirkung von Kurarevergiftung und Radiumbestrahlung. *Skand. Arch. Physiol.* **72**, 35–50.

Buchthal, F. and Lindhard, J. (1937). Elektrostatische Messungen an einzelnen, motorischen Endplatten und Muskelfasern; Änderung der Potentialdifferenz bei Erregung und Kontraktion. *Skand. Arch. Physiol.* **77**, 224–250.

Buchthal, F. and Lindhard, J. (1939). The physiology of striated muscle fibre. *Biol. Meddr* **14**, 61–185.

Buchthal, F. and Lindhard, J. (1942). Transmission of impulses from nerve to muscle fibre. *Acta physiol. scand.* **4**, 136–148.

Burke, R. E. (1978). Motor units: Physiological/histochemical profiles, neural connectivity and functional specializations. *Am. Zool.* **18**, 127–134.

Burke, R. E., Levine, D. N., Tsairis, P. and Zajac, F. E., III (1973). Physiological types and histochemical profiles in motor units of the cat gastrocnemius. *J. Physiol., Lond.* **234**, 723–748.

Burnstock, G. (1969). Evolution of the autonomic innervation of visceral and cardiovascular systems in vertebrates. *Pharmac. Rev.* **21**, 247–324.

Burnstock, G. (1972). Purinergic nerves. *Pharmac. Rev.* **24**, 509–581.

Burnstock, G. and Berger, P. J. (1979). The autonomic nervous system. *In* "Biology of the Reptilia." (C. Gans, P. Ulinski and R. G. Northcutt, eds). Academic Press, London and New York. **10**, 1–57.

Caldwell, P. C. (1953). The separation of the phosphate esters of muscle by paper chromatography. *Biochem. J.* **55**, 458–467.

Candiollo, L. and Guglielmone, R. (1968). Innervazione motoria e propriocettiva dei muscoli costo-cutanei inferiori in *Boa constrictor* (L.). *Rc Ist. lomb. Sci. Lett., Cl.* 2, **102**, 105–112.

Canfield, S. P. (1971). The mechanical properties and heat production of chicken latissimus dorsi muscles during tetanic contractions. *J. Physiol., Lond.* **219**, 281–302.

Carlson, F. D. and Wilkie, D. R. (1974). "Muscle Physiology." Prentice-Hall, Englewood Cliffs, New Jersey.

Chinoy, N. J. and J. C. George (1965). Cholinesterases in the pectoral muscle of some vertebrates. *J. Physiol., Lond.* **177**, 346–354.

Chlebowski, J. S., Przybylski, R. J. and Cox, P. G. (1973). Ultrastructural studies of lizard (*Anolis carolinensis*) myogenesis *in vitro*. *Devl Biol.* **33**, 80–99.

Cipollone, L. T. (1898). Nuevo ricerche sul fuso neuromuscolare. *Annali Med. nav. colon.* **4**, 461–514.

Cliff, G. S. and Ridge, R. M. A. P. (1973). Innervation of extrafusal and intrafusal fibres in snake muscle. *J. Physiol., Lond.* **233**, 1–18.

Close, R. I. (1965). The relation between intrinsic speed of shortening and duration of the active state of muscle. *J. Physiol., Lond.* **180**, 542–572.

Close, R. I. (1972). Dynamic properties of mammalian skeletal muscles. *Physiol. Rev.* **52**, 129–197.

Cole, W. V. (1951). Some observations on the comparative histology of the motor endplate (a preliminary report). *Trans. Am. microsc. Soc.* **70**, 239–244.

Cole, W. V. (1955a). The comparative morphology of sensory endings in striated muscle. *Trans. Am. microsc. Soc.* **74**, 302–311.

Cole, W. V. (1955b). Motor endings in the striated muscles of vertebrates. *J. comp. Neurol.* **102**, 671–716.

Conway, D. and Curtis, B. (1960). The effect of K^+, Ca^{++}, I^-, and temperature on the contracture of turtle muscle. *Proc. natn. Acad. Sci. U.S.A.* **46**, 903–910.

Conway, D. and Sakai, T. (1960a). Caffeine contracture. *Proc. natn. Acad. Sci. U.S.A.* **46**, 897–903.

Conway, D. and Sakai, T. (1960b). The sensitivity of nonpropagating muscle to longitudinal current. *Proc. natn. Acad. Sci. U.S.A.* **46**, 910–916.

Cooper, S. (1960). Muscle spindles and other muscle receptors. *In* "Structure and Function of Muscle." (G. H. Bourne, ed.). Academic Press, New York. **1**, 381–420.

Couteaux, R. (1947). Contribution à l'étude de la synapse myoneurale. *Revue can. Biol.* **6**, 563–711.

Crowe, A. and Ragab, A. H. M. F. (1970a). The structure, distribution and innervation of spindles in the extensor digitorum brevis I muscle of the tortoise *Testudo graeca*. *J. Anat.* **106**, 521–538.

Crowe, A. and Ragab, A. H. M. F. (1970b). Studies on the fine structure of the capsular region of tortoise muscle spindles. *J. Anat.* **107**, 257–269.

Crowe, A. and Ragab, A. H. M. F. (1972). A histochemical investigation of intrafusal fibers in tortoise muscle spindles. *J. Histochem. Cytochem.* **20**, 200–204.

Crush, K. G. (1970). Carnosine and related substances in animal tissue. *Comp. Biochem. Physiol.* **34**, 3–30.

Csapo, A. I. (1960). Molecular structure and function of smooth muscle. *In* "The Structure and Function of Muscle." (G. H. Bourne, ed.). Academic Press, New York. **1**, 29–64.

Dart, R. A. (1924). Some notes on the double innervation of mesodermal muscle. *J. comp. Neurol.* **36**, 441–494.

Demaille, J., Dutruge, E., Eisenberg, E., Capony, J. O. and Pechère, J. F. (1974). Troponins C from reptile and fish muscles and their relation to muscular parvalbumins. *FEBS Lett.* **42**, 173–178.

Dionne, V. E. and Parsons, R. L. (1978). Synaptic channel gating differences at snake twitch and slow neuromuscular junctions. *Nature, Lond.* **274**, 902–904.

Distèche, A. (1960a). pH changes during muscle twitch and tetanus. *Nature, Lond.* **187**, 1119–1120.

Distèche, A. (1960b). Contribution à l'étude des échanges d'ions hydrogène au cours du cycle de la contraction musculaire. *Mém. Acad. r. Belg., Cl. Sci.* **32** (1), 1–169.

Dogiel, A. S. (1890). Methylenblautinktion der motorischer Nervenendingungen in den Muskeln der Amphibien und Reptilien. *Arch. mikrosk. Anat.* **35**, 305–320.

Drachman, D. B. and Johnston, D. M. (1975). Neurotrophic regulation of dynamic properties of skeletal muscle: effects of botulinum toxin and denervation. *J. Physiol., Lond.* **252**, 657–667.

Dubowitz, V. and Pearse, A. G. (1960). A comparative histochemical study of oxidative enzymes and phosphorylase activity in skeletal muscle. *Histochemie* **2**, 105–117.

Dubuisson, M. (1953). Sur l'extractibilité des protéines de structure des muscles de tortue et ses modifications au cours de la contraction. *Bull. Acad. r. Belg., Cl. Sci.* **39**, 35–41.

Edwards, G. A., de Souza Santos, P., de Souza Santos, H. L., Hoge, A. R., Sawaya, P., and Vallejo-Freire, A. (1954). Estudos electronmicroscopicos de musculos estriados de répteis. *Mems. Inst. Butantan* **26**, 169–180.

Eisenberg, B. R. and Kuda, A. M. (1975). Stereological analysis of mammalian skeletal muscle. II. White vastus muscle of the adult guinea pig. *J. Ultrastruct. Res.* **51**, 176–187.

Eisenberg, B. R. and Kuda, A. M. (1976). Discrimination between fiber populations in mammalian skeletal muscle by using ultrastructural parameters. *J. Ultrastruct. Res.* **54**, 76–88.

Eisenberg, B. R., Kuda, A. M. and Peter, J. B. (1974). Stereological analysis of mammalian skeletal muscle. I. Soleus muscle of the adult guinea pig. *J. Cell Biol.* **60**, 732–754.

Evans, C. L. (1925). CLX. Studies on the physiology of plain muscle. IV. The lactic acid content of plain muscle under various conditions. *Biochem. J.* **19**, 1115–1127.

Fedde, M. R. (1969). Electrical properties and acetylcholine sensitivity of singly and multiply innervated avian muscle fibers. *J. gen. Physiol.* **53**, 624–637.

Filogamo, G. and Marchisio, P. C. (1961). Sulla sede delle placche motrici della musculatura della coda rigenerata dei Sauri. *Atti. Accad. naz. Lincei Rc.* **30**, 933–936.

Finol, M. and Ogura, M. (1972). Observaciones subre dos tipos de fibras "twitch" en el reptil *Cnemidophorus lemniscatus*. *Acta cient. venez.* **23**, 203–209.

Finol, H. and Ogura, M. (1977). Estudio sobre los tipos de fibras musculares esqueleticas de la iguana. *Acta cient. venez.* **28**, 213–219.

Fischer, E. (1935). Is internal work a factor in the variation of heat production of muscle at different lengths? *J. cell.comp. Physiol.* 5, 441–455.

Fischer, H. (1971). "Vergleichende Pharmakologie von Überträgersubstanzen in tiersystematischer Darstellung." Springer-Verlag, Berlin. (Handb. exp. Pharmakol., vol. 26).

Floyd, K. and Smith, I. C. (1971). The mechanical and thermal properties of frog slow muscle fibres. *J. Physiol., Lond.* 213, 617–631.

Focant, B. and Pechère, J.-F. (1965). Contribution à l'étude des protéines de faible poids moléculaire des myogènes de vertébrés inférieures. *Arch. int. Physiol. Biochim.* 73, 334–354.

Forbes, M. S., Plantholt, B. A., and Sperelakis, N. (1977). Cytochemical staining procedures selective for sarcotubular systems of muscle: Modifications and applications. *J. Ultrastruct. Res.* 60, 306–327.

Ford, L. E., Huxley, A. F. and Simmons, R. M. (1977). Tension responses to sudden length change in stimulated frog muscles near slack length. *J. Physiol., Lond.* 269, 441–515.

Fowler, W. S. and Crowe, A. (1976). Effect of temperature on resistance to stretch of tortoise muscle. *Am. J. Physiol.* 231, 1349–1355.

Franqué, O. von (1890). Beiträge zur Kenntnis der Muskelknospen. *Verh. phys.-med. Ges. Würzb.* 24, 19–48.

Fukami, Y. (1970a). Tonic and phasic muscle spindles in snakes. *J. Neurophysiol.* 33, 28–35.

Fukami, Y. (1970b). Accommodation in afferent nerve terminals of snake muscle spindle. *J. Neurophysiol.* 33, 475–489.

Fukami, Y. (1972). Electrical and mechanical factors in the adaptation of reinnervated muscle spindles in snakes. *In* "Research in Muscle Development and the Muscle Spindle." (Banker, B. Q., Przybylski, R. J., Van Der Meulen, J. P., Victor, M., eds). Excerpta Medica, Amsterdam. pp. 379–399.

Fukami, Y. (1977). Affinity of zinc iodide-osmium stain for sensory endings of snake muscle spindles. *Brain Res.* 128, 527–531.

Fukami, Y. and Hunt, C. C. (1970). Structure of snake muscle spindles. *J. Neurophysiol.* 33, 9–27.

Fukami, Y. and Hunt, C. C. (1977). Structures in sensory region of snake spindles and their displacement during stretch. *J. Neurophysiol.* 40, 1121–1131.

Fukami, Y., Ichiki, M. and Konishi, A. (1976). Responses of snake muscle spindles to mechanical and electrical stimulation. *Brain Res.* 103, 477–486.

Fukami, Y. and Ridge, R. M. A. P. (1971). Electrophysiological and morphological changes at extrafusal endplates in the snake following chronic denervation. *Brain Res.* 29, 139–145.

Fukami, Y. and Ridge, R. M. A. P. (1972). The effects of chronic denervation on spindle discharge and morphology in isolated costocutaneous muscles of garter snakes. *J. comp. Neurol.* 143, 137–156.

Gabella, G. (1966). Sulla sede della placche motrici nei sauri (*Lacerta muralis* Laur. e *Lacerta viridis* Laur.) *Boll. Soc. ital. Biol. sper.* 42, 405–408.

Gans, C., Dessauer, H. C. and Baic, D. (1978). Axial differences in the musculature of uropeltid snakes: The freight-train approach to burrowing. *Science* 199, 189–192.

Garven, H. S. D. (1925). The nerve endings in the *panniculosus carnosus* of the hedgehog, with special reference to the sympathetic innervation of striated muscle. *Brain* 48, 380–441.

Gauthier, G. F. and Lowey, S. (1977). Polymorphism of myosin among skeletal muscle fiber types. *J. Cell Biol.* 74, 760–779.

Gemelli, A. (1905). Sur la structure des plaques motrices chez les reptiles. *Névraxe* 7, 105–115.

George, J. C. and Berger, A. J. (1966). "Avian Myology." Academic Press, New York.

Giacomini, E. (1898). Sui fusi neuro-musculari dei Sauropsidi. *Atti Accad. Fisiocr. Siena* Ser. 4, **9**, 215–230.

Gilson, A. S., Jr., Schoepfle, G. M., and Walker, S. M. (1947). The time course of tension development in the muscle response. *Ann. N.Y. Acad. Sci.* **47**, 697–714.

Ginetzinsky, A. G. and Itina, N. A. (1938). Effect of eserine upon skeletal muscle of tortoise. *Bull. Biol. Med. exp. U.S.S.R.* **5**, 382–385.

Ginetzinsky, A. G. and Shamarina, N. M. (1942). The tonomotor phenomenon in denervated muscle. (DSIR, translation RTS 1710). *Adv. mod. Biol. (USSR)* **15**, 283–294.

Ginsborg, B. L. and Mackay, B. (1961). A histochemical demonstration of two types of motor innervation in avian skeletal muscle. *Biblthca anat.* **2**, 174–181.

Goodall, M. C. (1957). Kinetics of muscular contraction—I. *Yale J. Biol. Med.* **30**, 224–243.

Goodall, M. C. (1958a). Kinetics of muscular contraction in heavy water. *Nature, Lond.* **182**, 677.

Goodall, M. C. (1958b). Dependence of latent period in muscle on strength of stimulus. *Nature, Lond.* **182**, 1737.

Goodall, M. C. (1960). Excitation coupling in muscle. *Jap. J. Physiol.* **10**, 340–350.

Gopalakrishnakone, P. and Jayatilaka, A. D. P. (1978). An electron microscopic study of the adductor externus superficialis muscle associated with the venom gland of the cobra (*Naja naja*). *J. Anat.* **126**, 59–63.

Gradwell, N. and Walcott, B. (1971). Dual functional and structural properties of the interhyoideus muscle of the bull frog tadpole (*Rana catesbeiana*). *J. exp. Zool.* **176**, 193–218.

Gregory, J. E., Luff, A. R., Morgan, D. L. and Proske, U. (1978). The stiffness of amphibian slow and twitch muscle during high speed stretches. *Pflügers Arch. ges. Physiol.* **375**, 207–211.

Gregory, J. E. and Proske, U. (1975). Responses of tendon organs in a lizard. *J. Physiol., Lond.* **248**, 519–529.

Haas, G. (1973). Muscles of the jaws and associated structures in the Rhynchocephalia and Squamata. *In* "Biology of the Reptilia." (C. Gans and T. S. Parsons, eds). Academic Press, London and New York. **4**, 285–490.

Hammond, G. R. and Ridge, R. M. A. P. (1978a). Properties of twitch motor units in snake costocutaneous muscle. *J. Physiol., Lond.* **276**, 525–533.

Hammond, G. R. and Ridge, R. M. A. P. (1978b). Post-tetanic potentiation of twitch motor units in snake costocutaneous muscle. *J. Physiol., Lond.* **276**, 535–554.

Hansen, R. (1927). Untersuchungen über die Beeinflussung der Muskelleitungs-geschwindigkeit durch den osmotischen Druck der umgebenden Lösung. *Z. Biol.* **87**, 72–76.

Hartree, W. (1926). An analysis of the initial heat production in the voluntary muscle of the tortoise. *J. Physiol., Lond.* **61**, 255–260.

Hartree, W. and Liljestrand, G. (1926). The recovery heat production in tortoise's muscle. *J. Physiol., Lond.* **62**, 93–97.

Hartzell, M. C., Kuffler, S. W., and Yoshikami, D. (1975). Post-synaptic potentiation: Interaction between quanta of acetylcholine at the skeletal neuromuscular synapse. *J. Physiol., Lond.* **251**, 427–463.

Haslett, W. L. and Jenden, D. J. (1961). A comparative study of the effect of ryanodine on muscle. *J. cell. comp. Physiol.* **57**, 123–133.

Haswell, W. A. (1889). A comparative study of striated muscle. *Q. Jl microsc. Sci.* **30**, 31–50.

Heinl, P., Kuhn, H. J., and Rüegg, J. C. (1974). Tension responses to quick length changes of glycerinated skeletal muscle fibres from the frog and tortoise. *J. Physiol., Lond.* **237**, 243–258.

Heistracher, P. and Hunt, C. C. (1969a). The relation of membrane changes to contraction in twitch muscle fibres. *J. Physiol., Lond.* **201**, 589–611.

Heistracher, P., and Hunt, C. C. (1969b). Contractile repriming in snake twitch muscle fibres. *J. Physiol., Lond.* **201**, 613–626.

Heistracher, P., and Hunt, C. C. (1969c). The effect of procaine on snake twitch muscle fibres. *J. Physiol., Lond.* **201**, 627–238.

Hess, A. (1961). Structural differences of fast and slow extrafusal fibres and their nerve endings in chickens, *J. Physiol., Lond.* **157**, 221–231.

Hess, A. (1963). Two types of extrafusal muscle fibres and their nerve endings in the garter snake. *Am. J. Anat.* **113**, 347–363.

Hess, A. (1965). The sarcoplasmic reticulum, the T system, and the motor terminals of slow and twitch fibers in the garter snake. *J. Cell Biol.* **26**, 467–476.

Hess, A. (1970). Vertebrate slow muscle fibers. *Physiol. Rev.* **50**, 40–62.

Hikida, R. S. and Bock, W. J. (1974). Analysis of fiber types in the pigeon's metapatagialis muscle. I. Histochemistry, end plates and ultrastructure. *Tissue & Cell* **6**, 411–430.

Hill, A. V. (1926a). Croonian lecture: The laws of muscular motion. *Proc. R. Soc.* **B100**, 87–108.

Hill, A. V. (1926b). The viscous elastic properties of smooth muscle. *Proc. R. Soc.* **B100**, 108–115.

Hill, A. V. (1938). The heat of shortening and the dynamic constants of muscle. *Proc. R. Soc.* **B126**, 136–195.

Hill, A. V. (1939). The mechanical efficiency of frogs' muscle. *Proc. R. Soc.* **B127**, 434–451.

Hill, A. V. (1949). The abrupt transition from rest to activity in muscle. *Proc. R. Soc.* **B136**, 399–419.

Hill, A. V. (1950a). Does heat production precede mechanical response in muscular contraction? *Proc. R. Soc.* **B137**, 268–273.

Hill, A. V. (1950b). The development of the active state of muscle during the latent period. *Proc. R. Soc.* **B137**, 320–329.

Hill, A. V. (1951). The earliest manifestation of the mechanical response of striated muscle. *Proc. R. Soc.* **B138**, 339–348.

Hill, A. V. (1964). The effect of load on the heat of shortening of muscle. *Proc. R. Soc.* **B159**, 297–318.

Hill, A. V. (1965). "Trails and Trials in Physiology". Williams & Wilkins, Baltimore.

Hill, D. K. (1968). Tension due to interaction between the sliding filaments in resting striated muscle. The effect of stimulation. *J. Physiol., Lond.* **199**, 637–684.

Hines, M. (1927). Nerve and muscle. *Q. Rev. Biol.* **2**, 149–180.

Hines, M. (1930). The innervation of the muscle spindle. *Proc. Ass. Res. nerv. ment. Dis.* **9**, 124–137.

Hines, M. (1932). Studies in the innervation of skeletal muscle. IV. Of certain muscles of the boa constrictor. *J. comp. Neurol.* **56**, 105–133.

Hinsey, J. C. (1934). The innervation of muscle. *Physiol. Rev.* **14**, 514–585.

Hoffmann, P. (1913). Einige Versuche zur allgemeinen Muskelphysiologie an einem günstigen Objekte (Retractor penis der Schildkröte). *Z. Biol.* **61**, 311–325.

Homsher, E. and Kean, C. J. (1978). Skeletal muscle energetics and metabolism. *A. Rev. Physiol.* **40**, 93–131.

Hoyle, G., McNeill, P. A., and Walcott, B. (1966). Nature of invaginating tubules in Felderstruktur muscle fibers of the garter snake. *J. Cell. Biol.* **30**, 197–201.

Huber, C. and DeWitt, L. M. A. (1897). A contribution on the motor nerve-endings and on the nerve-ending in the muscle-spindles. *J. comp. Neurol.* 7, 169–230.

Hunt, C. C. and Wylie, R. M. (1970). Responses of snake muscle spindles to stretch and intrafusal muscle fibre contraction. *J. Neurophysiol.* 33, 1–8.

Huxley, A. F. (1971). The Croonian lecture, 1967. The activation of striated muscle and its mechanical response. *Proc. R. Soc.* B178, 1–27.

Huxley, A. F. (1974). Review lecture. Muscle contraction. *J. Physiol., Lond.* 243, 1–43.

Huxley, A. F. and Simmons, R. M. (1971). Proposed mechanism of force generation in striated muscle. *Nature, Lond.* 233, 533–538.

Huxley, A. F. and Straub, R. W. (1958). Local activation and interfibrillar structures in striated muscle. *J. Physiol., Lond.* 143, 40P–41P.

Ivanova, S. F. (1973). Morphological and diffusion parameters in the muscles performing different functions and loading (In Russian). *Arkh. Anat. Gistol. Embriol.* 64, Part 3, 18–27.

Isojima, C. and Bozler, E. (1963). Role of calcium in initiation of contraction in smooth muscle. *Am. J. Physiol.* 205, 681–685.

Itina, N. A. (1938). The transmission of excitation in the myoneural synapsis of the skeletal muscle in the turtle. *Fiziol. Zh. SSSR* 25, 664–672.

James, N. T. and Meek, G. A. (1973). An electron microscopic study of avian muscle spindles. *J. Ultrastruct. Res.* 43, 193–204.

Jewell, B. R. and Wilkie, D. R. (1958). An analysis of the mechanical components in frog's striated muscle. *J. Physiol., Lond.* 43, 515–540.

Jewell, B. R. and Wilkie, D. R. (1960). The mechanical properties of relaxing muscle. *J. Physiol., Lond.* 152, 30–47.

Jöbsis, F. F. (1956). "The pH Relations of Muscular Contraction." Ph.D. Thesis, The University of Michigan.

Jöbsis, F. F. (1963a). Spectrophotometric studies in intact muscle. I. Components of the respiratory chain. *J. gen. Physiol.* 46, 905–928.

Jöbsis, F. F. (1963b). Spectrophotometric studies on intact muscle. II. Recovery from contractile activity. *J. gen. Physiol.* 46, 929–969.

Jöbsis, F. F. and O'Connor, M. J. (1966). Calcium release and reabsorption in the sartorius muscle of the toad. *Biochem. biophys. Res. Commun.* 25, 246–252.

John, K. O. (1966). Cholinesterase activity in the muscles of two lizards—a glider and a runner. *J. Anim. Morph. Physiol.* 13, 126–132.

John, K. O. (1970). Studies on the histophysiology of the muscles of the south Indian flying lizard, *Draco dussumieri* (Dum. & Bib.). *J. Anim. Morph. Physiol.* 17, 44–55.

Jonecho, A. (1962). Die Ringbinden als eine allgemeine unspezifische Reaktion der quergestreiften Muskulatur. *Experientia* 18, 166–167.

Julian, F. J. (1969). Activation in a skeletal muscle contraction model with a modification for insect fibrillar muscle. *Biophys. J.* 9, 547–570.

Julian, F. J. and Sollins, M. R. (1975). Variation of muscle stiffness with force at increasing speeds of shortening. *J. gen. Physiol.* 66, 287–302.

Kaczmarski, F. (1969). The fine structure of extraocular muscles of the lizard, *Lacerta agilis* L. *Z. mikrosk.-anat. Forsch.* 80, 517–531.

Kaczmarski, F. (1974). The motor end plates in extraocular muscles of the lizard, *Lacerta agilis* L. *Z. mikrosk.-anat. Forsch.* 88, 1045–1060.

Kahn, E. B. and Simpson, S. B., Jr. (1974). Satellite cells in mature, uninjured skeletal muscle of the lizard tail. *Devl Biol.* 37, 219–223.

Katz, B. (1939). The relation between force and speed in muscular contraction. *J. Physiol., Lond.* 96, 45–64.

Kerschner, L. (1888). Bemerkungen über ein besonderes Muskelsystem im willkürlichen Muskel. *Anat. Anz.* 3, 126–132.

Khan, M. A. (1976). Histochemical sub-types of three fibre-types of avian skeletal muscle. *Histochemistry* **50**, 9–16.

Köhler, H. (1938). Histologische Untersuchungen an Skeletmuskeln von Reptilien. *Z. Zellforsch. mikrosk. Anat.* **28**, 597–613.

Kuffler, S. W. and Yoshikami, D. (1975a). The distribution of acetylcholine sensitivity at the post-synaptic membrane of vertebrate skeletal twitch muscles: Iontophoretic mapping in the micron range. *J. Physiol., Lond.* **244**, 703–730.

Kuffler, S. W. and Yoshikami, D. (1975b). The number of transmitter molecules in a quantum: An estimate from iontophoretic application of acetylcholine at the neuromuscular synapse. *J. Physiol., Lond.* **251**, 465–482.

Kühne, W. (1883). Die Verbindung der Nervenscheiden mit dem Sarkolemm. *Z. Biol.* **19**, 501–534.

Kühne, W. (1887). Neue Untersuchungen über motorische Nervenendigungen. *Z. Biol.* **23**, 1–148.

Kulchitsky, N. (1924). Nerve endings in muscles. *J. Anat.* **58**, 152–169.

Kushmerick, M. J. (1977). Energy balance in muscle: A biochemical approach. *Curr. Tops. Bioenerg.* **6**, 1–37.

Lännergren, J. (1978). The force-velocity relation of isolated twitch and slow muscle fibers of *Xenopus laevis. J. Physiol., Lond.* **283**, 501–522.

Lapicque, L. (1933). Alpha and gamma curves in slow muscles. *J. Physiol., Lond.* **78**, 381–403.

Lapicque, L. and Lapicque, M. (1927). Sur la chronaxie des muscles squelettiques de la tortue. *C. r. Seanc. Soc. Biol.* **96**, 1368–1371.

Lebedinskaya, I. I. (1963). Some characteristics of skeletal muscle tonus in reptiles. *Fiziol. Zh. S.S.S.R.* **49**, 596–602.

Lebedinskaya, I. I. (1964). Mechanism of sustained muscle contraction in the tortoise. *Fiziol. Zh. S.S.S.R.* **50**, 1350–1357. (Transl. in *Fed. Proc.* **24**, T1096–1100 (1965).)

Lededinskaya, I. I. (1965). On the morphological and functional differentiation in the peripheral motor apparatus of reptiles. *Fiziol. Zh. S.S.S.R.* **51**, 1199–1209.

Lebedinskaya, I. I. (1973). The ultrastructure of functionally differentiated skeletal muscle fibers of the tortoise *Emys orbicularis. Tsitologiya* **15**, 1458–1465.

Lebedinskaya, I. I. and Nasledov, G. A. (1977). Action potentials of fast and slow muscle fibers of the swamp tortoise *Emys orbicularis. Zh. evol. Biokhim. Fiziol.* **13**, 473–478. (Transl. in *J. evol. Biochem. Physiol.* **13**, 316–321.)

Lebedinskaya, I. I. and Ogorodnikova, L. G. (1978). Certain metabolic features of fast and slow muscles of the bog-turtle *Emys orbicularis. Zh. evol. Biokhim. Fiziol.* **14**, 461–466. (Transl. in *J. evol. Biochem. Physiol.* **14**, 380–385.)

Lee, S. Y. (1971). A histochemical study of twitch and tonus fibers. *J. Morph.* **133**, 253–271.

Lehky, P., Blum, H., Stein, E. A. and Fischer, E. H. (1974). Isolation and characterization of parvalbumins from the skeletal muscle of higher vertebrates. *J. biol. Chem.* **249**, 4332–4334.

Lemus, D., Zurich, L., Paz de la Vega-Lemus, Y. and Wacyk, J. (1970). Actividad espontanea y efecto de oxitocina en el utero aislado de *Liolaemus gravenhorsti* y *Liolaemus tenuis* T. *Archos. Biol. Med. exp.* **7**, 11–13.

Levin, A. and Wyman, J. (1927). The viscous elastic properties of muscle. *Proc. R. Soc.* **B101**, 218–243.

Levine, L. (1966). An electrophysiological study of chelonian skeletal muscle. *J. Physiol., Lond.* **183**, 683–713.

Licht, P., Dawson, W. R. and Shoemaker, V. H. (1969). Thermal adjustments in cardiac and skeletal muscles of lizards. *Z. vergl. Physiol.* **65**, 1–14.

Lindhard, J. (1931). Der Skeletmuskel und seine Funktion. *Ergebn. Physiol.* **33**, 337–557.

Luff, A. R. and Atwood, H. S. (1972). Membrane properties and contraction of single muscle fibers in the mouse. *Am. J. Physiol.* 22, 1435–1440.

Lukomskaya, N. Ya. and Rozhkova, E. K. (1970). Cholinoreception of tonic fibers in mixed muscles of the steppe tortoise *Testudo horsfieldi* and lizard *Agama caucasica. Zh. evol. Biokhim. Fiziol.* 6, 303–309. (Transl. in *J. evol. Biochem. Physiol.* 6, 240–244.)

Mackay, B. and Peters, A. (1961). Terminal innervation of segmental muscle fibres. *Biblthca anat.* 2, 182–193.

Maier, A. and Eldred, E. (1971). Comparisons in the structure of avian muscle spindles. *J. comp. Neurol.* 143, 25–40.

Maier, A., DeSantis, M. and Eldred, E. (1974). The occurrence of muscle spindles in extraocular muscles of various vertebrates. *J. Morph.* 143, 397–408.

Martin, J. H. (1972). The ultrastructure of rattlesnake shaker muscle. *Amer. Zool.* 12, xxvii.

Martin, J. H. and Bagby, R. M. (1973). Properties of rattlesnake shaker muscle. *J. exp. Zool.* 185, 293–300.

Maruyama, K., Murakami, F. and Ohashi, K. (1977). Connectin, an elastic protein of muscle: comparative biochemistry. *J. Biochem., Tokyo* 82, 339–345.

Mavrinskaya, L. F. (1962). Evolutionary and morphological changes in vertebrate junctions. *Arkh. Anat. Gistol. Embriol.* 43, #12, 3–28. Transl. in *Fed. Proc.* 22, T994–1008 (1963).

Mayeda, R. (1890). Ueber die Kaliberverhältnisse der quergestreiften Muskelfasern. *Z. Biol.* 27, 119–152.

Mays, K. (1884). Histo-physiologische Untersuchungen über die Verbreitung der Nerven in den Muskeln. *Z. Biol.* 2, 449–530.

Mays, K. (1893). Ueber die Entwicklung der motorischen Nervenendigungen. *Z. Biol.* 11, 41–85.

Meyer, H. (1893). Ueber einige pharmakologische Reaktionen der Vogel-und Reptilieniris. *Arch. exp. Path. Pharmak.* 32, 101–123.

Miller, A. T. and Hale, D. M. (1968). Comparisons of lactic dehydrogenase in rat and turtle organs. *Comp. Biochem. Physiol.* 27, 597–601.

Miura, N. (1886). Untersuchung über die motorischen Nervenendigungen der quergestreiften Muskelfasern. *Virchows Arch. path. Anat. Physiol.* 105, 129–135.

Momin, V. M. (1975). The influence of fasting and pancreatectomy on some glycolytic enzymes in the muscle of garden lizard, *Calotes versicolor. Z. mikrosk.-anat. Forsch.* 89, 744–757.

Mommaerts, W. F. H. M. (1954). Is adenosine triphosphate broken down during a single muscle twitch? *Nature, Lond.* 174, 1083–1084.

Mommaerts, W. F. H. M. (1955). Investigation of the presumed breakdown of adenosinetriphosphate and phosphocreatine during a single muscle twitch. *Am. J. Physiol.* 182, 585–593.

Mommaerts, W. F. H. M. (1969). Energetics of muscular contraction. *Physiol. Rev.* 49, 427–508.

Mommaerts, W. F. H. M., Olmsted, M., Seraydarian, K. and Wallner, A. (1962). Contraction with and without demonstrable splitting of energy-rich phosphate in turtle muscle. *Biochim. Biophys. Acta* 63, 82–92.

Moss, R. L., Sollins, M. R. and Julian, F. J. (1976). Calcium activation produces a characteristic response to stretch in both skeletal and cardiac muscle. *Nature, Lond.* 260, 619–621.

Müller, H. K. (1927). Die Verhältnisse der Zuckungssummation am quergestreiften Muskel bei Reizung mit dem galvanischen Strom. *Z. Biol.* 86, 301–308.

Munch-Petersen, A. (1953). Dephosphorylation of adenosine triphosphate during the rising phase of twitch. *Acta physiol. scand.* 29, 202–219.

Naeije, M. and Crowe, A. (1974). The response of chelonian muscle spindles to mechanical stimulation. *Life Sci.* 15, 131–136.

Naeije, M. and Crowe, A. (1977a). Responses of the chelonian muscle spindles to mechanical stretch and fusimotor stimulation. *J. Neurophysiol.* 40, 814–821.

Naeije, M. and Crowe, A. (1977b). Model for the motor stimulation in chelonian muscle spindles. *Biol. Cybern.* **26**, 73–79.

Nothmann, F. (1932). Beiträge zur Kenntnis der Acetylcholinkontraktur. *Pflügers Arch. ges. Physiol.* **229**, 588–593.

Ogata, T. and Mori, M. (1963). A histochemical study of hydrolytic enzymes in muscle fibers of various animals. *J. Histochem. Cytochem.* **11**, 645–652.

Ogata, T. and Mori, M. (1964). Histochemical studies of oxidative enzymes in vertebrate muscle. *J. Histochem. Cytochem.* **12**, 171–182.

Ottoson, D. (1972). Functional properties of a muscle spindle with no fluid space. *Brain Res.* **41**, 471–474.

Ovalle, W. K. (1976). Fine structure of the avian muscle spindle capsule. *Cell Tiss. Res.* **166**, 285–298.

Padykula, H. A. and Gauthier, G. F. (1966). Morphological and cytochemical characteristics of fiber types in normal mammalian muscle. *Excerpta med. int. Cong. Ser.* **147**, 117–128.

Page, S. G. (1965). A comparison of the fine structure of frog slow and twitch muscle fibres. *J. Cell Biol.* **26**, 477–497.

Page, S. G. (1968). Fine structure of tortoise skeletal muscle. *J. Physiol., Lond.* **197**, 709–715.

Page, S. G. (1969). Structure and some contractile properties of fast and slow muscles of the chicken. *J. Physiol., Lond.* **205**, 131–145.

Pakhomov, A. N., Aronshtam, A. A. and Borkin, L. Ya. (1973). The fractional composition of multiple forms of esterases and proteins in tortoise tissues. *Zh. evol. Biokhim. Fiziol.* **9**, 470–473. (Transl. in *J. evol. Biochem. Physiol.* **9**, 408–410.)

Pallot, D. J. (1974). The structure and motor innervation of intrafusal fibres in snakes of *Natrix* sp. *J. Anat.* **118**, 281–293.

Pallot, D. J. and Ridge, R. M. A. P. (1972). The fine structure of the long-capsule muscle spindles in the snake *Natrix* sp. *J. Anat.* **113**, 61–74.

Pallot, D. J. and Ridge, R. M. A. P. (1973). The fine structure of the short capsule muscle spindles in snakes of *Natrix* sp. *J. Anat.* **114**, 13–24.

Pallot, D. J. and Taberner, J. (1974). Histochemistry of muscle spindles in snakes of *Natrix* species. *J. Histochem. Cytochem.* **22**, 881–886.

Palmieri, G., Panu, R., Asole, A. and Branca, A. (1977). Sulla innervazione propriocettiva della muscolature di *Caiman sclerops*. *Quad. Anat. prat.* **33**, 181–190.

Patzl, M. (1932). Vergleichende Untersuchungen über die Wärmekontraktur und Wärmelähmung der quergestreiften Muskeln von Eidechsen und Fröschen. *Pflügers Arch. ges. Physiol.* **321**, 90–101.

Panzica, G. C. (1979). The ultrastructure of the capsule of the neuromuscular spindles from *Python reticulatus* (Schneid.). *Anat. Anz.* **145**, 276–285.

Panzica Viglietti, C. and Panzica, G. C. (1978). Extrafusal motor endings in *Python reticulatus* (Schneider) costocutanei inferiores muscles (Serpentes: Boidae). *Monitore zool. ital.* **12**, 29–40.

Paz de la Vega-Lemus, Y., Lemus, D. and Zurich, L. (1971). Efectos de acetilcolina, histamina, y 5-hidroxitriptamina sobre la motilidad del utero aislado de *Liolaemus gravenhorsti* y *Liolaemus tenuis* T. *Archos Biol. Med. exp.* **8**, 26–29.

Perroncito, A. (1901). Sur la terminaison des nerfs dans les fibres musculaires striées. *Archs ital. Biol.* **36**, 245–254.

Perroncito, A. (1902). Études ultérieures sur la terminaison des nerfs dans les muscles à fibres striées. *Archs ital. Biol.* **38**, 393–412.

Peter, J. B., Barnard, R. J., Edgerton, V. R., Gillespie, C. A. and Stempel, K. E. (1972). Metabolic profiles of three fiber types of skeletal muscle in guinea pigs and rabbits. *Biochemistry, Wash.* **11**, 2627–2633.

Pierobon Bormioli, S., Sartore, S., Vitadello, M. and Schiaffino, S. (1980). "Slow" myosins in vertebrate skeletal muscle. An immunofluorescence study. *J. Cell Biol.* **85**, 672–681.

Plattner, F. and Krannich, E. (1932). Über das Vorkommen eines acetylcholinartigen Körpers in den Skelettmuskeln. II. *Pflügers Arch. ges. Physiol.* **230**, 356–362.

Pollock, M. and MacAvoy, E. S. (1978). Morphological and metabolic changes in muscles of hibernating lizards. *Copeia* 1978, 412–416.

Proske, U. (1969a). An electrophysiological analysis of responses from lizard muscle spindles. *J. Physiol., Lond.* **205**, 289–304.

Proske, U. (1969b). The innervation of muscle spindles in the lizard *Tiliqua nigrolutea*. *J. Anat.* **105**, 217–230.

Proske, U. (1973). The muscle spindles in slow and twitch skeletal muscle of the lizard. *J. Physiol., Lond.* **230**, 429–448.

Proske, U. and Gregory, J. E. (1976). Multiple sites of impulse initiation in a tendon organ. *Expl Neurol.* **50**, 515–520.

Proske, U. and Rack, P. M. H. (1976). Short-range stiffness of slow fibers and twitch fibers in reptilian muscle. *Am. J. Physiol.* **231**, 449–453.

Proske, U. and Ridge, R. M. A. P. (1974). Extrafusal muscle and muscle spindles in reptiles. *Prog. Neurobiol.* **3**, 1–29.

Proske, U. and Vaughan, P. (1968). Histological and electrophysiological investigation of lizard skeletal muscle. *J. Physiol., Lond.* **199**, 495–509.

Proske, U. and Walker, B. (1975). Responses of muscle spindles in a tortoise. *Brain Res.* **91**, 79–88.

Prosser, C. L. (1973). "Comparative Animal Physiology." 3rd edn, Saunders, Philadelphia.

Pushpendran, C. K. and Eapen, J. (1972). Electrophoretic studies on proteins of tail of house lizard. *J. Anim. Morph. Physiol.* **13**, 169–188.

Rack, P. M. H. and Westbury, D. R. (1974). The short range stiffness of active mammalian muscle and its effect on mechanical properties. *J. Physiol., Lond.* **240**, 331–350.

Rahman, S. A., Ozaki, A. and Jahn, A. A. (1974). Innervation of the ventral costocutaneous muscles of the Egyptian flowered snake (*Coluber florulentus*). *Acta anat.* **90**, 539–549.

Rall, J. A. and Schottelius, B. A. (1973). Energetics of contraction in phasic and tonic skeletal muscles of the chicken. *J. gen. Physiol.* **62**, 303–323.

Rall, J. A., Homsher, E., Wallner, A. and Mommaerts, W. F. H. M. (1976). A temporal dissociation of energy liberation and high energy phosphate splitting during shortening in frog skeletal muscles. *J. gen. Physiol.* **68**, 13–27.

Raviola, E. and Raviola, G. (1967). Striated muscle cells in the thymus of reptiles and birds: an electron microscopic study. *Am. J. Anat.* **121**, 623–646. Also in *Rc. Ist. lomb. Sci. Lett.* **B101**, 134–138 (1967).

Regaud, C. and Favre, M. (1904). Les terminaisons nerveux et les organes nerveux sensitifs de l'appareil locomoteur. *Rev. gén. Histol.* **1**, 1–140.

Reger, J. G. (1966). The fine structure of iridial constrictor pupillae muscle of *Alligator mississippiensis. Anat. Rec.* **155**, 197–216.

Reichel, H. and Bleichert, A. (1955). Die Dehnbarkeit des Skelett- und Herzmuskels der Schildkröte während der Latenzzeit. *Experientia* **11**, 286–288.

Reichel, H. and Bleichert, A. (1958). Der zeitliche Ablauf der Aktivierung im Skeletmuskel der Schildkröte. *Pflügers Arch. ges. Physiol.* **265**, 416–424.

Reichel, H. and Zimmer, F. (1956). Der Erfolg plötzlicher Entdehnungen während der Erschlaffung des Skelett- und Herzmuskels. *Z. Biol.* **108**, 284–293.

Reichel, H., Zimmer, F. and Bleichert, A. (1956). Die elastischen Eigenschaften des Skelett- und Herzmuskels in verschiedenen Phasen der Einzelzuckung. *Z. Biol.* **108**, 188–195.

Reichel, H., Zimmer, F. and Bleichert, A. (1958). Die statischen Eigenschaften der elastischen Serienelemente im kontrahierten Muskel. *Pflügers Arch. ges. Physiol.* **265**, 410–415.

Reid, G. (1941). The reaction of muscle to denervation in cold-blooded animals. *Aust. J. exp. Biol. med. Sci.* **19**, 199–206.

Renard, S. (1952). Sur la distribution des protéines aisément extractibles des muscles de divers vertébrés. *Bull. Acad. r. Belg. Cl. Sci.* **38**, 1195–1210.

Rice, M. J. (1973). Supercontracting striated muscle in a vertebrate. *Nature, Lond.* **243**, 238–240.

Ridge, R. M. A. P. (1971). Different types of extrafusal muscle fibres in snake costocutaneous muscles. *J. Physiol., Lond.* **217**, 393–418.

Roberts, E. and Lowe, I. P. (1954). Occurrence of the O-phosphodiester of L-serine and ethanolamine in turtle tissue. *J. biol. Chem.* **211**, 1–12.

Robertson, J. D. (1956a). Some features of the ultrastructure of reptilian skeletal muscle. *J. biophys. biochem. Cytol.* **2**, 369–380.

Robertson, J. D. (1956b). The ultrastructure of a reptilian myoneural junction. *J. biochem. biophys. Cytol.* **2**, 381–393.

Roddie, I. C. (1962). The transmembrane potential changes associated with smooth muscle activity in turtle arteries and veins. *J. Physiol., Lond.* **163**, 138–150.

Roddie, I. C. and Kirk, S. (1961). Transmembrane action potentials from smooth muscle in turtle arteries and veins. *Science, N.Y.* **134**, 736–737.

Rojas, P., Szepsenwol, J. and Resta, L.-S. (1939). Influence du curare et de l'excitation sur la structure de la plaque motrice. *C. r. Séanc. Soc. Biol.* **131**, 293–296.

Romanul, F. C. A. (1964). Enzymes in muscle. *Archs Neurol.* **11**, 355–368.

Rosemann, H.-V. (1936). Die wellenförmige Aktionsstromausbreitung im Muskel. *Z. Biol.* **97**, 55–77.

Rossi, H. (1902). Sur les filaments nerveux (fibrilles nerveux ultraterminales) dans les plaques motrices de *Lacerta agilis*. *Névraxe* **3**, 341–346.

Rouget, C. (1862). Note sur la terminaison des nerfs moteurs dans les muscles chez les reptiles, les oiseaux et les mammifers. *C. r. hebd. Séanc. Acad. Sci., Paris* **55**, 548–551.

Rückert, W. (1931). Die phylogenetische Bedingtheit tonischer Eigenschaften der quergestreiften Wirbeltiermuskulatur. *Pflügers Arch. ges. Physiol.* **226**, 323–346.

Ruffini, A. (1894). Considerazzioni critiche sui recenti studi dell'apparato nervoso nei fusi muscolari. *Anat. Anz.* **9**, 80–88.

Schoepfle, G. M. and Gilson, A. S., Jr. (1945). Some observations on the configuration of the free loaded and after loaded muscle twitch. *J. cell. comp. Physiol.* **26**, 119–130.

Schoepfle, G. M. and Gilson, A. S., Jr. (1946). Elasticity of muscle in relation to actively developed twitch tension. *J. cell. comp. Physiol.* **27**, 105–114.

Serebrenikova, T. P. and Lyzlova, E. M. (1977). Some characteristics of molecular evolution of glycogen phosphorylase and aminotransferases of vertebrate muscle tissue. *Zh. evol. Biokhim. Fiziol.* **13**, 125–133.

Shah, R. V. and Chakko, T. V. (1966a). Histochemical localization of acid phosphatase in the adult normal and regenerating tail of *Hemidactylus flaviviridis*. *J. Anim. Morph. Physiol.* **13**, 169–188.

Shah, R. V. and Chakko, T. V. (1966b). Mitochondrial localization of alkaline phosphatase in the adult and regenerating lizard muscle (*Hemidactylus flaviviridis*). *J. Anim. Morph. Physiol.* **13**, 206–209.

Shah, R. V. and Chakko, T. V. (1967a). The histochemical demonstration of alkaline phosphatase in the normal (non-amputated) and regenerating tail of the common house lizard, *Hemidactylus flaviviridis*. *J. Anim. Morph. Physiol.* **14**, 69–88.

Shah, R. V. and Chakko, T. V. (1967b). Histochemical localization of glycogen and phosphorylase in the normal and regenerating tail of the house lizard, *Hemidactylus flaviviridis*. *J. Anim. Morph. Physiol.* **14**, 257–264.

Shah, R. V. and Chakko, T. V. (1968). Histological observations on the normal and regenerating tail of the house lizard, *Hemidactylus flaviviridis*. *J. Anim. Morph. Physiol.* **15**, 26–39.

Shah, R. V. and Chakko, T. V. (1969). Histochemical localization of succinate dehydrogenase in the normal and regenerating tail of the house lizard, *Hemidactylus flaviviridis. J. Anim. Morph. Physiol.* **16**, 89–96.

Shah, R. V. and Chakko, T. V. (1971). Histochemical localization of cholinesterase in the normal and regenerating tail of the house lizard, *Hemidactylus flaviviridis. J. Anim. Morph. Physiol.* **18**, 158–163.

Shah, R. V. and Chakko, T. V. (1972). Histochemical localization of nucleic acids in the normal and regenerating tail of the house lizard, *Hemidactylus flaviviridis. J. Anim. Morph. Physiol.* **19**, 28–33.

Shah, R. V. and Magon, D. K. (1969). Histochemical demonstration of a-glycerophosphate dehydrogenase (a-GPH) in the normal and regenerating tail of the house lizard, *Hemidactylus flaviviridis. J. Anim. Morph. Physiol.* **16**, 97–105.

Shah, R. V. and Ramachandran, A. V. (1972). Aldolase activity in the normal and regenerating tail of the scincid lizard, *Mabuya carinata. J. Anim. Morph. Physiol.* **19**, 43–49.

Sihler, C. (1895). Ueber Muskelspindeln und intramusculäre Nervenendigungen bei Schlangen und Fröschen. *Arch. mikrosk. Anat.* **46**, 709–723.

Sihler, C. (1900). Die Muskelspindeln. Kerne und Lage der motorischen Nervenendigungen. *Arch. mikrosk. Anat.* **56**, 334–353.

Smith, G. E. (1926). Discussion on the sympathetic innervation of striated muscle. *Proc. R. Soc. Med.* **19**, (*Neurol.*) 18–23.

Smith, R. S. and Ovalle, W. K., Jr. (1973). Varieties of fast and slow extrafusal muscle fibres in amphibian hind limb muscles. *J. Anat.* **116**, 1–24.

Snyder, C. D. (1927). Heat production in smooth muscle. *Am. J. Physiol.* **79**, 719–724.

Snyder, C. D. and Light, F. W., Jr. (1928). Initial and recovery heat production in smooth muscle based upon experiments on a urinary bladder-nerve preparation from terrapin. *Am. J. Physiol.* **86**, 399–422.

Somlyo, A. P., Devine, C. E., Somlyo, A. V. and North, S. R. (1971). Sarcoplasmic reticulum and the temperature-dependent contraction of smooth muscle in calcium-free solutions. *J. Cell Biol.* **51**, 722–741.

Somlyo, A. P. and Somlyo, A. V. (1968). Vascular smooth muscle. I. Normal structure, pathology, biochemistry and biophysics. *Pharmac. Rev.* **20**, 197–272.

Somlyo, A. P. and Somlyo, A. V. (1970). Vascular smooth muscle. II. Pharmacology of normal and hypertensive vessels. *Pharmac. Rev.* **22**, 249–353.

Stein, J. M. and Padykula, H. A. (1962). Histochemical classification of individual skeletal muscle fibers of the rat. *Am. J. Anat.* **110**, 103–124.

Stolk, A. (1962a). Muscular dystrophy in fishes, amphibians and reptiles. *Acta morph. neer.-skand.* **5**, 117–139.

Stolk, A. (1962b). Muscular dystrophy in lower vertebrates. *Revue can. Biol.* **21**, 445–456.

Subbasow, G. H., Maslow, A. P. and Burnaschewa, D. W. (1964). Vergleichend morphologische und einige histochemische Beobachtungen an besonderen Rezeptoren der Augenmuskeln bei Wirbeltieren. *Anat. Anz.* **114**, 27–37.

Suzdalskaya, I. P. and Kiro, M. B. (1957). The effects of temperature on the excitability of muscle of the turtle *Emys orbicularis. Bull. exp. Biol. Med. USSR* **43**, 28–31.

Szepsenwol, J. (1959). The motor end-plate of a lizard *Anolis cristatellus. Cellule* **60**, 153–167.

Szepsenwol, J. (1960). The neuromuscular spindle in the lizard *Anolis cristatellus. Cellule* **61**, 21–39.

Takeda, J. (1965). Zur Kenntnis der N-haltigen Muskelextraktivstoffe der japanischen Schlange *Natrix tigrina tigrina. J. Biochem.* **57**, 1–6.

Talesara, C. L. (1972). Three types of muscle fibers histochemically identified in the Indian snake, *Xenochrophis piscator. Copeia* **1972**, 176–177.

Talesara, C. L. and Mala, V. (1976). Histochemical analysis of the regional variation of fibre type composition in snake skeletal musculature. *Annls Histochim.* **21**, 321–328.

Talesara, C. L. and Mala, V. (1978). A comparative study of histochemical profile of pectoralis and gastrocnemius muscles of the frog *Rana tigrina*, the lizards *Hemidactylus flaviviridis* and *Uromastix hardwickii* and the turtle *Lissemys punctata. Indian J. exp. Biol.* **16**, 561–564.

Tiegs, O. W. (1932a). A study by degeneration methods of the muscles of a lizard (*Egernia*). *J. Anat.* **66**, 300–322.

Tiegs, O. W. (1932b). The innervation of the striated musculature in *Python. Austr. J. exp. Biol. Med. Sci.* **9**, 191–201.

Tiegs, O. W. (1953). Innervation of voluntary muscle. *Physiol. Rev.* **33**, 90–144.

Totland, G. K. (1976). Three muscle fibre types in the axial muscle of axolotl (*Ambystoma mexicanum* Shaw). A quantitative light- and electron microscopic study. *Cell Tiss. Res.* **168**, 65–78

Trinchese, S. (1891). Contribution à la connaisance des fuseaux musculaires. *Archs ital. Biol.* **14**, 221–230.

Tschiriew, S. (1879a). Sur les terminaisons nerveuses dans les muscles striées. *Archs Physiol. norm. path.*, 2 sér. **6**, 89–116.

Tschiriew, S. (1879b). Études sur la physiologie des nerfs des muscles striées. *Archs Physiol. norm. path.*, 2 sér. **6**, 295–329.

Tsunoo, S., Horisaka, K., Montonishi, K. and Takeda, J. (1964). Über das Ophidin in den Muskeln von den Seeschlangen *Laticauda semifasciata* und *laticaudata. J. Biochem.* **56**, 604–606.

Ullrick, W. C., Toselli, P. A., Chase, D. and Dasse, K. (1977a). Are there extensions of thick filaments to the Z line in vertebrate and invertebrate striated muscle? *J. Ultrastruct. Res.* **60**, 263–271.

Ullrick, W. C., Toselli, P. A., Saide, J. D. and Phear, W. P. C. (1977b). Fine structure of the vertebrate Z-disc. *J. molec. Biol.* **115**, 61–74.

Ushakov, V. B. (1969). The relationship between the resting potential and thermostability of muscle fibers of amphibians and reptiles. *Zh. evol. Biokhim. Fiziol.* **5**, 547–555.

van Gehuchten, A. (1888). Étude sur la structure intime de la cellule musculaire striée chez les vertébrés. *Cellule* **4**, 247–316.

Verratti, E. (1902). Ricerche sulla fine struttura della fibra muscolare striata. *Mem. Ist. lomb. Sci. Lett.* **19**, 87–133. (Transl. and reprinted in *J. biophys. biochem. Cytol.* **10**, suppl. 1, 1–59 (1961).)

Wachholder, K. (1931). Unterschiede in der Fähigkeit "tonischer" und "nichttonischer" Muskeln zur Superposition der Einzelzuckungen bei tetanischer Reizung. *Pflügers Arch. ges. Physiol.* **229**, 143–152.

Wachholder, K. and von Ledebur, J. (1930). Untersuchungen über "tonische" und "nichttonische" Wirbeltiermuskeln. I. Die Umklammerungshaltung des Frosches und die Schutzhaltung der Schildkröte; ihre spezifische Nachahmung durch muskuläre Acetylcholinwirkung. *Pflügers Arch. ges. Physiol.* **225**, 627–642.

Walsh, T. H. and Woledge, R. C. (1970). Heat production and chemical change in tortoise muscle. *J. Physiol., Lond.* **206**, 457–469.

Washio, H. (1973). The effect of glycerol treatment of voltage-clamped snake muscle fibers. *J. gen. Physiol.* **61**, 176–184.

Washio, H. (1974). Effect of external calcium and of temperature on contraction in snake muscle fibers. *J. gen. Physiol.* **63**, 415–431.

Weeds, A. G. (1976). Light chains from slow-twitch muscle myosin. *Eur. J. Biochem.* **66**, 157–173.

Weinstein, J. H. and Ralph, P. H. (1951). Myofilaments from smooth muscle. *Proc. Soc. exp. Biol. Med.* **78**, 614–615.

Wells, J. B. (1965). Comparison of mechanical properties between slow and fast mammalian muscles. *J. Physiol.*, *Lond*. 178, 252–269.

Wilkie, D. R. (1960). Thermodynamics and the interpretation of biological heat measurements. *Progr. Biophys. biophys. Chem.* 10, 260–298.

Wilkinson, H. J. (1929). The innervation of striated muscle. *Med. J. Aust.* 1929, 2, 768–793.

Wilson, P. (1975). Contractile activation, inactivation and repriming in denervated short scale muscles of the garter snake. *Expl Neurol.* 46, 244–256.

Witalinski, W. (1974). Structure of muscle fibres and motor end-plates in the intercostal muscles of lizard, *Lacerta agilis* L. *Z. mikrosk.-anat. Forsch.* 88, 796–808.

Witalinski, W. and Loesch, A. (1976). Structure of muscle fibres and motor end plates in extraocular muscles of the grass snake, *Natrix natrix*. *Z. mikrosk.-anat. Forsch.* 89, 1133–1146.

Woledge, R. C. (1968). The energetics of tortoise muscle. *J. Physiol.*, *Lond*. 197, 685–707.

Woledge, R. C. (1972). In vitro calorimetric studies relating to the interpretation of muscle heat measurements. *Cold Spring Harb. Symp. quant. Biol.* 37, 629–634.

Wyman, J. (1926). Studies on the relation of work and heat in tortoise muscle. *J. Physiol.*, *Lond*. 61, 337–352.

Yakovlev, N. N. (1965). Comparative biochemical estimation of the energetic metabolism of the striated muscles depending on the functional profile. *Ukr. Biokhem. Zh.* 37, 137–150 (reviewed by author with some additional material in 1975).

Yakovlev, N. N. (1975). Biochemistry of sport in the Soviet Union: Beginning, development, and present status. *Med. Sci. Sports* 7, 237–247.

Zacks, S. I. (1973). "The Motor End Plate." 2nd edn., Saunders, Philadelphia.

Zhukov, Ye. K. (1965). Evolution of physiological mechanisms of tonus in the vertebrates. *In* "Essays on Physiological Evolution." (J. W. S. Pringle, hon. ed.). Pergamon Press, N.Y., pp. 339–349.

Zhukov, Ye. K. (1967). Some progress in studying the tonic function of a skeletal muscle. *Zh. evol. Biokhim. Fiziol.* 3, 472–481.

CHAPTER 3

Axial Musculature

J.-P. Gasc

Laboratoire D'Anatomie Comparée
Muséum National d'Histoire Naturelle, Paris

I. Introduction

Recent reptiles are descendants of the first truly terrestrial vertebrates. Invasion of the land posed new mechanical problems and the Amphibia are the group that first provided direct attachments of the muscular bundles to the vertebrae; this tendency continued in the reptiles. The patterns shown by the diverse adaptations of various reptiles are best presented after a brief general description based on embryological and comparative data.

Scleromeric segmentation leads to an alternation of skeletal elements (proto-vertebrae) and muscular blocks (myotomes). The embryological processes in the Sauropsida differ from those in the Anamniota principally in the loss or indistinctness of the horizontal septum in the trunk. Thus, as shown below, the distinction between epaxial and hypaxial muscles requires more than purely topographic criteria. There is, furthermore, no clear separation in later stages between the dorsal segmented mesoblast (myomeric portion) and the ventral unsegmented mesoblast (lateral plate). Earlier workers differ on that topic (compare, for instance, Strauss and Rawles, 1953, with Maurer, 1896), probably because of different topographical interpretations. The mesoblast seems more plastic, possibly due to cellular migration, to judge from results with similar problems in the limb bud.

The complete restructuring of the relatively simple myoseptal arrangement of amphibians represents one of the most striking features of reptilian muscular organization. In fishes the myosepta are complexly folded; this leads to the overlapping of several vertebral segments by one myomere. Most, but not all, muscle fibers are parallel to the long axis. All amphibians have separate deep and superficial muscles. The former attach to the vertebrae and ribs; the latter have only myoseptal attachments. The dorsal expansion of the amniote iliac blade divides the epaxial muscles into a medial (M. transversospinalis and M. longissimus) and a lateral mass (M. iliocostalis). Each mass is internally split into individual musculo-tendinous bundles that span several vertebral segments; the mysoseptal intersections tend to be lost, especially in the medial part of the epaxial region.

Tendencies for delamination into several layers and stretching of bundles (substituting a longitudinal segmentation for the primitive transverse one) characterize the reptilian axial musculature. The distinctions observed among the various groups of reptiles reflect different degrees in the expression of these tendencies.

The general plan here followed is based upon the distribution of the main branches of the spinal nerves. Each spinal nerve emerges between two successive vertebrae and then divides into a dorsal and a ventral ramus, reflecting the old differentiation into episome and hyposome. Such a neural criterion for the epaxial and hypaxial muscles is safer than a purely topographic one, particularly in view of the extreme reduction of the horizontal septum. For instance, the ribs cannot be assumed to represent the old limit, as the absence of any trace of the horizontal septum makes suspect their homology with either the dorsal or the ventral ribs of fishes (Emelianov, 1936). We can distinguish the muscles belonging to each portion of the muscular system by following the neural rami. The muscle masses may be further subdivided by the level at which their innervation departs from the main ramus and by the pattern of their delamination.

The difficulties in the establishment of homologies, and subsequently of the nomenclature (Davis, 1936), are mainly with regard to the hypaxial musculature. This discussion is based on the literature and on my own dissections listed in Table I.

TABLE I

List of species dissected

Testudines
  Cheloniidae: *Chelonia mydas*
  Dermochelyidae: *Dermochelys coriacea*
  Testudinidae: *Geochelone radiata; Testudo graeca*
  Emydidae: *Emys orbicularis; Mauremys leprosa*
  Trionychidae: *Trionyx triunguis*

Crocodilia
  Crocodylidae: *Alligator mississippiensis; Crocodylus niloticus*

Rhynchocephalia
  Sphenodontidae: *Sphenodon punctatus*

Squamata
 Sauria
  Dibamidae: *Dibamus novaeguineae*
  Pygopodidae: *Lialis burtonis; Pygopus lepidopodus*
  Gekkonidae: *Hemidactylus mabouya; Gekko gecko*
  Iguanidae: *Anolis carolinensis; Basiliscus vittatus; Crotaphytus collaris; Ctenosaura acanthura; Iguana iguana; Plica plica; Sceloporus undulatus; Tropidurus torquatus; Uracentron azureum*
  Agamidae: *Agama agama; Uromastyx hardwickii*
  Chamaeleonidae: *Chamaeleo dilepis; C. parsonii*
  Teiidae: *Ameiva ameiva; Bachia intermedia; Cnemidophorus lemniscatus; Tupinambis teguixin*
  Lacertidae: *Lacerta lepida; L. viridis; Nucras tessellata; Ophisops elegans*
  Cordylidae: *Chamaesaura anguina; Cordylus jonesii; Platysaurus intermedius*
  Gerrhosauridae: *Tetradactylus tetradactylus; Zonosaurus madagascariensis*
  Scincidae: *Afroblepharus wahlbergii; Acontias lineatus; A. meleagris; A. plumbeus; Chalcides chalcides; Eumeces schneideri; Feylinia currori; Mabuya quinquetaeniata; Scelotes arenicolor; S. bidigittata; S. brevipes; S. inornata; Typhlosaurus aurantiacus; T. vermis*
  Anguidae: *Anguis fragilis; Barisia coerulea; Ophisaurus apodus*
  Anniellidae: *Anniella pulchra*
  Varanidae: *Varanus griseus; V. niloticus; V. rudicollis*
  Helodermatidae: *Heloderma suspectum*
 Amphisbaenia
  Amphisbaenidae: *Amphisbaena alba; Blanus cinereus; Rhineura floridana*
  Trogonophidae: *Trogonophis wiegmanni*
 Serpentes
  Typhlopidae: *Typhlops punctatus*
  Aniliidae: *Anilius scytale; Cylindrophis rufus*
  Xenopeltidae: *Xenopeltis unicolor*
  Acrochordidae: *Acrochordus javanicus*
  Boidae: *Acrantophis madagascariensis; Boa constrictor; Calabaria reinhardti; Chondropython viridis; Corallus enydris; Epicrates cenchria; Eryx jaculus; Eunectes murinus; Python molurus; P. regius; P. sebae*
  Colubridae: *Coluber viridiflavus; Coronella austriaca; Dasypeltis scabra; Elaphe longissima; Grayia smythii; Heterodon platyrhinos; Malpolon monspessulana; Mehelya capensis; Natrix natrix; N. maura; Oxybelis argenteus; Philodryas viridissimus; Psammophis sibilans; Spilotes pullatus; Xenodon merremii*
  Elapidae; *Dendroaspis jamesoni; Micrurus lemniscatus; Naja haje; N. nigricollis*
  Hydrophiidae: *Laticauda colubrina; Pelamis platurus*
  Viperidae; *Agkistrodon contortrix; Atheris squamiger; Atractaspis bibroni; A. reticulata heterochilus; Bitis arietans; Bothrops alternatus; B. atrox; B. jararacussu; Causus rhombeatus; Cerastes cerastes; Crotalus durissus; C. viridis; Echis carinatus; Lachesis muta; Sistrurus catenatus; Vipera ammodytes; V. aspis*

II. General Organization

A. EPAXIAL MUSCULATURE

1. *General*

The epaxial muscles differs significantly between amphibians and reptiles. This may closely reflect the differences in vertebral mechanics which are much more complex in forms with terrestrial modes of locomotion. It is generally said that the volume of epaxial as compared to hypaxial muscles decreased as cantilevered limbs developed. Nevertheless most reptiles still show horizontal rather than vertical bending of the vertebral column (Olson, 1936; Romer, 1956); the epaxial musculature is particularly important for this and remains extensive. In chamaeleonids, movements of the girdles substitute for bending of the column (Peterson, 1973), and the epaxial musculature is reduced.

Many features of the reptilian vertebro-costal elements reflect muscular attachments or special mechanical devices (Hoffstetter and Gasc, 1969). They relate to actions in which epaxial muscles play an important role.

Works emphasizing the epaxial musculature are those of Nishi (1919) and Vallois (1922) who reviewed them for the vertebrates. Mosauer (1935) and Auffenberg (1958, 1959, 1961, 1962) discussed those of snakes, and Gasc (1965, 1966, 1967a, b, 1968, 1970a) those of amphisbaenians and other snake-like squamates.

The epaxial muscles are devided into three longitudinal columns, namely the medial, central, and lateral one, that run close to the vertebral axis and seem isolated from each other by fibrous sheets (Fig. 1).

2. *The Medial Column or M. transversospinalis Group*

The medial column is innervated by the medial branch of the dorsal nerve ramus. This nerve passes dorsally into the muscles which it innervates and from which it emerges into the subcutaneous area of the back. The M. transversospinalis shows the following three main layers from a medial to a dorsolateral position:

a. a deep layer lies close to the neural spine and neural arch and, in the Squamata, is further differentiated into Mm. interneurales, multifidus, and interarticulares superiores;

b. a middle layer (the M. spinalis) lies dorsal to this, and in it each bundle joins (from rear to front) a medio-dorsal point on the neural spine to a ventrolateral one on the neural arch; and

c. a superficial layer consists of bundles crossing the preceding, i.e. from a posterior point on the zygapophysial wing to an anterior site near the tip of the neural spine, and can be differentiated into the Mm. semispinalis and tendino-articularis.

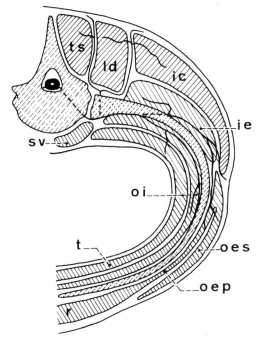

FIG. 1. Schematic transverse section of the muscles in the trunk of a reptile (after Gasc, 1967b). Diagonal lines to the upper right indicate epaxial muscles. Bone is shown stippled. ic, M. iliocostalis; ie, M. intercostalis externus; ld, M. longissimus dorsi; oep, M. obliquus externus profundus; oes, M. obliquus externus superficialis; oi, M. obliquus internus; r, M. rectus; sv, M. subvertebralis; t, M. transversus; ts, M. transversospinalis.

3. *The Central Column or M. longissimus Group*

The lateral branch of the epaxial nerve passes distally within the intercostal space, and then turns dorsally to pass between the central and lateral epaxial columns; halfway up the lateral column it divides into three nerves, the middle one supplying the mass of the M. longissimus. This muscle occupies the space defined by the extremities of the zygapophysial wing, and runs anteriolaterally to attach to a generally flat tendon at the surface of the column.

4. *The Lateral Column or M. iliocostalis Group*

The lateralmost ramus of the lateral branch of the epaxial nerve penetrates the M. iliocostalis. The differentiation of this group of muscles is related to the dorsal extension of the iliac blade (Romer, 1956). It consists primarily of opaque fibers that pass anteriolaterally covering the proximal half of the ribs; most of the myoseptal intersections remain inside this mass.

When differentiated, the mass is divided into a deep M. supracostalis and a more superficial M. iliocostalis; the length of individual bundles of the M. iliocostalis can be considerable, often spanning twenty ribs, particularly in snakes.

B. HYPAXIAL MUSCULATURE

1. *General*

The hypaxial musculature forms much of the body wall and is, therefore, often associated with breathing. However, as some of its elements attach to the skeleton (the deepest and subvertebral layers) or to the skin (the most superficial layers), it is, like the epaxial musculature, also involved in moving the trunk. Most authors classified epaxial and hypaxial muscles differently, probably because they believed that there was a clear functional distinction among these several muscles.

Following the descriptive work of Gadow (1882), the basic classification of hypaxial muscle was established by Maurer (1896, 1898) on the basis of embryological studies. Later Smirnowsky (1930) and Dombrowski (1930a, b) attempted to establish their homologies for all tetrapods upon purely topographical relationships.

The hypaxial Anlage has three main portions (Maurer, 1896, 1898): (1) the medial layer (lamella medialis) that later forms the internal lining of the rib cage, (2) the lateral layer (lamella lateralis) that later covers the outside of the rib cage, and (3) the subvertebral muscle (M. subvertebralis) that runs along the ventral aspect of the vertebral column. The rectus system seems to evolve independently from ventral portions of the first two layers.

2. *The Medial Layer*

The nerve to the medial layer of the hypaxial muscles arises from the ventral ramus (hypaxial nerve) at the origin of the latter and extends along the medial side of the preceding rib to its distal tip. It is distributed to the thin M. transversus, which is often divided into a proximal part with the fibers crossing the ribs (M. subcostalis) and a distal part with the fibers parallel to the ribs. It also reaches the Mm. obliquus internus and intercostalis internus. The latter sometimes consists of two sheets differing in the length of their bundles; these extend obliquely from posterodorsal to anteroventral. The distal tip of the medial nerve reaches both the skin and the M. rectus.

3. *The Lateral Layer*

The M. intercostalis externus lies between successive ribs. The lateral branch of the hypaxial nerve appears proximally, posterior to the costal head, and runs on the dorsal aspect of this muscle. In many limbless forms the proximal part of the M. intercostalis externus may form distinctly differentiated bundles, the Mm. intercostalis quadrangularis and tuberculocostalis. In snakes and amphisbaenians the distal cartilaginous tips of the ribs are united by fibers of the M. intercartilaginosi (Mosauer, 1935) which are scarcely distinct from the M. intercostalis externus. This sheet, which is sometimes called the M. intercostalis ventralis is innervated by the end of the medial branch as is the M. rectus of lizards (see Fig. 23).

The intercostal nerve passes between the preceding layer and the deepest part of the M. obliquus externus (= M. obliquus externus profundus). The latter is generally differentiated into a M. levator costae and various supracostal bundles such as the Mm. supracostales laterales of snakes. In snakes the M. supracostalis lateralis inferior is, surprisingly, not innervated by the intercostal nerve, but by one coming from the medial branch and passing through the M. intercostalis externus (see Fig. 25). This suggests that the M. supracostalis lateralis differentiated, at least in part, from the M. rectus abdominus. The superficial layer (M. obliquus externus superficialis) connects the skeletal elements to the integument. Two types of bundles (Mm. costocutanei superior and inferior) may be recognized in snakes (see Fig. 34). Both are innervated by a twig of the medial branch of the hypaxial nerve, which passes laterally through the intercostal sheet between the Mm. intercostalis quadrangularis and intercostalis externus proprius.

4. *The Subvertebral Layer*
The subvertebral layer is generally restricted to the neck as the M. longus colli. It is especially well developed in snakes in which it is differentiated into long bundles (=M. transversohypapophyseus of Mosauer, 1935) at least in the precardiac region (see Fig. 43).

III. Structural Patterns in Recent Orders

A. TESTUDINES

1. *General*
The muscular organization of turtles differs from that of most reptiles, mainly in relation to their peculiar topography with ankylosed vertebral column and ribs and a specialized head–neck system. The nomenclature used by the earliest authors (Wiedemann, 1802; Cuvier, 1800–05, 1835; Bojanus, 1819–21; Meckel, 1821–33; Rathke, 1848) was based essentially on the human anatomical terms and comparisons with the neck of birds. Later Hoffmann (1879–90) tried to establish synonymies. Ogushi (1911–13) accurately described the muscles, their innervation, and skeletal relations in

Trionyx sinensis. Nishi (1919) and Vallois (1920–22) attempted general reviews of the vertebrate axial musculature, establishing a classification in which the various bundles in the chelonian neck are homologized with those in other reptiles. Furthermore Vallois emphasized systematic differences between the Pleurodira and Cryptodira.

The difference in the type and degree of mobility of the neck among the three major taxonomic divisions of the suborder Cryptodira is here documented by the cervical regions of *Testudo*, *Trionyx*, and *Chelonia*; more species need to be examined before we can adequately characterize the suborder.

2. The Epaxial Muscles of Cryptodires

a. The M. transversospinalis group. The neural distribution near the head is complex, and it is difficult to determine whether bundles belong to the medial or to the middle epaxial column. The attachment of muscles to the nuchal plate of the carapace further confuses the arrangement.

The Mm. interneurales extend anteriorly from one neural arch to the posterior border of the preceding one and fill the space between the neural spines and the zygapophyses. These muscles represent an undifferentiated mass of Mm. interneurales (intercuales). In the Trionychidae a more superficial layer crosses each vertebra, running from a prezygapohysial wing to fuse anteriorly with the deepest layer (Mm. cervicospinales laterales breves dorsales, Ogushi, 1911). This layer seems to correspond to the M. multifidus of squamates.

M. interarticularis superior. The Mm. articulo-transversales longus et brevis (Ogushi, 1911) were described as muscular bundles that span up to four vertebrae, running from the prezygapophyses to the tip of the transverse process. The innervation of the most superficial layer of the epaxial musculature (M. semispinalis in the Cryptodira) passes between the long and the short portions. Both portions may be homologous to the M. interarticularis superior of other reptiles, which is sometimes bicipital in snakes.

Mm. spinalis and semispinalis. The important M. cervicocapitis medialis (Vallois, 1922) spreads superficially between the neural spines of the anterior vertebrae and the skull. The M. testo-cervicalis medialis (Fig. 2) is a muscle of the same layer that links the nuchal plate to the postzygapophysial wings of the cervical vertebrae (except of course the eighth); it attaches only to the third through the fifth vertebrae in the Cheloniidae. Nishi (1919) considered both of these muscles to be parts of the M. spinalis; he called them respectively the Mm. spinalis capitis and testospinalis cervicis. In the Trionychidae the cranial head of the M. spinalis is composite. The anterior

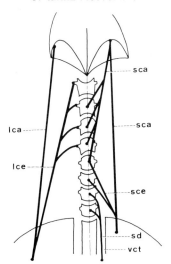

FIG. 2. Diagram of the cervical epaxial muscles in a cheloniid turtle (after Vallois, 1922). The longissimus group are shown on the left and the transversospinalis group on the right. lca, M. longissimus capitis; lce, M. longissimus cervicis; sca, M. spinalis capitis (cervicocapitis medialis); sce, M. spinalis cervicis (testocervicalis medialis); sd, M. spinalis dorsi; vct, vertebro-costal tunnel.

part reaches the posterior hyoid horn and is innervated by hypaxial nerves (M. cervico-hyocapitis, Ogushi, 1911), and the other part is more caudal (M. cortico cervicalis).

The transversospinalis group includes the M. testocapitis medialis (Vallois, 1922; = M. testospinalis capitis of Nishi, 1919) which arises from the nuchal plate and follows the mid-dorsal line of the neck to the skull. It is absent in the Trionychidae. In the Testudinidae and Cheloniidae, it appears to differentiate from the layer formed by the M. cervico-capitis medialis (possibly homologous to the M. spinalis capitis) and the M. testo-cervicalis medialis (possibly homologous to the M. spinalis cervicis).

The interpretation of the sheet underneath the bundles called Mm. articulocrurales longi by Ogushi (1911) and Mm. articuloneurales by Vallois (1922) is difficult. It spreads obliquely from the prezygapophysis of one vertebra to the postzygapophysial wing of the neural spine two or three vertebrae more anteriorly (Figs. 3 and 4). This course is very similar to that shown by the M. semispinalis of squamates and crocodilians. However if these are indeed homologous, a positional inversion of the M. spinalis and M. semispinalis must have occurred, as the former now lies superficial to the latter. Ogushi (1911) calls the most cranial bundle M. rectus lateralis. In mammals, the M. rectus capitis lateralis is homologized to the most anterior bundles of the Mm. intertransversarii laterales, here called the Mm.

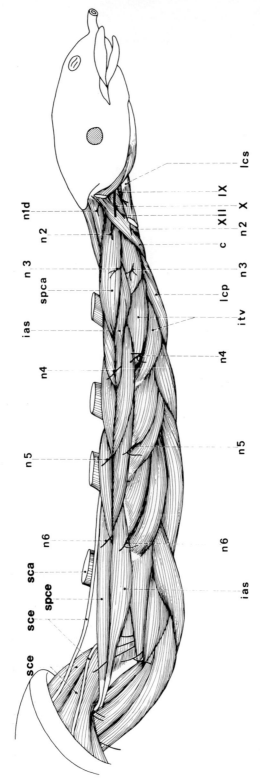

FIG. 3. Lateral view of the superficial cervical muscles of *Trionyx sinensis* (after Ogushi, 1913). c, Part of M. cucullaris (?); ias, M. interarticularis superior; itv, M. intertransversarius ventralis; lcp, M. longus colli profundus; lcs, M. longus colli superficialis; nld, dorsal branch of first spinal nerve; n2–6, second through sixth spinal nerves; sca, M. spinalis capitis; sce, M. spinalis cervicis; spca, M. semispinalis capitis; spce, M. semispinalis cervicis; IX, glossopharyngeal nerve; X, vagus nerve; XII, hypoglossal nerve.

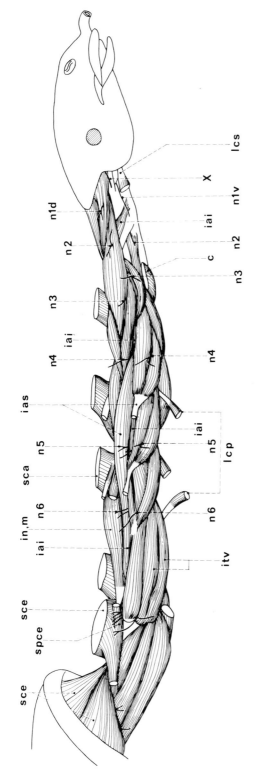

FIG. 4. Lateral view of the deep cervical muscles of *Trionyx senensis* (after Ogushi, 1913). c, Part of M. cucullaris (?); iai, M. interarticularis inferior; ias, M. interarticularis superior; in, m, Mm. interneurales and multifidus; itv, M. intertransversarius ventralis; lcp, M. longus colli profundus; lcs, M. longus colli superficialis; nld, dorsal branch of first spinal nerve; n2–6, second through sixth spinal nerves; sca, M. spinalis capitis; spec, M. semispinalis cervicis; X, vagus nerve.

interarticulares inferiores; these are hypaxial muscles. Therefore, only the
M. epistropheo-atlantis dorsalis (Ogushi, 1911) may logically be homologized with the M. rectus capitis lateralis.

A small muscle, called the M. epistropheo-squamosus dorsalis by Ogushi
(1911) and innervated by the dorsal branch of the first cervical nerve,
spreads between the neural arches of the axis and atlas and the posterior
margin of the skull roof. The muscle has two distinct bellies in *Trionyx*. It
clearly belongs to the occipital muscles and may be homologous to the rectus
capitis posterior major.

b. The M. longissimus group. The M. longissimus group is absent in the
Testudinidae and Trionychidae (Shah, 1963, describes under the name of
M. longissimus cervicis, what I call here the M. interarticularis superior). In
the Cheloniidae a layer of epaxial muscles runs along the neck superficial to
the transversospinalis group. Laterally this fleshy mass arised from the
internal aspect of the carapace just posterior to its anterior edge. It is
subdivided further cranially. The deepest portion (M. testo-capitis lateralis
= M. testotransversalis capitis of Nishi, 1919) reaches the parietal and
squamosal bones. Vallois (1922) homologizes these muscles with the M.
longissimus, an assignment that seems logical. There is, on the contrary,
some difficulty in following Nishi's (1919) decision to incorporate the Mm.
articulo-transversales longi et breves (of Ogushi, 1911) into this system;
these muscles more properly pertain to the M. interarticularis superior. It is
not surprising to find some ambiguity about a region as specialized as the
neck of turtles, particularly concerning the distinction between the Mm.
transversospinalis and longissimus, which are primitively very closely
associated in tetrapods.

c. The M. ilio-costalis group. Turtles lack a lateral column of epaxial
muscles.

3. *Hypaxial Muscles of Cryptodires*

a. General. Most of the hypaxial musculature is associated with the ribs
and body wall. Its arrangement should be simplest in the neck, but it is
difficult to explain in turtles which lack a transition between the trunk and
neck. One can, nevertheless, recognize the major divisions of the hypaxial
musculature known in other amniotes.

b. The lateral layer. Three types of deep segmental muscles (Mm.
intertransversarii) occur in mammals (Lessertisseur, 1968). The dorsalmost
belongs to the episome and is innervated by the dorsal spinal branch; it is
probably homologous to the M. interarticularis superior found in the trunk
of some reptiles. The other two correspond to the Mm. intertransversarii

laterales and ventrales, and are highly differentiated at the level of the craniocervical hinge.

Small bundles of the Mm. intertransversarii ventrales attach to the dorsal aspect of the bases of adjacent transverse processes and pass between the epaxial and hypaxial nerves. Ogushi (1911) calls these Mm. intertransversales (Fig. 5). Anteriorly, the lateral sheet forms the M. epistropheo-atlantis dorsalis and the M. atlanto-opisthoticus, which may be equivalent to the M. rectus capitis posterior of mammals.

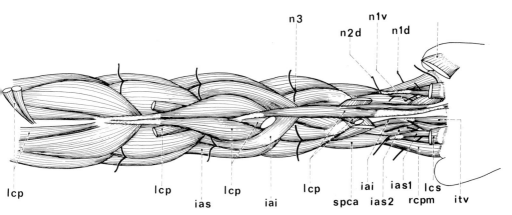

Fig. 5. Ventral view of the cervical muscles of *Trionyx sinensis* (after Ogushi, 1913). iai, M. interarticularis inferior; ias, M. interarticularis superior; iasl, first M. interarticularis superior; ias2, second M. interarticularis superior; itv, M. intertransversarius ventralis; lcp, M. longus colli profundus; lcs, M. longus colli superficialis; nld, dorsal branch of first spinal nerve; nlv, ventral branch of first spinal nerve; n2d, dorsal branch of second spinal nerve; n3, third spinal nerve; rcpm, M. rectus capitis posterior major; spca, M. semispinalis capitis.

c. The subvertebral system. The subvertebral system consists of two layers. The deeper one comprises a pair of bundles that originate from the midventral crest of the centrum by a short tendon and reach forward by fleshy heads to insert on both sides of the ventral crest two vertebrae ahead. The muscles arising from the second and first vertebrae fuse before inserting near the midline on the ventral surface of the basioccipital bone. Ogushi (1911) calls this layer the M. cervico-spinalis medialis; however, it seems advisable to call it a M. longus colli, or more specifically a M. longus colli profundus, to avoid confusion with elements of the epaxial musculature. Each segment is V-shaped the sharp point being the posterior tendinous origin and the legs being the anteriorly directed fleshy insertions. This arrangement is comparable, but inverse, to that of the M. parapophyseo-hypapophyseus (= M. transversohypapophyseus of Mosauer, 1935) in some snakes; that too is a portion of the subvertebral system (*vide infra*).

The two fleshy external and smaller median strips of the M. carapaco-basioccipitalis (Ogushi, 1911) run superficially and symmetrically dorsal to the digestive and respiratory tracts (Figs. 3 and 6). This layer can be considered the M. longus colli superficialis. The several families of cryptodires differ in details of insertion, probably due to the various mechanisms for retracting the neck. These muscles pass laterally from the internal aspect of the carapace and medially from the ventral surface of the pectoral girdle; the bundles reach the posterior processes of the basioccipital bone.

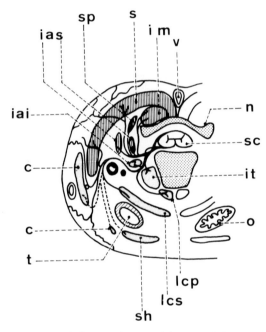

FIG. 6. Transverse section through the posterior part of the neck of *Trionyx sinensis* (after Ogushi, 1913). Epaxial muscles are shown in vertical lines, and hypaxial muscles are shown in outline. c, M. cucullaris; iai, M. interarticularis inferior; ias, M. interarticularis superior; im, Mm. interneuralis and multifidus; it, M. intertransversarius; lcp, M. longus colli profundus; lcs, M. longus colli super-ficialis; n, neural arch; o, oesophagus; s, M. spinalis cervicis; sc, spinal cord; sh, M. sternohyoideus (?); sp, M. semispinalis cervicis; t, trachea; v, median vein.

4. *Epaxial Muscles of Pleurodires*

a. The M. transversospinalis group. The Pleurodira have all the layers found in cryptodires and also the division in two portions (M. spinalis cervicis, M. spinalis capitis), one anterior and the other posterior to a

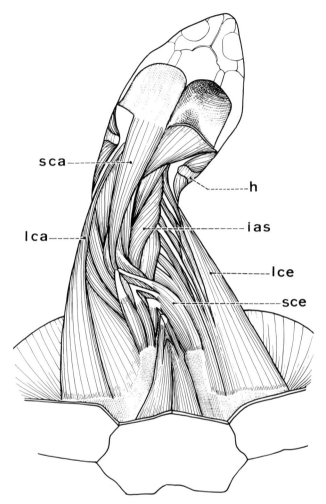

FIG. 7. Dorsal view of the neck of *Pelomedusa subrufa* (after Vallois, 1922). The nuchal and first costal plates have been removed. h, Hyoid apparatus; ias, M. interarticularis superior; lca, M. longissimus capitis; lce, M. longissimus cervicis; sca, M. spinalis capitis; sce, M. spinalis cervicis.

vertebra, generally the fifth cervical. Since this arrangement also occurs in the M. interarticularis superior, Vallois (1922) calls the two parts in the Pelomedusidae the M. transversarius obliquus cervici (from the eighth to sixth cervical to the sixth to fourth cervical) and M. transversarius cervicis (from the fifth to third cervical to the skull; Fig. 7). Pleurodires lack a M. testospinalis capitis (Nishi, 1919) which, in the Testudinidae and

Cheloniidae, follows the mid-dorsal line of the neck from the nuchal plate to the skull.

b. The M. longissimus group. The M. longissimus group originates from three areas, the ventral side of the nuchal plate, the ventral side of the first costal plate, and the anterior border of the first rib (Vallois, 1922). In the Pelomedusidae it forms a single mass distributed by tendons on the successive transverse processes from the fourth up to the first cervical vertebra and on to the skull; its cranial attachment passes ventral to the short suboccipital muscles. The fibers are not divided into two layers, with short deep ones and superficial long ones, as in the Cryptodira.

5. *Hypaxial Muscles of Pleurodires.*

There are relatively few differences between the hypaxial muscles of pleurodires and cryptodires.

The Mm. intertransversarii ventrales consist of two bellies, having a common origin on the ventral aspect of the posterior part of the centrum, near the midline (Fig. 8). The short medial head runs anteriorly to the preceding vertebra and attaches near the base of the posterior edge of its transverse process. The longer lateral head crosses the preceding vertebra to insert on the ventral surface of the transverse process of the next anterior one.

The M. longus colli of pleurodires has two layers, with the M. longus colli profundus being deeper and restricted to the anterior half of the neck. The fibers originate on the ventral keel, pass the anterior part of the centrum, and insert by a laterally tendinous attachment to the lateral portion of the basioccipital blade (Fig. 8).

The M. longus colli superficialis (= M. retractor capitis collique of Shah, 1963) inserts by a flat tendon on the ventral surface of the basioccipital

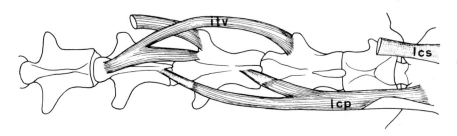

FIG. 8. Ventral view of the anterior part of the neck of *Pelomedusa subrufa*. The head is to the right. Only a few bundles are left so that the exact sites of the attachments are clear. itv, Deep M. intertransversarius ventralis consisting of a long and a short head; lcp, anterior bundle of the M. longus colli profundus which covers the preceding mantle; lcs, longus colli superficialis.

bone, and its fibers arise directly from the dorsal side of the anterior edge of the plastron. When the neck bends laterally, both right and left parts seem to pass on the same side, like the string of a bow.

The muscular organization of the Pleurodira is less complicated and, in some ways, reduced relative to that of the Cryptodira. On the other hand, cryptodires do not retain the horizontal flexure of the neck common among early vertebrates. The differences between suborders are most striking in the transversospinalis group; that of the Cryptodira is much more complex, as the cervical vertebrae of those show vertical flexure, otherwise seen only in birds and mammals.

Both suborders of turtles almost completely lack muscles in the dorsal region. Nevertheless, when the ribs are still distinct the epaxial mass (= M. dorsalis of Vallois, 1920) runs between them and the costal plates to reach the postzygapophyses of the eighth cervical. Some elements of the hypaxial musculature do occur in many forms (Shah, 1963; Gaunt and Gans, 1969; Fig. 9). In the Cheloniidae the different layers of intercostal and oblique muscles form shiny tendinous sheets. Furthermore, the Mm. transversus abdominus and obliquus internus still occur in the posterior part of the

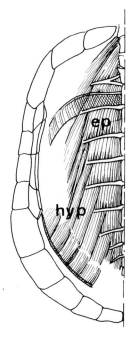

FIG. 9. Internal view of the carapace of *Deirochelys reticularia* (after Shah, 1963). ep, Epaxial muscles; hyp, hypaxial muscles.

carapace in *Testudo* and function in respiratory mechanisms (Gans and Hughes, 1967).

B. CROCODILIA

1. *General*

In early anatomical works (e.g., Cuvier, 1835) the axial musculature is generally treated with and considered similar to that of the Sauria. There are, however, important differences. The trunk is more rigid in the Crocodilia. The skin may be strengthened and reinforced by plates of dermal bone, but their pattern differs drastically from that in anguids and other Sauria. The tail is highly modified as propulsive organ. The trunk muscles show a mixture of scarcely differentiated states (M. longissimus dorsi) and complicated dispositions (M. transversospinalis group). Furthermore the musculature of all crocodilians is similar, whereas the squamates are highly heterogeneous.

The epaxial musculature occupies a significant volume of the trunk. It is firmly connected by a strong aponeurosis to the inner side of the dermis.

The hypaxial musculature, as in most lizards, reflects the subdivision into "thoracic" and "lumbar" subregions (Hoffstetter and Gasc, 1969).

2. *Epaxial Musculature*

a. The M. transversospinalis group. The Mm. interarcuales connect successive neural spines. They are immediately covered by a complicated muscular arrangement, the dorsal indications of which are crossed oblique tendons. The general pattern of this complex (Fig. 10) is best expressed by discussing it as four separate sets of muscular slips, a, b, c, and d.

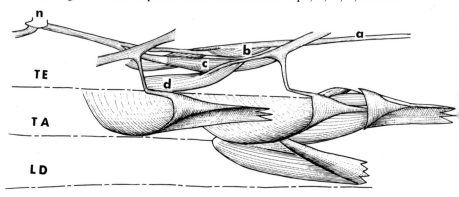

FIG. 10. Lateral view of the epaxial muscles of *Caiman*. Anterior is to the right. a, M. multifidus; b and c, M. spinalis; d, M. semispinalis; LD, M. longissimus dorsi (only one segment is figured); n, neural spine; TA, M. tendino-articularis (the tendinous frame is shown on the left and the muscular fibers of one segment on the right); TE, M. transversospinalis.

The deepest group (a) originates anteriorly by a thin tendon from the base of a neural spine, passes over three vertebrae, and inserts by fleshy fibers into the dorsal aspect of the post-zygapophysial wing of the two following vertebrae. Thus it crosses five segments. Vallois (1922) called this muscle the M. neurospinalis dorsi, interpreting it as a subdivision of the interneural layer, but rejecting its homology with the mammalian M. multifidus. However, it occupies the same place and shows the same arrangement as the M. multifidus; it consists of muscular bundles running obliquely ante-rodorsomedially between the Mm. interneuralis and spinalis. The differences in shape and function between reptilian and mammalian vertebral elements do not allow the use of purely topographical criteria for homology. However the special relationships introduced by differentiation within the main muscular masses are indeed similar. I shall, therefore, use the term M. multifidus for the superficial part of interneural layer which tends to be differentiated into bundles crossing over two or more vertebrae. Deep to it, strong bundles join the successive zygapophysial joints. Vallois calls them Mm. interarticulares dorsi. I consider them to be the Mm. interarticulares superiores, as they form the deepest part of the dorsal layer.

A thin tendon arises from the anterior side of the tip of a neural spine, crosses anterolaterally over two vertebrae, and is divided into an internal and an external slip. The internal slip passes over two more vertebrae and then becomes fleshy. Some fibers are attached to the tendon of the M. multifidus (group a) while others reach the neural arch (group b). The external slip is prolonged by fleshy fibers (group c) which, after crossing over two vertebrae, reach the tendon of the superficial layer.

In view of the disposition of the M. transversospinalis in other groups (e.g., the Squamata), it seems logical to homologize groups b and c to the M. spinalis. The internal part conserves the most primitive relationship; the external part shows a tendency illustrated by the M. spinalis in many Squamata.

Only the anterior end of the superficial layer (M. semispinalis = group d) attaches to bone. A relatively wide tendon fixed to the dorsal surface of the neural spine obliquely covers the muscles from groups a, b, and c from front to rear and laterally. At the level of the following vertebra it divides into two branches. The external one extends transversely to the internal tip of the arrow-like tendon of the M. tendino-articularis; the internal branch passes over one vertebra, receives the fleshy fibers of group c (external head of the M. spinalis), and is joined by the fleshy belly of group d, which crosses over two posterior vertebrae to insert on the lateral branch of the anterior origin of the muscles associated with the third vertebra more posteriorly (Fig. 10). The internal organization of the M. transversospinalis is thus marked by the interlinking of the different layers as well as by the fusion of bellies and tendinous continuity; bony insertions are limited.

This pattern is particularly striking in view of the differentiation of a lateral layer, the M. tendino-articularis, unknown in other reptiles. This layer shares an innervation with the M. semispinalis. The latter forms a longitudinal column set between the zygapophyses and the costal articulations. Superficially it appears as a succession of anteriorly pointing tendinous arrows. To explain its rather complicated spatial distribution, I must first describe its tendinous framework. The posteromedial tip of the arrow, joined to the anterior tendon of the group, is actually the exposed edge of the medial septum of the M. tendino-articularis. The posterolateral tip similarly represents the emergence of the lateral septum. This extends under the muscular fibers to reach the medial side of the column, forming a floor for the latter. The sharp point of the tendinous arrow belongs to a raphe which passes deep to the preceding arrow, separated from it by the muscular mass.

The muscular fibers lie inside the space described by those tendinous walls. Distally they are slightly oblique dorsoventrally, a small, distinct bundle joining the posteromedial tip of the arrow to the external tendon of the preceding group d (Fig. 10); ventrally, their obliquity is the inverse. Within the mass some fibers join the anterior raphe to the preceding one. The whole system crosses over four vertebral segments.

   b. The M. longissimus group. Superficially the column of the M. longissimus is marked by a succession of flat, V-shaped tendons. The larger external branch reaches the skin and the surface of the M. iliocostalis; the internal branch fuses with the posterolateral tip of the arrow from the M. tendino-articularis. The elementary units are conical; the strongly oblique, tendinous base faces anteriorly and receives the internal surface of the preceding cone. The fibers converge posteriorly to insert on the distal aspect of the diapophyses. Each cone extends over three vertebral segments (Fig. 10).

   Within the muscle, some fibers, which lie close to the deepest fibers of the corresponding cone, connect successive diapophyses. As these belong to the epaxial musculature, and even to the M. longissimus group, they have been called the Mm. intertransversarii dorsi by Vallois (1922). Such a term recalls the dorsal parts of the Mm. intertransversarii cervicis of mammals which are better compared with the Mm. interarticulares superiores of the reptilian trunk. However, the latter are a portion of the M. transversospinalis (represented in crocodilians and turtles by the Mm. articulo-transversales of Ogushi, 1911). As these bundles are so close to the M. longissimus, it does not seem useful to give them a special name.

   The disposition of the Mm. intercostales externi and M. obliquus muscular fibers fill the space between two successive myosepta. The whole column lacks any special connections with the M. longissimus.

3. *Hypaxial musculature*

The M. transversus, with its thin sheet of fibers, does not show any remarkable features compared to the generalized reptilian plan described above; it spreads proximodistally along the ribs.

The M. obliquus internus consists of bundles joining the proximal part of each rib to the internal surface of the rectus system. It forms a continuous sheet in the lumbar region.

Mm. intercostales interni also conform to the usual plan.

The disposition of the Mm. intercostales externi and M. obliquus externus, which form the lateral layer, is relatively simple in the Crocodilia; there is no differentiation of this muscle near the proximal or distal portion of the ribs, nor in its cutaneous relations (Fig. 11).

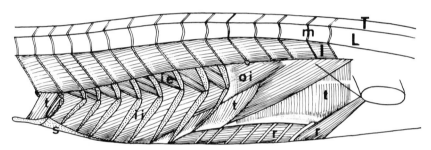

FIG. 11. Lateral view of *Crocodylus niloticus* showing the deeper hypaxial muscles (after von Wettstein, 1937–54). Anterior is to the left. L, M. iliocostalis; ie, M. intercostalis externus; ii, intercostalis internus; L, M. longissimus; oi, M. obliquus internus; r, M. rectus; s, sternum; T, M. transversospinalis; t, M. transversus.

There is no subvertebral system posterior to the powerful M. longus colli, the origin of which is marked on the skeleton by hypapophyses.

C. LEPIDOSAURIA IN GENERAL

The patterns of axial musculature within the extremely diverse Lepidosauria are highly variable. Authors generally studied the axial muscles of but a single order or suborder and devised special terminologies for each. The great plasticity of the muscular system, especially in the Squamata, is due both to its important role in motion and to the great variety of lepidosaurian locomotor adaptations. Limb reduction will obviously require increased participation by the vertebral column in locomotion. It is possible to establish the muscular characteristics of limbless forms. Among the snakes one may also characterize the major systematic divisions and the adaptive radiations.

D. RHYNCHOCEPHALIA

1. General

The axial muscles of *Sphenodon* have been described by Maurer (1896), Nishi (1919), and Byerly (1925) and reviewed by Wettstein (1931). They are classically characterized by the permanence of the myomeric segmentation. Few bundles cross more than one vertebrocostal segment, and most of the epaxial mass is feebly differentiated.

2. Epaxial Musculature

   a. The M. transversospinalis group. The medial layer of the M. transversospinalis is composed of interneural fibers which show no trace of differentiation into isolated bundles.

   The middle (M. spinalis) and lateral (M. semispinalis) layers are quite distinct; their fibers form acute angles with each other and cross more than two segments. The bundles of the M. semispinalis take their posterior origin from a tendinous sheet attached to the lateral side of the postzygapophyses. The succession of these sheets forms a continuous wall between the columns of the M. transversospinalis and the M. longissimus. The anterior tendons pass medially to the neural spines; their attachments to those surfaces reflect the pattern of the more lateral myosepta. The fleshy fibers of the M. spinalis are attached to the medial aspect of these tendons (Fig. 12). Before their tendinous attachment to the neural spine they send laterally other small tendons. These tendons join a tendinous bridge between the anterior myoseptal sheet, on which the M. longissimus inserts, and the more posterior insertion of another bundle from the M. semispinalis.

   b. The M. longissimus group. The M. longissimus remains partially segmented in the trunk, as shown by the continuous tendinous inscriptions on its surface. The superficial fibers are disposed longitudinally inside the space bounded by the neighbouring myosepta and the more lateral M. iliocostalis. Deeper in the bundle, the fibers cross three vertebral segments; passing posteromedially, they insert on the anterior side of a prezygapophysial wing.

   c. The M. iliocostalis group. The lateral epaxial mass, the iliocostalis, is the largest and shows complete segmental division by myosepta which are rather elevated and folded posteriorly (Fig. 12).

   The main bundles of each epaxial column have complex relations with the

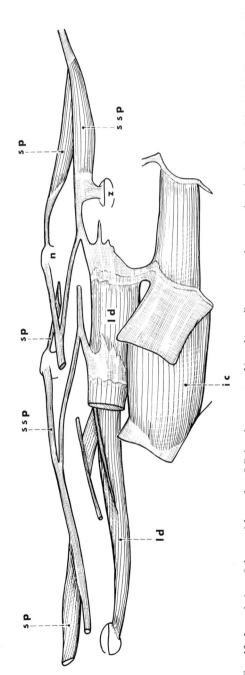

FIG. 12. Lateral view of the epaxial muscles of *Sphenodon punctatus*. Note the tendino-myoseptal system. Anterior is to the right. ic, M. iliocostalis; ld, M. longissimus dorsi (the deepest fibers cross three vertebral segments); n, neural spine; sp, M. spinalis; ssp, M. semispinalis; z, zygapophysial joint.

bundles belonging to the other columns. Thus the muscular pattern is the same from the neural spine to the base of the uncinate process. This same pattern occurs in the squamates (e.g., *Pygopus*, Fig. 21), particularly the linking by the tendinous sheet of the M. longissimus, which appears homologous to the anterior tendon of the same muscle in the Squamata.

3. Hypaxial Musculature

a. General. Sphenodon shows only a few specializations in its hypaxial musculature. These are mainly due to the morphology of the ribs, which bear uncinate processes, and the occurrence of a system of gastralia within the M. rectus abdominis.

b. The medial layer. The M. transversus extends dorsoventrally from the level of the uncinate processes dorsally to the midventral line ventrally.

The more superficial M. obliquus internus forms a continuous sheet ventrally with a serrated dorsal limit, while its dorsal part is composed of bundles extending over two intercostal spaces, between the ventral surface of one vertebra and a more anterior rib. The M. intercostalis internus is differentiated into two layers. Dorsally, bundles of the M. intercostalis externus longus originate on the anterior edge of one rib and extend anteriorly and ventrally to the posterior edge of another rib, passing over two segments. Muscular fibers of the M. intercostalis internus brevis spread from the head to the tip of successive ribs close to their internal aspect.

c. The lateral layer. The lateral layer consists of six different muscles (Byerly, 1925, Fig. 13). The deepest are the M. intercostalis externis brevis

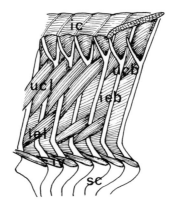

FIG. 13. Lateral view of the superficial hypaxial muscles of *Sphenodon punctatus* (after Byerly, 1925). ic, M. iliocostalis (epaxial); ieb, M. intercostalis externus brevis; iel, M. intercostalis externus longus; iv, M. intercostalis ventralis; sc, sternocostal segment of ribs; ucb, M. uncinocostalis brevis; ucl, M. uncinocostalis longus.

(proprius) and the M. uncino-costalis brevis, a small bundle from the uncinate process to the following rib. In the superficial layer, the M. intercostalis externus longus lies ventrally, and the M. uncio-costalis longus covers the space between the M. iliocostalis and the preceding muscle. Fibers of both the intercostalis externus longus and the M. uncio-costalis longus span two intercostal spaces. Distally, short bundles of the M. intercostalis ventralis link the adjacent, paddle-like extremities of the ribs. The tip of the paddles are joined by fibers of the M. abdomino-costalis which joins the rectus-gastralia system.

The M. abdomino-costalis can be compared with the costocutaneus inferior of the Squamata, which belongs to the M. obliquus externus superficialis. Similarly, the M. intercostalis ventralis, which also occurs between the tips of ribs in some squamates (M. intercartilaginosus of Mosauer, 1935, in snakes), is considered to belong to the rectus system because of its innervation. This region is complex so there are difficulties in attributing the muscles to one or the other of Maurer's (1896) lamellae.

The M. obliquus externus profundus is a thin sheet formed by fibers originating on the uncinate processes and inserting posteroventrally on the lateral side of the rectus.

The M. obliquus externus superficialis covers the M. obliquus externus profundus ventral to the uncinate processes from which it originates. It inserts directly in the inner side of the skin and can be considered a costocutaneous muscle.

Maurer (1896) described a trunk muscle, the M. intercostalis internus dorsalis longus, which is continuous anteriorly with the M. longus colli and posteriorly with the so-called M. quadratus lumborum. Each constituent bundle originates on the ventral surface of a vertebra and runs ante-rolaterally to insert on a rib near the base of the uncinate process. Wettstein (1931) referred to this muscle as the M. ilio-costo-costalis as did Byerly (1925), while others have called it the M. retrahens costarum. The description corresponds exactly to the dorsal part of the M. obliquus internus. The question is not purely one of terminology. Camp (1923), who uses the term M. intercostalis internus dorsalis longus, considers this muscle to be part of the M. subvertebralis because it is innervated by the ventral branch of the ventral spinal nerve. In fact, all the derivatives of the medial layer also possess this type of innervation (see section on General Organization above). Furthermore, when all the hypaxial constituents occur in the trunk, as in those snakes with hypapophyses in the postcardiac subregion, the bundles differentiated from the M. subvertebralis, which originate medially on a vertebra, point obliquely posterolaterally, i.e., the reverse orientation of the bundles in the dorsal part of the M. obliquus internus which cover them ventrally. One can, therefore, assume that the subvertebral system is lacking in the trunk of *Sphenodon*.

The midventral surface of the vertebral column is covered by a strong tendon.

E. SAURIA

1. *General*

The vast diversity of locomotor, feeding, and other patterns in lizards is responsible for the differences observed in the muscular arrangement around the vertebral column and ribs. Despite Camp's (1923) attempt, the present state of our ignorance keeps us from using such characteristics in systematics. Even adaptive aspects are difficult to disentangle from the great amount of variation which occurs, sometimes even within a single family of lizards. The classical descriptions of lizards remain those of Mivart (1867, 1870) and Sanders (1870).

2. *Epaxial Musculature*

a. The M. transversospinalis group. Except in some rare limbless forms in which the Mm. multifidus and interarticularis superior become distinct (Fig. 14), the deep layer is poorly differentiated.

Fibers of the M. spinalis generally cross three vertebrae. The muscle arises from the side of the neural arch by a short tendon, often with two short heads, one of which lies farther dorsally on the neural spine. Anteriorly the M. spinalis reaches the posterior edge of a postzygapophysial wing; sometimes it fuses with the M. semispinalis (Fig. 14).

The individual bundles of the middle layer are always longer than those of the deep layer. Each has a fleshy origin from the wing of a postzygapophysis and extends anteriorly and dorsomedially to a neural spine. As stated above, the M. semispinalis sometimes receives fibers from the M. spinalis. In the Pygopodidae, there is a linkage between the most superficial fibers of the M. semispinalis, which sometimes receives fibers from the M. spinalis, and the medial branch of the iliocostalis tendon (Fig. 21). This arrangement, already noted in *Sphenodon* (Fig. 12), is also characteristic of colubrids among the snakes.

b. The M. longissimus group. In the Sauria the M. longissimus does not show myomeric segmentation. Nevertheless the most generalized arrangement is directly derivable from that found in *Sphenodon*. It is characterized by a deep posterior origin on the tip of the postzygapophysial wing from which it courses anterolaterally to the superficial anterior tendon. This tendon is divided into two sheets. The medial one contributes to the thin superficial aponeurosis covering the column of the M. transversospinalis,

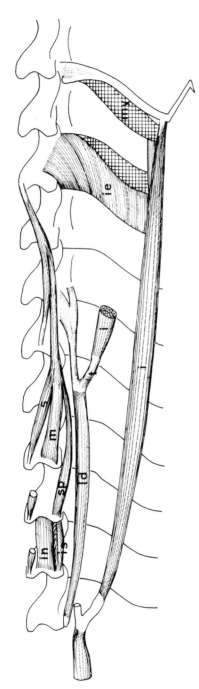

Fig. 14. Lateral view of the epaxial muscles of the scincid *Feylinia currori* (after Gasc, 1967b). Anterior is to the right. i, M. iliocostalis; ie, M. intercostalis externus (especially thick); in, M. interneuralis; is, M. interarticularis superior; ld, M. longissimus dorsi; m, M. multifidus; my, myoseptum; s, M. spinalis; sp, M. semispinalis; t. bifurcated anterior tendon of the M. longissimus dorsi.

and the lateral is continued by the origin of a bundle of the M. iliocostalis. The bundles are rarely very long; most span seven to eight segments. The length of the tendinous part relative to the total length of the bundle varies, being longest in apodous anguids. As each bundle covers the preceding, the surface of the column of the M. longissimus appears segmented because of the succession of anterior tendons. In varanids the anterior ends of the bundles insert on the dorsal surfaces of the ribs by thin tendons; there are no bifurcated tendons (Fig. 15).

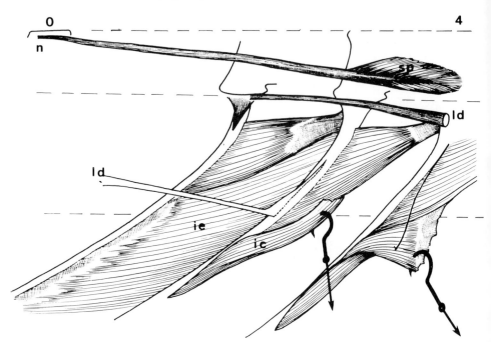

FIG. 15. Lateral view of the epaxial muscles of the varanid *Varanus griseus*. The numbers mark the vertebral segments. ic, M. iliocostalis; ie, M. intercostalis externus; ld, M. longissimus dorsi; n, neural spine; sp, M. spinalis.

c. *The M. iliocostalis group*. The Sauria show a wide range of iliocostal arrangements from the myomeric (similar to that in *Sphenodon*) to multisegmental longitudinal bundles (similar to those in snakes). Vallois (1922) speculated that the loss of myoseptal inscriptions and the shift to a longitudinal segmentation were related to the serpentine type of loco-motion, but this relationship is not always shown. Many limbless forms (*Pygopus, Anguis, Ophisaurus*) keep those inscriptions in the lateral portion of the column of the M. iliocostalis, while such quadrupedal forms as *Mabuya* lack them (Fig. 16). Examination of the course of an individual bundle shows that the inscriptions are related to the shape of the myosepta (cf. Gasc, 1967, b; Fig. 20) and to the thickness of the intercostal layer set in the interseptal space. Besides, the length of the bundles is greater in those limbless species in which some inscriptions remain (ten vertebral segments in *Pygopus* and *Ophisaurus*, nine in *Anguis* and eight in *Chalcides*, as opposed to nine in *Feylinia*, seven in *Acontias meleagris*, and three in *Typhlosaurus vermis*, the latter being especially snake-like). As the bundles are simply juxtaposed in lizards, possibly the conservation of the myoseptal inscriptions assures the attachment of the muscles to the costal frame when the body is bent laterally. However, the complicated spatial relations between successive bundles in snakes simultaneously permit much elongation with the absence of inscriptions.

The arrangement in varanids is quite unusual in that differentiation is transverse rather than longitudinal. Each bundle covers the ribs, as do the Mm. serrati of mammals (Fig. 17).

3. Hypaxial Musculature

a. The medial layer. The M. transversus is always very thin and intimately joined to the peritoneum.

The M. obliquus internus is weakly differentiated into a dorsal and a ventral portion. In the anterior part of the costal frame the M. intercostalis internus is often divided into unisegmental (M. intercostalis internus brevis) and multisegmental (M. intercostalis internus longus) bundles. The former are restricted to the dorsal parts of the ribs. In the posterior part of the frame (i.e., the lumbar region), the free ribs are short or absent and the Mm. intercostales interni longi form a continuous sheet that reaches the pelvic girdle and is analogous to the M. retractor costae ultimae of mammals.

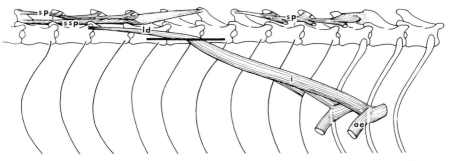

Fig. 16. Lateral view of the epaxial muscles of the scincid *Mabuya quinquetaeniata.* Anterior is to the right. The Mm. iliocostalis and longissimus are not continuous, but separated by a strong fibrous sheet. i, M. iliocostalis; ld, M. longissimus dorsi; oe, M. obliquus externus; sp, M. spinalis; ssp, M. semispinalis.

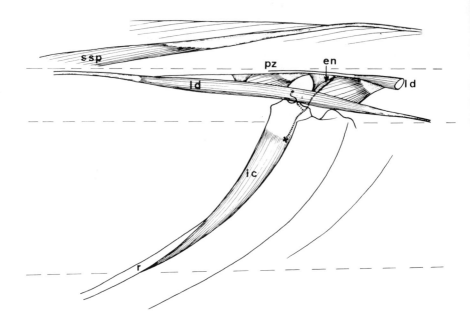

Fɪɢ. 17. Lateral view of the epaxial muscles of the varanid *Varanus griseus*. Anterior is to the right. en, Epaxial nerve; ic, M. iliocostalis; ld, M. longissimus dorsi; pz, prezygapophysis; r, rib; ssp, M. semispinalis.

   b. The lateral layer. The M. intercostalis externus is typically formed of two sheets. The M. intercostalis externus brevis consists of short intercostal bundles and tends to be differentiated dorsally (as in a M. intercostalis quadrangularis with more oblique fibers). A series of superficial supracostal bundles forms a M. intercostalis externus when, as in *Feylinia* (Fig. 18), the M. obliquus externus forms only a single sheet (Gasc, 1967b).
   The M. obliquus externus consists of two sheets in the anterior portion of the rib cage. The deep and generally long one originates on the last two presternal ribs; the superficial arises on the first pair of sternal ribs. Both sheets occur in the Lacertidae and Iguanidae (Smirnowsky, 1930). Only the superficial occurs in the Scincidae and Varanidae, and only the deep in Agamidae and Gekkonidae. Posteriorly, the M. obliquus externus, which is more or less subdivided, reaches the lateral process of the pubis.
   c. The subvertebral system. As in *Sphenodon*, the M. subvertebralis is restricted to the neck where it forms a M. longus colli. A tendinous strip lies along the ventral surface of the vertebral column in the trunk region.

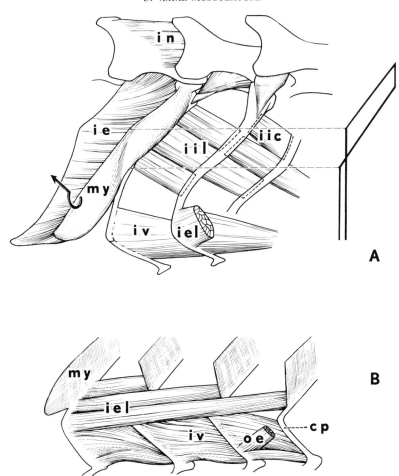

Fig. 18. Lateral views of the intercostal muscles of the scincid *Feylinia currori* (after Gasc, 1967b). A shows the anterior part of the trunk and B the posterior part; anterior is to the right. cp, Parasternal cartilage; ie, M. intercostalis externus proprius; iel, M. intercostalis externus longus; iic, M. intercostalis internus brevis; iil, M. intercostalis longus; in, M. interneuralis; iv, M. intercostalis ventralis; my, myoseptum; oe, M. obliquus externus.

d. The rectus abdominis problem. Camp (1923) stated that a M. rectus superficialis was characteristic of the families of lizards including limbless species (his group Autarchoglossa). His major argument was functional: he predicted that such a muscular sheet on the inner aspect of the ventral skin was necessary for limbless locomotion. However, as he himself emphasized, some Ascalabota (*Uromastyx, Physignathus, Leiolepis*) also have a M. rectus superficialis; furthermore, the assignment of the pygopodids to the Gekkota

(Underwood, 1957) places limbless forms among the Ascalabota. The role of the M. rectus abdominus in undulation is far from obvious. Consequently, neither development nor differentiation of the M. rectus system are clearly related to either systematic or functional considerations, although the presence of a parasternal apparatus does introduce special conditions for the M. rectus profundus, as this then continues posteriorly as an intercostal sheet between the ventral chevrons. Posterior to the chevron region the muscular bundles join the tips of the ribs; they show an arrangement similar to that of the Mm. intercartilaginosi (Mosauer, 1935) in snakes.

4. Special Adjustments in the Limbless Sauria

a. General. Morphologically, limblessness is related to the lengthening of the body; functionally, apodous locomotion is performed mainly by lateral undulations of the body, and not by the action of appendages. Many authors have treated the problem in general, but they give few details concerning the axial muscles. In reviewing this problem, Auffenberg (1962) noted the lack of such data. Sewertzoff (1931) and Stokely (1947) were more concerned with the relative transformation of body parts, and Gans (1962) with the analysis of the mechanical basis of limbless locomotion. Gasc (1967a,b,c; 1968) attempted to fill the gap with osteological and myological studies of several apodous lizards, and to consider the problem from a general evolutionary point of view (Gasc, 1970b).

All follow the general saurian pattern, but some general features may briefly be summarized here.

b. Epaxial musculature. Transversospinalis: Links between the different layers are often present. In some scincids, *Feylinia*, the pygopodids, and *Dibamus*, the M. spinalis joins and fuses with the M. semispinalis anteriorly. The crossed pattern of tendons disappears and the whole system is inserted anteriorly by a single tendon (Fig. 19). When it is completely differentiated,

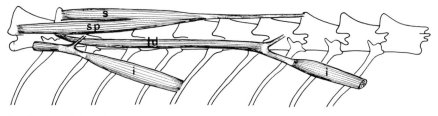

FIG. 19. Lateral view of the epaxial muscles of the dibamid *Dibamus novaeguineae* (after Gasc, 1967b). Anterior is to the right. i, M. iliocostalis; ld, M. longissimus dorsi; s, M. spinalis; sp, M. semispinalis.

the M. multifidus is also associated with this system (Fig. 14). Thus the tendency toward the formation of deep intervertebral muscles covered by a layer of musculotendinous chains, seen generally in the Sauria, is fully expressed in the apodous forms.

Longissimus: Again there is only a simple modification of the pattern derived from that of *Sphenodon*. In snake-like lizards, the length of the constituent bundles is generally larger (up to 10 segments in *Ophisaurus*; Fig. 20). The most striking feature is the linkage with adjacent masses, especially the continuity with the M. iliocostalis via the lateral tendon and even medially with the M. semispinalis (as in *Pygopus*; Fig. 21).

Sometimes the tendinous portions of the bundles are much elongated (e.g., in *Ophisaurus*). The deep posterior origin shows a tendency to be more punctiform, even set on a special process of the prezygapophysial wing (e.g., in *Dibamus*).

Iliocostalis: The M. iliocostalis contains fibers which are generally lengthened; remarkable exceptions occur, for instance in *Typhlosaurus* and *Dibamus*. The greatest length is seen when the fibers remain interrupted transversely by myosepta in a part of their course (*Anguis, Ophisaurus, Pygopus*, and *Chalcides*; Fig. 22), that is when the fibers are bound to the ribs between their extremities. However, even when myosepta persist in part of the M. iliocostalis, the transverse segmentation of an indistinct mass is clearly replaced by a longitudinal subdivision into individual bundles.

c. Hypaxial musculature. Medial layer: there are no special modifications of the Mm. transversus, obliquus internus, or intercostalis internus that can clearly be related to limblessness.

Lateral layer: The hypaxial muscles lying mainly on the rib cage are, on the other hand, modified in many snake-like forms.

The sheets of the M. obliquus externus form supracostal bundles which are often thick. Superficially, connections are sometimes established with the skin, especially when a parasternum is absent. In *Dibamus*, the M. obliquus externus is highly differentiated dorsally. Each constituent bundle arises by a short tendon on the prezygapophysial process; its fibers spread laterally and posteriorly on the dorsal quarter of the next posterior rib. As a similar muscle, the M. levator costae, is present in the Amphisbaenia and Serpentes, its occurrence can be related to a high degree of limblessness.

Subvertebral system: Even in the most snake-like lizards, there is no peculiar development of the subvertebral muscles posterior to the region where the vertebrae bear hypapophyses; furthermore, there is no relation between the extension of this region and the level at which the heart is located (Gasc, 1967c).

Thus it is difficult to define a precise and unique muscular pattern related

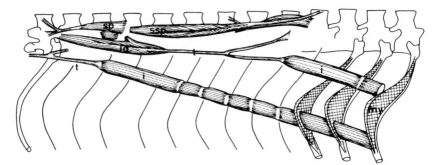

Fig. 20. Lateral view of the epaxial muscles of the anguid *Ophisaurus apodus* (after Gasc, 1967b). Anterior is to the right. i, M. iliocostalis; ld, M. longissimus dorsi; my, myoseptum; sp, M. spinalis; ssp, M. semispinalis; t, bifurcated anterior tendon of the M. longissimus.

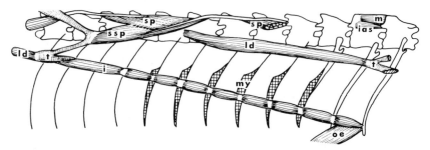

Fig. 21. Lateral view of the epaxial muscles of the pygopodid *Pygopus lepidopodus* (after Gasc, 1967b). Anterior is to the right. i, M. iliocostalis; ias, M. interarticularis superior; ld, M. longissimus dorsi; m, Mm. multifidus and interneuralis; my, myoseptum; oe, M. obliquus externus; sp, M. spinalis; ssp, M. semispinalis; t, anterior tendon of the M. longissimus linking it with the Mm. semispinalis and iliocostalis.

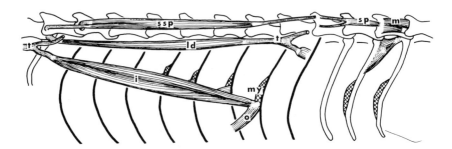

Fig. 22. Lateral view of the epaxial muscles of the scincid *Acontias meleagris*. Anterior is to the right. i, M. iliocostalis; ld, M. longissimus dorsi; m, Mm. multifidus and interneuralis; my, myoseptum; o, M. obliquus externus; sp, M. spinalis; ssp, M. semispinalis; t, anterior tendon of the M. longissimus.

to the absence of limbs and correlated lengthening of the trunk. However, beyond the different modalities due to taxonomic differences, general features or tendencies can be recognized. When all the Squamata are compared, certain trends that are emphasized in snake-like lizards find their full expression in the snakes themselves: differentiation within the inner layer of the M. transversospinalis, formation of musculo-tendinous chains, and concentration of the insertions on certain skeletal sites.

F. AMPHISBAENIA

1. *General*

The typical vermiform shape of the subterranean amphisbaenians might suggest a very peculiar muscular organization. However, Smalian (1885) showed that the homology of their axial muscles could be established by comparison with limbless lizards and snakes. His work remains the basic one on the subject; his comparative data are largely from Heusinger (1833) and Humphry (1872), and he used the method of homologizing later employed by Gegenbaur (1896). Since Smalian's time much more has been learned about the axial muscles of limbless squamates, so it is necessary to discuss some of his proposed homologies and to extend his observations.

2. *Epaxial Musculature*

a. General. When amphisbaenians (especially the Amphisbaenidae) are skinned, a relatively thick muscular layer is taken off; this represents the cutaneous muscles. The axial muscles appear rather indistinct, except near the mid-dorsal line where tendons are clearly visible.

b. The M. transversospinalis group. In the trunk, neural spines are absent, and a strong vertical septum extends above the neural arches which are covered on each side of the septum by a muscular sheath. The short fibers usually extend from the dorsal part of one neural arch to the posterior edge of the preceding one. These represent the Mm. interneurales. Laterally the layer is divided by a strong tendon set on the posterior edge of the neural arch; two muscular bellies insert on this tendon.

The lateral belly crosses two vertebrae and reaches a tendinous sheet attached to the prezygapophysial process of the third vertebra posteriorly. Smalian (1885) homologized this bundle to the M. multifidus, but with hesitation because its course is the reverse of the typical course of this muscle in the other squamates (extending posteromedially to its insertion in a neural spine). He tried to justify this anomaly by the absence of neural spines, but this is difficult to accept because the other muscles normally linked to the neural spines, the Mm. spinalis and semispinalis, do not show

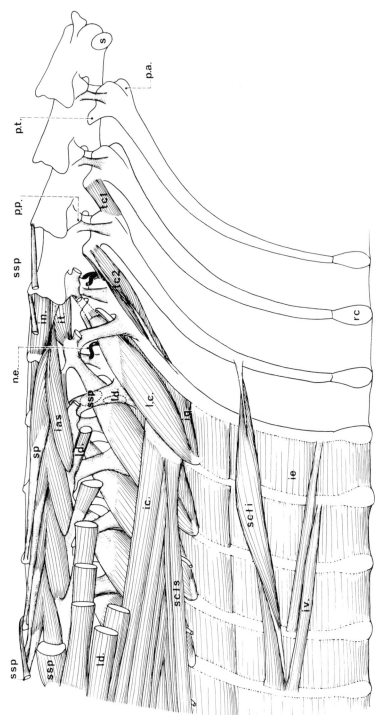

FIG. 23. Lateral view of the axial muscles of *Amphisbaena alba*. Anterior is to the right. ias, M. interarticularis superior; ic, M. iliocostalis; ie, M. intercostalis externus; in, M. interneuralis; iq, M. intercostalis quadrangularis; it, M. intertransversarius; iv, M. intercostalis ventralis; lc, M. levator costae; ld, M. longissimus dorsi; ne, epaxial nerve; pa, anteroventral process of rib; rc, cartilaginous ventral end of rib; s, costal facet of vertebra; scli, M. supracostalis ventralis inferior; scls, M. supracostalis ventralis superior; sp, M. spinalis; ssp, M. semispinalis; tcl, deep part of M. tuberculocostalis; tc2, superficial part of M. tuberculocostalis.

any modifications in their courses. I think that this bundle represents the M. interarticularis superior. Comparison with snakes allows the recognition of the ventral portion of this muscle. This is often bicipital (the so-called M. digastricus; Mosauer, 1935) and also joins the posterior edge of a neural arch to the prezygapophysial tendinous complex, near the origin of the M. longissimus dorsi (as in *Xenodon*, Fig. 29). The M. multifidus is not differentiated in the deep part of the transversospinalis group.

The second belly, attached on the medial aspect of the tendon described above, extends posteriorly over one vertebra and becomes tendinous; it is inserted two vertebrae posteriorly, on the side of the posterior tip of the neural arch (a possible remnant of the neural spine). This is the M. spinalis. Thus, in the amphisbaenians, the linkage within the transversospinalis group, which is characteristic of snake-like forms, is shown between the lateral part of the deep layer (M. interarticularis superior) and the middle layer (M. spinalis). Laterally the Mm. interneurales become Mm. intertransversarii between successive prezygapophysial processes (Fig. 23).

The superficial layer, the M. semispinalis, consists of bundles attached to the dorsal tip of the neural arch by a tendon. This extends posteriorly over six vertebrae and becomes fleshy, to insert mainly on the tendinous sheet which joins the prezygapophysial process to the proximal part of the preceding rib (Fig. 23). The total length of the individual bundles is 12 segments in the middle of the trunk. The succession of the tendons is reponsible for the silvery appearance near the mid-dorsal line.

c. The M. longissimus group. The column formed by the M. longissimus is not clearly visible on the surface. Each bundle has a deep tendinous origin from the posterior border of a prezygapophysial process; it passes anteriorly over four vertebrae, reaching the oblique tendinous sheet between a prezygapophysial process and the proximal part of the preceding rib. The fibers are attached to this sheet, lateral to the insertion of the M. semispinalis. Amphisbaenians lack the anteriorly bifurcate tendon present in so many Sauria and even, in rudimentary form, in *Sphenodon*.

d. The M. iliocostalis group. The most lateral part of the epaxial muscles consists of thin lamellar bundles which originate superficially, close to the anterior insertion of the M. longissimus dorsi. Each bundle crosses over six ribs and inserts on a rib, near the most lateral level of the attachment of the M. levator costae. There are no myoseptal inscriptions.

3. Hypaxial Musculature

a. The medial layer. There are two portions of the M. transversus. The pars ventralis consists of a very thin sheet extending transversely from the middle of the ribs to their ventral ends; the medial half of the rib is covered

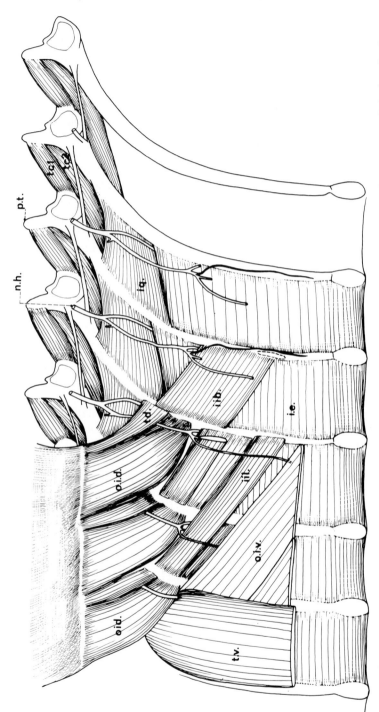

FIG. 24. Medial view of the axial muscles of *Amphisbaena alba*. Anterior is to the right. ie, M. intercostalis externus; iib, M. intercostalis internus brevis; iil, M. intercostalis internus longus; iq, M. intercostalis quadrangularis; nh, hypaxial nerve; oid, M. obliquus internus pars dorsalis; oiv, M. obliquus internus pars ventralis; pt, posterodorsal process of rib; tcl, deep part of M. tuberculocostalis; tc2, superficial part of M. tuberculocostalis; td, M. transversus pars dorsalis; tv, M. transversus pars ventralis.

by thick bundles which originate from a rib and reach posteriorly to the aponeurosis at the midventral line. The course of the medial branch of the hypaxial nerve permits the recognition of the most medial part as the M. transversus pars dorsalis with the nerve passing ventral to it (Fig. 24). Both probably correspond to the Mm. retrahentes costarum of Smalian (1885).

Ventral to the M. transversus pars ventralis a very thin sheet of oblique fibers spans two intercostal intervals from the ends of the ribs to their midpoints. These fibers represent the M. obliquus internus pars ventralis.

Deep to the Mm. transversus and obliquus internus are two kinds of intercostals. The fleshy ribbon-like M. intercostalis internus longus extends obliquely posteromedially over two segments, from the distal quarter of a rib to the level at which the M. obliquus internus pars dorsalis inserts.

The M. intercostalis internus brevis, a wide and almost square sheet, fills the intercostal space between the levels of the origins and insertions of the long intercostal muscles (Fig. 24).

In the amphisbaenians, therefore, the medial layer is fully differentiated.

b. The lateral layer. The M. intercostalis externus brevis is differentiated proximally into a M. intercostalis quadrangularis, with oblique fibers between the shafts of successive ribs, and a M. tuberculocostalis, which consists of two bundles. A deep bundle extends from a posterodorsal process to the anteroventral process of the following rib, and a more superficial one reaches from the posterodorsal process to the proximal quarter of the shaft to the following rib (Fig. 23; see also Gasc, 1968, Fig. 14, and Hoffstetter and Gasc, 1969, Fig. 62).

The M. obliquus externus includes the M. levator costae, which arises by a tendon from the posterior aspect of a prezygapophysial process and spreads ventrolaterally over the following rib ventrally to the level of the anterior insertion of the M. iliocostalis. The same pattern is found in *Dibamus* (Fig. 19; see also Gasc, 1967a, 1968, Fig. 14) and snakes. Closely connected to the anterior insertion of the M. iliocostalis, a ribbon-like bundle spreads over six intercostal spaces to insert in the subcutaneous muscular sheath. This is the M. supracostalis lateralis superior and is also a part of the M. obliquus externus profundus. The successive bundles of the Mm. iliocostalis and supracostalis lateralis superior look like chevrons jointed anteriorly (Fig. 23). More ventrally the ribs are covered by a thick supracostal sheet: the M. supracostalis lateralis inferior the constituent bundles of which cross five intercostal spaces as they extend posteroventrally from a tendon on the posterior border of a rib to a fleshy insertion not far from the end of a rib. Each bundle covers a following one in the anterior part of its course and is covered posteriorly by the same bundle, the path of the fibers being helicoidal.

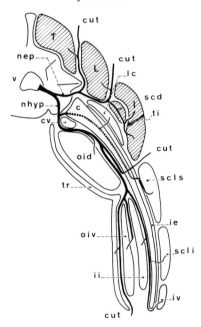

FIG. 25. Schematic transverse section of the muscles in the trunk of a snake (after Gasc, 1971). Compare with Fig. 1. Epaxial muscles are hatched. c, Rib; cut, cutaneous nerve; cv, M. costovertebrocostalis; I, M. iliocostalis; ie, M. intercostalis externus; ii, M. intercostalis internus; iv, M. intercostalis ventralis; L, M. longissimus; lc, M. levator costae; nep, epaxial nerve; nhyp, hypaxial nerve; oid, M. obliquus internus pars dorsalis; oiv, M. obliquus internus pars ventralis; scls, M. supracostalis ventralis pars dorsalis; scli, M. supracostalis ventralis pars ventralis; ti, intermediate tendon of M. iliocostalis; tr, M. transversus; v, vertebra.

Between the last muscle and the cartilaginous tips of the ribs (possibly homologous to sternocostal elements), small flat bundles cross anterolaterally over three intercostal spaces. I call these the Mm. intercostales ventrales, using this term only in a topographic sense, for the homology with the muscles of the same kind in the snakes (probably derived from the rectus) is not sure. Smalian (1885) considered them simply as a third part of the M. obliquus abdominis externus.

The M. obliquus externus superficialis is probably totally included within the subcutaneous sheath, which has no direct relation with the axial skeleton.

c. The subvertebral system. As in the Sauria, the subvertebral muscles of amphisbaenians are restricted to the cervical region as the M. longus colli. Their posterior limit is probably related to the number of vertebrae bearing hypapophyses, but I could not check forms like *Ancylocranium* in which there are no hypapophyses posterior to the third vertebra.

G. SERPENTES

1. General

The earliest descriptions of the muscular anatomy of snakes are those of Tyson (1682–83) and d'Alton (1834); a recent review is that by Lüdicke (1962–64). The division of snakes into three major types, boids, vipers, and colubrids, used by Cuvier (1835) and emphasized by Mosauer (1935), is hardly the current view (Bellairs and Underwood, 1951; Underwood, 1967; Hoffstetter, 1968); it does not seem to correspond strictly to the patterns of muscular organization. Some features underlined as characteristic of one of those types are shown also by snake-like lizards (for instance the linkage between the Mm. semispinalis and longissimus), and Auffenberg (1958, 1966), who increased the number of snakes studied among the smaller families (*Sanzinia*, *Chersydrus*), thought it necessary to recognize variant subtypes within each of Mosauer's types. I think that it is impossible to make an intelligent comparison of snakes by themselves without considering the entire order Squamata. A recent study is that of Pregill (1977).

A diagrammatic cross-section of the axial muscles of a snake is shown in Figure 25.

2. Epaxial Musculature

a. The M. transversospinalis group. The different states of union between the three layers of the M. transversospinalis have been stressed by Auffenberg (1961) who tried to establish a morphological sequence among them, describing this as a series from the completely fused to the fully

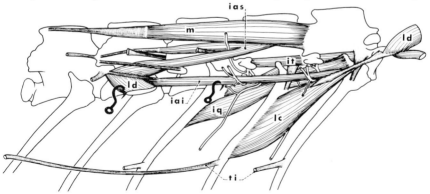

FIG. 26. Lateral view of the deep axial muscles of the colubrid *Coluber* (after Gasc, 1967b). Anterior is to the right. iai, M. interarticularis inferior; ias, M. interarticularis superior; iq, M. intercostalis quadrangularis; it, M. intertransversarius; lc, M. levator costae; ld, M. longissimus dorsi; m, M. multifidus; ti, anterior tendon of the M. iliocostalis.

differentiated state. However, as already noted for other Lepidosauria, the undifferentiated state (i.e., one in which the deep layer forms a simple interneural sheet) must be distinguished from the fused state (in which the bundles of the Mm. multifidus or interarcularis superior span more than one segment and are joined at one end to the Mm. spinalis or semispinalis). Therefore I consider the different modalities of union as tendencies expressed in different lines.

The M. multifidus appears generally to be the basic element; it is a single, triangular bundle which originates posteriorly by a tendon from the lateral surface of the dorsal edge of a neural spine and inserts anteriorly by fibers on the posterior border of a postzygapophysial wing (Fig. 26).

In boids, fibers from the interneural layer join the medial aspect of the M. multifidus. Laterally, the M. spinalis always reaches the flat posterior tendon of the M. multifidus. There, the Mm. multifidus and spinalis are so closely connected that it is difficult to know to which one the tendon belongs: it could represent the posterodorsal tendon of the M. spinalis found in some Sauria (Fig. 20).

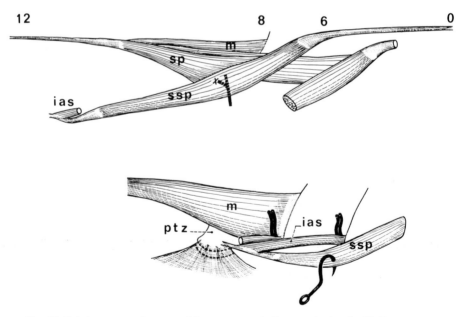

Fig. 27. Relations among the parts of the transversospinalis group in the viperid *Cerastes cerastes* (after Gasc, 1974). Vertebral intervals are indicated on the top part; the lower shows the tendinous fan attached to the postzygapophysis and forming an apononeurosis between the Mm. transversospinalis and longissimus. ias, M. interarticularis superior; m, M. multifidus; ptz, postzygapophysial wing; sp, M. spinalis; ssp, M. semispinalis.

The M. interarticularis superior is always well differentiated, and its constituent bundles are multisegmental. It originates by a tendon from the posterior border of the postzygapophysial wing, lateral to the fleshy insertion of the M. multifidus. It consists of two bellies in many species, and not only in colubrids as reported by Mosauer (1935). The nerve of the M. transversospinalis passes between both bellies at their separation. The dorsal (medial) belly runs longitudinally posterior to the lateral surface of a

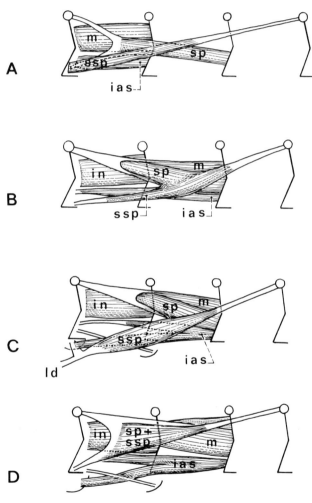

FIG. 28. Principal arrangements of the transversospinalis group in limbless squamates (after Gasc, 1974). A, Apodous anguid; B, viperid or elapid; C, colubrid; D, boid; ias, interarticularis superior; in, M. interneurales; ld, end of the dorsal branch of the anterior tendon of the M. longissimus dorsi; m, M. multifidus; sp, M. spinalis; ssp, M. semispinalis.

postzygapophysial wing (Fig. 26). In *Cerastes* and boids it joins the tendon of the M. semispinalis (Fig. 27). In *Crotalus* and *Tropidophis* it is absorbed by the M. multifidus (Auffenberg, 1961).

The ventral (lateral) belly runs ventrally from anterior to posterior, passing the zygapophysial articulation (except in *Cylindrophis* in which it is the shortest belly and inserts on the postzygapophysial wing). It may attach to the prezygapophysial process directly (e.g., in the colubrid *Grayia*) or, more commonly, after a tendinous intersection of the M. longissimus dorsi and often the M. semispinalis; therefore the ventral belly of the M. interarticularis superior tends to insert on the tendon of the M. longissimus (Fig. 28).

The evolutionary significance of the relationships between the M. interarticularis superior and the neighboring muscles is not as simple as

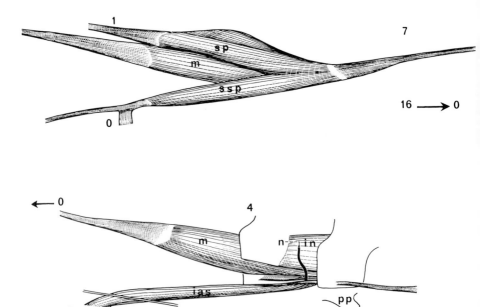

FIG. 29. Relations among the parts of the transversospinalis group in the colubrid *Xenodon merremii* (after Gasc, 1974). The numbers indicate the number of vertebral segments spanned by parts of the musculo-tendinous system. The top drawing shows the relations among the Mm. multifidus, spinalis, and semispinalis; the lower those among the Mm. multifidus, interneurales, and interarticularis. iai, M. interarticularis inferior; ias, M. interarticularis superior; in, M. interneuralis; m, M. multifidus; n, nerve to the transversospinalis group; pp, prezygapophysial process; sp, M. spinalis; ssp, M. semispinalis.

Auffenberg (1961) assumed. *Anilius*, *Eryx*, *Tropidophis*, and especially *Chondropython*, all members of the Henophidia (sensu Underwood, 1967), show much more similarity on this point with *Coluber* than do some Caenophidia, such as *Homalopsis* and *Xenodon* which lack the dorsal belly (Fig. 29). Thus, in this feature, contrary to the statement of Weaver (1965), *Xenodon* and *Heterodon* do not resemble the viperids at all closely.

The connection between the Mm. interarticularis superior and longissimus dorsi in *Anilius*, which resembles that in *Coluber*, does not indicate a process of "colubridization", but only reflects the great development of the prezygapophysial process; this feature is characteristic of some Caenophidia as well as those Henophidia in which lateral mobility is important in determining vertebral mechanisms (Gasc, 1971, 1974).

b. The M. longissimus group. The relationships and the general shape of the M. longissimus dorsi are strikingly stable among snakes (and even squamates) except the Scolecophidia. From a deep origin on the lateral tip of a prezygapophysial wing, it forms a fleshy vertical sheet of the whole longissimus column. The differences among the diverse forms of snakes are marked only by the various linkages with the neighboring muscular groups and by the ratio between tendinous and fleshy parts. Following the general tendency, noted by Vallois (1922), the constituent bundles can be continuous laterally with the M. iliocostalis (Fig. 30) and medially with the M. semispinalis (Fig. 31). The situation of the M. longissimus, set between the medial (M. transversospinalis) and lateral (M. iliocostalis) masses, favors the formation of musculo-tendinous chains, by linking of the constituent bundles with intermediate tendons. I call a series of such individual chains, repeated from anterior to posterior along the trunk, a musculo-skeletal pattern (Fig. 32); however, the continuity is never complete. In colubrids, for instance, a transverse tendinous ribbon always attaches the tendon uniting the Mm. longissimus and semispinalis to the prezygapophysial process. When the ribbon is short, the bundles look as if they were independently inserted on the process, thus resembling the henophidian and viperid patterns. Mosauer (1935) thought it possible to distinguish several types of colubrids, A, B, and C, based precisely on the degree of looseness of attachment to the prezygapophysial process: free continuity in type A, continuity with the attachment to the tendinous sheet in type B, and a fleshy origin of the M. semispinalis in type C.

Underwood (1967) also emphasized this classification, but it is based on too minor a feature and one which is difficult to observe objectively. As noted above there is no free continuity of the muscles and the vertebrae, and the attachment is always performed by a tendinous ribbon (Fig. 31), which, more or less loose, forms the base of the septum isolating the M. longissimus

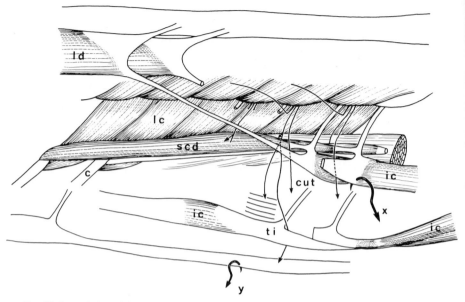

FIG. 30. Lateral view of the epaxial muscles of the boid *Python sebae* (after Gasc, 1974). The bundles of the M. iliocostalis have been turned laterally at X so that the medial surface is seen; one bundle of the M. iliocostalis is shown in lateral view (Y). c, Rib; cut, cutaneous nerve; ic, M. iliocostalis; lc, M. levator costae; ld, M. longissimus dorsi; scd, M. supracostalis dorsalis; ti, intermediate tendon of M. iliocostalis.

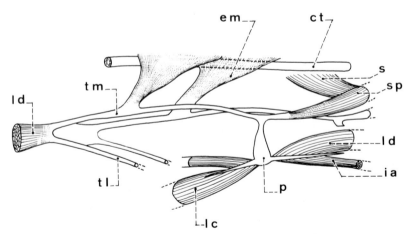

FIG. 31. Lateral view of the tendinous system linking the epaxial muscles of the colubrid *Coluber viridiflavus* (after Gasc, 1967b). Anterior is to the right. ct, Cord formed by tendons of M. semispinalis; em, superficial membranous fan; ia, M. interarticularis inferior; lc, M. levator costae; ld, M. longissimus dorsi; p, tip of prezygapophysial process; s, M. spinalis; sp, M. semispinalis; tl, lateral branch of anterior tendon of the M. longissimus dorsi; tm, medial branch of anterior tendon of the M. longissimus dorsi.

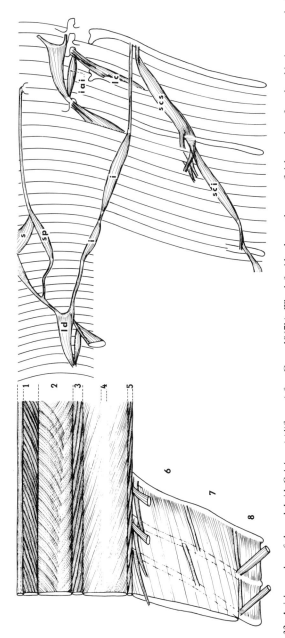

Fig. 32. Axial muscles of the colubrid *Coluber viridiflavus* (after Gasc, 1967b). The left side shows the superficial muscles after the skin is removed; the right side shows details of the musculoskeletal pattern. Lining up the two sides shows the origin of the superficial pattern. i, M. iliocostalis; iai, M. interarticularis inferior; lc, M. levator costae; ld, M. longissimus dorsi; s, M. spinalis; sci, M. supracostalis inferior; scs, M. supracostalis lateralis superior; sp, M. semispinalis.

from the M. transversospinalis. Therefore types A and B correspond only to a vague degree of looseness.

The differences observed in the ratio between fleshy and tendinous parts are more interesting, and probably have a functional basis. For instance, among colubrids, in the American vine-snake *Oxybelis*, as in the Asiatic *Ahaetulla*, the tendons are three to five times longer than the fleshy portions, but the ratio is the reverse in the rather aquatic *Grayia* (Fig. 44).

c. The M. iliocostalis group. For the M. iliocostalis group also, a more extensive survey leads me to criticize the statements of Mosauer (1935; that the M. iliocostalis = M. retractor costae biceps) and of myself (Gasc, 1967b, p. 96). The constituent bundles of the M. iliocostalis, arising from the lateral branch of the anterior tendon of the M. longissimus to reach anterolaterally to a rib, are not always formed by two bellies separated by a short tendon (cf.

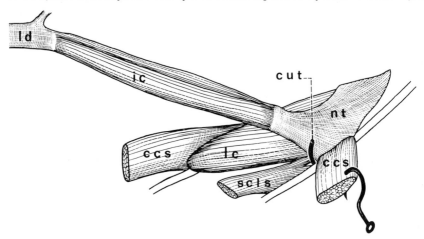

Fig. 33. Relationships of one bundle of the M. iliocostalis in the aniliid *Cylindrophis rufus* (after Gasc, 1974). ccs, M. costocutaneous superior; cut, cutaneous branch of the medial hypaxial nerve; ic, M. iliocostalis; lc, M. levator costae; ld, anterior tendon of the M. longissimus dorsi; nt, superficial tendinous sheet; scls, M. supracostalis lateralis superior.

Gasc, 1967b, Fig. 23). In some cases (e.g., Xenopeltidae and Aniliidae, Fig. 33), there is no essential difference from the arrangement seen in some limbless lizards like *Feylinia*; i.e., uninterrupted bundles are simply juxtaposed (Fig. 14) and span fewer than ten segments (seven in *Cylindrophis*; eight in *Xenopeltis*).

However, in most snakes an intermediate tendon is present, although it is minute in some cases (viperids), and is generally joined to the adjacent rib. The total length of both bellies can be considerable (20 to 25 segments), and their course is helical, each bundle being covered posteriorly by the next posterior bundle and covering the same bundle anteriorly.

Inversion of the spatial relations between the M. longissimus and the caudal belly of the M. iliocostalis occurs at the level of the lateral tendon of the former which appears woven.

Nishi (1919) and later Vallois (1922) tried to interpret the presence of two successive bellies in each bundle of the M. iliocostalis. If the muscles of a segment are specifically innervated by the nerve of the same segment (see Cunningham, 1890; Haines, 1936; Strauss, 1946; and many others), there may be either a mononeural or a diploneural supply for these bundles. In the former case, a bundle results entirely from the lengthening of unisegmental (myomeric) elements; in the latter, it results in part from the fusion of successive segments, and the intermediate tendon represents a myoseptum. Unfortunately both patterns are found (Gasc, 1967b, 1970a).

In boids the diploneury is the rule (Fig. 34): each belly is supplied by a different spinal nerve, and the distance between them is about six segments. Thus the parts of the muscular system supplied by one spinal nerve can be considered as a unit; i.e., in place of the musculo-skeletal pattern, the neuro-muscular pattern can be studied (Fig. 35).

Thus each nerve may supply first the posterior belly of a bundle and secondly the anterior belly of a bundle which originate six segments posterior to the first. In viperids, elapids, and hydrophiids (Fig. 36), a simple nerve supplies both bellies (mononeury), and the pattern of distribution is simple (Fig. 37).

Colubrids possess a complex system formed by an interlacing between pairs of successive nerves. The branches innervating the bellies thus arise from true plexuses, so that the area supplied by one nerve exceeds one segment (Fig. 38).

Aniliids and *Xenopeltis* possess only a single belly in each bundle of the M. iliocostalis; it may be homologous with the anterior or with the posterior belly of other forms. The type of anterior attachment and the relationships with the M. levator costae recall the complicated intermediate tendon of boids (Fig. 33). This suggests that the anterior belly of the latter is a new structure and so supplied by a different nerve, and that in opisthoglyphs and proteroglyphs the anterior belly is secondarily supplied by the original nerve which, in the colubrids, tends to pass into the territory of the neighboring segment.

Such an interpretation is tempting and recalls the evolutionary series of Xenopeltidae-Boidae-Viperidae-Colubridae proposed by Underwood (1967), but very important methodological obstacles prevent its easy acceptance. First, such a series is really a morphological one and not evolutionary, because all those forms are contemporaneous; secondly; the series is based on the conception of a linear arrangement of forms; and, thirdly, the direction of the line supposes a causal linkage between the neural

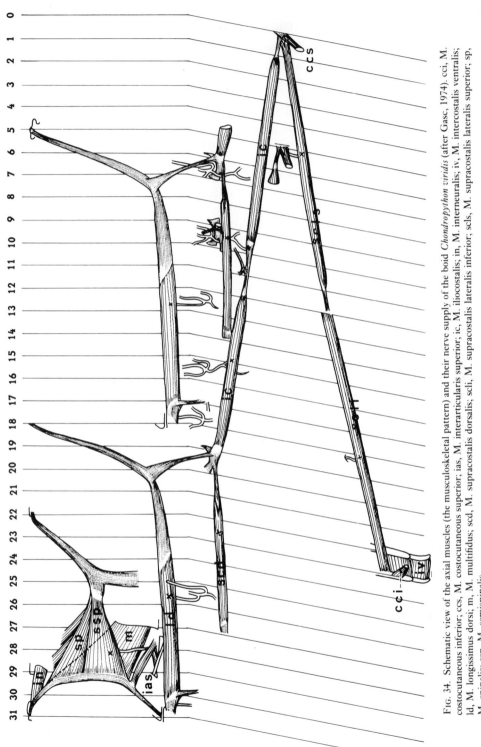

Fig. 34. Schematic view of the axial muscles (the musculoskeletal pattern) and their nerve supply of the boid *Chondropython viridis* (after Gasc, 1974). cci, M. costocutaneous inferior; ccs, M. costocutaneous superior; ias, M. interarticularis superior; ic, M. iliocostalis; in, M. interneuralis; iv, M. intercostalis ventralis; ld, M. longissimus dorsi; m, M. multifidus; scd, M. supracostalis dorsalis; scli, M. supracostalis lateralis inferior; scls, M. supracostalis lateralis superior; sp, M. spinalis; ssp, M. semispinalis.

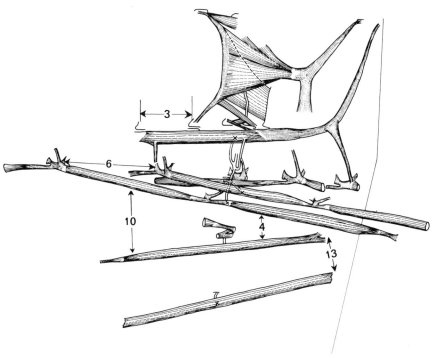

FIG. 35. Neuro-muscular pattern showing the spacial extension of the territory supplied by a nerve in the boid *Chondropython viridis* (after Gasc, 1974). The numbers indicate the segments between the attachments of successive elements supplied by the same nerve; they are greatest laterally, between the Mm. supracostales ventrales inferior and superior. For the identification of the muscles see Fig. 34.

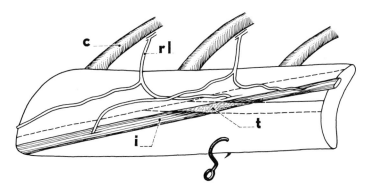

FIG. 36. Nerve supply of the M. iliocostalis in the viperid *Atheris squamiger* (after Gasc, 1967b). The entire iliocostalis system is drawn laterally by its dorsal edge to expose its medial aspect; anterior is to the right. c, Rib; i, one bundle of the M. iliocostalis; rl, lateral branch of the epaxial nerve; t, intermediate tendon of the M. iliocostalis.

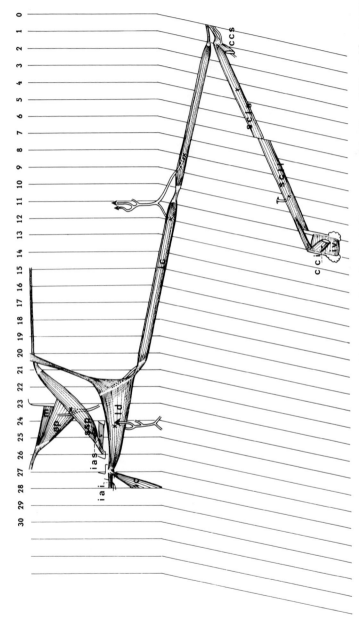

FIG. 37. Schematic lateral view of the musculoskeletal pattern and its nerve supply in the viperid *Cerastes cerastes* (after Gasc, 1974). cci, M. costocutaneous inferior; ccs, M. costocutaneous superior; ic, M. iliocostalis; iv, M. intercostalis ventralis; lc, M. levator costae; ld, M. longissimus dorsi; m, M. multifidus; scli, M. supracostalis lateralis inferior; scls, M. supracostalis lateralis superior; sp, M. spinalis; ssp. M. semispinalis.

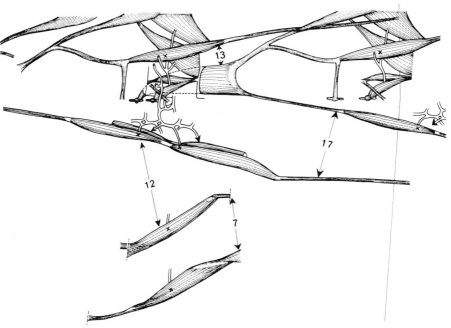

FIG. 38. Neuro-muscular pattern of the axial muscles in the colubrid *Coluber viridiflavus* (after Gasc, 1974). The numbers indicate the segments between the attachments of successive elements supplied by the same nerve; they are greatest in the epaxial mass between the Mm. semispinalis and longissimus and the Mm. longissimus and iliocostalis. For the identification of the muscles, see Fig. 32.

pathways and the muscular organization, which is not proved. Finally, I do not think that the question of the nerve supply to the M. iliocostalis can be separated from the other different features shown in the various parts of the musculo-skeletal apparatus.

d. The M. supracostalis dorsalis problem. Nishi (1919) described an epaxial muscular column lying on the ribs of *Python*, deep to the dorsal part of the iliocostalis. Mosauer's (1935) work figured this muscle in boids, but surprisingly the occurrence of this special muscle was not considered in the discussion. The term he used, M. supracostalis dorsalis, is unfortunate because it recalls bundles of the hypaxial muscles called the M. supracostalis lateralis (= part of the M. obliquus externus). Nevertheless, it is easiest to keep this name. As its innervation is by the iliocostalis nerve, which passes through the column (Fig. 39), this muscle is probably best considered to be a differentiated slip of the iliocostalis group, which appears, therefore, to be most complicated in the Boidae and Xenopeltidae.

The constituent bundles originate from a rib and extend anteriorly over

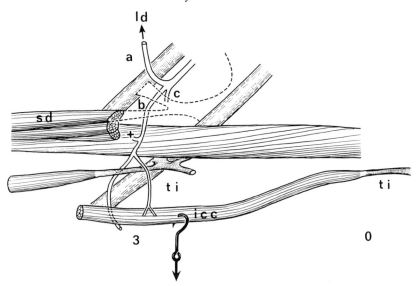

FIG. 39. Schematic view of the musculo-skeletal pattern of the epaxial muscles and its nerve supply in the boid *Chondropython viridis* (after Gasc, 1974). Anterior is to the right. a, Branch of epaxial nerve to M. longissimus dorsi; b, branch of epaxial nerve to Mm. iliocostalis and supracostalis dorsalis; c, cutaneous branch of epaxial nerve (cf. Fig. 25); icc, posterior part of bundle of M. iliocostalis; lc, M. longissimus dorsi; sd, M. supracostalis dorsalis; ti, intermediate tendon of the M. iliocostalis.

six segments (five in *Xenopeltis*) to join the posterior tendinous origin of the M. iliocostalis (Fig. 30).

3. *Hypaxial Layer*

a. The medial layer. The Mm. transversus and obliquus internus (= M. costalis internus of Mosauer, 1935) both show a clear-cut division into dorsal and ventral portions, the fibers of each portion being joined at the level of the middle of the ribs. The medial branch of the hypaxial nerve runs between the Mm. transversus and obliquus internus at the level of the anterior insertions of their respective dorsal portions (Fig. 45).

In the dorsal portion, the fibers of the M. transversus run obliquely from posteromedial to anterolateral, crossing the ribs; in the ventral portion the fibers are fewer and parallel to the ribs (Fig. 40). In most snakes the full development of the M. transversus is seen only in the postcardiac region.

The M. obliquus internus is generally thicker than the former (Fig. 41) except in some forms with thick body walls (e.g., *Grayia*; Fig. 44). Its dorsal and ventral portions have been called, respectively, the M. costalis internus superior and M. costalis internus inferior by Mosauer (1935). The term M.

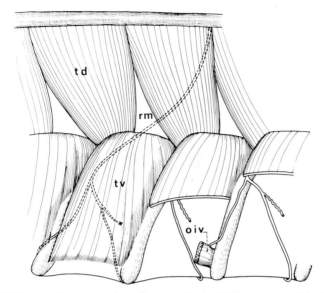

FIG. 40. Medial view of the muscles of the rib cage in the viperid *Cerastes cerastes* (after Gasc, 1974). Anterior is to the right. oiv, M. obliquus internus pars ventralis; rm, medial branch of the hypaxial nerve; td, M. transversus abdominis pars dorsalis; tv, M. transversus abdominis pars ventralis.

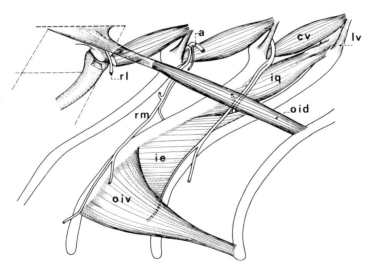

FIG. 41. Medial view of the deeper muscles of the rib cage posterior to the heart in the colubrid *Coluber viridiflavus* (after Gasc, 1967b). Anterior is to the right. a, Intercostal artery; cv, M. costovertebro-costalis; ie, M. intercostalis externus; iq, M. intercostalis quadrangularis; lv, ventral ligament of the head of a rib; oid, M. obliquus internus pars dorsalis; oiv, M. obliquus internus pars ventralis; rl, lateral branch of the hypaxial nerve; rm, medial branch of the hypaxial nerve.

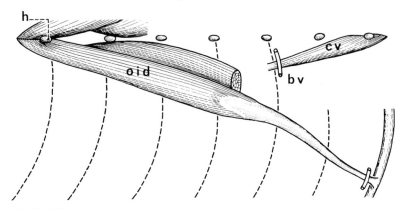

FIG. 42. Medial view of the muscles of the rib cage posterior to the heart in the boid *Chondropython viridis* (after Gasc, 1974). Superficial muscles are shown on the left side, deeper ones on the right; dotted lines indicate the positions of the ribs. bv, Ventral branch of the hypaxial nerve (cf. Fig. 39); cv, M. costo-vertebro-costalis; h, tip of hypapophysis; oid, M. obliquus internus pars dorsalis.

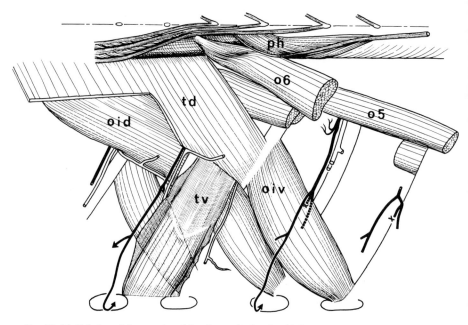

FIG. 43. Medial view of the muscles of the rib cage in the viperid *Cerastes cerastes* (after Gasc, 1971). Anterior is to the right. oid, M. obliquus internus pars dorsalis; oiv, M. obliquus internus pars ventralis; o5, short bundle of the M. obliquus internus pars dorsalis; o6, long bundle of the M. obliquus internus pars dorsalis; ph, M. parapophyso-hypapophyseus; td, M. transversus pars dorsalis; tv, M. transversus pars ventralis.

retrahens costarum had been also used for the dorsal portion (see the discussion of *Sphenodon* above). Each bundle of the dorsal portion reaches the lateral surface of the hypapophyses or the ventral surface of the centrum where there are no subvertebral muscles (Fig. 42), or the base of a parapophysial process if a M. parapophyso-hypapophyseus is present (Fig. 43).

The fibers cross the ribs (up to six segments) and are relayed by those of the pars ventralis. The nerve innervating the M. transversus pars ventralis and the skin on the ventral surface of the body passes ventral to the M. obliquus internus pars ventralis. The fibers of the M. obliquus internus often converge on the tip of the rib.

A distinct M. intercostalis internus, i.e., one with bundles that span one or two ribs on their internal aspect, seems to be rare in snakes. Only the boids show clearly a muscular layer between the M. obliquus internus and the distal portion of the ribs.

b. The subvertebral layer. The development of the subvertebral layer in the trunk of snakes is debatable. Some snakes possess hypapophyses in the post-cardiac part of the trunk; others do not (see the review in Hoffstetter and Gasc, 1969). In the Sauria, Amphisbaenia, and Scolecophidia, the occurrence of subvertebral muscles is restricted to the region with hypapophyses which extends only a short distance posteriorly. This correlation might also be expected among snakes. However, Mosauer (1935) did not find a true M. transverso-hypapophyseus (= M. parapophyso-hypapophyseus of Gasc, 1971) in boids, even in the precardiac subregion in which hypapophyses are developed. On the other hand, the correlation does hold in all Caenophidia. Auffenberg (1966) denied this distinction and recognized the equivalent of the M. transverso-hypapophyses in the ventral belly of the M. costo-vertebro-costalis of boids. This belly is clearly separated from the dorsal one in the precardiac subregion and extends over several segments. Indeed these bundles recall the M. parapophyso-hypapophyseus although they reach the ribs laterally, and not the parapophysial processes which are absent in boids.

The problem is more complex when the relations between elements of the medial layer are taken into account. In viperids and some elapids (I have not checked all the species), the subvertebral band is not covered ventrally by the M. obliquus internus pars dorsalis (Fig. 42), but the constituent bundles of the latter pass along the dorsal aspect of the subvertebral muscles, between the successive bundles, to insert on the base of the parapophysial process. In the precardiac subregion of boids, the ventral belly of the M. costo-vertebro-costalis (thought to be the M. transverso-hypapophyseus by Auffenberg, 1966) is covered ventrally by the Mm. transversus and obliquus internus (Fig. 43). In the precardiac subregion of those colubrids that lack

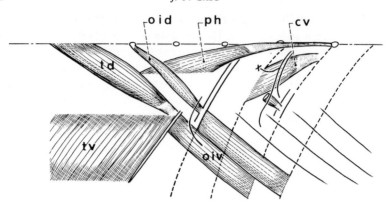

Fig. 44. Medial view of the rib cage anterior to the heart in the colubrid *Grayia smythii* (after Gasc, 1974). Anterior is to the right. cv, costo-vertebro-costalis; oid, M. obliquus internus pars dorsalis; oiv, M. obliquus internus pars ventralis; ph, M. parapophyso-hypapophyseus; td, M. transversus pars dorsalis; tv, M. transversus pars ventralis.

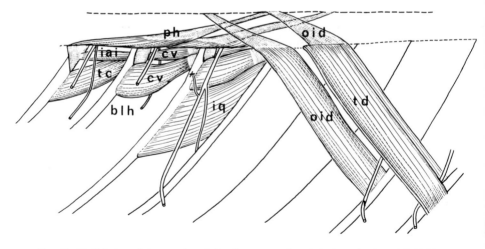

Fig. 45. Medial view of the muscles of the rib cage anterior to the heart in the colubrid *Natrix natrix* (after Gasc, 1974). Superficial muscles are shown on the right side, deeper ones on the left; anterior is to the right. blh, Lateral branch of the hypaxial nerve; cv, M. costo-vertebro-costalis (with two heads); iai, M. interarticularis inferior; iq, M. intercostalis quadrangularis; oid, M. obliquus internus pars dorsalis; ph, M. parapophyso-hypapophyseus; tc, M. tuberculocostalis; td, M. transversus pars dorsalis.

hypapophyses posteriorly (Fig. 44) and along the entire trunk in others (Fig. 45), a third pattern appears: The M. costo-vertebro-costalis is divided into two heads, is covered by the posterior tendons of the M. obliquus internus pars dorsalis, and coexists with a true M. parapophyso-hypapophyseus.

Thus Mosauer (1935) was right: only the Caenophidia possess a M. parapophyso-hypapophyseus, the presence of which is not automatically linked to the development of hypapophyses. However, two major types of relations are found with the medial layer (Fig. 46): the subvertebral column

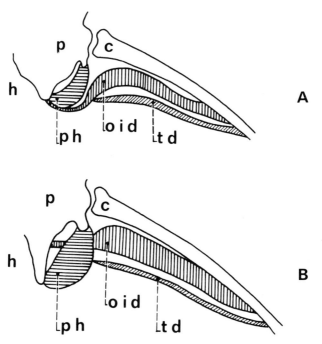

FIG. 46. Transverse sections showing the relations between the subvertebral and medial hypaxial muscles (after Gasc, 1974). A, Colubrid; B, viperid; c, rib; h, hypapophysis; oid, M. obliquus internus pars dorsalis; p, parapophysis and its ventral process; ph, parapophyseo-hypapophyseus; td, M. transversus pars dorsalis.

pushes the M. obliquus internus pars dorsalis laterally in viperids and some elapids, or the latter reaches the midventral line by a thin aponeurosis in colubrids, hydrophiids and American elapids. Malnate (1972) describes an intermediate stage in which the M. obliquus internus (the M. costalis internus superior of Malnate) is adjacent to the M. parapophyso-hypapophyseus. I think this is only a modality of one or the other type of relation; the fibers are adjacent but prolonged either dorsally to the centrum or ventrally to the hypapophysial tip by an aponeurotic slip. As noted above, the so-called aponeurotic sheath enclosing the muscular columns in squamates is generally formed by the juxtaposition of individual slips from the ends of bundles of the neighboring muscles (see Gasc, 1967b, especially for the method of dissection).

c. The lateral layer. The M. intercostalis externus does not show great variation in its dorsal position. A M. intercostalis quadrangularis is always distinctly visible, its limit being marked by the lateral passage of the lateral cutaneous nerve. In colubrids with thick body walls, such as *Grayia*, the intercostal layer tends to become supracostal, forming a M. intercostalis externus longus. In henophidians and viperids the thickness is due mainly to the M. obliquus externus and M. iliocostalis.

Ventrally, the cartilaginous tips of the ribs are linked by longitudinal fibers, which sometimes span several ribs (as in *Coluber*; Fig. 41). Mosauer (1935) calls them the Mm. intercartilaginosi and includes them in the M. rectus abdominis. As we saw above in the Amphisbaenia and *Sphenodon*, the nature of the M. rectus of squamates is still obscure. I call these bundles the Mm. intercostales ventrales.

The M. obliquus externus profundus is differentiated dorsally to form a M. levator costae, a fan-like muscle originating from a prezygapophysial process and spreading ventrolaterally onto the following rib. Present in all snakes, as well as in *Dibamus* and the Amphisbaenia, it appears to be an important functional element of the snake-like forms (Gasc, 1967c, 1971).

The M. supracostalis lateralis superior appears to be a specialized ventral portion of the M. obliquus externus profundus. Its constituent bundles originate anteriorly from a rib, lateral to the anterior insertion of the M. iliocostalis; the lateral cutaneous nerve passes between them (Fig. 25). They extend obliquely posteriorly over several ribs. The number crossed is highly variable, even within one family, but is generally greater in boids (Fig. 34) and smaller in colubrids (Fig. 32).

The M. supracostalis lateralis inferior does not receive the same innervation as the preceding muscle; although it looks topographically to be an element of the same layer (the M. obliquus externus profundus), its innervation suggests an origin from the rectus system. The question is still open, as I do not see positive reasons to prefer either solution over the other. The constituent bundles of the M. supracostalis lateralis inferior span several ribs and continue posterolaterally along the course of the M. supracostalis lateralis superior. They reach the distal bony tips of the ribs. The development of the whole supracostal system, which is probably heterogeneous, is generally related to the shape of the body: the bundles are fleshy in the thick walled and stout snakes, but mainly tendinous or reduced in the thin walled and slender ones (Figs. 47 and 48).

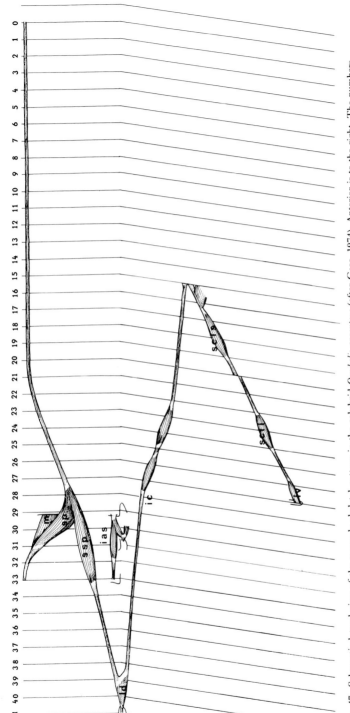

FIG. 47. Schematic lateral view of the musculo-skeletal pattern in the colubrid *Oxybelis argenteus* (after Gasc, 1974). Anterior is to the right. The numbers indicate the vertebral segments. In this vine snake tendinous portions of the muscles are more prominent than the fleshy ones. ias, M. interarticularis superior; ic, M. iliocostalis; iv, intercostalis ventralis; ld, M. longissimus dorsi; m, M. multifidus; scli, M. supracostalis lateralis inferior; scls, M. supracostalis lateralis superior; sp, M. spinalis; ssp, M. semispinalis.

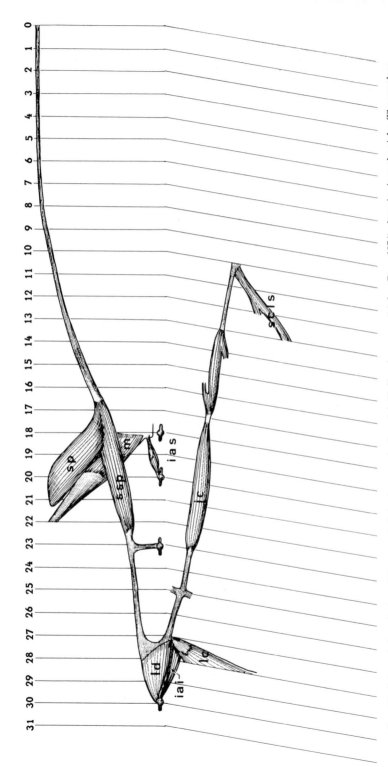

FIG. 48. Schematic lateral view of the musculoskeletal pattern in the colubrid *Xenodon merremii* (after Gasc, 1974). Anterior is to the right. The numbers indicate the vertebral segments. iai, M. interarticularis inferior; ias, M. interarticularis superior; ic, M. iliocostalis; lc, M. levator costae; ld, M. longissimus dorsi; m, M. multifidus; scls, M. supracostalis lateralis superior; sp, M. spinalis; ssp, M. semispinalis.

The M. obliquus externus superficialis always joins the ribs to the skin. This disposition is presumably related to the mobility of the skin in respect to the axial skeleton. The M. costo-cutaneous superior consists of oblique bundles which arise from the lateral surface of a rib, sometimes by a tendon, and insert more posteroventrally into the internal aspect of the skin at the lateral margin of the ventral scales. The M. costo-cutaneus inferior runs anteriorly from the bony tips of the ribs to the ventral part of the integument (Buffa, 1905; Guibé, 1970, Fig. 146; Fig. 50). Sometimes both Mm. costo-cutanei are highly developed and their fibers run longitudinally (*Laticauda*; *Cylindrophis*, Fig. 49).

H. SCOLECOPHIDIA

1. *General*

As noted above, the separate treatment of this infraorder has no special systematic meaning. It is simply more convenient to compare those specialized forms to the general pattern of organization for the whole suborder after a general treatment of other snakes. Very little is known about the axial muscles of the Leptotyphlopidae. Their small size does not allow sufficient precision in dissections, and the use of serial sections does not show complex three-dimensional relationships among muscles, tendons, and aponeuroses. Therefore this account is based on the Typhlopidae; the noticeable differences in movements between the two families suggest a difference in muscular arrangement, with the Leptotyphlopidae probably having a more conventional one.

Although scolecophidia are highly modified, compared with squamates in general or even with other snakes, the general plan defined at the beginning and used in the above descriptions is still followed. In fact, in many features the typhlopids fit easily into the series. They are not closer to the Sauria than to the Serpentes, as Mosauer (1935) claimed, but show some convergent characters with the Amphisbaenia on an osteo-myological background which is typically ophidian.

2. *Epaxial Muscles* (Fig. 51)

a. The M. transversospinalis group. The deep layer of the M. transverso-spinalis group is not differentiated. The Mm. interneurales form a thick sheet linking the successive dorsal aspects of the neural arches (there are no neural spines).

The M. interarticularis superior is multisegmental, spanning three vertebrae, and consists of one belly which appears to represent the ventral one of other snakes. Except for the difference due to the absence of neural

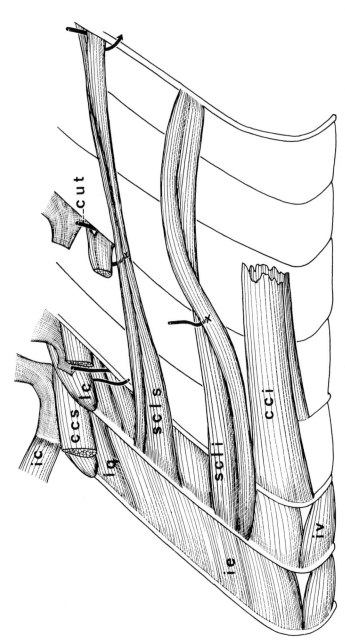

FIG. 49. Lateral view of the hypaxial muscles of the aniliid *Cylindrophis rufus* (after Gasc, 1974). Anterior is to the right. cci, M. costocutaneus inferior; ccs, M. costocutaneus superior; cut, lateral cutaneous nerve; ic, anterior insertion of a bundle of the M. iliocostalis (cf. Fig. 33); ie, M. intercostalis externus; iq, M. intercostalis quadrangularis; iv, M. intercostalis ventralis; lc, posterior insertion of the M. levator costae; scli, M. supracostalis lateralis inferior; scls, M. supracostalis lateralis superior.

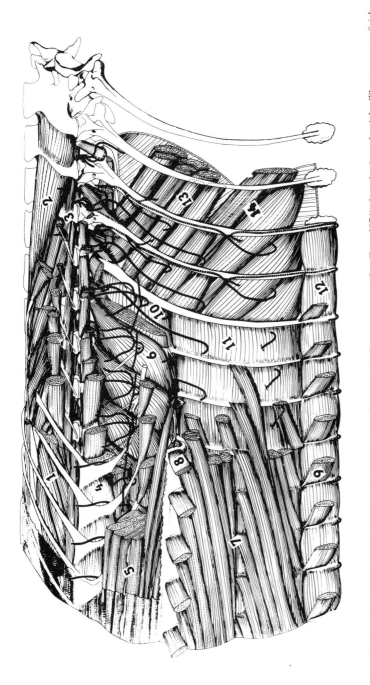

FIG. 50. Anterolateral view of the axial muscles of the trunk of the viperid *Cerastes cerastes* (after Gasc, 1974). Anterior is to the right. The more superficial muscles are shown to the left, deeper ones to the right. 1, Mm. spinalis and semispinalis; 2, M. multifidus; 3, M. interarticularis superior; 4, M. longissimus dorsi; 5, M. iliocostalis; 6, M. levator costae; 7, M. supracostalis lateralis; 8, M. costocutaneus superior; 9, M. costocutaneus inferior; 10, M. intercostalis quadrangularis; 11, M. intercostalis externus proprius; 12, M. intercostalis ventralis; 13, M. obliquus internus pars dorsalis; 14, M. obliquus internus pars ventralis.

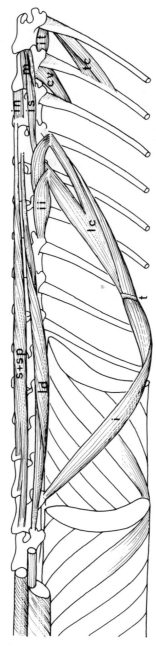

Fig. 51. Schematic lateral view of the dorsal axial muscles of the typhlopid *Typhlops punctatus* (after Gasc, 1966). On the left the relative proportions of the muscular columns and the directions of the fibers are shown; note the generally helical pattern of the bundles. cv, M. costovertebralis; i, M. iliocostalis; is, M. interarticularis superior; it, M. intertransversarius; lc, M. levator costae; ld, M. longissimus dorsi; m, M. multifidus; s + sp, Mm. spinalis and semispinalis (fused together); t, intermediate tendon of the M. iliocostalis; tc, M. tuberculocostalis.

spines, the arrangement of the deep layer is very like that found in viperids or elapids (Fig. 28B). The constituent bundles of the middle and lateral layers are fused anteriorly. Because of the lack of true neural spines and the flatness of the neural arches, the fibers of the dorsal part (M. spinalis) are parallel to those of the ventral part (M. semispinalis) posteriorly. The bundles describe a helix, span eleven vertebrae, and insert by tendons on the posterior edges of the neural arches, near the mid-dorsal line.

b. The M. longissimus group. Although it is relatively constant in shape and relationships among the Squamata in general, the M. longissimus of typhlopids shows a very peculiar arrangement. Each bundle originates posteriorly from the very prominent prezygapophysial process and, passing in an helical path over ten vertebrae, reaches the mid-dorsal surface of a neural arch. Two features are remarkable: the anterior insertion medially on a vertebra rather than laterally on a rib, and the absence of any relation with the M. iliocostalis at this level.

c. The M. iliocostalis group. The constituent bundles of the M. iliocostalis originate posteriorly in common with the M. longissimus from a tendon fixed to the prezygapophysial process. The fibers describe a helix making one complete turn anteriorly, the lateral ones passing medially, and attaching to a rib by a short tendon; seven segments are crossed. In the precardiac subregion, the bundle is interrupted by a small intermediate tendon after the third vertebra anteriorly, and this tendon forms a deep attachment with the adjacent rib.

3. Hypaxial Muscles

a. Medial layer. In contrast with the external, the internal aspect of the rib cage shows a simple pattern of muscles causing no problems in interpretation. The M. transversus is well developed in the post-cardiac subregion and is continuous down to the mid-ventral line so that it extends beyond the tips of the ribs in lateral view.

The M. obliquus internus is divided into dorsal and ventral portions, with the same relationships as in other snakes (see Figs. 41 and 43). There is no M. intercostalis internus.

b. Subvertebral layer. The subvertebral group is restricted to the most anterior vertebrae that possess well developed hypapophyses. In typhlopids, the hypapophyses are few (List, 1966; Hoffstetter and Gasc, 1969) and not correlated with the precardiac subregion; in this character, they resemble the Sauria.

c. Lateral layer. The M. intercostalis externus is dorsally differentiated

into several bundles: Mm. costo-vertebralis, tuberculo-costalis, interarticularis inferior, and intercostalis quadrangularis. The last extends ventrally
to the middle of the ribs.

Distally, supracostal bundles of the M. intercostalis externus longus cross
posteroventrally over three ribs (Fig. 52). In this they resemble the M.
intercostalis externus longus in *Feylinia* and the Scincidae (Gasc, 1967b,
Fig. 26B).

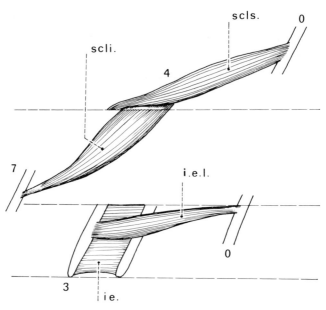

FIG. 52. Schematic lateral view of superficial muscles of the typhlopid *Typhlops punctatus*. Anterior
is to the right. The numbers indicate the number of segments spanned by the bundles of the muscles.
ie, M. intercostalis externus; iel, M. intercostalis externus longus; scli, M. supracostalis lateralis inferior;
scls, M. supracostalis lateralis superior.

Dorsally the M. obliquus externus profundus forms the very powerful M.
levator costae. Some fibers leave the main muscular mass to extend ventrally
along the adjacent rib. They resemble the M. iliocostalis of varanids (Mm.
supracostales dorsales breves of Nishi, 1938), but are clearly innervated by
the hypaxial nerve. The similarity to other snakes in its relations with the M.
interarticularis inferior is noteworthy (compare Figs. 51 and 26). The status
of the M. interarticularis inferior in snakes is debatable: it could be related to
the same layer as the M. levator costae, i.e., part of the M. obliquus externus
profundus, and not of the M. intercostalis externus, a theory which I have
adopted here.

Ventrally the M. obliquus externus profundus forms the two parts of the M. supracostalis lateralis (Fig. 52). The dorsal part (M. supracostalis lateralis superior) consists of fleshy bundles crossing four segments and extending posteroventrally. They originate near the anterior tendon of the M. iliocostalis. The bundles of the ventral part (M. supracostalis lateralis inferior) span only three ribs and insert by a short tendon. In the precardiac subregion, the M. supracostalis lateralis inferior covers the ventral margin of the M. supracostalis lateralis superior, and the external boundary between both is marked by a ridge.

A remarkable feature is the absence of the Mm. costo-cutanei, that is of a M. obliquus externus superficialis. This layer is probably incorporated into the very well developed subcutaneous musculature of typhlopids. Therefore the axial and cutaneous muscles are clear-cut and independent. This feature has great significance in explaining the worm-like method of burrowing used by these animals (Gasc, 1971).

IV. Summary and Conclusions

A. GENERAL

Although the living orders of reptiles arose from different lines which diverged a very long time ago and are very diversified, especially the Squamata, a general plan of organization in the axial musculature can be recognized. From this plan, which was probably established in the first truly tetrapodal terrestrial vertebrates, arose modifications closely connected with the vertebrocostal morphology; some of the arrangements shown by the entire musculo-skeletal apparatus are clearly related to the shape and way of life of the animals, for example in forms enclosed in a carapace or deprived of limbs.

Nevertheless, the homologies are rarely completely clear, and perhaps will never be, especially near the boundaries of two muscular layers which are closely associated during morphogenesis.

Tables II and III give a synoptical view of the homologies and important synonyms for the neck of the Testudines and the trunk of the Crocodilia and Lepidosauria. These tables show how varied the level of differentiation is among the orders and suborders.

In general, the transversospinalis group is the most differentiated of the epaxial muscles, consisting of at least three layers; these become secondarily connected in snakes and are very complex in the testudinian neck (seven sheets in the Cryptodira). The M. longissimus dorsi is the most conservative group, with its oblique orientation, extending anteriorly and superficially from a deep origin. The myomeric segmentation is often lost in the

TABLE II

Epaxial muscles of reptiles showing homologies and major synonyms

		Cryptodira	Pleurodira	Crocodilia
TRANSVERSOSPINALIS GROUP	M. interneuralis	M. interneuralis (Vallois, 1922)	M. interneuralis	M. interneuralis
	M. multifidus	M. cervicospinalis lateralis brevis dorsalis (Ogushi, 1913, in Trionychidae)	(absent)	M. neurospinalis (Vallois, 1922)
	M. interarticularis superior	Mm. articulo-transversales longus et brevis (Ogushi, 1913; = Mm. transversarius obliquus cervicis et transversarius cervicis, Vallois, 1922)	M. intertransversarius dorsalis cervicis (?; Vallois, 1922)	M. interarticularis (Valloi 1922)
	M. spinalis	M. spinalis dorsi (Ogushi, 1913) M. testospinalis cervicis (Nishi, 1938; = M. corticocervicalis, Ogushi, 1913; = M. testocervicalis medialis, Vallois, 1922; = M. spinalis cervicis)	M. spinalis cervicis	M. spino-articularis (Vallois, 1922)
		M. testospinalis capitis (Nishi, 1938; = M. testocapitis medialis, Vallois, 1922)	(absent)	
		M. spinalis capitis (Nishi, 1938; = M. cervico-capitis medialis, Vallois, 1922; = part of M. cervico-hyo-capitis, Ogushi, 1913)	M. spinalis capitis	
	M. semispinalis	M. articulocruralis longus (Ogushi, 1913; = M. articuloneuralis, 1922)	M. semispinalis cervicis	M. articulospinalis (Valloi 1922) M. tendino- articularis (Vallois, 1922)
LONGISSIMUS GROUP		M. testo-cervicalis lateralis (Hoffman, 1879–90; = M. testo transversalis cervicus, Nishi, 1938)	M. longissimus	M. longissimus
		M. testo-capitis lateralis (Vallois, 1922; = M. testo-transversalis capitis, Nishi, 1938; in Cheloniidae)		
ILIOCOSTALIS GROUP		(absent)	(absent)	M. iliocostalis

Rhynchocephalia	Sauria	Amphisbaenia	Serpentes
	M. interneurales	M. intervertebralis (Smalian, 1885)	
M. interarticularis	M. multifidus ⎤ ⎪ rarely ⎬ distinct M. interarticularis ⎪ superior ⎦	(absent) M. multifidus spinae (Smalian, 1885; partially fused with M. spinae)	M. multifidus M. digastricus (Mosauer, 1935; = M. interarticularis superior partes dorsalis et ventralis)
M. spino-articularis (Vallois, 1922; = M. spinalis, Nishi, 1938)	M. spino-articularis (Vallois, 1922)	M. spinalis (Smalian, 1885)	M. spino-articularis (Vallois, 1922; = M. spinalis, Mosauer, 1935)
M. articulospinalis (Vallois, 1922; = M. semispinalis Nishi, 1938)	M. articulospinalis (Vallois 1922; = M. semispinalis Nishi, 1938)	M. semispinalis (Smalian, 1885)	M. articulospinalis (Vallois, 1922; = M. semi- spinalis, Mosauer, 1935)
M. longissimus	M. longissimus	M. longissimus	M. longissimus
M. iliocostalis	M. iliocostalis (= supracostalis dorsalis brevis of Varanus; Nishi, 1938)	M. sacrolumbalis (Smalian, 1885)	M. iliocostalis (Vallois, 1922, and Nishi, 1938; = retractor costae biceps, Mosauer, 1935) M. supracostalis dorsalis (Nishi, 1938)

TABLE III

Hypaxial muscles of reptiles showing homologies and major synonyms

		Cryptodira	Pleurodira	Crocodilia
MEDIAL LAYER	M. transversus	?	?	M. transversus abdomin
	M. obliquus internus	?	?	M. obliquus internus
	M. intercostalis internus		?	M. intercostalis internus
LATERAL LAYER	M. intercostalis externus	M. intertransversalis (Ogushi, 1913; = M. epistropheo-atlantis dorsalis = M. atlanto-opisthoticus	M. intertransversarius colli (Shah, 1963)	
	M. interarticularis inferior	M. transversocorporis (Ogushi, 1913; = M. epistropheo-atlantis ventralis = M. atlanto-basioccipitalis		
	M. intercostalis externus proprius	0	0	M. intercostalis externu
	M. obliquus externus profundus	?	?	M. obliquus externus profundus
	M. obliquus externus superficialis	?	?	M. obliquus externus superficialis
SUBVERTEBRAL SYSTEM	Neck	M. longus colli profundus (= M. cervico-spinalis medialis, Ogushi, 1913) M. longus colli superficialis (M. carapaco-basioccipitalis, Ogushi, 1913) M. retrahens capitis collique (Shah, 1963)	M. longus colli (Shah 1963) M. retrahens capitis collique (Shah, 1963)	M. longus colli
	Trunk	(absent)	(absent)	(absent)

Rhynchocephalia	Sauria	Amphisbaena	Serpentes
M. transversus abdominis	M. transversus abdominis	M. transversus pars dorsalis (= part of M. retrahens costae, Smalian, 1885) M. transversus pars ventralis	M. transversus dorsalis (Mosauer, 1935) M. transversus ventralis (Mosauer, 1935)
M. intercostalis internus dorsalis longus (Maurer, 1896; = M. ilio-sacro-costo-costalis Byerly, 1925; = M. retrahens-costarum)	M. quadratus lumborum	M. obliquus internus pars dorsalis (= M. retrahens costae, Smalian, 1885) M. obliquus internus pars ventralis	M. obliquus internus pars dorsalis (= M. costalis internus superior, Mosauer, 1935) M. obliquus internus pars ventralis (= M. costalis internus inferior, Mosauer, 1935)
M. intercostalis internus brevis (Byerly, 1925)	M. intercostalis internus brevis	M. intercostalis internus brevis	M. intercostalis internus brevis
M. intercostalis internus longus (Byerly, 1925)	M. intercostalis internus longus	M. intercostalis internus longus	M. intercostalis internus longus
M. uncinocostalis brevis (= M. intercostalis externus brevis, Byerly, 1925) M. uncinocostalis longus (= M. intercostalis externus longus, Byerly 1925)	M. intercostalis externus brevis M. intercostalis externus longus	M. intertransversarius (Smalian, 1885) M. tuberculocostalis	M. intertransversarius M. interarticularis inferior M. tuberculocostalis M. costovertebrocostalis ? M. intercostalis quadrangularis (Mosauer, 1935) M. intercostalis externus
M. obliquus externus profundus (Maurer, 1896)	M. obliquus externus profundus	M. levator costae M. obliquus abdominis M. externus (3 layers) (Smalian, 1885)	M. levator costae M. supracostalis lateralis superior (Mosauer, 1935)
M. obliquus externus superficialis (Maurer, 1896)			M. supracostalis lateralis inferior (Mosauer, 1935)
M. abdomino-costalis (Byerly, 1925)	M. obliquus externus superficialis	?	M. costocutaneus superior M. costocutaneus inferior
M. longus colli	M. longus colli	M. longus colli	M. longus colli
(absent)	(absent)	(absent)	M. parapophy sohypapophysells

formation of a flat tendon which, in fact, constitutes the tendinous wall between the Mm. longissimus and iliocostalis.

The M. iliocostalis often remains segmental, its fibers lying between myosepta arising from the ribs. However, in the Sauria, and not only the limbless ones, the fibers tend to lose their myoseptal attachments and become multisegmental; this is the rule in the Amphisbaenia and in snakes in which the constituent bundles are very long and have helical courses.

The hypaxial muscles are more constant. The most striking differentiation is shown by limbless forms; for example the lateral layer, with numerous dorsal bundles, may be linked to specific parts of the vertebrae and ribs (M. levator costae and the prezygapophysial process; M. tuberculo-costalis and the posterodorsal costal process). Snakes, especially some Caenophidia, show special differentiation of the subvertebral system in the trunk.

In conclusion I will summarize the characteristics of each major group.

B. Testudines

(1) The axial muscles of the trunk are extremely reduced or even absent.

(2) The M. transversospinalis group is highly differentiated in the neck as the M. testospinalis capitis of Nishi (1938), especially in the Cryptodira.

(3) The M. longissimus also shares in the complicated linkage between the head, the vertebrae, and the carapace; it is divided into two layers in the Cryptodira.

(4) The M. iliocostalis system appears to be absent.

(5) Among the hypaxial muscles, the M. intertransversarius and the subvertebral muscles are well developed in the neck, while in the trunk the parietal muscles are present in some cases, but may be reduced to fibrous sheets.

C. Crocodilia

(1) Few crocodilians have been investigated, but it would be surprising if the uniformity of the vertebral morphology did not reflect identical muscular dispositions.

(2) The different layers of the epaxial and hypaxial muscles, for instance the three layers of the M. transversospinalis, are well developed.

(3) The M. semispinalis consists of two layers, the external or M. tendino-articularis being found only in the Crocodilia.

(4) The M. longissimus keeps a myomeric pattern, but the complicated folding of the myosepto-tendinous system transforms each segmental unit into a cone spanning three segments.

(5) The M. iliocostalis is completely segmental and has no connection with the M. longissimus.

(6) The hypaxial muscles show the generalized reptilian condition.

(7) The subvertebral muscles are limited to the cervical region.

D. RHYNCHOCEPHALIA

(1) The assumption that *Sphenodon* shows the primitive organization of the Lepidosauria is not entirely justified with regard to the axial muscles.

(2) The medial layer of the M. transversospinalis is undifferentiated and consists of interarcual fibers.

(3) The Mm. spinalis and semispinalis are distinct, and each crosses more than two segments.

(4) Fibers of the M. longissimus are interrupted by myosepta at the surface and cross three vertebral segments.

(5) The M. iliocostalis is completely segmental.

(6) All the epaxial muscles are transversely linked dorsoventrally by a complicated system of tendons and aponeuroses; the patterns resemble those shown by the Squamata.

(7) The presence of uncinate processes introduces differentiation in the layers of the M. intercostalis externus.

(8) There are no subvertebral muscles in the trunk, the M. intercostalis internus dorsalis longus of Maurer (1896) being, in fact, the dorsal portion of the M. obliquus internus.

E. SAURIA

(1) In many ways, the muscular dispositions in the Sauria are intermediate between those seen in *Sphenodon* and the snakes.

(2) The deep layer of the M. transversospinalis is differentiated into Mm. multifidus and interarticularis superior only in a few limbless forms.

(3) Both the middle and lateral layers, the Mm. spinalis and semispinalis, consist of multisegmental bundles which are rarely fused anteriorly.

(4) Generally (though not in varanids) bundles of the M. longissimus are multisegmental and end anteriorly in a bifurcate superficial tendon, the ventral branch of which is continued by the origin of a bundle of the M. iliocostalis.

(5) There is a great diversity in the morphology of the M. iliocostalis, but the general trend is toward uninterrupted bundles; this is not directly related to the serpentine type of locomotion.

(6) The M. iliocostalis is unusual in varanids, the bundles being transverse.

(7) In the lateral layers of the hypaxial muscles, the degree of differentiation varies, probably because of the different types of respiratory mechanisms.

(8) The subvertebral system is restricted to the neck, even in the most snake-like lizards.

(9) Apodous forms tend to develop deep intervertebral muscles covered by layers of musculo-tendinous chains.

F. Amphisbaenia

(1) The Amphisbaenia clearly differ in their muscular organization from limbless Sauria, even from such peculiar forms as dibamids.

(2) The differentiated inner layer of the M. transversospinalis includes a multisegmental M. interarticularis superior.

(3) The M. spinalis is linked with the M. interarticularis superior, but completely separate from the M. semispinalis.

(4) There are no anteriorly bifurcate tendons for the bundles of the M. longissimus.

(5) The M. iliocostalis consists of long bundles without any tendinous inscriptions.

(6) The medial hypaxial layer is clearly divided into dorsal and ventral portions.

(7) The lateral layer is differentiated proximally, in relation to the presence of processes on the vertebrae and ribs, into Mm. tuberculo-costalis and levator costae.

(8) The M. obliquus externus forms long supracostal bundles which fill the space between the lateral limit of the M. iliocostalis and the Mm. intercostales ventrales.

(9) The subvertebral muscles are restricted to the cervical region.

G. Serpentes

(1) The gross division into boid, viperid and colubrid types of muscular organization, briefly noted by Cuvier (1835) and more precisely documented by Mosauer (1935), is not completely acceptable.

(2) As far as I can observe, there is no reason to consider the Scolecophidia to have a saurian type of organization. Although they have highly specialized axial muscles, the main musculoskeletal relations shown by other snakes and summarized below appear. In the future the different

types of organization should be considered to have functional as well as taxonomic significance.

(3) The M. transversospinalis group includes three layers, and the deepest one is well differentiated into the Mm. interneuralis, multifidus, and interarticularis superior.

(4) These elements are secondarily fused, but there is no uniform pattern of fusion. The multisegmental M. multifidus appears to form the base of the system.

(5) The M. interarticularis superior, also multisegmental, consists in many species of two bellies; the ventral one often reaches the prezygapophysial process or tendon. Its joining the M. longissimus has no special systematic meaning, but characterizes forms in which the prezygapophysial processes are peculiarly prominent (some Henophidia and Caenophidia).

(6) The M. longissimus is remarkably constant in its disposition, except in the Scolecophidia in which the helical constituent bundles extend anteriorly to the neural arch, and not the ribcage. By its situation the M. longissimus constitutes the main link in the formation of musculotendinous attachment to the prezygapophysial process, even when the M. semispinalis joins the posterior tendon of the M. longissimus.

(7) The M. iliocostalis, generally linked to the M. longissimus as in many Sauria, has two bellies and helical fibers, except in the Typhlopidae, Xenopeltidae, and Aniliidae, in which the disposition is not very different from that in some limbless lizards.

(8) When digastric, the constituent bundles of the M. iliocostalis are innervated by a single spinal nerve distributed to both bellies (viperids, elapids, and hydrophiids), or by two different spinal nerves separated from each other by several segments (boids). A complex innervation is found among colubrids, in which one spinal nerve is distributed to two successive bundles through a type of plexus.

(9) A special epaxial muscle, the M. supracostalis dorsalis, is present in the Boidae and Xenopeltidae. It probably belongs to the M. iliocostalis group.

(10) The medial layer of hypaxial muscles is divided into dorsal and ventral portions, and only boids have the complete series of sheets with a M. intercostalis internus.

(11) The dorsal part of the lateral hypaxial layer is always differentiated into several bundles joining prezygapophysial processes and heads and shafts of ribs.

(12) Ventrally the M. obliquus externus shows supracostal differentiation, as in the Amphisbaenia.

(13) Two sets of costocutaneous muscles represent the M. obliquus externus superficialis.

(14) The subvertebral layer is present in the trunk of only the Caeno-phidia (as the M. parapophyseo-hypapophyseus) and absent in others, even when hypapophyses are developed. This is quite unlike the situation in the Sauria.

(15) Two types of relations can be found between the subvertebral layer and the dorsal portion of the medial hypaxial layer. In viperids, for example, the M. obliquus internus pars dorsalis does not reach the median line, while in colubrids it reaches this line, covering the M. parapophyso-hypapophyseus as a thin aponeurosis. Both types occur among the elapids.

References

d'Alton, E. (1834). Beschreibung des Muskelsystems einer *Python bivittatus*. *Archiv. Anat. Wiss. Med.* **1834**, 346–364, 432–450, 528–543.

Auffenberg, W. (1958). The trunk musculature of *Sanzinia* and its bearing on certain aspects of the myological evolution in snakes. *Breviora* (82), 1–12.

Auffenberg, W. (1959). The epaxial musculature of *Siren, Amphiuma* and *Necturus* (Amphibia). *Bull. Florida St. Mus. Biol. Sci* **4**, 253–265.

Auffenberg, W. (1961). Additional remarks on the evolution of trunk musculature in snakes. *Am. Midl. Nat.* **65**, 1–16.

Auffenberg, W. (1962). A review of the trunk musculature in the limbless land vertebrates. *Am. Zool.* **2**, 183–190.

Auffenberg, W. (1966). The vertebral musculature of *Chersydrus* (Serpentes). *Quart. J. Florida Acad. Sci.* **29** (2), 155–162.

Bellairs, A. d'A. and Underwood, G. (1951). The origin of snakes. *Biol. Rev.* **26**, 193–237.

Bojanus, L. H. (1819–21). "Anatome Testudinis Europaeae." Vilno.

Buffa, P. (1905). Richerche sulla muscolatura cutanea dei serpenti e considerazione sulla locomozione di questi animali. *Atti Acad. Ven. Trent.* n.s. **1**, 145–237.

Byerly, T. C. (1925). The myology of *Sphenodon punctatum*. *Univ. Iowa Stud. Nat. Hist.* **48**, 289–481.

Camp, C. L. (1923). Classification of the lizards. *Bull. Am. Mus. Nat. Hist.* **48**, 289–481.

Cunningham, D. J. (1890). The value of nerve supply in determination of muscular homologies and anomalies. *J. Anat. Phys.* **25**, 31–40.

Cuvier, G. (1800–05). "Leçons d'Anatomie Comparée. Vol. 1. Les Organes du Mouve-ment." C. Duméril, Paris.

Cuvier, G. (1835). "Leçons d'Anatomie Comparée." 2nd edn, Crochard et Cie., Paris, 8 vols.

Davis, D. D. (1936). The terminology of reptilian musculature. *Herpetologica*, **7**, 12–17.

Dombrowski, B. (1930a). Ein Versuch der Klassifikation der Brust- und Bauchmuskeln der Amnioten. *Anat. Anz.* **70**, 416–436.

Dombrowski, B. (1930b). Zur Phylotektonik des respiratorischen Muskulatur der Reptilien und Säugetiere. *Z. Anat. EntwGesch* **93**, 353–369.

Emelianov, S. W. (1936). Die Morphologie der Tetrapodenrippen. *Zool. Jb.* (*Anat.*) **62**, 173–274.

Gadow, H. (1882). Untersuchungen über die Bauchmuskeln der Krokodile, Eidechsen und Schildkröten. *Morph. Jb.* **7**, 57–100.

Gans, C. (1962). Terrestrial locomotion without limbs. *Am. Zool.* **2**, 167–182.

Gans, C. and Hughes, G. M. (1967). The mechanism of lung ventilation in the tortoise *Testudo graeca* Linné. *J. exp. Biol.* **47**, 1–20.

Gasc, J.-P. (1965). Les adaptations anatomiques du lézard apode *Feylinia currori* Gray au fouissage par reptation ondulante *C. r. hebd. Séanc. Acad. Sci., Paris* **260**, 1248–1251.

Gasc, J.-P. (1966). "Les Modalités Anatomiques de l'Adaptation à la Locomotion Rampante." Thèse de 3ème cycle, Paris, 166 pp.

Gasc, J.-P. (1967a). Un cas particulier de l'adaptation à la vie souteraine: le lézard serpenti-forme *Dibamus* Duméril et Bibron. *C. r. hebd. Séanc. Acad. Sci., Paris* **265**, 41–43.

Gasc, J.-P. (1967b). Introduction à l'étude de la musculature axiale des squamates serpenti-formes. *Mém. Mus. natn. Hist. nat., Paris.* N.S. **48A**, 69–125.

Gasc, J.-P. (1967c). Retentissement de l'adaptation à la locomotion apode sur le squelette des squamates. *In* "Problèmes Actuels de Palèontologie. Evolution des Vertébrés." (J.-P. Lehman, ed.) *Colloques Int. Cent. Natn. Res. Scient.* No. **163**, 373–394.

Gasc, J.-P. (1968). Contribution à l'ostéologie et à la myologie de *Dibamus novaeguinea* Gray (Sauria, Reptilia). *Annls Sci. nat. (Zool).* (12) **10**, 127–150.

Gasc, J.-P. (1970a). Les différents types d'innervation du muscle ilio-costal du tronc chez les serpents. *Bull. Ass. Anat.* 54ème Congr. (Sofia) **145**, 168–175.

Gasc, J.-P. (1970b). Réflexions sur le concept de "régression" des organes. *Rev. Questions sci. Louvain* **141**, (2), 175–195.

Gasc, J.-P. (1971). "L'interprétation Fonctionelle de l'Appareil Musculo-squelettique de l'Axe Vertébral ches les Serpents (Reptilia)." Thèse Sci., Paris, 189 pp.

Gasc, J.-P. (1974). L'interprétation fonctionelle de l'appareil musculo-squelettique de l'axe vertébral chez les Serpents (Reptilia). *Mém. Mus. nat. Hist. nat., Paris. Ser. A, Zool.* **83**, 1–182.

Gaunt, A. S. and Gans, C. (1969). Mechanics of respiration in the snapping turtle *Chelydra serpentina* Linné. *J. Morph.* **128**, 195–228.

Gegenbaur, C. (1896). Zur Systematik der Rückenmuskeln. *Morph. Jb.* **24**, 205–208.

Guibé, J. (1970). La locomotion. *In* "Traité de Zoologie." (P. P. Grassé, ed.) Masson et Cie., Paris, **14**(2), 186.

Haines, R. W. (1936). A consideration of the constancy of muscular nerve supply. *J. Anat.* **70**, 33–35.

Heusinger, C. F. (1833). Untersuchungen über die Extremitäten der Ophiden, nebst Bemerkungen über die Extremitäten-Entwicklung im Allgemeinen. *Zeitsch. Org.-Physic.* **3**, 481–523.

Hoffmann, C. K. (1879–1890). Reptilien. *In* "Bronn's Klassen und Ordnungen des Thier-Reichs." C. F. Winter'sche Verlagshandlung, Leipzig, **6**(3), 3 vols.

Hoffstetter, R. (1968). Review of: A contribution to the classification of snakes. *Copeia* **1968**, 201–213.

Hoffstetter, R. and Gasc, J.-P. (1969). Vertebrae and ribs of modern reptiles. *In* "Biology of the Reptilia." (C. Gans, A. d'A. Bellairs and T. S. Parsons, eds). Academic Press, London and New York, **1**, 201–310.

Humphry, G. M. (1872). Note on the muscles of the glass-snake (*Pseudopus pallasii*). *J. Anat.* **6**, 287–292.

Lessertisseur, J. (1968). Musculature hyposomatique des Mammifères. *In* "Traité de Zoologie." (P. P. Grassé, ed.). Masson et Cie., Paris, **16**(2), 549–732.

List, J. C. (1966). Comparative osteology of the snake families Typhlopidae and Lepto-typhlopidae. *Illinois biol. Mongr.* **(36)**, 1–112.

Lüdicke, M. (1962–64). Ordnung der Klasse Reptilia, Serpentes. *In* "Handbuch der Zoologie." (W. Kükenthal, T. Krumbach, J.-G. Helmcke, H. von Lengerken and D. Stark, eds). **7**([1]5–6), 1–298. Walter de Gruyter, Berlin.

Malnate, E. V. (1972). Observations on the vertebral hypapophyses and associated musculatures in some snakes, with special reference to the Colubridae. *Zool. Meded., Leiden* **47**, 225–239.

Maurer, F. (1896). Die ventrale Rumpfmuskulatur einiger Reptilien. Eine vergleichend-anatomische Untersuchung. *In* "Festschrift für Gegenbaur." **1**, 181–256.

Maurer, F. (1898). Die Entwicklung der ventralen Rumpfmuskulatur bei Reptilien. *Morph. Jb.* **26**, 1–60.

Meckel, J. F. (1821–33). "System der vergleichenden Anatomie." Renger, Halle, 6 vols.

Mivart, S. G. (1867). Notes on the myology of *Iguana tuberculata*. *Proc. zool. Soc. Lond.* **1867**, 766–797.

Mivart, S. G. (1870). On the myology of *Chamaeleon parsonii*. *Proc. zool. Soc. Lond.* **1870**, 850–890.

Mosauer, W. (1935). The myology of the trunk region of the snakes and its significance for ophidian taxonomy and phylogeny. *Publ. Univ. Calif. Los Angeles* **1**, 81–120.

Nishi, S. (1919). Zur vergleichenden Anatomie der eigentlichen (genuinen) Rückenmuskeln. *Morph. Jb.* **50**, 168–318.

Nishi, S. (1938). Muskeln des Rumpfes. *In* "Handbuch der vergleichenden Anatomie der Wirbeltiere." (L. Bolk, E. Göppert, E. Kallius, and W. Lubosch, eds) Urban und Schwarzenberg, Berlin and Wien, **5**, 351–446.

Ogushi, K. (1911). Anatomische Studien an der japanischen dreikralligen Lippenschild-kröte (*Trionyx japanicus*). I. Mitteilung. *Morph. Jb.* **43**, 1–106.

Ogushi, K. (1913). Anatomische Studien an der japanischen dreikralligen Lippenschild-kröte (*Trionyx japanicus*). II. Mitteilung. *Morph. Jb.* **46**, 299–562.

Olson, E. C. (1936). The dorsal axial musculature of certain primitive Permian tetrapods. *J. Morph.* **59**, 265–311.

Peterson, J. A. (1973). "Adaptation for Arboreal Locomotion in the Shoulder Region of Lizards." Thesis: Univ. Chicago, Ill.

Pregill, G. P. (1977). Axial myology of the racer *Coluber constrictor* with emphasis on the neck region. *Transact. San Diego Soc. Nat. Hist.* **18**(11), 185–206.

Rathke, M. H. (1848). "Ueber die Entwicklung der Schildkröten." Vieweg, Braunschweig.

Romer, A. S. (1956). "Osteology of the Reptiles." Univ. Chicago Press, Chicago.

Sanders, A. (1870). Notes on the myology of *Platydactylus japonicus*. *Proc. zool. Soc. Lond.* **1870**, 413–426.

Sewertzoff, A. N. (1931). Studien über die Reduktion der Organe der Wirbeltiere. *Zool. Jb.* (*Anat.*). **53**, 611–699.

Shah, R. V. (1963). The neck musculature of a cryptodire (*Deirochelys*) and a pleurodire (*Chelodina*) compared. *Bull. Mus. Comp. Zool. Harv.* **129**, 343–368.

Smalian, C. (1885). Beiträge zur Anatomie der Amphisbaeniden. *Z. wiss. Zool.* **42**, 126–202.

Smirnowsky, B. W. (1930). Zur Morphologie der respiratorischen Musculatur der Lacertilien. *Anat. Anz.* **70**, 58–77.

Stokely, P. S. (1947). Limblessness and correlated changes in the girdles of a comparative morphological series of lizards. *Am. Midl. Nat.* **38**, 725–754.

Strauss, W. L. Jr. (1946). The concept of nerve muscle specificity. *Biol. Rev.* **21**, 75–91.

Strauss, W. L. Jr. and Rawles, M. E. (1953). An experimental study of the origin of the trunk musculature and ribs in the chick. *Am. J. Anat.* **92** (3), 471–509.

Tyson, E. (1682–83). Vipera caudisona Americana, or the Anatomy of a Rattle snake, dissected at the repository of the Royal Society in January 1682–1683. *Phil. Trans. R. Soc.* **13**, 25–88.

Underwood, G. (1957). On lizards of the family Pygopodidae. A contribution to the morphology and phylogeny of the Squamata. *J. Morph.* **100**, 207–268.

Underwood, G. (1967). "A Contribution to the Classification of snakes." British Museum (Nat. Hist.), London, 179 pp.

Vallois, H. V. (1920). Les muscles de l'épisome chez les Chelonians. *Bull. Soc. Sci. Med. Biol. Montpellier* **41**, 323–326.

Vallois, H. V. (1922). Les transformations de la musculature de l'épisome chez les vertébrés. *Arch. Morph. gen. exper.* **13**, 1–538.

Weaver, W. G. Jr. (1965). The cranial anatomy of the hog-nosed snakes (*Heterodon*). *Bull. Florida St. Mus.* **9**, 275–304.

Wettstein, O. von (1931). Rhynchocephalia. *In* "Handbuch der Zoologie." (W. Kükenthal and T. Krumbach, eds). de Gruyter, Berlin, 7(1), 1–128.

Wettstein, O. von. (1937–54). Crocodilia. *In* "Handbuch der Zoologie." (W. Kükenthal and T. Krumbach, eds). de Gruyter, Berlin, 7(1) (1937), 225–320; 7(1) (1954), 321–424.

Wiedemann, C. R. W. (1802). Anatomische Beschreibung der Schildkröten überhaupt und der getäfelten Schildkröte (*T. tessellata*, Schneid; *T. tabulata*, Walbaum) insbesondere. *Arch Zool. Zootomie*, **2**, 177–210 and 3, 78–102.

Author Index

Van der Merwe, N. J., 65, 70, 225, *262*
van Gehuchten, A., 337, *353*
Van Pletzen, R., 70, *262*
Vaughan, P., 271, 277, 278, 285, 287, *350*
Verratti, E., 337, *353*
Versluys, J., 2, 31, 34, 126, *262*
Visser, J. G. J., 95, 96, 97, 99, 102, 136, 157, 158, 163, *262*
Vitadello, M. 292, *349*
Voeltzkow, A., 228, *262*
Von Gueldern, C., 91, *262*

W

Wachholder, K., 338, *353*
Wacyk, J., 314, *347*
Walcott, B., 271, 274, 276, 278, *344, 345*
Walker, A. D., 245, *262*
Walker, B., 321, 327, 331, 332, 333, *350*
Walker, S. M., 285, 288, 338, *344*
Wallner, A., 309, 310, *348, 350*
Walsh, T. H., 266, 271, 309, 310, *353*
Washio, H., 289, *353*
Weaver, W. G., Jr, 399, *435*
Webb, M., 73, 75, *262*
Weeds, A. G., 267, 291, *353*
Wegner, R. M., 223, 228, 244, *262*
Weinstein, J. H., 314, *353*
Wells, J. B., 271, 300, 301, *354*
Wermuth, H., 228, *262*
Werner, G., 114, 117, 118, 120, 121, 123, *262*
Werner, Y. L., 34, 35, 38, 73, 80, 90, *262, 263*
Westbury, D. R., 302, *350*
Westoll, T. S., 6, 61, *258*
Wettstein, O., von, 5, *262*, 375, 376, 379, *435*
Wever, E. G., 5, 9, 31, 34, 35, 40, 65, 67, 71, 73, 80, 83, 86, 90, 91, 95, 100, 101, 102, 104, 105, 106, 107, 108, 109, 113, 114, 118, 126, 132, 133, 134, 136, 145, 147, 148, 169, 174, 180, 183, 205, 223, *252, 262, 263*
Whetstone, K. N., 246, *263*
Wiedemann, C. R. W., 361, *435*
Wilkie, D. R., 266, 288, 298, 301, 302, 303, 304, 309, *341, 346, 354*
Wilkinson, H. J., 337, *354*
Willard, W. A., 86, *263*
Williams, E. E., 39, 172, 180, *250, 263*
Wilson, P., 290, *354*
Winchester, L., 39, *263*
Witalinski, W., 278, 294, *354*
Woledge, R. C., 266, 271, 285, 288, 301, 305, 306, 307, 308, 309, 310, *353, 354*
Wyeth, F. J., 114, 125, *263*
Wylie, R. M., 323, 327, 330, *346*
Wyman, J., 338, *347, 354*

Y

Yakovlev, N. N., 309, *354*
Yntema, C. L., 8, 220, 221, *263*
Yoshikami, D., 278, 285, 290, *344, 347*
Young, E. A. E., 71, 72, *263*

Z

Zacks, S. I., 266, *354*
Zada, S. K., 91, 92, 94, *256, 263*
Zaher, M. M., 136, 157, 159, 161, *250*
Zajac, F. E., 271, 280, *341*
Zalusky, S. B., 86, *263*
Zangerl, R., 126, 130, 131, 134, *263*
Zehr, D. R., 136, *263*
Zhukov, Ye, K., 290, *354*
Zimmer, F., 302, *350*
Zimmermann, S., 101, 102, *263*
Zurich, L., 314, *347, 349*

Subject Index

A

A band, 269, 273, 293
Abducens canal, 76, 93, 98, 106, 110, 112, 144, 154, 159, 162, 168, 170, 174, 187, 203
Abducens nerve, 15, 21, 22, 24, 41, 42, 43, 44, 52, 56, 66, 74, 105, 106, 124, 137, 138, 140, 144, 154, 155, 158, 160, 162, 163, 168, 173, 174, 187, 189, 203, 206, 210, 211, 212, 217, 224, 236, 237
Ablepharus, chondrocranium, 65, 70
Acanthodactylus, chondrocranium, 39, 40–57, 58, 60, 62, 64, 75, 150, 203
Accessory nerve, 26, 45, 109, 112, 145, 170, 213, 238
Accessory olfactory bulb, 170
Acetylcholine, 290, 291, 296
Acontias, axial muscles, 357, 383, 388
chondrocranium, 23, 65, 67, 68, 70, 107, 188, 197, 203
Acrantophis, axial muscles, 357
Acrochordal, *see* Crista sellaris
Acrochordidae, axial muscles, 357
chondrocranium, 152
Acrochordus, axial muscles, 357
Acrodonty, 95, 135
Action potential, 268, 271, 284, 285, 286, 289, 295, 297
Activation, 303
Adenine nucleotide, 309
Aditus conchae, 12, 15, 17, 19, 46, 49, 52, 57, 68, 72, 75, 76, 77, 84, 86, 88, 103, 104, 106, 127, 138, 140, 160, 163, 166, 173, 231, 233
Adventitious cartilage, *see* Secondary cartilage
Aerobiosis, 281, 292, 309, 335, 338
Afferent axons, 317, 333
Afroblepharus, axial muscles, 357
chondrocranium, 65
Afroedura, chondrocranium, 73, 75
Agama, axial muscles, 357

chondrocranium, 91, 92, 93, 94, 203
muscle tissue, 279
Agamidae, axial muscles, 357, 384
chondrocranium, 8, 61, 63, 91–95, 196, 197
Agamodon, chondrocranium, 126, 132, 134, 135
Agkistrodon, axial muscles, 357
muscle tissue, 283, 336
Agnatha, chondrocranium, 7
Ahaetulla, axial muscles, 402
Ala temporalis, 190
Alar process of basisphenoid, 58, 112
Albumin, 291
Alisphenoid, 5, 6, 23, 31, 32, 185, 190, 191, 242
Alligator, axial muscles, 356
chondrocranium, 228, 232, 234, 235, 237, 240, 244, 245
muscle tissue, 275, 278, 290, 294, 297, 317, 325, 336
Ambystoma, muscle tissue, 267
Ameiva, axial muscles, 357
chondrocranium, 71
Amphibia, axial muscles, 355, 358
chondrocranium, 21, 39, 222
muscle tissue, 265, 266, 267, 268, 271, 277, 282, 291, 292, 295, 298, 328, 338
Amphibolurus, chondrocranium, 91
Amphicoely, 82
Amphikinesis, 64, 113, 198
Amphisbaena, axial muscles, 357, 390, 392
chondrocranium, 126, 132, 133, 135, 201
muscle tissue, 283, 336
Amphisbaenia, axial muscles, 357, 358, 361, 387, 389–394, 411, 414, 417, 425, 427, 428, 430, 431
chondrocranium, 6, 23, 53, 107, 125–135, 149, 155, 180, 188, 191, 192, 193, 197, 199–200, 201, 202
muscle tissue, 268, 283, 336

Burrowing, *see* Fossorial adaptation

C

Caenophidia, axial muscles, 399, 411, 413, 428, 431, 432
  chondrocranium, 136–169, 172, 174, 203, 204
Caiman, axial muscles, 372
  muscle tissue, 273, 317, 333, 336
Calabaria, axial muscles, 357
Calcium, 8, 267, 273, 274, 288, 289, 292, 296, 299, 304, 305, 306, 308, 314, 315, 316, 335
Callisaurus, chondrocranium, 86
Calotes, chondrocranium, 91, 92, 94, 95
  muscle tissue, 278, 282, 283, 293, 336
Canalis cavernosus, 219
Capacitance, 284, 287, 288, 289
Capsule, 322–323
  long, 319, 321, 322, 327, 330, 331
  short, 319, 320, 321, 330, 331, 334
Carapace, 362, 366, 368, 372, 423, 428
Cardiac muscle, *see* Muscle, cardiac
Cardiovascular system, 267
Carnosine, 292
Carotid foramen, *see* Internal carotid artery
Cartilage, 5, 7, 10
Cartilage bone, 5, 10, 19, 58–59, 123, 150–151, 216–218, 241–243
Cartilage of Jacobson's organ, 18, 48, 54, 72, 79, 88, 89, 92, 93, 97, 121, 138, 139, 140, 141, 142, 152, 157, 160, 162, 163, 164, 165, 166, 167, 171, 176, 177, 182, 193, 194, 202, 225, 232
Cartilago hypochiasmatica, 21, 45, 52, 55, 66, 76, 93, 112
Cartilago transiliens, 216
Casque, 100, 101
Caudal autotomy, 272
Causus, axial muscles, 357
  chondrocranium, 164, 166, 167, 168
Cavia, muscle tissue, 280, 281, 282
Cavum acustico-jugulare, 213
Cavum cochleare, 25, 26, 55, 213
Cavum conchale, 19, 46, 49, 50, 57, 71, 77, 86, 88, 89, 92, 102, 104, 109, 120, 142, 171, 178
Cavum epiptericum, 24, 30, 31, 32, 105, 106, 116, 123, 124, 144, 155, 186, 188, 190,

212, 214, 219, 225, 226, 238, 241
Cavum nasi proprium, *see* Nasal cavity
Cavum vestibuli, 25, 55, 56, 121, 203, 213
Cavum vestibuli anterius, 55, 203
Cavum vestibuli posterius, 26, 55, 203
Central column of epaxial muscles, *see* M. longissimus
Centrum, 36, 82, 240, 367, 370, 411
Cephalic condyle of quadrate, *see* Otic process of quadrate
Cerastes, axial muscles, 357, 396, 398, 406, 409, 410, 419
  chondrocranium, 146, 164, 166, 167, 168, 186, 202
Ceratobranchial, 28, 36, 40, 42, 46, 57, 58, 72, 79, 83, 85, 90, 91, 95, 98, 107, 110, 117, 119, 123, 133, 134, 136, 138, 141, 150, 159, 160, 168, 170, 174, 178, 180, 183, 196, 198, 204, 205, 211, 214, 215, 216, 231, 240, 241
Ceratohyal, 15, 24, 28, 33, 34, 36, 40, 42, 45, 46, 47, 79, 80, 82, 90, 98, 110, 117, 118, 119, 123, 124, 133, 134, 136, 147, 150, 159, 183, 196, 198, 204, 205, 211, 215, 231, 233, 237, 239, 240, 241, 243
Ceratophora, chondrocranium, 91
Ceratopsia, chondrocranium, 9
Cerebellum, 28, 237, 240
Cerebral carotid artery, 11, 25, 99, 138, 160
Cerebral hemisphere, 22, 24, 32, 155, 187, 240
Cerebral vein, 187
Cervical mechanism of turtles, 361, 362, 363, 368, 371
Cervical vertebra, 362
Cetacea, muscle tissue, 292
Chalcides, axial muscles, 357, 383, 387
  chondrocranium, 65, 66, 67
  muscle tissue, 277, 336
Chamaeleo, axial muscles, 357
  chondrocranium, 36, 95, 100
  muscle tissue, 278, 293, 336
Chamaeleonidae, axial muscles, 357, 358
  chondrocranium, 63, 95–101, 102, 108, 121, 195, 196, 197
Chamaesaura, axial muscles, 357
  chondrocranium, 70
Chelidae, chondrocranium, 218
Chelodina, muscle tissue, 320, 327, 331, 332, 336

Sanzinia, axial muscles, 395
  chondrocranium, 169, 171, 172, 174, 186
Sarcolemma, 268, 276, 293
Sarcomeres, 267, 268, 273, 274, 277, 302, 312, 320
Sarcoplasmic reticulum, 267, 269, 273, 276, 293, 294, 297, 298, 299, 305, 308, 310, 315, 216, 338
Sarcotubules, 265, 267, 268, 271, 274, 275, 279, 284, 288, 293, 294, 295, 296, 297, 305, 321, 335
Satellite cell, 266, 320
Sauria, axial muscles, 357, 361, 372, 380–389, 391, 394, 395, 396, 402, 411, 417, 421, 425, 427, 429–430, 431, 432
  chondrocranium, 2, 3, 4, 7, 9, 12, 18, 20, 22, 23, 27, 29, 30, 31, 32, 33, 34, 36, 39–114, 116, 118, 120, 121, 123, 125, 130, 131, 132, 134, 139, 142, 144, 145, 146, 147, 149, 150, 151, 154, 155, 156, 157, 158, 159, 161, 162, 167, 169, 171, 172, 174, 177, 178, 182, 184, 188, 190, 192, 193, 194–199, 200, 201, 202, 203, 204, 206, 210, 216, 219, 221, 226, 232, 234, 236, 239, 245, 246
  muscle tissue, 272, 275, 278, 283, 284, 285, 288, 290, 291, 294, 295, 322, 323, 325, 327, 330, 332, 336, 338
Saurischia, chondrocranium, 246
Scale organ, 84
Sceloporus, axial muscles, 357
  chondrocranium, 86, 87, 88, 89, 90, 92, 96
Scelotes, axial muscles, 357
  chondrocranium, 65
Scincella, muscle tissue, 266
Scincidae, axial muscles, 357, 384, 386, 422
  chondrocranium, 7, 19, 23, 57, 61, 65–70, 71, 78, 85, 105, 146, 159, 188, 197
Scincomorpha, chondrocranium, 39–73, 102
Sclera, 84, 143, 157, 170, 179, 220, 244
Scleral cartilage, 17, 24, 39, 50, 53, 63, 105, 106, 124, 128, 157, 203, 212
Scleral ossicle, 17, 24, 39, 63, 84, 105, 106, 128, 157, 203, 220, 244
Sclerotomal segmentation, 38, 355
Scolecophidia, axial muscles, 399, 411, 417–423, 430, 431

chondrocranium, 4, 152, 180–185, 200, 201, 202
Secondary cartilage, 5, 10
Secondary palate, 61, 70, 120, 218, 244, 245
Secondary tympanic membrane, 27, 28, 29, 69, 145, 146, 237, 238, 246
Selachii, muscle tissue, 292
Sense organs, 7, 9, 228
Sensory axon, 320, 324
Sensory organs of muscles, 316–334
  see also Muscle spindle
Septomaxilla, 17, 20, 22, 48, 50, 59, 60, 71, 72, 73, 75, 79, 81, 88, 89, 100, 106, 119, 122, 123, 126, 129, 143, 152, 153, 161, 165, 171, 175, 176, 179, 181, 184, 218, 244
Septosphenoid, 23, 58, 84, 241
Serine, 292
Serpentes, *see* Ophidia
Shortening rate, 298, 299, 300, 301, 303, 308
  see also Contraction time
Siphonium, 237, 239, 243, 245
Sistrurus, axial muscles, 357
Skeletal muscle, *see* Muscle, skeletal
Skin, 360, 361, 372, 374, 379, 385, 387, 411, 417
Skull, 1–263, 362, 363, 366, 369, 370
  embryology of, 1–263
  vertebral theory of, 1
Sliding filaments, 265
Smooth muscle, *see* Muscle, smooth
Solum supraseptale, *see* Planum supraseptale
Space constant, 287
Spectacle, 84, 143, 170, 201
Speed, 268, 273
Sphaerodactylus, chondrocranium, 77, 79
Sphenethmoid, 21, 22, 130
Sphenethmoid commissure, 12, 15, 16, 17, 18, 19, 20, 22, 43, 44, 45, 46, 52, 66, 68, 72, 76, 77, 83, 84, 87, 88, 90, 93, 96, 103, 105, 106, 110, 115, 116, 117, 119, 124, 127, 131, 142, 161, 196, 197, 202, 208, 209, 212, 229, 231, 232, 233, 235, 240
Sphenodon, axial muscles, 356, 376, 377, 378, 379, 380, 382, 384, 387, 391, 411, 414, 429
  chondrocranium, 29, 30, 32, 33, 36, 38, 39, 48, 61, 71, 80, 89, 105, 114, 115,

Tongue, 17, 35, 36, 64, 95, 96, 100, 110, 129, 133, 143, 215, 226, 235, 240

Tonic fibers, *see* Fibers, tonic

Trabecula, 3, 10, 11–14, 15, 19, 20, 22, 23, 24, 30, 32, 39, 40, 41, 42, 44, 50, 52, 53, 54, 62, 66, 68, 74, 75, 93, 98, 106, 112, 114, 115, 116, 117, 119, 124, 127, 128, 129, 130, 132, 136, 137, 138, 140, 142, 143, 144, 150, 154, 155, 158, 160, 161, 163, 164, 166, 167, 168, 170, 171, 172, 173, 179, 180, 181, 182, 185, 187, 189, 193, 194, 195, 200, 201, 202, 205, 206, 207, 209, 210, 211, 212, 214, 216, 219, 220, 221, 223, 224, 229, 230, 231, 236, 237, 241, 242

Trabecula communis, 11, 15, 20, 23, 24, 42, 44, 50, 54, 55, 74, 76, 83, 84, 85, 88, 90, 110, 115, 116, 127, 128, 129, 130, 131, 132, 137, 138, 140, 141, 161, 163, 166, 170, 173, 180, 181, 182, 194, 195, 200, 201, 202, 217, 223, 224, 229

Trabecular crest, 110, 112

Trabecular groove, 153, 154, 185

Trabecular plate, 11, 19, 41, 42, 74, 75, 114, 115, 116, 136, 138, 141, 143, 194

Trabecular structure of bone, 241

Trachea, 24, 28, 170, 187, 214, 368

Trachyboa, chondrocranium, 169

Trachydosaurus, chondrocranium, 65

Transpalatine, *see* Ectopterygoid

Transverse anastomotic vein, *see* Anastomotic vein

Transverse process, 362, 367, 370

Triad, 269, 274, 275, 276, 316

Trigeminal foramen, 85, 90, 112, 216, 219, 224, 242

Trigeminal ganglion, 15, 26, 30, 31, 32, 68, 106, 127, 129, 131, 132, 160, 163, 186, 187, 188, 189, 190, 210, 217, 237, 243

Trigeminal nerve, 12, 15, 21, 22, 23, 26, 32, 106, 144, 187, 188, 210, 216, 243

Trigeminal notch, 12, 98, 110, 112, 124, 138, 140

Trimeresurus, chondrocranium, 164

Trionychidae, axial muscles, 356, 362, 363, 366, 424
chondrocranium, 222–223

Trionyx, axial muscles, 356, 362, 364, 365, 366, 367, 368
chondrocranium, 222

muscle tissue, 283, 294, 336

Trochlear nerve, 15, 21, 24, 41, 42, 74, 90, 105, 115, 116, 121, 124, 155, 160, 163, 187, 189, 195, 206, 210, 224, 229, 230, 231, 233, 236, 237, 243

Trochlear process, 216

Trogonophidae, axial muscles, 357
chondrocranium, 126

Trogonophis, axial muscles, 357
chondrocranium, 126, 127, 128, 129, 130, 131, 132, 134, 135, 200, 201

Tropibasic condition, *see* Tropitrabic condition

Tropidophinae, chondrocranium, 174

Tropidophis, axial muscles, 398, 399

Tropidurus, axial muscles, 357

Tropiocolotes, chondrocranium, 74, 75, 77

Tropitrabic condition, 11, 116, 128, 132, 144, 182, 193, 195, 200, 201, 206, 225, 241

Troponin complex, 292

Tryptic peptides, 291

Tubocurarine, 329

Tubular system, 267, 273, 274, 288, 289, 293, 294, 296, 297, 304, 313, 316

Tupinambis, chondrocranium, 71, 72
muscle tissue, 273, 336

Turbinal, *see* Nasal concha

Twitch, 299, 304–314

Twitch fiber, *see* Fibers, twitch

Tympanic cavity, 28, 31, 79, 99, 100, 103, 113, 132, 147, 148, 214, 215, 226, 243

Tympanic crest, 33, 34, 59, 76

Tympanic membrane, 28, 31, 33, 59, 65, 67, 84, 91, 95, 99, 100, 104, 105, 113, 114, 118, 132, 147, 196, 215, 222, 237, 239

Tympanic process, *see* Insertion plate of extracolumella

Typhlopidae, axial muscles, 357, 417, 421, 431
chondrocranium, 158, 180–185

Typhlopinae, chondrocranium, 182, 183

Typhlops, axial muscles, 357, 420, 422
chondrocranium, 180, 181, 182, 183, 184, 201, 202, 204

Typhlosaurus, axial muscles, 357, 383, 387
chondrocranium, 85

Xenopeltis, axial muscles, 357, 402, 403, 408
    chondrocranium, 169, 171, 176, 177–178,
    182
Xenopus, muscle tissue, 289, 300, 301
Xenosauridae, chondrocranium, 108
Xenosaurus, chondrocranium, 108

Y

Yolk, 8

Z

Z line, 269, 273, 274, 275, 276, 278, 293,
    294, 295, 321
Zinc iodide-osmium, 323
Zona annularis, 18, 48, 57, 72, 73, 75, 76, 92,
    103, 104, 109, 120, 142, 157, 169, 175,
    176, 177, 178, 182, 196, 197, 202, 208,
    209, 225, 232, 233
Zonosaurus, axial muscles, 357
Zygapophysis, 37, 358, 359, 362, 373, 374,
    377, 398